ISLAMIC ARCHITECTURE
Form, function and meaning

The lavish illustration of this book would have been impossible but for generous grants from the Aga Khan, the World of Islam Festival Trust, the Barakat Trust and the Carnegie Trust for the Universities of Scotland; and for the photographic archives of Ernst Cohn-Wiener, Archibald Creswell, and Bernard O'Kane.

ISLAMIC ARCHITECTURE

Form, function and meaning

Robert Hillenbrand

EDINBURGH UNIVERSITY PRESS

For Carole, with love

© Robert Hillenbrand, 1994
Edinburgh University Press
22 George Square, Edinburgh

Typeset in Monotype Garamond
by Alden Multimedia Ltd, Northampton
and printed and bound in Great Britain by
BPC Hazell Books Ltd, Aylesbury

A CIP record for this book is available
from the British Library

ISBN 0 7486 0479 0

Contents

Preface and Acknowledgements		vi
List of Captions for Black and White Plates		xi
List of Captions for Line Drawings		xiv
I	The Scope of the Enquiry: Problems and Approaches	1
II	The Mosque	31
III	The Minaret	129
IV	The Madrasa	173
V	The Mausoleum	253
VI	The Caravansarai	331
VII	The Palace	377
Composite Catalogue of Line Drawings		463
Glossary of Islamic Terms		598
Select Bibliography		601
Sources of Line Drawings Accompanying the text		608
Sources of Line Drawings at the back of the book		609
Index of Individual Monuments		613
Index of Terms in Foreign (Principally Islamic) Languages		626
Index of Proper Names		629
Subject Index		635

Key to the numbering system for Illustrations

12   refers to a colour plate

12   refers to a black and white plate

2.15 refers to a three-dimensional drawing located nearby

2.15 refers to a line drawing of the relevant monument

Preface and Acknowledgements

This book contains only one man's view of Islamic architecture; it does not pretend to summarise the accepted views of the subject – if indeed they exist. To survey so vast a field is certainly daunting; and since a desirably high level of competence across it is impossible, there are bound to be mistakes. Nevertheless, the exercise does have its advantages. Chief among them, perhaps, is that recurrent themes and patterns gradually manifest themselves and take on a more than local significance. Hence the creeping diffusionism of some of the text – a persistent reminder that the Islamic faith and the paarticular type of society which it engendered could make light of vast gulfs of time and space. One further advantage of the survey method, though more personal, is worth mentioning. It is quite impossible to maintain a steady degree of objectivity when confronted with such a vast quantity and variety of monuments. One cannot feel equally enthusiastic about them all. Accordingly – with the exception of the chapter on palaces, where the scattered nature of the material and the total absence of any earlier general survey made a sequence of detailed analyses well-nigh mandatory – I have felt free within reason to make my own selection of buildings for discussion. Often this has involved ousting the familiar to make way for the unfamiliar. In the same spirit, I have not attempted to shy away from value judgements, for to make them is part and parcel of being an art historian. Besides, they are enjoyable.

Most earlier surveys of Islamic architecture, whether long or short, have opted for the chronological mode, which is indeed how the subject is taught at universities. I have no quarrel with this method, but thought it would be interesting to attempt instead a typological approach, and thus avoid unnecessary repetition and clarify the evolutionary process of the major Islamic building types. In the event, the desire to do justice to the sheer scope and variety of monuments within these general categories has led me to place much emphasis on detailed architectural analysis. It has also dictated a rather piecemeal approach, involving sustained focus on one building type at a time. A by-product of this approach has been that a good deal of material in this book has already appeared in print in somewhat different guise. Architectural decoration is discussed throughout the book in the immediate context of the buildings themselves, as are materials and structural techniques. These three topics are, after all, secondary to the principal aim of the book.

My formal scholarly debts are only partially discharged in the bibliography at the end of the book. The decision to write a general book aimed at students and – yes – amateurs, rather than at scholars, has excluded the use of footnotes and, as a consequence, an exhaustive bibliographical apparatus. The titles have therefore been selected on the basis of their suitability for further reading. In this I have followed the general practice in the Edinburgh *Islamic Surveys* series, within which this book was conceived and written. To those readers who look in vain for the source of this or that statement, I can only apologise. Similar considerations have dictated the omission of diacritical points in the main text, though I am happy to refer *aficionados* to the index, where the fully transliterated form of every proper and Islamic name can be ascertained. Specific dates are given in the Islamic calendar first, with the Christian equivalent following after an oblique stroke; approximate dates and centuries are given in the Christian calendar only.

The inordinately long gestation of this book has been shortened by the encouragement and genial prodding of numerous friends and colleagues, among them James Allan, Robin Bishop, Sheila Blair, Jerome Clinton, Abbas Daneshvari, John Higgitt and Bernard O'Kane. Thank you all. Special thanks go to Jonathan Bloom, who generously provided pages of valuable criticism and data when he read Chapter III in draft, and above all to David Gye, a dear friend of more than twenty years' standing, who devoted many hours of his time to discussing and criticising several of the chapters, and whose sterling good sense and feel for buildings has not only saved me from numerous errors but also educated my eye. My parents took a lively interest in the book from the beginning, and their never-failing encouragement was a constant reassurance to me. More recently, my father freely gave precious help with the preparation of the index. Further back in time, my brothers Peter and Dieti shared and enriched my induction to the architecture of the Maghrib and Afghanistan respectively; I cherish those memories. But my longest-standing debt is to my old friend Richard Chinn, whose contagious enthusiasm drew me to Islamic architecture in the first place, and with whom I first saw many of the buildings described in this book.

Special attention has been paid to the choice of the illustrations used in this book. Indeed, to assemble all the visual material and to integrate it into the text in orderly fashion has taken longer than it did to write the text itself – though it has been a labour of love. Some preliminary remarks on this topic may therefore be in order. In writing the text, I inevitably found myself consulting earlier general surveys of Islamic architecture, and I was struck by the degree to which these works tended to cite the same buildings – not simply because of their status as unchallenged masterpieces but also to make some quite general points. The cumulative result of this persistent over-exposure of a few buildings is to obscure the sheer quantity and variety of Islamic architecture. It seems to me desirable that students as well as specialists should be aware of these characteristics, and the illustrations have been chosen with that aim in mind. I have not, for instance, tried to make them merely an elegantly presented appendage to the text. Accordingly the range of ground plans is designedly wide, and should highlight the extensive options open to a medieval Islamic architect operating within his local tradition, whether that was Andalusian or Central Asian. They are intended to flesh out some of the generalisations of the text, though there was not room to discuss all of them in the text itself.

A related aim has been to provide ground plans for most – though by no means all – of the buildings mentioned in the text and for virtually all of the three-dimensional drawings. But the sheer quantity of the illustrative material (1249 line drawings in all) has made it impossible always to place the illustrations close to the relevant discussion in the text. Since the book uses a typological framework, the drawings are, wherever possible, gathered into groups – not just for ease of reference but also to allow a quick assessment of the salient characteristics of the type in question. The order of the captions follows the page layout of the illustrations (most of them assembled together at the back of the book) as closely as possible. For that reason, different views of the same building are sometimes marginally separated from each other. Often a wide range of ground plans of a given building were available; in such cases I have tried to choose the plan that gave the most information even if, for example, it was unscaled. Similarly, I have preferred unscaled plans to those whose clarity was marred by a surfeit of measurements recorded on the drawing itself, or which gave less information. In virtually every case where the drawing has no scale this is because the original drawing itself lacked a scale. Sometimes only plans of relatively poor quality were available; in many such cases I have chosen to reproduce these rather than provide no plan at all for the building in question. These decisions were not made lightly. The great range of drawing styles in the illustrations reflects the variety of sources trawled for them. Some variations of quality are thus only to be expected, but an attempt has been made to ensure as high a standard of reproduction as was practicable. Thus many published illustrations of poor quality were redrawn or reproduced by several different means to get the best result.

Ideally, of course, all these illustrations would have been redrawn according to a single convention and reproduced on a generous scale. But, quite aside from the daunting problems of time and finance that this would have caused, the resultant body of material could not possibly have been accommodated in a book of this size. After much thought, therefore, it seemed preferable to me (and to accord with the prime function of this volume as a handbook, a work of reference) to accept some loss in the quality of reproduction, in the interests of presenting as much material as possible – much more than in any previous one-volume work on Islamic architecture. The variations in tone and quality, and the sometimes postage-stamp scale of the illustrations gathered together at the back of the volume, are the regrettable and inevitable price to be paid for this decision. But the presence of nearly 1600 illustrations should be ample compensation for these drawbacks and should to a great extent liberate readers from the need constantly to consult other works of reference. In order to help readers find their way amidst this mass of illustrative material, two cloth tabs have been provided and a supplementary index of monuments has been prepared which gives page numbers for the drawings and photographs of each building. The marginal numbers throughout the text are designed to help readers to locate the illustrative material that bears on any given monument; for the significance of the various type-faces, readers are referred to page v.

The 282 three-dimensional drawings – whether isometric, axonometric or perspectival – go still further towards underlining the often under-rated but still protean variety of Islamic architecture, for the majority of them have been specially commissioned for this book and therefore present wholly new material. Many of the rest of these three-dimensional drawings are taken from publications which are not easily accessible and thus they, too, especially when seen in the context of the other illustrative material, should shed new light on the buildings and the styles they illustrate. The aim throughout has been to make such three-dimensional drawings – a type of presentation hitherto largely ignored in surveys of Islamic architecture – the visual core of the book. Over twenty years' experience of teaching Islamic architecture has persuaded me that ground plans have an arcane flavour for most undergraduates, who indeed often find them positively rebarbative, while three-dimensional drawings are readily grasped and give a real idea of the building's impact. Islamic architecture – like all architecture – is about space, and not (as is often maintained) principally about decoration; and that point can best be reinforced by three-dimensional drawings. In the captions I have used the portmanteau and non-technical term "three-dimensional view" in preference to "axonometric", "isometric" or "perspectival". Ground plans have been provided for all but 20 of the three-dimensional drawings; in most of these exceptional cases, published ground plans were unavailable, incomplete or inadequate.

It should be emphasised that many of these three-dimensional drawings should be treated as sketches (indeed, some are specifically identified as such), and that no claim is made or implied here for their absolute accuracy in matters of detail. I hope this statement will not be misunderstood as a cavalier disregard for getting things right. Even a casual glance will reveal that some of them have taken many hours of concentrated thought and dedication, and are as accurate as they well could be; others are designedly more impressionistic in character, and their freehand execution underlines this point. I wish merely to ensure that drawings of the latter kind are not interpreted (in the words of Myron Bement Smith) as "a definitive record of the monument" in question, but are properly recognised as documents for discussion, documents which future research should supersede. The varied styles of draughtsmanship in these drawings reflect the individual styles of those who executed them; I deliberately made no attempt at standardisation. Lynx-eyed readers will perhaps note several cases in which mutually contradictory interpretations of a single building have been presented in the drawings. That too is no accident; it will serve as a necessary reminder that reconstructions cannot, of their very nature, claim to be totally accurate. If the drawings make the buildings speak, they will have served their purpose.

The black and white plates, like the other forms of illustration in this book, have been chosen to emphasise the unfamiliar rather than the familiar. Of course this trend has not been pursued to the extent of omitting such central masterpieces as the mosques of Damascus, Samarra, Cordoba; but it would have been all too easy to fill up the quota of illustrations with hackneyed plates of monuments whose very familiarity has blunted some of their impact. Accordingly I have tried to introduce some surprises. A secondary aim has been to use, wherever possible, historic photographs – since these are often able to recreate the original setting of the monument much better than more recent photographs. Two major archives, those of Professor K. A. C. Creswell, the founding father of studies of Islamic architecture, and Professor Ernst Cohn-Wiener, provided the bulk of the black and white plates, and I hope that their venerable photographs – taken for the most part in the 1920s – will not only add their own distinctive flavour to the book, but will bring these archival treasures the wider attention they deserve. This is all the more desirable since the aspect of some of these monuments has changed beyond recognition since the photographs were taken.

It is a pleasant task to record my debt to all those who have helped in the arduous task of assembling this body of visual information. Various scholars and publishers readily gave their assent to the copying of published or unpublished drawings, and my gratitude to them is profound, since these drawings lie at the very heart of the book. Helen Leacroft generously gave permission for some of her late husband's drawings to be reworked for this book; and numerous undergraduate and postgraduate architectural students at the University of Edinburgh prepared between them the bulk of the three-dimensional drawings. Individual acknowledgments are listed at the end of the book, but I must single out Ahmad Antar, Farnoush Hayati, Simon Shaw, Jeremy Sherring and Andrew Thomson for their devoted work on this part of the project. Through Alastair Duncan, The World of Islam Festival Trust shouldered the financial burden for most of these drawings; the Trust's open-handed support was absolutely indispensable, and was readily given at a critical juncture. Other drawings were prepared with the help of a grant from the Moray Fund at the University of Edinburgh. The Barakat Trust made a very generous contribution towards the cost of using the negatives from the Creswell Archive, and I am deeply grateful to my old friends Teresa Fitzherbert and James Allan for so selflessly facilitating my work in that collection. I am also much beholden to Mrs Nancy Kaiser for putting the Cohn-Wiener archive at my disposal. A very special "thank you" goes to Bernard O'Kane, who has freely allowed me the pick of his superb colour slides and his black and white negatives to help illustrate this volume – would that the interested reader could have seen the ones that got away! This is only the most recent of many such acts of munificence, and I truly appreciate his self-effacing generosity. Joe Rock has spared no pains to produce the best photographic plates

possible from these and other negatives. I would like to thank him in particular for his unflagging persistence and ingenuity in devising ways of printing the line drawings to best advantage. A timely and generous grant from the Aga Khan Foundation in Switzerland, through Said Zulfikar, made it possible to illustrate the book with colour plates, and – given the importance of colour in Islamic architecture – I am deeply grateful for this help. A supplementary grant from The Carnegie Trust for the Universities of Scotland provided further welcome help to this end. Without all these kind and helpful people the book would have had to be illustrated on a much more modest scale and in a much more conventional manner. I hope they can all take pleasure in the result.

I would not have been able to write this book without undertaking numerous visits to virtually all parts of the Islamic world. These journeys began some thirty years ago and have been a source of abiding happiness and intellectual stimulus. It is a great pleasure, therefore, to thank the official bodies whose financial support have made these field trips possible: the British Academy, the British Council, the British School of Archaeology in Jerusalem, the Carnegie Trust and the Universities of Cambridge, Edinburgh and Oxford. Thanks to them, I have been able to see and study at first hand the Islamic architecture of every country (except Niger) whose buildings are represented in this book. It was in fact this extensive and vivid experience of the sheer variety of Islamic architecture which prompted me to base this book on building types rather than on chronology. Last, but most emphatically not least in this connection, my heartfelt gratitude goes out to those hundreds of people throughout the Islamic world whose kindness and hospitality have not merely made it possible to visit all these buildings but have also given those visits an unforgettable personal dimension.

I am very grateful indeed to Mrs Gloria Ketchin for typing most of the manuscript; and warm thanks also go to Mrs Mona Bennett who did much supplementary typing at short notice.

My thanks to Archie Turnbull extend far beyond the customary civilities offered by author to publisher. When he commissioned this book some fifteen(!) years ago he not only gave a welcome personal boost to yet another junior academic; he also made the project sound exciting and worthwhile, and so it proved. It is a pleasure to know that the book bears his imprimatur. After his retirement, Vivian Bone took on the thankless task of seeing the work through the press, a task made especially complex because of the number and variety of illustrations. Like him, she managed always to stay on the right side of that invisible dividing line between encouragement and importunity, and in the closing stages of production she has been consistently helpful in ways great and small. I am very grateful to Ian Davidson for so carefully overseeing the progress of the book in general, especially at what turned out to be a tricky proof stage. Gillian Waugh, the designer of the book, deserves special plaudits for imposing her innate sense of style on it, for her unfailing ingenuity in meeting the many challenges it posed, and for her solid commitment to quality.

My final and most heartfelt thanks go to my wife Carole. She has been behind the project the whole way and has given selflessly of her time and energies to encourage, to give constructive criticism and to help out with historical and linguistic queries. In the past year especially I have drawn great solace from the support which I have received from her, and also from my daughters Margaret and Ruth, who both typed seemingly unending lists of unfamiliar names. Without Carole, the book might actually have taken twice as long; and it is dedicated to her from a full heart.

Robert Hillenbrand

List of Captions for Black and White Plates

1 Cairo, funerary *madrasa* and *khanqah* of Barsbay, 835/ 1432
2 Sivas, Çifte Minare *madrasa*, stonework detail
3 Divriği, castle mosque, dome
4 Samarqand, Shah-i Zinda, mausoleum dated 758/1360
5 Cairo, mausoleum of Toghay, inscription on drum
6 Dauran, Friday Mosque, zone of transition
7 Samarqand, Shah-i Zinda, mausoleum of Shad-i Mulk
8 Samarqand, Shah-i Zinda, anonymous mausoleum I, known as that of Ustad 'Alim. Detail of portal façade
9 Divriği, mosque and hospital, façade
10 Ardistan, Friday Mosquae, zone of transition
11 Incir Han, covered hall
12 Ta'izz, Muzaffariya mosque, *qibla* façade
13 Bidakhavid, shrine of Shaikh 'Ali Binyaman, alabaster *mihrab*
14 Yazd, Friday Mosque, dome
15 Jerusalem, Aqsa mosque, façade
16 Jerusalem, Ashrafiya *madrasa*, upper floor
17 Aleppo, Great Mosque, courtyard with ablutions fountain
18 Aleppo, Great Mosque, central aisle from the west
19 Ramla, White Mosque, minaret
20 Marrakesh, Qubbat al-Barudiyin, mosque fountain, interior
21 Marrakesh, Qubbat al-Barudiyin, mosque fountain, exterior
22 Baghdad, Mirjaniya *madrasa*, *waqfiya*
23 Susa, Great Mosque, original sanctuary
24 Damghan, Tari Khana mosque, *mihrab* and *minbar*
25 Hama, Great Mosque, *minbar* of Nur al-Din
26 Jerusalem, Aqsa mosque, *minbar*, entrance
27 Jerusalem, Aqsa mosquae, *minbar*, east side
28 Abyana, Friday Mosque, *minbar*
29 Qairawan, Great Mosque, interior of dome over *mihrab*
30 Kufa, Great Mosque, portal
31 Mosul, Nuri mosque, *mihrab* façade
32 Jerusalem, Aqsa mosque, main arch with Fatimid mosaics
33 Cairo, mosque of Baibars, *maqsura*
34 Qairawan, Great Mosque, *minbar* and *maqsura*
35 Damascus, Great Mosque, aerial view
36 Hama, Great Mosque, *bait al-mal*
37 Ma'arrat al-Nu'man, Great Mosque, courtyard, fountain and minaret
38 Qairawan, Great Mosque, *mihrab* area with *minbar*, *maqsura*, dome and polycandelon
39 Muhammadiya, Masjid-i Sar-i Kucha
40 Konya, 'Ala' al-Din mosque, interior
41 Ta'izz, Ashrafiya mosque, dome
42 Damascus, Great Mosque, interior before the fire of 1893
43 Samarra, Great Mosque, outer wall
44 Cordoba, Great Mosque, sanctuary showing Christian chapel
45 Toledo, mosque at Bar Mardum, façade
46 Mahdiya, Great Mosque, façade
47 Cordoba, Great Mosque, interior
48 Tunis, Zaituna mosque, interior
49 Cordoba, Great Mosque, exterior façade
50 Cordoba, Great Mosque, window
51 Qairawan, Mosque of Muhammad b. Khairun, façade
52 Fez, Qarawiyin mosque, façade of sanctuary
53 Marrakesh, Kutubiya mosque, general view
54 Marrakesh, Kutubiya mosque, lateral façade
55 Cordoba, Great Mosque, Capilla de Vilaviciosa, interlacing arches
56 Seville, Great Mosque, façade of sanctuary
57 San'a', Great Mosque, courtyard
58 Asnaf, Masjid al-'Abbas. interior
59 Ibb, Great Mosque, courtyard
60 Dhu Ashraq, mosque, courtyard
61 Asnaf, Masjid al-'Abbas, ceiling
62 Diyarbakr, Great Mosque, sanctuary façade
63 Konya, 'Ala' al-Din mosque, main façade
64 Beyşehir, Eşrefoghlu Süleyman Bey Cami, interior
65 Divriği, mosque and hospital, interior of hospital
66 Divriği, mosque and hospital, exterior sculpture
67 Divriği, mosque and hospital, south-west portal
68 Konya, Sahib 'Ata' mosque, portal
69 Cairo, Mosque of al-Mu'ayyad, vault in portal
70 Abyana, Friday Mosque, ceiling
71 Sujas, Friday Mosque, dome chamber
72 Ardistan, Friday Mosque, bays leading to dome chamber
73 Herat, Friday Mosque, *iwan*
74 Ashtarjan, Friday Mosque, courtyard façade looking north-east
75 Ashtarjan, Friday Mosque, *mihrab* and zone of transition
76 Varamin, Friday Mosque, courtyard arcade
77 Samarqand, Bibi Khanum mosque, sanctuary *iwan*
78 Samarqand, Bibi Khanum mosque, corner minaret
79 Bukhara, Masjid-i Kalyan, arcade
80 Samarqand, Bibi Khanum mosque, lateral dome chamber
81 Anau, mosque, east side
82 Anau, mosque, sanctuary *iwan*
83 Istanbul, Selimiye mosque, arcade
84 Istanbul, Sultan Bayazid mosque, pier
85 Istanbul, Şehzade mosque, interior
86 Istanbul, Mihrimah mosque, general view
87 Istanbul, Süleymaniye complex, model
88 Cairo, Aqmar mosque, façade
89 Tlemcen, Sidi al-Halwi mosque, courtyard

90 Yazd, Friday Mosque, interior of dome chamber
91 Uzgend, minaret
92 Aleppo, Great Mosque, minaret
93 Qairawan, Great Mosque, minaret
94 Marrakesh, Kutubiya mosque, upper part of minaret
95 Rabat, Mosque of Hassan, minaret
96 Seville, Great Mosque, Giralda minaret
97 Mujda, minaret
98 Samarra, Great Mosque and minaret
99 Samarra, Mosque of Abu Dulaf, minaret
100 Cairo, Mosque of Ibn Tulun, minaret
101 Hama, Great Mosque, minaret
102 Miskina, minaret
103 Bukhara, Masjid-i Kalyan, minaret, upper part
104 Vabkent, minaret
105 Bukhara, Masjid-i Kalyan, minaret, lower part
106 Ta'uq/Daquq, minaret
107 Irbil, minaret
108 Isfahan, Saraban minaret
109 Isfahan, Chihil Dukhtaran minaret
110 Zavara, Masjid-i Pa Minar, minaret
111 Ghazna, minaret of Mas'ud III
112 Jam, minaret
113 Jam, minaret, upper section
114 Sivas, Great Mosque, minaret
115 Mardin, Great Mosque, minaret
116 Antalya, Yivli mosque, minaret
117 Luxor, Mosque of Abu'l-Hajj, minaret
118 Cairo, Mosque of al-Hakim, northern salient and minaret, from the west
119 Cairo, minaret of Bashtak
120 Cairo, Ghanim al-Bahlawan mosque, minaret
121 Cairo, Mughalbay Taz mosque, base of minaret
122 Cairo, Mughalbay Taz mosque, minaret
123 Baghdad, Mirjaniya *madrasa*, sanctuary façade
124 Samarqand, Rigistan, *madrasa* of Ulugh Beg, side view
125 Samarqand, Rigistan, Shir Dar *madrasa*, roof
126 Isfahan, Madrasa-yi Imami, courtyard
127 Bukhara, *madrasa* of 'Abd al-'Aziz Khan, courtyard
128 Tabas, Madrasa-yi Du Dar, courtyard
129 Zuzan, *madrasa*, north *iwan*
130 Zuzan, *madrasa*, south *iwan*, general view
131 Zuzan, *madrasa*, south *iwan*, detail
132 Zuzan, *madrasa*, dating inscription
133 Baghdad, Mirjaniya *madrasa*, entrance to upper-floor room
134 Baghdad, so-called " '´Abbasid palace": vault
135 Aleppo, al-Firdaus, *jami`* and *madrasa*
136 Aleppo, Sharifiya *madrasa*
137 Cairo, *madrasa* of Qa'it Bay at   al'at al-Kabsh
138 Rada`, Madrasa al-'Amiriya
139 Ta'izz, Mu'tabiya *madrasa*, interior
140 Cairo, complex of Sultan Qala'un
141 Cairo, mosque-*madrasa* of Sultan Hasan, exterior
142 Cairo, mosque-*madrasa* of Sultan Hasan, student cells
143 Cairo, *madrasa* of Barsbay, 828/1425
144 Cairo, funerary *madrasa* of Qa'it Bay, general view
145 Cairo, funerary *madrasa* of Qa'it Bay, north-west *iwan*
146 Jerusalem, Is'ardiya *madrasa*
147 Jerusalem, Ashrafiya *madrasa*, portal
148 Jerusalem, Ashrafiya *madrasa*, Haram façade
149 Konya, Qaratai *madrasa*, interior
150 Konya, Ince Minare *madrasa*, portal
151 Sivas, Gök *madrasa*, main façade
152 Sivas, Gök *madrasa*, detail of portal sculpture
153 Tokat, Gök *madrasa*, courtyard
154 Amasya, Kapi Aghasi *madrasa*, general view
155 Baghdad, Mustansiriya *madrasa*, corridor
156 Baghdad, Mirjaniya *madrasa*, courtyard looking north
157 Baghdad, Mirjaniya *madrasa*, prayer hall
158 Yazd, Shamsiya *madrasa*, inscription
159 Khargird, Madrasa-yi Ghiyathiya: lecture hall, vaulting
160 Turbat-i Jam, shrine complex, courtyard
161 Bukhara, *madrasa* of 'Abd al-'Aziz Khan, vaulting
162 Samarqand, Rigistan, *madrasa* of Ulugh Beg, façade
163 Samarqand, Rigistan, *madrasa* of Ulugh Beg, portal
164 Samarqand, Rigistan, *madrasa* of Ulugh Beg, corridor
165 Samarqand, Rigistan, Shir Dar *madrasa*, niche
166 Samarqand, Rigistan, Shir Dar *madrasa*, courtyard
167 Samarqand, Rigistan, Tila Kari *madrasa*, side view
168 Bukhara, *madrasa* of 'Abdallah Khan, portal
169 Bukhara, Mir-i 'Arab *madrasa*, portal
170 Fez, Madrasa al-'Attarin, carved woodwork
171 Sale, Zawiya al-Nussak, portal
172 Sale, *madrasa*, of Abu'l-Hasan, covered arcade on south side
173 Marrakesh, Ben Yusuf *madrasa*, *mihrab* in oratory
174 Fez, Madrasa al-'Attarin
175 Samarra, Qubbat al-Sulaibiya
176 Samarqand, Shah-i Zinda (in foreground: tomb of Chujuk Bika)
177 Linjan, shrine of Pir-i Bakran, niche with *muqarnas* hood
178 Bukhara, tomb of Bayan Quli Khan, interior
179 Safid Buland, tomb of Shaikh Fadl
180 Aswan, mausolea
181 Uzgend, tomb dated 582/1186–7, detail of portal
182 Samarqand, Shah-i Zinda, tomb of Chujuk Bika, portal
183 Samarqand, Shah-i Zinda, tomb of Shad-i Mulk, interior
184 Samarqand, Gur-i Amir
185 Cairo, tomb of Yunus al-Dawadar
186 Marrakesh, tombs of the Sa'dians, interior
187 Rabat, Chilla necropolis
188 Zafar Dhibin, mausoleum within the mosque
189 Abarquh, Gunbad-i 'Ali
190 Samiran, anonymous mausoleum
191 Kharraqan, later tower
192 Merv, mausoleum of Sultan Sanjar
193 Bust, Shahzada Sarbaz
194 Gunbad-i Qabus
195 Kashmar, tomb, vaulting of interior
196 Qumm, tomb of 'Imad al-Din, interior
197 Qumm, tombs in the Bagh-i Sabz
198 Natanz, shrine of 'Abd al-Samad, interior of tomb chamber
199 Bukhara, "Tomb of the Samanids"
200 Bukhara, "Tomb of the Samanids", detail of gallery
201 Bukhara, "Tomb of the Samanids", interior, zone of transition
202 Safid Buland, tomb of Shaikh Fadl, interior
203 Uzgend, tomb of Jalai al-Din Husain

204 Uzgend, tomb associated with Nasr b. ʿAli, squinch
205 Bukhara, complex at Fathabad, shrine of Saif al-Din Bakharzi
206 Kirman, Jabal-i Sang
207 Sultaniya, mausoleum of Öljeitü
208 Sultaniya, mausoleum of Öljeitü, tilework in the interior
209 Yazd, tomb of Rukn al-Din, interior
210 Samarqand, Shah-i Zinda, tomb of Qadizada Rumi
211 Samarqand, Shah-i Zinda, tomb of Chujuk Bika, interior, dome
212 Samarqand, Shah-i Zinda, tomb of Chujuk Bika, interior
213 Samarqand, Shah-i Zinda, tomb of Qutham b. ʿAbbas, interior, zone of transition
214 Samarqand, Shah-i Zinda, street in the necropolis
215 Samarqand, Gur-i Amir, portal
216 Samarqand, Gur-i Amir, tilework in portal
217 Turkistan, shrine of Khwaja Ahmad Yasavi, portal
218 Turkistan, shrine of Khwaja Ahmad Yasavi, side view
219 Turkistan, shrine of Khwaja Ahmad Yasavi, doors
220 Bukhara area, Char Bakr shrine
221 Mahan, shrine of Ni ʿmatallah Wali, vaulting
222 Kalar-i Nadiri, tomb of Nadir Shah
223 Tokat, tomb of Nur al-Din b. Sentimur
224 Kayseri, Döner Kümber
225 Kirşehir, tomb of Melik Ghazi
226 Cairo, Sabʿa Banat
227 Aswan, *mashbad*
228 Cairo, tombs of al-Jaʿfari (foreground) and Sayyida ʿAtiqa
229 Cairo, aerial view of Mamluk tombs (lower centre: *khanqah* of Faraj b. Barquq; upper centre: Mosque of Sultan Inal; top right: tomb of Qansub Abu Saʿid; bottom left: tomb of Jani Bay al-Ashrafi)
230 Cairo, tomb of Toghay
231 Cairo, tomb of Yunus al-Dawadar, interior
232 Cairo, tomb of the ʿAbbasid caliphs, niche and window
233 Cairo, tomb of Sultan al-Salih Najm al-Din
234 Damascus, *madrasa* and mausoleum of ʿIzz al-Din
235 Damascus, tomb of Shaikh ʿAli al-Faranthi, zone of transition
236 Aleppo, tomb of Khair Bay (Jamiʿ Shaikh ʿAli Shatila)
237 Damascus, *madrasa* and mausoleum of Nur al-Din, interior of *muqarnas* dome
238 Imam Dur, tomb of Muslim b. Quraish
239 Imam Dur, tomb of Muslim b. Quraish, interior
240 Baghdad, tomb known as that of Sitt Zubaida
241 Cairo, funerary complex of Sultan Qalaʾun, interior of mausoleum
242 Maʿarrat al-Nuʿman, caravansarai, courtyard
243 Aleppo, Khan Utchan, portal
244 Cairo, *wakala* of Qaʾit Bay at Bab al-Nasr
245 Urfa, Khan Shifta, gateway
246 Ribat-i Malik, portal
247 Ribat-i Sharaf, courtyard
248 Ribat-i Sharaf, interior, detail
249 Ribat-i Sipanj, main façade
250 Sultan Han near Kayseri, courtyard with mosque
251 Sultan Han near Kayseri, main façade
252 Qaratai Han, portal
253 Cairo, Khah al-Khalili, vaulting
254 Damascus, Süleyman Pasha *khan*, interior
255 Damascus, Asʿad Pasha *khan*, interior
256 Fez, Funduq, al-Titwaniyin, courtyard
257 Cairo, *wakala, sabil* and *sabil kuttab* of Qaʿit Bay near al-Azhar
258 Cairo, *wakala* complex of Qaʿit Bay near al-Azhar
259 Aleppo, Khan al-Sabun, courtyard
260 Aleppo, Khan al-Wazir, gateway
261 Aleppo, Khan al-Sabun, window over entrance
262 Baghdad, Khan Mirjan, corbels for interior gallery
263 Baghdad, Khan Mirjan, main façade
264 Baghdad, Khan Mirjan, interior
265 Baghdad, Khan Mirjan, general view
266 Sin, caravansarai, lateral façade
267 Zaʿfaraniya, caravansarai, vaulted passage
268 Sangbast, caravansarai
269 Bisutun, caravansarai, entrance complex from courtyard
270 Gaz, caravansarai, courtyard
271 Incir Han, general view
272 Shahr-i Sabz, Aq Saray, main portal, detail
273 Shahr-i Sabz, Aq Saray, main portal, upper part
274 Mshatta, façade, detail
275 Mshatta, royal quarters
276 Ctesipon, palace
277 Ukhaidir, aerial view
278 Ukhaidir, east façade
279 Ukhaidir, vault
280 Samarra, stucco, Style 1
281 Samarra, stucco, Style 2
282 Samarra, stucco, Style 3
283 Samarra, Jausaq al-Khaqani, Bab al-ʿAmma
284 Samarra, Qasr al-ʿAshiq
285 Lashkar-i Bazar area, arch at Bust
286 Mosul, Qara Saray
287 Sinjar, niche
288 Shahr-i Sabz, Aq Saray, main portal
289 Shahr-i Sabz, Aq Saray, main portal, rear view
290 Shahr-i Sabz, Aq Saray, main portal, detail
291 Naʾin, palace, vaulting
292 Isfahan, Hasht Bihisht, entrance façade
293 Isfahan, Chihil Sutun, fresco of a royal audience
294 Cairo, palace of Yashbak, vaulting
295 Cairo, Sikkat al-Mardani or house of Qaʿit Bay
296 Jerusalem, palace of Sitt Tunshuq
297 Madinat al-Zahra, Dar al-Mulk, audience hall
298 Granada, Alhambra, Court of the Lions
299 Granada, Alhambra, Court of the Lions, north façade
300 Granada, Alhambra, Hall of the Abencerrajes, *muqarnas*
301 Granada, Generalife, garden
302 Istanbul, Topkapi Saray, Baghdad Kiosk

List of Captions for Line Drawings

1.1 Map of the Islamic world.
1.2 Chronological chart of the Islamic dynasties.
2.1 Merv, mausoleum of Sultan Sanjar, brickwork.
2.2 Turkmenistan, brick joint plugs, 11th–12th centuries.
2.3 Merv, mausoleum of Muhammad b. Zaid, brickwork.
2.4 Typical medieval mosque, three-dimensional cutaway schema.
2.5 Transept mosque, three-dimensional schema.
2.6 Medina, Umayyad *minbar*, reconstruction.
2.7 Rusafa, mosque, diagram showing visibility of *mihrab*.
2.8 Typical early *maqsuras*, three-dimensional sketches: Damascus, Great Mosque.
2.9 Jerusalem, Aqsa mosque.
2.10 Qairawan, Great Mosque.
2.11 Cordoba, Great Mosque.
2.12 Isfahan, Friday Mosque.
2.13 The Ka'ba, three-dimensional reconstruction of the original form.
2.14 Diyarbakr, mosque of Bahram Pasha, *shadirvan*, plan and elevation.
2.15 Ma'arrat al-Nu'man, fountain in *jami'*, three-dimensional view.
2.16 Jerusalem, Dome of the Rock, cutaway three-dimensional view.
2.17 Jerusalem, Dome of the Rock, plan (scale at 1:3000).
2.18 Fezzan, outdoor *minbar*.
2.19 Persepolis, *apadana*, bull-headed capital.
2.20 Baghdad, Jami' al-Khassaki, *mihrab*.
2.21 Tinmal, mosque, *mihrab*.
2.22 Aleppo, Maqam Ibrahim, *mihrab*.
2.23 Sultan Han near Aksaray, *mihrab*.
2.24 Divriği, Great Mosque, *mihrab*.
2.25 Niğde, mosque of 'Ala' al-Din, *mihrab*.
2.26 Cordoba, Great Mosque, *mihrab*, simplified elevation.
2.27 Qairawan, Great Mosque, door, simplified elevation.
2.28 Marrakesh, Kutubiya mosque, first *mihrab*.
2.29 Marrakesh, Kutubiya mosque, second *mihrab*.
2.30 Cairo, *madrasa* of Qadi 'Abd al-Basit, *zuraya*.
2.31 Cairo, mosque lamps (polycandelon).
2.32 Asnaf, Masjid al-'Abbas, schema of ceiling.
2.33 Cairo, copper dome finials.
2.34 Cairo, minaret finial.
2.35 Cairo, typical door-knockers.
2.36 Arcades in a hypostyle mosque, three-dimensional sketches: Parallel to the *qibla* wall.
2.37 Perpendicular to the *qibla* wall.
2.38 Converging arcades in both directions.
2.39 Mesopotamian mosques, plans: Kufa, as rebuilt in 50/670.
2.40 Harran.
2.41 Wasit.
2.42 Raqqa.
2.43 Baghdad: A, 192/807.
2.44 Baghdad: B, 260/873–4.
2.45 Kufa, Great Mosque and *dar al-imara*, plan.
2.46 Hama, Great Mosque, modern state.
2.47 Kufa, Great Mosque in its original form, plan.

2.48 Kufa, Great Mosque in its original form, cutaway three-dimensional view.
2.49 Abu Dulaf, Great Mosque, palatial suite of the Caliph al-Mutawakkil, cutaway three-dimensional view.
2.50 Samarra, Great Mosque, plan.
2.51 Samarra, Great Mosque, three-dimensional view.
2.52 Medina, House of the Prophet, first state, plan.
2.53 Medina, House of the Prophet, second state, plan.
2.54 Medina, House of the Prophet, three-dimensional view.
2.55 Umayyad mosques, schemata: Kufa.
2.56 Medina.
2.57 Harran.
2.58 Damascus.
2.59 Rusafa.
2.60 Aleppo.
2.61 Hama.
2.62 Busra.
2.63 Jerusalem.
2.64 Cordoba.
2.65 Medina, Mosque of the Prophet as rebuilt by al-Walid I: two interpretations.
2.66 Medina, Mosque of the Prophet as rebuilt by al-Walid I, three-dimensional view.
2.67 Hama, Great Mosque, Umayyad state, plan.
2.68 Damascus, Great Mosque, plan.
2.69 Damascus, *temenos* at the time of the Muslim conquest, reconstructed three-dimensional view.
2.70 Damascus, Great Mosque, three-dimensional view.
2.71 Damascus, Great Mosque, decoration of west *riwaq*.
2.72 Busra, Umayyad mosque, reconstructed plan.
2.73 Jarash, Umayyad mosque.
2.74 Cordoba, Great Mosque, scheme of its development at the end of the 10th century.
2.75 Jerusalem, Aqsa mosque, plan.
2.76 Jersualem, Aqsa mosque, three-dimensional view.
2.77 Cordoba, Great Mosque, present state, plan.
2.78 Cordoba, Great Mosque, original state.
2.79 Cordoba, Great Mosque, sketch cutaway three-dimensional view.
2.80 Cordoba, Great Mosque, area of *mihrab* and *maqsura*, plan and section.
2.81 Cordoba, Great Mosque, *sabat* of 'Abdallah, reconstruction.
2.82 Cordoba, Great Mosque, *sabat* of al-Hakam II, plan and reconstruction.
2.83 Cordoba, Great Mosque, arch systems.
2.84 Cordoba, Great Mosque, arcade, elevation.
2.85 Toledo, mosque at Bab Mardum, plan.
2.86 Toledo, mosque at Bab Mardum, vaults.
2.87 Toledo, mosque at Bab Mardum, south-west façade, elevation.
2.88 Egyptian mosques, plans to same scale (1:3000): Cairo, mosque of 'Amr, first rebuilding.
2.89 Cairo, mosque of Ibn Tulun.
2.90 Cairo, mosque of al-Hakim.
2.91 Cairo, mosque of al-Azhar, original state.

2.92 Cairo, mosque of al-Azhar, extension c. 700/1300.
2.93 Cairo, mosque of Ibn Tulun, sketch three-dimensional view.
2.94 Cairo, mosque of al-Hakim, three-dimensional view.
2.95 Cairo, mosque of al-Azhar, façade of sanctuary, elevation.
2.96 Cairo, mosque of Baibars, plan.
2.97 Cairo, mosque of Baibars, three-dimensional view.
2.98 Cairo, mosque of al-Aqmar, plan.
2.99 Cairo, mosque of al-Salih Tala'i', plan.
2.100 Maghribi mosques of T-shaped form: Tinmal.
2.101 Tlemcen, Mansura mosque.
2.102 Algiers, Friday Mosque.
2.103 Marrakesh, mosque of Ben Salih, plan.
2.104 Tunis, mosque of the Qsar, plan.
2.105 Tinmal, mosque, reconstructed three-dimensional view.
2.106 Marrakesh, mosque of the Qasba, plan.
2.107 Tunis, Great Mosque, plan.
2.108 Arab mosques, plans: Abu Dulaf, Great Mosque.
2.109 Tlemcen, Great Mosque.
2.110 Sfax, Great Mosque.
2.111 Fez, Qarawiyin mosque.
2.112 Fez, Qarawiyin mosque, three-dimensional view.
2.113 Rabat, mosque of al-Hassan, plan, proposed reconstruction.
2.114 Rabat, mosque of al-Hassan, three-dimensional view.
2.115 Seville, Great Mosque.
2.116 Rabat, mosque of al-Hassan, present state.
2.117 Taza, Great Mosque, first state, c. 537/1142.
2.118 Marrakesh, second Kutubiya mosque, c. 540–56/1146–62.
2.119 Fez, Jami' al-Andalus.
2.120 Taza, Great Mosque, second state, 692/1292.
2.121 Taza, Great Mosque, sketch three-dimensional view.
2.122 Fas al-Jadid, Jami' Hamra'.
2.123 Tlemcen, al-'Ubbad mosque.
2.124 Bône, mosque of Sidi Bu Marwan, plan.
2.125 Madinat al-Zahra, Great Mosque, plan.
2.126 Madinat al-Zahra, Great Mosque, three-dimensional view.
2.127 Marrakesh, Qubbat al-Barudiyin, mosque fountain, plan.
2.128 Marrakesh, Qubbat al-Barudiyin, mosque fountain, three-dimensional view.
2.129 Marrakesh, Qubbat al-Barudiyin, cutaway three-dimensional view.
2.130 Qal'a of the Banu Hammad, mosque, plan.
2.131 Axial naves in Arab mosques, plans: Damascus, Great Mosque.
2.132 Cordoba, Great Mosque.
2.133 Qairawan, Great Mosque.
2.134 Jerusalem, Aqsa mosque.
2.135 Fez, Qarawiyin mosque.
2.136 Qairawan, Great Mosque, Bab Lalla Raihana, three-dimensional view.
2.137 Mahdiya, Great Mosque, reconstructed plan.
2.138 Mahdiya, Great Mosque, sketch three-dimensional view.
2.139 Tlemcen, Mosque of Sidi Abu Madyan, plan.
2.140 Tlemcen, Mosque of Sidi al-Halwi, plan.
2.141 Tlemcen, Mosque of Sidi al-Halwi, sketch three-dimensional view.
2.142 Qairawan, Great Mosque, plan.
2.143 Qairawan, Great Mosque, three-dimensional view.
2.144 Ajdabiya, mosque, plan.
2.145 Susa, Tunisia, mosque of Bu Fatata, plan.
2.146 Susa, Tunisia, Great Mosque, plan.
2.147 Susa, Tunisia, Great Mosque, sketch three-dimensional view.
2.148 Madinat Sultan, mosque, plan.
2.149 Qairawan, mosque of Muhammad b. Khairun, plan.
2.150 Fez, Qarawiyin mosque, plan of *muqarnas* vault.
2.151 Fez, Qarawiyin mosque, elevation of *muqarnas* vault.
2.152 Marib, Masjid Sulaiman b. Da'ud, plan.
2.153 Ta'izz, al-Muzaffariya mosque, plan.
2.154 Thula, Masjid Ghurza, plan.
2.155 Thula, Great Mosque, plan.
2.156 Zafar Dhibin, mosque, plan.
2.157 Shibam, Friday Mosque, plan.
2.158 Dhu Ashraq, mosque, plan.
2.159 Tithid, mosque, plan.
2.160 Tamur, mosque, plan.
2.161 Zafar Dhibin, mosque, sanctuary façade, elevation.
2.162 Zafar Dhibin, mosque, three-dimensional sketch.
2.163 Jibla, mosque of Arwa bint Ahmad, plan.
2.164 San'a', Great Mosque, plan.
2.165 San'a', Great Mosque, three-dimensional sketch.
2.166 Ibb, Friday Mosque, plan.
2.167 Dhamar, Friday Mosque, plan.
2.168 Dhibin, Friday Mosque, plan.
2.169 Huth, Masjid al-Saumi'a, plan.
2.170 Sivas, Great Mosque, plan.
2.171 Urfa, Great Mosque, plan.
2.172 Divriği, Castle mosque, plan.
2.173 Anatolian domed mosques of the Saljuq period, plans: Akşehir, Ferruh Shah.
2.174 Konya, Hajji Ferruh.
2.175 Konya, Hoca Hasan.
2.176 Kayseri, Hajii Kilic mosque and *madrasa*, plan.
2.177 Niğde, mosque of Sunqur Beg, plan.
2.178 Niğde, mosque of Sunqur Beg, sketch three-dimensional view.
2.179 Kayseri, Khwand Khatun complex, plan.
2.180 Kayseri, Khwand Khatun complex, three-dimensional view.
2.181 Kayseri, Great Mosque, plan.
2.182 Kayseri, Han Cami, plan.
2.183 Kayseri, Han Cami, three-dimensional view.
2.184 Erzurum, mosque in citadel, plan and section.
2.185 Niksar, Friday Mosque, plan.
2.186 Konya, Sahib 'Ata' mosque, three-dimensional view.
2.187 Konya, Sahib 'Ata' mosque, plan.
2.188 Bitlis, Great Mosque, plan: two interpretations.
2.189 Ankara, Akhi Elvand mosque, plan.
2.190 Birgi, Friday Mosque, plan.
2.191 Afyon Karahisar, Great Mosque, plan.
2.192 Dunaysir, Great Mosque, plan.
2.193 Dunaysir, Great Mosque, three-dimensional view.
2.194 Mardin, Great Mosque, plan.
2.195 Erzurum, Great Mosque, plan.
2.196 Van, Great Mosque, plan.

2.197 Van, Great Mosque, three-dimensional view.
2.198 Beyşehir, Eşrefoghlu Süleyman Beg mosque, plan.
2.199 Selcuk (Ephesus), mosque of 'Isa Beg, plan.
2.200 Selcuk (Ephesus), mosque of 'Isa Beg, sketch three-dimensional view.
2.201 Harput, Great Mosque, plan.
2.202 Malatya, Great Mosque, plan.
2.203 Malatya, Great Mosque, *qibla iwan*.
2.204 Mayyafariqin, Great Mosque, plan: present and original state.
2.205 Siirt, Great Mosque, plan.
2.206 Diyarbakr, Great Mosque, plan.
2.207 Diyarbakr, Nebi mosque, three-dimensional view.
2.208 Sivrihisar, Great Mosque, plan.
2.209 Divriği, mosque and hospital, plan and section.
2.210 Divriği, mosque and hospital, three-dimensional view.
2.211 Konya, mosque of 'Ala' al-Din, plan.
2.212 Niğde, mosque of 'Ala' al-Din, plan and section.
2.213 Niğde, mosque of 'Ala' al-Din, three-dimensional view.
2.214 Niriz, Friday Mosque, plan.
2.215 Zavara, Friday Mosque, plan.
2.216 Siraf, Friday Mosque, Phase I, cutaway three-dimensional view.
2.217 Siraf, Friday Mosque, Phase II, cutaway three-dimensional view.
2.218 Yazd, Friday Mosque, cutaway three-dimensional view.
2.219 Yazd, Friday Mosque, original state, reconstructed plan.
2.220 Damghan, Tari Khana mosque, plan.
2.221 Damghan, Tari Khana mosque, three-dimensional view.
2.222 Yazd-i Khast, *chahar taq* converted into a mosque, plan.
2.223 Fahraj, Friday Mosque, plan.
2.224 Fahraj, Friday Mosque, three-dimensional view.
2.225 Naisar, fire temple (*chahar taq*), plan.
2.226 Naisar, fire temple (*chahar taq*), three-dimensional view.
2.227 Istakhr, mosque, plan.
2.228 Tirmidh, Char Sutun mosque, plan.
2.229 Susa (Iran), mosque, three-dimensional view.
2.230 Central Asian *namazgah* mosques, 11–12th centuries, plans: Dahistan.
2.231 Talkhatan Baba.
2.232 Nisa.
2.233 Central Asian Friday Mosques, plans: Mosque near Chihilburj.
2.234 Bashan.
2.235 Dahistan.
2.236 Lashkar-i Bazar, mosque, plan.
2.237 Balkh, Masjid-i Nuh Gunbad or Hajji Piyada, plan.
2.238 Balkh, Masjid-i Nuh Gunbad or Hajji Piyada, sketch three-dimensional view.
2.239 Bukhara, mosque of Maghak-i 'Attari, plan.
2.240 Hazara, Masjid-i Diggarun, plan and section.
2.241 Iranian Saljuq dome chambers, plans: Marand, Friday Mosque.
2.242 Isfahan, Friday Mosque, south dome chamber.
2.243 Qurva, Friday Mosque.

2.244 Gulpayagan, Friday Mosque.
2.245 Sujas, Friday Mosque.
2.246 Burujird, Friday Mosque.
2.247 Barsiyan, Friday Mosque.
2.248 Rida'iya (Urmiya), Friday Mosque.
2.249 Haidariya mosque, Qazvin.
2.250 Qurva, Friday Mosque, three-dimensional view.
2.251 Sujas, Friday Mosque, three-dimensional view.
2.252 Burujird, Friday Mosque, three-dimensional view.
2.253 Barsiyan, Friday Mosque, sketch three-dimensional view.
2.254 Siraf, mosque at site P2, three-dimensional view.
2.255 Siraf, mosque at site M2, three-dimensional view.
2.256 Siraf, Friday mosque, phase I, plan.
2.257 Susa (Iran), mosque, plan.
2.258 Na'in, Friday Mosque, plan.
2.259 Ardistan, Friday Mosque, plan.
2.260 Siraf, mosque at site P2 in its third period, plan.
2.261 Gulpayagan, Friday Mosque, plan.
2.262 Isfahan, Friday Mosque, Saljuq period, reconstructed plan.
2.263 Isfahan, Friday Mosque, south dome chamber and surrounding bays, cutaway three-dimensional view.
2.264 Isfahan, Friday Mosque, sketch three-dimensional view.
2.265 Varamin, Friday Mosque, plan.
2.266 Varamin, Friday Mosque, three-dimensional view.
2.267 Isfahan, Friday Mosque, schemata of typical vaults.
2.268 Dome chamber of typical Saljuq mosque showing squinch and zone of transition.
2.269 Isfahan, Friday Mosque, plan.
2.270 Isfahan, Friday Mosque, Buyid period, plans of piers.
2.271 Rida'iya (Urmiya), Friday Mosque, plan, section and elevation.
2.272 Turbat-i Shaikh Jam, "Old Mosque", plan and reconstructed cutaway three-dimensional view.
2.273 Farumad, Friday Mosque, plan.
2.274 Siraf, restored plan of mosque at site C.
2.275 Siraf, restored plan of mosque at site M2.
2.276 Ardabil, Friday Mosque, plan and section.
2.277 Simnan, Friday Mosque, plan.
2.278 Tabriz, Masjid-i 'Ali Shah, plan.
2.279 Mashhad, Masjid-i Shah, plan.
2.280 Mashhad, Masjid-i Shah, three-dimensional view.
2.281 Isfahan, Masjid-i Shah (now Masjid-i Imam), plan and section.
2.282 Isfahan, *maidan*, three-dimensional view.
2.283 Mashhad, Mosque of Gauhar Shad, plan.
2.284 Tabriz, Masjid-i Muzaffariya (Blue Mosque), plan.
2.285 Tabriz, Masjid-i Muzaffariya (Blue Mosque), three-dimensional view.
2.286 Ghalvar, Masjid-i Haud-i Karbas: sketch plan.
2.287 Persian *iwan*s, elevations: Mashhad, mosque of Gauhar Shad.
2.288 Isfahan, Masjid-i Shah (now Masjid-i Imam).
2.289 Mashhad, shrine of Imam Rida.
2.290 Isfahan, Masjid-i Shaikh Lutfallah, plan.
2.291 Samarqand, mosque of Bibi Khanum, plan.
2.292 Samarqand, mosque of Bibi Khanum, sketch three-dimensional view.
2.293 Anau, mosque façade, elevation.

2.294 Ziyaratgah, Friday Mosque, plan.

2.295 Ziyaratgah, Friday Mosque, three-dimensional view.

2.296 Herat, Friday Mosque, plan.

2.297 Bukhara, Masjid-i Kalyan, plan.

2.298 Bukhara, Masjid-i Kalyan, sketch three-dimensional view.

2.299 Anau, mosque, plan.

2.300 Early Ottoman mosques, plans: Bursa, 'Ala' al-Din.

2.301 Bilecik, Orhan Ghazi.

2.302 Iznik, Yeşil Cami.

2.303 Iznik, Yeşil Cami, three-dimensional view.

2.304 Bursa, Great Mosque, plan.

2.305 Bursa, Great Mosque, three-dimensional view.

2.306 Bursa, Yeşil Cami, plan and section.

2.307 Bursa, Yeşil Cami, three-dimensional view.

2.308 Bursa, Bayazid Yildirim mosque, plan.

2.309 Manisa, Great Mosque, plan.

2.310 Dimetoka, mosque of Chelebi Sultan Mehmed, plan.

2.311 Antalya, Yivli Minare mosque, plan.

2.312 Ottoman mosques, simplified plans: Edirne, Üç Şerefeli.

2.313 Istanbul, Mehmed II Fatih.

2.314 Istanbul, Sultan Bayazid II.

2.315 Istanbul, Şehzade.

2.316 Edirne, Eski (Ulu) Cami, plan.

2.317 Ottoman mosques, sections and elevations, 1:500. Bursa, 'Ala' al-Din.

2.318 Iznik, Haci Ozbek.

2.319 Iznik, Yeşil Cami.

2.320 Bilecik, Orhan Ghazi.

2.321 Istanbul, Shamsi Pasha.

2.322 Amasya, Sultan Bayazid II.

2.323 Istanbul, Selimiye.

2.324 Bursa, Great Mosque.

2.325 Edirne, Sultan Bayazid II.

2.326 Istanbul, Murad Pasha.

2.327 Edirne, Üç Şerefeli.

2.328 Istanbul, Zul Mahmud.

2.329 Istanbul, Rüstem Pasha.

2.330 Istanbul, Sokollu Mehmed Pasha.

2.331 Istanbul, Qara Ahmed.

2.332 Istanbul, Mihrimah.

2.333 Ottoman mosques, sections and elevations, 1:500. Istanbul, Şehzade.

2.334 Edirne, Selimiye.

2.335 Istanbul, 'Atiq 'Ali.

2.336 Istanbul, Süleymaniye.

2.337 Istanbul, Sultan Ahmed.

2.338 Edirne. Üç Şerefeli mosque, cutaway three-dimensional view.

2.339 Edirne. Üc Şerefeli mosque, three-dimensional view.

2.340 Edirne, Üç Şerefeli mosque, plan.

2.341 Istanbul, mosque of Mehmed II Fatih, plan.

2.342 Edirne, Selimiye, plan.

2.343 Istanbul, Şehzade mosque, plan, section and simplified three-dimensional view.

2.344 Edirne, külliye of Sultan Bayazid II, plan.

2.345 Edirne, külliye of Sultan Bayazid II, three-dimensional view.

2.346 Istanbul, complex of Mehmed II Fatih, plan.

2.347 Amasya, mosque of Sultan Bayazid II, plan.

2.348 Amasya, mosque of Sultan Bayazid II, sketch three-dimensional view.

2.349 Edirne, Selimiye, cutaway three-dimensional view.

2.350 Istanbul, Mihrimah mosque, plan.

2.351 Istanbul, mosque of Sultan Bayazid II, plan.

2.352 Istanbul, mosque of Sultan Ahmed, cutaway three-dimensional view

2.353 Istanbul, mosque of Sultan Ahmed, plan.

2.354 Edirne, Selimiye complex, three-dimensional view.

2.355 Istanbul, Şehzade mosque, three-dimensional view.

2.356 Istanbul, Süleymaniye complex, plan.

3.1 Table of 25 minarets arranged according to scale, sketch elevations. Rabat, Mosque of al-Hassan (reconstruction).

3.2 Mecca, al-Haram.

3.3 Cairo, Mosque of Muhammad 'Ali.

3.4 Cairo, mosque and madrasa of Sultan Hasan.

3.5 Delhi, Qutb Minar.

3.6 Jam.

3.7 Khiva, Masjid-i Jami'.

3.8 Urgench, Masjid-i Jami'.

3.9 Lednice, Czech Republic.

3.10 Hyderabad (Deccan), Char Minar.

3.11 Bursa, Great Mosque.

3.12 Samarra, Great Mosque.

3.13 Isfahan, Manar-i Saraban.

3.14 Aleppo, Great Mosque.

3.15 Bijapur, Jum'a Masjid.

3.16 Mosul, Jami' al-Nuri.

3.17 Cairo, Ibn Tulun mosque.

3.18 Delhi, Jum'a Masjid.

3.19 Bursa, Mosque of Murad I.

3.20 Qairawan, Great Mosque.

3.21 Karbala', al-Mashhad al-Husaini.

3.22 Algiers, Jami' al-Sammak.

3.23 Agadez mosque, Niger.

3.24 Ghardaya Jami'.

3.25 Al-Janad, Yemen.

3.26 Seville, Giralda minaret, as represented in a medieval Christian sculpture.

3.27 Fas al-Jadid, Great Mosque, minaret, elevation.

3.28 Typical minarets, simplified elevations to same scale: Samarra, Great Mosque.

3.29 Qairawan, Great Mosque.

3.30 Sfax, Great Mosque.

3.31 Marrakesh, Kutubiya mosque.

3.32 Aleppo, Great Mosque.

3.33 Qal'a of the Banu Hammad, Great Mosque.

3.34 Bukhara, Masjid-i Kalyan.

3.35 Ghardaya, Great Mosque.

3.36 Ramla: minaret, elevation.

3.37 Tlemcen, Mansura mosque, minaret, sections.

3.38 Tlemcen, Agadir, mosque: minaret, elevation.

3.39 Sfax, Great Mosque, minaret, section.

3.40 Qal'a of the Banu Hammad, minaret, elevation.

3.41 Qal'a of the Banu Hammad, minaret, plans.

3.42 Susa (Tunisia), the manar, plans and section.

3.43 Qal'a of the Banu Hammad, minaret, section.

3.44 Granada, minaret of San Juan de los Reyes, plan and section.

3.45 Cordoba, Great Mosque, minaret, south face, reconstructed elevation.

3.46 Cordoba, Great Mosque, minaret, east face, reconstructed elevation.

3.47 Sfax, Great Mosque, minaret, elevation.

3.48 Qairawan, Great Mosque, minaret, section.

3.49 Almohad minarets, elevations (to same scale): Marrakesh, Kutubiya mosque.

3.50 Seville, Giralda (reconstruction).

3.51 Rabat, minaret of al-Hassan, north side (reconstruction).

3.52 Rabat, mosque of al-Hassan, minaret, elevations: south side (reconstruction), west side (present state) and north side (present state).

3.53 Rabat, mosque of al-Hassan, reconstruction of north side.

3.54 Madinat al-Zahra, Friday Mosque, minaret, elevation.

3.55 Marrakesh, Kutubiya mosque, minaret, elevation.

3.56 Marrakesh, Kutubiya mosque, minaret, paired windows.

3.57 Marrakesh, Kutubiya mosque, south-west face of minaret, arch detail.

3.58 Marrakesh, Kutubiya mosque, minaret, interlaced arches.

3.59 Yemeni minarets, sketch elevations: San'a', Masjid al-Abhar.

3.60 San'a', Great Mosque, western minaret.

3.61 Sa'da, Masjid al-Shamri.

3.62 Sa'da, Masjid 'Ulayyan.

3.63 Zabid, Friday Mosque, minaret: plans, section and elevation.

3.64 Delhi, Qutb Minar complex, three-dimensional view.

3.65 Dunaysir, minaret, plan.

3.66 Antalya, Yivli Minare, elevation.

3.67 Aleppo, Great Mosque, minaret, elevation.

3.68 Ma'arrat al-Nu'man, Great Mosque, minaret, elevation.

3.69 Ahmadabad, Shah 'Alam Mosque, minaret, elevation.

3.70 Edirne, Selimiye, minaret, elevation.

3.71 Istanbul, Süleymaniye, minaret, elevation.

3.72 Indian minarets, simplified elevations of upper parts: Ghazni (Afghanistan), minaret of Mas'ud III.

3.73 Delhi, Qutb Minar.

3.74 Delhi, Khirki mosque.

3.75 Gaur, Firuz Minar.

3.76 Ahmadabad, Shah 'Alam mosque.

3.77 Bidar, *madrasa*.

3.78 Daulatabad, Chand Minar.

3.79 Champaner, Jami' Masjid.

3.80 Burhanpur, Bibi ki Masjid.

3.81 Hyderabad (Deccan), Char Minar.

3.82 Bijapur, tomb.

3.83 Bijapur, Gol Gumbaz.

3.84 Agra, Sikandra, tomb of Akbar.

3.85 Lahore, Shahdara, tomb of Jahangir.

3.86 Delhi, Jum'a Masjid.

3.87 Agra, Taj Mahal.

3.88 Lahore, mosque of Wazir Khan.

3.89 Aurangabad, tomb of Rabi'a Daurani.

3.90 Karabaghlar, funerary complex with twin-minaret portal, plan.

3.91 Khusraugird, minaret, plan.

3.92 Uzgend, minaret, plan and section.

3.93 Bukhara, Manar-i Kalyan, plan and section.

3.94 Jar Kurgan, minaret, plan and elevation.

3.95 Nigar, Friday Mosque, minaret, plan and elevation.

3.96 Isfahan area, minarets, plans: Manar-i Saraban.

3.97 Ziyar.

3.98 Karabaghlar, twin-minaret portal, elevation.

3.99 Dhu'l-Kifl, minaret, elevation.

3.100 Irbil, minaret, elevation.

3.101 Ta'uq (Daquq), minaret, elevation.

3.102 Zarand, Friday Mosque, minaret, plan and elevation.

3.103 Ghazna, minaret of Mas'ud III, horizontal sections at various heights.

3.104 Kirman, Masjid-i Malik, minaret, plan and elevation.

3.105 Ghazna, minaret of Bahramshah, section.

3.106 Ghazna, minaret of Bahramshah, structural components.

3.107 Ghazna, minaret of Mas'ud III, section.

3.108 Ghazna, minaret of Mas'ud III, sketch of elevation.

3.109 Ghazna, minaret of Mas'ud III, 19th-century sketch of elevation.

3.110 Ghazna, minaret of Mas'ud III, structural components.

3.111 Jam, minaret, plans and elevation.

3.112 Alexandria, the Pharos, reconstructed elevation.

3.113 Cairo, mosque of al-Ashraf Barsbay, minaret, elevation.

3.114 Cairo, mosque of al-Hakim, western minaret, cap.

3.115 Isna, Jami' al-'Amri, minaret, elevation 1:100.

3.116 Cairo, minarets, elevations: Mosque of 'Amr.

3.117 Iskandar Pasha mosque.

3.118 Ibn Tulun mosque.

3.119 Mosque of al-Azhar, minarets of Qa'it Bay (left) and al-Ghuri, elevations, general view.

3.120 Mosque of Qala'un in the citadel, minaret, elevation.

3.121 Minaret of Aqbugha, elevation.

3.122 Qala'un complex, minaret.

3.123 Sultan Hasan complex, minaret.

3.124 Minarets of al-Mu'ayyad at Bab Zuwaila, elevation.

3.125 *Khanqah* of Faraj b. Barquq, minaret, plans, section and elevation.

3.126 Mosque of al-Azhar, minaret of Qa'it Bay, plans and section.

3.127 Mosque of al-Hakim, western minaret, elevation.

3.128 Mosque of al-Hakim, northern minaret, elevation.

3.129 Minaret of Sarghitmish, elevation.

3.130 Mosque of Muhammad Bay Abu'l-Dhahab, minaret.

3.131 Qa'it Bay mosque, minaret.

4.1 Khargird, Nizamiya *madrasa* (?), plan.

4.2 Danestama, plan.

4.3 Samarqand, *madrasa* of Ibrahim I: plan, section and elevation.

4.4 Ak Beshim, Buddhist temple, plan.

4.5 Ak Beshim, Buddhist temple, sketch three-dimensional view.

4.6 Zuzan, *madrasa*, plan.

4.7 Shah-i Mashhad, *madrasa*, plan.

4.8 Rayy, *madrasa* (?), plan.

4.9 Pasargadae (Madar-i Sulaiman), *madrasa*, plan.

4.10 Bamiyan, house, plan.

4.11 Syrian and Iraqi *madrasa*s, plans to the same scale: Busra, *madrasa* of Abu Muhammad Gumushtegin.

4.12 Damascus, Madrasa al-Nuriya al-Kubra.

4.13 Damascus, Madrasa al-'Adiliya.

4.14 Aleppo, *madrasa* of Ma'ruf Shadbakht.

4.15 Ma'arrat al-Nu'man, *madrasa* of the Shafi'ites.

4.16 Damascus, Madrasa al-Maridaniya.

4.17 Aleppo, Madrasa al-Zahiriya.

4.18 Aleppo, Madrasa al-Sultaniya.

4.19 Baghdad, Madrasa al-Mustansiriya.

4.20 Aleppo, *jami'* and *madrasa* of al-Firdaus.

4.21 Damascus, Madrasa al-Sahibiya.

4.22 Damascus, *dar al-hadith* of Nur al-Din.

4.23 Aleppo, Madrasa al-Sharafiya.

4.24 Damascus, Madrasa al-Zahiriya.

4.25 Damascus, Madrasa al-Kamiliya.

4.26 Baghdad, Madrasa al-Mirjaniya.

4.27 Damascus, Madrasa al-'Adiliya, three-dimensional view.

4.28 Aleppo, Madrasa al-Sultaniya, three-dimensional view.

4.29 Baghdad, Madrasa al-Mustansiriya, sketch three-dimensional view.

4.30 Aleppo, *jami'* and *madrasa* of al-Firdaus, sketch three-dimensional view.

4.31 Baghdad, Madrasa al-Mirjaniya, three-dimensional view.

4.32 Baghdad, anonymous *madrasa* ("the 'Abbasid palace"), plan.

4.33 Baghdad, anonymous *madrasa* ("the 'Abbasid palace"), three-dimensional view.

4.34 Damascus, Madrasa al-Atabakiya, plan.

4.35 Aleppo, Madrasa al-Zahiriya, portal, section and elevation.

4.36 Aleppo, Khanqah fi'l-Farafra, plan.

4.37 Natanz, shrine and *khanqah* of 'Abd al-Samad, plan.

4.38 Jerusalem, Madrasa al-Ashrafiya, porch.

4.39 Damascus, *madrasa* of Shaikh Hasan Ra'i al-Himma, plan.

4.40 Aleppo, Madrasa al-Zahiriya, *qibla* wall, section.

4.41 Damascus, Salihiya, Madrasa al-Jaharkasiya, plan.

4.42 Jerusalem, Madrasa al-Ashrafiya, ground floor plan.

4.43 Jerusalem, Madrasa al-Ashrafiya, main floor plan.

4.44 Jerusalem, Madrasa al-Ashrafiya, three-dimensional view.

4.45 Cairo, funerary *madrasa* of Zain al-Din Yusuf, plan.

4.46 Cairo, *madrasa* of Tatar al-Hijaziya, plan.

4.47 Cairo, mosque, *madrasa* and *khanqah* of Sultan Barquq, plan.

4.48 Cairo, funerary *khanqah*, of Baibars al-Jashankir, plan.

4.49 Cairo, *madrasa* of Ilgay Yusufi, plan.

4.50 Cairo, Madrasa al-Mithqaliya, plan.

4.51 Cairo, Madrasa al-Mithqaliya, three-dimensional view.

4.52 Cairo, funerary *madrasa* of Sultan Qala'un, plan.

4.53 Jerusalem, Madrasa al-Kilaniya, plan.

4.54 Jerusalem, Madrasa al-Kilaniya, three-dimensional view.

4.55 Cairo, funerary *madrasa* of Sultan al-Malik al-Nasir Muhammad, plan.

4.56 Cairo, funerary *madrasa* of Salar and Sanjar al-Jauli, plan.

4.57 Cairo, funerary *madrasa* of Salar and Sanjar al-Jauli, three-dimensional view.

4.58 Thula, funerary *madrasa* of al-Hadi, plan.

4.59 Cairo, *madrasa* of Il-Malak al-Jukundar, plan.

4.60 Cairo, funerary *khanqa* of Sultan Faraj b. Barquq, plan.

4.61 Cairo, funerary *khanqah* of Sultan Faraj b. Barquq, three-dimensional view.

4.62 Cairo, Madrasa al-Salihiya, plan.

4.63 Cairo, Madrasa al-Salihiya, mausoleum, cutaway three-dimensional view.

4.64 Cairo, complex of Sultan Hasan, plan.

4.65 Cairo, complex of Sultan Hasan, three-dimensional view.

4.66 Zabid, Madrasa al-Sikandariya, plan.

4.67 Ta'izz, Madrasa al-Mu'tabiya, plan.

4.68 Ta'izz, al-Ashrafiya mosque and *madrasa*, plan.

4.69 Rada', Madrasa al-'Amiriya, north-south section.

4.70 Zabid, Madrasa al-Jabartiya, plan.

4.71 Rada', Madrasa al-'Amiriya, plan.

4.72 Erzurum, Çifte Minare *madrasa*, plan.

4.73 Erzurum, Çifte Minare *madrasa*, three-dimensional view.

4.74 Akşehir, Taş *madrasa*, plan.

4.75 Sivas, Gök *madrasa*, plan of first floor.

4.76 Erzurum, Yakutiye *madrasa*, plan.

4.77 Atabey, Ertokuş *madrasa*, plan.

4.78 Diyarbakr, Zinciriye *madrasa*, plan.

4.79 Sivas, Gök *madrasa*, plan (ground floor).

4.80 Konya, Sırçalı *madrasa*, plan.

4.81 Sivas, Buruciye *madrasa*, plan.

4.82 Qaraman, *madrasa* of Ibrahim Beg, plan and sections.

4.83 Mardin, Sultan 'Isa *madrasa*, plan.

4.84 Urfa, *madrasa* of Great Mosque, plan.

4.85 Kayseri area, Köşk *madrasa*, plan.

4.86 Kayseri area, Köşk *madrasa*, sketch three-dimensional view.

4.87 Konya, Ince Minare *madrasa*, plan.

4.88 Konya, Ince Minare *madrasa*, three-dimensional view.

4.89 Niksar, *madrasa* of Yaghi-basan, plan.

4.90 Kayseri, Külük Cami *madrasa*, plan.

4.91 Amasya, Gök *madrasa* and Cami, plan.

4.92 Amasya, Gök *madrasa* and Cami, sketch three-dimensional view.

4.93 Konya, Qaratai *madrasa*, plan.

4.94 Konya, Qaratai *madrasa*, cutaway three-dimensional view.

4.95 Çay, Yusuf b. Ya'qub *madrasa*, plan.

4.96 Tokat, Çukur (Yaghibasan) *madrasa*, plan.

4.97 Kayseri, Çifte Minare *madrasa*, plan.

4.98 Diyarbakr, Mas'udiya *madrasa*, plan.

4.99 Kirşehir, Caca Bey *madrasa*, plan.

4.100 Niğde, Ak *madrasa*, sketch three-dimensional view.

4.101 Mardin, *madrasa* of Sultan Qasim, plan.

4.102 Diyarbakr, *madrasa* of 'Ali Pasha, plan.

4.103 Boyaliköy, *khanqah*, three-dimensional view.

4.104 Pir Sa'dat, *khanqah*, plan.

4.105 Istanbul, *madrasa* of Rüstem Pasha, plan.

4.106 Bursa, mosque and *madrasa* of Murad I, plan.

4.107 Boyaliköy, *khanqah* and mausoleum, plan.

4.108 Pir Sa'dat, *khanqah*, sketch three-dimensional view.

4.109 Medieval Anatolian *khanqah*s, plans: Marash, *ribat* of Eshab-i Keyf.

4.110 Tokat, *zawiya* of Sünbül Baba.

4.111 Bursa, complex of Bayazid Yildirim, *madrasa*, plan.

4.112 Istanbul, *madrasa* of Sultan Bayazid II, plan.

4.113 Istanbul, *madrasa* of Sultan Bayazid II, three-dimensional view.

4.114 Tokat, Khatuniye *madrasa*, plan.

4.115 Bitlis, Ihlasiye *madrasa*, plan.

4.116 Iznik, Süleyman Pasha *madrasa*, plan.

4.117 Bursa, *madrasa* of Lala Salin Pasha, plan.

4.118 Amasya, Sultan Bayazid II *madrasa*, plan.

4.119 Bursa, Muradiye *madrasa*, plan.

4.120 Bursa, Muradiye *madrasa*, sketch three-dimensional view.

4.121 Amasya, Kapi Aghasi *madrasa*, plan.

4.122 Amasya, Kapi Aghasi *madrasa*, sketch three-dimensional view.

4.123 Merzifon, *madrasa* of Sultan Mehmed II, plan.

4.124 Merzifon, *madrasa* of Sultan Mehmed II, sketch three-dimensional view.

4.125 Bursa, *madrasa* in Yeşil Külliye, plan.

4.126 Diyarbakr, *madrasa* of Muslih al-Din Lari, plan.

4.127 Tabas, Du Minar *madrasa*, plan.

4.128 Isfahan, Madrasa-yi Imami, plan.

4.129 Yazd, *madrasa* of Diya' al-Din, plan.

4.130 Chahar Dih, *madrasa*, plan.

4.131 Yazd, *madrasa* of Mir Shams al-Din, plan.

4.132 Khwaja Mashhad (Tajikistan), *madrasa*, elevation.

4.133 Isfahan, Friday Mosque, Suffa-yi 'Umar (*madrasa?*), plan.

4.134 Samarqand, Rigistan, plan.

4.135 Samarqand, Rigistan, sketch three-dimensional view.

4.136 Khargird, Madrasa-yi Ghiyathiya, plan.

4.137 Bukhara, Mir-i 'Arab *madrasa*, plan and elevation.

4.138 Bukhara, Mir-i 'Arab *madrasa*, sketch three-dimensional view.

4.139 Bukhara, *madrasa*s of 'Abdallah Khan and Madar-i Khan, plans.

4.140 Bukhara, *madrasa* of 'Abdallah Khan, sketch three-dimensional view.

4.141 Bukhara, *madrasa* of 'Abd al-'Aziz Khan, plan.

4.142 Bukhara, *madrasa* of 'Abd al-'Aziz Khan, sketch three-dimensional view.

4.143 Mashhad shrine, *madrasa*s of Parizad and Bala Sar, plans.

4.144 Bukhara, *madrasa* of Ulugh Beg, plan.

4.145 Bukhara, *madrasa* of Ulugh Beg, sketch three-dimensional view.

4.146 Ghujduvan, *madrasa*, entrance block, plan.

4.147 Mashhad shrine, Du Dar *madrasa*, plan.

4.148 Turbat-i Shaikh Jam, *madrasa* of Amir Firuzshah, plan.

4.149 Isfahan, Madar-i Shah *madrasa*, section of portal and general plan.

4.150 Isfahan, Madar-i Shah *madrasa* and caravansarai, sketch three-dimensional view.

4.151 Maghribi *madrasa*s, plans: Fez, al-Saffarin.

4.152 Fez, al-Misbahiya.

4.153 Tlemcen, al-Tashfiniya.

4.154 Fez, al-Sahrij.

4.155 Fez, al-'Attarin.

4.156 Sale, Abu'l-Hasan.

4.157 Fez, al-Suba'in.

4.158 Tlemcen, al-'Ubbad, Shaikh Sidi Abu Madyan.

4.159 Fez, Sharratin *madrasa*, plan.

4.160 Fez, Abu 'Inaniya *madrasa*, plan.

4.161 Fez, Abu 'Inaniya *madrasa*, three-dimensional view.

4.162 Marrakesh, Ben Yusuf *madrasa*, plan and section.

4.163 Marrakesh, Ben Yusuf *madrasa*, three-dimensional view.

4.164 Tripoli, *madrasa* of 'Uthman Pasha, plan.

4.165 Sale, *madrasa* of Abu'l-Hasan, façade, elevation.

5.1 Mashhad, shrine of Imam Rida', plan.

5.2 Qumm, shrine of Fatima, plan.

5.3 Ardabil, shrine of Shaikh Safi, site plan.

5.4 Ardabil, shrine of Shaikh Safi, mosque and mausoleum, plan.

5.5 Maghribi *marabouts*, sketch three-dimensional views.

5.6 Tlemcen, *qubba* of Sayyidi Ibrahim, plan.

5.7 Rabat area, mausoleum of 'Abdallah b. Yasin, section.

5.8 Rabat area, mausoleum of 'Abdallah b. Yasin, plan.

5.9 Marrakesh, Tombs of the Sa'dians, plan.

5.10 Granada area, Rabita de San Sebastian, plan and section.

5.11 Tlemcen, *qubba* of Sayyidi Abu Madyan, plan.

5.12 Rabat, Chilla, plan.

5.13 Tlemcen, "Tomb of the Sultana," plan.

5.14 Tlemcen, "Tomb of the Sultana," cutaway three-dimensional view.

5.15 Iranian tomb towers, plans: Maragha, Gunbad-i Surkh.

5.16 Maragha, Gunbad-i Surkh, crypt.

5.17 Maragha, round tower.

5.18 Nakhchivan, mausoleum of Mu'mina Khatun.

5.19 Maragha, Gunbad-i Ghaffariya.

5.20 Maragha, Joi Burj.

5.21 Maragha, Gunbad-i Surkh, cutaway three-dimensional view.

5.22 Radkan West, three-dimensional view.

5.23 Gunbad-i Qabus, schema of proportions.

5.24 Gunbad-i Qabus, three-dimensional view.

5.25 Kharraqan, later mausoleum, plan and section.

5.26 Varamin, Imamzada Husain Rida', plan.

5.27 Gunbad-i Qabus, plan and explanatory drawing.

5.28 Gurgan, Imamzada Nur, plan.

5.29 Kashmar, tomb tower, horizontal section at crown of plinth.

5.30 Kashmar, tomb tower, cutaway three-dimensional view.

5.31 Mil-i Radkan (Radkan East), plan, section and elevation.

5.32 Varamin, mausoleum of 'Ala' al-Din, plan, section and elevation.

5.33 Natanz, mausoleum of Shaikh 'Abd al-Samad, plan.

5.34 Natanz, mausoleum of Shaikh 'Abd al-Samad, cutaway three-dimensional view.

5.35 Damavand, Imamzada 'Abdallah, reconstructed plan.

5.36 Qumm, Shahzada Ibrahim, plan.

5.37 Qumm, Imamzada 'Imad al-Din, plan.

5.38 Darjazin, Imamzada Hud, plan.

5.39 Rida'iya (Urmiya), Sa Gunbad, plan.

5.40 Haidariya, Imamzada Kamal al-Din, plan and section.

5.41 Sultaniya, "mausoleum of Chelebi Oghlu", plan.

5.42 Bukhara, "Tomb of the Samanids": plans at ground and gallery level, sections and elevation.

5.43 Bukhara, "Tomb of the Samanids", section showing interior brickwork.

5.44 Bukhara, "Tomb of the Samanids": sketch three-dimensional view.

5.45 Uzgend, mausolea, plan.

5.46 Safid Buland, funerary complex, plan.

5.47 Mausoleum and mosque types from Transoxiana.

5.48 Fudina, mausoleum of Ishaq 'Ata', cutaway three-dimensional view.

5.49 Central Asian, Iranian and Iraqi domed buildings, three-dimensional views, all to the same scale: Naisar, fire temple.

5.50 Bairam 'Ali, ossuary.

5.51 Pavilion on bronze salver in Berlin.

5.52 Sabian temple as described by al-Dimashqi.

5.53 Bairam 'Ali, ossuary with portal.

5.54 Samarra, Qubbat al-Sulaibiya.

5.55 Bukhara, "Tomb of the Samanids".

5.56 Merv, mausoleum of Shir Kabir.

5.57 Tim, 'Arab 'Ata' mausoleum.

5.58 Mihna, mausoleum of Abu Sa'id.

5.59 Sarakhs, mausoleum of Abu'l-Fadl.

5.60 'Alambardar, mausoleum.

5.61 'A'isha Bibi, mausoleum.

5.62 Merv, mausoleum of Sultan Sanjar.

5.63 Merv, mausoleum of Muhammad b. Zaid, plan.

5.64 Central Asian mausolea: typical plans and elevations.

5.65 Merv, mausoleum of Sultan Sanjar, plans at various levels.

5.66 Merv, mausoleum of Sultan Sanjar, cutaway three-dimensional view.

5.67 Tim, 'Arab 'Ata' mausoleum, elevation.

5.68 Mihna, mausoleum of Abu Sa'id, plan.

5.69 Sarakhs, mausoleum of Abu'l-Fadl, plan.

5.70 Merv, *mazar* of Shir Kabir, plan.

5.71 Central Asian mausolea, 11th–12th centuries, plans: Yarti-Gunbad.

5.72 Chugudur-Baba.

5.73 Vakil Bazar, 'Abdallah b. Buraida.

5.74 'Alambardar.

5.75 Dahistan (Mashhad-i Misriyan), mausolea, plans: Mausoleum No. 1.

5.76 Mausoleum No. 2.

5.77 Mausoleum No. 3.

5.78 Vakil Bazar, mausoleum of 'Abdallah b. Buraida, section and elevation.

5.79 Tim, 'Arab 'Ata' mausoleum, plan and section.

5.80 Urgench, mausoleum of Tekesh, elevation.

5.81 Urgench, mausoleum of Tekesh, ground plan.

5.82 Bust, Shahzada Sarbaz, plan.

5.83 Bust, Shahzada Sarbaz, cutaway three-dimensional view.

5.84 Urgench, mausoleum of Tekesh, cutaway three-dimensional view.

5.85 Manas (Kyrgyzstan), mausoleum, plan and section.

5.86 Manas (Kyrgyzstan), mausoleum, elevation.

5.87 Urgench, mausoleum of Tekesh, plan of drum.

5.88 Sar-i Pul, mausoleum of Imam-i Kalan, plan.

5.89 Sar-i Pul, mausoleum of Imam-i Kalan, three-dimensional view.

5.90 Kharraqan, earlier mausoleum, fresco of tree with birds.

5.91 Hamadan, Gunbad-i 'Alawiyan, plan.

5.92 Kalkhuran, mausoleum of Shaikh Jibra'il, cutaway three-dimensional view.

5.93 Nakhchivan, mausoleum of Yusuf b. Kuthair, section and elevation.

5.94 Kharraqan, earlier mausoleum, fresco of lamp.

5.95 Tabriz, mausoleum of Ghazan Khan, reconstructed elevation.

5.96 Sultaniya, mausoleum of Öljeitü, plan.

5.97 Sultaniya, mausoleum of Öljeitü, three-dimensional view.

5.98 Sultaniya, mausoleum of Öljeitü, cutaway three-dimensional view.

5.99 Mashhad area, mausoleum of Khwaja Rabi'a, plan.

5.100 Nakhchivan, mausoleum of Yusuf b. Kuthair, plan.

5.101 Kirman, Jabal-i Sang, plan.

5.102 Kirman, Jabal-i Sang, three-dimensional view.

5.103 Multan, mausoleum known as "Shah Rukn-i 'Alam", plan.

5.104 Multan, mausoleum known as "Shah Rukn-i 'Alam", sketch three-dimensional view.

5.105 Takistan, "Pir" mausoleum, plan.

5.106 Takistan, "Pir" mausoleum, sketch three-dimensional view.

5.107 Yazd, Davazdah Imam mausoleum, plan.

5.108 Yazd, Davazdah Imam mausoleum, cutaway three-dimensional view.

5.109 Nakhchivan, mausoleum of Mu'mina Khatun, crypt.

5.110 Samarqand, Ishrat Khana, plan and section.

5.111 Samarqand, Ishrat Khana, elevation.

5.112 Urgench, mausoleum of Turabek Khanum, plan.

5.113 Urgench, mausoleum of Turabek Khanum, section.

5.114 Urgench, mausoleum of Turabek Khanum, cutaway three-dimensional view.

5.115 Urgench, mausoleum of Turabek Khanum, three-dimensional view.

5.116 Bukhara area, Char Bakr ensemble, plan.

5.117 Bukhara area, Char Bakr ensemble, sketch three-dimensional view.

5.118 Samarqand, Gur-i Amir, tomb chamber, section.

5.119 Samarqand, Gur-i Amir, three-dimensional view.

5.120 Gazur Gah, shrine of 'Abdallah Ansari, plan.

5.121 Samarqand, Gur-i Amir, plan.

5.122 Tirmidh, Sultan Sa'adat ensemble, plan.

5.123 Samarqand, Shah-i Zinda necropolis, plan.

5.124 Samarqand, Shah-i Zinda necropolis, sketch three-dimensional view.

5.125 Turkistan, shrine of Khwaja Ahmad Yasavi, plan.

5.126 Turkistan, shrine of Khwaja Ahmad Yasavi, sketch three-dimensional view from the south-east.

5.127 Turkistan, shrine of Khwaja Ahmad Yasavi, three-dimensional view from the north-east.

5.128 Balkh, mausoleum of Khwaja Abu Nasr Parsa, plan.

5.129 Sivas, "Güdük Minare" (mausoleum of Shaikh Hasan Bair), plans.

5.130 Niğde, mausoleum of Khudavand Khatun, plan.

5.131 Amasya, mausoleum of Turumtay, plan.

5.132 Medieval Anatolian mausolea, plans: Erzurum, Amir Saltuq.

5.133 Konya, Qilij Arslan II.

5.134 Kayseri, Döner Kümbet.

5.135 Ahlat, Ulu Kümbet.

5.136 Ahlat, Ulu Kümbet, sketch three-dimensional view.

5.137 Kayseri, mausoleum of 'Ali b. Ja'far, plan.

5.138 Ahalt, mausoleum of Bayindir, plan.

5.139 Gevaş, mausoleum, plan.

5.140 Tokat, tomb of Nur al-Din b. Sentimur, plan.

5.141 Tercan, mausoleum of Mama Khatun, plan.

5.142 Tercan, mausoleum of Mama Khatun, sketch three-dimensional view.

5.143 Ottoman mausolea, plans: Iznik, Khair al-Din Pasha.

5.144 Bursa, Bayazid Yildirim.

5.145 Bursa, Yeşil Türbe.

5.146 Bursa, Murad II.

5.147 Istanbul, Mahmud Pasha.

5.148 Istanbul, Süleyman the Magnificent.

5.149 Istanbul, Selim II.

5.150 Istanbul, Barbaros.

5.151 Bursa, Yeşil Türbe, cutaway three-dimensional view.

5.152 Tagisken, ancient Turkic mausolea, sketch three-dimensional view.

5.153 Ani, Shepherd's Chapel, plans and elevation.

5.154 Tekor, Armenian church, drum.

5.155 Kayseri, Döner Kümbet, cutaway three-dimensional view.

5.156 Kirşehir, mausoleum of Melik Ghazi, plans, section and elevation.

5.157 Kayseri, Döner Kümbet, elevation.

5.158 18th-century drawing of Mongol tents as described by Rubruquis.

5.159 Kayseri, mausoleum of 'Ali b. Ja'far, cutaway three-dimensional view.

5.160 Hisn Kaifa, mausoleum of Zainab, plan and section.

5.161 Guroymak near Bitlis, tomb tower, restored elevation.

5.162 Khachen Dorbatly, mausoleum, section.

5.163 Khachen Dorbatly, mausoleum, sculptures.

5.164 Khachen Dorbatly, mausoleum, plan including vault.

5.165 Cairo, Sab'a Banat, plans.

5.166 Cairo, Sab'a Banat, third mausoleum from the east, sketch three-dimensional view.

5.167 Aswan, *mashhad*, plan.

5.168 Aswan, *mashhad*, three-dimensional view.

5.169 Qus, mausoleum, plan.

5.170 Qus, mausoleum, sketch three-dimensional view.

5.171 Cairo, mausoleum of Sayyida Ruqayya, plan.

5.172 Aswan, mausolea Nos. 33, 19, 18, 17, 10 and 47 (scale 1:100), plans.

5.173 Aswan, mausoleum No. 3, plans and section.

5.174 Aswan, anonymous mausoleum, sketch three-dimensional view.

5.175 Cairo, *mashhad* (or mosque or *zawiya*) of al-Juyushi, plan.

5.176 Cairo, *mashhad* (or mosque or *zawiya*) of al-Juyushi, three-dimensional view.

5.177 Cairo, mausolea of Muhammad al-Ja'fari and al-Sayyida 'Atiqa, plan.

5.178 Cairo, mausoleum of Umm Kulthum, plan.

5.179 Cairo, mausoleum of Jani Bay al-Ashrafi, plan.

5.180 Cairo, mausoleum of Jani Bay al-Ashrafi, cutaway three-dimensional view.

5.181 Cairo, mausoleum of Imam al-Shafi'i, plan.

5.182 Cairo, mausoleum of Imam al-Shafi'i, three-dimensional view.

5.183 Cairo, *mashhad* of Sharif Tabataba, reconstructed plan.

5.184 Cairo, *mashhad* of Sharif Tabataba, sketch three-dimensional view.

5.185 Cairo, mausoleum of Qasim Abu Tayyib, plan.

5.186 Cairo, mausoleum of the 'Abbasid caliphs, plan.

5.187 Cairo, mausoleum of Shaikh Yunus, plan.

5.188 Aleppo, Mashhad al-Husain, plan.

5.189 Aleppo, Mashhad al-Dikka, plan.

5.190 Damascus, Salihiya, Abu Jarash ('Abdallah al-Raqqi), plan.

5.191 Damascus, mausoleum in funerary *madrasa* of Nur al-Din, section of *muqarnas* dome.

5.192 Damascus, mausoleum of Nur al-Din, *muqarnas* dome, sketch.

5.193 Damascus, Farrukhshahiya mausoleum, plan.

5.194 Damascus, Shibliya mausoleum, plan.

5.195 Aleppo, Turbat Umm Malik al-Afdal, plan.

5.196 Aleppo, Turbat 'Ali al-Harawi, plan.

5.197 Damascus, Turbat al-Najmiya, plan.

5.198 Jerusalem, *sabil* of Qa'it Bay, plan.

5.199 Jerusalem, *sabil* of Qa'it Bay, sketch cutaway three-dimensional view.

5.200 Baghdad, mausoleum of Sitt Zubaida, plan.

5.201 Baghdad, mausoleum of Sitt Zubaida, three-dimensional view.

5.202 Samarra, Qubbat al-Sulabiya, plan.

5.203 Samarra, Qubbat al-Sulaibiya, cutaway three-dimensional view.

5.204 Damascus, Rukniya *madrasa*, plan.

5.205 Damascus, mausoleum in Rukniya *madrasa*, sketch three-dimensional view.

5.206 Imam Dur, mausoleum of Muslim b. Quraish, plans and section.

5.207 Imam Dur, mausoleum of Muslim b. Quraish, three-dimensional view.

5.208 Mosul, mausoleum of 'Aun al-Din, plan and elevation.

5.209 Iwan-i Karkha, Imamzada Tu'il, plan and section.

5.210 Cairo, funerary complex of Qa'it Bay, plan.

5.211 Cairo, mosque-*madrasa* and mausoleum of Qansuh al-Ghuri, plan.

5.212 Cairo, funerary complex of Sultan Inal, plan.

5.213 Cairo, funerary complex of Sultan Qala'un, three-dimensional view.

6.1 Tripoli, *funduq*, section and elevation.

6.2 Tripoli, *funduq*, plan.

6.3 Susa (Tunisia), *ribat*, plan.

6.4 Susa (Tunisia), *ribat*, three-dimensional view.

6.5 Monastir, *ribat*, plan.

6.6 Granada, Corral del Carbon (*al-funduq al-jadid*), plan and section.

6.7 Granada, Corral del Carbon (*al-funduq al-jadid*), façade, elevation.

6.8 Fez, Funduq al-Titwaniyin, plan and section.

6.9 Darzin, Fort No. 2, plan.

6.10 Darzin, Fort No. 2, cutaway three-dimensional view.

6.11 Ribat-i Malik, reconstructed plan of first period.

6.12 Ribat-i Malik, three-dimensional view.

6.13 Ribat-i Karim, plan.

6.14 Ribat-i Karim, cutaway three-dimensional view.

6.15 Ahuvan, Ribat-i Anushirvan, plan.

6.16 Qush Ribat, plan.

6.17 Dair-i Gachin, caravansarai, plan.

6.18 Dair-i Gachin, caravansarai, three-dimensional view.

6.19 Ribat-i Sharaf, plan.

6.20 Ribat-i Sharaf, three-dimensional view.

6.21 Daya Khatun, caravansarai, plan.

6.22 Ode-Mergen', caravansarai, plan.

6.23 Al-'Askar, caravansarai, plan.

6.24 Dahistan, caravansarai, plan.

6.25 Daya Khatun, caravansarai, three-dimensional view.

6.26 Akcha Qal'a, caravansarai, reconstructed three-dimensional view.

6.27 Manakeldi, caravansarai, plan.

6.28 Zindan-i Harun, plan.

6.29 Zindan-i Harun, cutaway three-dimensional view.

6.30 Akyr-Tash near Dzhambul, caravansarai (?), plan.

6.31 Akcha Qal'a, caravansarai, plan.

6.32 Hurmuzfarra, caravansarai, plan.

6.33 Tash Ribat (Kyrgyzstan), plan.

6.34 Zindan-i Harun, restored sections.

6.35 Manakeldi, caravansarai, reconstructed cutaway three-dimensional view.

6.36 Darb Zubaida, fort of Ummu Qurun, plan.

6.37 Darb Zubaida, residential unit at al-Thulaima, plan.

6.38 Qasr al-Khabbaz, plan.

6.39 Sultan Han near Aksaray, plan.

6.40 Qaratai Han, plan.

6.41 Hakim Han, plan.

6.42 Ağzikara Han, plan.

6.43 Ağzikara Han, three-dimensional view.

6.44 Sultan Han near Kayseri, plan.

6.45 Sultan Han near Kayseri, three-dimensional view.

6.46 Kirşehir, Kesik Köprü Han, plan.

6.47 Kirşehir, Kesik Köprü Han, three-dimensional view.

6.48 Zazadin (Sa'd al-Din) Han, plan.

6.49 Ertokuş Han, plan.

6.50 Çardak Han, plan.

6.51 Evdir Han, plan.

6.52 Horozlu Han, plan.

6.53 Incir Han, plan.

6.54 Kargi Han, plan.

6.55 Dolay Han, plan.

6.56 Dolay Han, three-dimensional view.

6.57 Öresin Han, plan.

6.58 Zivarik Han, plan.

6.59 Yeniceköy Han, plan.

6.60 Kuru Han, plan.

6.61 Şarafşa Han, plan.

6.62 Kuruçeşme Han, plan.

6.63 Dokuzum Derbent Han, plan.

6.64 Medieval Armenian caravansarais, plans: near Zora.

6.65 Vagarshavan.

6.66 Akhkend.

6.67 Aruch.

6.68 Nerkiyi Dzhrapi.

6.69 Khan al-Inqirata, plan.

6.70 Khan al-Inqirata, three-dimensional view.

6.71 Staging post of al-Manakhir near Mshatta, plan.

6.72 Staging post known as "The Cistern" near al-Qaryatain, plan.

6.73 Staging post "at the fork" near al-Qutaifa, plan.

6.74 Staging post of al-Hair, Syria, plan.

6.75 Balis area, staging post, plan.

6.76 Medieval Syrian *khans*, plans: Al-Qutaifa.

6.77 Al-Qusair.

6.78 Khan al-'Arus.

6.79 Khan Tuman.

6.80 Khan al-'Arus, three-dimensional view.

6.81 Qasr al-Hair West, *khan*, plan.

6.82 Khan al-Sabil, plan.

6.83 Qasr al-Hair East, small enclosure (caravansarai?), plan.

6.84 Qasr al-Hair East, small enclosure (caravansarai?), three-dimensional view.

6.85 Khan Barur, Tektek area, plan.

6.86 Raqqa area, *khan*, plan.

6.87 Jerusalem, Ribat Kurt and Madrasa al-Jauhariya, plan.

6.88 Aleppo, Khan al-Wazir, plan.

6.89 Aleppo, Khan Abrak, plan.

6.90 Aleppo, Khan of Khair Bay, plan.

6.91 Jerusalem, Ribat Kurt and Madrasa al-Jauhariya, three-dimensional view.

6.92 Damascus, Khan As'ad Pasha, three-dimensional interior view.

6.93 Damascus, Khan Süleyman Pasha, plan.

6.94 Damascus, Khan As'ad Pasha, section.

6.95 Damascus, Khan As'ad Pasha, plan.

6.96 Damascus, Khan Jaqmaq, plan.

6.97 Bursa, Emir Han, plan.

6.98 Bursa, Emir Han, three-dimensional view.

6.99 Erdirne, Rüstem Pasha caravansarai, plan.

6.100 Diyarbakr, Khan Delaler, plan.

6.101 Qal'at al-Mudiq, plan.

6.102 Mardin, *khan*, section.

6.103 Bursa, Ipek Han: mosque in courtyard, plans and elevation.

6.104 Khan al-Qutaifa, plan.

6.105 Bursa, market and caravansarai area, plan.

6.106 Eski Malatya, caravansarai, plan.

6.107 Ulukishla, caravansarai of Okuz Mehmed Pasha, plan.

6.108 Istanbul, Hasan Pasha Han, plan.

6.109 Bursa, Bey Han, plan.

6.110 Bursa, Bey Han, three-dimensional view.

6.111 Ottoman caravansarais, plans: Bursa, Fidan Han.

6.112 Bursa, Geyve Han.

6.113 Bursa, Koza Han.

6.114 Bursa, Pirinç Han.

6.115 Istanbul, Valide Han.

6.116 Istanbul, Kürkçuler Han.

6.117 Istanbul, Rüstem Pasha Han, Galata.

6.118 Payas, Sokollu Mehmed Pasha Han, plan.

6.119 Mardin, *khan*, plan.

6.120 Incesu, Kara Mustafa Pasha caravansarai, three-dimensional view.
6.121 Edirne, Rüstem Pasha caravansarai, three-dimensional view.
6.122 Erzurum, Rüstem Pasha caravansarai, three-dimensional view.
6.123 Istanbul, Ibrahim Pasha Saray, three-dimensional view.
6.124 Istanbul, Büyük Yeni Khan, plan.
6.125 Cairo, *wakala* and *rub'* of Qa'it Bay near Bab al-Nasr, elevation.
6.126 Cairo, *wakala* and *rub'* of Qa'it Bay near Bab al-Nasr, plans at ground floor and first floor level.
6.127 Cairo, *wakala* and *rub'* of al-Ghuri, plan at ground floor level.
6.128 Cairo, *wakala* and *rub'* of al-Ghuri, fourth floor plan.
6.129 Cairo, *wakala* and *rub'* of al-Ghuri, three-dimensional view.
6.130 Cairo, Wakalat Bazar'a, plan.
6.131 Cairo, Wakalat Bazar'a, three-dimensional view.
6.132 Baghdad, Khan Mirjan, short section.
6.133 Baghdad, Khan Mirjan, long section.
6.134 Baghdad, Khan Mirjan, plan.
6.135 Baghdad, Khan Mirjan, three-dimensional view.
6.136 Khan Hamat, Iraq, three-dimensional view.
6.137 Khan Mashahida, Iraq, sketch three-dimensional view.
6.138 Mosul area, al-Khan, relief in spandrel of gateway.
6.139 Chah-i Siyah-i Nau, caravansarai, plan and section.
6.140 Tabriz road, Shibli caravansarai, plan.
6.141 Gaz, caravansarai, plan.
6.142 Mahyar, caravansarai, plan.
6.143 Sarcham, caravansarai, reconstructed plan.
6.144 Natanz, caravansarai, plan.
6.145 Ribat-i Ziza, plan.
6.146 Kuhpaya, caravansarai, plan.
6.147 Aminabad, caravansarai, plan and elevation.
6.148 Aminabad, caravansarai, three-dimensional view.
6.149 Bisutun, caravansarai, plan.
6.150 Bisutun, caravansarai, three-dimensional view.
7.1 Fourth-century Roman forts, plans: Qasr al-Azraq.
7.2 Dair al-Kahf.
7.3 Qasr Bashir.
7.4 Qasr al-Quwaira.
7.5 Mukhatat al-Hajj.
7.6 Eski Hisar.
7.7 Khirbat al-Khan.
7.8 Mughayir.
7.9 Qasr al-Tuba, reconstructed three-dimensional view.
7.10 Qasr al-Tuba, plan.
7.11 Mshatta, palace, plan.
7.12 Mshatta, palace, proposed reconstruction of façade.
7.13 Mshatta, palace, throne room complex, three-dimensional view.
7.14 Qasr Kharana, plan.
7.15 Kufa, palace, plan.
7.16 Usais, palace, elevation of gateway.
7.17 Usais, palace, plan.
7.18 Qasr al-Hair West, palace, plan.
7.19 Qasr al-Hair West, palace, three-dimensional view.
7.20 Qastal, palace, plan.
7.21 Qastal, palace, three-dimensional view.

7.22 Khirbat al-Minya, plan.
7.23 Dura Europos, palace of the Dux Ripae, cutaway three-dimensional view.
7.24 Qasr al-Hair East, site plan.
7.25 Rusafa, palace, plan.
7.26 Rusafa, palace, three-dimensional view.
7.27 Qasr al-Hair East, large enclosure, restored plan.
7.28 Split, palace of Diocletian, plan.
7.29 Jerusalem, Umayyad palatial complex: tentative reconstruction, three-dimensional view.
7.30 Jerusalem, Umayyad palatial complex, tentative plan.
7.31 Hammam al-Sarakh, plan.
7.32 Hammam al-Sarakh, three-dimensional view.
7.33 'Amman, citadel with Umayyad palatial buildings, plan.
7.34 'Amman, citadel with Umayyad palatial buildings, three-dimensional view of the site.
7.35 'Amman, ceremonial building, reconstruction with dome, three-dimensional view.
7.36 'Amman, ceremonial building, reconstruction without dome, three-dimensional view of the interior.
7.37 'Amman, ceremonial building, reconstruction without dome, three-dimensional view of the exterior.
7.38 Qusair 'Amra, cutaway three-dimensional view.
7.39 Qusair 'Amra, plan.
7.40 Khirbat al-Mafjar, palace, main façade and fountain, reconstructed three-dimensional view.
7.41 Khirbat al-Mafjar, palace courtyard, three-dimensional view.
7.42 Khirbat al-Mafjar, doorway to the palace, three-dimensional reconstruction.
7.43 Khirbat al-Mafjar, fountain, three-dimensional view.
7.44 Khirbat al-Mafjar, palace complex, plan.
7.45 Khirbat al-Mafjar, bath hall, three-dimensional view.
7.46 Sasanian pavilion (Taq-i Taqdis?) on bronze salver in Berlin, Museum für Islamische Kunst.
7.47 'Amman, palace, plan.
7.48 'Amman, palace: *bait*, cutaway three-dimensional view.
7.49 Sasanian pavilion (Taq-i Taqdis?), proposed reconstruction and plan deduced from the Berlin salver.
7.50 'Amman, reconstructed plan of palace.
7.51 Ctesiphon, Taq-i Kisra, reconstructed elevation.
7.52 Ctesiphon, Taq-i Kisra, plan.
7.53 Firuzabad, palace, plan.
7.54 Firuzabad, palace, three-dimensional view.
7.55 Damghan, Sasanian building, plan.
7.56 Qasr-i Shirin, 'Imarat-i Khusrau, reconstructed three-dimensional view.
7.57 Qal'a-yi Zahhak, Parthian (?) pavilion, plan.
7.58 Qal'a-yi Zahhak, Parthian (?) pavilion, sketch three-dimensional view.
7.59 Qasr-i Shirin, 'Imarat-i Khusrau, plan.
7.60 Ukhaidir, plan of entire enclosure.
7.61 Baghdad, Round City of al-Mansur, plan (after Grabar).
7.62 'Atshan, stopover, plan.
7.63 'Atshan, stopover, three-dimensional view.
7.64 Jayy (Isfahan), reconstructed schema of Round City.
7.65 Ukhaidir, palace, central tract, plan.
7.66 Ukhaidir, palace, three-dimensional view.

7.67 Baghdad, Round City of al-Mansur, plan (after Herzfeld).

7.68 Sabra/al-Mansuriya, hypothetical site plan of the city.

7.69 Samarra, Qasr al-Jiss, plan.

7.70 Samarra, site plan.

7.71 Uskaf Bani Junaid, palace, plan.

7.72 Samarra, al-Istabulat, palace, plan.

7.73 Samarra, Qasr al-'Ashiq, plan.

7.74 Samarra, Balkuwara palace, plan.

7.75 Samarra, Balkuwara palace, reconstruction of main part, sketch three-dimensional view.

7.76 Samarra, Jausaq al-Khaqani, palace, plan.

7.77 Samarra, Jausaq al-Khaqani, three-dimensional sketch.

7.78 Raqqa, palace G, plan.

7.79 Raqqa, palace B, plan.

7.80 Tulul al-Sha'iba, palace, plan.

7.81 Raqqa, palace D, plan.

7.82 Darb Zubaida, residential unit at al-Hamra', plan.

7.83 Darb Zubaida, residential unit at al-Shahuf, plan.

7.84 Berkut Qal'a, Khwarizm, donjon, three-dimensional view.

7.85 Afrasiyab, palatial building, section of dome, reconstruction.

7.86 Merv area, palatial houses, 11th–12th centuries, plans.

7.87 Merv area, palatial houses, elevations.

7.88 Shirdak Beg castle, Kyrgyzstan, post-6th century A.D., three-dimensional view.

7.89 Moyuncur Qaghan (Uighur *ordu*), three-dimensional view.

7.90 Merv, Saljuq palace, plan.

7.91 Varakhsha, palace, three-dimensional reconstruction.

7.92 Merv area, palatial houses, 9th–11th centuries, plans.

7.93 Merv, kiosk, plan.

7.94 Merv area, Haram kiosk, plan.

7.95 Merv, Dar al-Imara, reconstructed plan.

7.96 Lashkar-i Bazar, simplified site plan.

7.97 Lashkar-i Bazar, Central Palace, cutaway three-dimensional view.

7.98 Lashkar-i Bazar, Northern Palace, plan.

7.99 Lashkar-i Bazar, Central Palace, plan and section.

7.100 Lashkar-i Bazar, garden, central pavilion, plan.

7.101 Lashkar-i Bazar, Southern Palace, plan.

7.102 Ghazna, palace of Mas'ud III, plan.

7.103 Tirmidh, Regent's Palace, site plan.

7.104 Kayqubadiye, smaller kiosk, plan.

7.105 Raqqa, Qasr al-Banat, plan.

7.106 Tirmidh, Regent's Palace, ceremonial *iwan*, plan.

7.107 Tirmidh, Kirk-Kiz, plans at ground floor and first floor level.

7.108 Qal'a-yi Dukhtar, Abaghlu area, palatial pavilion, plan.

7.109 Qal'a-yi Dukhtar, Abaghlu area, palatial pavilion, cutaway three-dimensional view.

7.110 Merv area, Sultan Qal'a kiosk, plan.

7.111 Kayqubadiye, larger kiosk, plan.

7.112 Kayqubadiye, kiosk by the lake, plan.

7.113 Qubadabad, palaces, site plan.

7.114 Qubadabad, Lesser Palace, plan.

7.115 Diyarbakr, Artuqid palace, plan.

7.116 Konya, Saljuq kiosk built into the castle wall, sketch three-dimensional view.

7.117 Qubadabad, Great Palace, plan.

7.118 Qubadabad, Great Palace, sketch three-dimensional view.

7.119 Erkilet (near Kayseri), kiosk of Hizr Ilyas, plan.

7.120 Kayseri area, Haidar Bey kiosk, plan.

7.121 Konya, Saljuq kiosk built into the castle wall, plan.

7.122 Mardin, Firdaus palace, plan.

7.123 Jerusalem, Dar al-Sitt Tunshuq, plan.

7.124 Aleppo, citadel, palace of al-Malik al-'Aziz, plan and elevation of portal.

7.125 Aleppo, Matbakh al-'Ajami, plan.

7.126 Jerusalem, Dar al-Sitt Tunshuq, three-dimensional view.

7.127 Aleppo, citadel, palace of al-Malik al-'Aziz, plan.

7.128 Takht-i Sulaiman, plan.

7.129 Takht-i Sulaiman, palace, south octagon, section.

7.130 Shahr-i Sabz, Ak Saray palace, plan of portal.

7.131 Takht-i Sulaiman, reconstruction of *muqarnas* vault, three-dimensional view.

7.132 Nardaran, palatial pavilion, plan and section.

7.133 Isfahan, 'Ali Qapu, three-dimensional view.

7.134 Baku, palace of the Shirvanshahs, three-dimensional view.

7.135 Baku, palace of the Shirvanshahs, plan.

7.136 Baku, palace of the Shirvanshahs, *divan khana*, plan.

7.137 Baku, palace of the Shirvanshahs, *divan khana*, section.

7.138 Baku, palace of the Shirvanshahs, *divan khana*, plan of entrance portal.

7.139 Isfahan, 'Ali Qapu, plan.

7.140 Isfahan, Hasht Bihisht, plan.

7.141 Isfahan, Hasht Bihisht, three-dimensional view.

7.142 Isfahan, Chihil Sutun, palace and garden, plan.

7.143 Isfahan, Chihil Sutun, three-dimensional view.

7.144 Isfahan, 'Ali Qapu, plan at *talar* level.

7.145 Isfahan, Hasht Bihisht, perspective drawing of the interior.

7.146 Isfahan, Chihil Sutun, plan.

7.147 Isfahan, palace precinct, reconstructed plan.

7.148 Safid Ab, palace plan.

7.149 Isfahan, palace precinct in the later 17th century, three-dimensional view.

7.150 Ashraf, Safavid gardens, plan.

7.151 Qazvin, Safavid royal pavilion, plan.

7.152 Qazvin, Safavid royal pavilion, three-dimensional view.

7.153 Cairo, Mamluk *qa'a*s, plans: Ahmad Kuhya.

7.154 Muhibb al-Din Yahya.

7.155 Shakir b. al-Ghannam.

7.156 Tashtimur.

7.157 Cairo, house no. VI at Fustat, plan.

7.158 Cairo, palace of Yashbak, plan.

7.159 Cairo, palace of Alin Aq, plan.

7.160 Cairo, palace of Sayyidat al-Mulk.

7.161 Cairo, anonymous *qa'a*.

7.162 Cairo, Qasr al-Ablaq, plan.

7.163 Cairo, Roda Island, palace of Sultan al-Salih, plan.

7.164 Cairo, Maq'ad Mama'i, plans at ground and first floor levels.

7.165 Cairo, Qasr al-Ablaq, three-dimensional interior view.

7.166 Cairo, palace of Qa'it Bay, courtyard façade, elevation.

7.167 Cairo, palace of Qa'it Bay, first-floor plan.

7.168 Cairo, palace of Bashtak, cutaway three-dimensional view.

7.169 Cairo, qa'a of 'Uthman Katkhuda, plans at ground floor and first-floor level.

7.170 Cairo, palace of Bashtak, plan.

7.171 Cairo, qa'a of 'Uthman Katkhuda, cutaway three-dimensional view.

7.172 Ashir, palace, plan.

7.173 Qal'a of the Banu Hammad, palace of Qasr al-Salam, plan.

7.174 Mahdiya, supposed palace of Abu'l-Qasim, entrance complex, plan.

7.175 Tahart, qasba, plan.

7.176 Qal'a of the Banu Hammad, palace of al-Manar, plan.

7.177 Qal'a of the Banu Hammad, palace of al-Manar, three-dimensional view.

7.178 Sadrata, palatial house, plan.

7.179 Qal'a of the Banu Hammad, site plan.

7.180 Fez, royal palace, harim, plan.

7.181 Madinat al-Zahra, plan of the city.

7.182 Palermo, La Cuba palace, plan and section.

7.183 Palermo, La Cuba palace, cutaway three-dimensional view.

7.184 Sabra/al-Mansuriya, palace throne room, plan.

7.185 Palermo, Favara palace, plan.

7.186 Raqqada, Qasr al-Sahn, plan.

7.187 Palermo, Ziza palace, plan.

7.188 Palermo, Ziza palace, three-dimensional view.

7.189 Palermo, Ziza palace, analytical cutaway three-dimensional view.

7.190 Ajdabiya, qasr, plan.

7.191 Malaga, Alcazaba, pavilion, plan.

7.192 Malaga, Alcazaba, pavilion, general cutaway three-dimensional view.

7.193 Malaga, Alcazaba, pavilion, detailed cutaway three-dimensional view.

7.194 Cordoba, Great Mosque, detail of façade east of the qibla.

7.195 Granada, the Alhambra: the Partal, oratory, elevation.

7.196 Zaragoza, Aljaferia: entrance gateway, restored elevation.

7.197 Seville, Alcazar, façade of the Patio de la Monteria, elevation.

7.198 Granada, the Alhambra: schema of the roofed area between the Court of Machucha and the hammam.

7.199 Madinat al-Zahra, simplified site plan.

7.200 Madinat al-Zahra, Majlis al-Gharbi, elevation of façade.

7.201 Granada, the Alhambra, plan.

7.202 Granada, the Alhambra, sketch three-dimensional view.

7.203 Cordoba area, al-'Amiriya palace, plan.

7.204 Granada, the Alhambra: Hall of the Two Sisters, analysis of the dome.

7.205 Granada, the Alhambra: Court of the Lions, sketch three-dimensional view.

7.206 Murcia, palace, plan.

7.207 Madinat al-Zahra, Dar al-Mulk ("Salon Rico"), plan.

7.208 Madinat al-Zahra, palace, reception hall (dar al-jund), plan.

7.209 Zaragoza, Aljaferia, plan.

7.210 Zaragoza, Aljaferia: general three-dimensional view.

7.211 Zaragoza, Aljaferia: courtyard, cutaway three-dimensional view.

7.212 Zaragoza, Aljaferia: mosque, cutaway three-dimensional view.

7.213 Seville, Alcazar, plan.

7.214 Granada, the Generalife, three-dimensional view.

7.215 Granada, the Generalife, plan of the gardens before reconstruction.

7.216 Granada, the Alhambra: hammam, three-dimensional view.

7.217 Granada, the Alhambra: residential quarter, plan and section.

7.218 Granada, the Generalife, plan of the gardens.

7.219 Granada, the Alhambra: the Partal, plan.

7.220 Granada, the Alhambra: the Partal, section.

7.221 Doğubayazit, Ishaq Pasha palace, three-dimensional view.

7.222 Istanbul, Anadolu Hisari, Köprülü Yalisi, reception hall, three-dimensional sketch.

7.223 Edirne, Jahan-Numa Kasiri, three-dimensional sketch.

7.224 Istanbul, Topkapi Saray, plan.

7.225 Istanbul, Topkapi Saray, sketch three-dimensional view.

7.226 Doğubayazit, Ishaq Pasha palace, plan.

7.227 Istanbul, Topkapi Saray, Revan Kiosk, plan.

7.228 Istanbul, Topkapi Saray, Çinili Kiosk, plan.

7.229 Istanbul, Topkapi Saray, Çinili Kiosk, cutaway three-dimensional view.

I The scope of the enquiry: problems and approaches

The limited scope of this book makes it impossible to do more than tilt at certain issues which do not particularly belong in any of the chapters devoted to architectural types but are none the less important for an understanding of Islamic architecture as a whole. In the belief that a few tentative remarks are better than total silence on such issues, attention may at any rate be drawn to their existence. The comments that follow are emphatically not to be regarded as *ex cathedra* generalisations, since they are not based on a sufficiently representative body of material, and to present such data would require a book in itself.

METHOD

Given that the prime intention of this book is to survey pre-modern Islamic architecture from Spain to Afghanistan in its entirety, the need for drastic selection of material is self-evident. What may require explanation, however, is the overall approach adopted here. The deliberate intention has been to highlight the function of the major Islamic building types within the medieval society which produced them. Accordingly each chapter deals with a single type of building. This is a relatively novel procedure in works on Islamic architecture, which are traditionally conceived within either a chronological or a regional framework. These approaches are of course perfectly adequate in themselves, but they entail bias towards strictly morphological and stylistic analyses at the expense of a proper emphasis on function. Brief and unavoidably superficial prefatory remarks on the purpose of individual building types quickly give way to an account of how architectural style as a whole developed over a given period. Subsequent information which bears on function is apt to be introduced at unpredictable intervals, and will thus be robbed of its full effect. The crucial advantage of treating a given building type at length is that its immanent characteristics and functions will stand out from a medley of less important regional and temporal variations. It

will, in short, be easier to distinguish the diagnostic from the contingent. Thus the typological approach adopted here may serve as a useful corrective to more conventional treatments of Islamic architecture.

The need to cover briefly, yet in as interesting a way as possible, over a thousand monuments scattered all over the vast Islamic world and often many centuries apart has made it impossible to maintain a consistent level of accuracy in this book. Inevitably there will be outright mistakes, to say nothing of shades of error in interpretation. The material is too copious for any single person to be able to control it with complete confidence, and such a situation goes far to explain the otherwise curious dearth of general books on Islamic architecture. On close examination, the middle ground between a brief superficial survey and a detailed monograph on the architecture of a given period or area turns out to be dangerously uncharted. The pioneering nature of the present book is still more pronounced because its emphasis is not on chronology but on the development of building types. Hence this is deliberately a broad-brush account of Islamic architecture. In view of the limitations of space imposed by the *Islamic Surveys* series, it could not hope to be more than this. But shortage of space has been treated here more as a challenge than as a disadvantage. Accordingly there is no attempt to be exhaustive in the choice of buildings. I have tried to follow the rule of thumb that the more buildings the book discusses, the less room there is to treat the really significant ones in appropriate detail or to address some of the underlying concerns of Islamic architecture and to delineate its historical, religious and social context. A continuing emphasis in this book is to show how the monuments operated in medieval Islamic society. This generalising approach has entailed a rigorous exclusion of minor building types such as baths or bridges, and of urbanism, while the emphasis on the medieval period has necessarily excluded discussion of vernacular arch-

1

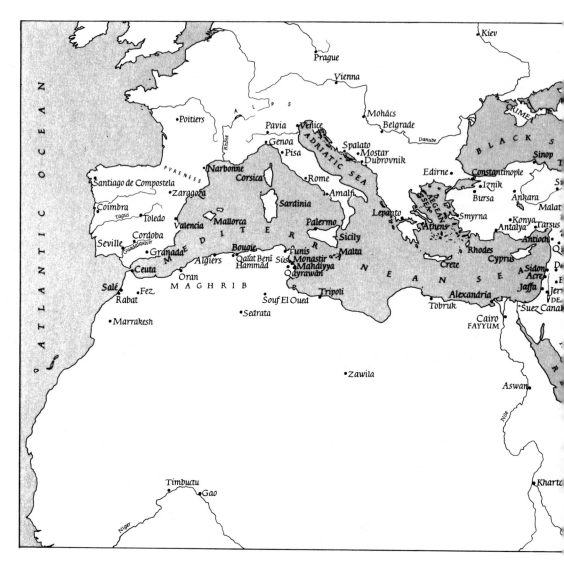

1.1 *The Islamic world, showing the area covered by this book, but not corresponding to any specific period. (5)*

itecture. Finally, the treatment of ornament has deliberately been pruned, so much so that many will perhaps regard the discussion of it here as inadequate. These decisions have been taken to allow the wood to be seen and not just the trees.

In two chapters of the book the approach followed in the other chapters has had to be modified quite drastically. In the case of mosques and mausolea the sheer quantity of surviving monuments is such that it is simply not feasible to undertake the detailed examination of more than, say, a dozen significant examples in the course of the chapter. Thus the emphasis in these two chapters shifts from individual buildings to regional trends, and from architectural analysis to an examination of the place of such buildings in medieval Islamic society. The somewhat generalising tenor of these chapters should help to offset the more narrowly technical and architectural emphases

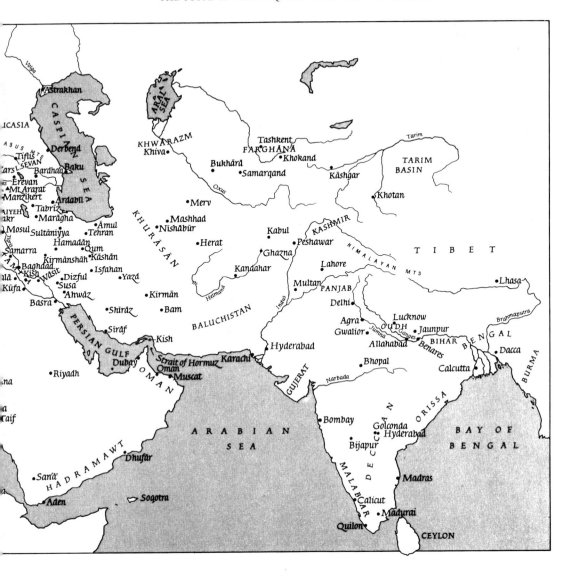

of the other chapters. A side effect of this decision is that in the book as a whole there cannot be a consistent attempt to describe only buildings of major significance. Some *madrasa*s or palaces rate an analytical account even though they are not of the first quality, whereas many unquestioned masterpieces among mausolea and mosques are mentioned only in passing. In periods or regions where examples of a given genre are scarce, the rare specimens to survive often have an evidential value which is clearly greater than their intrinsic quality. Hence the paradoxically uneven coverage of *madrasa*s and palaces–which are in any case neglected areas in Islamic architectural scholarship–as against mosques and mausolea. At the other end of the scale, the material on palaces, while not over-whelmingly copious, is yet so variegated as to require a very narrowly focused approach in which the buildings of a given period or area are

3

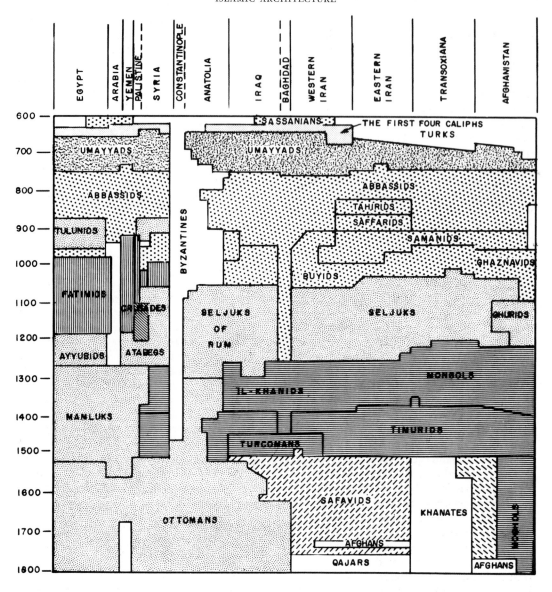

1.2

examined in sequence. So different are these various buildings that they absolutely forbid the kind of generalisation that presents itself so naturally in the case of minarets, caravansaris and even–though to a lesser extent–*madrasa*s. Umayyad desert residences, 'Abbasid palace-cities, Safavid garden pavilions–all are not only *sui generis* but also devoid of any more substantial connecting thread than that in each case princes built them to live in. Each of these three types alone–and the examples could be multiplied–ministered to a substantially different life-style.

The decision to examine most of the important surviving palaces in turn, and the desire to include examples from all over the Islamic world from Spain to Afghanistan so that if possible no area is unrepresented, have resulted in this chapter attaining a perhaps disproportionate length. In mitigation it might be pointed out that the palace is perhaps the most neglected genre of Islamic architecture, and thus an attempt to see its development over the centuries steadily and as a whole is long overdue.

The mosque lies at the very heart of Islamic architecture. It is an apt symbol of the faith which it serves. That symbolic role was understood by Muslims at a very early stage, and played its part in the creation of suitable visual markers for the building: dome, minaret, *mihrab* and *minbar* among others. Yet it is even more the practical significance of the mosque in Muslim society that explains its pre-eminence. Alone among Islamic buildings, the mosque can gather to itself the functions of all the architectural types discussed in detail in this book. Naturally, if every mosque did this in practice, Islamic architecture would have come to a full stop with the invention of the mosque: an obvious *reductio ad absurdum*. Nevertheless, it is a salutary thought that the mosque can provide a place to live, food and accommodation for travellers, and facilities for teaching, administration and burial; all this in addition to its principal function of worship. It could also serve a host of purposes apart from those specified above, and could do so on a regular or an occasional basis. Here, then, the life of the Muslim community was concentrated.

The all-embracing importance of the mosque makes it quite natural that this should be the medieval building type preserved in the greatest number. The upkeep of *madrasa*s, mausolea, palaces and caravansarais was the responsibility of specific groups of interested parties, and where their interest waned, or if fashions changed, or when they themselves died, their buildings suffered accordingly. But the whole community had a permanent stake in ensuring that the local mosque was kept in good repair. Hence it is not surprising that the sole surviving representative of a given local style should be a mosque. For the architectural historian this plethora of buildings, though in itself wholly

desirable, poses problems not encountered in the other Islamic building types. Quite apart from the sheer quantity of mosques to survive, the range of scale, of architectural form, and of style which they represent puts this particular building type in a category by itself. This in turn imposes a different type of treatment from that employed in the other chapters of this book. Shortage of space forbids the detailed analysis of individual mosques. It seems preferable to highlight the major stages in the early evolution of the mosque. This will entail what might seem to be a disproportionate emphasis on the first three centuries of mosque architecture, but there is ample justification for such an approach. The mosque was the one building type which perforce spread throughout the entire Muslim world, and did so from the very beginning. This ensured that the characteristics of the earliest mosques imposed themselves on local traditions. With the passage of time those traditions asserted themselves, but they retained the impress of the early influences. It is this factor which explains the presence of identical mosque types at opposite ends of the Islamic world. Accordingly it is important to examine in detail the early history of the mosque: only thus will it be possible to assess correctly the role of the numerous local traditions in the Islamic world. The later developments of mosque architecture will therefore be treated in more summary fashion, with a view to picking out and explaining the individual traits which distinguish one regional tradition from the next.

CHRONOLOGICAL SCOPE

Some brief explanation of the choice of time 1.2 span covered by this book may be useful at this stage. This is essentially a history of *medieval* Islamic architecture, covering the millennium between *c*.81/700 and *c*.1112/1700. Such a time span is shorter than that of Western architecture by well over a millennium; nevertheless this perspective is sufficiently broad to reveal a fairly steady progression in Islamic architecture. Some areas emerge from obscurity to create their own style, which flourishes more or less briefly. Thus it is with Umayyad Syria, early 'Abbasid Iraq, Nasrid Granada, even Ottoman Turkey. Other areas, such as Egypt and Iran, exhibit a seamless development with virtually no lacunae. These two regions are in fact the prime sources of inspiration for most of the Islamic world in the period from *c*.236/850 onwards, though Egypt gave up this role in 922/1517 on becoming an Ottoman province.

Short as this time span may be, it reflects not only the particular interests of the author but also the generally accepted opinion that the best Islamic architecture dates from before the 18th century. University courses on Islamic art are also predicated on this assumption. The medieval bias of the book means that many a building type is deliberately not followed up in its later developments. Frequently the requisite information for such a study, in the form of published drawings, photographs and descriptions, is not available. Yet even when this information can be obtained, it is not to be given the same emphasis as material clarifying the earlier evolution of the genre in question, when form and function were often still in flux. The derivative nature of much post-medieval Islamic architecture, whether it be in the Maghrib, Egypt, Anatolia, Iran or India, is readily apparent. In some cases, as in Turkish baroque or Qajar architecture, the material is beginning to attract a degree of scholarly attention; but the time is not yet ripe for a full-scale history of the last three centuries in Islamic architecture. The conscious decision to restrict the scope of this book to the medieval period does less violence to the history of Islamic architecture than might appear at first sight, since 'medieval' is by common convention a somewhat more elastic term as applied to Islamic art than it is in the West. In fact, in many parts of the Islamic world it is only as late as the years around 1112/1700 that medieval styles come to an end. Their demise ushers in a period of political and cultural decline. Islam then found itself forced to come to terms with the West, and the experience was traumatic. The impact of Western influence was as destructive to indigenous modes in painting or pottery as it was in architecture. The impact of colonialism was not only political but also cultural. Ottoman mosques spawn baroque detailing, city plans echo Haussmann's Paris, the Delhi of the Raj is re-shaped along neo-Roman lines by Lutyens. Such developments took place against the backdrop of a society no longer medieval, and of new political systems. The intrinsic interest of this long-drawn-out process of change and adjustment deserves something more than a mere postscript in a book focused exclusively on an earlier period, and a full-length study of this pre-modern architecture is a major desideratum of Islamic art history.

INTRINSIC PROBLEMS

It will be seen that there are formidable difficulties to be overcome in a book of this kind. At the most basic level there is the problem of maintaining a proper balance between the analysis of the buildings themselves and the analysis of their function in medieval Islamic society. I have tried never to lose sight of the latter aspect, but this book nevertheless remains squarely an architectural history: formal analysis is its keynote, and most of the text is therefore devoted to that topic. The sheer physical extent of the Islamic world, and the chronological span of an entire millennium which marks the parameters of the buildings to be discussed, makes that task difficult enough in all conscience. These considerations alone make it impossible to embark on a profound study of the functions of Islamic buildings in a book of this length. Yet there are at least two other reasons which make it imperative to adopt a cautious approach in this matter. The first is that a pat description of how any given building type functioned, unless hedged about with disclaimers and qualifications, would tend to give the impression that medieval Islamic society was monolithic and fixed. Yet the exact opposite is the case. 8th-century Syria and 15th-century Spain are worlds apart. Only by the crudest simplification of complex historical processes can generalisations be fashioned as to the role of Islamic buildings in their parent society, for that society, seen as a whole, was in a state of constant flux. Generalisations as to the function of, say, 'Islamic mausolea' rather than 'Egyptian mausolea of the 14th century' therefore need to be framed with proper caution.

The second reason for such caution lies, paradoxically enough, precisely in the multi-functional nature of Islamic architecture. Muslims did not worship only in mosques; they received their religious education not only in *madrasa*s: they were buried not only in mausolea; when travelling they lodged not only in caravansarais.

1 Cairo, funerary *madrasa* and *khanqah* of Barsbay, 835/1432

gradual incrustation of scholarship, the accumulated work of many generations, on which the discipline of Western art history is founded.

Nor is the problem confined to the lack of art-historical enquiry as developed in 19th-century Europe. It extends to the Muslim attitude to the architecture of the past. In Western Europe adequate techniques for recording architecture were well developed by the time of the High Renaissance, so much so that drawings made at that time are used by modern scholars as reliable evidence of vanished structures. The interest in earlier buildings that such developed techniques of recording architecture imply finds no echo in the Islamic world. There is no equivalent of the patient recording of ancient sites carried out by 18th-century European savants. The direct consequence of this late start in the professional study of architecture is that a mere handful of Islamic buildings have received the sort of detailed treatment long accorded to Western architectural masterpieces as a matter of course. Unfortunately, careful studies of the Alhambra, the Dome of the Rock and the Taj Mahal are an entirely inadequate foundation on which to build up the science of Islamic architectural history. The most urgent need confronting modern specialists in this field is a systematic country-by-country survey and recording of the extant medieval Islamic buildings, with the data being fed into a generally accessible central store.

The phenomenon of multiple foundations–for example, the erection of a mosque, a *madrasa* and a mausoleum each adjoining the next–is a formal pointer in that direction: but it was much commoner for a given building to serve more than one purpose. This helps to explain, too, the otherwise puzzling imprecision of Islamic architectural terminology. Small wonder that one and the same building could be designated by a string of descriptive terms if each did in truth refer to some aspect of its regular function.

These are by no means the only difficulties which confront any attempt to write a history of Islamic architecture, and the fact that so few such histories have been written suggests that they are by no means negligible. Some are extrinsic to the subject; others are inseparable from it. In the first category is the plain fact that the study of Islamic architecture, seen as a whole, is barely out of its infancy. It is a relatively recent field of study, and the number of serious scholars engaged in it over the past eighty years or so has been far too few. Thus it lacks that

As for the intrinsic difficulties in the way of a reliable history of Islamic architecture, it must suffice here to draw attention to only two of the most important: the number of lost buildings, and the practical obstacles to extended work in the field. Over the last century and a half the rapid industrialisation of much of the Islamic world, and a concomitant increase in population, has resulted in increasing destruction of the urban fabric in order to provide more room for new building. In the decades since the Second World War the pace of this destruction has followed a geometrical progression. Government and municipal authorities, faced with the plight of cities bursting at the seams, are under constant pressure to erode the architectural heritage of the past. According to some estimates, Delhi has lost approximately half of its

2.344-2.345

ancient Islamic monuments in the last thirty years, and that same period has witnessed the transformation of Jedda from a small town crammed with its own special brand of vernacular architecture to a modern concrete jungle with much less specific regional character. Such a loss is all the more poignant since it follows on the heels of a continuous cycle of destruction and rebuilding throughout the medieval period, a process of which echoes can be heard in the medieval literary sources. Before the Mongol invasion, we are told, the city of Rayy in Iran (near modern Teheran) had 2700 mosques, of which not one has survived. In its golden age during the 17th century, Isfahan had upwards of 2000 urban caravansarais; these too have vanished almost without trace, as have Palermo's 300 mosques. Such figures are likely to be exaggerated, but their cumulative testimony as to the prodigal quantity of public buildings in medieval Islamic cities cannot lightly be set aside. Here, it may be argued, is a quantative difference between the medieval Islamic world and medieval Europe, and it is a difference which the wholesale destruction of the buildings in question has all but effaced.

Finally, among the practical problems which impede the progress of research into Islamic architecture one may cite the remoteness and virtual inaccessibility of so many key monuments. It is often an expensive and time-consuming task to reach them and in some cases political considerations forbid access to them by all but natives of the country in question. Similarly, political factors within the Islamic world have prevented Muslim scholars from travelling freely throughout the area. The result is that Middle Eastern scholars in this field tend to know the monuments of their native countries intimately, while their acquaintance with the monuments of most other Islamic countries is largely second-hand. In such a situation it is not surprising that Western scholars, impeded by no such restrictions, should dominate the field so far as published work is concerned, and it is important to be aware of the distortions of the Eurocentric approach which can easily result.

TERMINOLOGY

It is as well to confront problems of terminology at the very outset. The architecture discussed in this book is advisedly termed 'Islamic'. Earlier generations might have preferred 'Saracenic', 'Moorish' or 'Muhammadan'–all of them terms which have long been very properly rejected as inadequate or positively misleading. 'Islamic' is both adequately wide and accurate. A simple parallel will make this clear. Western art historians, when describing in general terms the architecture of their culture, would tend to avoid the term 'Christian' in favour of 'Western' or 'Western European'. The advantage of the word 'Islamic' is that it refers as much to a culture–a culture as self-contained as that of Western Europe–as to a faith. As a descriptive term it is therefore a good deal more useful and expressive than 'Christian', even if the pictures it most readily evokes may smack of cliché. Thus there is no need to complicate the issue with such neologisms as 'Islamicate' or 'Islamdom'. Throughout this book, then, 'Islamic' should be taken to refer to both a religious and a cultural entity, and thus to embrace caravansarais, bridges, cities and other forms of secular architecture just as much as religious buildings.

'Islamic' will work satisfactorily also because, to a remarkable extent, Islamic architecture does have a distinctive quality, even if that quality is not easily definable. In this it resembles Islamic decoration or, for that matter–to borrow an analogy from much further afield–Chinese painting. That individuality is less a matter of architectural forms, even if an 'Eastern' city may most readily be evoked by a vista of domes and minarets, than of decoration. This decoration avoided figural sculpture and classical detailing, the two staples of external architectural ornament in the West. Instead it exploited differences in texture by contrasting stone, brick, wood, plaster and tilework; developed endless *2, 3, 4* colour harmonies, whether bold or recondite; brought abstract geometrical and vegetal themes to new peaks of complexity; and gave inscriptions, executed in many different styles, a visual importance vouchsafed to them in no *5* other architectural tradition. In the interplay of these various elements must be sought the distinguishing mark of Islamic architecture.

Finally, it is worth remembering that, for all the convenience of 'Islamic' as a blanket term, Spain and Egypt, Syria and Iran, Turkey and India all have their own local traditions. The differences between each of these entities can be as wide, as irreconcilable, as those between England and Italy, France and Russia, or Germany and Portugal. It is, in short, as justified–and as unjustified, probably more so–to speak of 'Islamic' as of 'European' architecture; precisely the same caveat applies in each case.

THE SNARE OF EXOTICISM

One further obstacle to the proper understanding of Islamic architecture by Westerners is of their own making: their tendency to see it as exotic. This may be linked to a total lack of interest in Islamic culture. Almost inevitably this hankering after the exotic involves a misunderstanding, sometimes on a gross scale, of the architecture in question. It panders to Western escapism rather than reflecting Islamic realities.

This exoticism is a complex phenomenon which has recently begun to attract much

2 Sivas, Çifte Minare *madrasa*, stonework detail

3 Divriği, castle mosque, dome

scholarly and polemic interest. It seems to work on several levels. Perhaps its most gross expression is the use of the name Mecca for dancing halls. The Alhambra is a popular name for night clubs, while the Taj Mahal has been adopted as a standard title for Indian restaurants. These are, so to speak, simple perversions of resonant names for banal ends.

The next level of exoticism is somewhat more respectable, but is no less the creation of a self-indulgent Western fantasy. It is an eagerness to submit to the spell of 'heart-beguiling Araby'. Washington Irving experienced it as he lived among the gypsies of Granada, steeping himself in the atmosphere and legends which he later, by a mysterious alchemy, transmuted into the *Tales of the Alhambra*. The *Arabian Nights*, often translated in the 19th century, perpetuated the myth. At the other end of the Islamic world, James Elroy Flecker was susceptible to the same enchantment, immortalised in his lines

"For lust of knowing what should not be known

We tread the golden road to Samarkand. . . ."

Traces of that same romantic affinity permeate much of Kipling's work on India, or, in the medium of book illustration, the evocative but finally precious imaginings of Dulac. Nor was the phenomenon confined to the English-speaking world. Pierre Loti, with his sensuous evocations of Grand Cairo and Stamboul, was its high priest in France, while more than a century earlier the peaceful rural landscape of Schwetzingen in Baden was the unlikely *mise-en-scène* for a passably accurate pastiche of an Ottoman mosque and a Turkish garden. The project even included a *hammam*, but this was never finished. The whole was part of a collection of architectural exotica including a Temple of Mercury, an obelisk and other structures with English, French, Egyptian and Chinese associations. Contemporary critics, it is true, found it a foolish and meaningless concept, and were quick to note its dependence on the quasi-Islamic buildings in Kew Gardens; but it might be remarked parenthetically that the Schwetzingen mosque carried the quest for verisimilitude further than its contemporaries, since it included accurately executed Arabic inscriptions of Qur'anic and proverbial content.

The third, and most 'scientific' level of exoticism is in some ways the most pernicious for a proper understanding of Islamic architecture, for it purports to pronounce on that subject in an objective way. It is demoralising to reflect on the thousands of Western architectural students whose acquaintance with Islamic monuments has never advanced beyond the trite or inaccurate *ex cathedra* pronouncements on that subject embodied in Banister Fletcher's *A History of Architecture on the Comparative Method* (original edition, 1896). The authority of that book is rendered virtually unassailable by its score of editions—a Gray's *Anatomy* for the student architect. Yet in his very nomenclature (for example, his use of the long-outdated term 'Saracenic' for 'Islamic'), to say nothing of his perverse genius in fixing on trivial or irrelevant features (such as horseshoe, cusped or interlaced arches) as indicators of style, Bannister Fletcher is a good century behind the times. Assuredly more scientific than this is the controversy which raged in the 1930s about the origins of the pointed arch and the rib vault, and the possibility that European developments in these techniques owed something to Muslim Spain, Egypt or even Iran. Yet the question of whether such influences were indeed operative is of marginal importance to the study of Islamic architecture. Worse still, it insinuates the notion that Islamic architecture is more interesting for the light it may shed on Western architecture than as a subject worthy of study in its own right.

The fascination with the exotic, then, in its several manifestations, can be seen to devalue Islamic architecture. It strikes the wrong chords–the antagonism between Muslim and Christian fuelled by the Crusades, the mutual incomprehension, the Western sense of superiority—even the readiness to see traces in Islamic buildings of that (to Western eyes) reprehensible self-indulgence symbolised by the institution of the harem.

Obviously Islamic architecture is to no small degree a somewhat accidental victim of attitudes born of the Western response to the Islamic world in general. Nevertheless it is fair to ask whether there are factors intrinsic to Islamic buildings which might attract the equivocal attentions of sensation-seekers self-confessedly in the thrall of the mysterious East–'the Omar

4 Samarqand, Shah-i Zinda, mausoleum dated 758/1360

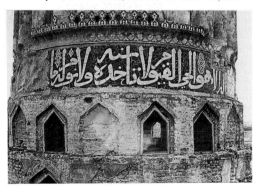

5 Cairo, mausoleum of Toghay, inscription on drum

Khayyam fiends' as Robert Byron disparagingly dubbed them. Perhaps Islamic decoration is partly responsible for such reactions, especially in its deliberate—and so un-European—assault on the eye. Acres of glowing tilework, thickets of arabesques, richly textured panels of geometric ornament which suggest a subtle underlying harmony, and finally the inscriptions which are inseparably part of this tradition—all conspire to disarm criticism. Such uncritical admiration of course has its pitfalls. It undervalues, for example, the mathematical element in Islamic architecture, and it responds to the purely visual (and excitingly alien) quality of Islamic inscriptions while remaining blind to their deliberately recondite nature, and to their role as a rebus for the faithful, as bearers of the Word and as signposts for the deeper meanings of the monuments they grace.

MUSLIM AESTHETICS

Function is of necessity one leitmotif of this study, but it is not the major one. Nonetheless, the decision to order the material according to building types rather than chronology—as is the normal practice—has useful side-effects. Prolonged concentration on a given building type does bring with it a closer focus on how its component parts worked, and it does help in setting stylistic and structural changes within a more detailed functional context. Thus even the most drily analytical passages have a wider horizon. The plain fact is that there was no less stylistic change in medieval Islamic monuments than, for example, in their counterparts in the medieval West—indeed rather more, as might be expected from the much greater geographical and ethnic extent of the Islamic world.

Closely related to the identification of successive styles is the much thornier problem of Muslim aesthetics. How did medieval Islamic architects intend their buildings to be experienced? Such a question is more easily posed than answered. Medieval Islam produced no Vitruvius or Alberti. The relevance of medieval literary sources for an understanding of Islamic architecture will be treated at some length later on in this chapter, but for the moment this absence of textbooks on architectural theory is worth pondering. Such theoretical writing must

not be confused with various practical aids designed to help architects in their work. Aids of this kind include ground plans, models, pattern books for architectural decoration, modules for erecting *muqarnas* vaults and diagrams showing how to construct arches. All this is helpful enough in showing how architects went to work, but it sheds little light on the particular kind of impact which they expected their buildings to exert.

Even without the evidence of such drawings and technical instructions, however, it would be possible to deduce from the buildings themselves some of the perennial concerns of Islamic architects and thus, by implication, their aesthetic preferences. This is a delicate operation, and it would be wise to retain an open mind on the somewhat dogmatic claims which have recently been bandied about as to the religious, and specifically Sufi, meaning of much Islamic architecture. Whatever the truth of such assertions, there can be no doubt that the unquestioning acceptance of the classical heritage, the one factor which gives a framework to the treatises of Vitruvius and Alberti, finds no sympathetic echo in Islam. No Muslim literary source has yet been discovered which proves the existence of any comparable standard of excellence. It is entirely possible that Islam as a religion played a significant—perhaps even *the* significant—role in inspiring Muslim architects, but in that case such inspiration was not explicitly acknowledged. Certainly the evidence that has been adduced to substantiate such a theory can be interpreted in more than one way. Nor can it be claimed that the views of modern Muslims have the same evidential value as medieval Islamic literary sources.

What, then, is the verdict of the buildings themselves? Pitifully few Islamic monuments have been subjected to the kind of rigorous analysis that would reveal the operation of underlying precepts of harmony and proportion. Yet the cases where such work has been done show that an emphasis on exact mensuration and on complex correlations stamps the best Islamic architecture of almost any place and period. Here, if anywhere, is a constant. Moreover, since it can be objectively documented it cannot be brushed aside, as can other judgements on the

6 Dauran, Friday Mosque, zone of transition

7 Samarqand, Shah-i Zinda, mausoleum of Shad-i Mulk

aesthetics of Islamic architecture, as an intrusion of Western art-historical method into a sphere where it does not belong. The square root of two is used to set up the design of the so-called

5.42–5.44 Tomb of the Samanids in 10th-century Bukhara,
4.19, 4.29 the 13th-century Mustansiriya *madrasa* in
4.53–4.54 Baghdad and the 14th-century tomb of the Amir Kilani in Jerusalem. Proportional ratios of 3:2 occur almost as a leitmotif in 9th-century 'Abbasid architecture in Iraq. A grid of equilateral triangles generates the designs of the

2.71 window grilles in the 8th-century Umayyad mosque in Damascus and the plan of the 14th-

2.265–2.266 century Friday Mosque of Varamin in northern Iran. The use of carefully correlated units accounts for the harmony of the hospital façade

9, 2.209 in 13th-century Divriği in eastern Anatolia, while the choice of a man's height as the modular elevation of a window in certain mature Ottoman mosques gives a new resonance to the aphorism that man is the measure of all things. The very first great Muslim

2.16–2.17 building, the Dome of the Rock, has a diameter which corresponds within a few centimetres to that of the dome above the Holy Sepulchre, the rival confessional monument in Jerusalem. Such examples could be multiplied indefinitely. Their value is to show that there is. ample empirical basis for the judgement that mathematical calculation is an integral part of the Muslim architectural aesthetic.

What other elements go to make up that aesthetic? Several might be proposed: a sense of hierarchy; a readiness to exploit symbolism; a love of lavish decoration whose functions go beyond mere display; and perhaps a leaning towards the use of colour. Even if none of these factors can be demonstrated with the same exactness as can the penchant for mathematical calculation, there is sufficient evidence to make a case for each of them. The present discussion will, however, confine itself to the questions of hierarchy and symbolism, since the other two factors have long attracted far more attention.

Hierarchy

The sense of hierarchy finds expression in two distinct ways. The first is, so to speak, neutral, as can be seen for example inside many a dome chamber, whether in a mosque, a *madrasa* or a
10 tomb. The tripartite arrangement of square

lower chamber, medial zone of transition and crowning dome embodies the notion that each successive element is of greater importance than the one below. Similarly, in the typical 13th-century caravansarai of Saljuq Anatolia, a rough 11 and ready hierarchy is implicit in the courtyard area immediately within the entrance being reserved for animals, while the people are housed in the covered hall leading off the courtyard. In the one case hierarchy is expressed vertically; in the other, horizontally. Yet in neither case is this hierarchy employed for especially portentous ends. It is primarily a means of sub-dividing the building functionally.

The other type of hierarchy is more complex, as befits the more exalted purposes for which it is employed. It is found most often in Friday mosques and in palaces–in other words, in buildings which have a pronounced royal character. Axial emphasis in crucial to its operation. This trend, too, can be traced back to the very beginning of Islamic architecture, where it occurs in both religious and secular buildings.

In the Great Mosque of Damascus the use of 2.69 a pre-existing site whose layout was far from ideally suited to serve as a mosque saddled the architect with sumptuous but almost redundant lateral entrances to the courtyard, and thus virtually excluded the possibility of creating a new principal entrance on the axis of the *mihrab*. 2.68, 2.70 Consequently there was an urgent need for visitors to be made aware of the *qibla* as soon as possible after entering the mosque. This was the principal function of the great raised gable with its elaborately articulated façade. It towers over the covered sanctuary and shears its way through to the *mihrab* by the most direct path: a path at right angles to the direction established by the pitched roofs and triple-aisled elevation. These preserve the basilical scheme of early Christian churches, even though that model is quite inappropriate for the needs of Muslim worship.

The gable was further singled out by a central dome and it is this feature which finally establishes the notion of hierarchy. The gable could be explained away as an ingenious but essentially practical means of visually asserting the *qibla*, the location of which would otherwise have remained in doubt. Not so the dome. It is not required to mark the *qibla* and is too far forward

8 Samarqand, Shah-i Zinda, anonymous mausoleum I, known as that of Ustad 'Alim. Detail of portal façade

to mark the *mihrab*. What, then, is its purpose? Briefly, it may be suggested that it is intended to mark a specific stage in a formal procession. Throughout the Middle Ages important mosques were used as settings for key official ceremonies. This very mosque in Damascus witnessed a triumph of Roman proportions when al-Walid I and his court assembled there in 95/714 to fête the conqueror of North Africa, Musa ibn Nusair. Some eight hundred years later the festive solemnity of Mamluk court ceremonial was well captured by an anonymous Venetian artist in the Louvre's *Reception of the Ambassadors*, where the setting incorporates the dome, gable and minarets of the very same mosque. When viewed as part of a whole consort of architectural elements with royal associations–such as the *mihrab, minbar* and *maqsura*–the dome can be seen as a device for appropriating the mosque as a royal monument and–unlike the other features just mentioned–proclaiming that association from afar. The office of caliph brought with it the obligation to lead the community in the Friday prayer, and there are frequent references in medieval sources to the pomp and circumstance which surrounded the discharge of this duty. Everything would be calculated to exalt the ruler: his headgear, clothing, mount, trappings and retinue. It was fitting that architecture should play its part in such calculated self-advertisement. What could be more likely that the caliph, when making his public entrance into the Damascus mosque, should enter the sanctuary on the axis of the gable, perhaps pausing under the dome on the way to the *mihrab*?

Early Islamic palaces tell the same story, though the architectural setting is perforce 7.44-7.45 somewhat different. In the bath hall of Khirbat al-Mafjar may be seen a comparable axial progression, combining the same elements of elaborate gateway, central dome and arcuated niche 7.11 disposed in sequence. At Mshatta the scale expands but is still controlled by a rigorous axiality, which propels the visitor along a predetermined path through a vestibule, and then through lesser and greater courtyards until the royal apartments are reached. Here a now 7.13 familiar schema operates. An elaborate entrance leads through a basilical hall to a domed triconch hall with an arcuated niche, presumably

holding the caliphal throne, at the far end. The sequence noted earlier is therefore maintained, though its intervals are telescoped, and constant changes of pace employed. 'Abbasid palaces use similar modes, while the formula of entrance gate–dome–*mihrab* employed in the Damascus mosque continued into Aghlabid, Fatimid, Saljuq and later mosque architecture. Naturally enough, the use of well-nigh identical formulae in Friday mosques and palaces meant that each building type derived an added charge from the other. A hierarchy expressed in a religious context received royal sanction, while the same hierarchy observed in palaces could be in some sense sanctified by its religious associations.

Symbolism

The question of how symbolism operated in Islamic architecture is somewhat more complex, and is rendered problematical by the lack of explicit supporting evidence in literary sources. The Muslim world has no equivalent for the medieval Christian obsession with religious symbolism, an obsession equally well illustrated in the Latin Bestiary, in middle Byzantine mosaic programmes and–most significantly in the present context–in Western ecclesiastical architecture. It commonly occurred that the parts of a church, the disposition of sculpture, the very steps that led to a cathedral, were organised within a rigid framework where almost every feature had an other-worldly as well as a practical significance. Islamic religious architecture–which of course accounts for most of the public buildings in the Muslim world–was denied nearly all these means of expression. It rejected sculpture and other figural decoration and there was, it seems, no consistent association between any particular type of plan or elevation and a deeper symbolic meaning. The interchangeability of functions for a given building type is further evidence in this direction. It was very different in the West, where the standard cruciform shape of Christian churches draws naturally on the whole nexus of Christian beliefs associated with the cross. Islam had no equivalent for this.

Such deliberately or potentially symbolic features as mosque architecture, in particular, incorporated were supplementary to the nuclear design of a courtyard and covered sanctuary.

9 Divriği, mosque and hospital, façade

This is not to suggest, of course, that they were merely tacked on to the standard schema; on the contrary, they are usually very well integrated into it. Yet the crucial point is that they are not a necessary part of the design. They include a whole battery of devices designed to lend extra impact to the sanctuary, and especially to the axis of the *mihrab*: a wider central aisle; a dome over the first bay of that aisle; a raised gable over most of the central aisle and sometimes its entirety; a dome over the bay preceding the *mihrab* and sometimes at each corner of the *qibla* wall; doubled columns along the central aisle, and more complex vaults or arch forms in the area of the *qibla*. The entrance portal of important mosques is another area that customarily attracts more complex treatment, and sometimes symbolic connotations can be read into this— for example a gateway set well back and flanked by splayed projecting wings, as it were welcoming worshippers inside. Beyond question, however, it is the *mihrab* that is the natural focus of religious symbolism in mosque architecture. Technically and theoretically, it is true, it may have been no more than a visual *aide-mémoire* of the location of the *qibla* wall. Popular belief obstinately held otherwise, and invested it with portentous significance as a shrine for divine illumination and as the gate to paradise. These ideas were fostered by its arched form, by the frequent depiction of a mosque lamp at its centre and by framing bands of Qur'anic quotations from the Sura of Light. The association of the *mihrab* with the Prophet and with royalty–for this was where the caliph stood to lead the Friday prayer–added yet another dimension of meaning to this already numinous form.

Mention of inscriptions serves to draw attention to another field which gave scope for religious symbolism, namely architectural decoration. It must suffice here to emphasise the double role played by much Islamic ornament. Inscriptions are usually so placed and executed as to embellish the building that bears them.

17

Their effectiveness is an amalgam of handsome lettering, texture and colour; added to this, their disposition in bands may serve to articulate a larger decorative scheme. Side by side with this already varied role there operates another dimension altogether–that of meaning. This is, of course, their primary function. In portal inscriptions, puns on Muhammad or 'Ali as the Gate of Knowledge are legion. Qur'anic epigraphy is often chosen for the relevance of the text to the type of building that it adorns or to its precise location there, as in the presence of the *shahada* at the top of a minaret. The patron of a building may have his name set in the place of honour precisely above the apex of the entrance arch. Historical inscriptions may include an inflated set of titles as a bid by some local notable to enhance his prestige. Non-epigraphic decoration may also have more than one meaning.

Peacocks or composite birds, the so-called 'birds of paradise', may occupy the spandrels of a portal arch in a mosque, simultaneously repelling evil and welcoming the faithful. Dragons, serpents, Sagittarius, or lions bringing down 6.130 bulls–all these with astrological content–are found in similar locations, as are depictions of isolated lions, a punning reference to the Prophet's cousin and son-in-law 'Ali (known as *haidar*, "lion"). Internal dome decoration often 10 exploits solar or stellar motifs and thus continues the age-old association between a vault 14 and the dome of heaven. The use of an oculus at the apex of a dome has similar connotations of great antiquity and prestige, stretching even further back than the Pantheon. More problematic, perhaps, is the equation of floral decoration–especially when it is predominantly green, as in Umayyad religious buildings–with fertility,

10 Ardistan, Friday Mosque, zone of transition

11 Incir Han, covered hall

or of the blue tilework of eastern Islam with notions of good luck or of heaven itself. Recent attempts to establish a symbolic dimension to the use of colour in Islamic architecture have foundered for lack of literary evidence, but it is only fair to add that such research is still at an early stage.

The foregoing remarks do not apply only to religious architecture; many of the same ideas were popular in secular buildings too. Moreover, some types of secular architecture developed their own distinctive symbolism. 7.61, 7.67 Thus the city of Baghdad was, it seems, self-consciously conceived as *imago mundi*, its concentric circular walls broken by four equidistant gates (one of them roughly aligned to Mecca). It is a concept of immemorial antiquity found alike in Europe, China and the Middle East. Roughly contemporary with the palace at Baghdad is a much-reduced variation on the same theme, the 7.95 palace of Abu Muslim in Merv. According to

literary descriptions, this vanished structure had a domed audience hall at the meeting point of four *iwan*s facing the cardinal points and in cruciform disposition. The symbolism is comparable in both cases, and is of a thorough-going secularity: the ruler presents himself as cosmocrator. Other types of royal symbolism that developed in palatial architecture will be discussed in more detail in the chapter on those buildings.

Among commemorative structures the Dome of the Rock is an obvious example of how the 2.16–2.17 Muslim builders deliberately took over an architectural form which in its parent culture was invested with symbolic significance; presumably they intended that a similar significance should attach to their building. In this instance the canopy or baldachin tomb had been used extensively in the early Christian centuries to mark a holy site, usually where a martyr or prophet lay buried or where a theophany had occurred. In other words, the form had itself come to symbolise sanctity and commemoration. The Dome of the Rock was thus able to profit from the built-in symbolic associations of its form. Suggestions have been made, too, that its designer enriched these associations by adding specifically Islamic ones in the number and placing of its supports, such as references to the Rashidun caliphs, to the pillars of the faith, and even, some say, to the number of Muslim saints to be found in each generation. Given the comparative rarity of Islamic buildings erected to commemorate a specific event, however, it would be prudent to leave open the question of what a given architectural form used in such a context might have signified to the medieval Muslim.

One very popular category of commemorative buildings, however, constitutes a special case: mausolea. Here, too, detailed discussion of the symbolic dimension of the forms employed will be reserved for the relevant chapter. For the purposes of the present discussion it must suffice simply to refer to the cluster of meanings which have been proposed for such structures: monumentalised versions of the Tree of Life, prefigurations of the shade which the blessed will enjoy in paradise, translations into brick and stone of the royal tents used by Turkic nomads, 5.158 vehicles for apotheosis, auguries of buildings in heaven itself. In the latter two interpretations, of course, the archetypal connection between the dome and the sky comes into its own once more. It is entirely likely that detailed research into other popular Islamic architectural forms will also disclose a stratum of symbolic significance— a significance which was perhaps never intended to be apparent to the populace at large. Recent research on the Great Mosque of Qairawan has revealed the existence of a plan within a plan, whereby the placing of columns of a given colour can be seen not to be random, but to create idealised versions of the plans of the Dome of the Rock and the Aqsa mosque. Thus the memory of the most prestigious sanctuaries of the Islamic East was perpetuated in a key mosque of the Islamic West. Yet this esoteric meaning of the ground plan has come to light only after a century and more of detailed study of this building. It had eluded all earlier Western scholars, and the memory of it had not been preserved locally. The obvious conclusion is

that from the first, this refined symbolism was not bruited abroad but was intended for the cognoscenti alone. It is worth bearing this implication in mind when considering other manifestations of Islamic architectural symbolism.

THE URBAN ENVIRONMENT

Only recently has the immediate environment within which medieval Islamic architects worked been subjected to close attention, and even then only in a few cases, such as later Mamluk Cairo. Yet some attempt to recover the milieu which encompassed the great masterpieces of Islamic architecture, and from which they sprang, is vital. They could no more afford to ignore rights of way, pre-existing buildings, the feeling of local people and basic services and amenities than can their modern counterparts. It is only in a very few cases that architectural historians have shown themselves to be aware of these wider horizons. The majority of Muslim

12 Ta'izz, Muzaffariya mosque, *qibla* façade

architecture is urban. At the outset, therefore, the architect usually has to surrender any ambition to secure full visibility for his structure on all sides. He learned to make the most of the difficulties with which a dense urban environment faced him.

These considerations help to explain why the plain domes of the Isfahan *jami'* or the *muqarnas* exterior domes of 12th-century Damascus seem to float comfortably above the huddle of surrounding rooftops. *Mashrabiya* balconies sprout from the external façades of Cairene houses at a level just sufficiently above the rough-and-tumble of the street. In Seville, the lower section of the Giralda minaret is plain up to a point about half-way up the shaft. Thereafter luxurious decoration envelops the tower. This point coincides with the present height of the cathedral, but it is permissible to assume that the roof of the now destroyed Almohad mosque also reached this height. Similarly, in Jerusalem the late Mamluk Ashrafiya *madrasa*, which fronts on the Haram al-Sharif, reserves its most elaborate architecture for the upper floor where the architect has much more freedom of manoeuvre and where the danger of upstaging the Haram itself is dissipated. The Fatimid mosque of al-Salih Tala'i' is constructed on comparable principles, though in that case the lower frontage consisted of shops.

Such cases are the norm. They show the architect making the best of a bad job. Sometimes his best is so ingenious that it produces its own felicities, and one may be grateful that he was set a problem so triumphantly overcome. Just occasionally, though, the innate significance of a building guaranteed it a privileged site, and this allowed its architect to exploit the free space around it. Outstanding examples are the Dome of the Rock, still the natural focus of attention in Jerusalem, and the caliphal palace at Baghdad, which could scarcely have had more untrammelled surroundings had it been in the open countryside. The Ka'ba partakes of this arrangement, as does the shrine of the Imam Rida at Mashhad in its most recent rebuilding. In most of these cases, the means chosen to highlight the building are the same–the whole area for scores of metres around is made *tabula rasa*. No other building is suffered to deflect attention from the structure in question. In general the Muslim

Margin references (left column): 2.264 · 5.192 · cf. 96 · 3.26, 3.50 · 16 · 4.43–4.44 · 2.99 · 2.16–2.17 · 7.61, 7.67

13 Bidakhavid, shrine of Shaikh 'Ali Binyaman, alabaster *mihrab*

world made little play with squares and piazzas, preferring to keep such open spaces within the private domain and thereby missing an opportunity to make them a natural focus for public life. The few examples just cited (al-Mansur's palace excluded) in some measure made up for this deficiency.

GEOGRAPHICAL AND CLIMATIC FACTORS

It is hard to exaggerate the role of geographical factors in moulding the evolution of Islamic architecture. By a pleasing symmetry, the effective limits of the medieval Islamic world from west to east are marked by two of the most famous buildings of that culture: the Alhambra and the Taj Mahal. The Islamic extensions into eastern Europe, i.e. the Balkans, and into the Far

Margin reference (right column): 7.201–7.202

East, namely Indonesia and China, are for our present purposes only footnotes. Paradoxically, these two celebrated monuments, whose glamour has sired innumerable clubs, theatres and restaurants, are themselves not central but peripheral. The heartlands of Islamic architecture lie in the area bounded to the west by Egypt, to the north by Turkey and Transoxiana and to the east by Iran. Black Africa and Arabia lie outside these heartlands. Such a definition may seem too rigorously exclusive. Its purpose, however, is to focus on those areas which over the centuries consistently produced significant monuments. Isolated masterpieces and brief periods of efflorescence are deliberately left out of account. By that reckoning the Maghrib and Muslim Spain must be omitted, although the achievements of the Muslim West make an honourable chapter in the history of Islamic architecture. The omission of India is even more disputable, and can only be justified by the general *a priori* exclusion of Indian material from the scope of this book, though a few Indian buildings make as it were a guest appearance here and there, especially in the chapter on minarets.

Even this admittedly contentious definition of the heartlands of Islamic architecture reveals a factor of crucial importance in determining how this tradition developed. The area thus defined measures some three thousand miles across and is thus of substantially greater extent than Europe. That distance can of course be tripled if the actual continuous extent of Islamic territory from Spain to Bengal is the basis of the calculation. This will help to explain why the concept of an 'Islamic' architecture is even more fraught with difficulties and dangerous simplifications than that of a 'Western' architecture. Of course, there was continuity—the adoption of a single faith ensured that—but this continuity also permitted remarkable variety, as might be expected from the many linguistic, ethnic and social divisions within the fold of Islam. Undue readiness to use the portmanteau term 'Islamic' predisposes one to gloss over the distinct local schools, even though these may maintain their individuality over the centuries as stubbornly as any national architecture in Western Europe. As the pace of scholarly research accelerates, provincial and chronological sub-schools can be

identified, just as they have long been in the West. Yet such knowledge is slow to percolate to the interested public, to whom the term 'Islamic architecture' is more likely to connote a few over-exposed masterpieces than sharply focused images of Maghribi, Rum Saljuq or Fatimid buildings.

Just as important a formative influence on Islamic architecture as the wide span and diversity of the Islamic world is its climate. It is above all the climate of Arabia and of the Fertile Crescent, rather than that of other parts of the Islamic world, which has in large part determined the evolution of Islamic monuments. The impact of the desert, with its heat, harsh sunlight, infrequent and therefore precious water, can be sensed in many a congregational mosque. It is quite true that the modular mosque of the first Islamic century was in time modified to take account of different climates, as also of different tastes and functions. Nevertheless, the prestige conferred upon it by its associations with the prophet Muhammad—whose house was the first mosque—ensured that few 2.52-2.54 drastic changes were introduced. By the time the 2.58 Great Mosque of Damascus was built, the com- 2.4 ponent parts of mosque design had assumed monumental form, and they bore the firm imprint of the Middle Eastern climate. The sanctuary was covered and thus gave shade. The courtyard was vast, open and uncluttered— perhaps an intentional evocation of the wide expanses of the desert. In its midst would be the ablutions pool or fountain, for all the world like 17 the watering hole at an oasis. At Damascus the idea of an oasis is suggested still more strongly by the overwhelming green tonality of the mosaics, in whose repertoire trees and streams 2.71 figure largely. Subsequently it became standard practice for arabesque or other organic ornament to be used in mosques.

There was often no attempt—why should there have been?—to conceal the links of such decoration with notions of growth, abundance and fertility. In later medieval Iran, for instance, it was common to embellish buildings with tilework whose principal theme was flowers. Cool restful tonalities, in which various shades of blue played a major part, were preferred. In pursuit of that same coolness—the necessary and much desired antidote to the harsh desert

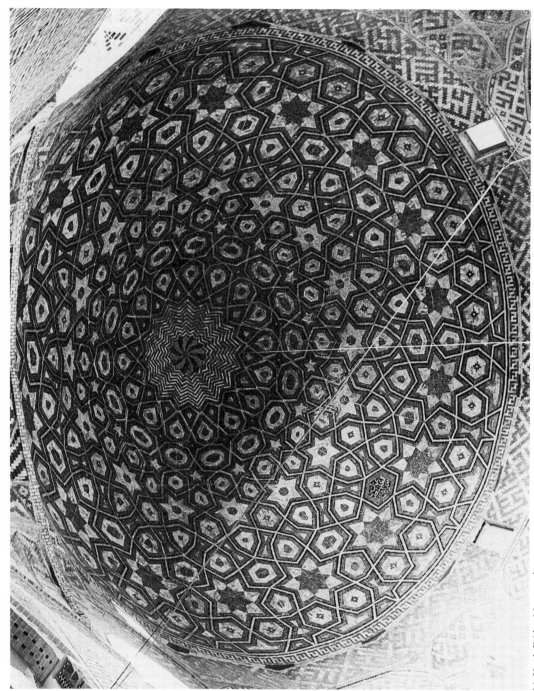

14 Yazd, Friday Mosque, dome

climate of much of the Middle East–as much as possible was done by means of shutters, grilles and bead curtains to mitigate the glare of such strong sunlight as penetrated into a building. Bare feet were soothed by floors which were *27* tiled, stone-flagged, carpeted or laid with matting. The absence of furniture helped currents of air to circulate more freely. Windows were few. All this combined to create that dim religious atmosphere which rested both body and soul. Open and roofed spaces are therefore able to complement each other to perfection. More than that, the distinctive attraction of each–of light, heat and clarity on the one hand *18* and a shadowed, cool obscurity on the other–is heightened by the close juxtaposition with its opposite.

AMBIGUITY IN FORM AND DECORATION

For many people, decoration provides the readiest identification tag for Islamic architecture. At a less obvious level, form can be almost as diagnostic. Some few forms are quintessentially Islamic and could be nothing else, notably the *muqarnas* in all its varieties, or the developed *6, 10, 2.268* zone of transition in a dome chamber. As a rule, though, Islamic architects were happy to use for their own purposes forms already long acclimatised in their parent culture. Thus certain minarets perpetuate a type of tower familiar for *19* centuries earlier as an ecclesiastical campanile, while the *iwan* so celebrated in Iranian architecture is found from Iraq to Central Asia in the pre-Islamic period. The Islamic architect, in short, was not restlessly experimenting with new forms the whole time; he preferred to refine existing ones (as the transition from Saljuq to Mongol architecture in Iran, or the history of the arch profile in the Maghrib, make clear) or to load them with extra decoration. These forms, then, are not enough in themselves to clinch the identification of a building as Islamic. Nor do they necessarily reveal the nature of the building. Paradoxically, it is this factor which by its very ubiquity stamps the buildings in question as Islamic. Interchangeability of types is the clue. Caravansarais, mosques and *madrasa*s may be difficult to tell apart. Virtually no form in Islamic architecture connotes a single exclusive function. This might in theory allow architecture to degenerate to the stage of reshuffling

a few building blocks; but this danger is more apparent than real. The need to work with a few well-defined building types no more fettered the creative imagination of Islamic architects than did a commitment to the classical orders inhibit their Western colleagues. A relatively constricted vocabulary acted as a spur to innovation rather than as a brake. The interchangeability of terms which marks Islamic architectural terminology will be examined in more detail later in this book; it is, incidentally, a natural concomitant of this flexible attitude to the interplay of form and function. For this reason a round dozen forms are used in literary sources to designate 'mausoleum', often on the basis of analogy (e.g. *rauda*, 'garden', hence paradise) or of *pars pro toto*; and similarly a whole battery of unrelated words is used to refer for example to a palace or a minaret.

One final common denominator of much–though by no means all–ambitious public architecture in the Islamic world may be ventured: a penchant for illusionism and ambiguity. This finds the most varied expression in both form and decoration. Examples of this trend in architectural forms include the pervasively two-dimensional quality of so much Persian and Mughal architecture from *c*.957/1550 onwards, with a corresponding emphasis on screening walls and *pishtaq*s. The true nature of a building *2.287–2.289* may easily be hidden by such means. Pools are so placed that they reflect the buildings nearby and thus double their size. Often it is not clear whether a form is decorative or structural–a *20* question that poses itself insistently when one contemplates the upper elevation of the sanctuary in the Cordoba *jami*ᶜ, especially in the area of *56* the *mihrab*. *Muqarnas* vaults and domes raise similar questions, and can be interpreted with equal plausibility as suspended or aspiring, to say nothing of their impact as decoration, which often blots out their structual role altogether. Similarly, is the cresting so often found on external walls in Islamic public buildings to be *21* read as a decorative feature or as an aggressively military one?

Ambiguity and illusionism are taken even further in the field of decoration. The tilework within the dome of the Masjid-i Shah creates light reflections within the dome that make it seem as though the sun were shining through.

15 Jerusalem, Aqsa mosque, façade

16 Jerusalem, Ashrafiya *madrasa*, upper floor

The aim seems to be that the dome should be as insubstantial as possible–indeed, as it were, transparent. Surfaces bedecked with tilework of floral design create the illusion of a building embowered in a garden. Above all, if a wall is richly embellished, attention is inevitably drawn in some measure to the decoration. By that same measure the impact of the building as pure architecture is diminished. Architecture and decoration are therefore permanently at war. The unusually important role which Islamic architecture allots to ornament encourages its victory and with it the dissolution of mass. It is as if a wall had become a vast canvas. It would not be

17 Aleppo, Great Mosque, courtyard with ablutions fountain

18 Aleppo, Great Mosque, central aisle from the west

hard to 'establish' tempting connections between this way of looking at architecture and the rejection of prosaic reality by Islamic mystics. In both cases metaphor clothes matter and renders it less material. Nevertheless such a connection is not susceptible of proof and without further evidence it is merely dogmatism to state that it exists. The Muslim predilection for ornament might just as well be founded on a love of colour or texture or design.

LITERARY SOURCES

Literary sources on the whole provide a disappointingly meagre range of information on medieval buildings. Yet this apparently discouraging statement must at once be qualified. Anyone leafing through K.A.C. Creswell's *Early Muslim Architecture* cannot fail to be struck by the wealth of literary documentation assembled there for such key buildings as the Dome of the Rock or the Great Mosque of Damascus. Are complaints about the lack of literary source material justifiable, then? Two general points need to be made at this stage and must be borne in mind subsequently in evaluating literary 'evidence'.

The first is that even information which is apparently comprehensive turns out on closer inspection to be full of lacunae, or, worse still, demonstrably inaccurate. To take as an example the pair of buildings just mentioned, there is no contemporary literary evidence *at all* which bears on them. The earliest extant sources date from almost two centuries later, and they are tantalisingly brief. They do not give even such basic information as the name of the architect, the size of the work-force, the source of the building material, and the like. Later writers quite shamelessly embroider the terse descriptions of their earliest predecessors, so that a chain of mutually dependent but increasingly inflated and unreliable accounts is fashioned.

The second observation bears on the tastes and interests of medieval writers. They very frequently ignore buildings which have since become key documents of a style, area or period. Often enough the buildings which they most admired have vanished, but this argument does not cover all cases. Not a single one of the major dozen Umayyad palaces, for example, can be identified with assurance in any medieval text

dealing with that period. Indeed, any building that is not a mosque is unlikely to be described in more than cursory fashion by medieval Islamic authors. The picture that emerges, then, is one of the somewhat unhelpful over-exposure of a few great monuments at the price of total neglect of the majority of buildings contemporary with these masterpieces.

These remarks do not by any means exhaust the tally of difficulties inherent in exploiting literary sources for specific information on architecture. In most cases the medieval author mentions buildings *en passant*. Such asides—whether in a geographical treatise, chronicle or poem—are often forced by modern scholars to bear a greater weight of significance than they really should. The collation of such scraps of information certainly helps to establish major trends, such as the continued existence of fire temples in Fars in early Islamic times, the custom of burying important personages in *madrasa*s in the Saljuq period, or the fortification of parts of the North African coast by numerous *ribat*s in the 9th century. It can also provide valuable information as to the existence of building types now entirely vanished, notably various kinds of palace or luxurious domestic architecture. It can establish, too, the architectural activity of areas or dynasties which have left no physical traces of their building operations. Most interestingly of all, such stray references can identify some of the great but lost buildings of the past. At the risk of labouring the point, however, it must be repeated that the material is so scanty that it is inherently inadequate as a reliable guide to what has gone for ever—and, as noted elsewhere in this chapter, the total of lost buildings is so great as to defeat the imagination.

It might be thought that the propensity to decorate Islamic buildings with inscriptions would ensure that Islamic architecture would have a much sounder documentary basis than most of medieval Western monuments. This is unfortunately not the case. Frequently historical inscriptions will give the date of the building, the name of the patron, and even that of the architect. In that respect the development of Islamic architecture is hearteningly well signposted. Nevertheless, the inscriptions rarely go any further. It is very little help to have the bare

name of the architect without any clue as to how long he worked on the building, who his assistants were, what his executive role was, how much he was paid and so on. Medieval Islam has produced nothing to equal the invaluable and endlessly revealing sketchbook of Villard d'Honnecourt. The conventions of epigraphy do not permit the inclusion of personal data on the architect and literary sources do little to make good this deficiency. It is only in the post-medieval period, and particularly in Ottoman Turkey, that biographical information about major architects becomes available. The nomenclature of inscriptions reveals, for example, that around the year 700/1300 the architect Muhammad from Damghan in eastern Iran built both a mosque and a tomb tower, designed a Kufic inscription and worked as a stucco

19 Ramla, White Mosque, minaret

20 Marrakesh, Qubbat al-Barudiyin, mosque fountain, interior

27

21 Marrakesh, Qubbat al-Barudiyin, mosque fountain, exterior

carver, and from the mention (again in an inscription) of his brother Hasan it is perhaps permissible to conclude that they belonged to a family of architects; but there is no literary evidence to flesh out this picture. Architects in their hundreds are known by name because they signed their buildings, but next to nothing is known about them. Their monuments might just as well be anonymous. Most tantalising of all is the discovery that many of the greatest buildings in the Islamic world—not just the Umayyad monuments mentioned above, but the Gunbad-i Qabus and the Alhambra—are anonymous. In the West, by contrast, the later Middle Ages produced such men as Brunelleschi and Alberti, whose activities are documented in detail or who published theoretical treatises on their art. Nor is there an equivalent in Islamic architectural history to Abbot Suger, a patron whose commitment to the arts and whose connoisseurship found extensive expression in writing. In this respect architecture fared much worse in the Islamic world than calligraphy,

which attracted much literary attention, or painting. Dust Muhammad, the prime literary source for the latter art, is a very poor exchange for Vasari. The history of Islamic architecture, then, suffers—as does Islamic history itself—from the absence of a documentary base. The raw material of charters, letters, judicial records and other legal documents, chancery archives and the like, on which so much Western medieval history is based, is largely missing in the medieval Islamic world. What can be offered in its stead?

Perhaps the most useful contemporary written source, so far as the social history of architecture is concerned, is the *waqfiya*. This is a record of the endowment (*waqf*) laid down by a patron in favour of a specified building. Such an endowment would stipulate the conditions of administration and upkeep, including the cost of maintenance and salaries, governing the monument in question. The deed of *waqf* would be legally attested and, in addition to being deposited with a *qadi* (judge), might be inscribed on the building itself. Monies, properties, rents or similar sources of income would be specified in the minutest detail—e.g. the income from certain shops, from one-sixth of a given village, the money derived from the sale of the produce of half an orchard – so that a building could be provided for in perpetuity. Curses would be called down on anyone who infringed these inalienable conditions. This system of endowment, though not altogether free of abuses, worked tolerably well in the medieval Islamic world. It became increasingly popular in the later Middle Ages, so that its history can best be reconstructed on the basis of Mamluk and Ottoman material. This material is usually in the form of deeds, but a few lengthy *waqf* inscriptions, such as that on the Mirjaniya *madrasa* in Baghdad, dated 756/1357, survive. It would be difficult to cite a system of financing architectural construction and maintenance which tied architecture to society in a more intimate way.

Other miscellaneous literary sources which have a bearing on architecture may be mentioned briefly. A 15th-century treatise by an Iranian from Kashan explains how to compute the surfaces of domes and how to construct arches of various spans and profiles. The manuals of *hisba*—codes of practice for the

5.23–5.24, 5.27

4.26, 4.31

22

22 Baghdad, Mirjaniya *madrasa, waqfiya*

various crafts and professions–sometimes shed light on such matters as the use and maintenance of mosques, the building of houses and shops in accordance with the need to avoid danger to life and limb and to ensure rights of way, or the regulation of the water supply. The outstanding example of this genre, so far as architecture is concerned, is the work of Ibn ʿAbdun, whose information relates to Seville in the early 12th century and covers such topics as the proper size of construction materials. Finally, attention should be drawn to the very occasional technical report–such as that of an otherwise obscure author, al-Maqdisi, who despite his name hailed from Bust in Afghanistan, and has left a description of the uses of wood in predominantly mud

architecture–and to the work of those geographers who happened to have a pronounced interest in architecture. Paramount among them is another, but celebrated, al-Muqaddasi (d.*c.*390/1000), who sprang from a line of architects in Jerusalem and in his travels throughout the Islamic world always had an eye for fine buildings. The Spaniard Ibn Jubair (d. 614/1217) runs him close for the quality of his connoisseurship and his capacity for detailed and accurate observation. Students of Islamic architecture have good reason to be grateful to such men, for they have preserved from oblivion literally thousands of buildings which have vanished without trace.

II The Mosque

What makes a mosque a mosque? The answer is forbiddingly simple: a wall correctly orientated towards the *qibla*, namely the Black Stone within the Ka'ba in Mecca. No roof, no minimum size, no enclosing walls, no liturgical accessories are required. Indeed, it might very properly be argued that even the single wall is unnecessary. After all, the Prophet himself is recorded as saying, 'Wherever you pray, that place is a mosque (*masjid*)'. Accordingly, to this day and throughout the Islamic world, when the hour for prayer arrives, pious Muslims stop whatever they are doing, orientate themselves towards the *qibla* and then and there undertake the formal ritual of prayer. Technically, therefore, it could be argued that the term *masjid*, normally translated into English as 'mosque', does not necessarily connote a building of any kind.

In fact, of course, Muslims began to build mosques from the very early days of Islam, and as the number of these mosques multiplied, patterns of architecture began to develop. Nevertheless, it is salutary to remember the willed austerity of the arrangements for worship as defined and practised by Muhammad. In the centuries to come Muslims never entirely forgot the starkness of his example, and periodically the forces of revivalism and pietism attempted at least a partial return to the pristine simplicity of the earliest Islamic worship. The mosques erected in Saudi Arabia by the Wahhabis typify the attempt to reconcile early Islamic practice with the accumulated traditions of a millennium and more of mosque architecture. The polarities are virtually irreconcilable, but it is highly significant that such consistent attempts have been made over the centuries to bring them together.

The salient fact, however, is that the mosque is the Islamic building *par excellence*, and as such the key to Islamic architecture. Moreover, the medieval Muslim world, like medieval Europe, was a theocentric society, and the mosque was the natural expression of that society. To examine its functions in detail therefore affords insights into the workings of medieval Islamic culture. For historians attuned to material culture as well as written evidence it is a primary source of the first quality.

There are other and still more practical reasons for investigating the history of the mosque. This was the building type which by and large produced the finest structures in Islamic architecture; it was built to last, whereas many secular monuments tended to be richly decorated but of flimsy construction. As a result, it has survived in larger quantities than any other type of medieval building. Indeed, the early period of Islamic architecture – from *c*.80/700 to *c*.390/1000 – is documented largely by mosques. It was the mosque which embodied the first timid Arab experiments in architecture and it was in the medium of the mosque above all that Muslim builders came to grips with the pre-Islamic architectural heritage. As a result, this is the building type which most frequently reflects – just like the church in the Christian world – the impact of the many distinct local architectural traditions which together shaped Islamic architecture.

DEFINITION

Before proceeding any further, it might be as well to attempt a definition less austere than the one proposed at the beginning of this chapter. The mosque is of course the principal religious building of Islam, and paramount among its many functions is communal prayer. In its simplest and most widespread form the medieval mosque comprised a courtyard bordered by arcades and adjoining a covered hall. Yet this definition, for all its deliberate inclusiveness, gives little idea of the well-nigh endless variety of forms and uses which characterised the most quintessentially Islamic building. Nor does the limited space available here permit even a reasonably detailed inventory of the significant mosque types and of the functions which they discharged. It is imperative rather to distance oneself from this wealth of detail, however alluring, the better to identify the immanent characteristics of the mosque and to appraise its unique role within Islamic culture. Accordingly this chapter will focus less on close analysis of individual mosques than on how this genre of building expressed the perennial concerns of Islamic religious architecture. These concerns or underlying principles governed and are reflected in the choice of component parts of mosque design, and their interaction; the functions which the mosque was called upon to perform; the role of decoration; and finally all that contributes to the visual and aesthetic impact of this building type. It would pre-empt the ensuing discussion to dilate on these principles at any length at this stage. Suffice it to say that mosque architecture is at base egalitarian, iconoclastic, inward-looking and – above all – profoundly religious in its intent.

The latter aspect deserves particular emphasis because of the much-vaunted identity of the sacred and the secular in medieval Islamic society. This theory, a favourite construction of some trends in modern scholarship, is ideally as true of Islam as of Christianity. It is, however, only a theory and a glance at common practice is enough to dispose of it. To this day no one walking from the bustle of a bazaar to the serenity of a mosque can seriously doubt that Islam clearly distinguishes between the dues of Caesar and those of God. The architecture proclaims that very distinction. The change to an orientation towards Mecca, so frequently noticeable as soon as one enters the building, is conceived in the same spirit. Finally, the believer takes off his shoes to enter a mosque and that simple homely action symbolises the transition from the secular to the spiritual realm. A saying of the Prophet reported by Abu Huraira makes the same point still more sharply: 'most favoured of God in cities are their mosques and most abhorred are their markets'. In just the same way, the physical evidence contradicts another fashionable concept: that all the mosque is equally sacred and that its architecture embodies no hierarchy of importance. In mosques provided with a courtyard – and such mosques are the predominant type throughout the Islamic world – a clear visual distinction is drawn between the courtyard with its surrounding arcades and the larger covered space containing the *mihrab*. Even the Arabic language has at times singled out this area from the rest of the mosque, calling it the *musalla* or 'place of

23 Susa, Great Mosque, original sanctuary

prayer'–though this usage is by no means universal, and indeed is distractingly ambiguous, because the same term is widely used of an enclosed open space, normally outside a town, in which communal prayer is celebrated at festivals and on other special occasions. A common term for this covered area in early texts is *al-mughatta*, a term (like *riwaq*) also used of tents. Similarly, it is in this area that the principal architectural and liturgical elements of the mosque are concentrated: the main dome, the largest continuous covered space in the building, the *mihrab*, the *maqsura* and the *minbar*. These elements will be discussed in more detail later. Finally, it is here that the most lavish ornament which the building can boast is to be found. These remarks are not intended to cast aspersions on the sanctity of the mosque as a whole. Nevertheless they do imply that one part of the mosque – the covered space containing the *mihrab*, conventionally rendered into English as 'sanctuary' – was accorded greater visual emphasis and status than the rest of the building.

So much for preliminaries. Impressionistic as such remarks may appear, they nevertheless help to delineate the background against which the evolution of the mosque over a millennium and more must be seen. Any considered analysis of this building type must, of course, go further than this. Certain crucial aspects of mosque architecture have a particular claim to extended discussion and this chapter will lay special emphasis on them. They are the origins of the mosque; its constituent parts, with their associated liturgical significance; its various functions; and its standard characteristics. Only when these matters have been sufficiently clarified will it be possible to move from the general to the particular and to flesh out the resultant rather stark generalisations with specific detail. The other section of this chapter will therefore be devoted to a discussion of the various types of mosque, illustrated by some of the major examples of the genre, and to the rôle played by the decoration of these buildings.

ORIGINS OF THE MOSQUE

2.52-2.54

The matter of origins is surprisingly straightforward. Islamic tradition champions the decisive impact of a single building on the evolution of the mosque: the house of the Prophet. Nor is this emphasis misplaced. The briefest acquaintance with Muslim liturgy is enough to explain why the places of worship employed by the other faiths of the time were fundamentally unsuitable for the needs of Islam. It is true that 2.222 many churches, some fire temples, and on 2.67 occasion even portions of classical, Hindu or Jain temples, were adapted to serve as mosques. But this was only a matter of expedience, and was never a long-term, deliberate policy. It did, however, have its uses; indeed, several motives could account for these conversions. In newly Islamised territory the pressing need for a place of worship could not always be met as quickly as might be wished. The advantages of using an already existing monument – convenience, cheapness, suitable location, the saving of time and effort and of course the less easily definable proselytising, propaganda and symbolic elements – outweighed the initial disadvantage of using an architectural form not designed to serve as a mosque. Nevertheless, these disadvantages made themselves felt in short order, and

already within the first decade of the Islamic conquests 'custom-built' mosques – if that is not too grand a term for such extremely simple structures – were being erected.

The informality of the earliest arrangements for communal worship in Islam irresistibly brings to mind the comparable situation among the early Christians. There, the first places where the nascent community foregathered for worship were the homes of the faithful, and Christ's words 'Where two or three are gathered together in my name, there shall I be among them' highlight the lack of outward forms, including architectural forms, in the early Church. The fact that much of Christ's teaching took place in synagogues is of a piece with this simplicity. Much later, when custom-built churches began to be erected in quantity, the basilicas and mausolea of the late antique world provided the models. It was only gradually that the forms of these pagan buildings were altered and refined so that they could discharge their new religious functions more effectively. Even then, there was no question of the word 'church' connoting exclusively one kind of building.

These reflections may help to clarify the early history of the mosque. In several crucial respects, however, the historical circumstances of the rise of Islam were totally different from those of early Christianity. Islam was spread by the sword, at great speed and over vast distances – from Spain to the borders of China. The consequences for the faith and for Islamic society are not relevant here, but the consequences for Islamic architecture could not be more crucial. Developments which in the Christian world proceeded in leisurely fashion over several hundred years were, in the world of Islam, telescoped into little more than half a century. Christianity began, grew and consolidated itself in the Mediterranean world, in the context of a high degree of political, cultural and even linguistic homogeneity. By contrast, the array of political, cultural, ethnic and linguistic entities which succumbed to Islam in such rapid succession is nothing short of bewildering. The range of architectural forms which the Muslims encountered was correspondingly wide. Christian architects had no such input of alien forms to absorb. Not only did the Muslims have to come to terms with the protean expressions of Christian religious architecture which they encountered; Zoroastrian, Jewish, Hindu, Jain and Buddhist religious buildings also challenged them. Finally, the military nature of the Islamic expansion requires emphasis. As the conquests progressed, the major body of Muslims in each new territory was initially the army itself. The need for some serviceable gathering place for these thousands of Muslims was acute, and a simple enclosure best fitted that need. The means chosen to enclose the desired space were not necessarily monumental: a line of scattered ashes, a reed fence, a shallow ditch and the like. In this informal way there arose the 2.45, 2.48 ancestors of the great congregational mosques 2.78, 2.88 of later times. As early as the year 21/642, after the conquest of Alexandria, a mosque was laid out in a garden where the commander-in-chief, 'Amr b. al-'As, had set up his standard–and he himself lived right next door. The same arrangement was followed at Mosul in northern Iraq. In some carefully selected centres these enclosures seem to have taken on a more permanent form, even within the first century of Islam. Once again, military motives provided the initial

stimulus for this development. The Muslim expansion could not be directed entirely from Mecca and Medina, or even from Damascus, and therefore intermediate headquarters were set up near the major fronts. Thus the invasion of eastern North Africa was spearheaded from Fustat (near modern Cairo), and that of western North Africa and Spain from Qairawan in Tunisia. Similarly, the campaigns against the northern and southern areas of the Iranian world were prosecuted from headquarters in Kufa and Basra respectively. Such settlements 2.39 became virtual garrison cities which saw the regular coming and going of thousands of troops. The Muslim authorities soon came to feel the desirability of separating such military camps from the symbiotic town which grew up beside each of them, and a separate mosque was an effective symbol of that segregation. With ample free space on which to build, and with the need to accommodate thousands of worshippers, it is no wonder that these early mosques should have been so huge.

Although no mosque from these early decades survives in anything like its original

24 Damghan, Tari Khana mosque, *mihrab* and *minbar*

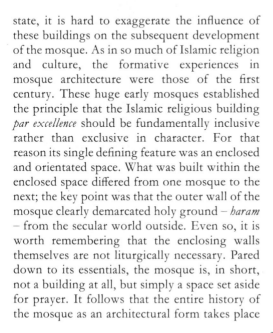

25 Hama, Great Mosque, *minbar* of Nur al-Din

26 Jerusalem, Aqsa mosque, *minbar*, entrance

state, it is hard to exaggerate the influence of these buildings on the subsequent development of the mosque. As in so much of Islamic religion and culture, the formative experiences in mosque architecture were those of the first century. These huge early mosques established the principle that the Islamic religious building *par excellence* should be fundamentally inclusive rather than exclusive in character. For that reason its single defining feature was an enclosed and orientated space. What was built within the enclosed space differed from one mosque to the next; the key point was that the outer wall of the mosque clearly demarcated holy ground – *haram* – from the secular world outside. Even so, it is worth remembering that the enclosing walls themselves are not liturgically necessary. Pared down to its essentials, the mosque is, in short, not a building at all, but simply a space set aside for prayer. It follows that the entire history of the mosque as an architectural form takes place

within the secular domain. This may sound an extreme statement, and perhaps an offensive one too. Yet until the absolute simplicity of the Muslim requirements for communal prayer are clearly understood, the subsequent complexity of mosque architecture is liable to be misinterpreted as a response to liturgical needs. Instead, that complexity resulted principally from the adoption of non-Islamic features and their integration into the new context created by the mosque. This point deserves a little further investigation.

Islam was able to draw on a much more varied range of models for religious buildings than was Christianity, which says much for the simplicity of Islamic communal worship and its refusal to be tied down to a narrow range of architectural expression. Its austerely simple liturgy meant that Islam could appropriate almost any kind of building for worship. Even so, there was – at least as far as the 7th-century

35

Arabs were concerned – an optimum design for mosques, and it is revealing that its roots should be in domestic rather than public architecture. This is not to say that the mosque is simply the Arab house writ large, for both Christian and Zoroastrian places of worship left their mark upon its design, as did the aulic architecture of late antiquity. These external influences took time to make an impact on mosque architecture, and even at their strongest they were only rarely the determining factor. Mature Ottoman mosques, which cannot be understood without reference to Byzantine churches of the 6th century, notably Haghia Sophia, are the exception that proves the rule. Muslim architects happily plundered, both literally and metaphorically, the religious architecture which they encountered in the Mediterranean, Arabian, Iranian and – nearly six centuries later – Indian worlds. Yet the materials and ideas which they 2.19 quarried from these buildings were not enough to make the mosque an Islamised church, fire sanctuary or temple. The places of worship used by the adherents of religions which Islam supplanted were basically ill-suited to Muslim needs. Churches emphasised depth rather than breadth, if they were of basilical form, and centrality if they were a variation of the martyrium 2.225-2.226 type. The sanctuaries of fire worship in the Iranian empire were built for ceremonies in-

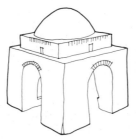

2.226 Naisar, fire temple

volving a few priests, not large congregations – indeed, the congregation foregathered in the open air – while the temples of Arabia and India also put no premium on housing great numbers of worshippers within a covered hall, let alone ensuring easy visibility between them. For these practical reasons the cultic centres of other religions were of limited value to early Muslim

architects, who looked elsewhere for inspiration.

LITURGY

The fact of the matter is that the Muslim liturgy does not demand any man-made structure for its celebration. When the early Muslims gathered for worship on their holy day – a Friday, not a Sunday – they performed ritual prayer together and listened as the *imam* ('prayer leader' is a somewhat inadequate translation) delivered the *khutba* – part sermon, part bidding prayer, but often with political content too. The various prescribed movements of prayer, involving as they did outstretched arms, kneeling and prostration, meant that each worshipper ideally required a minimum space of 1 × 2 metres. Moreover, prayer was communal. It was thus clearly desirable that its constituent movements should be synchronised. The alternative would be visually chaotic and might even suggest spiritual discord. The functions of the *imam* included the leading of communal prayer, and to this end it was important that he should be as widely visible as could be. Thus there developed the custom of disposing the worshippers in long lines parallel to the *qibla*. In this way it was possible for hundreds, not scores, of people to follow the movements of the *imam*. By contrast, the disposition of worshippers within most Christian churches is in lines perpendicular to the altar. The consequent loss of visibility is only partially compensated for by the raising of the altar. These remarks are not intended to suggest that the *imam* was visible in a large mosque to a congregation of, say, several thousand. But the grouping of worshippers in comparatively few long and well-spaced lines, rather than in many short lines close together, did ensure the easy intervisibility of worshippers 2.7 and thus facilitated precise timing in the movements prescribed for prayer. A chance remark of Ibn Hauqal *à propos* the Great Mosque of Palermo casts some light on the organisation of the communal prayer: 'I estimated the congregation, when it was full, at over 7,000 persons. Not more than 36 rows stand in prayer, with not more than 200 men in each row'.

This lateral grouping of worshippers, which might fairly be termed a liturgical convenience, but was in no sense a doctrinal imperative,

27 Jerusalem, Aqsa mosque, *minbar*, east side

proved to be the single vital factor in the layout of future mosques. At a stroke it forbade the simple transformation into Friday mosques of pre-Islamic places of worship. It forced Muslim architects desirous of making such transformations to rearrange the constituent elements of the sequestrated building – lateral thinking, indeed. Such conversions of existing structures, though obviously convenient in the short term, were no adequate solution to the needs of a new, powerful and rapidly growing religious community with its own distinctive forms of worship. Thus the earliest custom-built mosques were erected at the very same time that existing non-Muslim buildings were being converted into mosques, and in them the lateral emphasis is already well-marked. From the very beginning Islamic architects rejected the basilica, and with it the standard Christian church of Western type, as a suitable source of inspiration for the mosque. Nevertheless, the idea of a central nave focused on an altar was eventually incorporated, suitably modified, into numerous mosques, and occasionally – as in the 2.8 Great Mosque of Damascus – an entire basilical form, once shorn of its telltale Christian axiality, could be integrated into a mosque. Similarly, it seems unlikely – although here the crucial archaeological evidence is still missing – that the 2.225–2.226 Zoroastrian fire temple, a domed square

chamber with four axial openings, was ever accepted as a suitable model for a congregational mosque built from scratch and intended to consist of no other structures. Yet as in the case of the basilica, this alien form–found also in 7.46, 7.49 Sasanian palaces–could lend itself very ade- 2.12 quately to mosque architecture. Sometimes, it seems, the mere addition of a courtyard was sufficient modification. The domed chamber proved to be a most striking method of singling out the sanctuary of a mosque, or even a particular area of the sanctuary. As with the basilica, it was not a necessary element in the congregational mosque but rather an optional extra.

In this respect the earliest large mosques, which have been convincingly analysed on the basis of the copious literary sources, offer telling evidence. At Basra, Kufa and Fustat the story is 2.45, 2.48 the same: the mosque comprises simply a large rectilinear enclosure of which one complete side, varying in scale from a quarter to a half of the entire enclosure, is taken up by a covered area, namely the sanctuary–a space thus rendered architecturally distinct from the rest of the mosque.

The decision to include a covered area in the mosque, and moreover to position it next to the *qibla* and therefore in the place of honour, was fraught with consequences for subsequent

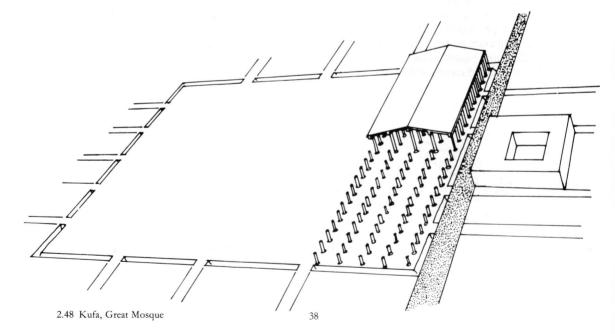

2.48 Kufa, Great Mosque

mosque architecture. Why was this feature included? It is clear from the discussion so far that there was no need for it from the point of view of doctrine or liturgy. It seems justified to invoke such other factors as custom, precedent and practicality – and this inevitably leads to the first mosque of all, Muhammad's house in Medina.

MUHAMMAD'S HOUSE

2.52-2.54 The first point to notice about this building, now entirely vanished but described in exhaustive detail in the Arabic sources, is that it was in Medina, and not in Mecca where Muhammad spent most of his life. It was only in 622, ten years before his death, that the hostility of the Meccans to his religious teaching caused him to move for safety to Medina. This emigration (*hijra*) marks the beginning of the Islamic calendar. In that same year he began to build a house for himself and his family. But he built that house not as a despised and persecuted religous outcast, which was how he was generally regarded in Mecca, but as the respected leader of a new and dynamic religious community. What could be more natural than that his new house should be designed at least in part to serve this community as well as his own family?

A second striking feature of the house is its very substantial size. It was a largely open square of some fifty-six metres per side. These dimensions speak for themselves. They were probably exceptional for that time and place. Nor did Muhammad keep the kind of state which called for a vast establishment; the *hadith*s on this subject sufficiently emphasise the sim-

plicity, indeed austerity, of his daily life. A house on this scale was far bigger, in short, than was required for a household as modest as that of the Prophet. Indeed, its domestic accommodation comprised no more than nine small rooms built side by side on the outer side of the east wall.

This last detail is very telling, and highlights the third notable characteristic of the house, namely that it is a house only incidentally. To judge by later domestic architecture, the obvious location for rooms intended to be lived in would have been inside, not outside, the enclosure. Thus the paradox emerges of a building which, though ostensibly intended to function as a house, is apparently designed with quite other ends in view. In other words, the evidence suggests that Muhammad's 'house' was intended from the first to serve as the focal point of the new Islamic community. That definition also includes its role as a mosque. It did not become the first mosque as it were by accident. Consequently the traditional interpretation which emphasises the origin of the mosque in domestic architecture is erroneous. The mosque was custom-built from the very beginning, though it is important to remember that the precise meaning of 'mosque' in the 620s is not readily definable today. The inclusive rather than exclusive nature of the concept at this early date requires emphasis.

These remarks place Muhammad's 'house' in a new light. They indicate that the random element in the building was its domestic rather than its religious appurtenances. For this reason, purely domestic accommodation was banished outside the building. By the same token every-

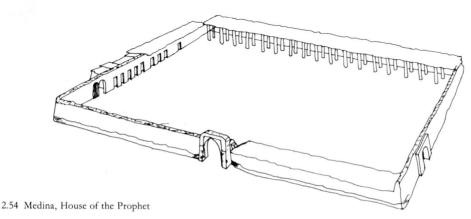

2.54 Medina, House of the Prophet

28 Abyana, Friday Mosque, *minbar*

Jerusalem to the Ka'ba, the *zulla* was pulled down and re-erected alongside the new *qibla*. it was large enough to accommodate at least a hundred people. Opposite the *zulla* was another covered area, half as deep and less than half as long, which was used by the most poverty-stricken followers of the Prophet. The court-yard contained no other structures, and the three gates which gave access to it were little more than openings in the wall.

Before the implications of this layout are assessed, it is necessary to confront the arguments marshalled by Creswell and others to the effect that this building was not intended to be a mosque. The burden of these arguments is that no special sanctity attached to the building in the Prophet's lifetime and that it was indeed used like, and exclusively referred to as, an ordinary house (*dar*). Moreover, on important occasions Muhammad prayed at the *musalla* outside Medina. There is no need to try to discredit these statements, but they fail to in-validate the assertion that the building was pri-marily intended as the focus of the new com-munity and only secondarily intended as Muhammad's house. The latter assertion, moreover, coincides with the Islamic tradition itself. Above all, there is no inherent contradic-tion between those who interpret the building as a mosque and those who see it as Muhammad's house. Clearly it served both purposes, and it was fully in the spirit of the earliest Islamic religious practice that it should.

For a full understanding of the mosque in the crucial early stages of its development it is neces-sary to remember its role as a community centre. It is that role which explains the apparently contradictory reports about how Muhammad's house was used. Both the spiritual and the secular life were pursued there simultaneously. This was the formative period of Islamic society, and so it is not surprising that the architecture which that society generated should also be in a state of flux. In later centuries, the development of specifically Islamic institutions removed from the mosque the functions which it had earlier, if only sporadically, performed: teaching, burial, the care of the sick, and many more. Some of these functions lingered for a long time. Thus in the 9th and 10th centuries mosques were usually open day and night, and the law permitted their

thing within the building was deliberately included because it had a function to fulfil in this primitive mosque. The evidential value of Muhammad's 'house' can scarcely be exag-gerated – for here, in the very lifetime of the Prophet, were laid down the norms for the central religious building type of the new com-munity.

The major features of the building may quickly be summarised. It was essentially a large and almost empty enclosed space. The enclosing walls were plain. Along the inner wall facing the *qibla* was the *zulla*, or shaded place, a double row of palm trunks carrying a roof of palm leaves plastered with mud. This feature was not part of the original design but was added within a year because some of the Companions (*sahaba*) of the Prophet had complained of the discomfort which the sun had caused them during prayer. When, very soon afterwards, a divine revelation caused Muhammad to change the *qibla* from

29 Qairawan, Great Mosque, interior of dome over *mihrab*

use to shelter travellers, penitents and the homeless. As the mosque grew more specialised in its functions, so it naturally developed its own specialised architecture. But in the first century of Islam all this lay in the future. The very informality of early Muslim practice militates against any dogmatic or exclusive interpretation of the mosque in the early decades of Islam. It is bad practice to apply concepts of the mosque derived from later buildings to the earliest structures of this kind, which were built at a time when the very idea of a mosque was not yet precisely defined. Thus the evidence adduced by Caetani as to spitting, sleeping, lounging, arguing, dancing and convalescing in the Prophet's house merely underlines the varied role which this building played in the early Muslim community. That same building was used for prayer on a regular basis by Muhammad and his family, by the Companions of the Prophet and by the impoverished 'People of the *suffa*'. The speedy demolition and re-erection of the *zulla* at the time of the change in *qibla* is entirely consonant with the regular use of the building for worship, and would be hard to explain otherwise.

The essentially multi-purpose nature of Muhammad's house helps to explain both its large size and its architectural design. Had Muhammad wished to live the modest and retired life of a private citizen, it seems unlikely that he would have built his *dar* in the form that he did. His mission of course dictated the public nature of his life-style and his house was a correspondingly public building. The design amply proved its worth during Muhammad's own lifetime and, so long as the mosque remained not only a place of worship but also the focal point of the Muslim community, there was no need for any fundamental reshaping of a plan already hallowed by the Prophet's use of it.

From the standpoint of design perhaps the most significant feature of Muhammad's house was the large empty courtyard. This took up some 75% of the available space even after the final expansion of the building, which involved the provision, outside the courtyard, of a total of nine dwellings for Muhammad's family. In fact, in the original design the 'house' consisted almost entirely of a vast empty courtyard. The austerity of this layout left its mark on subse-

quent mosques, while its flexibility needs no further emphasis.

The trend in subsequent centuries was towards an increasing specialisation of the mosque. The gradual shedding of many of its earlier functions opened the way for quite radical changes in design, and it became the practice to meet a specific function not directly connected to worship by adding an appropriate custom-built element to the nuclear design. This practice explains why so many later mosques seem encumbered by the multiple appendages clustered around them. 2.269

MASJID AND JAMI^c

The foregoing remarks are intended not so much to fuel the long-standing controversy about the role of the Prophet's house as to shed some light on the prehistory of the mosque and to explain the reasons behind that simplicity which has remained its abiding characteristic. The vast courtyard sufficed to proclaim the essentially public nature of the building. It quickly became the nerve centre of the burgeoning Muslim community. Here worship was conducted, public announcements made, ambassadors lodged, meetings held, parades reviewed, cases tried, the treasury housed and councils of war convened. Like the religion of which it quickly became a potent symbol, then, it encompassed both the spiritual and the secular domain. Later mosques in theory maintained this dual allegiance, and the lack of formal urban institutions in the Muslim world, with a corresponding lack of certain types of formal public building such as town halls or law courts, put a premium on this double role. Thus by a natural process it became the community centre of the new faith. Larger mosques in particular continued throughout the medieval period to offer a more or less wide range of facilities unconnected with worship. Smaller mosques on the whole did not. This functional distinction reflects a difference in status and purpose which became established within a century of the Prophet's death, and was formalised by the adoption of two quite separate terms both meaning mosque: *masjid* and *jami^c*. *Masjid*, derived from the root *sajada*, 'to prostrate oneself', is used in the Qur'an itself, though in rather a broad sense, to denote a place of worship. Its meaning was quickly refined,

30 Kufa, Great Mosque, portal

however, to indicate more specifically a mosque for daily private prayer. The simplest architecture, right down to a single unadorned room, sufficed for such oratories, though it was not rare for a splendidly embellished *masjid* to be erected at the behest of some wealthy patron. No Muslim community was without a *masjid*, even if it was no more than a small space set aside in some larger building. In towns it was common practice for each individual quarter to have its own *masjid*, and yet other *masjid*s were built specifically for members of a certain tribe, sect, profession or other exclusively defined community. Finally, the growing popularity of joint foundations from the 10th century onwards meant that *masjid*s were built in association with a wide range of buildings whose prime emphasis was secular, such as caravansarais, mausolea, and palaces, as well as buildings with an overt religious significance, such as *ribats* – fortified structures which housed warriors for the faith – and *madrasa*s or theological colleges. This association of the *masjid* with secondary places of worship ensured that the physical form of the *masjid* became more and more varied.

The *jami'* was an altogether more ambitious kind of building, and this was entirely in keeping with its much grander function. The religious obligation imposed on every adult male and free Muslim to meet for communal worship every Friday for the public service or *salat* created a need for a building conceived on a much larger scale than the *masjid*. The very word *jami'*, which derives from the Arabic root meaning 'to assemble', recalls and perpetuates this crucial function of the building. It had to accommodate thousands instead of scores or a couple of hundred. It had in addition a public role, with undertones of symbol and propaganda denied to the *masjid*. It was in some sense a showpiece for the faith and often for the person, dynasty or area most closely associated with it. Not surprisingly, then, the crucial experiments in the evolution of the mosque, as well as the finest realisations of that type, have been reserved for the *jami'*. The Western term 'cathedral mosque', though obviously a solecism, is thus an appropriate transference of ideas. The building of a *jami'* was no more to be undertaken lightly than was that of a cathedral – indeed, until the 10th century the express

approval of the caliph himself was required before a *jami'* could be erected, and for centuries normally only one such building per city was permitted. This had much to do with the fact that possession of a Friday Mosque conferred upon a settlement the status of a town: 'How the citizens of Baikand tried and tried', notes al-Muqaddasi *à propos* this village in Central Asia, 'until they were allowed to put up a *minbar*'. The Hanafi *madhhab* allowed the Friday *salat* to be performed only in large towns, while the Shafi'ites allowed the Friday *salat* in only one mosque per town. Hence the disapproval which met al-Hajjaj, the Umayyad governor of Iraq, when he built a *jami'* for Wasit, his capital, even though the town already had one on the other side of the river. Gradually however, the population pressure in the major cities forced a relaxation of this rule.

Despite the clear functional distinction between *masjid* and *jami'*, there was not necessarily any corresponding distinction between the two building types so far as their basic layout was concerned. The generalisations ventured at the beginning of this chapter therefore hold good for both these genres of mosque. True, the *jami'* normally had an extra dimension not only literally, by virtue of sheer size, but also metaphorically through its extra degree of embellishment. Yet often *masjid*s were built which yielded nothing in decorative splendour to the finest *jami'*s of the same style.

INNOVATIONS

Certain types of *jami'*, especially in the early centuries of Islam, did develop certain distinctive features not encountered in *masjid*s, though it must be emphasised that these features represent only minor modifications to the basic schema of open courtyard and covered sanctuary common to both *masjid* and *jami'*. Their introduction is of key importance to the history of the mosque, however, for it heralds an influx of foreign ideas, techniques and materials which decisively transformed the primitive Arabian simplicity of the mosque. Henceforward mosque architecture evolved against a backcloth of classical, Byzantine and Iranian influences. As a result, from the later Umayyad period onwards the physical form of the mosque was unmistakably rooted, at least in part, in the millennial traditions of the Near East and the Mediterranean world. The *masjid* in its original form was well able to do without these addenda, but there is no doubt that their incorporation into mosque design substantially enriched the whole subsequent development of the genre.

These new features were five in number: the *mihrab* or prayer niche, the *minbar* or pulpit, the *maqsura* or royal box, the raised gabled transept, and the dome over the *mihrab* bay. Not all of them were to remain of equal importance, nor indeed were all five often to be encountered in one and the same building. In the context of the present general discussion it is less their individual evolution than the motive behind their introduction which is relevant. Their origins are unmistakably classical, filtered and in some measure distorted though they are through the medium of Byzantine art. This latter connection is significantly both religious and secular, whereas in classical art proper it was the secular milieu in which these features were most at home. Their final incarnation in a Muslim religious building is therefore simply the logical

31 Mosul, Nuri mosque, *mihrab* façade

fulfilment of a process begun many centuries before. The readiness with which Islam adopted these five features, and the natural way in which they acquired a liturgical *raison d'être*, speaks volumes for the powers of assimilation possessed by the new religion.

The choice of these particular alien features is interesting on quite other grounds too. All of them have a close connection with palace architecture and court ceremonial, an element which was overlaid by an ecclesiastical veneer in the Byzantine period but still retained its original potency. The evocative power of these architectural symbols was thus virtually undimmed when Islam adopted them, as a brief analysis of each will reveal.

The mihrab

The *mihrab* is perhaps the clearest case of all. The *31* deeply recessed arcuated niche could hold a cult statue in a Graeco-Roman temple or the emperor in person in a late antique palace. Writ large, as an apse, it contained the altar of a Christian church; correspondingly reduced in size, it did duty as a *mihrab*, or niche indicating the direction of prayer – though even in the context of a mosque some vestigial memory of its original function lingers, in that at the Friday *salat* the *imam* stands within the *mihrab* to lead the worshippers. The fact that it was part of the caliph's duties to act as *imam* vividly illustrates the capacity of the new faith to reconcile in a new synthesis the hitherto conflicting demands of church and state. The innate interchangeability of this feature is perhaps most revealingly illustrated in the late Umayyad palace of Mshatta. The triconch form of the throne room *7.11* which terminates the main processional axis finds its closest counterparts in a 6th-century cathedral and bishop's palace in Bosra, in southern Syria. The architectural form is the same in all three cases, even though the great central niche is put to different uses in each – to hold the altar, a bishop's and a caliph's throne respectively. In due course the same form entered the vocabulary of mosque design, with a *mihrab* set within the central niche. Lest it be thought that the *mihrab* was an absolute requirement of any functioning mosque, it should be remembered that the earliest example dates from as late as 86/705, when the rebuilt Mosque of the

2.65–2.66

Prophet at Medina was furnished with one, perhaps to commemorate the place where Muhammad himself had led prayers. There is no question of the earlier mosques which lacked *mihrab*s being regarded as somehow deficient for that reason. In a properly orientated mosque the entire wall which faces the Black Stone in Mecca – the so-called *qibla* wall – serves as a directional indicator. It thereby makes the *mihrab* super-fluous. Thus it was no liturgical necessity which called the *mihrab* into being. The evidence suggests rather that a growing desire to secularise the mosque, or at any rate to bring it more into line with the highly developed arch-itecture of the ancient Near East and of the classical and Byzantine world, was the decisive factor. Once 'invented', the *mihrab* was so ob-viously a signal success as a symbol and as the cynosure of worship that its future was assured. Accordingly, it soon became the focus for elabo-rate decoration in mosaic, marble and other costly materials. Pious Muslims regarded all this splendour with mixed feelings. The 'just' Caliph 'Umar II wanted to remove the gold mosaic from the *mihrab* of the Damascus mosque because it distracted the mind from prayer. But then the head of a Byzantine embassy visited it and praised it, saying 'whoever built this is a great king'; so 'Umar said 'Let it be left alone, since it annoys the enemy'. The various genres of *mihrab* which were ultimately developed – flat, concave, or recessed so as to form a separate chamber – are so varied as to demand a study in themselves, and therefore fall beyond the remit of this account. So too does its formal and symbolic relationship to the portal.

The minbar

The *minbar* never attained the well-nigh univer-sal popularity of the *mihrab* in Islamic architec-ture. To begin with, its function is much more specifically concentrated on the Friday *salat*, and thus on the *jami'*, whereas the *mihrab* quickly became an essential component of even the humblest *masjid*, and is frequently to be found also in *madrasa*s, mausolea, caravansarais and other buildings. An integral part of the Friday service was the *khutba*, part bidding prayer, part sermon and part formal address. This element of the service had a strong political flavour. Indeed, a ruler's claim to legitimacy depended,

inter alia, on the formal mention of his name in the *khutba*. Like the diptych in Byzantium, the *khutba* thus became an instrument for affirming allegiance. Clearly it was important for the *khatib* who pronounced the *khutba* to be easily visible and audible; hence the development of the *minbar*, which was customarily placed im-mediately to the right of the *mihrab*, though in Umayyad times its position was within the *mihrab* itself. The obvious analogy to it in Christ-ian practice is of course the pulpit, and in fact the closest known prototype to the *minbar* is the *ambo*, a word used to describe the lectern and pulpit in early medieval churches as well as the bishop's throne in Byzantine ones. Coptic churches in particular had *ambo*s with the same striking simplicity of form found in *minbar*s: a primitively stepped right-angled triangle set against a wall. No *minbar*s securely datable before the early 9th century have survived, however, so that the precise relationship between the Muslim form and its presumed Christian prototype is hard to determine.

This problem is compounded by the existence of alternative hypotheses on the origin of the *minbar*. One of these holds that the later *minbar* is simply a monumental version of the raised chair from which Muhammad was wont to address his followers; but no trace of this has survived. The other theory associates the *minbar* with the raised throne from which the Sasanian commander-in-chief reviewed the Persian army. Here again, the lack of physical evidence scotches any extended discussion. The irritating gap of two centuries and more between pre-Islamic Christian *ambo*s and the earliest precisely datable *minbar* – generally held to be the teakwood specimen in the Great Mosque at Qairawan – may not be quite the obstacle it seems. A comparison of the example at Qairawan with the *ambo* of a typical Coptic monastery like that of Apa Jeremias at Saqqara reveals sufficient basic similarity of form to justify the analogy. The built-in *minbar* in the Tari Khana mosque at Damghan, perhaps as early as the 8th century and scarcely likely to be any later than the year 900, provides an even closer parallel to the Coptic *ambo* and is moreover of mud brick rather than wood. Since mud brick is a traditional Iranian substitute for stone, the stepped triangular form used at

2.6
34
24

32 Jerusalem, Aqsa mosque, main arch with Fatimid mosaics

Damghan can most conveniently be interpreted as a translation of the Coptic stone *ambo* into the most closely related material available. Perhaps the simple stone, brick or mud *minbar* (still known today, for example in Libya) co-existed with a more elaborately developed version executed in wood. The latter type was sometimes wheeled, and could therefore be brought out into the courtyard when a specially large congregation had foregathered. The link with princely life was already established in the early Umayyad period, for it is recorded that the caliph Mu'awiya I took his *minbar* with him on his travels. It is tempting to assume that it was a *minbar* of this type which Muhammad himself had used. Certainly the *minbar* served in early Islamic times as a kind of throne from which the ruler could address his subjects or receive their allegiance, often in the form of an oath (*bay'a*). In such situations the mosque functioned essentially in a political way as an appendage to the palace.

The example at Qairawan is typical of the subsequent development of the whole genre, though of course minor modifications and improvements were introduced over the centuries. Thus in order to boost the acoustic properties required by the nature of the *minbar*, a canopy, often polyhedral in shape, capped the upper platform or landing, performing very much the same function as the tester in European pulpits. A hinged gate often gave access to the steps, again somewhat in European fashion though there is no need to postulate any direct influence in either direction. Supplementary *minbar*s – and for that matter supplementary *mihrab*s – were sometimes placed elsewhere in a *jami'*, for example in the courtyard, or might be carved out of rock in an open-air mosque or in an *'idgah*, otherwise known as *musalla*– both terms usually denoting a mosque for extraordinary intercessory prayer at the time of the two great *'id*s (festivals) or in times of drought, famine and the like. The decoration of *minbar*s was, by some quirk of tradition, remarkably stereotyped. Their wooden construction laid a premium on the use of many small modular units which on being fitted together created the overall pattern. This was nearly always of geometric type, though some of the early surviving *minbar*s, such as those at Fez and Marrakesh, favour floral designs. From the 14th century onwards more varied types of *minbar* appeared. Examples sheathed in tilework were erected in Iran and increasingly in Ottoman Turkey. The latter area also favoured stone or marble *minbar*s with banisters of elaborately fretted openwork tracery. *Minbar*s in baked brick and iron are also known. In general the use of durable materials brought in its train a markedly simplified design; as late as the 17th century, in Safavid Isfahan, a *minbar* could be built which exactly repeated the shape of the Damghan example of a millennium earlier, but in costly marble instead of mud brick.

The *maqsura*

Far fewer examples of the *maqsura* survive, and it is likely that this situation reflects their relative scarcity in medieval times. The reason is not far to seek. Much more explicitly than either the *mihrab* or the *minbar*, the *maqsura* implies the presence of a ruler. By contrast, every *jami'* requires an *imam* and a *khatib*. In form, the

33 Cairo, mosque of Baibars, *maqsura*

48

34 Qairawan, Great Mosque, *minbar* and *maqsura*

maqsura is a separate, usually square, enclosure within the mosque and close to the *mihrab*. Its walls may be of masonry but a lattice-work of wood or metal is more common. This suffices to screen the occupant from the other worshippers but allows him to see and participate in the *salat*. Several reasons may be proposed for this seclusion. One is a desire straightforwardly to adapt the Byzantine practice of housing the emperor in a royal box, the *kathisma*, and thereby to emphasise his high rank and his essential apartness. Another, related motive might have been to secure privacy of worship for the ruler. This might explain the frequent provision, as at Damascus, of a door beside the *mihrab* communicating both with the royal palace and with the *maqsura* or with a suite of rooms reserved for the caliph, as at the mosque of Abu Dulaf. At Cordoba a vaulted passage (*sabat*) serving this purpose is recorded in the texts both for the mosque as it was *c.*287/900 and for its enlarge-

ment in 350/961. Thus the ruler would be absolved of the need to mingle with other worshippers. Such exclusiveness would be of a piece with the growing emphasis in the Umayyad period on the remoteness of the caliph, a far cry from the unpretentious democracy of Arabian practice. A third reason might well have been a naked fear of assassination. Two of the first four caliphs, 'Umar and 'Ali, were murdered in a mosque, and a third, 'Uthman, was killed while reading the Qur'an. Behind the *maqsura* screen the caliph was visible but not vulnerable. The emphasis on openwork screens in the typical *maqsura* opens up the possibility of a formal connection with the choir screens which were so marked a feature of Byzantine architecture. These too were of course located close to the liturgical focus of the building.

Whatever the origins of the *maqsura*, its symbolic function can scarcely be in doubt. It was a visible exaltation of the ruler's rank, and

2.68

2.49

2.81–2.82

34

therefore an integral part of the strong secular element in the early Islamic *jami'* and of its intimate connection with royal pomp and ceremony. The subsequent history of the *maqsura* betrays a weakening of these associations. The word came to mean the detached part of a mosque set aside for communal as distinct from private prayer. As such, its form underwent a major change. From the 11th century onwards, *maqsura*s in the form of large domed chambers incorporated into the sanctuary of a mosque began to proliferate, especially in the eastern Islamic world, as in the Great Mosque of Isfahan. They were usually preceded by an emphasised central aisle. The example of the mosque of Baibars in Cairo shows that this fashion penetrated to western Islam too. As with the *minbar*, the *maqsura* appears in a variety of forms and contexts, among them mobile examples in wood (as at Qairawan) and others in multi-purpose foundations such as the complex of Sultan Qala'un in Cairo.

2.12, 2.204
2.241–2.249
2.252, 2.263

33, 2.97

34

241

The raised gabled transept

For all its symbolic importance, and of course the physical impact which its sheer size guarantees, the *maqsura* cannot claim to have any significant liturgical role, even when it came to connote the domed sanctuary itself. The same applies even more strongly to the two remaining features of foreign origin which were incorporated more and more often into large urban *jami'*s: the raised gabled transept and the dome over the *mihrab*. The transept never attained any great popularity, if only because it was not a form which could be imposed on all kinds of mosque. Far from it; to make its desired effect the transept called for a sanctuary whose roofing system extended parallel to the *qibla*, not perpendicular to it. The whole purpose of the transept was to assert an axis at variance with the preponderant one in the sanctuary and thereby to emphasise the *mihrab* which terminated the axis thus highlighted. The extra height of the gabled transept, towering above the sanctuary and

29

2.5

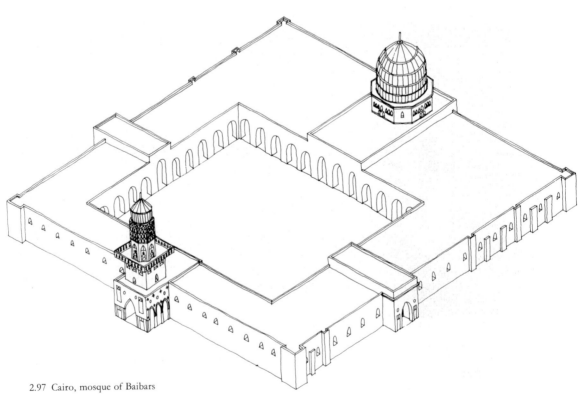

2.97 Cairo, mosque of Baibars

driving at right angles across its roof-line, was the outward visual embodiment of this processional way.

By a fortunate chance the mosque which first expressed this idea was one of the absolutely seminal buildings of Islamic architecture, the Great Mosque of Damascus. The transept was at once recognised as an integral part of the Damascus schema, and in one form or another it is reproduced in all the mosques which depend upon that prototype. By the same token, however, it has no locus in mosques which derive from other sources, and these are by far in the majority. Clearly, then, it is in no sense an obligatory or even customary part of a mosque. Accordingly the obvious question is why it was introduced in the first place. Lack of space forbids the requisitely detailed discussion here, and it must suffice to summarise in barest outline the two most likely possibilities. First, it could be argued that the wholesale transposition of the west front of a typical Syrian church to serve as the centrepiece for an interior mosque façade must have overtones of triumph in political and religious terms, if indeed it is not to be interpreted as outright parody. It must be admitted that such a deliberate reformulation of the components of an established style is a typically Umayyad proceeding. Even so, the second possibility – a connection with princely ceremonies – seems more likely. By that reckoning the key parallel would lie not in religious architecture at all but in palaces, whether gubernatorial as at Ravenna, episcopal as at Bosra or imperial as at Constantinople. In all these contexts the gabled façade encloses an arched entrance which gives on to a processional way. The latter customarily leads to a throne room. There is of course no throne room in a mosque, nor is there any provision in the Qur'an or in the earliest Islamic practice for formal royal receptions in the mosque. Nevertheless the processional entry of

35 Damascus, Great Mosque, aerial view

the caliph or sultan into the *jami‘* for the Friday *salat* was a long-established tradition in the medieval Islamic world. The gabled raised transept, the dome over the *mihrab* and eventually over the *maqsura*, and the *mihrab*, would together create an architectural *mise-en-scène* which would be the natural corollary to such pomp and circumstance. A comparable and much better documented process may be observed in Western medieval architecture.

The significant progeny of the transept in the Great Mosque at Damascus is to be traced almost exclusively in the western Islamic world. The easternmost limit of its influence is **2.206** probably the Great Mosque of Diyarbakr in Anatolia. Interestingly enough, the mosques in Egypt which repeat the transept motif, though relatively few in number, include some of the finest mosques of their time – those of al-Azhar, **2.94-2.97** al-Hakim and Baibars. This suggests that when the transept motif travelled outside the confines of Syria it retained its royal associations. In time its form became simplified so as to allow a smoother integration with the courtyard façade of which it was the cynosure. This is particularly noticeable in the major Maghribi mosques, **2.109, 2.112** where the greater breadth of the "transept" **2.118, 2.149** *vis-à-vis* the flanking aisles is maintained intact, but its external silhouette rises much less markedly above the rest of the roof-line. Most

2.112 Fez, Qarawiyin mosque

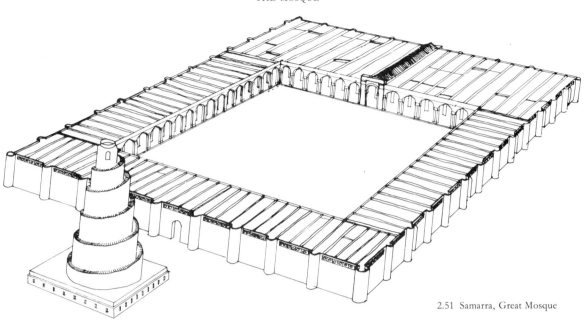

2.51 Samarra, Great Mosque

significantly of all, the basic notion of conflict-
ing axes so crucial to the transept form is lost. It
seems likely that this was already the case in the
Umayyad mosque at Medina and, a little over a
century later, at the Great Mosque of Samarra.
In these Maghribi mosques the aisles tend to be
perpendicular to the *qibla* and it is only by its
greater width, height and vaulting that the
central one stands out. In the long run,
therefore, the concept of a transept proved to be
an aberration within the context of Islamic
architecture as a whole; the axial nave replaced it.

The dome over the mihrab

Finally, what of the dome over the *mihrab*–or
alternatively, over the bay preceding it? Roman
architecture had decisively established the
honorific character of the dome by giving it
pride of place in palatial architecture, and it is no
accident that the greatest of all Roman religious
edifices, the Pantheon, makes the dome its focal
point. These lofty associations did not of course
prevent the Romans from using the dome in
humbler contexts, but a pattern had been set and
was confirmed in Byzantine architecture by the
large-scale use of the dome in churches and
monasteries. It was therefore a natural transition
to employ it in mosques, and incidentally in key
locations within Islamic palaces. Within the

mosque the obvious place for it was near the
mihrab, as part of the intricate nexus of royal
associations established by that feature, the
minbar, the *maqsura* and the transept. Each of
these elements derives added impact from the
nearness of the others. In a mosque which uses
principally flat or pitched roofs or at most
shallow vaulting, the presence of a full-scale
dome is obviously intended to emphasise some
liturgical focus if not to express some religious
or political symbolism. Given the fact that the
mihrab, even if it does on occasion project
slightly beyond the rest of the external *qibla* wall,
is essentially part of the interior formulation of
the mosque and that its position is therefore not
readily identifiable from the outside, the value of
the dome as an outward sign of that spot is
obvious. More than that, its very form, with its
rich inbuilt secular associations, emphasises the
princely role of the *mihrab*. Finally, it marks the
location of the *qibla* – an important consideration in a crowded urban setting otherwise
devoid of fixed directional points.

   The dome over the *mihrab* proved to be one
of the most durable and versatile aspects of
medieval Islamic architecture. By degrees its
usefulness as a distinguishing mark won such
recognition that the idea was applied on a more
extensive scale. Pairs or trios of domes over the

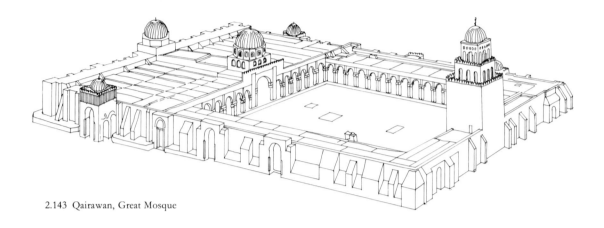

2.143 Qairawan, Great Mosque

mihrab, maqsura and transept area, or along the centre stretch of the *qibla* wall, multiplied the effect. A favourite combination was to mark the erstwhile transept, now reduced to simply a larger central aisle, by a dome at each extremity, *12* or to assert the *qibla* wall by a dome at each end and one in the middle. Such devices show *2.94, 2.143* Islamic architects composing their buildings with an eye to the overall design, and using domes like grace notes to punctuate the regular beat of an articulated wall or a peristyle. This specialised architectural context, however, did not entirely divest the dome of its traditionally weighty secular and religious associations. That situation obtained even when the popularity of domical architecture was at its zenith. As late as the high Ottoman period a clear hierarchy based on gradations of size ensured that the principal *2.333-2.337* domes were suitably highlighted by the diminutive scale of the surrounding ones.

These, then, are the five features of the *jami'* for which a foreign origin of at least partially royal character may be claimed. As mentioned earlier, however, none of them are to be regarded as vital to the proper functioning of a mosque. Since both *mihrab* and *minbar* have the sanction of an unbroken tradition stretching back some thirteen hundred years, it might well be argued that they are now indissolubly part of the *jami'*. It would indeed be pedantic to discount the force of custom entirely in these

two cases, whatever a strict interpretation of Muslim liturgy might suggest. The other three features obviously lacked this direct appeal to Muslim taste, and by degrees fell into disuse, or at best maintained their popularity in a few areas only. This decline from their earlier importance is almost certainly attributable to the gradual divorce between the caliph and the conduct of the Friday *salat*. As the caliph delegated those of his functions which bore directly on the Friday service to the *imam* and the *khatib*, the motive for singling out those parts of the mosque specially connected with the royal presence disappeared. But the close connection between politics and the mosque was perennial. When Ikhshid, the 10th–century ruler of Egypt, was confirmed in his position by the caliph, the doors of the chief mosque in Cairo were covered with gold-embroidered brocade. Reverence for the ruler went further still in Fatimid times, for the mere mention of any of the Fatimid rulers in the Azhar mosque resulted in the people prostrating themselves.

OTHER COMPONENTS OF THE MOSQUE

The five princely components of the mosque are far from exhausting the tally of its constituent parts, some of which are of equal or even greater importance. The minaret (which forms the subject of the next chapter), the courtyard, the covered sanctuary, facilities for ablution – all play a significant role in the overall design of a mosque, to say nothing of such lesser facilities as a *dikka* (a raised platform), carpets or other floor coverings, latrines and even doorknockers.

2.35

There is little to be said about the courtyard, although paradoxically this is in some ways the most striking aspect of mosque design for the casual observer. Its impact is largely due to its size: the huge empty space gives the visitor pause and serves notice that he has left the workaday world behind him. Like the *atrium* of an early Christian church, it heralds the sanctuary proper and defines an area which is holy even if it is not regularly used for worship. There was no set form for the courtyard, but the

2.55–2.64 rectangle dominates, whether the emphasis lies on depth or on width. Arcades or a flat-roofed portico customarily articulate its inner façades, while the open space itself may be punctuated by

2.46; 36 a small domed treasury as at Damascus, Hama

57 and San'a', a shrine or other aedicule and perhaps a *minbar*, a pool or a *dikka*. These additional elements, however, are not suffered to impinge too strongly on, or to detract from, the sense of unbroken space which the courtyard creates. In the larger towns the courtyard held the overflow of worshippers from the sanctuary

at the Friday *salat*, and even in smaller centres its capacity might be required on the occasion of the '*id*s or extraordinary prayers. It was never a dead space.

Islamic worship demanded ritual ablution (*wudu*') as a necessary preliminary to prayer.

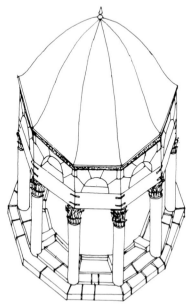

2.15 Ma'arrat al-Nu'man, fountain in *jami*'

Facilities for washing are therefore standard in 2.14 most mosques. They take various forms. 37 Sometimes they comprise a domed or open 2.15 fountain within the mosque, intended for washing only. When Ibn Tulun was ruler of Egypt he was criticised for adding a fountain (now long gone) to the courtyard of his mosque. Ten marble columns supported a dome, beneath which was a marble basin some four metres in diameter. In the centre of this basin a fountain played, its waters bordered by trellises. Perhaps all this was too close for comfort to the life of the court–indeed, one such fountain, the Qubbat al-Barudiyin in Marrakesh, has been 21 interpreted by some as a palace pavilion. An 2.127 alternative tradition is for ritual ablution to be 2.128–2.129 carried out near the latrines outside the mosque, in which case drinking water may be provided by a fountain in the courtyard. The influence of the classical house with its *impluvium* in the

36 Hama, Great Mosque, *bait al-mal*

37 Ma'arrat al-Nu'man, Great Mosque, courtyard, fountain and minaret

groups of muezzins would perform the movements of prayer in time with the *imam* and in full view of the worshippers further back. Not surprisingly, this became distracting and the practice was largely discontinued, except in mosques whose layout made it imperative. Although Baghdad reputedly had some 27,000 places of worship in the year 300/912, and according to some reports even more, the Friday *salat* was held exclusively in three mosques. These were quite insufficient to hold the vast numbers of people that had gathered, so the rows of worshippers spilled out week after week beyond the mosque portals, lining the streets all the way to the Tigris – and latecomers arrived in canoes to join the congregation. In such circum-

atrium may perhaps be detected in those mosques (such as some of Ottoman date at Bursa) where the ablutions facility is placed below a skylight in the sanctuary itself. In Iran and India especially, much of the courtyard is taken up by a large pool, which acts also as a landscaping feature, alleviating the bare expanse of the courtyard and introducing a broad band of contrasting colour. Elsewhere, in areas where the dominant *madhhab* or law school was Hanbali, this was not permitted on the grounds that ablution had to be performed with running water. Water in Hanbali mosques is therefore provided by taps. None of these practices, incidentally, excludes the possibility of performing ablutions by means of sand where water is scarce.

In the larger mosques the burgeoning size of congregations gradually highlighted a problem not previously encountered: the press of people tended to make it hard to see the *imam* leading the worship. The solution adopted in such mosques, from about the 9th century onwards, was to build a raised platform or *dikka* on which

2.128 Marrakesh, Qubbat al-Barudiyin

2.129 Marrakesh, Qubbat al-Barudiyin

stances supplementary *imam*s posted at intervals were required to synchronise the actions of worship. Sometimes, of course, mosques would outlive their purpose; thus the Spanish traveller Ibn Jubair, visiting Baghdad in the late 12th century, found eleven Friday mosques even though 'almost nothing was left of Baghdad except its famous name'.

This virtually exhausts the tally of items which together constitute a typical mosque. It will be abundantly clear that Islamic tradition had no place for the furnishings which are so

38 Qairawan, Great Mosque, *mihrab* area with *minbar*, *maqsura*, dome and polycandelon

regular a feature of Christian churches – pews, fonts, monuments, altars, and various kinds of ecclesiastical sculpture such as the retable, reredos, tester, choir screen and the like. Provision could sometimes be made for music; al-Muqaddasi notes that in Khurasan it was the custom for a choir to sit on a bench opposite the *minbar* and sing music 'with skill and melody'. Stained glass – abstract rather than figural, of course – seems to have been used more frequently than is generally supposed, but virtually the only objects to break the puritanically bare expanse of the average sanctuary are lamps. In the larger mosques these lamps, in form like a triangular candelabra, were hung in their hundreds or even thousands, suspended on long chains to just above the height of a man. The symbolic value of such lighting as a metaphor for spiritual illumination is made explicit by the habit of depicting a simple lamp (*qandil*) on *mihrab*s and enclosing it by a quotation from the Sura of Light (Qur'an 24:35): 'God is the light of the heavens and the earth; the likeness of his light is as a niche wherein is a lamp, the lamp in a glass, the glass as it were a glittering star.' On special occasions *mihrab*s and minarets were decked with lights. According to al-Baihaqi it was the 'Abbasid caliph al-Ma'mun who ordered that mosques should be illuminated in a more costly fashion than had been the practice earlier. By the 10th century, huge oven-shaped lamps (appropriately called *tanur*) had come into fashion for this purpose. One such object, made of silver and donated by the Fatimid caliph al-Hakim, weighed 100,000 drachms and the doors of the 'Amr mosque in Cairo had to be removed to let it in.

Apart from mosque lamps the only other furnishing commonly found in mosques was some kind of floor covering. Mats of woven reeds were the most popular solution in much of the Arab world; the particular type of matting varied from sect to sect. The custom no doubt evolved from the religious requirement that all must enter the mosque unshod. Muhammad himself sometimes used a carpet when he was praying and it is therefore not surprising that in Iran and Turkey especially – countries with an immemorial tradition of carpet weaving – mosque floors were bedecked with rugs, whether these were of pile or flat-weave (e.g.

*kilim*s or *zilu*s). Luxury carpets were reserved for the great feasts, a custom which ensured that they suffered much less wear and that helps to explain why some of the finest and oldest carpets have been found in mosques. The puritan lobby naturally rejected such luxury as being unIslamic. The use of sweet-smelling spices in the mosque was also frowned on in some quarters. Nevertheless, in the 10th century the Azhar mosque had Indian aloe, camphor and musk available to perfume the building during Ramadan and on other festive occasions.

SUBSIDIARY FUNCTIONS OF THE MOSQUE

Such are the component parts of a typical mosque in medieval times. Most of them bear on the essential *raison d'être* of the building, namely communal worship, but they are susceptible of other uses too. Moreover, still other features might be added to serve additional purposes of a less explicitly religious nature. In the case of the great urban *jami*'s a host of such satellite functions had to be catered for, thereby greatly extending the surface area of the complex. The ancillary buildings thus called into being might themselves serve dual or even multiple functions. There is no space in this chapter to investigate such subsidiary structures in any detail, and it must suffice to list them somewhat baldly, with only a passing comment here and there.

Education and scholarship

Education was perhaps the principal secondary function of the mosque, especially in the first four centuries of Islam. The term connoted a wide range of religious activities: the study of Islamic law and of the so-called 'religious sciences' such as *tafsir* and *fiqh*; the memorisation of the Qur'an, often carried out in a building known as *dar al-qur'an* or *dar al-huffaz*; and the study of *hadith*, or sayings of the Prophet, for which a *dar al-hadith* was sometimes provided. The *kuttab* – schools with a very strong emphasis on religious teaching – were also sometimes sited within the precincts of the mosque. Teaching customarily took place in the sanctuary; the lecturer would seat himself against a pillar and the class would squat around him. The geographer al-Muqaddasi noted 120 such 'circles' (*khalqa*s) in the chief mosque of

Cairo in the 10th century. Lecturers in jurisprudence could have an audience of as many as 500 people. The popularity of the different *madhhab*s could be gauged by the number of students they attracted in the mosque. Ibn Sa'id says that in 326/938 the Shafi'ites and Malikites each had 15 circles of students in the chief mosque of al-Fustat, while the Hanafites had only three. Al-Suyuti notes that at this time the audience which formed around the Maliki *imam* al-Na'ali extended to 17 pillars of the mosque. In time, purpose-built *madrasa*s took over the role of teaching institutions which mosques had formerly discharged, though even these *madrasa*s might on occasion be located next to or within a mosque. To this day, of course, certain outstanding mosques are more famous for their roles as universities than as places of worship: al-Azhar in Egypt, founded in 361/970 and beyond doubt the oldest continuously functioning university in the world; the Qarawiyin mosque in Fez, an educational institution without peer in the western Maghrib; and the Zaituna in Tunis, its equivalent in the eastern Maghrib.

The mosque maintained, throughout the Middle Ages and in some cases right up to modern times, close links with a particular facet of education: the world of scholars, scholarship and books. It was in the mosque above all that scholars foregathered for discussion, lectures and to hear the latest works being read. Publication before the advent of the printing press meant a public reading of the work in question, validated by the presence of the author himself or by someone authorised by him in writing to do so. Everyone thus authorised could in turn authorise others by the same process, for which the mosque was the obvious public forum. Every mosque of importance had a library, and books were often bequeathed to them. They could also act as the venue for sales; it is recorded that when the *qadi* Abu'l-Mutrif died in Cordoba in 420/1029 his library was sold in his mosque for an entire year, fetching a total of 400,000 *dinars*. Wandering scholars, who were as much a feature of medieval Islam as of medieval western Christendom, were accustomed to seeking shelter in mosques. These effectively took over the functions of hostelries and might have additional features such as soup kitchens, hospi-

tals and even morgues. That inveterate scholar-traveller Ibn Battuta travelled the length and breadth of the Muslim world in the 14th century expecting – and finding – free board and lodging at a wide range of religious institutions, foremost among them being the mosque. By a natural extension of usage the mosque was an obvious early port of call for foreigners – that is, Muslims from another part of the Islamic world.

Additional religious functions

While worship was of course the primary function of the mosque, it was the natural setting for a series of related activities. These included sermons or theological lectures, retreats – especially popular in the last third of Ramadan and taking the form of nocturnal vigils – the systematic teaching of Qur'an recitation, the practice of *dhikr*, namely the ritual repetition of stock formulae, especially of praise and adoration of God; and finally the offering of special prayers – in cases of barrenness, for instance – the sealing of oaths or covenants and the celebration of rites of passage: birth, circumcision, marriage, divorce and burial. A form of higher piety was to live in the mosque; the caliph al-Qadir (d.422/1031) daily distributed to those living in mosques one-third of the food provided for his own table.

Mosques were also the obvious places in which to preserve relics: a shoe of the Prophet at Hebron, and numerous copies of Qur'ans which had passed through the hands of 'Uthman. In the State treasury in the mosque of Cordoba, for instance, there was a Qur'an which contained four folios of that caliph's own copy. They even bore his bloodstains. It was so heavy that two men were required to carry it – a detail which perhaps casts a certain doubt on the authenticity of this relic. It was fetched out early on Fridays by two servants of the mosque while a third preceded it with a candle. It had a finely embroidered cover and used to be placed on a stool in the sanctuary.

Foremost among these 'lesser' religious or semi-religious purposes was the use of the mosque as a place of pilgrimage. This special distinction applied only to certain mosques, usually those associated in some particular way with Muhammad or with some notable saint. Naturally such mosques are more numerous in the Levant and Saudi Arabia than in the rest of the Muslim world; the most important are those of Mecca, Medina and Jerusalem. *Hadith*s averred that prayers offered in 'pilgrimage' mosques were much more meritorious than those offered in other mosques, while prayer offered in an ordinary mosque was itself worth twenty times as much as that offered elsewhere. By degrees such special sanctity was extended to mosques somewhat further removed from the heartlands of Islam, such as those of Qairawan in Tunisia and Konya in Turkey. To this day large numbers of Shi'ites from Iran, Iraq and the Arabian peninsula make pilgrimages to the Great Mosque of Damascus.

2.142

Justice

There is a long and honourable connection between the mosque and the administration of justice; Muhammad himself had used the mosque for this purpose. The use of the mosque as a venue for the taking and registration of oaths and notarial acts is only one aspect of this association. Much more important in the medieval period was the custom of turning over a part of the mosque for use as a law court on set days, with the *qadi* presiding. According to the *Kitab al-Aghani*, it was originally the custom for the *qadi* to sit in the chief mosque leaning against a pillar, since this was a public place open to entire community. Later attempts (in the 9th century) to stop this practice on the grounds that it desecrated God's house failed, though a century later it is recorded that a crowd of Egyptians, indignant at a *qadi*'s injustice, flung his prayer mat out of the mosque into the street. During the Fatimid period the chief *qadi* of Cairo sat on Tuesdays and Saturdays in the wing of the mosque of 'Amr ibn al-'As. He occupied a dais and had a silken cushion. To the left and right of him sat his assessors, in order of seniority. In front of him sat five court servants and four court clerks, facing each other in twos. A silver inkpot from the citadel treasury was placed before him. That the mosque was not the only place where cases were tried is revealed by the report that the 'Abbasid caliph al-Muhtadi built a special domed hall with four doors where he administered justice, as was the caliph's duty in early Islamic times. It was called 'The Dome of Justice' (*qubbat al-mazalim*) and was erected in

255–6/868–9. The caliph even arranged, so al-Baihaqi says, for coal-pans to heat it on cold days 'so that the suitors may not be turned into stone by cold together with His Majesty's presence'. The fact that caliph and *qadi* alike used a *minbar* like that of the *khatib* is an eloquent testimony, as indeed is the use of the mosque for so many different purposes, of the underlying unity of so much of Islamic civilisation. Equally revealing is the fact that while cases concerning Muslims were heard in the mosque, these concerning Christians were held on the steps leading up to it.

Politics

Due emphasis should be laid on the political dimension within which the mosque evolved and functioned. This aspect finds manifold expression in the mosque: the five alien elements mentioned earlier as being incorporated into its schema are far from exhausting the range of relevant connections. One might point, for example, to the location of many early mosques in the middle of the camp where the Arab soldiery lodged, and right next to the dwelling-place of the commander-in-chief, ultimately the palace of the ruler. The *khutba* was one of several ways whereby this close relationship was expressed. It functioned as a mark of legitimacy, and participation in it was equivalent to a collective oath of allegiance. In times of civil strife or other kinds of political instability there was no quicker way of informing the populace of who the true ruler and his accredited deputy might be than the *khutba*. Hence the high feelings which, despite the sanctity of the mosque, vented themselves on occasion in the stoning or even murder of the *khatib*, or conversely in the ritual cursing from the pulpit of enemies of the régime. Just as in later times the captain of a British warship had to read himself in before his authority had official confirmation, so too in medieval Islam a governor's first task on taking up office was to mount the *minbar*, glorify God, and read out the Caliph's letter of appointment, or simply announce the fact that he had been invested with that dignity. That same *minbar* was also the scene for political announcements and harangues of all kinds. When it was announced from the pulpit that the *de facto* ruler of Baghdad, the Buyid 'Adud al-Daula, had assumed the ancient

Persian title of Shahanshah, the people rebelled and pelted the preacher with stones. The mosque was frequently the forum for sectarian disputes, which of course often had a political edge. The Buyid ruler Mu'izz al-Daula decorated the mosques of Baghdad with the usual Shi'ite inscriptions of curses and imprecations, but these were blotted out overnight. Similarly, in 395/1005 the Fatimid caliph al-Hakim enjoined curses on Abu Bakr, 'Uthman, Mu'awiya and the 'Abbasids to be inscribed on the exteriors of mosques. Sometimes the curses inscribed on mosques had nothing to do with sectarian disputes; in Baghdad in 425/1034 the repeal of the unpopular but lucrative tax on salt was announced in a sermon in the mosque, and curses were inscribed on the door of the mosque on anyone who imposed this tax again. The tradition that the mosque was a place of political asylum, like the church in western Europe, was deeply ingrained in Islam. In some cases provision was even made to employ the mosque as a military building, with fortifications behind which the faithful could take refuge in times of uprising or war. Such bastions were apt to become a traditional feature of mosque architecture even when Muslim society had long outgrown the need for them. Sometimes the mosque discharged a policing function, for example at the time of the rebellion of Zaid b. 'Ali in 123/741, when the people of Kufa were ordered to proceed to the Great Mosque, with the clear implication that anyone who did not turn up would be treated as a rebel. Once they were safely inside, the gates of the mosque were locked. In another episode during Zaid's rebellion, the role of the mosque moved from the defensive to the offensive; al-Tabari relates that 'the Syrian troops looked down on them [the rebels] and they began throwing stones at them from the top of the mosque'. Finally, in yet another uprising during this period, the successful one led by Yazid b. al-Walid, it was the Great Mosque of Damascus which was chosen as a meeting place by the conspirators, perhaps not least because they knew that many weapons were stored there.

2.143

Mosques with special functions

These wider and in large part secular functions could in theory be discharged by *masjid*s and *jami*'s alike, though in practice they tended to bulk larger in the latter. There was, however, a further category of mosques (usually *masjid*s) which responded to the needs of particular groups of people. Among these were mosques reserved for certain tribes, which flourished especially in Arabia in the first century of Islam and were a potent force for disunity; and mosques for separate quarters in a town or, as a logical extension of this, for certain crafts or occupations. Sometimes mosques reflected theological differences – not only the obvious schism between Sunni and Shi'i, but also the relatively minor distinctions between the various *madhhab*s. These mosques, like the tribal ones, also fostered dissension and their legality was open to question on these grounds.

Finally there was a category of mosque which could broadly be termed memorial. This type

39 Muhammadiya, Masjid-i Sar-i Kucha

included mosques built on sites sanctified by certain events in the life of the Prophet – including places where he had prayed as well as locations where some seminal event had taken place, like the Aqsa mosque in Jerusalem which commemorated his *mi'raj*, namely his night journey to Hell and the Seven Heavens. Also in this category were mosques with specific Biblical associations, such as the mosque of Abraham at Hebron; both types recall (functionally though not architecturally) the Christian martyrium. With them may be classed funerary mosques, a type denounced in numerous *hadith*s but which drew its vitality from pre-Islamic tradition in which the graves of ancestors often became sanctuaries. Muhammad's own tomb at Medina, around which there developed the Mosque of the Prophet, is an example of this. By a natural transition mosques were built over the tombs of some of the great men of early Islam, such as the Companions of the Prophet, and pilgrimages – admittedly unorthodox – were made to them. In time a whole complex of buildings might evolve around the tomb of the notable in question. The case of the Masjid-i Sar-i Kucha at Muhammadiya in central Iran (perhaps 4th/10th century), with its monumental Kufic inscription listing Companions of the Prophet, shows that commemorative as well as funerary mosques were built in their honour.

It was of course appropriate that a building which ministered to the community as a whole should be a financial charge on that community; hence the practice (recorded at Isfahan for example) of enlarging a mosque by means of public subscription. Ibn Hauqal, in the course of his account of Sicily, notes as a prodigy that 'in Palermo and Khalisa, together with the quarters outside the walls, there are more than 300 mosques, most of them in good condition, with their roofs, walls and doors intact . . . I have never seen so many mosques in any place or great city, even in cities double the size, nor have I heard anyone claim such a number, except for the claim of the Cordovans that their city has 500 mosques. I was not able to verify this in Cordova and mentioned it in its place with some expression of doubt, but I can confirm it for Sicily because I personally saw the greater part. One day I was standing near the house of . . . .al-Qafsi, a jurist and notary. From

his mosque I could see, at the distance of a bowshot, about ten mosques, all within view, some of them facing one another and separated only by the breadth of the street. I inquired about this and was informed that these people are so puffed up with pride that each one of them wants to have his own mosque, reserved to him and shared by no-one apart from his own family and retinue. It even happened that two brothers, whose houses were adjoining with party walls, each built a mosque for himself in which to sit alone.'

GROWING SANCTITY OF THE MOSQUE

These remarks are far from exhausting the subject of how the mosque functioned in medieval times. Nevertheless, they at least hint at the variety of functions which characterised the medieval mosque and which explains the popularity of a nuclear plan onto which extra elements could easily be grafted. This innate flexibility can be traced to the very origins of the mosque; for it cannot be emphasised too strongly that the mosque did not begin life as a primarily religious centre. Muhammad's house was more of a political headquarters than a place of worship; people camped, argued and even fought there. It was only by degrees that the sanctity of the mosque asserted itself. Under the Umayyads, for example, it was still permissible for Christians to enter mosques. For a long time only specified parts of the mosque were held to be fully sacred – the *mihrab*, the *minbar* and the tomb of a saint who might be buried there, which would be venerated for the holiness (*baraka*) emanating from it. Rules of behaviour gradually imposed themselves: the removal of shoes became obligatory, and worshippers were enjoined not to spit (or to spit only to the left), to preserve silence and decent conduct – a provision aimed at the unruly Bedouin – to ensure their ritual cleanliness, to wear best clothes on a Friday and to observe a host of similar prescriptions. By the 9th century booksellers were forbidden to trade in mosques, but such practices (like preaching for money) were hard to eradicate. So too was the practice, noted by the 10th-century geographer Ibn Hauqal at Fustat, of eating meals in mosques. Hence, no doubt, arose the practice whereby bread– and water-sellers freely plied their trade in the mosque precincts. The *Maqamat* of al-Hariri, written in the 12th century, shows how swindlers proliferated in mosques. The 10th-century geographer al-Muqaddasi speaks disparagingly of Ahwaz in south-west Iran: 'there is no sanctity in its mosque. I mean thereby that it is full of swindlers, low and ignorant people who arrange to meet there. Thus the mosque is never free of people who sit there while others are engaged in prayer. It is the gathering-place of importunate beggars and a home of sinners'. The role of women in the mosque became more sharply defined. They were to sit apart from the men, to leave before them, not to wear perfume and not to enter the mosque during menstruation. Often a specific part of the mosque, such as the upper galleries around the courtyard or an area at the back of the sanctuary, was reserved for them. Announcements in mosques about lost property were forbidden on the grounds that the Prophet had said of such conduct 'May Allah not return it to you; mosques are not built for this'. In the same vein, a *hadith* transmitted by al-Tirmidhi records Muhammad as saying 'when you find someone selling and buying in the mosque, say 'May Allah not allow you profit in this trade'.' Other *hadith*s forbade the use of the mosque for purposes as various as the administration of punishment, the reciting of poetry, the unsheathing of swords and the treatment of wounds – though in the latter case another *hadith* states that the Prophet made provision for a tent to be pitched within the mosque at Medina for the treatment of the sick, and a nurse named Rufaida was appointed to look after them.

PROBLEMS OF CLASSIFICATION

The necessary pendant to the foregoing generalities is a detailed survey of the major schools of medieval mosque architecture. Shortage of space imposes a broad-brush approach in this account. Hence it is necessary to gloss over the particular genres of mosque which became associated with specific dynasties or provinces and to force an inordinate variety of types on to the Procrustean bed of three 'ethnic' architectural traditions: Arab, Turkish and Persian. If this proceeding were applied to all mosques in the Islamic world it would involve such gross simplifications as treating the mosques of the Indo-Pakistan subcontinent, which account for perhaps half of those preserved from medieval times in the entire Muslim world, as offshoots of the Arab or Persian types insofar as they are mentioned at all. It would also entail ignoring the many vigorous if quasi-vernacular sub-schools of Islamic architecture, such as those of Africa south of the Maghrib; China; and south-east Asia. As it happens, these areas fall outside the purview of this book; what follows is therefore intended to encompass the significant basic types of medieval mosque in the central Islamic lands. This material does lend itself tolerably well to analysis within the framework of the three 'ethnic' traditions.

One solution to this problem of misrepresentation, although it is admittedly a compromise, is to select a few of the most celebrated mosques, to imply in more or less arbitrary fashion that they are typical, and to base the requisite generalisations on them. This approach has at least the merit of clarity, and it could indeed be argued that it is in the finest mosques of a given period and region that local peculiarities are apt to find their fullest expression. Nevertheless, such a broad-brush approach, for all its superficial attractions, is simply not specific enough. Another approach, which might be termed typological, cuts across regional and temporal boundaries in order to isolate the significant variants of mosque design and trace their development. Yet, precisely because it ignores such boundaries, this approach tends to minimise the significance of regional schools and fashions. The categories and sub-species which it proposes tend to have a somewhat academic flavour; while technically defensible, they somehow miss the point. A third approach might be to rely on statistics and, by chronicling all known mosques of premodern date, to discover the types and distribution of the most popular varieties. The picture to emerge from such a study might indeed be literally accurate, but it would not distinguish between the *jami'* and the *masjid*, that is, between the major religious building of a town or city and the neighbourhood mosque. Since virtually all the mosques under discussion here fall into the category of *jami'*, such a study would be of limited value in this context, and would

40 Konya, 'Ala' al-Din mosque, interior

assuredly blur the sharp outlines of regional peculiarities of mosque design. After all, the simplest types of mosques not only vastly outnumber the more complex ones but are also to be found throughout the Muslim world. It is such mosques, therefore, which make up the standard distribution of this building type. They dominate by sheer weight of numbers, but – by the same token – they distort the overall picture, suggesting a uniformity that actually exists only at the level of the most primitive buildings. Only when a statistical survey of this kind is relieved of the effectively dead weight of such buildings can regional and temporal distinctions stand out in their full clarity.

Such are the difficulties attendant on venturing a *tour d'horizon* of formal developments in the pre-modern mosque. What, then, is the best way of tackling this problem? The most promising line of approach is probably to identify those mosque types which are most distinctive of a given area and period, describing their constituent features but avoiding a detailed analysis of individual buildings. It should be emphasised that the overriding aim of highlighting significant regional developments entails the suppression of much corroborative detail and, more importantly, of those periods when a given region was simply continuing to build mosques in a style already well established. Admittedly the lulls in innovation have their own part to play in the history of mosque architecture; but that part is too modest to rate any extended discussion here.

For that same reason, areas in which the pace of change was sluggish are allotted less attention

in the following account than those which were consistently in the forefront of experiment. The Maghrib, for example, receives less space than Iran, while Iraq and the Levant take second place to Egypt and Anatolia. These emphases, moreover, reflect the basic truth that the design of a mosque was often less liable to take on a distinctively local colouring than were its decoration, its structural techniques or even specific components of that design, such as the minaret. One final caveat should be sounded: the ensuing generalisations deliberately exclude the "peripheral" areas of the Islamic world, not least because nearly all the mosques in these areas are of post-medieval date, and therefore lie in the shadow of developments in the Islamic heartlands. There is, moreover, a strong vernacular element in these regional traditions, for often they draw very heavily on a reservoir of ideas, practices and forms which owe very little to Islam. Thus for reasons which are as much historical and cultural as geographical they do not belong in the mainstream of mosque architecture.

This survey, then, will cover the central Islamic lands from Andalusia to Afghanistan. The very nature of the material, however, makes it undesirable to embark directly on a series of regional summaries: the sheer lack of surviving monuments would require each summary to start at a different date. In most areas of the Islamic world it is not until the 11th century that mosques survive in sufficient quantities for the lineaments of a local style to emerge. To explain that style would in most cases entail reference to earlier mosques in other regions, with consequent repetition and overlap. The crucial decisions which dictated the subsequent formal development of the mosque were taken in the early centuries of Islam; and the buildings which embodied those decisions are themselves thinly scattered over the entire area bounded by Andalusia and Afghanistan. Yet the inter-connections between these buildings are such as to make light of their geographical remoteness from each other.

It will be clear from what has been said so far that to give a sufficiently full account of the subsequent development of the mosque in its various regional guises without obscuring or falsifying the major issues is no easy task. The mosque is, after all, the most frequently encountered of Islamic buildings, and the one which over the centuries has attracted the most attention from travellers, historians and scholars. Not surprisingly, it is the building type which has experienced the widest range of variations in Islamic architecture. Within the compass of the present study it is impossible to describe these variations at length while at the same time remaining alert to their basic kinship, and thus it would be impossible to see the wood for the trees. Perhaps the most convenient solution, then (despite the attendant difficulties noted above) is to identify the three major categories of mosque architecture – Arab, Iranian and Turkish – and to attempt to accommodate all regional and formal variations within one or other of them. It would of course be possible to propose other kinds of category, such as those based more precisely on building types, on chronology, on more detailed regional sub-divisions or on function. All these categories have much to recommend them, but they would all tend to obscure the one salient fact that in mosques, as in no other type of Islamic architecture, an extraordinarily consistent distinction was maintained between the developed Arab, Persian and Turkish types. Naturally there are numerous buildings in which these distinctions are somewhat blurred, and there are examples where one ethnic tradition adopted a feature characteristic of another. Examples may also be cited of mosques being built in a foreign style quite different from the prevalent local one – 'Arab' mosques in India, or 'Turkish' ones in Algeria. Moreover, in the early stages of Persian and Turkish mosque architecture it was inevitable that strong Arab influences should make themselves felt, since it was of course in the Arab lands that the first mosques were built. Then there are those mosques – comparatively few in number as it happens – which obstinately refuse to fit into any ethnic, political or geographical pigeon-hole and which were built in response to specific functions or occasions, or owed their form to the personal inspiration of the architect. Nevertheless, to accept all these qualifications is not to deny the validity of the three categories proposed. *Faute de mieux*, they will provide the framework for an account of the manifold development of the one building central to the Islamic faith.

ARAB MOSQUES

Since all the really early mosques to survive, namely those securely datable to the seventh and eighth centuries, are of Arab plan, no matter where they were built, it will be convenient to tackle that category first. Such a procedure recommends itself on other grounds too. The Arab concept of the mosque was decisive in determining its architectural form, and the changes wrought on the mosque in Turkish and Persian territory were grafted on to that pre-existing form. Broadly speaking, no fundamental re-thinking of mosque forms occurred in either the Turkish or the Persian tradition. Thus the Arab form of the mosque may fairly claim not only chronological precedence but also an absolute pre-eminence in that most subsequent mosques were derived more or less closely from it. Besides, the Arab mosque plan not only had the widest diffusion but also covers the longest chronological span. Next in length will be the survey of the Persian tradition, almost as ancient as that of the Arab plan but more restricted in geographical scope. Shortest of all will be the discussion of the Turkish mosque type, whose creative development is confined in time to the 14th–17th centuries and in space to Anatolia.

The term 'Arab plan' will be used frequently in the discussion which follows and a close definition of it is therefore desirable. The irreducible minimum which the term connotes is a walled rectilinear enclosure comprising an open courtyard and a covered area near the *qibla*. The sanctuary comprises either multiple columns supporting a flat roof, or arcades supporting a pitched roof. The emphasis on regularly spaced supports fairly close together has led to this type of mosque being called 'hypostyle'. All three elements – enclosing walls, courtyard and sanctuary – were to undergo changes later; but those changes were inconsistent and spasmodic, and both the pace and the degree of change differed from one element to another.

The earliest Arab mosques

Not surprisingly, the constituent elements of the Arab mosque plan are found at their starkest in the earliest mosques built in the generation after the death of the Prophet. The best-known examples are the mosques of Fustat, Qairawan,

41 Ta'izz, Ashrafiya mosque, dome

Kufa and Basra. But it is highly significant that their austerity of plan and elevation ran increasingly counter to contemporary taste. Thus it was that the mosques of both Kufa and Basra were rebuilt on a much larger scale within a generation. Some of the changes introduced in the course of these and still later rebuildings were clearly improvements and were thus incorporated into the normal vocabulary of the mosque. Thus it seems that the simple juxtaposition of empty courtyard and enclosing walls found little favour, and a columned arcade or portico was set around the courtyard, at once articulating the space in a more directed way than hitherto and providing worshippers with extra protection from the weather. Thereafter it was a natural step gradually to increase the amount of covered space within the mosque. This was done by increasing the number and depth of the arcades (*riwaq*) both around the

67

three sides of the courtyard – for the open courtyard remained a standard element of the design – and within the sanctuary. Thus by easy degrees the mosque acquired extra articulation, and new relationships between open and covered space emerged. Unfortunately, no mosque datable before the early eighth century has survived in largely unaltered form, and it is therefore not possible to state definitively what forms such extra articulation took. But there are a few clues. In the time of Ziyad b. Abihi, for example, who as the Umayyad viceroy of Iraq (d.53/673) had the task of delivering the *khutba* in the Friday service, the congregation in the great mosque at Kufa customarily expressed its disapproval at his announcements by gathering up handfuls of pebbles and throwing them at him. Accordingly he gave orders for the floor of the mosque to be paved throughout. The same governor introduced brick-built piers into mosque architecture, and crowned them with capitals of 'Persian' type, namely those with *protomai* of addorsed bulls or other creatures. This argues an indifference to iconoclastic ideas which casts an interesting sidelight on the alleged Islamic interdiction of the portrayal of living creatures within religious architecture, although it must be admitted that this fashion did not catch on. It was Ziyad b. Abihi, too, who according to Ibn al-Faqih briefly experimented with circular mosques in Basra. Clearly there was ample scope for variety in this first century of the faith. Even so, the adoption of each new feature meant reduced room for manoeuvre, and it is therefore not surprising that within a hundred years of the Prophet's death the guidelines for the future development of the Arab mosque plan had been laid down. Much of the credit for this speedy development belongs to the Umayyad caliph al-Walid I, who was responsible for a trio of strategically sited mosques which consolidated earlier experiments and introduced several features which were quickly to become canonical–though numerous other mosques founded in the Umayyad period (e.g. Busra, Jarash, Ramla and Aleppo) were of significantly different character.

The major Umayyad mosques

On the basis of the literary evidence it seems justified to draw a clear distinction between these three consciously imperial mosques and all others produced in the later Umayyad period, that is from the death of al-Walid I in 96/715. Such a distinction is not intended to minimise the role of the major mosques erected (and often enlarged) between 11/632 and 81/700. Their role was even more crucial in that they roughed out the general principles of Arab mosque design; but it fell to the mosques of al-Walid I to demonstrate that these principles need not necessarily produce utilitarian structures, but could inspire buildings splendid enough to vie with the best of Christian architecture. Thus al-Walid's building programme had significant political and symbolic implications, and this importance is underlined by the expense of the programme, the speed with which it was carried out, and the precise location of each mosque within the city in which it was built. This achievement stamps him as the major patron of the Umayyad dynasty.

The three mosques in question were sited in Jerusalem, Damascus and Medina. Damascus, as the caliphal capital, was the political nerve-centre of the empire. Medina had sacrosanct status because of its close assocation with the Prophet, its pivotal role in early Islamic history and its continuing function in the Pilgrimage. Jerusalem ranked as the third holiest city in the Islamic world, after Mecca and Medina, and had indeed been the *qibla* at one stage of Muhammad's ministry. After Mecca, then, whose sanctuary had been rebuilt within the previous century, these were the three most important centres of the Muslim world. To underline that importance by means of splendid buildings expressed a new dimension of commitment to architecture. That commitment transcended purely practical motives and pointed the way for the mosque to function more fully and more subtly both within the Islamic community and *vis-à-vis* the outside world.

It is of a piece with this new role of architecture that the choice of site for these special mosques should be carefully considered. In the case of the two Syrian monuments, the sites had religious, symbolic and political resonances, while at Medina the mosque was built over the very spot where the Prophet's house had stood. It is worth examining this general issue in more

42 Damascus, Great Mosque, interior before the fire of 1893

35, 42 detail. For the mosque at Damascus the option of selecting a hitherto unexploited site, presumably on the outskirts of the built-up area, was not taken up. Instead, the caliph set his heart on the prime site in the whole city: the huge enclosure (*temenos*) which had earlier been the emplacement of the Temple of Hadad and then–many centuries later–of Jupiter Damascenus and which currently contained the church of St. *2.69* John the Baptist, and in which the Muslims too had a temporary place of prayer. The terms of the peace treaty which had been signed with the Christians some seventy years earlier denied him the options of compulsory purchase or confiscation, so he was compelled to apply to the Christian community in order to buy the whole site. Perhaps he made them an offer they could not refuse; at all events, having bought the site lock, stock and barrel, he promptly demolished the

Christian church. He was thus left with a huge empty space, markedly oblong (157 m. by 100 m.) and bounded by the Roman walls of the *temenos*, which were broken to the west by the Roman monumental entrance or *propylaeum* and to the east by a lesser entrance. These elements could be incorporated readily enough into the new mosque, but not so the west-east progression which they implied. Indeed, by insisting on an oblong site which was already defined by extant walls, and which incorporated an axiality at odds with the *qibla*, al-Walid had surrendered most of his freedom of manoeuvre. That the mosque built with these inconvenient preconditions in mind should nevertheless have become a seminal influence in Islamic architecture is perhaps incidental. It is hard to believe that the Damascus mosque would have taken the form it did if the architect had been presented

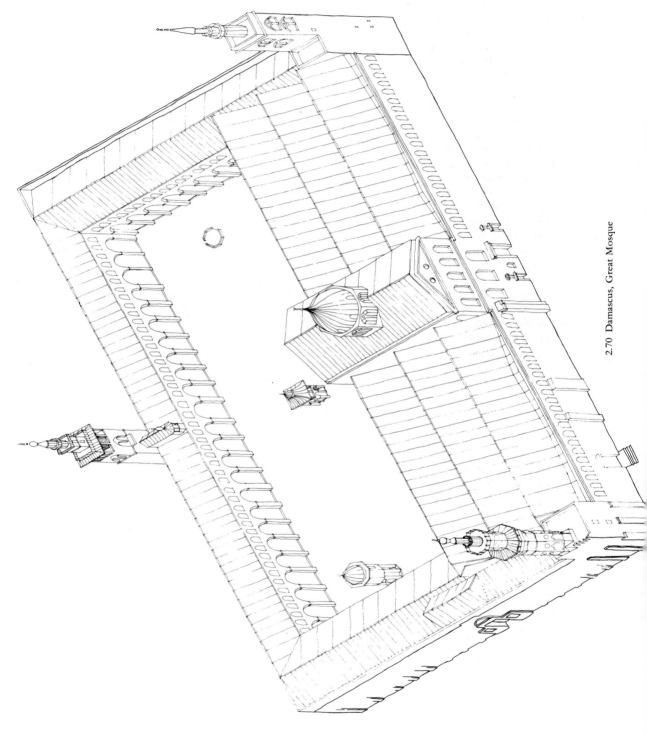

2.70 Damascus, Great Mosque

with an unencumbered site. Certainly the mosques at Jerusalem and Medina, where the architects had a free hand, were much more traditional in their design than was the Damascus mosque. Presumably, then, the latter would have followed suit if the site chosen for it had been entirely clear. It is worth noting that the sequence of events at Damascus was it seems repeated with very little change half a century later at Cordoba, perhaps in a deliberate attempt to evoke the vanished glories of Umayyad Syria.

Thus it seems clear that the innovations incorporated into the design of the Damascus mosque were a response to the challenge offered by its unprecedented and in some ways unsuitable site. By triumphantly overcoming these inherent difficulties the architect showed that mosque design could be much more flexible than earlier buildings might suggest, and forestalled the danger of a premature conservatism. The success of the design and its numerous interesting features should not be allowed to obscure the fundamental question of why this particular site was chosen, and what that choice reveals about the role of this mosque in its historical context. Al-Walid, like his father 'Abd

al-Malik before him and the 'Abbasid caliph al-Mansur after him, was fully alive to the propaganda role of impressive architecture. By physically superimposing his mosque on the ruins of a pagan temple and a Christian church – both structures having symbolised their respective faiths in the centre of Damascus – he was asserting that Islam had superseded earlier religions. In short, the Damascus mosque was a victory monument, and that victory was proclaimed five times a day from the corner towers of the *temenos*, which served as minarets for the call to prayer. The splendour of its embellishments in marble, glass mosaics and cut stone rammed home the message. Al-Muqaddasi describes them in glowing terms: 'The whole area is paved with white marble. The walls of the mosque for twice the height of a man are faced with variegated marble; and above this, even to the ceiling, are mosaics of various colours and in gold, showing figures of trees and towns and beautiful inscriptions, all most exquisitely and finely worked. And rare are the trees and few the well-known towns that will not be found figured on these walls.' No medieval Christian building of east or west could rival the sheer

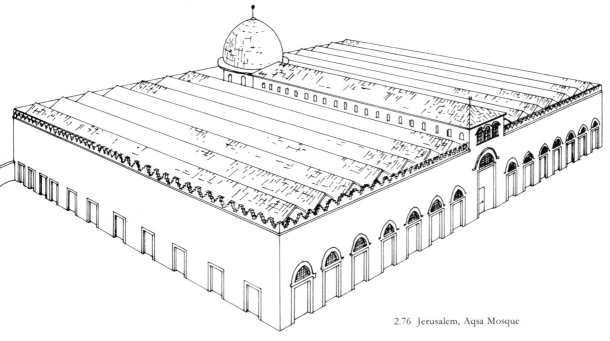

2.76 Jerusalem, Aqsa Mosque

expanse of the wall mosaics in the Damascus mosque. The Arab historians report that al-Walid lavished on this mosque the entire tax revenue for Syria – almost the richest of all the Umayyad provinces – over a period of seven years. Such expenditure could be regarded as wanton extravagance if it were not for the political dimension of the mosque. It was a visible statement of Muslim supremacy and permanence. It was in the middle of the city, with the caliphal palace right next to it, and it simply could not be ignored.

Similar motives help in part to explain the siting of the Aqsa mosque. Placed not far from the Dome of the Rock and on the same axis as that building – a physical and typological juxtaposition which invites comparison with the Constantinian basilica and the adjoining Rotunda of the Holy Sepulchre in the same city – it too enjoys a central site of unrivalled topographical importance. As at Damascus, that site was already hallowed by many centuries of worship – here Abraham had prepared to sacrifice Isaac, here Solomon's Temple had stood, and of course Christians as well as Jews venerated these associations. But a new and distinctive-

2.75, 2.76

2.16–2.17

7.29

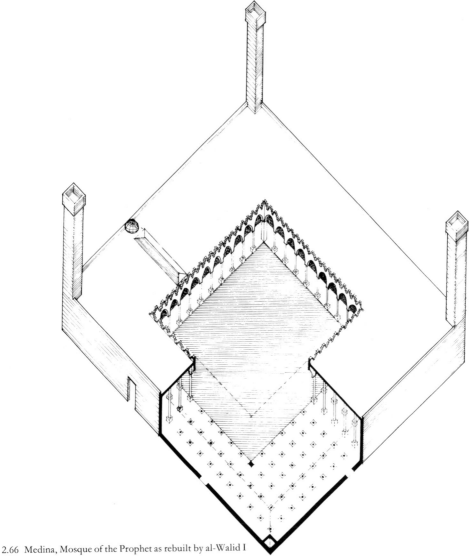

2.66 Medina, Mosque of the Prophet as rebuilt by al-Walid I

ly Muslim factor brought added sanctity to the spot – for this was the 'furthest' (*aqsa*) place which Muhammad had visited in the course of his miraculous Night Journey (*mi'raj*) from Mecca. The Aqsa mosque is therefore as much a commemoration of this specific episode in Muhammad's life as (in common with the Dome of the Rock) it is an acknowledgement of the continuity of Islam with Christianity and Judaism, an assertion of its superiority over them as a religion, and an expression of its political supremacy.

The mosque of Medina constitutes a very different but also unique case. It was built on the site of Muhammad's house and derived much added prestige from this, especially as the Prophet had also been buried there. Interestingly enough there was strong local opposition to the proposed total demolition of the simple primitive buildings, but this was disregarded on the explicit orders of the caliph. As at Damascus, there was much emphasis on splendid decoration, and here too corvée labour was widely employed, for the decoration was the work of Greek and Coptic craftsmen. As al-Tabari recounts:

'We began to pull down the Mosque of the Prophet in Safar 88 (January 707). Al-Walid had sent to inform the Lord of the Romans (the Byzantine Emperor) that he had ordered the demolition of the mosque of the Prophet, and that he should aid him in this work. The latter sent him 100,000 *mithqal*s of gold, and sent also 100 workmen, and sent him 40 loads of mosaic cubes; he gave orders also to search for mosaic cubes in ruined cities and sent them to al-Walid'. A similar tale is told by al-Muqaddasi about the building of the Great Mosque of Damascus:

'And it is said that for building it al-Walid gathered the skilled workmen of Persia, India, al-Maghrib and Byzantium and spent on it the tax revenue of Syria for seven years as well as the gold and silver load of eighteen ships that had called from Cyprus, let alone the implements and the mosaic cubes which the King of the Romans had sent him as a gift.' Thus the very heartland of the faith received a mosque which could bear comparison with those concurrently being built in Jerusalem and Damascus. The transfer of the seat of power from the Hijaz to Syria had long rankled with the Medinese, and

the desire to appease them may have been a contributory factor in al-Walid's decision to build the mosque there.

Thus it could be argued that these imperial foundations established once and for all the principle that the mosque was potentially more than a place of worship or a focus of communal life–it could be used as an instrument of policy too. These three key buildings publicly expressed al-Walid's piety. They were also an acknowledgment of his own roots and those of Islam itself in the Hijaz, and specifically in the city which had witnessed Muhammad's later ministry. By singling out Jerusalem and Damascus as especially favoured sites, al-Walid could broadcast the commitment of his dynasty to Syria, the nerve centre of his empire and the linchpin of his military power. Finally, these Syrian buildings, erected in a pervasively Christian environment, were a statement of intent: Islam had come to stay, it was superior to the religions which it replaced, and its mosques could challenge the finest churches that the Christians might boast. Perhaps the foundations of al-Walid could even be interpreted as documenting the emancipation of the Muslims from Christian cultural tutelage, a process begun in the sphere of architecture by the Dome of the Rock and expressed almost simultaneously in other spheres, for example by the substitution of Arabic for Greek as the language of chancery administration, or by the minting of a spectacular new coinage in which Arabic inscriptions replaced the royal image. This is the wider background to the creation of mosque forms which were later to become canonical. Yet the essential components of these three great mosques were not, after all, so very different from those of Muhammad's house at Madina–an enclosed square or rectangular space with a courtyard and a covered area for prayer on the *qibla* side. The essential fact is that these elements could be varied at will so as to transform the aspect of the building.

'Abbasid mosques

The changes undergone by the courtyard and its articulation help to bear out these remarks. The sunny climate of the southern Mediterranean and the Near East allowed the courtyard to accommodate the huge numbers of extra wor-

43 Samarra, Great Mosque, outer wall

shippers attending the Friday service. This was when its large expanse justified itself. For the rest of the week it was largely empty, and the heat and light emitted by this expanse could cause discomfort. This was especially likely if there were no provision for shade on three of the four sides, as in the early versions of the

2.78 Great Mosques of Cordoba (170/786), Qairawan
2.142, 2.107 (221/836) and Tunis (250/864). Hence there arose the practice of adding arcades along the three subsidiary sides, so that people could walk around the mosque in cool shade. In time these
2.40-2.44 arcades could be doubled, tripled or even quadrupled. A change in the alignment of their vaulting from one side of the mosque to another brought welcome visual relief and excluded the

danger of monotony; so too did variations in the depth or number of the arcades (the second 'Amr mosque in Cairo). As the surface area of 2.88 the covered sanctuary was increased, so did new spatial refinements suggest themselves, such as the progressive unfolding of seemingly endless vistas in all directions. Rows of supports (often *spolia*) with fixed intercolumniations created hundreds of repetitive modular units, perhaps deliberately mirroring the long files of worshippers at prayer.

Externally, the accent was on simplicity, with regular buttresses giving the structure a warlike air. At the Great Mosque of Samarra (completed *43* 238/852) there are a dozen of these on each long 2.50-2.5 side, not counting the corners, with doorways after every second buttress. At Susa the exterior 2.146-2 dispenses with buttresses in favour of rounded corner bastions, while in the mosque of al-Hakim in Cairo (381/991 onwards) the minarets 2.90, 2.9 at the corner of the façade rise from two gigantic square salients. The emplacement of the *mihrab* was marked by a corresponding rectangular projection on the exterior wall. Entrances were commonly allotted a measure of extra decoration – as in the series of shallow porches along *49* the flank of the Cordoba mosque – but massive portals on the scale of those in Western cathedrals found no favour in the early mosques of Arab plan. The absolute scale of some mosques 2.108 (the mosque of Samarra, for instance, could have accommodated 100,000 people) encouraged the adoption of fixed proportional

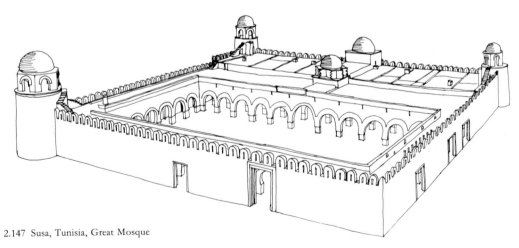

2.147 Susa, Tunisia, Great Mosque

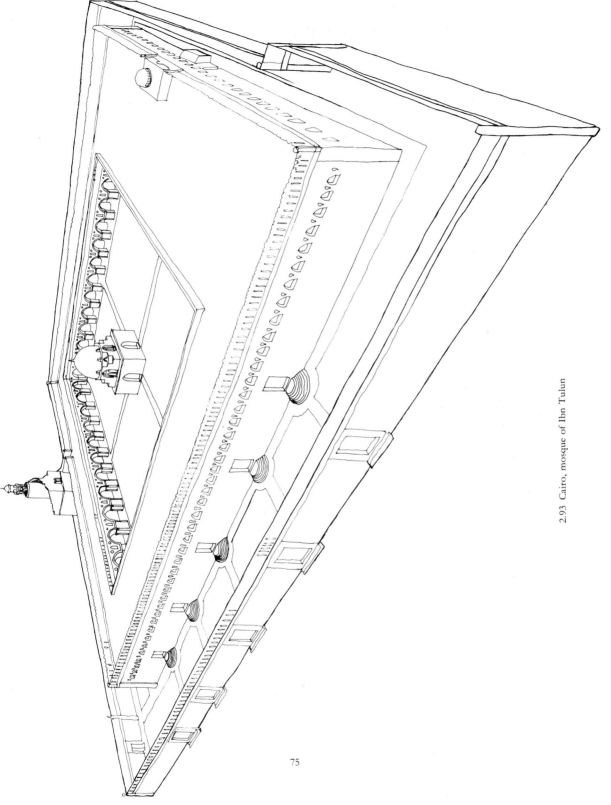

2.93 Cairo, mosque of Ibn Tulun

ratios such as 3:2, which contributed in large measure to the impression of satisfying harmony which these mosques produced. The Qara-khanid mosque of Samarqand (11th century) illustrates the continuing use of such ratios. Sometimes the scale of the mosque was illusion-istically increased by the addition of a broad open enclosure (*ziyada*) on three of the four sides 2.93, 2.89 (mosque of Ibn Tulun, Cairo, finished 264/877, presumably copying the mosques of Samarra). In comparison with later mosques of similar scale, which catered for multiple subsidiary functions by adding appropriate purpose-built structures to the central core, these early mosques maintain simple and symmetrical lines,

especially for their outer walls (mosque of Abu Dulaf).

The architectural vocabulary of these early mosques brought further scope for diversity. In the first half-century of Islamic architecture, the system of roofing was still primitive, and even when columns and roof-beams had replaced palm-trunks and thatching, the basic scheme remained trabeate (Basra; Kufa; and Wasit, 83/ 2.39, 2.4 702) whether the roof was flat or pitched, and even so seminal a monument as the Great Mosque of Samarra continued this system, though probably not for its courtyard façade. 2.50-2.5 Thus the post-and-lintel system long familiar from Graeco-Roman buildings was perpetuated,

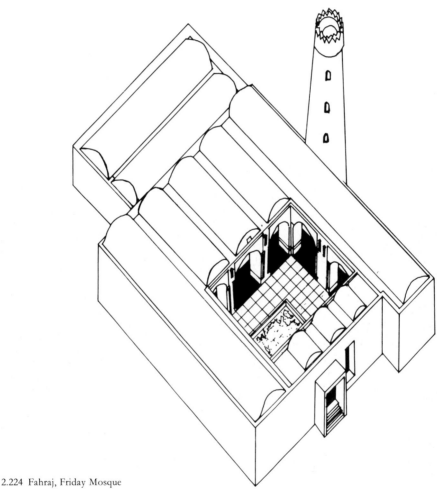

2.224 Fahraj, Friday Mosque

and the pervasive classical flavour was strengthened by the lavish use of *spolia*. Sometimes, however, as in the bull-headed capitals of the Istakhr mosque, these were of Achaemenid origin.

By degrees, wooden roofs resting on arcades gained popularity, and this was the prelude to full-scale vaulting in durable materials (especially in Iran: Tari Khana mosque, Damghan, and Fahraj *jami'*, both perhaps 9th century; Na'in *jami'*, perhaps 10th century). The earliest mosques all use columns, and were thereby restricted to relatively low roofs. By the 9th century the pier had ousted the column as the principal bearing member, though it occurs as early as the mosques of Damascus, Ba'labakk and Harran, and though the column was still used for some mosques (Qairawan; al-Azhar, Cairo, 362/973). This change made it possible to raise the height of the roof, an important development given the oppressive sensation produced by a low roof extending over a large surface area. At the Cordoba mosque the column shafts bore piers braced by strainer arches; but this device, for all its ingenuity, could not rival the popularity of superposed arcades in the fashion of Roman aqueducts (Damascus mosque, finished 96/715).

The apparently minor detail of whether the arcades ran parallel to the *qibla* or at right angles to it was sufficient to transform the visual impact of the roof. In the latter case, it focused attention on the *qibla*, and this was the solution that recommended itself to Maghribi architects (mosques of Cordoba, Tunis and Qairawan). Syrian architects, on the other hand, with only one major exception (Aqsa mosque, Jerusalem), preferred arcades parallel to the *qibla* (Damascus; Qasr al-Hair East, *c*.109/728; Ba'labakk, *c*.12th century; Harran, *c*.133/750; and Raqqa, *c*.9th century), possibly reflecting in this the influence of the Christian basilica ubiquitous in that region; several Egyptian mosques followed suit, including those of Ibn Tulun, al-Azhar and al-Hakim. It was a natural development to build mosques with arcades running in both directions (Great Mosques of Sfax and Susa, both finished 236/850), but with

44 Cordoba, Great Mosque, sanctuary showing Christian chapel

45 Toledo, mosque at Bab Mardum, façade

10th century. These buildings inaugurate the much more ambitious use of vaults in later mosques. No such solutions are to be found in the larger mosques built before the 11th century. This early Islamic vaulting drew its ideas impartially from the Romano-Byzantine tradition and from Sasanian Iran, and quickly developed its own distinctive styles, in which the pointed vault soon dominated.

these exceptions the early experiments with this idea are all on a relatively modest scale which betrays some uncertainty of purpose. They comprise a small group of 9-bayed mosques *45* with a dome over each bay and no courtyard: a *2.85–2.87,* type represented in Toledo, Susa, Qairawan, *2.145, 2.149* Cairo and Balkh and dating mainly from the *2.237–2.238*

In some mosques, the desire to emphasise the covered sanctuary was achieved simply by adding extra bays and thus increasing its depth. In other mosques, especially those with royal associations, the requisite emphasis was achieved by some striking visual accentuation of *55* the sanctuary: a more elaborate façade (as at *2.95* Mahdiya), a higher and wider central aisle, a *2.137–2.1* gable or a dome. Once this idea of glorifying the sanctuary had taken root it was enthusiastically exploited, for example by furnishing this area with several carefully placed domes as at the

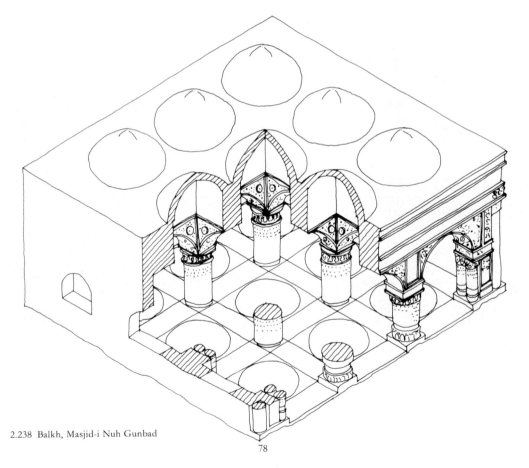

2.238 Balkh, Masjid-i Nuh Gunbad

46 Mahdiya, Great Mosque, façade

4, 2.77,
2,80,
1–2.92 mosques of Cordoba and al-Azhar. On occasion, indeed, the sanctuary – complete with such distinguishing features as wider central aisle, dome in front of the *mihrab* and transversely vaulted bays adjoining the *qibla* – could itself become the mosque, with no attached courtyard, as at the 2.75–2.76 Aqsa Mosque.

The transformation of the sanctuary

The effect of singling out the sanctuary by these

47 Cordoba, Great Mosque, interior

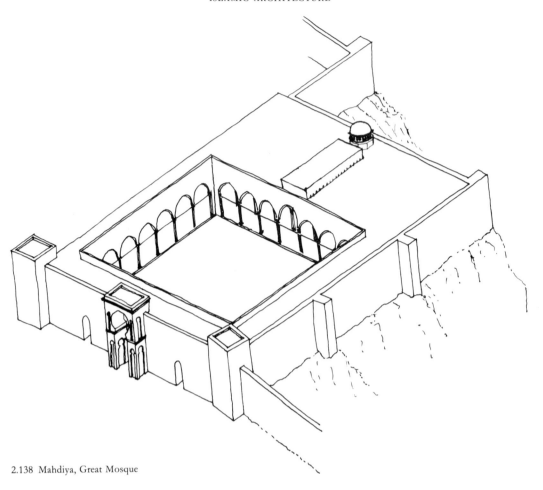

2.138 Mahdiya, Great Mosque

various means is to emphasise that this area is more important than any other in the mosque. Since this latter notion runs counter to the widely-expressed belief that all parts of the mosque are equally sacred, and that gradations of sanctity within it run counter to the spirit of Islam, its origins are worth investigating. This will involve a brief recapitulation of material presented in much greater detail earlier in this chapter, but that material will now be examined from a slightly different angle. It should be stressed at the outset that these various articulating devices cannot all be explained as attempts to draw attention to the *qibla*. Some measure of emphasis for this purpose was certainly required. Hence, no doubt, the greater depth of arcade on that side and the provision of an

elaborate façade for the sanctuary alone. Similarly, the use of a different alignment or type of vaulting for the bays immediately in front of the *qibla* would make sense as a means of signposting this crucial area. Yet the addition of a dome or gable, or both, along the central aisle of the sanctuary, and the greater width and height of 2.183 that aisle, cannot be explained – as is so often the case – simply as a means of highlighting the *mihrab*. After all, the entire *qibla* wall served to mark the correct orientation for prayer, so that the *mihrab* was technically redundant. The relatively late appearance of the *mihrab* further suggests that it was not devised to meet some liturgical imperative.

The evidence points rather to the desire to assert, in as public a way as the dictates of

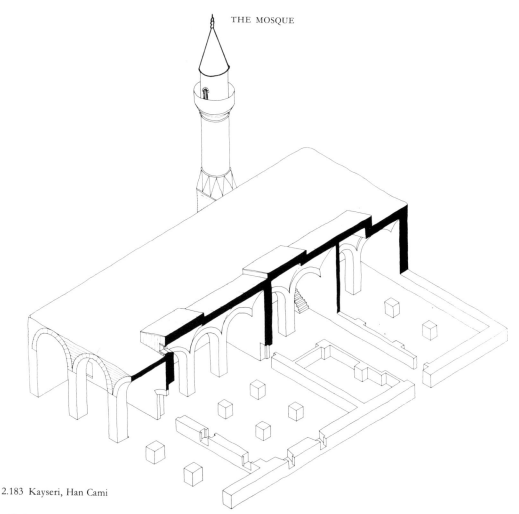

2.183 Kayseri, Han Cami

religious architecture would permit, the importance of the ruler in religious ceremonies. It was the duty of the caliph or of his representative to lead his people in prayer and to pronounce the *khutba*. The political overtones of this ritual, which proclaimed allegiance to the ruler, in large part explain the physical form of the *minbar* from which the *khutba* was pronounced. Similarly, the *mihrab*, another latecomer to mosque architecture, can be interpreted in secular terms, most conveniently as a throne apse transposed into a religious setting. These royal connotations could only be intensified by the addition of a dome over the bay directly in front of the *mihrab*. Underneath that same dome was the preferred location for the *maqsura*, usually a square enclosure of wood or stone reserved for the ruler, and ensuring both his privacy and his

physical safety. Each of these elements in the mosque – *mihrab, minbar, maqsura,* dome – drew *38* added power from the proximity of the others, and together they stamped a secular and princely significance on this particular area of the mosque.

The earliest surviving mosque which illustrates this emphasis, the Great Mosque of Damascus, adds – as noted earlier – a further refinement: a high transverse gable with a *35* pitched roof cuts across the lateral emphasis of the sanctuary and thus highlights not just the *mihrab* area but also the way to it. The extra height of the gable and the way it cleaves across *cf. 52* the grain of the mosque underscore its proclamatory role. Sometimes, as in the *jami*'s of Tunis *2.107, 48* and Qairawan, another dome over the central *2.142–2.143* archway of the sanctuary façade sufficed to

81

48 Tunis, Zaituna mosque, interior

create an axis focused on the *mihrab*. As at Damascus, this axis asserted itself both inside the sanctuary and – by virtue of its greater width and the consequent break in the even tenor of the roofing – externally, at roof level. The Great Mosque at Samarra probably had some such device, to judge by the extra width of the central aisle in its sanctuary. In later mosques, such as those of al-Azhar and al-Hakim (which possibly derive in this from al-Aqsa) the notion of the external gable is toned down to a broad flat strip projecting only modestly above roof level; but internally, the emphasis on the broader central nave terminating in the dome over the *mihrab* remains unchanged. It seems likely that these articulating devices were intended to mark out a processional way, presumably the formal route by which the ruler approached the *mihrab*.

So much, then, for the various elements in mosque design for which princely associations have been proposed. Yet their mere enumeration does not tell the full story. For it is above all the occurrence of these features in mosques located next to the residence of the ruler that places their political associations beyond doubt. This close juxtaposition of the secular and the religious may well have had its roots in the Prophet's house. Be that as it may, at Basra, Kufa, Fustat, Damascus, to name only a few very early examples, the principal mosque and the private residence of the ruler adjoined each other, and the viceroy Ziyad b. Abihi said of this arrangement 'it is not fitting that the *imam* should pass through the people' – a sentiment, incidentally, not shared by many later Islamic rulers and indeed contradicted by the development outlined in the previous paragraph. The analogy with the palatine chapel in Byzantium and medieval Europe – at Constantinople and Ravenna, Aachen and Palermo – is striking. Perhaps the most public expression of the idea in the medieval Islamic world was in the Round City of Baghdad, where the huge and largely empty space at the heart of the city held only two buildings: the palace and the mosque, next door to each other. It would be hard to find the concept of Caesaropapism expressed more explicitly, or on a more gargantuan scale, than this.

The rôle of structure and ornament

The local expression of the articulating features

49 Cordoba, Great Mosque, exterior façade

under discussion varied from one part of the Islamic world to another, but they had come to stay. Henceforth, the *jami'* of Arab plan only rarely returned to the simplicity of the 7th century. Such, however, was the strength of the traditions formed at that time that the basic nature of the earliest mosques remained substantially unchanged. They were proof, for example, against immense increases in size and against a growing interest in embellishment by means of structural innovations and applied ornament. Even the conversion into mosques of pre-Islamic places of worship, as at Damascus and Hama, was powerless to affect their essential nature. The component parts of the Arab mosque could be redistributed and re-arranged almost at will without impairing their functional effectiveness.

In much the same way, their idiosyncrasies of structure and decoration were purely cosmetic. The range of options in these areas was gratifyingly wide. Windows and lunettes bore *ajouré* grilles in stone or plaster with geometric and vegetal designs (Damascus mosque); wooden ceilings were painted or carved and coffered (San'a' mosque, 7th century onwards); a wide range of capitals, at first loosely based on classical models but in time becoming almost unrecognisably debased (Samarra) was developed; and piers with engaged corner colonnettes (Ibn Tulun mosque, Cairo; Great Mosque of Isfahan) rang the changes on the traditional classical column. A few mosques (e.g. Cordoba and the Three Doors mosque at Qairawan) had elaborately articulated façades or portals. Finally, the aspect of these early mosques could be varied still further by the type of flooring employed –

stamped earth, brick, stone or even marble flags
– by applied decoration in carved stone or
stucco, fresco, painted glass, embossed metalwork or mosaic, and even by finials on domes.

2.33

The essentially simple components of the
Arab plan set a limit to the degree of diversity
that could be achieved within these specifica-
2.68, 2.75, tions. Most of the room for manoeuvre had been
2.77–2.78, exhausted within the first four centuries of
2.88–2.92 Islamic architecture. Thus the subsequent
history of the Arab plan cannot match the early
period for variety and boldness; the later
mosques, moreover, lie very much in the
shadow of their predecessors, to such an extent
that it is hard to single out significant new
departures in these later buildings. It can
scarcely be doubted that the presence of the
great Umayyad and ʿAbbasid mosques, built at
the period when the Islamic world was at the
peak of its material prosperity, acted as a signal
deterrent to later architects with substantially

50 Cordoba, Great Mosque, window

51 Qairawan, Mosque of Muhammad b. Khairun, façade

less money, men and materials at their disposal. In these early centuries the caliphal permission, not readily granted, had been required for the construction of a *jami'*, making it a major undertaking and correspondingly hard to emulate. By the 11th century, moreover, most of the major Muslim cities had their own *jami'*, so that the need for huge mosques had much declined.

Although mosques of Arab plan have continued to be built throughout the Islamic world until the present day, in the medieval period there were only two areas where they achieved dominance: in the Western Islamic lands before they fell under Ottoman rule, and in pre-Ottoman Anatolia. These areas will therefore provide the material for most of the discussion which follows. Nevertheless, sporadic references will be made to mosques elsewhere, for instance in Egypt and the Yemen.

Maghribi mosques

The Maghrib rightfully takes pride of place in this account because for almost a millennium virtually no mosque that was not of Arab type was built there. Here, then, is to be found the most homogeneous and consistent development of that type. Its sources lie, like so much of Maghribi art, in Syria, and specifically in the Great Mosque of Damascus. Its transverse gable becomes a leitmotif in Maghribi mosques, and in some cases (such as the Qarawiyin Mosque, Fez, *52* founded 226/841 but largely of the 12th century) is associated with the same proportions as the 2.111–2.112 Syrian building, including the relatively shallow oblong courtyard imposed on the Damascus mosque by the classical *temenos* but copied thereafter in other mosques as a deliberate feature. In the Mosque of the Andalusians at Fez (600–4/ 2.119 1203–7) the Damascus schema is retained despite a jaggedly irregular perimeter and trapezoidal courtyard; and, as at the Qarawiyin mosque, the main entrance to the mosque is aligned to it, a refinement not found at Damascus. The length of the gable has also increased considerably, though its height is modest.

52 Fez, Qarawiyin mosque, façade of sanctuary

53 Marrakesh, Kutubiya mosque, general view

54 Marrakesh, Kutubiya mosque, lateral façade

In later Maghribi mosques especially, the emphasis shifted from the exterior elevation of the gable to its impact from within the building. It attracts unusually intricate vaulting, often of *muqarnas* type, as in the Qarawiyin mosque, or may be marked by domes ranging in number from two (Tlemcen, 531/1136) to six (second Kutubiya, Marrakesh, mid-12th century). The latter mosque has a further five cupolas placed three bays apart along the transverse *qibla* aisle. Thus by means of vaulting alone is created a T-shape which combines the secular and religious emphases of the *jami'*. Fewer vaults or domes, more strategically placed – for example at the *mihrab*, the sanctuary entrance and the corners of the *qibla* wall – could suffice to carry the T-shape into the elevation, but the form

could be created at ground level alone by means of a wider central nave and by ensuring that the vaults stopped one bay short of the *qibla*, thus opening up dramatically the space immediately in front of it. The T-shape can indeed claim to be the principal Maghribi contribution to the development of mosque form, though horseshoe arches and square minarets were equally characteristic of the style. This T-shape also made its way, presumably via Libya (e.g. the mosques of Ajdabiya and Madinat Sultan) to Egypt.

Three other features distinguish Maghribi mosques from those found elsewhere in the Islamic world, though all have their origins in al-Andalus: the use of pierced, ribbed or fluted domes, especially over the *mihrab*; the manipulation of arch forms to create hierarchical distinctions by means of gradual enrichment; and a readiness to alter the size, shape and location of the courtyard in response to the imperatives of a specific design. The ribbed domes (e.g. *jami'*s of Taza, 537/1142 and 691/1291–2, and Algiers, *c.*490/1097) derive from those of the Cordoba mosque, but elaborate on them by cramming them with vegetal designs in carved stucco or by increasing the number of ribs from the usual eight to twelve (Tlemcen *jami'*) or even sixteen

(Taza *jami'*). This practice gives free rein to the characteristically Maghribi obsession with non-structural arched forms, here used as a lace-like infill between the ribs; the overall effect is one of feathery lightness and grace. The light filtered through these domes suffuses the area of the *mihrab* with radiance, perhaps as a deliberate metaphor of spiritual illumination, an idea rendered still more potent when, as is often the case, that *mihrab* bears the popular text of Sura 24:35, 'God is the light of the heavens and the earth; the likeness of His light is as a niche wherein is a lamp . . .'

15   Long files of arcaded columns stretching in multiple directions and generating apparently endless vistas are a particular feature of Maghribi mosques. The distinctive 'forest space' thereby created finds its fullest expression *47* in the fourth major rebuilding of the Cordoba mosque, the unchallenged masterpiece of Western Islamic architecture, and the major Almoravid and Almohad mosques are best interpreted as reflections of this great original. Where the Cordoba mosque, however, employed systems of intersecting arches and carefully differentiated types of capital to establish hierarchical distinctions, later Maghribi *jami'*s typically use a wide range of arch profiles

2.74, 2.77-2.79

2.80, 2.83-2.84 55

to the same end. These include, besides the ubiquitous horseshoe type already noted, lobed, multifoil, interlaced, cusped, trefoil, lambrequin and other varieties. They spring from piers, not columns, and this, coupled with the low roof, dim lighting and the general absence of ornament unconnected with vaulting, lends these interiors a ponderous austerity. Against this general background of parsimonious simplicity, the sudden switch from plain arch profiles for most of the sanctuary to elaborate ones for the axial nave alone constitutes a dramatic enrichment of the interior. Sometimes the transverse aisle in front of the *qibla* wall attests a third type of arch profile, and thus a further gradation of importance is emphasised.

In most western Islamic mosques the courtyard is something of an appendage. It is almost always very much smaller than the covered space. Custom decreed that it was isolated at the opposite end of the mosque from the *mihrab*, and that it should either be contiguous to the outer wall or be separated from it by no more than a single aisle. By contrast, the sanctuary tended to be of disproportionate depth and extent. This meant that the courtyard was never able to function as the heart of the mosque. Only when

2.103-2.104

2.124-2.126,

2.130

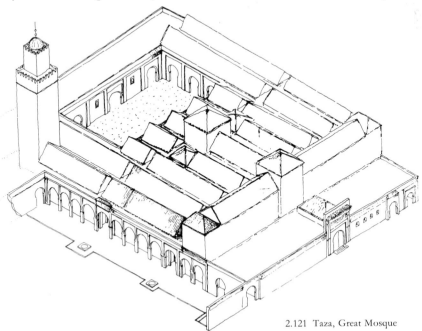

2.121 Taza, Great Mosque

55 Cordoba, Great Mosque, Capilla de Vilaviciosa, interlacing arches

2.106 the sanctuary was reduced, as in the Qasba mosque in Marrakesh (581–6/1185–90), with its pronounced cruciform emphasis, was the court-yard able to play a more central role, both liter-ally and figuratively. In narrow rectangular plans it can be a diminutive square box hemmed

56 Seville, Great Mosque, façade of sanctuary

2.101 in by deep lateral aisles (mosque of al-Mansura, 704–45/1304–44), or an extended shallow
6, 2.115 oblong (mosque of Seville, c.571/1175). In oblong plans it faithfully mirrored that emphasis
45, 2.110 on a diminutive scale (Tinmal, 548/1153; second
05, 2.118 Kutubiya, Marrakesh, c.555/1160). Exceptional
3–2.114, on all counts is the gigantic but unfinished
2.116 mosque of Hassan, Rabat (c.591/1195), whose scale of 180 × 139 m. makes it the second largest medieval mosque in the world, after the Great Mosque of Samarra. Here the typical shallow

oblong courtyard is supplemented by two lesser and narrow courtyards perpendicular to the *qibla* and along the lateral walls. These were, it seems, intended for men and women respectively, but they would also have served for ventilation and lighting, besides offering visual relief to the endless march of columns. Later medieval 2.139–2.141, Maghribi mosques decisively rejected such gar- 2.122–2.123 gantuan scale in favour of a more domestic atmosphere, as shown by numerous examples at Fez and Tlemcen. 2.141

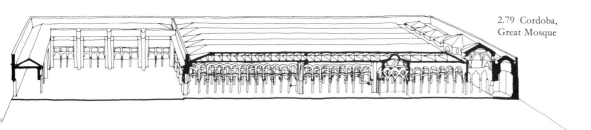

2.79 Cordoba, Great Mosque

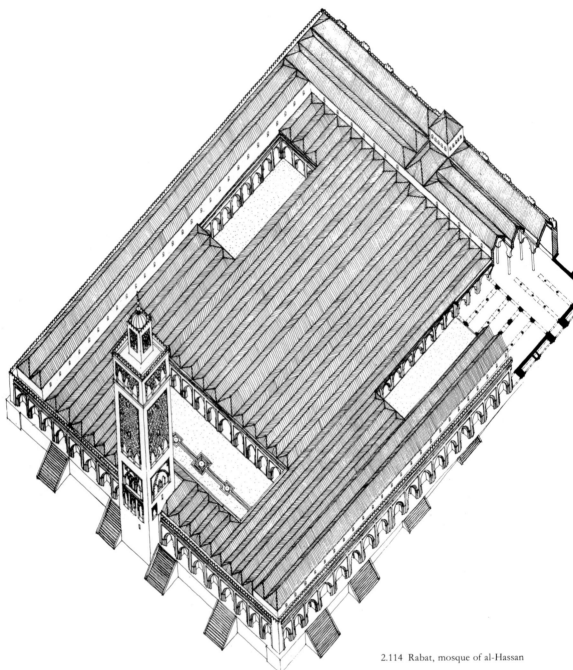

2.114 Rabat, mosque of al-Hassan

Yemeni mosques
Apart from the Maghrib, it was principally in the Yemen that the large hypostyle mosque maintained its popularity throughout the medieval period. Inadequate publication has meant that these buildings are less well known than they deserve, and without excavation the dating of many of them will remain problematic. This is particularly regrettable because several of them were built on the sites of pre-Islamic

90

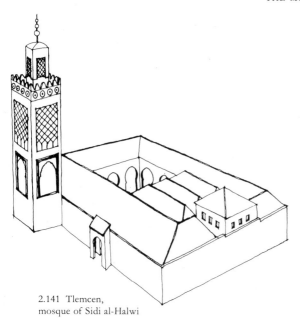

2.141 Tlemcen,
mosque of Sidi al-Halwi

The commonest form, however, comprises a structure that is rectangular or trapezoidal (Masjid al-Saumi'a, Huth, 13th century) with a *2.169* central courtyard and extensive covered *riwaq*s on all sides (Rauda *jami'*, 13th century; Asnaf). Often this formula is enriched by a lavishly carved or painted wooden ceiling over the sanctuary area alone (Shibam *jami'*, 10th century; *2.157* Asnaf) or by the incorporation of mausolea *2.32, 58, 61* (Zafar Dhibin, 13th century; funerary mosque *2.156, 2.162, 188* of the Imam al-Hadi Yahya, Sa'da, 10th century and later) or of minarets (Jibla, 480/1087; Dhu *60* Ashraq, 410/1019). Influences from the central Islamic lands explain the use of wider central aisles in the sanctuary (Zafar Dhibin, Ibb, Jibla, *2.161, 2.166,* Dhu Ashraq) and a concentration of domes *2.163, 2.158* along the *qibla* wall (enlargement of Ibb *jami'*; mosque-*madrasa*s of al-Muzaffariya and al- *2.153, 12* Ashrafiya, both 13th century, Ta'izz). The glory *4.68, 41* of these Yemeni mosques as a group lies in their decoration: exceptionally long bands of stucco inscriptions (mosques of Dhamar and Rada', *2.167*

57 San'a', Great Mosque, courtyard

2.152 temples (e.g. mosque of Sulaiman ibn Da'ud, Marib), churches or synagogues (e.g. al-Jila mosque, San'a'), and *spolia* from these earlier buildings – such as columns, capitals, inscriptions and even sculptures of birds – are used very widely. Persistent local tradition attributes 2.164–2.165 the *jami'*s of San'a' and al-Janad to the time of the Prophet; both were probably rebuilt by al- *18, 57* Walid I. The former has preserved much more of its original appearance: perimeter walls of finely cut stone in stepped courses enclose a roughly square shape with a central courtyard, with the sanctuary only slightly deeper than the other sides. The Sa'da mosque, another early foundation, has had its similar original layout transformed by a domed transept and numerous subsidiary buildings. This gradual transformation by the addition of prayer halls, mausolea, ablutions facilities and the like is a recurrent 2.155 pattern in the Yemen (*jami'*s of Zabid, Thula 2.166 and Ibb).

Small hypostyle mosques of square form *58, 2.32,* (Asnaf, 13th century), or of rectangular shape, 2.154, 2.159 whether broad and shallow oblongs (Tithid, 2.160 13th century) or narrow and deep (Tamur, 11th century or earlier), are common, and a few larger mosques of this kind, still without a 2.168 courtyard, are known (Dhibin, after 648/1250).

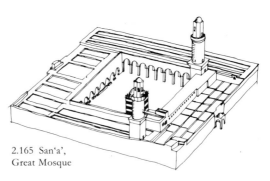

2.165 San'a',
Great Mosque

58 Asnaf, Masjid al-'Abbas, interior

59 Ibb, Great Mosque, courtyard

13th century and later), frescoes with epigraphic, floral and geometric designs (Rasulid mosques of Ta'izz), and a matchless series of carved and painted wooden ceilings (Zafar Dhibin, Asnaf, Sarha, Dhibin, Shibam, San'a' and others). Their minarets, too (Zabid; Zafar Dhibin; al-Mahjam) are some of the most varied in the Islamic world.

8, 41

24, 58, 61

3.59–3.63

59, 60

Anatolian hypostyle mosques

For all that pre-Ottoman Anatolia was a fertile field for innovation in later medieval experiment with the hypostyle mosque, its contribution cannot seriously match that of the Maghrib and al-Andalus, not least because of the much shorter time span, a mere three centuries; discussion of it will accordingly be brief. The earliest surviving mosques well illustrate the dependence of local builders on more developed traditions of Arab and Persian origin. The Great Mosque of Diyarbakr (484/1091) follows the transept schema of Damascus, while those of Mayyafariqin (550/1155), Dunaysir (601/1204)

2.206

7, 62

11, 17, 2.204,
2.192–2.193

60 Dhu Ashraq, mosque, courtyard

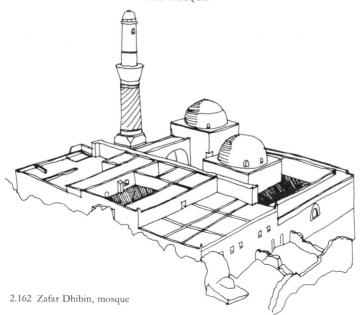

2.162 Zafar Dhibin, mosque

2.194 and Mardin (largely 12th century) follow Iranian precedent in their emphasis on a monumental dome rearing up out of the low roofing 2.188, 2.205 of the sanctuary and set squarely in front of the *mihrab* bay. Their foreshortened courtyards, however, owe nothing to Iranian precedent and instead presage later developments. So too did the increasing tendency to use domical forms rather than modular trabeate units as the principal means of defining space.

61 Asnaf, Masjid al-'Abbas, ceiling

62 Diyarbakr, Great Mosque, sanctuary façade

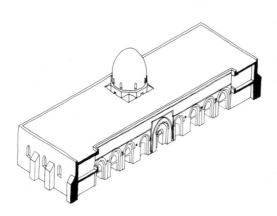

2.193 Dunaysir, Great Mosque

63 Konya, 'Ala' al-Din mosque, main façade

The buildings of the 12th and 13th centuries sufficiently demonstrate the embryonic state of mosque design in Anatolia, for the variety of plans is bewildering and defies easy categorisation. The absence of direct copies of the classical Arab type of plan is striking, though modifications of it were legion. A common solution was to do without the courtyard altogether – perhaps a response to the severe Anatolian

65 Divriği, mosque and hospital, interior of hospital

winter – and reduce the mosque to a wooden-roofed hall resting on a multitude of columns or pillars ('Ala' al-Din mosque, Konya, 530/1135 to 617/1220; Sivas, c.494/1100; Afyon Karahisar, 672/1273; Beyşehir, 696/1296). Usually the minaret was outside the mosque and therefore not integrated into the layout. Sometimes a similar design was executed in multiple small vaults (Divriği, castle mosque, 576/1180; Niksar, 540/1145; Urfa, 12th century), and indeed the preference for vaulted as distinct from trabeated construction is well marked even at this experimental stage. Whatever the roofing system adopted in these enclosed mosques, the scope for development in either direction was small, while poor lighting, a sense of cramped space and inadequate ventilation were virtually inevitable. Huge piers and low vaults gave many of these mosques a crypt-like appearance ('Ala' al-Din mosque, Niğde, 620/1223; Sivas, Ulu Cami).

40, 63, 2.111
2.170, 2.191
64, 2.198

2.172, *9*
2.185, 2.171

2.212–2.213
2.170

64 Beyşehir, Eşrefoghlu Süleyman Bey Cami, interior

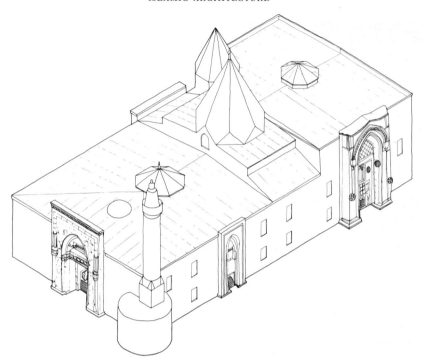

2.210 Divriği, Great Mosque and hospital

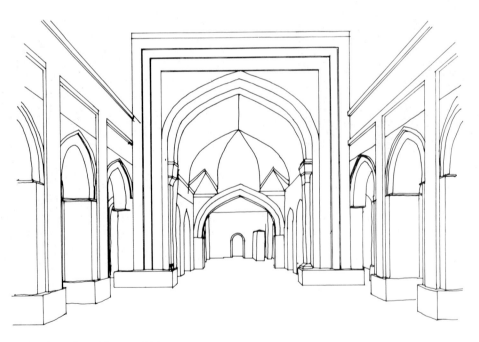

2.203 Malatya, Great Mosque, *qibla iwan*

66 Divriği, mosque and hospital, exterior sculpture

feature of Turkish mosque architecture, and as a natural corollary fostered a compact and integrated style. Sometimes a small courtyard is squeezed into this design (Malatya, 635/1237; Kayseri, Mosque of Khwand Khatun, 635/1237; Harput, 560/1165). By degrees, however, the courtyard was relegated to one of two functions: as a forecourt, akin to the atrium of Byzantine churches and thus heralding the mosque proper, instead of being co-equal to the sanctuary; and as a bay within the sanctuary, furnished with a skylight and a fountain as a symbolic reminder of the world outside. Sometimes these two uses coincided. The skylight bay (*shadirvan*) was normally placed along the axis of the *mihrab* and thus served as a secondary accent for it, in much the same manner as a central dome.

The 14th century saw no major developments in hypostyle plans. Flat-roofed prayer halls –

67 Divriği, mosque and hospital, south-west portal

The obvious way forward was to allot a more significant role to the dome, a decision made at an early stage (Great Mosque of Erzurum, 530/1135; Kayseri, 535/1140; and Divriği, 626/1229), but by no means universally accepted. In such mosques the domed bay is invariably the largest of all and is placed along the axis of the *mihrab*. This emphasis on the totally enclosed covered mosque, sometimes – as in the Konya region – reduced to a single domed chamber, occasionally with a porch, was to remain the principal

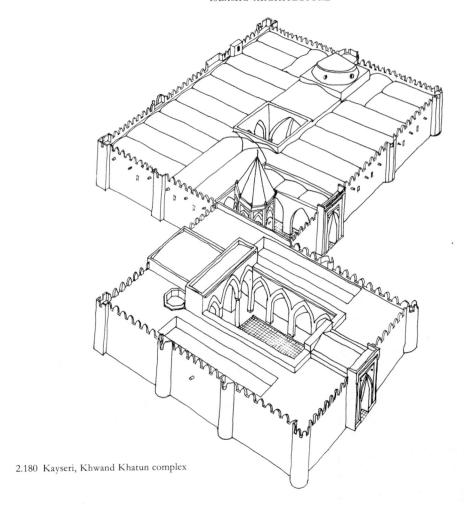

2.180 Kayseri, Khwand Khatun complex

some with wooden-roofed porches (Meram mosque, Konya, 804–27/1402–24), others, especially in the Qaraman region, without them – continued to be built. So too did hypostyle mosques with vaulted domical bays (Yivli *5, 2.311* Minare mosque, Antalya, 775/1373; the type recurs both in eastern Anatolia and Ottoman *2.304–2.305* territory in Bursa and Edirne). Variations on the Damascus schema, with the transept replaced by one or more domes, a raised and wider central aisle, a skylight bay, or any combination of *2.199–2.200* these, were frequent ('Isa Beg mosque, Selcuk, *2.190* 776/1374; Ulu Cami, Birge, 712/1312; mosque of *2.189* Akhi Elvand, Ankara, *c.*780/1378). Finally, mosques with an enlarged domed bay in front of

the *mihrab* spread from their earlier base in south-eastern Anatolia, an area bounded to the east by the Ulu Cami in Van (791–803/1389– *2.196–2.19* 1400?) and to the west by that of Manisa (778/ *2.309* 1376). In the latter mosque the *qibla* side is dominated by the dome and takes up almost half the mosque; a large arcaded courtyard with a portico accounts for the rest. With such buildings the stage is set for Ottoman architecture and Arab prototypes are left far behind.

These Anatolian mosques depart still further from the norm of the hypostyle type in their predilection for elaborate integrated façades. *2.186–2.18* While earlier mosques of Arab type frequently *68* singled out the principal entrance by a mon-

98

umental archway, often with a dome behind it, the tendency was to keep the façade relatively plain. Only in the highly built-up areas of the major cities of the Near East, such as Cairo, Jerusalem, Damascus and Aleppo, did the extreme shortage of space, and often the small scale of the mosques themselves, oblige architects to decorate mosque façades if they wished *88* to draw attention to them (e.g. the Aqmar *2.98* mosque, Cairo, 519/1125). Portals were especially favoured for this purpose (e.g. mosque of *69* al-Mu'ayyad, Cairo). In Anatolia the tenacious Armenian tradition, which favoured extensive external sculpture and articulation, may well have predisposed Muslim architects in this area to develop integrated decorative schemes for the main façades of their mosques. A monumental

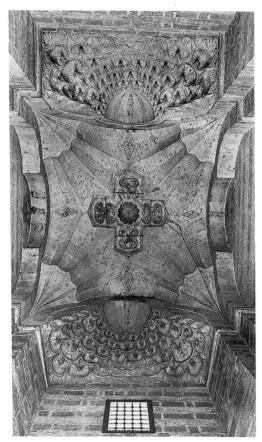

69 Cairo, Mosque of al-Mu'ayyad, vault in portal

stone portal or *pishtaq*, often an *iwan*, was the *2.177–2.178* standard centrepiece for such designs. It could be strongly salient and tower well above the roof-line (Divriği Cami). Further articulation *2.209–2.210* was provided by ranges of recessed arches with decorative surrounds (Dunaysir), open or blind *2.193* arcades along the upper section of the façade (Mayyafariqin and 'Ala' al-Din mosque, Konya), and windows with densely carved frames ('Isa Beg mosque, Selcuk).

Egypt

It seems possible that some of the more elaborate Mamluk mosque façades in Cairo, such as those of Baibars (660/1262) and Sultan Hasan *2.97* (757/1356) may derive, if at several removes, *4.65* from Anatolian prototypes of the kind discussed above. It is noteworthy, however, that in general the mosques of the Ayyubid and

68 Konya, Sahib 'Ata' mosque, portal

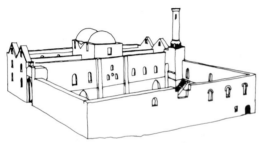

2.200 Selcuk (Ephesus), mosque of 'Isa Beg

time, not surprisingly, joint foundations became the norm, in which the mosque was a mere oratory, a component in some larger complex, a development foreshadowed in Fatimid times by the mosque (or *zawiya*?) of al-Juyushi. Eventually, too, the forms of mosques came to reflect those of contemporary *madrasa*s more than the hypostyle plans of earlier periods. Hence the dominance of small domed mosques such as the 14th-century Mamluk *jami*'s of Tripoli. Such buildings have no bearing on the history of the Arab mosque plan.

5.175–5.1

MOSQUES IN IRAN

i. The early period

Such was the prescriptive power of the 'Arab

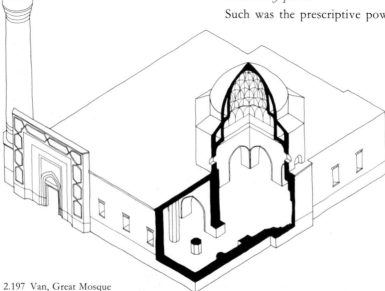

2.197 Van, Great Mosque

Mamluk period offer little scope for large-scale reworking of the hypostyle plan, since they were too small. The mosque of Baibars and that of al-Nasir Muhammad b. Qala'un in the Cairo citadel (718/1318), which is a free copy of it, provide exceptions to this rule; in both cases a monumental dome over the *mihrab* bay is the principal accent of an extensive covered space. The relative scarcity of major mosques in this period not only reflects the primacy of the great early *jami*'s still in use, which made further such buildings redundant; it also marks a shift in patronage away from mosques towards mausolea, *madrasa*s, *khanqah*s and the like. In

2.96–2.97

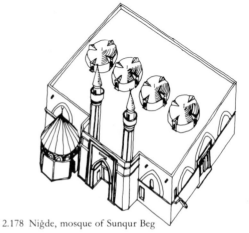

2.178 Niğde, mosque of Sunqur Beg

70 Abyana, Friday Mosque, ceiling

(Bishapur, Abyana, Istakhr, Siraf, Susa, Yazd) were of Arab plan. Some also had the square minarets which were an early feature of that plan (Damghan; Siraf). Rather did the Iranian mosque acquire its distinctive character by enriching the hypostyle form by two elements deeply rooted in pre-Islamic Iranian architecture: the domed chamber and the *iwan*, a vaulted open hall with a rectangular arched façade. The domed chamber derived either from Sasanian palace architecture or from the much more widespread and mostly diminutive Sasanian fire temple with four axial arched openings, the so-called *chahar taq*. Set in the midst of a large open space, it served to house the sacred fire. This layout obviously lent itself to Muslim prayer, and literary sources recount how such temples were taken over and converted into mosques (e.g. at Bukhara) by the simple expedient of blocking up the arch nearest the *qibla* and replacing it with a *mihrab*; but conclusive archaeological evidence of this practice is still lacking, though the mosques of Yazd-i Khast and Qurva may be examples of it. Such domed chambers, whether converted fire temples or

2.227;
2.216–2.217,
2.256;
2.229, 2.257;
2.218, 2.219
2.220, 2.216

7.56, 7.59

2.225–2.226

2.222
2.243, 2.250

plan' that its influence permeated mosque architecture in the non-Arab lands too. It would therefore be an artificial exercise to consider the development of the Iranian mosque in isolation, the more so as many early mosques in Iran

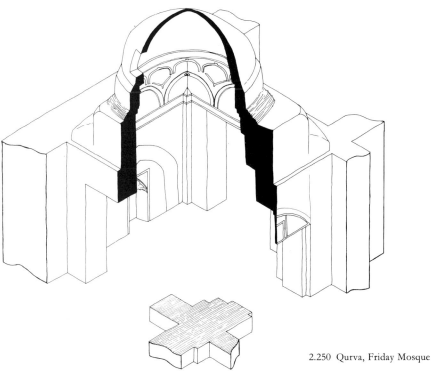

2.250 Qurva, Friday Mosque

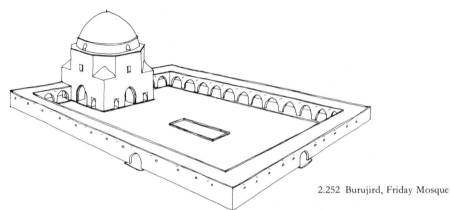

2.252 Burujird, Friday Mosque

purpose-built Muslim structures, may conceivably have served as self-contained mosques, with or without an attached courtyard (Burujird); certainly the earliest part of many medieval Iranian mosques (e.g. Sujas) is precisely the domed chamber. Only excavation will solve this perennial problem.

The associations of the *iwan*, by contrast, were markedly more secular than religious; its honorific and ceremonial purpose in Sasanian palaces is epitomised by the great vault at Ctesiphon, where it announced the audience chamber of the Shah. The *iwan* form was therefore well fitted to serve as a monumental entrance to the mosque, to mark the central entrance to the sanctuary (Tari Khana at Damghan; Na'in) or, indeed, itself to serve as the sanctuary (as at

Niriz, perhaps 363/973 onwards). Thus both the domed chamber and the *iwan* quickly found their way into the vocabulary of Iranian mosque architecture, and by their articulating power gave it a wider range of expression than the Arab mosque plan could command. It was in the interrelationships between the domed chamber, the *iwan* and the hypostyle hall that the future of the Iranian mosque was to lie, though much simpler *masjid*s, as at Siraf, were no doubt the norm.

ii. Saljuq mosques

The tentative experiments of early Iranian mosque architecture crystallised in the Saljuq period, especially between *c.* 473/1080 and *c.* 555/1160. The major mosques built or enlarged

2.246, 2.252
2.245, 2.251
71

7.51–7.52

2.220–2.221,
2.258

2.214

2.254–
2.260,
2.274–

2.270

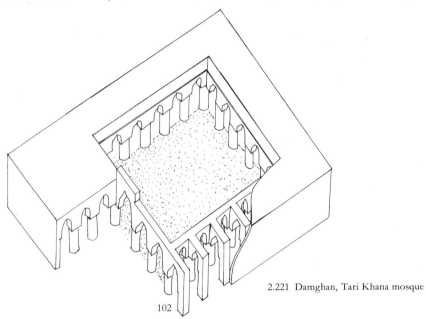

2.221 Damghan, Tari Khana mosque

102

71 Sujas, Friday Mosque, dome chamber

bination of old forms created the classical, definitive version of the already ancient four-*iwan* courtyard plan that was to dominate Iranian architecture for centuries to come, infiltrating not only other building types such as *madrasa*s and caravansarais, but also spreading as far west as Egypt and Anatolia and eastwards to Central Asia and India. The four-*iwan* mosque thus became in time the dominant mosque type of the eastern Islamic world.

Up to the end of the Saljuq period, however, the way was still open for numerous other combinations of hypostyle hall, domed chamber and *iwan*. Bashan, for example (10th century) has a square layout with courtyard, hypostyle hall, domed sanctuary and sanctuary *iwan*, but lacks any further articulation of the courtyard façade by *iwan*. Among many others, the mosques of Dandanqan and Mashhad-i Misriyan (both 11th century) are typologically related to it. At Urmiya/Rida'iya (13th century) the mosque is an extensive shallow oblong with the domed

at this time (such as the Isfahan and Ardistan *jami*'s) have as their focus a monumental domed chamber enclosing the *mihrab* and preceded by a lofty *iwan*. This double unit is commonly flanked by arcaded and vaulted prayer halls. This arrangement represents the final transformation of the sanctuary in Iranian mosques, using the vocabulary of Sasanian religious and palatial architecture for new ends. The sanctuary *iwan* opens on to a courtyard with an *iwan* at the centre of each axis punctuating the regular sequence of *riwaq*s. These arcades attain a new importance as façade architecture by their arrangement in double tiers. Yet the focus of attention is undoubtedly the great domed chamber, as at Barsiyan. The simplicity of the prototypical *chahar taq* is scarcely to be recognised in these massive Saljuq *maqsura* domes, with their multiple openings in the lower walls and their complex zones of transition. They are frequently the result of princely patronage, and perhaps connoted political authority. This concentration on the domed chamber was often achieved at the expense of the rest of the mosque (Gulpayagan *jami*', *c*.510/1116). The new com-

72 Ardistan, Friday Mosque, bays leading to dome chamber

103

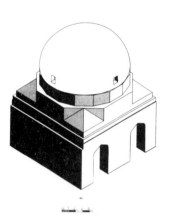

2.251 Sujas, Friday Mosque

chamber at one end of a hypostyle hall, and no *iwan*. Sometimes the mosque is entirely covered 2.240 by five (Masjid-i Diggarun, Hazara, 11th century) 2.228 or nine domed bays (Char Sutun mosque, 2.237–2.238 Tirmidh, 10th century; Balkh, Masjid-i Nuh *cf.* 2.239 Gunbad, 9th century; Masjid-i Kucha Mir, Natanz, 12th century). In its Saljuq form the 2.276 mosque at Ardabil comprised a domed chamber with an *iwan* in front of it, while at Sin (528/1133) the sanctuary, comprising a deep *iwan* with *muqarnas* vaulting, engulfs one side of the diminutive courtyard. The huge courtyard of the

Firdaus *jami'* (597/1200) is dominated by its single *iwan* which heralds a low vaulted sanctuary. The *jami'*s of Farumad (13th century?) and 2.273 Gunabad (606/1209) have only two *iwan*s facing each other across a narrow courtyard, and no domed chamber. Other mosques in Khurasan are simpler still, comprising only the domed chamber itself (Sangan-i Pa'in, 535/1140; Birrabad and 'Abdallahabad, both possibly Saljuq) or with insignificant bays adjoining it (Talkhatan Baba, 12th century). Often too, the 2.231: various elements were added in an unpredictable *cf.* 2.230 sequence, for instance at Simnan where a 2.277 probably 11th-century columned hall had a complete mosque 'unit' comprising a domed chamber, *iwan* and courtyard tacked on to its side. Even within the classical four-*iwan* model, considerable diversity could be attained by varying the scale of the components: from long narrow courtyards (Simnan) or small square ones of domestic scale (Zavara, 530/1135) to 2.215 huge open expanses broken up by trees (Shiraz *jami'*, mainly 16th century), pools or fountains.

The principal emphasis on the internal façade was, however, unchanging. The exterior, by contrast, was unadorned and unarticulated to the point of austerity, through portal *iwan*s were a common exception to this rule, as at Herat. Variations in the height or breadth of *iwan*s reinforced axial or hierarchical distinctions. By 73 common consent the sanctuary *iwan* was the largest and deepest; the opposite *iwan* was next in size, though often very shallow, while the two lateral *iwan*s were usually the smallest. Minarets

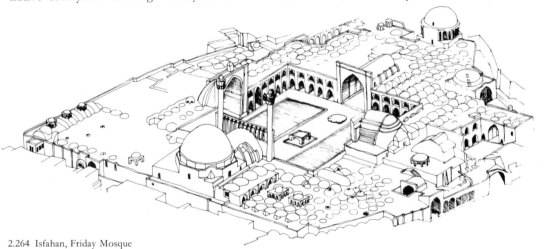

2.264 Isfahan, Friday Mosque

at the corners of the sanctuary *iwan* underlined its importance, while the twin-minaret portal *iwan* first encountered in the Saljuq period (Nakhchivan, 582/1186; Ardistan, Masjid-i Imam Hasan, 553/1158) became increasingly monumental and elaborate in later centuries

cf. 3.9

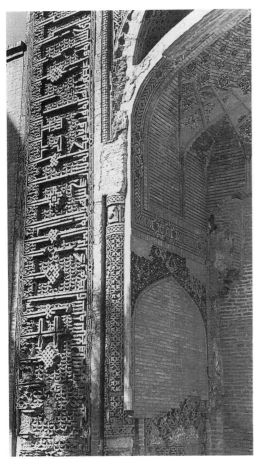

73 Herat, Friday Mosque, *iwan*

74 Ashtarjan, Friday Mosque, courtyard façade looking north-east

2.253 Barsiyan, Friday Mosque

105

75 Ashtarjan, Friday Mosque, *Mihrab* and zone of transition

76 Varamin, Friday Mosque, courtyard arcade

75 (*jami*'s of Ashtarjan, 715/1315, and Yazd, 846/ 1442). *Iwan* minarets of this kind gradually replaced the freestanding cylindrical minarets so popular in the Saljuq period.

iii. Ilkhanid mosques

As in Mamluk Egypt, so too in Iran the later medieval history of the mosque is sometimes hard to disentangle from that of the *madrasa-*, tomb- or shrine-complex. Prayer and communal worship were, after all, integral to the operation of such 'little cities of God' as the shrines of *5.3, 4.37, 2.272* Ardabil, Natanz, Turbat-i Jam, Bastam and Linjan – all of them the scene of much building activity in the 14th century – to say nothing of *5.1–5.2* the great shrines of Qumm and Mashhad. Such

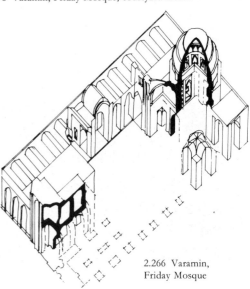

2.266 Varamin, Friday Mosque

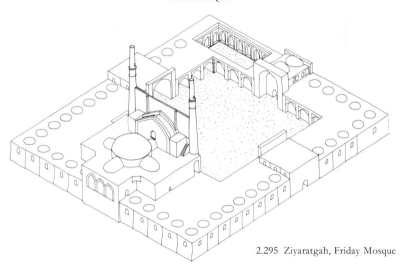

2.295 Ziyaratgah, Friday Mosque

new foundations as there were simply perpetuated Saljuq models (Hafshuya, early 14th
century), though these were subtly altered by
having their proportions attenuated or otherwise modified. At Ashtarjan everything is subordinated to the principal axis announced by the
double-minaret façade, an emphasis which is
taken up and intensified by the single great *iwan*
which takes up the full width of the courtyard
and leads into the domed sanctuary. At
Varamin, too (722/1322 onwards), which is of
standard four-*iwan* type, the sense of axial pro-

gression is strong, and is made rather more
effective than at Ashtarjan by the absolute length
of the mosque and the extended vestibule. The
jami' of 'Ali Shah in Tabriz, by contrast (*c.*
710–20/1310–20) seems a deliberate return to
much earlier models, for it comprised essentially
a huge cliff-like *iwan* preceded by a courtyard
with a central pool and clumps of trees in the
corners – perhaps a deliberate reference to the
Taq-i Kisra itself. For smaller mosques, Saljuq
models were again at hand; hence, for example,
the trio of domed chamber mosques with *iwan* at
Aziran, Kaj and Dashti, all datable *c.* 725/1325.
Yet another compliment to earlier masters was
the Ilkhanid tendency to add new structures to
existing mosques: a *madrasa* to the Isfahan *jami'*
(776–8/1374–7), an *iwan* to the mosque at Gaz
(715/1315), and so on.

iv. Timurid mosques

The Timurid period took still further ideas
which had been no more than latent in earlier
centuries. While some mosques of traditional
form were built – such as the Mosque of Gauhar
Shad, in Mashhad, of standard four-*iwan* type
(821/1418) – attention focused particularly on
the portal and *qibla iwan*, which soared to new
heights. Turrets at the corners magnified these
proportions still further. This trend towards
gigantism is exposed at its emptiest in the four-
iwan jami' of Ziyaratgah, near Herat (887/1482),
where the absence of decoration accentuates the

77 Samarqand, Bibi Khanum mosque, sanctuary *iwan*

107

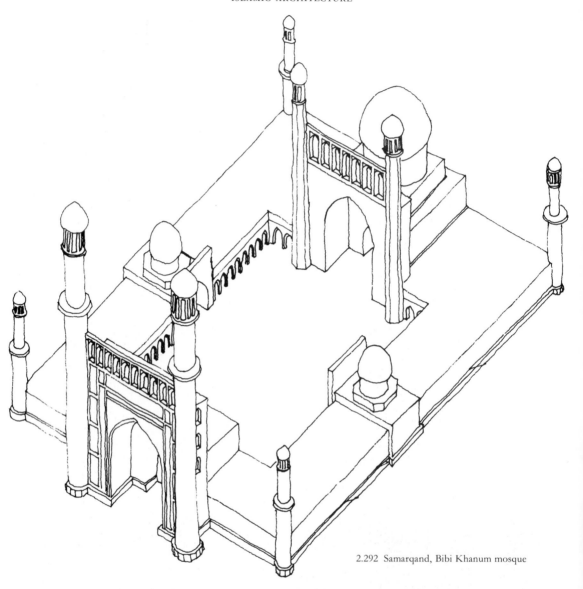

2.292 Samarqand, Bibi Khanum mosque

sheer mass of the sanctuary *iwan* looming over the courtyard. At its best, however, as in the mosque of Bibi Khanum, Samarqand (801/ 1399), where these exceptional proportions are consistently carried through to virtually every part of the mosque, the effect is overwhelming. Here the four-*iwan* plan is transformed by the use of a domed chamber behind each lateral *iwan*; by the profusion of minarets – at the exterior corners and flanking both portal and sanctuary *iwan* – and by the four hundred-odd domes which cover the individual bays. The slightly later Masjid-i Kalyan at Bukhara is clearly in its thrall.

As in the Mongol period, however, the fashion for building *khanqah*s, *madrasa*s and funerary monuments, all of them capable of serving as places of worship (shrine of Ahmad Yasavi, Turkistan, begun 797/1394; the Rigistan complex, Samarqand, begun in its

2.291-2.292
77
80
78

79, 2.29?
5.125-5.1?
4.134-4.1?

Timurid form in 820/1417; Gauhar Shad complex, Herat (821/1418), excluded an equal emphasis on mosque architecture. This may explain the continued popularity of so many standard mosque types – the domed hypostyle (Ziyaratgah, Masjid-i Chihil Sutun, *c*.890/1485) and the two-*iwan* type so long familiar in

78 Samarqand, Bibi Khanum mosque, corner minaret

79 Bukhara, Masjid-i Kalyan, arcade

80 Samarqand, Bibi Khanum mosque, lateral dome chamber

Khurasan (Bajistan and Nishapur *jami*'s, both later 15th century) – to say nothing of the emphasis on refurbishing earlier mosques (*jami*'s of Isfahan, 880/1475 and Herat, 903–5/1497–9), which, in accordance with the Timurid predilection for innovative vaulting, often took the form of adding transversely vaulted halls (*jami*'s of Abarquh, 818/1415; Yazd, 819/1416; Shiraz, *c.* 820/1417; Maibud, 867/1462; Kashan, 867–8/

1462–3; and the mosques of Sar-i Rik, 828/1425 and Mir Chaqmaq, 840–1/1436–7, at Yazd). There was still ample room for surprises. The winter prayer hall added to the Isfahan *jami*' in 851/1447 has multiple aisles of huge pointed arches springing directly from the ground and lit by ochre alabaster slabs let into the vaults and diffusing a golden radiance. The hoary four-*iwan* formula was given a new twist by the addition

110

81 Anau, mosque, east side

of twin domed chambers flanking the sanctuary *iwan* (Herat *jami'*, 15th century), an idea which infiltrated other plan types too (Rushkhar *jami'*, 859/1455 and Anau mosque). At Jajarm (late 15th century?) the central axis marked by the domed chamber and the courtyard is flanked on each side by a trio of vaulted bays.

Yet perhaps the most original mosque designs of the period were those which focused on the single dome and thus echoed, if only distantly, the preoccupations of contemporary Ottoman architects. This concept manifested itself in several different ways. In the Masjid-i Gunbad, Ziyaratgah (*c.* 887–912/1483–1506) a square exterior encloses small corner chambers and a cruciform domed central area, a layout more reminiscent of a palace pavilion than a mosque. The core of the Masjid-i Shah,

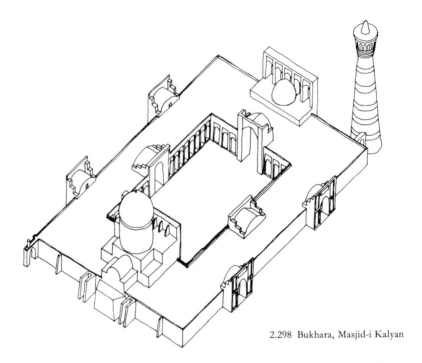

2.298 Bukhara, Masjid-i Kalyan

2.279–2.280 Mashhad (855/1451) is again a large domed chamber, but this is enclosed by a vaulted ambulatory and preceded by a long façade with corner minarets and a portal *iwan*. Most ambitious of all is the Blue Mosque in Tabriz (870/1465), in which a similar idea is given much more integrated expression by virtue of the open-plan arrangement of the central space. The dome springs from eight massive piers, but this octagon has further piers in the corners, making it a square with twelve openings, and thus offering easy access to the multi-domed ambulatory. A similar openness characterises the gallery area and ensured that this mosque, though entirely covered, was airy, spacious and flooded with light. The range and subtlety of its polychrome tilework makes this mosque an apt coda for a period which exploited to an unprecedented degree the rôle of colour in architecture.

v. Safavid mosques

The restoration and enlargement of existing mosques, a trend already noted in Timurid times, continued apace in the Safavid period, and involved over a score of mosques in the 16th century alone. Yet not one new mosque of the first importance survives from this century, though the Masjid-i 'Ali in Isfahan (929/1522), a classic four-*iwan* structure, has a sanctuary whose open-plan dome on pendentives provides a bridge between the Blue Mosque in Tabriz and the Lutfallah mosque in Isfahan (1011–28/1602– 19). The latter, a private oratory for Shah 'Abbas I, makes a very public break with tradition, for it is simply a huge square chamber. Its lofty dome rests on eight arches via an intermediary zone of 32 niches. The whole interior is sheathed in glittering tilework, whose smooth surfaces simplify all structural subtleties. Though the mosque is correctly oriented towards Mecca, it is set at an angle to the great square (*maidan*) from which it is entered, an angle dissimulated by the portal *iwan* which instead obeys the orientation of the *maidan* towards the cardinal points of the compass. A low vaulted passage linking *iwan* and dome chamber, but invisible from either, resolves

2.284–2.2

2.290

112

82 Anau, mosque, sanctuary *iwan*

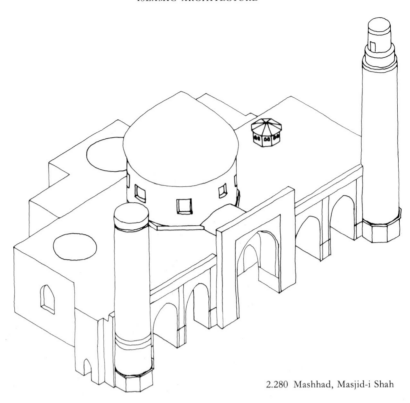

2.280 Mashhad, Masjid-i Shah

these conflicting axes. It also draws attention to a discrepancy which could easily have been avoided and is therefore deliberate.

2.281–2.282 In the nearby Masjid-i Shah (1021–40/1612–30), which also fronts the *maidan*, the problem of discordant axes is solved with sovereign ease, for the portal leads into a diagonal vestibule which in turn opens into a four-*iwan* courtyard, now correctly orientated. Both portal and *qibla iwan* have paired minarets to assert their importance. The scale is vast, but the entire mosque is conceived in due proportion to it. As at the 2.291–2.292 comparably large mosque of Bibi Khanum, dome chambers behind the lateral *iwan* give extra space for prayer, while two *madrasa*s with courtyards flank the main courtyard to the south. Thus even at the height of its popularity the four-*iwan* mosque could accommodate quite major innovations without impairing its essential character. Later Safavid mosques, such as the *jami*'s of Sarm and Chashum, the Masjid-i Vazir in Kashan and that of 'Ali Quli Agha in Isfahan, serve by their very modesty to highlight

the altogether exceptional status of the two mosques on the Isfahan *maidan*. Even such a spacious and handsome version of the traditional four-*iwan* schema as the Masjid-i Hakim, Isfahan (1067/1656) could not fail to be an anticlimax in their wake.

THE TURKISH TRADITION

Early domed mosques

The earliest Anatolian mosques follow Arab prototypes, and by degrees some of them take on an Iranian colouring, especially in their free use of *iwan*s for portals and for sanctuary entrances. By the 13th century, however, an emphasis on the isolated domed chamber as a mosque type began to make itself felt. This idea too might have had Iranian origins, but it soon developed in ways that owed nothing to Iran, since the contemporary preference for entirely covered mosques with no courtyard was itself enough to encourage experiments in the articulation of interior space (e.g. mosques in

114

2.285 Tabriz, Masjid-i
Muzaffariya (Blue Mosque)

2.213 Niğde,
mosque of 'Ala' al-Din

Ottoman architecture before 857/1453

The sequence begins very modestly with a series of mosques comprising a simple domed cube with a lateral vestibule ('Ala' al-Din mosque, Bursa, 736/1335, a structure typical of well over a score of such Ottoman mosques built in the course of the 14th century); and minor variants of this schema, such as the mosque of Orhan Ghazi, Bilecik, and the Yeşil Cami, Iznik, 780/1378, abound. Such structures have a natural affinity with larger mausolea throughout the Islamic world, and with the simplest forms of Iranian mosques. It is only with hindsight that their significance for later developments, in which the theme of the single, and (above all) central, dominant dome of ever-increasing size becomes steadily more important, can be appreciated. This, then, is the main line of evolution in Ottoman mosque architecture, and the discussion will return to it shortly.

Meanwhile two other types of mosque, in which the dome also loomed large, deserve brief investigation, especially as they bade fair in the formative early years to oust the domed, centrally planned mosque as the favoured Ottoman type, and also because they had their own part to play in the final synthesis of the 16th century. The presence of three major types of domed mosque in the same century is a reminder that the pace of change was uneven. Several mosques conceived on an altogether larger scale rejuv-

2.300, 2.3
2.301, 2.3
2.302–2.3
2.319

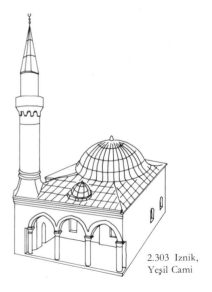

2.303 Iznik,
Yeşil Cami

2.184
2.182–2.183
2.177–2.178;
2.208

Erzurum, Kayseri, Niğde and Sivrihisar). The dome quickly became the most favoured device to this end. In Iran, by and large, the domed chamber behind the *qibla iwan* remained spatially isolated from the rest of the mosque. In Anatolia, by contrast, architects were always seeking new ways of integrating the main domed space with the area around it (e.g. Nebi mosque, Diyarbakr). A consistent emphasis on domical forms created the necessary visual unity to achieve this. Already in the Saljuq period tentative experiments in this direction may be noted, for example the 'Ala' al-Din mosque, Niğde (620/1223), whose *qibla* is marked by three domed and cross-vaulted bays with further parallel aisles behind. In the Ulu Cami of Bitlis (545/1150), a single great dome replaces these smaller bays, while in the Gök mosque and *madrasa*, Amasya (665/1266), the *masjid* comprises a series of triple-domed aisles. Experiment with domical forms was therefore deeply rooted in Anatolian architecture from the beginning. It is above all the hallmark of mosques erected by the Ottomans, and can be traced to the very earliest years of that dynasty.

2.207

2.212–2.213

2.188

4.91–4.92

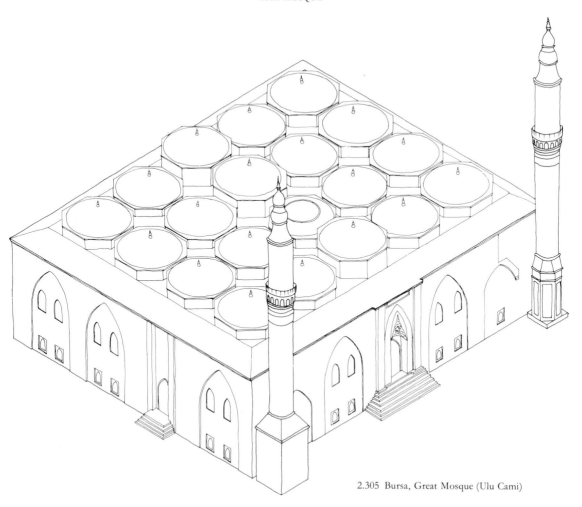

2.305 Bursa, Great Mosque (Ulu Cami)

enated the hypostyle form by investigating the impact of multiple adjoining domes. In some cases, like the Ulu Cami, Bursa, of 797/1395, a simple square subdivided into twenty domed bays of equal width though of varying height—the choice of the dome as the agent of vaulting is a diagnostic Ottoman feature—the effect was distinctly old-fashioned. At ground level this is an Arab mosque, even if its elevation is Anatolian. Contemporary with this, but marking a very different attitude to interior space, are two other mosques in Bursa, that of Yildirim Bayazid, 794/1392, and the Yeşil Cami of 816/1413, which use the dome motif on various scales and thus far more imaginatively. They represent a second preparatory stage on the way to the mature Ottoman mosque, and their

spacious layout is by turn cruciform, stepped or of inverted T-type. Their distinguishing feature is the use of several domes of different sizes. In the two cases under discussion, or at the mosque of Sultan Bayazid at Amasya, the inverted T-plan highlights the *mihrab* aisle by two adjoining domes along the central axis flanked by a trio of domed or vaulted bays on each side, all this knit together laterally by a five-domed portico. Sandwiched between these two buildings in date is the Ulu Cami of Edirne, 806/1403, where the square is subdivided into nine equal bays, eight of them domed, with a domed and vaulted portico tacked on. At the mosque of Chelebi Sultan Mehmed, Dimetoka, this arrangement is refined by an increased concentration on the central dome, which is enveloped by vaults on

117

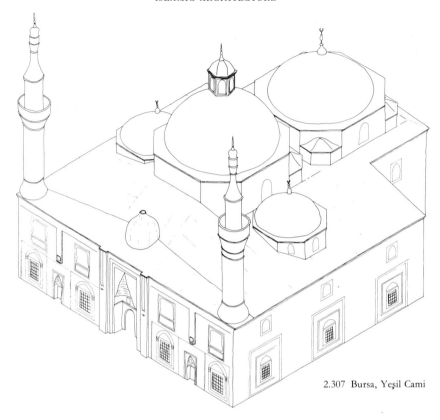

2.307 Bursa, Yeşil Cami

the main axes and diagonals, the whole preceded by a three-domed portico. Such a combination cannot fail to recall the standard quincunx plan, complete with narthex, of mid-Byzantine churches, and it was of course these buildings which dominated the Anatolian countryside in the early centuries of Turkish occupation. Steady Byzantine influence can be seen to have affected the evolution of Ottoman architecture, even before the capture of Istanbul brought Turkish architects face to face with Haghia Sophia. Yet it would be grossly mistaken to regard mature Ottoman mosques as mere derivatives of Haghia Sophia. The Üç Şerefeli mosque, Edirne, of 851/1447, with its huge central dome on a hexagonal base flanked on either side by a pair of much smaller domes and preceded by a lateral courtyard enclosed by twenty-two domed bays, makes excellent sense within a purely Ottoman perspective as a key stage in the evolution which terminated in the great masterpieces of Sinan. The divergence between the great dome and the lesser ones

2.312, 2.327, 2.338–2.339, 2.340

flanking it has already become acute and was to end in their total suppression.

Yet one significant element, crucial to Haghia Sophia and a cliché of Ottoman architecture after 857/1453, had not yet entered the architectural vocabulary of the Turkish mosque before that date. This was the use of two full semi-domes along the *mihrab* axis to buttress the main dome. The long-rooted Islamic custom of marking the *mihrab* bay by a great dome rendered such a feature otiose. Once the decision had been taken to make the largest dome the central feature of a much larger

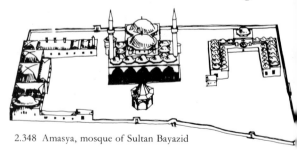

2.348 Amasya, mosque of Sultan Bayazid

118

square, the way was open for the adoption of this Byzantine feature, and then the transformation and enrichment of interior space was a foregone conclusion. Otherwise, most of the architectural vocabulary used in mature Ottoman mosques was already to hand by 857/1453: flying buttresses, the undulating exterior profile created by multiple domes, tall pencil-shaped minarets and a certain parsimony of exterior ornament allied to exquisite stereotomy. It has to be admitted that these features *83, 84* had yet to find their full potential, notably in the failure to develop a suitably imposing exterior to match the spatial splendours within. That potential could be realised only when these features were used in association with each other by masters seeking to express a newly-won confidence and bent on creating an integrated style for that purpose. The mosque was, moreover, their chosen instrument; indeed, Ottoman architecture is, first and foremost, an architecture of mosques.

The mature Ottoman style

The capture of Constantinople in 857/1453 provided both a terminus and an impetus to a radical rethinking of mosque design. Appropriately enough, the first building to express the

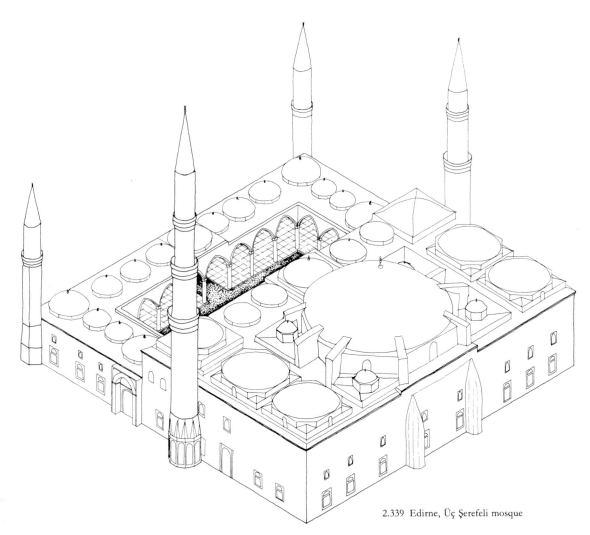

2.339 Edirne, Üç Şerefeli mosque

83 Istanbul, Selimiye mosque, arcade

84 Istanbul, Sultan Bayazid mosque, pier

new mood was a victory monument, as its name indicates: the Fatih Mosque (867–75/1463–70). This has a single huge semi-dome buttressing the main one but also displacing it off the main axis; clearly, the spatial, aesthetic and structural implications of such a semi-dome had not yet been fully grasped. Within a generation, this anomaly at least had been rectified; the mosque

2.313,

2.341, 2.

85 Istanbul, Şehzade mosque, interior

of Bayazid II (completed 913/1507) has two such semi-domes on the *mihrab* axis, with four lesser domes flanking this central corridor on each side. On the other hand, the projecting portico sandwiched between dome chamber and court-yard is a clumsy and lopsided expedient with little functional justification. Yet the resultant emphasis on the portico is wholly typical of a period in which this feature re-appeared under

84

2.314, 2.

86 Istanbul, Mihrimah mosque, general view

numerous guises, especially in doubled form
(Mihrimah mosque, completed c. 973/1565).
The Şehzade mosque (955/1548) presents a
much more streamlined appearance, with dome
chamber and courtyard of approximately equal
proportions. Within the sanctuary, the great
central dome opens into semi-domes on all four
sides, with small diagonal semi-domes opening
off the main ones and with smaller domes. It is
instructive thus to see Ottoman architects developing the possibilities of the centralised plan
like the builders of Christian churches and
martyria a millennium before, and coming to
very similar conclusions. Smaller mosques with
domes on hexagonal (Ahmed Pasha, completed
c. 970/1562) or octagonal bases (Mihrimah
mosque) were scarcely less popular than domed
squares. A small number of wooden-roofed
mosques perpetuating earlier modes, especially
in Anatolia and Iran (e.g. Afushta), and with
their roots in the Arab tradition, survive (e.g.
Ramazan Efendi in Kocamustafapasha, 994/

1586, and Takkeci Ibrahim Aga, 999/1591) as
reminders of a very widespread type of Ottoman
mosque now almost entirely eclipsed by more
durable structures.

In the ferment of experiment which marks
16th – century Ottoman architecture, the key
figure was undoubtedly Sinan, an Islamic equivalent of Sir Christopher Wren, who transformed the face of the capital city as of the provinces
with some 334 buildings (mostly mosques)
erected in his own lifetime. His pivotal role as
chief court architect (effectively Master of
Works) allowed him to stamp his ideas on public
architecture from Algeria to Iraq and from
Thrace to Arabia in the course of a phenomen-
ally long career which spanned virtually the
entire century. His finest mosques are nearly all
in Istanbul, scattered prodigally throughout the
city; they are his epitaph, which might fittingly
read *si monumentum requiris, circumspice*. The
Süleymaniye mosque in Istanbul (963/1556) is by
common consent the masterpiece of his middle

2.314, 2.351
2.315, 2.333,
2.343, 2.355

age. It takes up and refines the model of the Bayazid II mosque by adding ideas taken from the Şehzade mosque, like the succession of semi-domed spaces billowing out from the main dome, though only along the principal axis. *87* Huge arches serve to compartmentalise the spatial volumes.

All these mosques are preceded by an open courtyard whose cloister is roofed by long files of adjoining domes. This standard feature typifies the new emphasis on subsidiary structures – mausolea, *imaret*s, *madrasa*s and the like 2.325 – and the consistent attempt to integrate them visually with the sanctuary itself, for example by subordinating them to the principal axes of the design. All this implies a marked increase in scale and a new sensitivity to the landscaping of 2.344–2.345 the ensemble (*külliye* of Bayazid II, Edirne). Hence the recurrent choice of dramatic sites for these mosques, especially in Istanbul with its built-in vistas along the Bosphorus. This aware-ness of topography as a feature of mosque 2.346 design is evident as early as the Fatih mosque; its three parallel axes are grouped around and

While the increase in the absolute height and breadth of these great domed chambers is striking, the amount of articulation and detail crammed into these spaces is scarcely less im-pressive. All is subordinated to a formidable concentration of purpose – for example, the carefully considered fenestration, surely a legacy from Haghia Sophia, with its superposed groupings of eights and sixes or of sevens, fives and threes. In the interests of creating the maximum untrammelled space, thrusts are con-centrated on to a few huge piers with spherical pendentives between them, and thus the layout is a model of clarity and logic. Flooded with light, their volumetric sub-divisions apparent at a glance, these interiors are at the opposite pole from the dim mysteries of Haghia Sophia. Frescoes reminiscent of manuscript illumination and of carpet designs vie with Iznik tiles to decorate the interior surfaces, and often (as in the case of fluted piers) to deny their sheer mass.

Externally, these mosques demonstrate a well-nigh fugal complexity by virtue of their obsessive concentration on a very few articulat-

87 Istanbul, Süleymaniye complex, model

2.334, 2.342
2.349, 2.354

within an enclosed open piazza measuring some 210 m. per side. The climax of mature Ottoman architecture is reached with Sinan's final master-piece, the Selimiye at Edirne (982/1574), in which the largest of Ottoman central domes (31.38 m. in diameter), hedged externally by the loftiest quartet of Ottoman minarets (70.89 m. high) rests on eight piers pushed as close to the walls as safety will allow so as to create the largest possible open space.

ing devices like windows, arches and domes. The repetition of the same forms on varying scales intensifies the sense of unity. Even the minarets which mark the outer limits of the mosque's surface area are brought into play; for example, those of the Sultan Ahmed Mosque 2.337, (completed 1025/1616) have the bases of their 2.352–2.3 balconies so calibrated as to coincide with the top of the main dome, its collar and the collar of the main subsidiary half-domes, while their

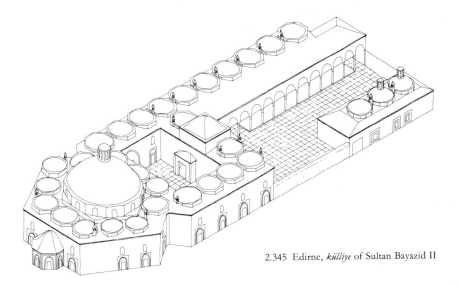

2.345 Edirne, *külliye* of Sultan Bayazid II

location at the corners of the building binds it together and defines the sacred space from afar. Detailing is sparse and crisp, with a strong linear emphasis, a flawless sense of interval and a pronounced attenuation of features like wall-niches and engaged columns (Süleymaniye mosque). Nothing is allowed to impair the primary aesthetic impact of cliff-like expanses of smooth grey stone. Most notable of all is a dramatic but ordered stacking of units, culminating in the great dome which crowns and envelops the entire ensemble. These individual units are each locked into place within a gently sloping pyramidal structure whose inevitable climax is the central dome. From this peak the subsidiary domes, semi-domes and domed buttresses cascade downwards to form a rippling but tightly interlocked silhouette. These highly articulated exteriors are a triumphant reversal of the standard Islamic preference in mosque architecture for stressing the interior at the expense of the exterior. As the viewpoint changes, so too does the profile of these mosques, from a continuous smoothly undulating line to a series of sharp angular projections formed by stepped buttresses and roof-turrets. The preference for saucer domes rather than pointed domes with a high stilt fosters the sense of immovable, rock-like stability, with the topmost dome clamped like a lid on to the mobile, agitated roof-lines beneath it.

This, then, can justly claim to be architects' architecture. It merits that term by virtue of its unbroken concentration on the single germinal idea of the domed centralised mosque. It is against that consistent unity of vision that the role of the Haghia Sophia must be assessed. Of course Turkish architects were not blind to its many subtleties, and they freely quarried it for ideas. But it was as much a challenge that inspired them to emulation as it was a source for technical expertise. Finally, it was the Ottomans who succeeded where the Byzantines had failed: in devising for these great domed places of worship an exterior profile worthy of the spendours within. The triumphant issue of their labours to that end can be read along the Istanbul skyline to this day.

CHARACTERISTICS OF MOSQUE DESIGN

The analysis given above has attempted to outline and explain the major components of mosque design, the various functions which the building served in medieval times and – admittedly in a very cursory fashion – to identify and describe the principal schools of mosque architecture. It is now time to relinquish the specific in favour of the general and to try to pinpoint

88 Cairo, Aqmar mosque, façade

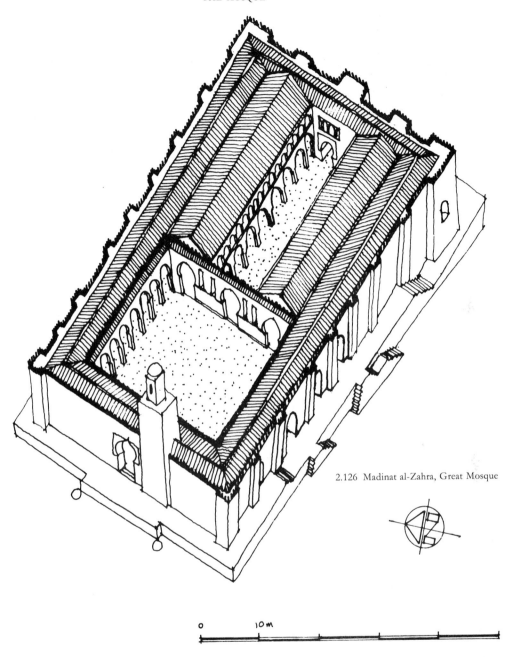

2.126 Madinat al-Zahra, Great Mosque

0   10 m

the abiding characteristics of mosque design throughout the Islamic world and over almost a millennium. Four trends may perhaps be singled out: an innate flexibility; an indifference to exterior façades; a corresponding emphasis on the interior; and a natural bent for applied ornament.

Flexibility

Mosque architecture owes its flexibility – which

125

is so pronounced a feature that it is not always possible to recognise the building as a mosque at first glance – to several distinct factors. Perhaps the most important of these is the lack of sacraments and formal ceremonies in Muslim worship, which means that there are few ritual requirements to be met. This has made it possible for a very wide variety of buildings to serve as mosques. The lack of a well-developed architectural tradition in Arabia meant that Muslims encountered the cultic buildings of other faiths with remarkably open minds, if only in the sense that they had no clearly defined notion of what constituted an appropriate kind of sanctuary. From this sprang a willingness to adopt alien traditions of architecture and to adapt them freely, indeed ruthlessly, to suit Muslim needs. This was equally true whether the mosque was a free variation on themes borrowed from pre-Islamic tradition, or whether its very structure was that of a pre-Islamic place of worship taken over by the Muslims for use as a mosque and subsequently modified. The net result of all this was to present Islamic architects, at least in theory, with a remarkably wide range of options in designing a mosque. In practice, of course, they tended to work within the limits of their own local school.

Indifference to exterior façades

Several reasons might be cited for the indifference which Muslim architects customarily display to the notion of a highly articulated exterior façade in mosque design. They might, for example, have been influenced by the stubborn insistence of orthodox opinion that the Prophet would himself have disallowed elaborate display in architecture. This attitude found expression in numerous *hadith*s. Alternatively one might cite the ingrained custom in Islamic lands whereby domestic and much public architecture presents an unyieldingly blank face to the world and thus preserves the privacy of those within. An even more practical consideration is the layout of most towns in the Islamic world. The absence of wheeled traffic meant that most streets were narrow. Moreover Islamic law safeguarded private property rights; and this, together with the absence of municipal corporations of European type, discouraged town planning on a spacious scale. The opera-

tion of these various factors ensured that the average medieval Islamic city was too labyrinthine in layout to contain much in the way of long straight avenues, crescents, piazzas or other similar features which might foster the development of elaborate façades. Thus the concept of the mosque as a major feature of the cityscape never took root in the Islamic world. Despite a few major exceptions, then, which include mosques built in open country as well as urban mosques like the Aqmar mosque in Cairo, 2.98, 8 it was standard practice for medieval mosques to have unpretentious exteriors. Very often they were located in the thick of bazaars and domestic housing, thus literally and metaphorically at the level of everyday life. So modest might the various entrances be that it would be quite possible to enter a mosque without immediately realising it – though elaborate porches 46 are not rare. In addition to all this the exterior perimeter of a mosque might well have grafted on to it, by a process of gradual accretion, whole clusters of subsidiary buildings – treasuries, 2.264 latrines, mausolea, halls for prayer in winter, *madrasa*s and even palaces. All would conspire to block any integrated exterior view of the mosque.

Emphasis on the interior

The relative neglect of the exterior façade brought in its train, by a pleasingly exact reciprocity, a consistent emphasis on the symmetrical planning of the interior. The façade, in short, moved inside the mosque. The role of the courtyard was crucial in all this, and significantly it is nearly always large enough to permit a full view 2.126 of the sanctuary façade. *Iwan*s, arcades, gables 89 and domes are the most popular methods of articulation, while the use of alternately projecting and recessed masses was also known. Islamic architects, in short, knew how to manipulate the masses of a building on the grand scale. The interaction of courtyard, *riwaq*s (covered arcades or cloisters) and enclosed sanctuary allowed them to experiment with various combinations of open, half-covered and enclosed space, and to exploit multiple contrasts between light and shade. Broad uncluttered surfaces helped to instil a peaceful atmosphere and prepared the worshipper to enter the cool, dark ambience of the sanctuary. The device of turning the mosque

89 Tlemcen, Sidi al-Halwi mosque, courtyard

90 Yazd, Friday Mosque, interior of dome chamber

88 outside in, as it were, has an appealing simplicity; but more than that, it allows the architect a freedom of manoeuvre which would be denied to him in the world outside the mosque. He can plan every detail of the façade, including the vital aspect of its interaction with its immediate surroundings, liberated from the constraints imposed by the secular architecture engulfing the exterior of the mosque on all sides.

Decoration

No account of mosque architecture would be complete without reference to the decoration which embellishes it. In the religious sphere, the unwavering Muslim hostility to figural decoration, with its accompanying overtones of idolatry, encouraged an intense focus on abstract ornament. This was soon valued in its own right as an aid to contemplation, which is why such care is lavished on panels just above floor level and therefore at the right height to be comfortably taken in by someone sitting on the ground. Whether the ornament is architectural or applied, its purpose is the same: to dissolve matter, to deny substantial masses and substitute for them a less palpable reality, whose forms change even as they are examined. This is done by repeating individual units indefinitely – columns, arcades, the cells of a honeycomb vault (*muqarnas*) and especially the various forms of

41 applied decoration: floral, geometric and epigraphic. That the craftsmen who produced this ornament experienced a sensuous delight in the mingling of colours, materials, textures and

design motifs is scarcely to be questioned. But there is much more to Islamic decoration than this. Each of the three categories noted above – floral, geometric and epigraphic – has a deeper dimension. The endless variations which Islamic craftsmen were able to conjure forth on the theme of floral motifs, and which brought the word 'arabesque' into European languages, of themselves suggest the inexhaustible richness of 22 God's creation, and are frequently interpreted in a symbolic religious sense as references to paradise and Allah himself. Geometrical ornament makes much play of multiple superimposed levels and of patterns which continue beyond the frame which encloses them; in both cases there are obvious suggestions of infinity. Finally, the epigraphic mode as encountered in 90 mosques is overwhelmingly and explicitly reli- 41 gious in content, comprising quotations from the Qur'an and the *hadith*, with historical matter 41 coming a poor second. These inscriptions are, quite simply, the Muslim answer (not equivalent) to icons. Their text, whether the mosque is in Spain or China, is in Arabic, a tribute to the potent unifying force of that language in the Muslim world.

Such, then, are the basic principles of medieval Islamic mosque architecture. So faithfully were they observed across vast gulfs of space and time that almost any medieval mosque is instantly recognisable as such, whether it be in 7th-century Iraq, 10th-century Cordoba or 17th-century Delhi. Here, if anywhere, is the ocular proof that Islam is one.

III The Minaret

INTRODUCTION

Unlike the other types of Islamic religious building, such as the mosque and the *madrasa*, the minaret is immediately and unambiguously recognisable for what it is. The reasons for this are worth investigating. They seem on the whole unrelated to its function of *adhan* (calling the faithful to prayer). The call to prayer can be made quite adequately from the roof of the mosque or even from a house-top. During the lifetime of the Prophet, his Abyssinian slave Bilal, whose stentorian voice became the stuff of legend, was responsible for making the call to prayer in this way. As the tale is told in the *hadith*, this happened in the most natural way: "When the Muslims came to Madina they used to gather for prayer without any given summons to it; a lack which they discussed one day, and some argued 'Let us have a bell like the Christians' and some said 'Let it be a trumpet like the horn of the Jews'. 'Umar said: 'Why not appoint a man to call the people to prayer?' And the Prophet said 'Rise, Bilal, and call people to prayer'." The practice continued for another generation, a fact which demonstrates that the minaret is not an essential part of Islamic ritual. To this day certain Islamic communities from Kashmir to the Sudan, especially the most orthodox ones like the Wahhabis in Arabia, avoid building minarets on the grounds that they are ostentatious and unnecessary. Others are content with the so-called 'staircase' minarets, which consist simply of a few broad external steps leading to a diminutive kiosk a little above roof level. These perpetuate a practice common in the first century of Islam. While such structures are obviously functional, it is very doubtful whether the same can be said for any minaret much more than fifty feet high. Without mechanical amplification the human voice simply cannot make itself heard, especially in a noisy urban setting, from the top of such celebrated minarets as the Giralda in Seville or the Qutb Minar in Delhi.

If, then, the ostensible function of the minaret is somewhat misleading, what other purposes might it have served? If the investigation confines itself in the first instance to the early minarets of the Islamic world – i.e. those predating 1000 A.D. – three possible approaches may be suggested, following in this van Berchem's lucid analysis of the genre. One is to examine the role of the very earliest minarets in their particular historical setting, on the theory that these examples laid down guidelines for the further development of the form. Another is to see what clues lie in the Arabic words used for minaret, and in their etymology. A third approach would focus on the forms of these early minarets and on their immediate sources, and would thus involve the assumption that at least traces of the earlier functions associated with these forms survived into the Islamic period. Yet each of these approaches is flawed, for each is riddled with inconsistencies, especially in the crucial early centuries when the very notion of the minaret was undergoing a complex evolution. Indeed, the early history of the minaret is particularly fraught with difficulties, exacerbated by a marked tendency to assess the early evidence in the light of later developments rather than in its contemporary context. Happily, a recent monograph on this subject by Jonathan Bloom revises many current misconceptions and puts scholarship in this field on to an entirely new footing.

THE CONTEXT OF THE EARLIEST MINARETS OR TOWERS

It will be convenient to begin by studying the circumstances in which the earliest minarets were built. According to the literary evidence, the first minaret was erected under the caliph Mu'awiya in *c.*45/665 at the instance of his governor in Iraq, Ziyad b. Abihi. A stone tower was accordingly added to the mosque at Basra – and if indeed it was a tower, it would certainly have been the most monumental feature of that mosque. Soon after, in 53/673, at the behest of the governor of Egypt, the mosque of 'Amr at Fustat was given a quartet of minarets, while minarets were also added to other mosques in Egypt. Although nothing remains of any of these structures, this literary evidence – for all

3.1   3.2   3.3   3.4   3.5   3.6   3.7   3.8   3.9   3.10 3.11

that it must be treated with some caution, since it is largely of 15th-century origin – is most revealing. The evidence indicates that the impetus to build minarets came from the highest power in the land. It may even have derived from the caliph himself, though this is admittedly speculation. Clearly this is not convincingly explicable as a matter of local initiative, nor was such a major innovation generated by some unique concatenation of local circumstances. The idea, found as it is well-nigh simultaneously in Iraq and Egypt, may well have come from Syria, a province equidistant from both of them and – more to the point – the centre of the Umayyad dynasty which was then newly in power and concerned to establish its position. The key to this momentous innovation seems to lie less in functional imperatives than in political ones. Mu'awiya's conception of his role as caliph is very relevant here. It was Mu'awiya who outraged orthodox opinion by minting coins depicting himself as an armed monarch, by using a *minbar* when still only governor of Syria, by arrogating to himself much of the panoply of

Byzantine royal ceremonial. His justification for these and similar actions never varied: the local population had to be conciliated, and their tradition demanded that rulers should hold state in splendour. And it was precisely in Mu'awiya's caliphate that his governor, Maslama, ordered the four "minarets" (*sawami*) for the Fustat mosque; though perhaps not for the *adhan*.

Against this background the introduction of the minaret acquires an unmistakably political colouring. Christian Syria, within which the Muslims formed a few small enclaves, was lavishly endowed with fine stone churches whose most striking external feature was a tall tower. At the top of these towers was struck the *simantron* – the Orthodox equivalent of the church bell – to summon worshippers for divine service. Mu'awiya, sensitively attuned to the discrepancies between Christian and Muslim culture, and to the need to reconcile them wherever possible, can scarcely have failed to compare this Christian practice with its much simpler Islamic equivalent. It would have been wholly in character for him to have decided to

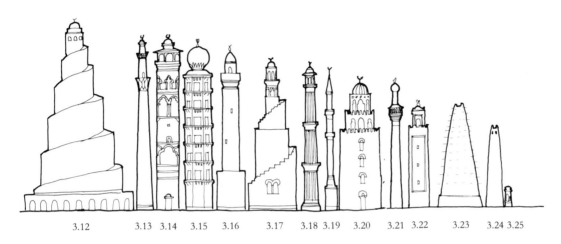

3.12 3.13 3.14 3.15 3.16 3.17 3.18 3.19 3.20 3.21 3.22 3.23 3.24 3.25

secure for the *adhan* a dignity and formality it had not hitherto possessed by giving it monumental expression. Typically, too, that expression borrowed a Christian form but imbued it with a new Muslim meaning. The slightly later case of the Dome of the Rock leaps to mind as the obvious parallel. The intrusion of political concerns into the forms of early Islamic religious architecture was to be a hallmark of the Umayyad period.

These arguments are susceptible to more than one interpretation. They could support the theory that these early, essentially redundant, minarets were intended simply to demonstrate to the local non-Muslims that the new faith was no less capable than its rivals of devising monumental architecture for its own glory. More simply, they could be seen as evidence of the gradually crystallising intention of the Muslims to find worthy outward expressions of their faith, directed primarily if not exclusively at the Muslim community itself. However, they could also imply the conclusion that from its very beginning the minaret was intended to function as an outward sign of Islam. After all, the Near East was still overwhelmingly non-Muslim in these early years of the new faith. A usage formulated in response to a hostile environment would then gradually have become canonical and would have persisted even when circumstances had overtaken the need for it. These two interpretations will be considered in more detail below, in the context of the form of the earliest minarets. For the moment, it is worth remembering that in all probability these early minarets were too small to carry much of a propaganda charge, irrespective of whether that charge were directed at the Muslims or the Christians, or both at once. They are therefore better interpreted as early and hesitant essays at an unfamiliar form, a form which Islam was later triumphantly to make its own.

ETYMOLOGY

The second possible approach to the original function of the minaret is through the etymology of the words used in Arabic to describe this kind of building. It is perhaps significant that

6-2.17

3.111

131

the three words most commonly used – *manara*, *saumaʿa* and *miʾdhana* – all seem to refer, so far as their etymology is concerned, to quite separate functional aspects of the building. Thus the notion that the minaret served multiple functions is embedded in the Arabic language itself. These functions quite naturally generated appropriate terms for themselves. Whether the prevalence of a given term in a given geographical area reflects the predominance of one function over another is, however, doubtful.

By far the commonest of the three terms is *manara* or *manar*, which is appropriately enough the source – via the Turkish version of the term – for the English word 'minaret'. It needs to be emphasised at the outset that the word carries no connotation of the call to prayer. Its basic meaning is a place of light or fire (*nur* or *nar* in Arabic). It is in no sense surprising that these two shades of meaning should converge in actual linguistic usage – though the evidence of the various verbs connected with the root *n.w.r.* suggests that the primary meaning is light. The word was used in pre-Islamic Arabia to designate high places from which signals of fire or smoke were made. For this reason the minaret has often been equated with a lighthouse, especially since such structures were widely used for military purposes by the Byzantines in North Africa and Syria well into Islamic times. The Pharos of Alexandria, which was of course one of the Seven Wonders of the ancient world, and which was damaged by the Arabs in 21/642, had this function among others and has remained the exemplar of all subsequent lighthouses. It has repeatedly been cited as the inspiration for certain types of minaret, a theory which will be discussed shortly. Moreover, the cylindrical towers attached to Islamic fortresses along parts of the North African coast (e.g. Tunisia) not only served as lighthouses and beacons but were actually called *manara*s. It need therefore occasion no surprise that *manara* has been etymologically derived from the Arabic word for light (*nur*). This connection with light has been used as the basis for a symbolic interpretation of the minaret as an emanation of divine light or as an image of spiritual illumination. More generally – and this point will be taken up later – the term *manara* was applied, by a familiar process of semantic depreciation, to sign-posts, boundary stones and watch-towers even when no particular association with light or fire was intended. Conversely, the connection with fire and light is especially emphasised in the use of *manara* to mean oil-lamp or lampstand. One

3.111

might summarise the discussion of *manara* by noting that the term combines two distinct concepts: the notion of light or fire and that of a marker. Neither meaning has any locus in Islamic ritual. However, while the lighting of a fire on the minaret of a mosque was an event of the utmost rarity in the early period (it is recorded to have occurred in the case of the Manarat al-ʿArus in the Damascus mosque), and is difficult to reconcile with any regular function of the mosque, the value of the minaret as a marker of the principal building of the Islamic community is self-evident. It may safely be conceded, therefore, that in the context of religious architecture the association between the minaret and light or fire is (in practical terms) an irrelevance. It will be necessary, however, to return to this association in the context of secular architecture.

The second term frequently used to designate the minaret – indeed, it is the standard usage in North Africa – is *sauma'a*. The word means a cell in which a Christian (usually a monk) secludes himself (with the particular gloss that the cell has a slender pointed apex). It is worth remembering in this context that when the greatest of medieval Islamic theologians, al-Ghazali, was undergoing his spiritual crisis he turned, like many a Christian anchorite before him, to seclusion in a building – though he calls it a *manara*. In his own words: 'for a period I confined myself in the mosque of Damascus, and stayed on the minaret all day long with the door barred'. This concept of shutting oneself off seems to be derived from the *sauma'a*s or cells which were a regular feature of pre-Islamic Byzantine architecture; they were incorporated into the tall rectangular towers with which churches, monasteries and houses were furnished. Once again, however, as in case of *manara*, the etymology is apt to mislead – for while the basic meaning of *sauma'a* is indeed 'hermitage', the word has come to designate, by a process of *pars pro toto*, the entire structure of which the cell was a small part. It might also be noted that, as with *manara*, which is often used of the lamp of a Christian monk, the connection with Christianity – a connection which is a recurrent feature of the history of the minaret – may simply reflect the Christian context of many of the early usages of the term. In other words, *sauma'a* may well

have been used to mean 'cell' rather than specifically 'a Christian's cell', which is the primary definition given by Lane. Among the meanings for the verb *sami'a* is to have an ear which is tapering or slender at the extremity. At all events, the specific connotation of *sauma'a* in the present context seems to be a tall rectangular minaret, rather than the minaret genre itself. Perhaps it developed its association with height not by the *pars pro toto* process but because – as the case of Fustat suggests – it originally connoted small rectangular box-like projections above the roof-line at the corners of the mosque. As time passed, such 'sentry-box' minarets, as Schacht has felicitously termed them, became taller and thus more prominent, and a free-standing minaret was the obvious climax to such an evolution. Be that as it may, *sauma'a* seems to be an entirely appropriate term for the minarets of North Africa. Moreover, unlike the word *manara*, and its Jewish cognate *menorah*, its connotations are religious, albeit with a Christian tinge. Possibly as a result of its association with the minaret, the word was also used more generally to mean ' a high place' or even 'a high building', and in the less specific sense its connection with *manara* in the sense of signal tower or marker is plain. In North Africa, however, a distinction clearly exists, for *manara* is used for signal towers and lighthouses. Appropriately enough in view of its Christian connotations, *sauma'a* has found a lodging in Europe, in the Spanish word *zoma* meaning 'minaret'.

It is a challenging reflection that the two Arabic words most frequently used to designate the minaret give no clue to the ritual function which for centuries has commonly been associated with the building. Instead they evoke respectively pre-Islamic and Christian associations. The term that does accurately render the ritual function of the building – *mi'dhana* – is, ironically enough, much rarer than the other two. It derives from *adhan*, 'the call to prayer', and means a place from which that call is made. The same root yields *mu'adhdhin* (more familiar as 'muezzin'), meaning 'he who makes the call to prayer'. Pre-Islamic traditions infiltrate even this word, for in those days the herald who made important proclamations was known as the *mu'adhdhin*. It must be admitted that the rarity of the term *mi'dhana* is pregnant with meaning, for if the etymologically obvious term is not used, a justifiable logical deduction would be that the early minaret, later tradition notwithstanding, did not serve primarily (or perhaps at all) as a place for making the call to prayer. That is indeed a momentous concept, and it leaves the way open for a thorough-going reassessment of the genre as a whole. By this reasoning, then, some connection with the ruler, presumably with his role as *imam*, would seem possible (a view most cogently proposed in recent years by Jonathan Bloom) – though the close interplay of secular and religious elements in the caliphal office should caution against a too narrowly political or secular interpretation of the minaret, as should its widespread popularity, from at least the tenth century onwards, in provincial contexts outside the orbit of the court and the major centres of power. The evidence of these later centuries unambiguously points to the use of the *manara/sauma'a* for the call to prayer, and that evidence cannot lightly be set aside. For the time being it must suffice merely to draw attention to these inconsistencies; for it cannot be denied that the persistent equation of the minaret with the proclamation of power is hard to reconcile with its widely assumed role as a tower for the *adhan*.

Before leaving the problem of etymology, it may be worth noting that several other words occur sporadically in literary or epigraphic texts as synonyms for at least some of the meanings of *manara*: *'alam/'alama* ('signpost', 'boundary marker', 'standing stone', 'flag'), *mil* (possibly derived from the Greek *miliarion*, 'milestone') and *asas*, 'a place of watching', a term especially popular in the Maghrib. The mere mention of these words in the context of the foregoing discussion is enough to emphasise yet again that etymology is a somewhat treacherous guide in determining the function of the minaret. Certainly these rarer words suggest that the minaret had other functions besides the call to prayer; but here too caution is required, since still more words are used for 'mausoleum' and are applied to structures which do contain a body and therefore incontestably function as mausolea. It can safely be asserted, however, that a review of Arabic terminology establishes that the minaret performed not one function but several in the medieval Islamic world. While the rarer Arabic

words used for 'minaret' may well reflect the function of the building in the particular context concerned, the most commonly employed word, *manara*, was obviously a blanket term which does not readily lend itself to precise elucidation, unless the context offers further, more specific, clues.

THE FORM OF THE EARLIEST MINARETS

The third possible approach to determining the function of the minaret in the early centuries of Islam is by way of morphology. The briefest survey of the formal characteristics of medieval minarets is enough to yield one very significant result: that virtually the whole body of surviving minarets belongs in one of two categories. One category comprises minarets with ample interior space; the other, minarets in which the interior space is reduced to the bare minimum required for a spiral staircase to ascend the structure. Minarets with external staircases obviously belong in neither category. Useful as this division is, it cannot shed light on the crucial first century of Islam. Any attempt to explain the function of the minaret by means of its form has to take some account of the earliest recorded minarets, even though none of these has survived. The interpretation placed on the tantalisingly brief literary accounts which refer to the earliest minarets is therefore crucial.

These accounts are unfortunately either ambivalent or too short to throw any light on the problem. For example, the historian al-Baladhuri refers to the minaret at Basra as being of stone. Since stone is specified, and the rest of the mosque was of mud brick, it seems legitimate to conclude that the minaret was important enough to have special care taken over its construction. This, then, seems to be a fairly straightforward case. The same cannot be said for the minarets of the mosque of 'Amr at Fustat. The source here is the 15th-century historian al-Maqrizi, who states – in a text that draws on several different sources and which for that reason may not be a true reflection of his own vocabulary – that Mu'awiya ordered the building of four *sawami'* (pl. of *sauma'a*) for the call to prayer, and that Maslama placed four *sawami'* in the corners of the mosque. Since this is not, in all probability, the first word for minaret that would have come naturally to al-

91 Uzgend, minaret

Maqrizi's mind, its use in this passage calls for some discussion, even if it is not possible to arrive at a totally convincing explation. Perhaps the most straightforward explanation is that the choice of word is not al-Maqrizi's but that of the particular source he was quoting. In that case, one must reckon with the changes of meaning to which this particular word was subjected over the medieval period. Put plainly, the word could mean 'rectangular box' if the source were of 7th- or 8th-century date and 'tall minaret' if it were half a millennium later. It is also possible, of course, as suggested earlier, that al-Maqrizi himself used the word deliberately because to him it connoted tall, rectangular minarets of the Syrian or Maghribi type (very unlike those which he saw all around him in Egypt). His choice of word would in that case have reflected either his own or his source's belief (perhaps even precise knowledge) of the form which these early Umayyad minarets took. Alternatively, he may have used the word *sawami'* with one of its other meanings in mind, such as a high place. In that case the sense of the passage might be more accurately rendered by translating the key passage as 'Maslama heightened the four corners of the Friday Mosque'. Such an interpretation would find further support in the literary accounts dealing with the construction of the Damascus mosque. Yet the difficulties attending any of these interpretations are legion.

The key point to bear in mind in a discussion of the Damascus minarets in their present form is that there is no evidence that they were the work of any early Muslim patron. Indeed the geographer Ibn al-Faqih, writing in 903, states specifically that the minarets (*mawadhin*) in the Damascus mosque 'were originally watch towers in the Greek days, and belonged to the Church of John. When al-Walid turned the whole area into a mosque, he left these in their old condition'. Similarly, his contemporary al-Mas'udi writes that in this rebuilding 'the *sawami'* were not changed, they serve for the *adhan* at the present day'. Thus strictly speaking there is no clear evidence even that these pre-Islamic towers were used for the call to prayer in Umayyad times, and one may especially doubt that they served this function before the reign of al-Walid, when the Muslims shared the site of the future Great Mosque with the Christians.

Nevertheless, the use of the word *sawami'* by the Iraqi al-Mas'udi, while it could mean simply that the Greek watch-towers contained chambers and happened in *that* sense to be like the *sawami'* at Fustat, could perhaps yield the meaning that, at Damascus as at Fustat, the *sawami'* – whatever their form – were indeed used for the *adhan*.

Reasonable grounds therefore exist for assuming that the corners of the mosque of 'Amr at Fustat were typologically very like those of the Damascus *temenos*, even though they would have been much smaller. Such *sawami'* would be no more than abrupt excrescences at roof level, possibly articulated a little further by crenellations. They would indeed resemble Christian towers, but only in a somewhat stunted fashion. They could not aspire to dominate the skyline or indeed make any marked physical impact on the urban landscape. If this motive had loomed large in the mind of al-Walid at the time that he was building the Damascus mosque it would have been a simple process to heighten the existing corner towers accordingly. That he chose not to do so is clear evidence that the symbolic role of the minaret was not yet generally accepted. Indeed, the mosques of Basra and Fustat are more prophetic of later developments even though they were built earlier. At Basra the minaret, whatever its form may have been, was clearly distinguished by its different material of construction, while at Fustat the *sawami'* were solid up to roof level, necessitating access by ladders. While this detail reflects the early Islamic practice of delivering the *adhan* from the roof, it also suggests that these corner *sawami'*, by virtue of the strength conferred by their solid walls and by virtue of their position at the corners of the mosque, also had an architectural function as buttresses for the whole building. Their location and strength in turn invites a symbolic interpretation of their function as cornerstones of the faith, although it has to be admitted that their modest projection above the roof-line would scarcely proclaim this. Even so, the impact of their placing can be gauged from the statement of al-Maqrizi that at the time of the dawn prayer a muezzin was stationed at each *sauma'a* and that their combined *adhan* resounded like thunder through the silent city. It might fairly be said, then, that despite the probably rather truncated nature of

2.69

their resemblance to Christian towers, the *sawami'* of the Mosque of 'Amr – like those of the mosque of Medina as rebuilt by al-Walid I – did operate as markers for the mosque. This function was certainly performed more effectively and elegantly by later minarets, but the crucial point is that it is already implicit in the earliest buildings of this genre.

The discussion so far has repeatedly assumed a close relationship between the Christian towers of Syria and the early minaret, but so far no physical evidence of this relationship has been adduced. Unhappily, the earliest surviving minaret of wholly Islamic construction, that of the so-called Mosque of 'Umar at Busra in southern Syria, dated by inscription to 102/720–1, does nothing to remedy this deficiency. It fits quite naturally into place alongside the long-since-vanished *sawami'* just discussed, with a staircase giving access to its summit. Attached to the same mosque is a tower boldly projecting from the otherwise regular perimeter wall of the mosque, which boasts a twin window with a columnar dividing shaft; this is of Mamluk date rather than Umayyad, as was formerly believed. Its presence raises pressing questions as to its own function if the 'sentry-box' minaret was still operative at that time. At all events, the Umayyad minaret was here unassumingly grafted into the body of the mosque, exactly as had been done in the Damascus mosque and probably also at Fustat.

The Damascus minaret

It will be clear from the evidence presented so far that in the first century of Islam the role of the minaret within the religious – let alone the secular – domain had not yet been defined in its essentials. Later centuries were to bring major changes, notably variations in form and new secular functions. The minaret in tower form was still to come, unless indeed one were to assume, as is legitimate enough, that the minaret covered with external glass mosaic at the north entrance of the Damascus mosque was erected by al-Walid I. This tower was unfortunately destroyed in 570/1174, and replaced soon thereafter by the present minaret on that site. Such a building could readily be paralleled by a long series of similar towers (though without the mosaic revetment) erected as part of pre-Islamic

92 Aleppo, Great Mosque, minaret

137

Christian churches, monasteries and houses in Syria – such as the examples of Sameh, Umm al-Rasas, Umm al-Surab and Qasr al-Banat. Before too much is made of this long-vanished tower at Damascus, however, it is only fair to point out that despite the evidence of four texts asserting that al-Walid I was responsible for it, its Umayyad date has been questioned. That said, the evidence of the external wall mosaic points unambiguously to the Umayyad period. Firstly, it was under that dynasty that glass mosaic reached its apogee in Islamic times. Secondly, the minaret of the Umayyad mosque in Cordoba, a mosque which embodied a thoroughly conscious recreation of Umayyad Syrian modes, was modelled on it. Thirdly, it is hard to imagine the 'Abbasid government of Syria embellishing, or allowing others to embellish, the Umayyad mosque in a style so expensively reminiscent of their hated predecessors. It may seriously be doubted, too, whether the skills required to execute wall mosaics on a large scale were available in the 10th century, which is the date which some scholars have proposed for this tower.

3.45-3.46

The mosaics of that tower ensured that attention was specifically drawn to it, perhaps already at street level, and certainly in the upper part of the elevation. It would not be going too far, perhaps, to suggest that the germ of the concept that the minaret is a symbol of the faith is already to be found in this tower at Damascus. For good measure that tower may also express the idea – particularly relevant in a predominantly Christian urban setting – of the mosque as a refuge for the faithful, with the minaret as its bulwark. In that case the defensive connotations of such towers in pre-Islamic Christian Syria – for example, the tower which is all that survives of the monastery on whose site the Umayyad palace of Qasr al-Hair al-Gharbi was built – would have been adopted and re-interpreted in a profounder sense by the new faith. The fact that such towers were a feature not only of Christian churches, but also of the larger pre-Islamic houses in Syria, may have helped to clinch the Muslim adoption of a similar form for their minarets, since the earliest mosque was of course the Prophet's house and the practice of using a house as a mosque is enshrined in Islamic tradition and practice to this day.

7.19

3.14

The Qairawan minaret

An early surviving example of the square form of minaret, probably established in Syria as a result of the evolution outlined above – though the surviving examples, including three at Aleppo and one in the mosque of al-Khidr in Busra, dated 528/1134, are much later – is to be found in Tunisia. Recent excavations have confirmed that the square substructure of the minaret of the Mosque of Sidi 'Uqba at Qairawan can be associated with a rebuilding of the mosque undertaken in 221/836, though the upper parts are later. The latter detail weakens a once popular theory – to which there will be occasion to return later – that this minaret reflects the influence of the Pharos of Alexandria, which had a three-tier elevation, each tier smaller than the previous one. However, it is quite possible that in its original form the minaret looked very much like it does now. Even if that were not so, the adoption of a three-tier elevation at a later period would still require explanation and would certainly not exclude the possibility that the influence of the Pharos was decisive. The stepped three-tier form is not known in the towers of pre-Islamic Syria. Moreover, it is quite plausible that the Arab conquerors of Tunisia, who began their campaign in Egypt, should have used the most celebrated tower of that country as a model for the minaret of the first mosque built in this newly Islamised territory. The prime function of the Pharos as a lighthouse would have dovetailed quite naturally with the pre-Islamic associations of the *manara* in pagan Arabia, and would therefore have rendered it an unusually appropriate model for a minaret. The distinctive triply-stepped silhouette of the Qairawan minaret, however, was, to remain something of a dead end in the later history of the minaret. Even if the specific link with the Pharos is difficult to sustain, a connection with the lighthouse genre (as already suggested by the etymology of *manara*) seems assured, for the researches undertaken by Lézine have identified as a likely model for the Qairawan minaret the Roman lighthouse of Salakta (the ancient Sullecthum), conveniently sited nearby on the Tunisian coast.

92,

93

3.29

3.11

The principal impact of the Qairawan minaret, whatever its ancestry, was local, as the Susa *manar* and the minarets of the Great

3.42

93 Qairawan, Great Mosque, minaret

of the mosque by setting the minaret at the opposite end of the courtyard to the sanctuary. The emptiness of that great rectangular courtyard threw into stark relief the sheer mass of the minaret and confirmed its vital role in the building. Moreover, the placing of the minaret broadly though not exactly on the axis of the *mihrab* announced, more clearly than ever before, a ceremonial and liturgical connection between them. Besides, since the two features are at opposite ends of the building, this positioning helps to knit the mosque together and puts all the interior space to work, energising what was previously inert.

The disposition of minarets at the corners of the mosque, as at Fustat, Medina and Damascus, 2.66, 2.70 had already established their use as an articulating device. Qairawan developed that function still further. It was only a matter of time before the last refinement was added and the minaret was exactly aligned with the *mihrab*. The Great Mosque of Samarra is the earliest and best 3.28 example of this culmination; the minaret at Madinat al-Zahra, near Cordoba, runs it close. 3.54 The minaret at Qairawan, as at Samarra, is 3.29 notable for its bold projection from the otherwise regular perimeter wall of the mosque. There is no evidence to suggest that some local peculiarity of the site, or for that matter any structural consideration, dictated such an arrangement, and this arresting departure from the otherwise unbroken continuity of the wall enclosing the mosque therefore invites explanation. No longer is the minaret unassumingly incorporated into the body of the mosque, as at Damascus and probably Fustat. Attention is specifically drawn to it in the ground plan – that is, effectively at street level – in the upper part of the elevation, and by its great height.

One might have thought that the substantial enclosed space of the Qairawan minaret (the 3.48 base is some 10 m. square and the height is *c*.35m.) would have encouraged the provision of chambers within the minaret itself. For some reason this was not done, and the minaret therefore has inordinately thick walls. Self-contained rooms in superposed storeys had long been characteristic of Syrian church towers, and it was only to be expected that this idea should eventually take root in Islamic architecture, whether as an independent invention or as an

30, 3.39, Mosques of Sfax and, to a lesser extent, Tunis 3.47 testify. In other respects, however, this building anticipates later developments. It serves notice of the increasingly important rôle which the minaret had come to acquire in the 9th century. Its enormous bulk (perhaps the result of inexperience and hence timidity on the part of the architect) was underlined in the original layout

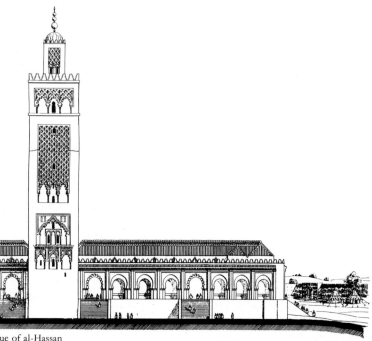

3.51 Rabat, mosque of al-Hassan

imitation of pre-Islamic prototypes. In the Syrian Christian tradition the floor of each storey was of wood, a practice also recorded in the corner towers of the Damascus mosque. Later Maghribi and Andalusian minarets not only revive the practice of furnishing the building – such as the minaret at the Qal'a of the Banu Hammad and the Almohad examples in Seville, Rabat and Marrakesh – with chambers, but also give them decorative vaults in stone or brick.

ALMOHAD MINARETS

This trio of minarets, all dated to the end of the 12th century, unquestionably registers the high-water mark of this genre in western Islam. Obedient to the strong undertow of conservatism in Maghribi architecture, they perpetuate the outer shell of pre-Islamic Syrian towers, of which the minarets of the mosques of Aleppo and Ma'arrat al-Nu'man preserve a distant memory. Given the geographical remoteness of these Maghribi minarets from Syria, and the fact that by the 12th century Syria was definitively sundered from the Maghrib in the political sphere, it is in the highest degree unlikely that

this postulated Syrian influence reached the far west of the Muslim world directly. Rather was it mediated through the filter of Umayyad Spain, which early established cultural dominance in the Maghrib. The archaising tendencies of Moorish architecture predisposed Spanish Muslim craftsmen to perpetuate Syrian archetypes. In the domain of architecture the Great Mosque of Cordoba was undoubtedly the centre from which such Syrian influences, re-interpreted in sometimes bizarre forms, radiated throughout the Maghrib.

The internal arrangements of the great Almohad minarets are significantly different from those of their distant Syrian ancestors, as in the vaulting of the chambers or the use of a ramp as the means of ascent; the 10th-century minaret (long since destroyed) of the Cordoba mosque even had two separate staircases. They are also very much larger than their Syrian models, approaching 65 m. (200 feet) in height, and – again unlike their prototypes – they display lavish decoration on all four sides. This is executed in a typically Maghribi idiom of cusped, horseshoe or multifoil arches, often generating a latticework design or enclosing yet

140

further variants on the arched form. Single or
paired windows on each storey are a standard
95 feature. Carved vegetal ornament is used to
96 provide secondary accents in the spandrels and
elsewhere. The few slightly earlier minarets in
the Maghrib are mostly plain and crowned with
a crenellated balustrade. The two in Fez obey a
1:4 proportional ratio of width to height; this is
changed to 1:5 in some of the greater Almohad
3.37 minarets (e.g. Mansura). A small pavilion, often
3.38 a diminutive replica of the main shaft of the
94 minaret, and crowned with a dome sometimes
bearing a finial or standard, completes the upper
elevation. Apart from a new emphasis on lavish
external tilework, this formula remains essentially unchanged in the later medieval period

95 Rabat, Mosque of Hassan, minaret

94 Marrakesh, Kutubiya mosque, upper part of minaret

throughout Spain and the Maghrib (e.g. Fas 3.39
al-Jadid, Great Mosque, 674/1275). Indeed, by 3.27
an ironic quirk of history the minarets of Andalusia exerted a decisive influence on the cam-
paniles of Spanish churches in this period. Thus
the wheel came full circle.

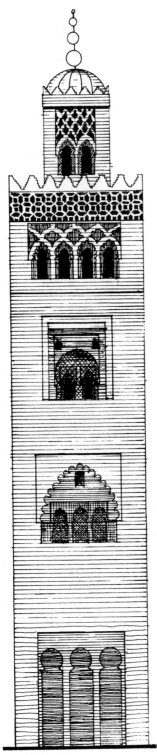

So strong was the tradition of the tall square-shafted Maghribi minaret that it even survived the advent of the Ottomans. Possibly under their influence, the minarets of Algeria and Tunisia erected under Turkish rule occasionally recaptured the grand scale of the Almohad minarets, though falling far short of the finesse of earlier decoration. A novel type of octagonal minaret, each face richly tiled and the whole crowned by a projecting balcony and steepled pavilion, enjoyed special popularity in Ottoman Tunis. It represents a somewhat awkward blend of the local tradition with the slender pencil-shaped Turkish minaret, and manages to forfeit 3.70–3.71 the distinctive qualities of both.

WEST AFRICAN MINARETS

An unexpected and distant by-product of the Syrian tradition is the Saharan or West African minaret. The Saharan type, often very high (e.g. the fairly recent example of Walad Jalal at Zibane) has a marked batter to its walls – a feature which had occurred at Qairawan but had not been exploited subsequently in the medieval period – and 's crowned by an open-plan kiosk. Given the pre-eminent religious status of Qairawan throughout North and Western Africa as a centre for pilgrimage and learning, it is not surprising that the celebrated mosque of that city should make its presence felt thousands of miles away. But that influence, if indeed it can be proved to exist, became steadily more at-tenuated over the centuries and overlaid by local ideas. Thus in West African minarets, most of which date from the last four centuries (e.g. Timbuktu and Agadez), the batter is so pro- 3.23 nounced that the minaret resembles a truncated cone, studded with projecting palm beams. These facilitate the constant repairs that such mud-brick structures require. Similar minarets are found as far north as the Mzab region in Algeria (e.g. Ghardaya). They leave far behind 3.24, 3.35 the putative model furnished by the Qairawan minaret.

The minarets of the Maghrib and Andalusia form a school unique in the Islamic world for its fidelity to an imported model and for its innate conservatism, which maintained a broadly con-sistent form throughout a vast area for over a millennium. The history of the minaret in the rest of the Islamic world, that is in Egypt and

3.55 Marrakesh, Kutubiya mosque

96 Seville, Great Mosque, Giralda minaret

Turkey and in the area to the east of them, is somewhat more varied. It embraces a very wide range of forms, of alien influences, and of functions both secular and religious.

MINARETS IN IRAQ

This wider canvas is immediately apparent in the immediately post-Umayyad minarets which survive in the eastern Islamic world. These are principally to be found in Iraq. Possibly the earliest among them is the so-called Manarat Mujda – though there is some dispute as to when it was built, and even a pre-Islamic dating has been canvassed. This undeservedly neglected building opens a new chapter in the history of the minaret. Both in form and function it departs decisively from the norms established in the previous century. It is a slender cylindrical structure of baked brick, with a diameter just large enough to accommodate a winding interior stair and with sparing external geometric decoration executed in baked brick. It is thus in all its essentials prophetic of the matchless series of minarets erected in Iran during the Saljuq period. Its location is even more revolutionary, for it is entirely freestanding and there is no evidence that there was ever any building adjoining it. Its *raison d'être* – like its date – may be established with reasonable confidence by virtue of its strategic location midway between two 'Abbasid palaces: the great princely residence of al-Ukhaidir (*c*.159/775–6?) and its lesser satellite 'Atshan. The direct route between Ukhaidir and Kufa, the nearest city with a Friday mosque, cut straight across the desert and the most likely function of this minaret was to mark the way. The non-classical form could conceivably be derived from the watch-towers that, according to Yaqut and al-Baladhuri, studded the Sasanian *limes* nearby, which faced Bedouin Arab territory in southern Iraq. An extension of that line of reasoning might suggest that this tower is part of the system of watch-towers which was erected in early 'Abbasid times to mark major desert routes, in particular the Darb Zubaida or pilgrim route from Kufa to the Holy Cities of the Hijaz.

The most celebrated of early 'Abbasid minarets are of course the helicoidal towers attached to the Great Mosque of Samarra (234–7/848–52) and the mosque of Abu Dulaf nearby

(245–7/859–61). Although their precise origin is a matter of dispute, the question of a classical or Christian source does not arise. Their forms are deeply rooted in ancient Near Eastern architecture. In both cases a square base carries an external ramp which spirals upwards, at first gently but then with increasing steepness, around a solid central cylinder. In the case of the minaret at Samarra (the *malwiya*) the ramp ends after five complete revolutions at an arcaded kiosk. A similar aedicule probably crowned the minaret of the Abu Dulaf mosque after the ramp had completed four revolutions. The Samarra minaret is therefore substantially larger, and at a height of 53 m. (174 feet) is indeed one of the highest minarets in the Islamic world. As befits its importance, the minaret has a new and imposing location. It is placed some 30 m. outside the mosque and is precisely on the axis of the *mihrab*. By this means its integration with the mosque and its liturgical function in relationship to the rest of the building is adequately stressed, while its isolation is sufficiently marked for the minaret to invite attention as a separate structure. It boosts the mosque visually too. The practice of placing the minaret on the *mihrab* axis was copied throughout the Islamic world, and in time the idea was still further developed, perhaps as an original local invention, by making the minaret abut the exterior wall of the mosque and incorporating into its base the major entrance to the mosque itself (Mosque of al-Mansura near Tlemcen, 703–6/1303–6).

How and why did this bizarre helicoidal form come to be chosen for a minaret? If the *malwiya* is considered in the context of other early 'Abbasid architecture in Mesopotamia, such as al-Ukhaidir, or the round city of Baghdad, the possibility of its dependence on Persian models will be readily apparent. There still survives, at Firuzabad in southern Iran – the first capital of the Sasanians – a square-shafted tower with the remains of an external ramp winding around it. This monument, known to the early Arabs by the obscure term *tirbal*, has been interpreted as a Zoroastrian monument, with a fire burning at its summit. The readiness of the early Muslims to take over for Islamic religious purposes the architectural forms sanctified by earlier religions makes it entirely plausible that the sacred function of the tower and its connection with fire rendered it (or others like it) an especially suitable model for a minaret. The anti-Umayyad bias of the early 'Abbasids would have disposed them against copying architectural forms that had strong Syrian associations, and might conversely have predisposed them in favour of Persian models.

The other possible source for the two minarets of *malwiya* form is the ancient Mesopotamian ziggurat or tower-temple. While most such buildings had stepped elevations comprising superposed squares of decreasing size, a few were characterised by a square base which carried a huge central cylinder encircled

97 Mujda, minaret

by a rising ramp. A four-storeyed building of this type, which probably once had seven stories in all, has been excavated at Khorsabad in northern Iraq, and medieval Arabic accounts indicate that a similar tower existed at the ancient site of Babylon until at least the 12th century. To have adopted this model would also have accorded well with the anti-Syrian tendencies of the time. If this kind of building provided the inspiration for the *malwiya*s of Samarra and *98* Abu Dulaf, this would be a very rare case of *99* Islamic architects deliberately drawing their ideas from the very distant, as distinct from the immediate, past. For this reason, and bearing in mind the pervasive Persian flavour of the early 'Abbasid court, there is a case for suggesting that the Persian rather than the ancient Mesopotamian model was the source of their inspiration. Even so, the Persian tower itself was in all probability dependent on the ziggurat form. Thus the *malwiya* stands revealed as the classic case in Islamic architecture of the continued sanctity of a given form, which maintained itself with remarkably little change over a period of millennia and through two changes of religion. However, subsequent generations seem to have regarded the *malwiya* as too bizarre to serve satisfactorily as a minaret, and it remained virtually without progeny. Nevertheless Islamic tradition cherishes the very secular memory of the caliph 'Ali Muktafi taking his constitutional and simultaneously enjoying the view over his domains by riding up to the top of a similar tower in Baghdad, on a donkey specially trained to amble.

The sole important descendant of the Mesopotamian *malwiya* – derived specifically from the example at Abu Dulaf rather than the grander version at Samarra – was, significantly enough, the minaret of the mosque built in *2.93, 2.89* Cairo by Ibn Tulun (263–5/876–9), a man *3.118* brought up at the 'Abbasid court in Mesopota- *100* mia. In Egypt too the minaret was perceived as a curiosity, and tradition – which disdains art history – relates that the genesis of the minaret's unusual shape lay in the patron demanding that his architect monumentalise the spiral shape he had casually created by twisting a piece of paper round his finger. Unfortunately the present minaret is a reconstruction of the late 13th - early 14th century, but earlier medieval his-

98 Samarra, Great Mosque and minaret

99 Samarra, Mosque of Abu Dulaf, minaret

torians agree that its original form was spiral, and an 11th-century historian even mentions its similarity to the Samarra minaret. Thus the spirit if not the letter of the Mesopotamian model is sufficiently well captured by the present Mamluk structure.

MINARETS IN IRAN

The origins

These spiral minarets, then, however fascinating in themselves, represent a by-way in the history of the minaret. In the eastern Islamic world the focus of attention in the following centuries was Iran, where an entirely different form of minaret developed, namely the lofty, slender, cylindrical type. The origins of this form have yet to be established satisfactorily, and widely divergent theories have been aired. Perhaps the most speculative of all was that advanced by Schroeder, in which he linked the Iranian minaret, in association with the mosque, to some of the ancient religious structures of mankind – Mycenean, pre-Buddhist Indian, pre-Achaemenid Iranian – and drew attention to suggestive similarities between modern shamanistic proto-architectural forms and the essentials of mosque architecture. Beneath the contingent differences of these various forms he traces an underlying unity: the pillar form is an immemorial symbol of 'the axis of the universe, and the direct way to Heaven.'

100 Cairo, Mosque of Ibn Tulun, minaret

This somewhat mythopoeic and anthropological approach, larded with nebulous ethnic and religious associations – an approach of which Strzygowski was the high priest in the first half of this century – may seem too fanciful for some tastes. Yet even a sober art-historical enquiry concentrating on the form alone points to some startling correspondences in pre-Islamic traditions. The crucial point to establish is that the tall cylindrical minaret owes nothing to the Syrian and western Islamic tradition, whereas the areas to the north and east of Iran offer a plethora of possible sources for that form. In China, for example, multi-storeyed eight- or twelve-sided pagodas were built in substantial numbers from the 5th century onwards, and the towers built by the Buddhist Kushans in Central Asia (e.g. the famous tower of King Kanishka near Peshawar) may have introduced these or very similar forms to an area that was soon to become Islamic territory. A second possible source is greater India, which is of course con-

tiguous with Central Asia. The lofty pillars raised for commemorative and political purposes by Asoka in the 3rd century B.C. immediately come to mind. Recent research suggests that these pillars perpetuated an earlier tree cult and intensified the deliberate cosmological symbolism associated with that cult. In short, they were intended to represent the axis of the universe. Nor was this the only relevant Indian form, for one kind of Buddhist *stupa*, especially popular in northern India and Central Asia, elongated the standard domical type to produce a domed cylinder on a high square base. The resemblance of such a form (indeed of the Buddhist *lat* or *stambha* form generally) to an Iranian minaret like that of Khusraugird is self-evident; its relevance is 3.91 perhaps another matter.

Finally, the indigenous tradition of the Turkic peoples of Central Asia and beyond must be considered. The term *idhiz eb*, 'sacred house', was used by the eastern Huns among others to denote high towers placed at the corners of temples or cities, marking the site of the Iokapala shrines. Significantly enough, height was a major desideratum for these towers so that their auspicious influence, represented by their shadows, could extend as far as possible. Such apotropaic concepts are also found in Islamic architecture, though they are not specifically associated with minarets. One further relevant form, recorded in the 8th-9th centuries in Minya Konka and Chotski, both in eastern Tibet, is a stellate watch-tower some 18–19 m. high, which reproduces the form of the otherwise virtually unparalleled 12th-century minarets of Ghazna. 3.103, 3.105–3.110

Thus the border regions of the eastern Islamic world provided a fertile source of inspiration for the builders of the early Iranian cylindrical minarets. At the very least, these areas on the periphery of Islamic territory provided ideas for the forms themselves; whether those forms travelled into the Islamic world with an accompanying set of ideas and beliefs is quite another matter. Yet it is a reasonable hypothesis that at least some of the many different functions and associations – religious, symbolic, political, commemorative and military – of these pre-Islamic towers survived the advent of Islam and in time infiltrated the Iranian minaret.

Even so, such fragmentary evidence as

101 Hama, Great Mosque, minaret

ses with it in elevation, setting an octagonal shaft on the square plinth – a form frequently found somewhat later in Syria (Hama; Miskina). *101, 102* Two-thirds of the elevation is taken up by this shaft, which thereafter becomes a tapering cylinder. The transition from octagon to circle is so muted as to be scarcely noticeable. A cavetto cornice carries a substantial trellised balcony and a small, cylindrical, domed shaft pierced by multiple apertures adds the finishing touch. Apart from a double chevron band near the top of the octagonal shaft, and palmette designs (probably executed in stucco) on the cornice, the minaret is devoid of ornament. This feature alone suggests that the minaret is pre-Saljuq, like the oldest part of the mosque, and the obviously transitional form offers further support for such a theory. Ample literary evidence indicates that extremely tall minarets were a familiar feature in Iranian towns by the 10th century, but it gives little specific information about their form.

Saljuq minarets

The 11th century, however, sees the opening of the great series of Iranian cylindrical minarets, and they are of such finished assurance in their formal and decorative qualities that a lengthy prior development of this type must be postulated. Some of the finest examples are in the towns of Damghan and Simnan on the western borders of Khurasan. These soaring minarets – they are all about 100 feet high – have a pronounced taper which further accentuates their height (a feature developed even more strongly *103* in Central Asian minarets such as the 12th- *3.7–3.8* century examples at Bukhara, Jar Kurgan, *3.93–3.94* Uzgend and Vabkent). Their internal stairways *102, 3.92,* wind around a central column. The Simnan minaret has preserved the original cornice, a precociously developed three-tier *muqarnas*, which presumably carried some kind of balcony; this part has not survived in the two minarets at Damghan. All three minarets are entirely covered with brick decoration, principally broad bands of geometric designs (such as lozenges or interlaced octagons) or inscriptions. Thin guard bands, themselves comprising rhomboids, inclined stretchers, discs or the like, separate the major bands (Kirman). This lavish *3.104* overall decoration is the hallmark of the

survives suggests that the very earliest minarets *2.220; 2.216,* in Iran, such as those at Damghan and Siraf, *2.256* followed the square tower format which was standard under the Umayyads. To judge by the minaret of the Na'in mosque, it was not long before this form underwent substantial modification. The Na'in minaret maintains the traditional square format in ground plan but dispen-

102 Miskina, minaret

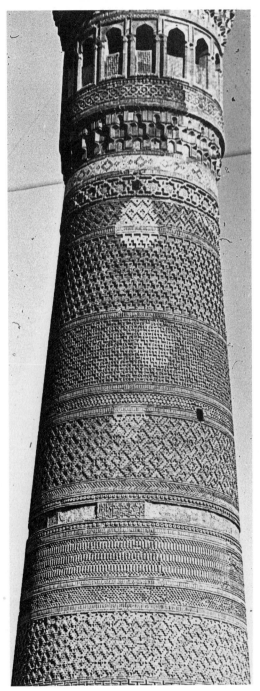

103 Bukhara, Masjid-i Kalyan, minaret, upper part

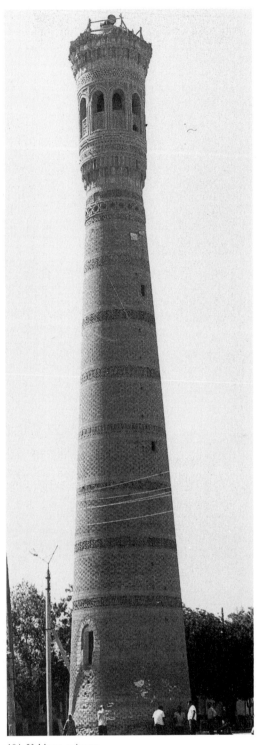

104 Vabkent, minaret

150

105 Bukhara, Masjid-i Kalyan, minaret, lower part

medieval Iranian minaret, though a few plain mud-brick examples survive. It stamps the building as a vehicle for external display. Moreover, this lavish decoration was not extended to the exterior walls of the mosques to which such minarets belonged. While the range and type of decoration is itself an absorbing topic, the principal questions raised by these monuments – and the related minarets of Bastam, Khusraugird, Sava, and the Isfahan area, to name only a few among the forty-odd which survive in Saljuq Iran – bear on the reason which prompted such decoration, and thus on the function of these buildings. It might be argued that the efflorescence of these elaborately ornamented minarets in the Saljuq period could be seen as the result of a particular, indeed unique, combination of circumstances.

The tally of surviving 11th- and 12th-century buildings in Iran indicates that this was a time of unprecedented building activity. This phenomenon has often been connected with the irruption of the Saljuq Turks into the eastern Islamic world. The Saljuq rulers, and their governing class, were celebrated for their Sunni orthodoxy. This orthodoxy is traditionally regarded as the prime impetus behind the official programme of building *madrasa*s throughout their empire. That same orthodoxy could equally have been the motivating force behind the building of other religious structures. What better method of proclaiming allegiance to the true faith than financing the construction of a place of worship? Mosques were the most obvious expressions of such official patronage, and indeed there is ample evidence of a major programme of mosque building and – more significantly – mosque extension in this period. Some of the major *amir*s of the Saljuq court were associated with such projects, as the mosques of Qazvin and Burujird show. The remarkably large number of such foundations in the Saljuq period attests the popular fashion for building monuments of religious function – even the mausolea of the time frequently contain *mihrab*s.

It is into this context that the typical Saljuq minaret seems to fit: a singularly appropriate means of publicly expressing allegiance to the faith. As such, of course, it would recommend itself equally well to Shi'ites, and indeed the city of Kashan (which was solidly Shi'ite at this

period) still has two lofty minarets dating from Saljuq times. But the bulk of Iran was Sunni, and it is therefore not surprising that minarets from Sunni areas far outnumber those from Shi'ite ones. Within the heated, disputatious religious atmosphere of the times the minaret readily lent itself to serve as a statement of faith. It was beyond question the prime architectural symbol of Islam. It was gratifyingly visible. Its rich decoration would testify to its patron's munificence. That same decoration could make doctrinal capital out of its inscriptions, whether these were Shi'ite in tenor or, as was much more frequently the case, Sunni. Some of them – for example the Saraban and Rahrun minarets in the

3.100 Irbil, minaret   3.101 Ta'uq/Daquq, minaret

Isfahan area – bear the *shahada*. Moreover, as an architectural project the minaret was substantially smaller in scope – despite its ostentation – than a mosque. This would obviously recommend it to less wealthy patrons. That these minarets did not necessarily have a straightforward liturgical function is suggested by the case of 12th-century Isfahan. Given that it is only the

106 Ta'uq/Daquq, minaret

107 Irbil, minaret

Friday mosque that according to custom (not dogma) requires a minaret, it is remarkable to note that this city, one of the Saljuq capitals of *109* Iran, had over a score of minarets in this period. In nearly every case, the mosque for which the minaret was originally intended has vanished. It is tempting to speculate that these mosques were very much simpler and humbler structures which in earlier times, before the fashion changed, would not have been furnished with minarets. One may justifiably assume that some evidence besides the minarets themselves would have remained if these minarets had been built contemporaneously with their adjoining mosques as integrated building projects.

According to this interpretation, then, many of the more elaborate Saljuq minarets are expressions alike of conspicuous consumption and conspicuous piety. Their historical and religious inscriptions tell the same story. No city of the period could have required for liturgical purposes the thickly clustered and extraordinari-

ly lofty minarets which are still such a feature of the townscape of Isfahan.

These considerations also have a bearing on the lavish decoration of so many Saljuq minarets – a feature found also on the Iraqi examples 3.100–3.101 (Ta'uq/Daquq, Sinjar, Mosul and Irbil). This 3.16, *106, 107* feature would naturally recommend itself to patrons who wished their buildings to make the maximum impact. The relatively restricted surface area of these narrow cylindrical *110* minarets, especially in comparison with the surface area of the Syrian and Maghribi type of minaret, was a further advantage; it obviously kept the cost of decoration down. If an explanation be sought for the use of such all-over brick decoration on a minaret, the case of the Samanid mausoleum at Bukhara may be cited. This shows that by the early 10th century, the effectiveness 5.42–5.44 of brick decoration as a mantle for a building of relatively small surface area had been discovered. It would have been quite natural to transpose this newly fashionable technique to the minaret. Considerations of time, expense and aesthetic judgement seem to have combined to ensure that the technique was rarely used on a much larger scale than this. The case of contemporary tomb towers, with their much larger diameter, is illuminating; overall brick decoration occurs only on the smaller buildings of that genre. Similarly, the exteriors of the great domed chambers of contemporary mosques are notably austere.

The cylindrical Iranian minaret – also found in Iraq, as at Ta'uq, Irbil and Dhu'l-Kifl – 3.99–3.101 proved capable of generating a surprising variety of forms, most of which were developed in the 12th century. They include low plinths that are flanged or lobed or a combination of both (Nigar; Zarand); others that are octagonal 3.95, 3.102 with elaborate blind arcading (Gulpayagan), or that are square in ground-plan but pylon-like in elevation (Khusraugird). Sometimes a very 3.91 plain square plinth carries an intermediate octagon on which the circular shaft rests (Chihil Dukhtaran, Isfahan). Frequently the plinth is *109* quite plain, thereby contrasting with the richly textured upper elevation. In some cases the plinth extends to such a height that it rivals the cylindrical shaft in importance (Kirat). In the case of the two minarets at Ghazna, where a low *111* circular plinth carries a dramatic and lofty

108 Isfahan, Saraban minaret

canyons of rock, it nevertheless manages to dominate the narrow secluded valley in which it is placed. Setting and monument mutually enhance each other, as was earlier the case with Achaemenid rock tombs or Sasanian reliefs.

It was probably the Saljuq period that saw the introduction of paired minarets, though pre-war excavations at the Sasanian city of Bishapur, unfortunately not fully published, revealed two massive drums with slots which might have been intended for a lintel. The idea seems not to have been further developed until the 12th century, when paired minarets established themselves as a means of lending extra importance to the entrance gate of a building (Nakhchivan; Ardistan). This articulating function further distanced the minaret from any liturgical purpose, but it allowed the minaret's long-traditional role as a marker to develop in new directions. Accordingly it was not long before paired minarets were brought into the mosque proper to flank the entrance to the sanctuary. Thus they were used as indicators of direction as well as of importance. There seems to have been no consistent practice governing the location of single minarets within the mosque. When the minaret was erected as an integral component of the mosque, provision was often made for it to be entered not at ground level but from the roof of the mosque. The otherwise puzzling existence of such doorways comparatively high up the shaft of minarets which are now freestanding are clear evidence that they were originally intended to be part of a mosque.

Two forms of staircase are commonly encountered in Saljuq minarets: those revolving around a central column and those built into the thickness of the exterior wall and carried on small vaults. The two techniques are even recorded as being used successively in a single minaret (Mil-i Qasimabad). Double spiral staircases, in which those ascending never meet those descending, are occasionally encountered (Jam; Samiran).

A few minarets of this period raise searching problems of function. Some are located along major routes or at the edge of the desert (Khusraugird; Ziyar; Mil-i Nadiri), which would lend support to the theory that they served, no doubt *inter alia*, as signposts. Since much caravan travel was by night, a lamp at the top of a minaret

cf. 3.98

3.111

3.91

3.97; *cf.*

3.103
3.105–3.110
3.72 flanged shaft bearing unusually elaborate ornament, which in turn originally gave way to a cylindrical shaft, the eight-pointed middle tier is undoubtedly the cynosure of the monument. Such minarets emphasise the scope for experiment in this period; clearly there was no canon governing the respective proportions of plinth and cylinder. Similarly, in minarets consisting essentially of two or three tiers of tapering cylinders, the proportional relationship between one tier and the next could vary quite markedly

108 (Manar-i 'Ali and Manar-i Saraban, both in Isfahan). The most ambitious of these multi-tier minarets are the examples at Ziyar, outside

112–113 Isfahan, and of Jam in central Afghanistan, the latter probably the masterpiece of the period. Substantial balconies divide the three tiers and

3.111 an open-plan arched aedicule perches at the summit of the building. Surrounded by sheer

would allow the building to serve as a land-locked lighthouse. A chance literary reference establishes that in 582/1186 the practice of placing a lamp at the top of a minaret was sufficiently familiar in Khurasan to occasion no comment. In a few cases the minaret is located on top of a hill where there is no room for an adjoining mosque (Kirat). Such a siting can only emphasise the role of the minaret as a signal-tower or watch-tower; in a small settlement like Kirat there would be little enough call for a minaret in any case, and therefore even less need to site the minaret well away from the mosque

109 Isfahan, Chihil Dukhtaran minaret

in the interests of making the *adhan* more audible.

Perhaps the most enigmatic as well as the most splendid minaret of the period is the minaret of Jam, mentioned earlier. Its height (*c.* 60 m.) is unprecedented among Iranian minarets. The main lower shaft is unique in that its principal decoration is an entire *sura* of the Qur'an – Surat Maryam, comprising ninety-seven verses. The other major inscriptions are all historical. They laud the achievements and proclaim the resounding (and self-appointed) titles of the Ghurid sultan of the time, who had emerged victorious from a protracted struggle with the declining Ghaznavids. A generation earlier, captive citizens of Ghazna had trekked to the mountain fastness of Firuzkuh, the Ghurid capital and site of the Jam minaret, to build the citadel by forced labour; they were then slaughtered and their blood mixed with mortar to build towers there. The sultan Muhammad b. Sam, the builder of the minaret, delivered the *coup de grâce* to his dynasty's ances-tral enemy and it is hard not to see his gigantic and wholly impractical minaret as a symbol of that victory, a *fathnama* memorialised in brick. The mountainous territory of Ghur had moreover only recently been Islamised, and it may therefore be suggested that the presence of a long Qur'anic *sura* on the minaret emphasised the equally important role of the building as a witness to the faith in potentially hostile territory.

Ilkhanid minarets

In later periods the Iranian minaret never re-covered the importance it had enjoyed under the Saljuqs. Even so, new uses and new types of decoration were found for it. At the mausoleum of Öljeitü in Sultaniya, for reasons still not ade-quately explained, eight minarets encircle the dome at roof level – the germ of an idea later to be exploited intensively in Ottoman architec-ture. In Ilkhanid times, too, the device of paired minarets flanking an important *iwan* – usually the entrance to the building – was enthusiastic-ally employed (Abarquh, Ashtarjan, Karabagh-lar, Sultaniya and two buildings in Isfahan). The scale of these minarets was, it seems, substan-tially larger than that of the tentative experi-ments with this feature made in the previous

3.111
112
113

5.97–5.98

3.98, 3.90, 74

110 Zavara, Masjid-i Pa Minar, minaret

two centuries. Moreover, the attenuated proportions of their parent portals serve to increase their apparent size still further. Quite often the minarets and portal are smoothly integrated so that the upper shafts of the minarets shoot up directly from the *iwan* roof; their lower portions are not separately emphasised (Ashtarjan; Natanz; Du Minar Dardasht, Isfahan). The *74* newly fashionable emphasis on large-scale glazed ornament caused such minarets to stand out with extra vividness against a somewhat drab urban setting of mostly mud-brick architecture.

The lower stages of the minaret were now deliberately highlighted, a feature only sporadically found in the Saljuq period, as at Gulpayagan, Kirat, and Jam. The advent of lavishly *3.111* applied tilework was a crucial factor in this change of emphasis, as two examples in Isfahan clearly demonstrate. The Manar-i Bagh-i Qushkhana has its two-tier cylinder borne, via an insignificant octagonal plinth, on a square mass of brickwork some 10 m. high and boldly ornamented with square Kufic inscriptions spelling out Allah and other sacred names. Even if this block served a double purpose as part of an entrance portal, presumably with a second flanking minaret on the other side, its ornament was, it seems, intended to articulate precisely the area beneath the minaret. Symbolically it is of course wholly appropriate that the minaret should in a literal, visual sense be founded upon the name of God. Such symbolism is of a piece with the use of the *shahada*, the very text proclaimed by the muezzin, in the inscription band encircling the upper part of such Saljuq minarets as the Manar-i Saraban in this same city of *108* Isfahan. Particularly appropriate inscriptions of this kind can easily be cited in other periods – thus the minarets of the Masjid-i Shah, Mashhad (probably 855/1451) bear *hadith*s in praise of muezzins. Others bear the Sura of Light.

Quite different in form was the lower part of the Manar-i Khwaja 'Alam, probably also of the 14th century, which collapsed in 1934. By a novel conceit the cantilevered *muqarnas* cornice normally found just below the topmost tier of post-Saljuq Iranian minarets is here used not only in the customary location, but also as the culmination of the lower shaft immediately above the plinth. This shaft, which rests on a tall

square socle again decorated with Kufic epigraphy bearing the name of Allah, is in the form
of a twelve-pointed star, and its body is entirely
covered with strapwork in high relief. The elevation of the Khwaja 'Alam minaret was thus in
four distinct stages, and while this is exceptional, the distinctive emphasis on the plinth or
lower elevation in Ilkhanid minarets does frequently result in a three-tiered form. Arched
openings in the topmost storey are standard, and
encourage the theory that these minarets could
have been used for signals.

Timurid and Safavid minarets

The 15th century brings nothing remarkably
new in its train so far as minarets are concerned.
Form and function alike faithfully follow established precedent. *Muqarnas* cornices, often five-
or six-tiered, are perhaps denser than before (as
various minarets in Herat show) or developed
bolder contrasts of solid and void than their
2.287 predecessors (minarets of the Gauhar Shad
mosque, Mashhad). Possibly the form of the
balcony also changed slightly in this period,
developing a distinctive overhanging canopy
above the railing; but this is the feature above all
others which is an obvious target for restoration, and a specific study would be needed to
establish the authentic date of these constructions. The surviving minaret of the Friday
Mosque of Gauhar Shad at Herat (completed
841/1437–8) has an unusual ten-sided base,
complete with an engaged marble column at
each angle, bearing the customary cylindrical
shaft. Perhaps the most significant of these
minor innovations is a slight change in the rôle
of the minarets flanking an *iwan*. As the
2.287 examples of the mosques of Gauhar Shad,
2.295 Mashhad, and the Ziyaratgah *jami'*, near Herat,
show, the common Saljuq and Mongol practice
of masking the lower sections of the minaret by
the façade of the building which it adjoined was
rejected. Instead the minaret maintained its elevation unbroken throughout, and was therefore
able to play its full role in articulating the
interior façades. Safavid architects continued to
use this device, though somewhat less boldly (as
2.282, 2.288 in the Masjid-i-Shah, Isfahan). The separateness
of the minaret could be further underlined by
decorative means, since the types of ornament
used on its cylindrical body were necessarily

different from those which were appropriate to
a flat façade. Indeed, it is in their decoration that 78
Timurid minarets assert their independence
from their precursors. The favoured technique
was to envelop the shaft with a lozenge grid in
brick whose interstices were each filled with a
medallion of high-quality tilework (e.g. the
minarets of the Masjid-i Shah and the mosque of 2.280
Gauhar Shad, both in Mashhad). Occasionally
the topmost storey of the minaret would bear a
similar grid, but of square plan, with square,
rectangular or L-shaped cartouches (as on the
minaret of the *madrasa* of Gauhar Shad, Herat,
completed 836/1432-3).

Subsequent centuries added even less of significance to the development of the Persian

111 Ghazna, minaret of Mas'ud III

157

minaret. From the 16th century onwards the corkscrew moulding already in frequent use for arch profiles was on occasion adopted for flanking minarets (e.g. the shrine of Khwaja Abu Nasr Parsa, Balkh), though there is no evidence that this novel form was continued beyond the top of the *pishtaq*. In Safavid times, too, the topmost storey of the minaret was standardised in the form of a tapering shallow-domed cylinder which, like the rest of the minaret, was entirely sheathed in glazed tilework. Occasionally – in the great shrines of Qumm and Mashhad – much of the shaft was tapering and gilded. By Qajar times minarets had come to sprout substantial tiled and arcaded balconies with a corona of miniature domed pinnacles (e.g. the shrine at Mahan). Qajar architects signalled the increasingly secular function of the minaret by using it to punctuate entrance portals to bazaars (Yazd), towns (Qazvin, Simnan) and palaces (Tehran). In earlier times minarets had normally been built singly or in pairs, but now they proliferated and thus became trivial. A typical 19th-century shrine, the Shahzada Husain at Qazvin, with its cluster of five slender three-tier minarets – at once absurd and charming – may serve as the sorry epitaph of a distinguished tradition.

THE MINARETS OF INDIA AND PAKISTAN

It is generally accepted that the Saljuq minarets of Iran included the greatest masterpieces in that tradition. It is not surprising, therefore, to encounter traces of their influence far beyond the borders of Iran proper. Indeed, the tallest minaret in the Islamic world – and to many the supreme monument of its genre – is unmistakably an offshoot of that same eastern Iranian culture which produced the minarets of Khurasan, Ghazna and – most significantly – Jam.

Quth Minar, Delhi

The Qutb Minar in Delhi was in fact the work of Qutb al-Din Aybak, a Turkish general who was the protégé of the self-same Ghurid sultan, Muhammad b. Sam, who had built the Jam minaret. Built in the same generation as the minaret of Jam (587–94/1191–8), similarly multi-tiered and surpassingly high, similarly

located in territory only recently claimed for Islam, and – to clinch matters – containing panegyrics of Muhammad b. Sam in its epigraphy, it offers such a close parallel to the minaret of Jam that the direct influence of the latter upon the Qutb Minar can scarcely be denied. The most striking element of comparison between the two monuments, however, is their association with victory. Whereas the minaret of Jam celebrates the victorious outcome of a conflict which, against the wider canvas of Islamic history, must be regarded as a minor local squabble, the Qutb Minar is a worthy memorial of a great theme: the Islamisation of northern India. The mosque which it serves is appropriately called Quwwat al-Islam ('Might of Islam') and the inscriptions on the minaret are executed not only in Arabic but also in Sanskrit. Indeed, a Nagari inscription on the minaret (admittedly added somewhat later) calls it the victory column (*vijaya-stambha*) of 'Ala' al-Din (reigned 639–44/1241–7). The theme of victory is taken up implicitly in the use of building material from some twenty-seven Indian temples in the construction of the mosque and minaret, and explicitly in the setting up of an iron column from a 4th-century Vishnu temple in the very courtyard of the mosque. The ten-fold contrast in size and majesty between these two towers (7.2 m. as against 72.5 m.) would have told its own story. The later additions, both structural and epigraphic, made to the minaret served of course to make the contrast even more pointed; but even in its original, slightly shorter, form the Qutb Minar must have been a very speaking symbol.

In the details of that form, too, the Qutb Minar acknowledges the influence of eastern Iranian minarets. Each of the three original storeys (the three upper ones were added *c.*626/1229 by the Delhi sultan Iltutmish) was laid out according to a different plan, and for each plan Persian prototypes can be cited. The lowest storey features an elevation of alternating flanges and engaged columns (cf. Zarand); the second an elevation of engaged columns (cf. Jar Kurgan) and the third a flanged elevation (cf. the Ghazna minarets). The continuity of vertical emphasis is maintained throughout all three storeys, which lends the elevation a formidable impetus.

112 Jam, minaret

Later minarets in India

Although a later sultan of Delhi, 'Ala' al-Din Khalji (695–715/1296–1316), conceived the megalomaniac ambition of building a minaret twice the size and height of the Qutb Minar, the project foundered after the building had risen to no more than seventy feet. No subsequent attempts to rival the Qutb Minar were made by Indian architects. Indeed, the importance of the minaret declined sharply in the Indian subcon-

tinent in later centuries. This is reflected above all in the functions assigned to it. These are so tied to the needs of articulation that it is more a matter of convenience than of strict accuracy to call them minarets, and on occasion that term may be positively misleading. It is of course hard to prove in any specific case that a mosque tower with an interior staircase was never used as a minaret – even if, as so often in Iran, there is also a *guldasta* perched on one of the *iwan*s – and for that reason alone the conventional term is used in this chapter. Nevertheless, it is well to remember that in the subcontinent in particular, where many areas never adopted the custom of building true minarets, the term 'minaret' may often be no more than a courtesy title.

Following Persian precedent, minarets were often used to flank entrances, though the fairly standard proportional relationship between entrance and minarets in Iran was frequently flouted in India. Staged tapering cylinders on polygonal plinths flank the entrances to the Begampuri and Khirkhi mosques in Delhi (both 14th century). Yet at Burhanpur the Bibi-ki-Masjid of *c*.998/1590 has its entrance overwhelmed by the sheer bulk and height of the mountainous domed minarets flanking it, whose elevation is by turns octagonal, hexadecagonal, cylindrical and domed, with balconies on brackets separating the various stages. In some imperial Mughal mosques (Jum'a Masjid, Delhi, 1054–68/1644–58; Badshahi Mosque, Lahore, 1085/1674), minarets are used unexpectedly to stress the four corners of the sanctuary, whose northern façade projects into the courtyard; this is a logical extension of their function as markers.

In such cases a hierarchy of size may make itself felt; at the Badshahi mosque, for example, further and larger minarets, tapering tiered octagons, establish the outer corners of the mosque. Alternatively, parts of the mosque that were traditionally somewhat neglected, such as the courtyard (e.g. Wazir Khan mosque, Lahore, 1044/1634), could be brought into prominence by using minarets to demarcate their boundaries. At the Abu Amjad mosque, Khairpur (899/1494), huge tapering minarets, their shafts displaying an alternation of flanged and gadrooned articulation, mark the angles of the *qibla* wall and the sides of the *mihrab*. In

3.83 mausolea such as the famous Gol Gumbaz, Bijapur (c.1060/1650), massive minarets provide a fitting culmination for the corners of the building, and they serve a similar purpose in gatehouses used as entrances to the gardens in which a mausoleum is set (tomb of Akbar at
3.84 Sikandra, Agra, 1016/1607) or as tetrapylons marking the intersection of major roads as in the
3.81, 3.10 classical world (Char Minar, Hyderabad, 999/1591).

113 Jam, minaret, upper section

It must be admitted, however, that almost from the beginning of Indo-Muslim architecture the minaret had been allotted a particular function as an articulating feature at roof level which effectively stunted its further growth.

The mausoleum of Rukn-i 'Alam at Multan 5.104 (c.720/1320) is illuminating as a transitional monument in this respect. The angles of its battered lower octagon are brought into bold relief by cylindrical buttress-minarets whose domical terminations project well above the coping of the first storey. Thus both the shaft of the minaret and its crowning dome have an important part to play. The second storey is also octagonal but incorporates a significant change: the domical terminations recur above the coping, but the parent shaft is absent. It is hard not to see this as a crucial devaluation of the minaret. It was precisely the independence of the minaret in the rest of the Islamic world which had allowed it to play such a variegated role in Islamic architecture. No similar locus existed for the Indian minaret, and this accounts for the rarity of the freestanding minaret in that country, apart from the area of Gujarat.

Other exceptions are the minaret or pillar in the fort at Fathabad (14th century) which records the lineage of Firuz Shah Tughluq, a cylindrical minaret at Daulatabad of c.840/1436, 3.78 and the five-tiered twelve-sided tower known as the Firuz Minar, built in Gaur in Bengal c.893/ 3.75 1488, possibly as a tower of victory. This special function might explain the exceptional form and location of the monument. The isolated Hiran Minar at Shaikhupura near Lahore was also the product of special circumstances: it was built at the order of the Mughal emperor Jahangir over the grave of an antelope. The association of minarets with the skulls of game animals was an ancient tradition in Iran, and a minaret festooned with the horns and skulls of game has survived to this day at Khuy in Azerbaijan. A small octagonal room set in the third storey of the Hiran Minar suggests that the building had a largely recreational function, as indeed its setting amidst gardens, lakes and pavilions would tend to confirm.

Perhaps the commonest form of minaret in the Indian subcontinent, which occurs in numerous guises throughout the northern part of the area, comprises a stocky cylinder resting on a high polygonal plinth and horizontally articulated by a farrago of annular mouldings 3.77, 3 (the latter feature possibly derived from pre-Islamic commemorative columns), balconies and niches (examples at Ahmadabad – where the 3.69, 3.

114 Sivas, Great Mosque, minaret

Sona Masjid, Gaur) or – in the later stages of this development – by an open turret, dome or kiosk (tomb of I'timad al-Daula, Agra, 1037/1628, among numerous other Mughal buildings). In such cases the minaret, while perhaps retaining a residue of religious significance, was used primarily as an articulating element. Moreover, these pinnacles are usually called *guldasta* rather than *manara*. Frequently they are solid, which of course excuses them from any religious function. Their use in mausolea such as the 3.89 tomb of Humayun in Delhi could cause little disturbance.

In the Taj Mahal the major minarets defining 3.87 the extent of the funerary complex are supplemented by a series of extremely slender minarets integrated into the façades of the tomb and barely breaking the roof-line; these show how the minaret could shrink to a symbolic presence only. Perhaps the ultimate degeneration of the Indian minaret, in form and function alike, is marked by the funerary architecture of 17th-century Bijapur, where one tomb after 3.82 another is festooned by a dozen or more tiny, bulbous-headed towers applied like candles to a birthday cake. These trivial constructions scarcely deserve the name of minaret. In its Indian form, indeed, the minaret was apt to be confused with the *chhatri* – the open-plan, domed, arcaded pavilion used as a means of animating the roof-line of a building. The similarity of function can readily be gauged by comparing a mausoleum which uses the *chhatri* form (e.g. the tomb of Muhammad Chaus, Gwalior, c.971/1564) with a roughly contemporary one which uses the minaret form in just the same way (tomb of Adham Khan, Delhi, c.968/1561). Curiously enough these *chhatri*s, though originally local, non-Islamic forms, irresistibly evoke the earliest corner minarets in Islamic architecture.

MINARETS IN TURKEY

The Saljuq and Beylik periods

The minaret genre enjoyed particular popularity in two areas of the Islamic world which have yet to be discussed in this context – Egypt and Turkey. The latter area has a tradition of minaret construction not only as distinguished and individual as that of Egypt, but also much

minarets are usually placed centrally, flanking the sanctuary or the *qibla iwan* – at Hyderabad 3.15 and at Bijapur). In the case of minarets used to mark the corners of a building, a wide range of practices developed. Sometimes the essential nature of the minaret was retained in that it projected from the building which it adjoined and was made to seem higher still by the low roof-line of the tomb proper (tomb of Jahangir 3.85 at Shahdara near Lahore). More often the minaret comprised a massive polygonal lower storey, serving also as a buttress, and would be crowned by a slender, insubstantial shaft (Chota

115 Mardin, Great Mosque, minaret

longer lived. The sequence begins in somewhat derivative vein with the minarets built in their scores by the Saljuqs of Rum in the thirteenth century. Following the practice of the Great Saljuqs in Iran, they placed minarets at the sides of portals to mosques, and expanded the use of this feature to *madrasa*s. The wider spread of paired portal minarets *vis-à-vis* the situation in Saljuq Iran makes it natural that the motif should have experienced substantial changes in Anatolia. The most striking of these changes is the emphasis on massive strength in these portal minarets. Their lower structure, while incorporated into the portal proper, does project from it in plan and elevation and is also singled out by decorative means. The upper elevation, too, offers novel features: fluted shafts, bowl-shaped balconies and slender conical terminations to the shaft (e.g. Çifte Minare Medrese, Erzurum, possibly *c.*640/1242; and the less well preserved Sahib 'Ata' mosque, Konya, 656/1258). At the Gök Medrese, Sivas (*c.*668/1270), the shafts are notably short, even stumpy, with a concomitant stress on stability; slender widely-spaced colonnettes articulate them. In this building, as in the Çifte Minare Medrese in the same town, the balconies are carried on corbelled tiers of facetted brickwork, a variation on the theme of the so-called Turkish triangle. In their upper sections all these minarets are of brick, which makes for a powerful contrast with the ashlar stone façade below. The material of these minarets betrays their ultimately Iranian origin.

Rather more individual, perhaps, was the Anatolian interpretation of what had long been a standard device of Islamic architects, namely employing a single minaret as an integral part of a mosque deserving special attention in its own right. The novelty lay in reducing the surface area of the mosque and thereby giving the minaret much more prominence. Nowhere in the Islamic world is the familiar silhouette of a compact mosque with a low dome and cylindrical minaret encountered as regularly as in Turkey. This is a schema which has attained well-nigh symbolic status, and was in Anatolia extended to *madrasa*s and *imaret*s. Their sturdiness and their location at a corner of the building lends these minarets the air of a bastion, well exemplified in the 'Ala' al-Din

4.73

2.186–2.187,

151

2

mosques at Konya and Niğde or the Ulu Cami at Divriği (all 13th century) and, in the following century or so, in the mosques of 'Isa Bey at Selcuk (777/1375) or Ilyas Bey at Miletus (806/1404). Such buildings kept the tradition alive, and ensured that it became canonical under the Ottomans from the time of their earliest buildings at Iznik (Yeşil Cami) and Bursa (Yeşil Cami and the Hudavendigar mosque among others). In the mature Ottoman masterpieces of Istanbul two or more minarets are standard equipment for mosque complexes, but in the provinces the old tradition continued unchanged, as mosques in Elbistan, Diyarbakr, Gebze and elsewhere testify.

Under the Saljuqs in Iran the concept of the minaret as a monument in its own right had been developed to perhaps a greater degree than in any other area of the Islamic world. This concept continued to operate, though on a lesser scale, in the architecture of the Rum Saljuqs. Completely free-standing minarets are rare (e.g. the Yivli Minare at Antalya, though its parent mosque is only a few metres away, or the isolated Artuqid minaret at Dunaysir), but numerous cases may be cited in which the minaret effectively achieves independence by virtue of its extreme height (e.g. the minaret of the Rizq mosque in Hisn Kaifa, the very similar minaret of the Mardin Friday Mosque, or the case of the Ince Minare Medrese, where the building is popularly named after its minaret, a common feature in Anatolia) or of its decoration (minaret of the Yaqutiye Medrese, Erzurum, whose shaft is enveloped by boldly three-dimensional lozenge interlace in brick). In their decoration, indeed, the minarets of Saljuq Anatolia clung to Iranian precedent, with much emphasis on patterned brickwork and inscription bands, often glazed. However, their use of two bowl-shaped balconies to articulate the elevation, and of a crowning stage comprising a slender cylinder with candle-snuffer roof (e.g. Taş Medrese, Akşehir) departs from Iranian models and foreshadows the mature Ottoman minaret. Among variant forms may be cited square bases with blind arcades or with chamfered upper corners (Bayburt, Ulu Cami), intermediate octagonal drums with blind arcades (Ereğli, Ulu Cami), and various types of gadrooning applied to the main shaft. The latter feature is best

116 Antalya, Yivli mosque, minaret

5.3.66 illustrated by the Yivli Minare at Antalya (early
116 13th century), where a cannular flange divides
the engaged columns from each other; the result
3.94 is remarkably similar to the Jar Kurgan minaret
built a century earlier in Central Asia. Perhaps
the most curious version of the theme is the
2.175 minaret of the Hoca Hasan mosque in Konya,
whose square shaft has a semi-circular buttress
at the centre of each side, and similarly placed
buttresses on the octagon above. High octagonal drums (Sırçalı mosque, Konya) and octagonal shafts (Zemburi mosque, Konya) are
also encountered occasionally, as are stalactite
cornices carrying a balcony (Zemburi mosque,
Konya). The motif of Turkish triangles so
widely used in zones of transition in this period
sometimes finds its way onto the drum of
mausolea which are visually very close to
5.129 minarets (Güdük Minare, Sivas).

Ottoman minarets

The discussion so far has emphasised the variety
of forms and decoration which characterise the
pre-Ottoman minarets of Anatolia. It must be
admitted, however, that these minarets give
little hint of the unique role which the minaret
3.11, 3.19 came to play in Ottoman architecture. It is especially striking that, apart from some minor
tinkering with form and decoration in the provinces (notably in the use of striped masonry),
the form of the minaret – for all the world like
86 a long, meticulously sharpened pencil – became
virtually fossilized after the Ottoman conquest
of Istanbul. Since much the same can be said for
the basic components of mosque design, if not
indeed for the form of the mosque in general,
the formal interest of these structures lies in
2.317-2.337 quite small variations from a generally accepted
norm. It might indeed be argued that such variations were not needed, for in its mature form the
standard Ottoman minaret has a slender
elegance which is rarely rivalled in the Islamic
2.323 world (Selimiye, Istanbul). Rising from a square
or polygonal base, its main cylindrical shaft is
punctuated by one, two or even three circular
balconies carried on *muqarnas* vaulting. Elongated conical roofs, sheathed in lead and ending
in finials, capped the shafts. Muezzins stationed
at each balcony would deliver the call to prayer
in the form of a canon. The acoustic impact of
these many voices would of course be intensified

significantly in a mosque with multiple
minarets, the voices interweaving in different
sonorities depending on the height and distance
separating the muezzins. Perhaps the sheer
quantity of voices involved, which would naturally generate a greater volume of sound (especially if the muezzins were stationed in pairs or
even groups), explains why the call to prayer in
the case of Ottoman minarets could be given
from a greater height than usual. It is still noticeable, however, that even the topmost balcony is
still far below the summit of the minaret.

Within this architectural formula there was
little room for manoeuvre. Sometimes the shaft
would carry extremely long and slender arcades
functioning as flutes, leading the eye upwards
and thus emphasising the height of the minaret.
Often the shaft is not a true cylinder at all but a
polygon, though the angles are so obtuse that
the visual effect is that of a cylinder. In a few
cases a diminutive arcade encircles the base of
the roof. Such variations are largely cosmetic.
More significant are the changes in the proportions of the shaft itself. Many Ottoman architects preferred a stumpy, even massive, minaret
to a very tall and slender one, and certainly that
solution, with the addition of a squat adjoining
dome chamber, ensures a more integrated silhouette. It would be hard to devise an apter
symbol, at once sturdy and simple, of the quint-
essential Islamic religious building. In minarets
of all kinds Ottoman architects were apt to lay
stress on the plinth. This was commonly square
in plan but in elevation its walls sloped sharply
inwards, as if to stack extra volume against the
shaft. This buttressing role was especially
appropriate if the minaret were located at a
corner of a building. In fact the standard
location of single Ottoman minarets was at the
north-west corner of the mosque, though many
are sited at the north-east corner. Possibly the
corner location was chosen because experience
had shown it to be the safest in the event of an
earthquake, or as a means of buttressing the
corner, always a vulnerable area.

Perhaps the most celebrated feature of
Ottoman minarets was not their outward form
but their use in pairs, quartets or sextets as a
device to proclaim the royal status of the
building – for only a reigning sultan could erect
more than one minaret per mosque. There can

be little doubt that such mosques represent the most sustained attempt in all of Islamic architecture to reconcile the divergent aims of royal and religious iconography. Planted as they are like lances in the sacred precinct, these minarets may be said to consummate a tradition stretching far back in time to the Prophet's long spear (*'anaza*) which he would thrust into the ground to indicate the direction of prayer. The wheel has turned full circle and the original form has become splendidly monumentalised. Whether or not this was a deliberate echo is an open question. At all events, it is hard to overlook the aggressive and ceremonial implications of these

117 Luxor, Mosque of Abu'l-Hajj, minaret

2.354 gigantic needle-sharp lances clustered protectively, like a guard of honour, around the royal
3.70 dome. Their impact depends to a large extent on their proportions, which are almost unprecedented; the pair of minarets flanking the
7, 3.71 Süleymaniye dome are each some seventy metres high. Such minarets function simultaneously to enrich the exterior silhouette of the

mosque – in the case just cited, for instance, the outer minarets flanking the principal façade of the building are shorter than those flanking the dome. Thus a pyramidal effect is achieved which is still further emphasised by the choice of a sloping site. The gently rolling skyline of Istanbul, with its extensive natural views, was ideally suited to this kind of display, and the political significance of the city as the Ottoman capital may partly have motivated this new use of the minaret as a component of urban design on a mammoth scale. Such minarets were also used in a more symbolic way as markers of the courtyard, of the sanctuary, or of the entire mosque, staking out the boundaries of the religious domain within a secular environment. Dome chamber and minaret alike thus acquire extra significance as symbols of the faith. This development was not new, but only in Ottoman architecture is it pursued with such singlemindedness. It is therefore entirely appropriate that these minarets, like the domes over the *mihrab*, should bear the emblem of the crescent, supported on a series of superposed orbs.

MINARETS IN EGYPT

If conservatism may be termed the hallmark of 3.3 the Ottoman minaret, its Egyptian counterpart is above all varied. This variety is all the more remarkable because the Egyptian school is to all 3.116, 3.117, intents and purposes concentrated on the 3.121 buildings of Cairo, though it is represented in some small measure in the provincial towns of Egypt and in the architecture of the Mamluks in Syria and the Levant. Unfortunately very few surviving pre-Mamluk minarets have escaped extensive alteration. Moreover, the most important examples to fall within this category are not metropolitan work at all but are found in various provincial towns: Isna, Luxor, Aswan 117, 3.115 and nearby Shellal. All date from the late 11th century. They already display the characteristic Egyptian division of the minaret into separately conceived superposed tiers. The Asna minaret 3.115 (474/1081–2) illustrates the type in its classic form. From a square base some thirty-five feet high, generously articulated by windows, rises a plain tapering truncated cylinder capped by an open pavilion whose eight concave sides bear a diminutive hexagonal domed aedicule, also of open plan. Inside the structure is a square newel staircase with a series of short, sharp ascents. Other minarets of this group maintain the three-fold division of the elevation but change the proportions (for example reducing the crowning pavilion, as at Luxor), the decoration *117* or the material (thus the Luxor minaret is of mud brick). Their material, and certain structural features, such as the lantern on free-standing columns and the tapered cylindrical shaft above a lofty square base, have been persuasively linked by Jonathan Bloom to contemporary *3.25,* architecture just across the Red Sea in the Hijaz. *3.59–3.62, 3.63* Yemeni minarets perpetuate some of these features.

Interesting as these minarets are stylistically, they are insignificant in comparison with the *3.127–3.128* great corner towers marking the main façade of the mosque of al-Hakim in Cairo, built between *118* 380/990 and 401/1010. With their massive, *2.90, 2.94* embattled – but later – square bases, whose taper, like that of an ancient Egyptian pylon, is so pronounced that it is almost a slope, they have all the appearance of bastions. In its original layout the Hakim mosque maintained a powerful consonance between minarets and portal. Very soon, however – by 401/1010 – each minaret was enclosed by a huge salient some 1.7 m. square, which allotted it a portentous, indeed revolutionary, role. Finally, in 480/1087, Badr al-Jamali enlarged the northern salient to gigantic proportions (some 25 m.

square) and thereby gave that minaret a military function. In so doing he also incorporated the principal façade of the mosque into the expanded fortifications of the city and gave it a quasi-military aspect; but he managed to make the minarets play a major part in this process without noticeable strain or incongruity.

Even so, it must be admitted that the bastions constitute brutal, unadorned masses of masonry; the minaret shafts above are not only dwarfed by the bulk of their substructure, but also by contrast loaded with architectural and applied ornament. The northern minaret observes the multiple division of parts so typical of the Egyptian style. Its lowest part is a cylinder resting on a cube. Then comes an octagonal shaft with a blind arch and windows on each side, which gives way to a heavy band of *muqarnas* decoration in three distinct tiers. A fluted keel-shaped dome crowns the whole; *3.114* within is a spiral staircase. In the western minaret the octagonal *muqarnas* zone is reduced in size and the square lower shaft is pierced by a double tier of arched windows. But its ornament, featuring two bands of epigraphy and two of arabesque, with numerous additional geometrical panels and cartouches, is significantly richer.

Since the minarets of the Hakim mosque survive in such an altered state, it is not easy to see where they belong in the corpus of Egyptian

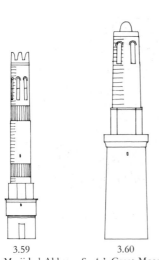
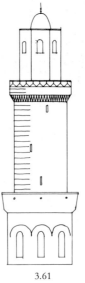

| 3.59 | 3.60 | 3.61 | 3.62 |
| San'a', Masjid al-Abhar | San'a', Great Mosque | Sa'da, Masjid al-Shamri | Sa'da, Masjid 'Ulayyan |

118 Cairo, Mosque of al-Hakim, northern salient and minaret, from the west

minarets. This is all the more serious a lacuna in view of the once-vigorous controversy over the role of the Pharos of Alexandria, which stood well-nigh intact until it was partially ruined by an earthquake in 180/796–7, in the evolution of the Egyptian minaret. *Pace* Creswell, who argued against any connection between the two building types, it can scarcely be overlooked that the surviving Egyptian minarets which date before 493/1100 all attest a pronounced multipartite division of the elevation.

Since this feature – though present in the minarets of Mecca and Medina, very possibly as a result of Egyptian influence – is absent alike in the Syrian, Iranian and Maghribi traditions (with two significant exceptions), some rationale for such an unusual division must be proposed. Interestingly enough, the two major Maghribi minarets with three superposed stories are those of Qairawan and Sfax. In the early Islamic period these sites were the first major Muslim settlements on the road west from Alexandria. Moreover, it was precisely in Tunisia, a maritime frontier area in the war against the Byzantines in southern Italy and Sicily, that the building of lighthouses is copiously recorded in the early Muslim sources. As noted above, the form of the Qairawan minaret has itself recently been linked with that of a Roman lighthouse nearby. Thus the idea of an association between lighthouses and minarets, which so mesmerised scholars earlier this century, has not entirely lost its relevance. Quite aside from this, the reasons adduced by Creswell for rejecting any link between the Pharos and Egyptian minarets are themselves not entirely sound. His narrowly chronological approach is superficially attractive because of its methodological rigour. Yet not all types of architectural evolution are entirely chronological. The case of the Holy Sepulchre indicates that the idea of a seminal building may find extremely varied expression at the hands of subsequent architects, and that references to it include copies both very faithful and very distant. Creswell's proposed evolution effectively ignores the likelihood that a monument as world-famous and as physically memorable as the Pharos would have exerted a continuing influence on Egyptian architecture long after its destruction.

If the Pharos can be proposed – though with all due reserve – as a possible source for certain three-staged minarets outside Egypt, its influence within that country is still more likely. This is not to say that any surviving Egyptian minaret is intended even as a reasonably close copy of the Pharos. Instead they might well be regarded as very free variations on the Pharos theme. The principal points of contact would then be the multiple (usually triple) division of the elevation, with superposed storeys of successively reduced diameter and size, and the provision of a crowning open-plan lantern. In conclusion, it is perhaps worth remembering that the Pharos was repeatedly rebuilt by the Muslims until its final disappearance some time between the early 13th and the mid-14th

tier example adjoining the mosque of al-Juyushi 5.175-5
(478/1085), does it follow that this influence was
continuous? The evidence of a host of minarets
beginning with that of the mausoleum of Abu'l-

119 Cairo, minaret of Bashtak

century. Indeed, as Butler noted, the account of
'Abd al-Latif indicates that in *c.*597/1200 the
Pharos comprised successively square, octagonal and round storeys and was crowned by
a lantern or small cupola. It may well be,
therefore, that this semi-Islamic Pharos rather
than the original building was the means of
establishing the tradition of the multi-staged
minaret in Egypt.

If, then, it is possible that the Pharos, whether
in its original guise or in one of its later transformations, exerted decisive influence on at least
some early Egyptian minarets, such as the four-

120 Cairo, Ghanim al-Bahlawan mosque, minaret

121 Cairo, Mughalbay Taz mosque, base of minaret

Ghadanfar (552/1157) suggests that this is not the case. In the early versions of such towers the emphasis is on a tall square shaft of Syrian type, which may be very plain (mausolea of Abu'l-Ghadanfar and Fatima Khatun) or richly decorated (minaret in *madrasa* of Sultan al-Nasir Muhammad). Crowning this shaft is the so-called *mabkhara*, a two-storey octagonal pavilion whose dome above a heavy *muqarnas* cornice is usually fluted and whose lower walls are broken by decoratively profiled arches (examples attached to the *zawiya* of al-Hunad and the *madrasa* of Sultan Salih).

Such buildings, which are mostly of the 13th century, do seem to be independent of the Pharos tradition. It is with their immediate successors that the problem becomes acute. Now the *mabkhara* is accorded much more emphasis than hitherto, with a consequent downgrading of the main shaft, and the internal divisions of the *mabkhara* are much more marked. In effect it becomes two separate storeys, whose formal and decorative independence from each other is underlined by the use of different ground-plans: an octagonal storey giving way to a circular one which bears the crowning dome and finial. Thus the Pharos pattern – of tiers which are in turn square, octagonal and circular and are capped by a roof with a crowning device – reappears. But does it issue from the Pharos itself, via such 5.176 transitional monuments as the Juyushi minaret, or is it a natural development of the Abu'l-Ghadanfar type? The minaret attached to the 5.213, 3.122 Sultan Qala'un complex suggests the first alternative, while the almost contemporary minaret 4.56–4.57 of the *madrasa*-mausoleum of Salar and Sanjar al-Jauli suggests the second. Yet for all that, the differences between them are slight. If these were indeed two separate strands in the evolution of the Egyptian minaret, these strands fused in the early 14th century in the minarets of the *madrasa*-cum-mausoleum of the Amir Sunqur Sa'di or of the *khanqah* of the Amir Qusun. By that time (735/1335) the tripartite division was standard.

The principle of altering the ratio of one tier *vis-à-vis* the other continued in later Cairene minarets. Its most striking expression may be seen in the continued reduction of the main shaft, which finally diminishes to the point where it is lost in the surrounding walls of the mosque. Thus the visible part of the minaret is an octagonal shaft with a cylindrical superstruc- *119* ture (minarets of Shaikhun and Sarghitmish, 3.129 both of the mid-14th century). The future course of the Egyptian minaret was now clear. With the rejection of the tall square shaft as the essential defining feature of the minaret, the way was open for quite radical changes in the proportional relationships between the various parts of the minaret (minaret of *khanqah* of Faraj b. Barquq). Sometimes the elevation was domin- 3.125 ated by a series of diminishing octagons. Multiple balconies on *muqarnas* corbelling mask these and other transitions. Such balconies inevitably recall those of Ottoman minarets, and indeed were used to secure the same antiphonal effects in the chanting of the *adhan* as in Turkey. Built into the crowning cupola were a series of projecting poles from which lamps were sus-

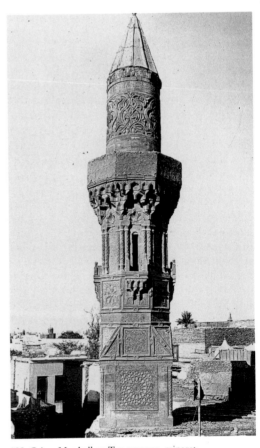

122 Cairo, Mughalbay Taz mosque, minaret

pended on the occasion of the great festivals (minaret of Bashtak, 737/1336). Thus the ancient associations built into the very name of the structure were perpetuated.

A new emphasis on absolute height may be discerned in the minarets of the later Mamluk period, such as that placed at the south-east corner of the Sultan Hasan mosque (757–60/ 1356–9), which soars to 280 feet, and is the tallest in Cairo. This example is also typical of the later period in that the crowning dome is carried on an open circular colonnade – a *tholos*, in fact, allotted a new and quite unexpected function (minaret of Aqsunqur, 748/1347). Sometimes these columns are doubled. The crowning element of the minaret also changes definitively under the rule of the Burji Mamluks, though the first examples of the new form date from the early 14th century. Earlier, the crowning feature was the diminutive two-storey *mabkhara* – so called because it resembled the top of an incense-burner, though they are also locally known as pepper-pots. Now this was replaced by the *qulla*, which owed its name to its resemblance to the upper half of the typical Egyptian water-container. The pear-shaped *qulla* usually bears at least two bronze finials whose crescents are orientated towards the *qibla*. In the final decades of Mamluk rule a playful variation on this theme makes its appearance: the minaret is crowned by a pair of pavilions, square in plan and crowned by a whole cluster of *qulla*s (funerary complex of al-Ghuri; one might compare the minaret of al-Ghuri in the Azhar mosque and the minaret of the Qani Bay mosque). It is entirely fitting that the evolution of the medieval Egyptian minaret should end on this fanciful note, for the previous five centuries had shown lavish decoration to be the keynote of this tradition. The changing succession of geometrical forms – principally cube, rectangle, octagon and cylinder – allowed free rein to this

decorative emphasis, which is unmatched in any other group of minarets.

Finally, the popularity of the minaret in Mamluk architecture invites explanation. In the 14th and 15th centuries the main building type in Cairo appears to have been the composite ensemble. Its constituent parts could vary from one ensemble to another, but their main functional elements were the mosque, *madrasa*, *khanqah* and mausoleum. Similar complexes had already become popular in Saljuq Anatolia. In Egypt, however, unlike Anatolia, the minaret was from the first regarded as an integral part of such complexes. Whether this was entirely for functional reasons may be doubted. In the dense urban fabric of Cairo nothing could more appropriately designate such a complex from afar than a minaret. In this sense it could be regarded as a public affirmation of its patron's munificence, and thus served a personal, quasi-totemic function. Their placing varied. Sometimes they were located at the two corners of the principal façade, or flanking a gateway (e.g. Bab Zuwaila); these were traditional locations. But many of the locations were unusual or even unprecedented. The *madrasa* of al-Salih has a single minaret above the central porch of the façade, and the two minarets in the mosque of al-Nasir Muhammad on the citadel are at one corner of the *qibla* wall and to one side of the main entrance. The latter location recurs in the funerary complex of Qa'it Bay. In this unpredictable positioning of the minaret one may recognise concerns similar to those of Ottoman architects. Now the minaret was, it seems, valued less for its actual or symbolic religious function and more for its rôle as a marker or articulating feature, both within the complex to which it belonged and, more broadly, within the cityscape itself. Once again, the flexibility of the forms developed by Islamic architects had asserted itself.

IV The Madrasa

The *madrasa* may briefly be described as an institute of higher education, usually residential, in which the traditional Islamic sciences – *hadith*, *tafsir*, *fiqh* and so on – were taught. Unlike most of the major Islamic building types, the *madrasa* did not issue from that century of ferment in which the nascent Islamic culture was coming to grips with neighbouring civilisations. The millennial traditions of the classical and Near Eastern worlds, as represented by the empires of Byzantium and Sasanian Iran, had left an indelible mark on mosque, minaret and mausoleum alike. The *madrasa*, however, was a response to the specific needs of the Muslim community; it was a custom-built structure tailored to serve an institution which was itself a deliberate innovation. Moreover, the *madrasa* was the creation of a self-confident, well-established civilisation near the peak of its achievement: the earliest *madrasa*s recorded in written sources are those of eastern Iran in the early 10th century. By this time Islamic architecture had developed its own styles and – equally important – the concept of the interchangeability of building types was already familiar, as the Tunisian *ribat*s show. Thus 10th-century architects had the option of seeking inspiration within their own architectural tradition. This interchangeability may well be rooted in Muslim belief, as can be inferred from a *hadith* reported by Abu Huraira: 'Whoever enters our mosque to learn good or to teach, he is like a warrior (*mujahid*) in the way of God'. Thus the activities of teaching, worship and holy war are specifically linked. As it happens, the somewhat cloudy origins of the *madrasa* suggest that the earliest examples were anything but state institutions operating in buildings specifically designed for that purpose.

The institution grew slowly and at a natural pace, and was probably fostered by a significant change in the method of teaching. In the first centuries of Islam information was transmitted by plain dictation. From the 10th century, if not before, this was supplemented by explanation and commentary (*tadris*) which in turn went hand in hand with disputation (*munazara*), for which the mosque was obviously not the ideal place. Nor was it an ideal solution for poor students to sleep in the minaret of the mosque in which they heard their lectures. At first the *madrasa* was simply a room in the house of the teacher himself; clearly its purpose was only to provide a setting within which to teach the students, not to house them too. How long it took for this *ad hoc* arrangement to burgeon into something more official and permanent cannot be calculated with any precision. But the evidence unearthed by modern historians working on the pre-Saljuq period in eastern Iran suggests that the 'prehistory' of the *madrasa* can be traced for at least one and a half centuries before the official Saljuq adoption of the institution. It is, however, highly unlikely that these earlier *madrasa*s were substantial public buildings. Their very number argues against it. By 416/1025–6 there were over twenty *madrasa*s in the modest provincial town of Khuttal, and each was fully endowed with *auqaf*. The missionary Karramiya movement, which was so strong in eastern Iran in the 10th and 11th centuries, had a marked educational and political bias and both *khanqah*s and *madrasa*s were built in quantity by the adherents of this sect. The Ghaznavids also used *madrasa*s endowed with *auqaf* in order to establish Islam in the stubbornly pagan territory of Ghur, possibly through the intermediary of missionaries from the Karamiya.

Above all, such foundations should be seen within the context of a well-established tradition of building *madrasa*s in the large cities of the eastern Iranian world. The best documented case is Nishapur, where no less than thirty-eight *madrasa*s predating the great Nizamiya of that city (founded *c*.450/1058) are recorded, though none of them survive. The earliest of them, apparently, to be mentioned in the sources, the Madrasa-yi Miyan-i Dahiya, was probably founded at the end of the 9th century, and Bulliet has presented cogent arguments to suggest that it was not the first. Some of these buildings were founded by the teachers who taught in them, by Sufis, or by wealthy notables who sometimes kept control of the *madrasa*

123 Baghdad, Mirjaniya *madrasa*, sanctuary façade

within their family over a period of generations. It was common for the *madrasa* to be attached to the house of the founder, and sometimes even the house itself was converted into a *madrasa*. Often the *madrasa* was located beside or within a mosque, and the founder or director might be buried in it. Several of these Nishapuri *madrasa*s have a particular importance in that they testify to the exercise of official patronage. Thus the Madrasa-yi Ibn Furak was built by the Simjurid governor some time before 372/982–3; the brother of Mahmud of Ghazna founded the Madrasa al-Sa'idi/Sa'diya in 390/999–1000; and the Saljuq sultan Tughril Beg founded the Madrasa al-Sultaniya in 437/1045–6. Within the next century other Saljuq princes were to found *madrasa*s in Marv, Baghdad, Isfahan and Hamadan. It seems, then, that there was ample precedent for the state to finance this kind of building, and what are perhaps the earliest sur-

viving *madrasa*s of all – the building in Samarqand attributed to the Qarakhanid Ibrahim I (444–60/1052–68) and the similar, perhaps contemporary, so-called Khwaja Mashhad *madrasa* in Tajikistan – illustrate the point. But the steadfast political purpose and the grand scale of the building programme inaugurated by Nizam al-Mulk was essentially new.

ARCHITECTURAL ORIGINS

The undoubtedly eastern Iranian origin of the *madrasa* makes that the obvious area in which to seek the architectural origins of the institution. Two major possibilities present themselves, and these are not mutually exclusive. The first, espoused by Bartol'd over sixty years ago with his typical perspicacity, would link the *madrasa* with the Buddhist *vihara* as seen in Central Asia and Afghanistan. This area had been saturated in Buddhism in the centuries immediately preceding the Muslim conquest and it is, to say the least, thought-provoking that a Buddhist institution combining the functions of worship, education, communal life and burial should have flourished in almost the very area associated with the earliest *madrasa*s. Bartol'd's prescience was confirmed by the discovery of one such site at Adzhina Tepe, just across the Oxus north-east of Balkh. This consisted of a monastery and *stupa* complex, the whole comprising two equal halves joined by a gangway and each measuring some 50 m. square. Both elements use a four-*iwan* plan focused on a central courtyard. The monastery element consisted of temple structures, cells for the monks, and a large assembly hall, plus various ancillary rooms. All this was linked by corridors. In its essentials, and even more in its four-*iwan* plan, this 7th-8th century monument comes remarkably close in spirit to a *madrasa*, though the Muslim emphasis on education is somewhat more marked. Numerous other Buddhist sites have been excavated in Soviet Central Asia over the last two decades, among them Ak-Beshim, Airtam, Kalai-Kafirmigan and Kuba, while perhaps the most important Buddhist site in the Iranian world was just south of the Oxus – the Naubahar of Balkh.

The other architectural source which has been proposed for the Iranian *madrasa* is the typical Khurasani house, like the medieval example at Bamiyan. Godard, the champion of this theory, was forced at the outset to assume an unbroken continuity of tradition between the medieval and the modern houses of the area. He then compared this domestic form with that of later *madrasa*s and concluded that it was the private

structure that had generated the public one. While the literary evidence gives ample warrant for the functions of a *madrasa* being carried out in private houses, no such houses which can be shown to have served this function have survived. Neat as Godard's theory is, it cannot be more than speculative.

STATE-SPONSORED MADRASAS IN THE EARLY SALJUQ PERIOD

The formal, as distinct from the informal, history of the *madrasa* is commonly taken to begin in 460/1068, when the great Nizamiya *madrasa* was inaugurated in Baghdad. In swift succession a whole series of *madrasa*s founded by private individuals and devoted to the teaching of jurisprudence according to one of the particular schools of Islamic law (*madhhab*s) were built. They sprang up throughout the Saljuq empire – for instance at Merv, Balkh, Herat, Nishapur, Tus, Rayy and Isfahan. Two related issues deserve special emphasis here. One is the question of whether there was indeed wholehearted state support for these buildings, as is so often maintained; or whether (as al-Muqaddasi suggests) the impetus came rather from individuals anxious to keep their personal autonomy in matters of religious law. Most prominent among these individuals was the great Saljuq vizier Nizam al-Mulk. Yet his endowment of a chain of *madrasa*s named Nizamiya after him is an ambivalent action in view of his rôle as the leading statesman of the age. It could be seen either as a state investment of the first magnitude or as the action of a powerful private citizen dedicated to the spread of his own Shafi'ite *madhhab*. As al-Subki said, 'he had a *madrasa* in every city of Iraq and Khurasan'. The other issue to be pondered is their carefully calculated location in the major cities of the Saljuq realm. From this one may deduce that each was designed to serve as a provincial centre with a wide catchment area embracing the smaller towns and villages of the region. Such a function presupposes buildings of considerable scale and capacity.

The reasons behind this sudden spate of building activity, which significantly enough was confined to the Saljuq empire, are largely political. A brief digression will make this clear. For centuries Muslim theologians, and for that

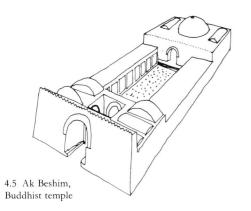

4.5 Ak Beshim,
Buddhist temple

124 Samarqand, Rigistan, *madrasa* of Ulugh Beg, side view

matter the '*ulama*' in general, had been content to pursue their higher studies in the mosque. Indeed, this practice has continued right into modern times. Typically the teacher sits with his back against a pillar and expounds to a circle (*khalqa*) of students. They move freely from one teacher to another and such education is free of charge. The even tenor of this tradition was disturbed when the Fatimids rose to power in North Africa and Egypt in the 10th century. They preached a militant missionary Sevener Shi'ism, which posed a direct political and reli-gious challenge to the orthodox Muslim world. Their *da'is* or missionaries were sent all over that world, often with instant and disturbing success. The powerhouse of Fatimid propagan-da was the great mosque of al-Azhar in Cairo, 2.91 founded in 361/970, only a year after the city itself, and intended from the first not only as a mosque but also as a centre of higher education. Only slightly later in date was the caliph al-Hakim's *dar al-hikma* and various smaller local centres of Fatimid propaganda.

Within a generation the Fatimids had seized

Palestine and much of Arabia, including the two Holy Cities. An enfeebled caliph at Baghdad was in no state to lead the opposition against them. Since 334/945 the caliphate had been under the dominance of the mayors of the palace, the Buyid clan – who were Twelver Shi'ites. Thus in the early 11th century the political situation looked bleak for Sunni Islam in western Asia. The reaction of orthodoxy was, however, imminent. Its intellectual foundations were prepared in Baghdad itself under the aegis of the theologian Ibn 'Aqil and the caliph al-Qa'im, and were associated with the spread of the Ash'ari *kalam* and a militant Hanbali *madhhab*, while the rise to power of the fanatically Sunni Mahmud of Ghazna in the easternmost Iranian world undermined Buyid hegemony. The *coup de grâce* occurred in 447/1055 when Baghdad (and the last Buyids) fell to the Saljuq Turks, themsel-

ves staunchly orthodox – who, leaving their Central Asian homelands, had in the previous two decades established themselves in northeast and central Iran at the expense of Ghaznavids and Buyids alike. With their rapid takeover of Iran, Mesopotamia and parts of Anatolia and Syria, the Saljuqs inevitably became the major challenge to Fatimid power. The struggle was waged on an ideological as well as political level and it might therefore be argued that the official *madrasa* movement was a delayed but deliberate reaction to al-Azhar. If so, it was clearly not long before the Shi'ites retorted in kind, for according to the *Kitab al-Naqd* the later twelfth century saw Shi'ite *madrasas* proliferate in Rayy, Qumm, Kashan, Ava, Varamin, Sabzavar and elsewhere. One of the *madrasas* at Rayy had indeed been founded as early as the mid-11th century. The form of these

125 Samarqand, Rigistan, Shir Dar *madrasa*, roof

126 Isfahan, Madrasa-yi Imami, courtyard

*madrasa*s is as obscure as that of their Sunni counterparts, but to judge by the later consonance between Sunni and Shi'ite *madrasa*s in the Iranian world there was probably no formal distinction between them.

The quantity of *madrasa*s erected within a short space of time and throughout the Saljuq empire at the order of Nizam al-Mulk is a clear indication that some kind of blueprint had been developed for this purpose. Unfortunately none of these very early Iranian *madrasa*s has survived; in fact until quite recently the earliest extant Iranian building of this type whose identification as a *madrasa* was unchallenged was the Madrasa-yi Imami of 725/1325 in Isfahan. This compact structure (some 92 m. × 72 m. at its widest extent) employs the standard Iranian four-*iwan* plan, but the modifications to the traditional layout are significant. The *iwan*s no longer rear high above their flanking arcades; the roof-line is only slightly broken. This simple change entirely reverses the traditional pattern, in which the *iwan* was the dominant feature – and dwarfed the flanking arcades. Two stories of

continuously niched façades, behind which the cells for student accommodation were located, form the principal accent of the elevation and engulf the central *iwan* on each side. The question is of course whether such massy, cliff-like façades also characterised the elevations of the first Nizamiyas. The example of the Madrasa-yi Imami, the known Saljuq predilection for the four-*iwan* plan, and the need to accommodate substantial numbers of students living in the building as distinct from visiting it – all combine to suggest that the first official Iranian *madrasa*s were indeed fairly similar to their Ilkhanid descendant.

So far the discussion has assumed that the more important of these early *madrasa*s were purpose-built structures, intended solely for the students accommodated in them. Other possibilities, however, have been aired. Perhaps the most extreme, propounded by Sauvaget, is that the buildings generally accepted as the major urban mosques of the Saljuq period – those of Ardistan, Qazvin, Gulpayagan and so on – were actually *madrasa*s. This theory runs counter to common sense, for it does not account for the resultant absence of Friday mosques in these centres, and does not assume a double function for these buildings. More intrinsically likely is the proposition that the larger mosques contained an inbuilt *madrasa* element in the provision of a second storey around the courtyard. This possibility will be discussed later in this chapter in the context of the subsequent development of the Iranian *madrasa*. Meanwhile it will suffice to note that on occasion the niched façades of these upper storeys could indeed lead to separate chambers, but the extremely diverse functions discharged by a Friday mosque in a large city means that a wide range of other purposes can be suggested for such rooms. Elsewhere in the Islamic world joint foundations were labelled as such; cases of mosque-*madrasa*s or mosque-mausolea and various other com-

binations abound in Mamluk Cairo. A further argument against the *madrasa* function of the upper storeys of large urban mosques in the Iranian world is provided by the well-documented practice of adding self-contained *madrasa*s to established mosques (e.g. Isfahan and Mashhad). There would have been little need for such new foundations if the mosques in question were already serving *inter alia* as *madrasa*s. If one bears in mind the noted imprecision of the Arabic terminology which bears on building types, and also the virtual interchangeability of these types, it will be clear that no firm conclusion as to the form of the pre-Mongol *madrasa* in Iran is warranted. Rather does the evidence suggest that the forms of the *madrasa* were scarcely less varied than those of the mosque itself. But the rarity of standing buildings impairs any discussion of these early

1, 143

2.269
5.1

127 Bukhara, *madrasa* of 'Abd al-'Aziz Khan, courtyard

*madrasa*s. Their organisation, personnel, curricula and financial arrangements can be followed up in minute detail in the literary sources; but the all-important question for the student of architecture, namely the precise form they took, remains obscure.

PROBLEM CASES: SURVIVING PRE-ILKHANID MADRASAS IN THE IRANIAN WORLD

With such a plethora of literary evidence available, it is ironic that Iran should retain so little in the way of pre-Mongol *madrasa*s and that perhaps the two earliest buildings thus identified – excluding such doubtful cases as the perhaps 12th-century monument of Danestama in Afghanistan – are not universally accepted as such. It will be convenient to begin with these two problem cases.

Khargird

The more controversial of them is a mud-brick ruin at Khargird, whose damaged inscription specifically identifies it as a foundation of Nizam al-Mulk; it must therefore date before 485/1092. Its principal surviving feature is a broad and deep *qibla iwan* with at least one room of comparable depth flanking it on either side. Little sense can be made of any other part of the structure, but the dimensions of the courtyard in front of the *iwan* might well be about 22 m. by 28 m. In favour of the identification as a *madrasa* may be cited the very fact that Nizam al-Mulk is cited in the inscription as the official founder, although a mere *shaikh* actually carried out the work of supervising construction. Why should this august personage, the pivot of the Saljuq state, take an interest in Khargird? The family of Nizam al-Mulk hailed from Sabzavar, and he himself was born in Tus, so there can be no question of explaining his connection with this monument by his desire to erect a public building in his native town. Khargird was a small town of secondary importance. Moreover, this structure is, as Herzfeld noted, very small for a courtyard mosque of its period, and the row of windows high up in the *qibla iwan* would make much better sense in the context of the cells on the first floor of a *madrasa* than as an element of mosque architecture. These various factors suggest that the most natural interpretation of the ruins is to see them as the sole surviving trace of Nizam al-Mulk's extensive programme of building *madrasa*s. As Ibn al-Athir says: 'The Nizamiya *madrasa*s are famous the world over, no town that had not one of them . . . ' Against this it must be admitted that the presence of supplementary *mihrab*s does suggest a mosque rather than a *madrasa*. The flanking halls have also been cited as evidence that this is a mosque, but this feature occurs consistently in Anatolian Saljuq *madrasa*s. To summarise, the evidence seems to incline towards interpreting the Khargird structure as a *madrasa*, but without fresh evidence there is no clinching the matter.

Rayy

The other disputed '*madrasa*' is a shoddily published structure found in excavations at

128 Tabas, Madrasa-yi Du Dar, courtyard

Rayy in the late 1930s. Godard himself, the source of all the information available, at first expressed himself with reserve as to its function but eventually he shed such caution and treated the identification as a certainty. Nevertheless he produced no arguments to offset his earlier qualms about the eccentric orientation of the structure and its equally atypical emphasis – by means of the differential size of the *iwan*s – on the east-west rather than the north-south axis. It must also be admitted that the sixteen habitable spaces which together parcel out the ground plan do not correspond in their layout to any known *madrasa*. All this being admitted, it would be still more accurate to say that no medieval house of this kind is known either; that ten of the ground-floor spaces could well have functioned as cells accommodating one or several students, to say nothing of the capacity of an upper floor; that cases of the faulty orientation of religious buildings are legion in medieval Islam, and that the difficulties of that kind presented by this building disappear if one assumes that the west *iwan* is intended to function as if it faced southwest, the direction of the *qibla*. This simplification is in fact characteristic of medieval religious buildings in eastern Iran, and it would not be surprising if the trend had spread westwards. Finally, and most significantly of all, the presence of a *mihrab* is not easily explained away. Unfortunately Godard's plan does not mark it, so that to identify the niche in question as a *mihrab* is itself somewhat hazardous. Nevertheless, despite the fact that in its present form, on display in the Teheran museum, it is largely a figment of the restorer's

imagination, the published photograph of it *in situ* shows clearly enough the Qur'anic Kufic inscription which it bore. The presence of a *mihrab* with a Qur'anic inscription in a private house takes somewhat more explaining than does the eccentric orientation of a *madrasa*. Even so, it may be felt that the building at Rayy presents rather more problems of identification than does its counterpart at Khargird. Whatever conclusion is reached, it is regrettable that the undoubtedly seminal role of Iran in the early development of the *madrasa* is obscured by the lack of early surviving specimens whose claims to be *madrasa*s are not disputed.

Tabas

Similar doubts as to function and dating weaken the value of the Madrasa-yi Du Minar at Tabas as a guide to the nature of lost Saljuq *madrasa*s. The major rebuilding which the monument experienced long after the erection of the minarets – perhaps in the Safavid period or later still – make it hazardous to draw even provisional inferences from the form it had in the 1970s. Recent reports indicate that the building collapsed in an earthquake several years ago, and its history is therefore liable to remain an enigma. For the record, the building was of markedly irregular 4-*iwan* plan. Following normal practice, the *qibla iwan* was the deepest; its counterpart at the opposite side of the courtyard was of the same width but a good deal shallower. Broader but still shallower *iwan*s marked the centres of the lateral sides. The arcaded facades linking the *iwan*s were in two storeys. A tree-lined pool occupied the centre of

129 Zuzan, *madrasa*, north *iwan*

130 Zuzan, *madrasa*, south *iwan*, general view

the courtyard. In all these respects the building fitted the model of many later *madrasa*s; but neither the architecture nor the decoration of the *madrasa* proper bore traces of medieval work. The only unmistakably Saljuq feature of the building was the pair of stumpy minarets with Kufic inscriptions in blue-glazed brick which flanked the portal. They indicated clearly enough that a substantial building lay behind them; but whether the modern identification of it as a *madrasa* was correct cannot be proved from the information available. The same can be said for two other putative *madrasa*s, apparently of Ilkhanid date, which have recently come to light: those at Pasargadae and at Chahar Dih near Tabas.

4.9, 4.130

Shah-i Mashhad

4.7 In the Iranian world the earliest *madrasa* identified as such by inscription is the recently discovered example dated 571/1175–6 at Shah-i Mashhad in north-western Afghanistan. Ruined as it is, it nevertheless yields much useful information. To begin with, its spendid ornament proclaims it to be a monument of the very first importance. The person responsible was, as the titulature reveals, a lady of high rank. In plan it is certainly a two-*iwan* and possibly a four-*iwan* structure, with two dome chambers of unequal size to the east of the entrance. Presumably these had their counterparts to the west. The façade is energetically articulated with niches, panels and archways, and is lavishly decorated; it centres on a lofty projecting arched portal. In size alone the building is remarkable for its time, measuring as it does some 44 m. per side. This far exceeds the dimensions of 12th-century *madrasa*s further west, but it was to find many subsequent parallels in the Iranian world. One further detail, which again is echoed in later Iranian *madrasa*s, is the bevel used in the only surviving corner of the courtyard.

Nothing on quite such an ambitious scale survives from the following two centuries, and the obvious question is why this exceptionally large and expensive building was erected in an area which was always remote. The minaret of Jam may provide the necessary clue. The role of that tower as a beacon of Islam in a context which until recently had been pagan goes far to explain its site, size and epigraphy. The *madrasa*

131 Zuzan, *madrasa*, south *iwan*, detail

of Shah-i Mashhad, with its fifteen inscriptions, may have been intended in similar vein to stamp an Islamic presence on a stubbornly pagan countryside. Its size and magnificence would assuredly impress, but might also have helped to convince waverers that Islam was the faith to embrace.

Zuzan

Of almost comparable importance is the great ruined *madrasa* of Zuzan, in north-eastern Iran, whose inscriptions state that it was built in 615/ 1218–9 by a local magnate, one Qiwam al-Din Mu'ayyad al-Mulk Abu Bakr b. 'Ali, who governed the town on behalf of the Khwarazm-shah Muhammad b. Tekesh. A huge inscription at the back of the south *iwan*, long known but only recently deciphered in full by Sheila Blair, states that it was 'for the followers of the great *imam*, light of the nations [a common title of the

129

4.6

130

131

132

founder of the Hanafite *madhhab*] Abu Hanifa Nu'man . . . ' – and two hundred years later the geographer Hamdallah Mustaufi reports that the people of Zuzan were still devoted Hanafites. Even the aberrant orientation of the *madrasa*'s *qibla* follows Hanafite norms, which in this case seem also to have determined the orientation of the governor's palace next door, on the west side of the *madrasa*. This close juxtaposition of secular and religious foundations, common enough in the case of royal palace and Friday mosque in the early Islamic period, is striking. Framing that same south (or rather *qibla*) *iwan* is a quotation from the beginning of Sura 23 of the Qur'an proclaiming the victory of the faithful. *129* The 'north' *iwan* directly opposite is substantially narrower in width and less than one-third as deep as the *qibla iwan*, thereby accurately reflecting the practice in contemporary and earlier mosques. Nevertheless it has one of the most spectacular *muqarnas* vaults of the period, rendered all the more splendid by its decoration in two-tone brick. Its outer portal bears an external *mihrab* so that passers-by can accomplish their devotions; a similar *mihrab* can be found on the façade of an earlier Saljuq caravan-sarai in this region, the Ribat-i Sharaf. This *6.19-6.20* recalls the practice of allowing public access from outside to the mosques in some Umayyad palaces.

It may be wondered whether the outer portal at Zuzan was in fact the main entrance to the building, for its size hardly seems commensurate with the gigantic scale of the rest of the monument. Even though its ruin is now far advanced, the *madrasa* towers colossally over the mean hamlet which is all that remains of medieval Zuzan, stranded in these miserable surroundings like some unexpected survival from a heroic age. This deliberately massive scale, whose splendour must have been inten-*131* sified by the *madrasa*'s wonderfully ornate terra-*132* cotta and glazed decoration, finds its natural *4.7* parallels in such buildings as the Garjistan *3.111* *madrasa* and the minaret of Jam. Seen in that wider context, the *madrasa* of Zuzan can be interpreted as an expression of royal power harnessed both to the defence of Islam from internal heterodoxy and to its proclamation to the heathen peoples which were then still surviving in pockets in the eastern Islamic world.

Given the quite unheralded scale and magnificence of this *madrasa*, for which the only useful parallel is the Garjistan *madrasa* in the same general area, it is indeed a pity that nothing is yet known of the rest of its architecture or of its precise relationship to the buildings which adjoin it. Together these two *madrasas*, and the superb decorative brickwork of the surviving pair of dome chanbers of the so-called Khwaja Mashhad *madrasa* in Tajikistan, make it clear *4.132* that in the period before the Mongol invasion *madrasas* in the Iranian world could be built on a scale which dwarfed that of their counterparts in Anatolia, Syria, Egypt and the Maghrib; and the quality of their decoration rose to the challenge of their scale. These buildings emphasise the enormous gap created in the architectural history of the *madrasa* by the virtual disappearance of pre-Mongol Iranian *madrasas*.

EARLY MADRASAS IN THE NEAR EAST:
THE CRESWELL THEORY

It is with some relief, therefore, that one turns to an examination of the surviving *madrasas* whose identification as such is incontrovertible. The earliest free-standing and independent example of these, the *madrasa* of Gumushtegin in Busra, *4.11* bears a disappointingly late date – 530/1136 – and is located in Syria, an area which has not yet entered the discussion. It is followed in brisk succession by a round score of surviving *madrasas* in Syria all dated or datable before 700/1300, and the literary evidence confirms that these are only a fraction of what was built in this period and has since vanished: eighty-two

132 Zuzan, *madrasa*, dating inscription

133 Baghdad, Mirjaniya *madrasa*, entrance to upper-floor room

134 Baghdad, so-called "'Abbasid palace": vault

*madrasa*s are mentioned in the detailed chronicle of medieval Damascus, for example, and forty-six in the more summary account of medieval Aleppo.

These numbers, impressive though they are, need not be interpreted as confirmation of the primacy of Syria in the architectural development of the *madrasa*. Nor, *pace* Creswell, can this honour be claimed by Egypt without further ado. This subject will be treated in appropriate detail later, but a few brief remarks are necessary here to introduce the perennially thorny problems about the architectural origins of the *madrasa* and the respective roles of Syria, Egypt, Anatolia and Iran in its development. Creswell lists some twenty-nine *madrasa*s in Cairo dated before 700/1300, and of these a scant four have remained. From the undoubted fact that the latter group includes the first cruciform four-rite *madrasa* to survive, he has built an elaborate edifice of argument designed to establish the innovatory role of the Egyptian *madrasa*.

As will shortly be apparent, however, the area with the largest number of surviving *madrasa*s datable before 700/1300 is Saljuq Anatolia, which boasts no less than fifty examples, nine of them datable to the 12th century. Egypt and Syria together cannot match the latter tally, and indeed have only a third as many *madrasa*s datable before 700/1300. Yet these buildings figure not at all in Creswell's history of this architectural type. Common sense dictates that the Anatolian *madrasa*s, built in an area culturally dependent on Iran and geographically close to it by patrons who themselves sprang from Great Saljuq stock, would be likely to reflect the Saljuq *madrasa*s of Iran, whose decisive role in the formation of the genre has never seriously been questioned. Iranian influence may in any case readily be detected in the plan types, brickwork and tile decoration of much of Rum Saljuq architecture. The historical background outlined above encourages the assumption that it is precisely in these unfortunately vanished Iranian Saljuq *madrasa*s that the essential original lineaments of the official *madrasa* are to

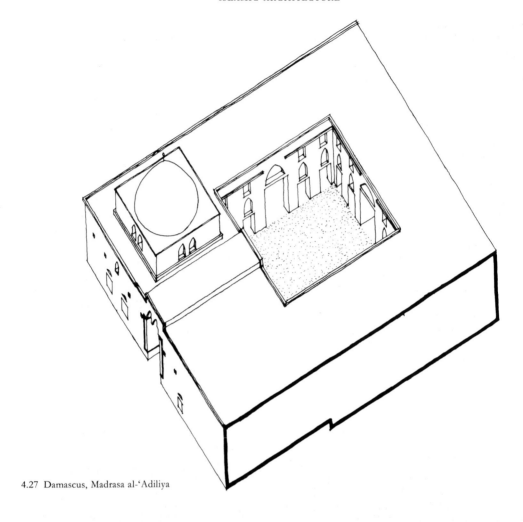

4.27 Damascus, Madrasa al-'Adiliya

be sought. Hence the paramount historical importance of the Anatolian Saljuq *madrasa*s as the closest surviving relatives of the Iranian type. Many of their features are duplicated in contemporary Syrian *madrasa*s, which may be seen as a parallel and co-eval group. It is not hard to recognise in Anatolian, Syrian and (perhaps thence) Egyptian *madrasa*s the ultimately Iranian origin of such elements as centrally domed sanctuaries or *iwan*s articulating a courtyard façade. When it is remembered, finally, that the four-*iwan* plan has an ancient lineage in Iran but no traditional place in Egyptian architecture, it becomes virtually impossible to accept Creswell's theories about the originality of the Egyptian school of *madrasa*s. It may perhaps be

conceded, however, that the concept of allocating each *madhhab* a single *iwan*, and thereby creating the cruciform four-rite *madrasa*, was, as Creswell argues, an Egyptian achievement – though recent research by Michael Meinecke casts doubt even on this.

SYRIAN MADRASAS TO *c.*648/1250

Enough has been said to illustrate the dangers of arguing exclusively on the basis of surviving structures, especially in the case of a building type already more than two centuries old. With this caveat in mind, then, one may return to a consideration of the Busra *madrasa*. Like most 4.11 Syrian *madrasa*s, it is diminutive; for all that its patron was a senior *amir* serving the *atabegs* of

Damascus, its external dimensions do not exceed 20 m. by 17 m. On this tiny scale there is scarcely room for a proper courtyard, and the space which would normally be designated as such is domed, a feature which was to recur a century later in some of the Saljuq *madrasa*s in Konya and elsewhere. Two lateral *iwan*s open off this space while a prayer hall and a kind of narthex to the south, the latter reached by narrow entrance vestibules to east and west, fill up most of the remaining area. In this single-storey building the only space left over is the area flanking the prayer hall, which yields two rooms per side. Since these each average less than 4 m. square, the total number of students accommodated in this *madrasa* can scarcely have exceeded a dozen. Such a building will simply not fit the popular image of officially sponsored *madrasa*s located strategically throughout the Saljuq empire and serving, at least in part, significant political ends.

Later Syrian *madrasa*s rejected many of the solutions found in the example at Busra: the small size, the pair of *iwan*s, the domed central space and the paired entrance vestibules. This is not to say that they fit the popular image any better. Perhaps the most distinctive local characteristic was to be the laterally developed prayer hall, entered by a triple archway and vaulted in a variety of ways (*dar al-hadith*, Damascus, between 549/1154 and 569/1174; Madrasa Khan al-Tutun, Aleppo, 564/1168–9; *madrasa* of Nur al-Din, Damascus, 567/1172; and *madrasa* of Shadbakht, Aleppo, 589/1193 among others). Sometimes the central bay of the sanctuary is domed, with groin vaults covering the flanking bays (Shafi'ite *madrasa*, Ma'arrat al-Nu'man, 595/1199), though tunnel vaults for these bays are commoner; but in other examples all three bays are groin-vaulted ('Adiliya *madrasa*, Damascus, completed 619/1222–3) or domed (Zahiriya *madrasa*, Aleppo, 616/1219–20; *jami'* and *madrasa* of al-Firdaus, Aleppo 633/1235–6). Recurrent features of these buildings include a

135 Aleppo, al-Firdaus, *jami'* and *madrasa*

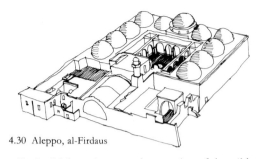

4.30 Aleppo, al-Firdaus

mihrab which projects on the exterior of the *qibla* wall, a mausoleum, and on occasion even two, occupying an angle of the building, a tank in the centre of the courtyard, and utilitarian accessories like wells and air-shafts. Most of these *madrasa*s have one *iwan*, but only one – the 4.11 example at Busra – has a pair of *iwan*s facing each other across an empty space. Altogether excep-135 tional is a joint foundation: the *jami'-cum-* 4.20, 4.30 *madrasa* of al-Firdaus, Aleppo, which not only has two large *iwan*s back to back but also two small but self-contained courtyard units, each with a pair of *iwan*s facing each other across the court, an intimately domestic arrangement encountered earlier in palaces and caravansarais.

FUNCTION OF SYRIAN MADRASAS

The emphasis on one rather than several *iwan*s may reflect the fact that the great majority of these buildings – all but seven of the 128 *madrasa*s in Damascus and Aleppo which pre-date 700/1300 and are recorded in the literary sources – were erected to serve a single *madhhab* and therefore required only one location for teaching. But this is purely supposition, for the 4.11 two-*iwan madrasa* at Busra was built to serve the Hanafite *madhhab* alone, while the two-rite Sul-4.18, 4.28 taniya *madrasa* at Aleppo (620/1223–4) has no *iwan*s at all. It therefore seems equally possible that any causal connection between the number of *iwan*s in a Syrian *madrasa* and the number of *madhhab*s which it served is more apparent than real. This conclusion seems all the more appropriate when it is remembered that neither Anatolian nor Iranian *madrasa*s attest any consistent connection between the number of *iwan*s in a *madrasa* and the number of *madhhab*s which it serves. Against this wider perspective, the Egyptian cruciform four-rite *madrasa* is nothing short of freakish, reflecting perhaps a conciliat-

ory religious policy on the part of the founder. Not surprisingly it remained very rare; the overwhelming majority of medieval *madrasa*s throughout the Islamic world were built to serve a single *madhhab*.

A cursory examination of the Syrian *madrasa*s is enough to establish that the provision of student accommodation was not a major priority. The information available on this score is unfortunately not very precise, for most of these buildings are long since disaffected and modern houses have encroached on them. But the Busra *madrasa*, as noted above, suggests in the gross disproportion between public and private space that the structure was purpose-4.11 built to accommodate no more than a handful of students. We have seen that it could not lay claim to the propaganda function and aura of official dignity enjoyed by larger and more prestigious institutions of this kind. Indeed, it is probable that its catchment area was no wider than Busra itself. Nur al-Din's *dar al-hadith* in 4.22 Damascus also seems to have had no more than four rooms, and although the other surviving Syrian *madrasa*s are more generously provided with student cells not one of them approaches the larger Maghribi *madrasa*s, let alone those of Iran, for capacity. The Khan al-Tutun *madrasa* in Aleppo probably had ten cells, while the Nur al-Din *madrasa* in Damascus, and the Zahiriya 4.12, 5 *madrasa* in Aleppo, had sixteen disposed in two 4.17, 4 storeys. If so, they had the most generous 4.40 housing capacity to be found in surviving contemporary Syrian *madrasa*s. The most unusual solution of all, as noted above, was the introduc-

136 Aleppo, Sharafiya *madrasa*

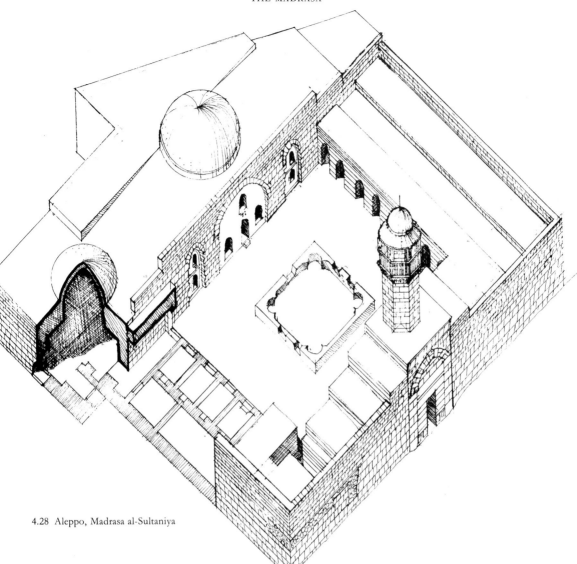

4.28 Aleppo, Madrasa al-Sultaniya

tion of two minute courtyard houses, each one complete with several irregularly shaped cells, on either side of the great double *iwan* of the 4.20, 4.30 *jami'-cum-madrasa* of al-Firdaus, Aleppo. But even this very carefully designed building leaves inexplicably little space in the layout for student cells, like a car with no engine.

One is driven to the conclusion, therefore, that the patronage directed towards the building of *madrasa*s in Syria deliberately kept them on a small scale. The fact that nearly all of them were built to serve (exclusively?) a single *madhhab* may itself be sufficient explanation, but other reasons

for this trend might be canvassed. Perhaps, for example, these *madrasa*s were intended to serve the needs of their immediate locality alone. Alternatively, they might have been meant more as oratories for the daily use of the local population, a practice recorded in Maghribi *madrasa*s, than as *madrasa*s *tout court*. Several of them incorporate a triple-bayed prayer hall (*madrasa* at Ma'arrat al-Nu'man; Kamiliya and Sharafiya 4.15, 4.25, 4.23 *madrasa*s, Aleppo). Or they might have been one of the results of the competitive urge to build *136* which seems to have seized the *amir*s of Ayyubid Syria and which was responsible for such a plethora of other buildings in this same period.

Some or all of these factors may well have been operative in Ayyubid Syria, but they are scarcely enough to account for the phenomenon of such large numbers of small *madrasas*. The answer seems rather to lie in local circumstances. To begin with, the topography of these *madrasas* is itself revealing. They are crammed into the nooks and crannies of ancient, densely populated cities, where building space was at a premium. There could be no question here of a state-inspired blueprint imposed regardless of local conditions. Sociologically, too, the picture differs from that presented by Iran, Iraq or Anatolia. The patrons are not the sultans themselves but lesser *amirs*, their wives or mothers, or local notables. Such people were well-to-do but not necessarily rich or with free access to public funds. Thus the buildings had a wider social base than their equivalents elsewhere in the Islamic world. Sometimes the endowment even specified the conditions of use: for example, that the teacher appointed was forbidden to teach anywhere else. This individual approach is reflected in the very varied layouts of these *madrasas*, which show the architects grappling with a unique site. For Ayyubid patrons, it seems, small was beautiful. Small was also functional. Since *madrasas* were built by the score in the larger cities it would have been wasteful to give them a large capacity, just as it would have been wasteful to decorate them lavishly. What decoration there is, however, maintains a high level of quality and is set off by the consistently fine stereotomy of Syrian tradition. The stone vaulting of the time deserves particular commendation. Thus these *madrasas* were firmly rooted in a topographical, sociological and artistic context which depended little on external influence – apart from the initial, though presumably indirect, stimulus from Iran.

FUNERARY MADRASAS

Perhaps the main distinguishing feature of these Syrian *madrasas* is the inclusion of a mausoleum (e.g. Damascus, 'Adiliya and Sahibiya *madrasas*). Indeed, it is doubtful whether the connection between the *madrasa* and the mausoleum was ever closer than it was in Ayyubid Syria. Once again epigraphy provides a clue, for inscriptions in the Sultaniya and Atabakiya *madrasas*, located

4.13, 4.27; 4.21

4.18, 4.28; 4.34

in Aleppo and Damascus respectively, refer to the recitation of the Qur'an there. Provision was made for this recitation to be unceasing – an Islamic parallel for the Christian custom of paying for masses to be said for the souls of the dead. Burial in a *madrasa*, then, like burial in the neighbourhood of a saint, was intended at least in part to confer *baraka* upon the dead. It was in Syria rather than in Egypt that the exaltation of the mausoleum at the expense of the *madrasa* proper can first be traced; time and again it is the mausoleum which has the favoured site of the street façade, with the *madrasa* modestly tucked away virtually out of sight. In sheer surface area the mausoleum is apt to rival, if not exceed, the *madrasa*. Small wonder, then, that it has even been suggested that the terms *turba* ('mausoleum') and *madrasa* were interchangeable in this period. On the other hand, the notion of ensemble which underlies a modern term like 'funerary *madrasa*' is belied by the epigraphic evidence, which often suggests that the *turba* element and the *madrasa* element both had their own foundation inscriptions. This practice has often obscured the original intention of the founder, for it has resulted in many now freestanding *turbas* being identified as simple mausolea rather than as part of a funerary *madrasa* (e.g. Farrukhshahiya and Amjadiya *turbas*, Damascus). Conversely, it sometimes happens that the inscription of a *turba* may mention the *madrasa* of which the mausoleum was part, and may indeed be the only surviving evidence that such a *madrasa* ever existed ('Izziya and Rukniya *madrasas*, Damascus).

5.193

5.204, 5.2

The intimate symbiosis of *turba* and *madrasa* is epitomised by a curious joint foundation in Damascus. The Farrukhshahiya *madrasa*, with the mausoleum of 'Izz al-Din Farrukhshah attached, dates from 578 or 579/1182–3. A generation later, in 628/1231, another *madrasa* was built beside it and this too was provided with a mausoleum, which housed the son of 'Izz al-Din, al-Malik al-Amjad. Father and son, then, are buried in adjacent *turbas*; the *turba* of the former is, perhaps appropriately, the larger of the two. Similar pairs of tombs survive in Damascus in the Jaharkasiya *madrasa* and later in Mamluk *madrasas*. If the *madrasas* of Ayyubid Syria were analysed from the purely formal point of view, with no backward glance at their

234

5.193

4.41

Eastern origins, the obvious conclusion would be that a major, if not indeed the primary, purpose of the institution was to contain a monumental mausoleum. Is it fair to assume, then, that the term 'madrasa' did not have a consistent meaning throughout the medieval Islamic world? Certainly Ayyubid Syria provides evidence suggesting that the term did not connote one single type of building. Thus the Dar al-Hadith al-Ashrafiya in Damascus (634/1236-7) is called a madrasa in its foundation inscription, and in its sequence of entrance vestibule, prayer hall and turba conforms to the standard type of contemporary madrasa as illustrated by the Murshidiya madrasa in Damascus. Conversely the Qilijiya, also in Damascus, is defined in its foundation inscription as an institution for teaching hadith, but is identical in form to the Murshidiya. As in Iran and Egypt, it was common for a private house to be converted into a madrasa, but more ambitious conversions are also recorded and it is these that testify yet again to the loose boundaries between

medieval Islamic building types. The Halawiya madrasa in Aleppo was successively a church and a mosque before it became a madrasa, while the Maridaniya served in turn as a madrasa, burial ground and mosque. Thus the mere fact that a structure was founded with a given purpose in mind was no guarantee that it would continue to function as such, especially if the value of its endowment fell; it might easily shed some functions or acquire additional ones. The absence of any sign of student cells in many of these admittedly half-ruined Ayyubid madrasas invites speculation that at least some of these foundations were never intended to be residential.

If the Syrian madrasa tradition, as it developed during the scant century of its heyday, is analysed as a whole, the sheer variety of types encountered cannot fail to make an impression. It is hard to avoid the conclusion that these differences are not casual or contingent on the local topograpy, but rather reflect a basic uncertainty about the ideal form such buildings

137 Cairo, madrasa of Qa'it Bay at Qal'at al-Kabsh

138 Rada', Madrasa al-'Amiriya

should take. For a long time Syrian architects were sidetracked by the influence exerted by the mosque. The prestige of that long-established model helps to explain why ideas derived from mosque design permeate these *madrasa*s. They were after all religious buildings. The 4.14 Shadbakhtiya *madrasa* in Aleppo (591/1195) is essentially a mosque writ small, especially in its laterally developed domed sanctuary. To judge by the plan alone, the teaching function of the building is plainly secondary. For that function the *qa'a* element of a private house – i.e. two deep *iwan*s facing each other across a courtyard, with individual rooms extending along the sides – was much better suited. This suitability was tacitly accepted by the widespread conversion of private houses into *madrasa*s. The curious fact is that, on the whole, Syrian architects baulked at redesigning the *madrasa* from scratch so that it could fulfil its primary function more effectively.

Nor was the dead weight of mosque design the only factor which hampered a rational development of the *madrasa*, for as already noted it was precisely in Syria that it became standard practice to incorporate a mausoleum into the *madrasa*. Obviously the mausoleum had even less to do with teaching than did the mosque, and its inclusion is apt to wreck the equilibrium of the building altogether. Probably it was the need to cater simultaneously for several mutually unrelated and not readily compatible functions that kept the Ayyubid Syrian *madrasa* in a state of flux and forbade any definitive solution to the design problems posed by such *madrasa*s. It was not until Mamluk architects in

Cairo tackled the problem that the experience of the *qa'a* was fully brought to bear on *madrasa* design. So successful was the Mamluk solution that the earlier process reversed itself and, as will shortly appear, the *madrasa* began to influence the mosque.

MADRASAS IN EGYPT AND THE YEMEN

Since Egypt was Shi'ite it was impossible for the explicitly Sunni *madrasa* movement to establish itself there, or for that matter anywhere else in the Fatimid domains, before the fall of that dynasty in 567/1171. Within five years of that date, however, under the militant orthodoxy of Saladin, there were already five *madrasa*s in Cairo, swiftly to be followed, no doubt at least partly for propaganda reasons, by examples at Mecca and Medina. However, the long start which Syria had enjoyed in building *madrasa*s seems to have resulted in a more lavish provision of these buildings in that area than in Egypt, where the total recorded before 700/1300 is only thirty-one, about a third of the comparable figure in Anatolia or in Damascus alone. These figures are enough in themselves to cast doubt on the supposed primacy of Egypt in the architectural development of the *madrasa*.

Even so, the few Ayyubid and early Mamluk *madrasa*s in Egypt –which were concentrated all but exclusively in Cairo – do count among them some of the masterpieces in this genre. The Salihiya of 639/1242, for example, is one of the 4.62–4.6 earliest *madrasa*s intended for all four rites; its architect adroitly met the challenge of a cramped and unpromising site by constructing the monument on either side of a busy thoroughfare and linking its two halves by a pair of arches which support the minaret. The latter feature was to become standard in Egyptian *madrasa*s, unlike their Syrian counterparts. To judge by the surviving half of the *madrasa*, the quirks of the site called for a series of ingenious shifts and compromises on the architect's part, including an entrance so bent as to be serpentine, rhomboidal cells and a royal mausoleum placed eccentrically off-axis. This is, incidentally, a slightly later construction but was presumably envisaged in the original layout; since it was the first royal tomb in the city itself, it might be argued that it was deliberately integrated into the *madrasa*, an undeniably useful public foundation, to disarm the criticism of the pious. Virtually every detail of the plan is conditioned by the fact that the correct religious orientation is at variance with both the public façades of the building. As so often happens in medieval Cairo, the façade is essentially a screen which conceals the rest of the building; it is not conceived as the logical corollary of what lies behind it.

Too little work has been done on the later medieval *madrasa*s of the Yemen to permit general conclusions to be drawn on the precise nature of this particular school. Nevertheless, significant Rasulid foundations at Rada' and Ta'izz show that the decoration of these multi-domed buildings yielded nothing in quality to that of the best contemporary work in Cairo, although much simpler *madrasa*s are also known (e.g. that of al-Hadi at Thula, 849/1445). Moreover, a much greater area of the interior wall surface was covered in decoration than was the norm in Egypt and Syria. The lower surfaces were ornamented in carved stucco, while bright frescoes in which epigraphy played a preponderant role enlivened the interiors of the domes (Mu'tabiya *madrasa*, Ta'izz).

4.66, 4.70
4.69, 4.71, 138
139, 4.68
4.67
4.58
8
4.67, 139

Mamluk madrasas in Cairo

The building of *madrasa*s in Cairo gathered new momentum with the coming of the Mamluks. The largely vanished Zahiriya *madrasa* (660–62/1262–4) of Sultan Baibars was a gigantic four-*iwan* structure with a stalactite portal probably of Syrian inspiration, a theme repeated in the deep niches with *muqarnas* hoods which articulated its

139 Ta'izz, Mu'tabiya *madrasa*, interior

façade. This building inaugurates, if indeed it was not preceded by some comparably magnificent earlier *madrasa*, the distinguished tradition of Cairene *madrasa*s with splendid façades and interiors to match. Anatolia was about a genera-

tion earlier in this development, so far as surviving evidence indicates, while Syria lagged behind.

This notable degree of splendour can be explained on both political and economic grounds.

140 Cairo, complex of Sultan Qala'un

institutions, is the *maristan*, tomb and *madrasa* of
Sultan Qala'un (683–4/1284–5). As in the case of
the Salihiya, its internal arrangements are at
odds with its façade, which at nearly 70 m. is
exceptionally long and to which in a sense the
whole building is subordinated. Mausoleum and
madrasa are sundered by a long corridor which
led to the now largely-vanished hospital. It is no
doubt significant that the mausoleum, now
enlarged by a functionally dispensable courtyard, occupies a far larger proportion of the
combined tomb and *madrasa* portion of the
ensemble than it did in the Salihiya. The *madrasa*
itself has a generous courtyard with two *iwan*s
on the longitudinal axis and cells disposed laterally. Its most notable feature is without doubt
the *qibla iwan*, which is divided into three naves
and therefore explicitly associated with the
traditional architecture of the mosque. Interestingly enough, Qala'un's son, al-Malik al-Nasir
Muhammad, himself built a mausoleum-*cum-*
madrasa cheek by jowl with his father's great
foundation, and in this later ensemble (695–703/

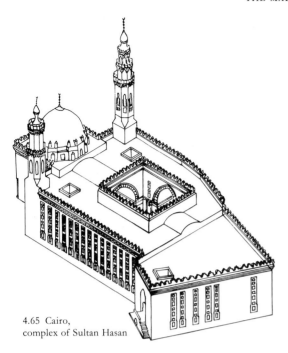

4.65 Cairo,
complex of Sultan Hasan

Mamluk *madrasa*s in Cairo are overwhelmingly
the product of royal or high official patronage,
a fact consistently reflected in the names they
bear and in their lavish decoration. Outward
splendour would be the natural corollary of such
patronage. But it would be inaccurate simply to
treat these buildings as instances of conspicuous
consumption, even though the lengths to which
an *amir* or sultan would go to secure a fashionable site with ample street frontage does suggest
such a conclusion. Many of them were endowed
far more generously than their size and therefore
the scope of their activities dictated, and while
these endowments (*auqaf*) were inalienable
under Islamic law, that same law permitted any
surplus from an endowment to be applied to the
benefit of the descendants of the original
endower. The more lavish the endowment,
therefore, the more such a foundation would
approximate to an investment. Not surprisingly
it was among the first concerns of an *amir*, upon
reaching power, to found some charitable institution, nor was there any bar to his adding
piecemeal to its endowment over the years.

Perhaps the most ambitious of these multi-
purpose Mamluk foundations, and the one
which seems to have set the fashion for such

141 Cairo, mosque-*madrasa* of Sultan Hasan, exterior

142 Cairo, mosque-*madrasa* of Sultan Hasan, student cells

1295–1303) the mausoleum is relegated to a subsidiary role beside a substantial four-*iwan madrasa*. This latter building has the peculiar distinction of being the first known cruciform *madrasa* intended to serve all four *madhhab*s.

By common consent the masterpiece among these Mamluk ensembles, and certainly the largest of them (150 m. × 68 m.), was the mosque, *madrasa* and mausoleum of Sultan Hasan (757–64/1356–63). Its lofty portal, originally designed to have flanking minarets, and with a spacious vestibule behind it, bears the unmistakable imprint of Anatolian Saljuq architecture, but most of the detailing within is typically Cairene. At first sight the layout seems familiar enough, focused as it is on an ample four-*iwan* plan. But – and here again foreign influence, this time from Iran, must be taken into account – this cruciform plan is employed, exceptionally in the case of Egypt, for a mosque, while each *madhhab* has its own *madrasa* in one of the corners between the arms of the cross. The

4.64–4.65

141

142

sultan's own mausoleum, a gigantic dome chamber, extends the full width of the *qibla iwan* and is placed (emphatically not in Iranian fashion) directly behind the *qibla* wall. It therefore usurps the position of the domed sanctuary in the classical Iranian mosque. The building thus epitomises the vitality and versatility of the traditional four-*iwan* formula.

Several prestigious Mamluk buildings in Cairo, such as the various funerary *madrasa*s of Sultan Sha'ban and his family, followed the lead of the Sultan Hasan ensemble. But its principal impact on later buildings was through its four-*iwan* schema, which henceforth was to be repeatedly used for mosque architecture until the Ottoman conquest. In other words, the architecture of the *madrasa* had now come to influence that of the mosque; indeed, the unprecedented expansion of the *qibla iwan* into a full-scale sanctuary in later Mamluk buildings (e.g. the Qa'it Bay complex) can best be explained by such a process. Presumably the decisive factor was that the mosque thereby gained a large unbroken space for the sanctuary, which – unlike mosques with arcaded or columned sanctuaries – allowed all the congregation to see the *imam*. This inherent advantage of the four-*iwan* schema had not been seized at the time that the Qala'un ensemble was built and thus the *qibla iwan* there is treated like a traditional sanctuary and parcelled out by arcades, a device continued in the mosque-*madrasa* of Barquq (786–8/1384–6). Moreover, even as late as the funerary *khanqah* of Faraj b. Barquq (completed 813/1410), a set of domed bays forming minature compartments take up the areas normally reserved for *iwan*s. The liturgical distinction between the *qibla iwan* and the subsidiary ones was expressed in architectural terms too. The former was vaulted, and thereby given the illusion of still greater spaciousness, while the scale of the latter was reduced and their ceilings were now flat.

For the *madrasa* to influence mosque design was indeed a momentous change; it signalled a new relationship between the two buildings. Earlier, the dependent status of the *madrasa* had been vividly expressed by the way it had been tacked on, very much in the manner of an afterthought, to the parent structure. Examples abound; they include the *madrasa* of 507/1113–4 beside the Great Mosque of Urfa (earlier than

5.210

4.52, 5.2

4.47

4.60–4.6

4.84

the example at Busra but differing from it in that, by virtue of its location, it was not an autonomous foundation) and a trio of *madrasa*s – those of the *amir*s Taibars (709/1309–10), Aqbugha (740/1340) and Jauhar (before 844/ 1440) – attached to the Azhar mosque in Cairo. Henceforth, however, these two institutions could combine their functions within a single building (which was highly desirable given the chronic shortage of space in Cairo) and with minimum trespass of one upon the other, as in the *madrasa-khanqah* of Barsbay. For it is noticeable that in the Sultan Hasan complex a novel solution for the *madrasa* has been devised: not only does each *madhhab* occupy a corner of the building, but certain aspects of the traditional full-scale *madrasa* are retained even on this miniature scale. The cells for students are clustered on two sides of a diminutive courtyard, except in the case of the Maliki *madrasa* situated in the western corner, where the exigencies of the site bisected the space available. Since the Maliki rite

enjoyed relatively less popularity than the other three (though the Maliki professor was allotted the prestigious *qibla iwan* in the funerary *madrasa* of al-Malik al-Nasir), this solution was not as unjust to that *madhhab* as might at first appear. Furthermore, the small size of the student cells meant that their numbers and dimensions could be readily adjusted to fill the space available, thereby obviating the need to encroach on the mosque proper. Presumably the four *iwan*s were used for teaching purposes outside the hours of prayer; the association between *iwan*s and teaching had been rooted for a good two centuries in Syria and thence Egypt. The Mamluk historian al-Maqrizi, in his description of the mausoleum and *madrasa* of al-Malik al-Nasir, lists the four lecturers – one from each *madhhab* – who were first appointed to teach there, and specifies the *iwan* allotted to each one. The lack of subsidiary *mihrab*s in the lateral *iwan*s is sufficient indication that their rôle as places for prayer was not paramount.

At the mosque-*madrasa* of Barquq, built a generation later (786–8/1384–6), the emphasis is reversed in favour of the *madrasa* without any fundamental change in plan. Thereafter, while true four-*iwan* mosques or *madrasa*s remained the exception rather than the rule in Egypt (e.g. the foundations of Jamal al-Din of 811/1408 and Sultan Inal of 860/1456), the principle that the same building could serve both functions was unassailable. It is not surprising, therefore, to discover in 13th- and 14th-century Mamluk architecture a marked propensity to use *iwan*s, though the combination varies widely – one, two or three *iwan*s may be used in conjunction with courtyards, halls, mausolea or sets of smaller chambers. Acute shortage of space was no doubt a contributory factor in these developments. It favoured the compact multiple foundation as the most economic use of scarce building land, and obviously put a premium on building types which could function in a variety of ways. Since an unwelcome sense of constriction was only to be expected in these ensembles, the combination of *iwan* and courtyard introduced a much-needed sense of space. Extremely elaborate exterior façades were therefore complemented by an interior arrangement which encouraged free circulation and provided the maximum of open areas. Some

143 Cairo, *madrasa* of Barsbay, 828/1425

144 Cairo, funerary *madrasa* of Qa'it Bay, general view

145 patrons were not above duplicating these well-tried formulae within a single group of buildings. Thus the mosque-*madrasa* of Qa'it *210* Bay (877–9/1472–5) with the royal mausoleum attached has, adjoining it on the northeast, a miniature version of the selfsame combination. It must be admitted that in many such buildings the four-*iwan* plan is more an illusion, or perhaps allusion, than a reality. Indeed, two *iwan*s are quite sufficient to articulate the courtyard. The width of the larger *iwan*s may be such as to take up all of that side of the courtyard. Another common device is to replace an *iwan* by a huge arched opening which gives on to an extensive transversely vaulted hall placed broadside on to the courtyard. Visually, such an arch is clearly intended to function as an *iwan* forming part of a cruciform schema (mosque-*madrasa* in complex of Qansuh al-Ghuri, 909–11/1503–6).

The diminutive scale of many Circassian *4.49* Mamluk foundations (such as those of Ilgay *4.46* Yusufi, 775/1373, and Tatar al-Hijaziya, 761/1360) necessarily excluded ample accommodation for students, but to make up for the difficulties inherent in lateral expansion many of these foundations extended upwards instead, comprising two or even – in the case of the four-*iwan* funerary *madrasa* of Amir Sarghitmish (757/1356) – three storeys which in the latter example all contain cells for students. The case of the tiny but elegant *madrasa* of the Amir *4.51* Mithqal, datable to the period between 762/1361 and 776/1374, and measuring a mere 20 m. per side, shows that the practice of allocating separate storeys to the functions of worship and to those of teaching and/or accommodation had already established itself in pre-Circassian times. Relieved of the requirement to fit student cells into the ground floor of a cramped, awkward site, the architect could create an ordered and even ample layout by expanding the four-*iwan* plan to take up virtually all the available space, with special emphasis on a laterally placed sanctuary which stretches the full width of the building. Without a comparably bold solution, such a building would be undesirably cloistered, indeed claustrophobic. An airshaft (*malqaf*) is another means of countering the unduly inward-looking quality of such buildings. In the Mithqaliya, store-rooms take up what little area remains on the ground floor, while the two

145 Cairo, funerary *madrasa* of Qa'it Bay, north-west *iwan*

upper floors are reserved for living and lecture rooms and a library. The mezzanine floor is not continuous but is confined to the lateral *iwan*s which have wooden ceilings at their springing and above this are closed by *mashrabiya* grilles giving into the rooms behind. Thus was created the so-called 'hanging' *madrasa*, a natural development from earlier 'hanging' or 'suspended' *2.99* mosques in the same city. The funerary *madrasa* of Zain al-Din (697/1298) may have been a *4.45* forerunner of this type.

Like many other Mamluk *madrasa*s, the Mithqaliya was sited close to the private quarters of its patron – indeed, as at Nishapur centuries earlier, a private house (*qa'a*) was frequently turned into a *madrasa* after its owner's death and named after him (e.g. the still-surviving Madrasa al-Ghannamiya in Cairo, dated 774/1372–3, and this case can be supplemented by a dozen literary references). In both types of building the two-*iwan* plan is normal though not mandatory. The interdependence of private

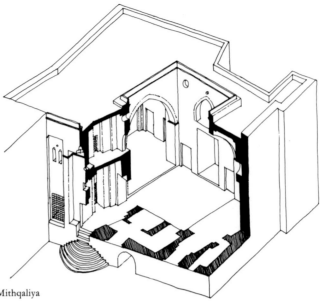

4.51 Cairo, Madrasa al-Mithqaliya

house and *madrasa* is highlighted by the absence of staircases between ground and first floor in the original composition. It seems, therefore, that the *madrasa* proper can only have been reached via such private quarters as adjoined it, presumably those of the *amir* himself. The *madrasa* in turn would have provided access for buildings behind it.

144   Among the surviving *madrasa*s in Cairo one type is clearly predominant: the funerary *madrasa*. So traditional was this kind of building in Cairo that (to judge by surviving structures) it was the *madrasa tout court* that remained exceptional. In the earlier funerary *madrasa*s the mausoleum occupied such a significant portion of the ensemble that it is appropriate to describe such structures as joint foundations. Five such monuments survive dated between 697/1298 and 715/1315 alone, and they were only gradually superseded by foundations of still wider scope. It is hard to avoid the conclusion that the *madrasa* was a convenient means of 'laundering' the mausoleum – for the latter building type of course flouted Islamic orthodoxy. An early example of this process is the vanished *madrasa* built in conjunction with a magnificent mauso-
6, 5.181–5.182 leum near the grave of the Imam al-Shafi'i (d.204/820) in 572–5/1176–80. This ensemble conferred an implied legal recognition on the

cult of mausolea; after all, if a funerary *madrasa* could be erected in honour of the founder of one of the four major *madhhab*s, the practice could henceforth safely be regarded as unimpeachable. The mausoleum continued to provide the true *raison d'être* of such monuments, and visually speaking it almost invariably usurps pride of place. This is particularly evident when the ensemble includes two mausolea instead of one (funerary *madrasa* of Salar and Sanjar al-Jauli, 4.56 703/1303–4), although later in the century such double mausolea appropriately enough take second place to the *madrasa* (*madrasa* of Khwand al-Baraka, also known as that of Sha'ban, 770/ 1368–9). The inclusion of minarets, which by this time were too common in the city for fresh ones to be anything but redundant, may also have been designed to ward off pious disapproval. Even so, it was the minaret and mausoleum, not the *madrasa* itself, which gave these buildings their distinctive stamp externally. Perhaps the competition of these already well-established building types was one of the factors which prevented the *madrasa* from developing its own instantly recognisable form. A modest edifice in the name of Il-Malak al-Jukandar (719/ 4.59 1319), described as a *masjid* in its inscription – even though the now demolished rooms on the roof, the striking resemblance to the slightly

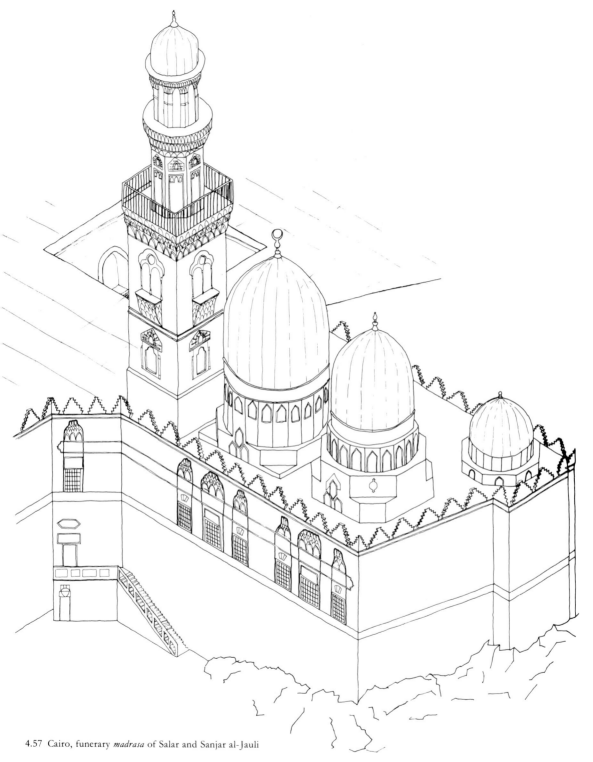

4.57 Cairo, funerary *madrasa* of Salar and Sanjar al-Jauli

later Mithqaliya and the historical evidence all point to its being a *madrasa* – epitomises the simplicity and austerity of the *madrasa* once shorn of such parasitic structures. It is the first Cairene *madrasa* to have the *sahn* roofed in the Anatolian manner. This feature continues in later *madrasa*s and results in the courtyard shrinking to the level of a large room (*madrasa* of Qa'it Bay, 880/1475).

137

These remarks should not be construed to suggest that Cairene *madrasa*s served exclusively educational, religious or funerary purposes. A casual reminiscence set down by al-Maqrizi indicates that the *madrasa*-mausoleum of the Amir Qarasunqur was used as a hostel by couriers of the *barid* service preparing for their return journey to Syria and elsewhere. The same source mentions a *ribat* for women attached to the *madrasa* and mausoleum of the Amir Sunqur Sa'di (715/1315). But above all the *madrasa* provided a focus both for the relentless emulation of the Mamluk *amir*s in architectural projects, and for their desire to make financial provision for their descendants.

SYRIAN MADRASAS AFTER 1250

Just as the *madrasa*s of Syria in the 12th and early 13th centuries yield valuable data not available from Egypt in the form of actual monuments, so do Mamluk Egyptian *madrasa*s fill the information gap in Syria. The sudden decline in *madrasa* building in Syria after 1250 can safely be associated with the fall of the Ayyubid dynasty whose power was centred there.

This decline is not reflected solely in *madrasa*s; it is a widespread characteristic of later medieval architecture in Syria, and is only to be expected given the henceforth provincial status of the area. After the death of Baibars, whose early career adequately explains his interest in Syria, it was very rare for a Mamluk sultan to undertake an important building project in the province. Jerusalem, on the other hand, by virtue of its exalted status in the Islamic world, continued to benefit from the architectural patronage of the Mamluk sultans right up to the death of Qa'it Bay.

Syrian *madrasa*s of the Mamluk period, then, are significantly below the level of contemporary work in Cairo. Moreover, they were built in significantly smaller numbers than under the Ayyubids, for under the Mamluks the emphasis of patronage shifted to mausolea and funerary mosques. Even so, it is well-nigh impossible to draw a clear line of demarcation between either of these categories and the *madrasa*. There is no significant difference in layout between the tomb of Shaikh Nakhlawi (730/1330), the funerary mosque of Sidi Shu'aib (*c*.800/*c*.1398) and the funerary *madrasa* of Shaikh Hasan Ra'i al-Himma (863/1459). In both the latter cases an entrance portal leading to a small courtyard is flanked on either side by a monumental mausoleum with a barrel-vaulted room or *iwan* behind each. In both these buildings, too, the latter elements are clearly secondary; indeed the *iwan*-based layout becomes so impoverished and reduced that in its later incarnations its origins are barely recognisable. Such later buildings are in fact essentially two-*iwan* structures; the third *iwan* is transmogrified into the entrance while the fourth is suppressed altogether. Sometimes the entrance remains uncovered and is broadened so as to enlarge the courtyard. In other cases (e.g. the funerary *madrasa* of Shaikh Hasan Ra'i al-Himma) the *iwan*s are replaced by a *turba* and a mosque. So flexible is the *iwan* in such buildings that in one and the same structure it can shrink to the status of a niche and expand to become a laterally conceived mosque (e.g. al-Sayyida *madrasa*, Damascus).

4.39

4.39

The courtyard becomes increasingly important in these later buildings and at the same time the earlier emphasis on regularity and symmetry declines. What now counts is the street façade with the domes of the *turba*s and the much narrower portal sandwiched between them forming a compact, symmetrical silhouette. The Rashidiya *madrasa* of 750/1349 in Damascus follows the same pattern, but single-tomb structures combined with a much larger laterally developed sanctuary, sometimes with a vestibule, continued to be built. These could equally well bear the name mosque (Turuziya, Damascus, 825/1422) or *madrasa* (Jaqmaqiya, Damascus, rebuilt and enlarged 822/1419). Thus in Mamluk as in Ayyubid times the term '*madrasa*' did not connote exclusively one kind of building or one particular function. Other continuities may readily be noted. The Zahiriya *madrasa* in Damascus, for example, dated 676/1277–8 and containing the mausoleum of

4.24

146 Jerusalem, Is'ardiya *madrasa*

with radial or *muqarnas* vaulting (Khatuniya, 784/1382 and Salamiya, *c*.700/1300 respectively) and entrance recesses with trefoil heads (Tashtimuriya, *c*.785/1383; Muzhiriya, 885/1480-1). These and other Jerusalem *madrasa*s (e.g. the Jauhariya, 844/1440, the Is'ardiya – before 760/ 1359 – and even the early Ottoman Rasasiya, 947/1540) concentrate attention upon the entrance. This feature is easily explained. Streets were very narrow and the buildings bordering them constituted a succession of cliff-like façades; no one building had a street frontage of any substantial length. Thus the custom developed of leaving most of the façade plain and confining applied and architectonic ornament to the entrance and perhaps the windows. The doorway itself tended to be much smaller than the slender, lofty entrance recess into which it was set, and was normally crowned by a *muqarnas* composition enclosing the inevitable epigraphic panel trumpeting the name and titles of the founder.

6.87, 6.91, *139*

The self-same shortage of space which had conditioned the characteristic local exterior façade ensured that in residential *madrasa*s the cells were disposed on two or even three storeys. There is even a case of a *madrasa* being extended over the roof of an adjoining *ribat* (Jauhariya

6.87, 6.91

Baibars, is essentially still in the Ayyubid architectural tradition. Its steep narrow portal, focused on a *muqarnas* vault ending in a scallop-shaped niche, does however find its natural parallels in other Bahri Mamluk buildings in Cairo. Some *madrasa*s, such as the Turunta'iya in Aleppo (794/1392) had two such portals, neither in any way integrated with the principal features of the building. This *madrasa*, incidentally, combines in a new way many of the standard features of earlier Syrian *madrasa*s: around its spacious central courtyard are disposed a sanctuary extending the entire width of the *qibla* side, arched colonnades with rooms above on the two long sides and a huge *iwan*, presumably for teaching, occupying all the north side. The rôle of mosque played by many Mamluk *madrasa*s in Syria is advertised by the addition of a minaret (Saffahiya *madrasa* built by the *qadi* Ibn al-Saffah in 868/1464, and Ansariya *madrasa*, both in Aleppo).

Attention so far has been focused on the Mamluk *madrasa*s of Damascus and Aleppo, and the evidence cited makes it clear enough that these buildings fall substantially below the standards set by contemporary Cairene *madrasa*s. Another local school flourished in Tripoli – *madrasa*s of al-'Ajamiya (766/1365) and al-Khatuniya (774/1372–3) – but this too could not rival Cairo. As noted above, it is in Jerusalem that most of the best provincial Mamluk architecture is to be found, and this is as true of *madrasa*s as of any other building type. Particularly worthy of note is the sparse but exquisite applied and architectonic decoration of these buildings, including stellar vaulting (Madrasa al-Dawadariya, *c*.697/1298), niches

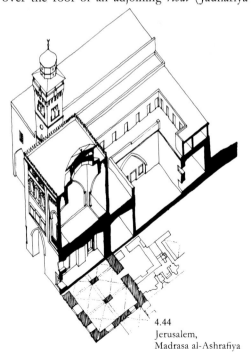

4.44
Jerusalem,
Madrasa al-Ashrafiya

147 Jerusalem, Ashrafiya *madrasa*, portal

madrasa, 844/1440). In such cramped conditions it is not surprising to find that the four-*iwan* plan used on more spacious sites in contemporary Cairo is apt to be reduced, for example by the suppression of lateral *iwan*s as in the Muzhiriya *madrasa*. Here the portal gives on to a vestibule which leads into an *iwan* facing a courtyard, probably once covered, with a *qibla iwan* opposite.

Ashrafiya madrasa, Jerusalem

There can be little question that the most important of these Mamluk *madrasa*s built outside Cairo is the Ashrafiya erected by Qa'it Bay in 887/1482. This was the third extension and rebuilding of the monument, which was already a major institution staffed by an indefinite number of *shaikh*s, *fuqaha* and sixty *sufi*s, all salaried. Several reasons combine to lend it special distinction. To begin with, it attests to the patronage of the sultan himself, a rare occurrence – as already noted – in provincial Mamluk *madrasa*s. Secondly, its location in a favoured

(margin: 4.42-4.44)
(margin: 147)
(margin: 148)

site along the inner façade of the Haram al-Sharif would confer *baraka* on it to an unusual degree. Earlier in the Mamluk period several *madrasa*s had been erected along the Haram, but the visual impact of the Ashrafiya is much greater. Qa'it Bay's patronage, however, must be assessed against a wider context than the purely local ambience of the Haram, or indeed of Jerusalem itself. A short time previously he had erected *madrasa*s within the precinct of the Haram in Mecca (882–4/1477–80) and the Mosque of the Prophet in Medina. Like his foundation in Jerusalem, these buildings are so designed that their windows look out upon the sacred enclosures in each case. Thus the Ashrafiya falls into place as one component in a religio-political master-plan expressing imperial Mamluk involvement in the holy places of Islam. Such links between Jerusalem and the Hijaz go back to the Dome of the Rock and thus to the very beginnings of Islamic architecture. The foundations of al-Walid I nearly eight centuries previously also provide an obvious parallel. Finally, the Ashrafiya possesses intrinsic distinction on account of its architecture. Seen as a whole, the inner façade of the Haram emphasises the motif of arcading above all others. The architect of the Ashrafiya was therefore constrained to reject the model presented by earlier Mamluk *madrasa*s in the city, with their emphasis on high blank façades and block-like design. Although an open-arcaded façade had no functional justification in a *madrasa*, this device did permit the Ashrafiya to blend fairly naturally with its surroundings. But the operative word here is 'fairly'. Not content with the prime site which the *madrasa* already occupied, as close as practicable to the Dome of the Rock, Qa'it Bay took the major step of sanctioning the extension of the *madrasa* façade, which until then had remained flush with the open arcade fronting the inner side of the Haram enclosure, so that it projected well beyond the arcade. It was a brutally simple way of drawing attention to his new foundation. Earlier *madrasa*s bordering the Haram enclosure and indeed forming with the Ashrafiya a continuous band of monuments, such as the Tankiziya (729/1329), the Baladiya (782/1380) and the 'Uthmaniya (840/1437), had by contrast all respected the extant portico. The Ashrafiya was regarded in its time as one of the three jewels of the Haram al-Sharif, with the Dome of the Rock and the Aqsa mosque, a distinction expressed in symbolic fashion in 882/1477 when, like these other two buildings, it was specially illuminated to celebrate the visit of a Mamluk *amir* to Jerusalem. Nor is this all. A detailed analysis of the building shows that its silhouette was very carefully designed to make an impact from a few selected viewpoints; it would be interesting to look for comparable evidence of sensitivity to the urban skyline on the part of Islamic architects elsewhere. The immediate source for this unwonted emphasis on the skyline, as for the presence of a minaret which is exceptional in the Syrian context, is likely to be Cairo. Cairo, too, as will be shown below, provides the fullest context for the recast, not to say deformed, cruciform *iwan* schema encountered at the Ashrafiya.

The ensemble takes an unusual form which is due only in part to the exigencies of the site. At ground floor level it comprises three elements. The most important of these is a large assembly hall (*majma'*) whose capacity and spatial extent are much reduced by the architect's decision to retain in his remodelling the original piers of the arcade enclosing the Haram. Here congregated the judges, *fuqaha* and other notables connected with the *madrasa*. This hall, measuring some 10.65 m. by 14.7 m., with a *mihrab* tucked away in one corner, constituted the major covered space in the building, but there is no indication that it was of anything more than peripheral importance to the daily functioning of the *madrasa* proper. Behind it are a series of three adjoining square or rectangular rooms, whose western walls abut the Baladiya *madrasa*; they neatly subdivide an awkward lateral corridor of space. At least two of these rooms served as mausolea. The third component of the ground-floor layout is the entrance complex, which comprises a vaulted porch open on all four sides and leading to the entrance itself flanked by stone benches (*mastaba*s), which opens into a tripartite vestibule within. A staircase reached from the southern section of the vestibule and making three right-angled turns gives access to the first floor. It will be noted that none of the features described so far lend themselves to the prime function of a *madrasa* – for there is no suggestion

in the literary sources that the *majma'* served as a lecture hall for students.

As if to make up for this neglect, the first floor is ingeniously and tightly planned to serve as a self-contained *madrasa*. As such it immediately recalls, for example, the Jauhariya *madrasa* in Jerusalem itself, which like the Ashrafiya is intimately dovetailed with a pre-existing structure, or the Mithqaliya *madrasa* in Cairo. The first-floor unit divides naturally into two areas, one north of the minaret above the staircase and the other west of it. The latter area consists of an L-shaped open-air terrace (*saha*) with twenty rooms, disposed roughly as uneven pairs to the south, and five identical rooms plus a washroom (*mutawadda'*) to the west. Even if the larger rooms are excluded and only symmetrically repetitive chambers are identified as student cells, the number of resident students which were catered for here can scarcely have been less than twenty. Its sister foundation in Mecca had (according to one account) forty students attended by four lecturers (*mudarrisun*) plus a jurisconsult (*faqih*), Qur'an reciter (*qurra*) and, somewhat surprisingly, muezzins.

The area north of the minaret comprises another open-air terrace to the west, lavatories with a reservoir, and a remarkably compact cruciform *madrasa* adjoining the terrace to the east and thus placed directly above the *majma'*. To describe this rectangular hall, measuring a mere 22.7 m. by 12.1 m., as a cruciform *madrasa* requires some justification. As so often in later Mamluk architecture, barely the skeleton of the four-*iwan* plan has survived. It would perhaps be more accurate to describe this part of the

148 Jerusalem, Ashrafiya *madrasa*, Haram façade

building as a continuous spatial unit with a powerful drive along the north-south axis. The lateral *iwans* are not only much narrower than the *qibla iwan* and its opposite number, but also project far less forcibly from the walls behind them. Their relative suppression of course serves to highlight the other two *iwans*. This technically cruciform unit is in fact essentially a two-*iwan qa'a* – a type already long familiar in Cairo but also encountered in Coptic architecture – and it may be relevant to note that the architect responsible for the re-fashioning of the *madrasa* into its final form was a Copt. The resultant layout suggests very strongly that it was the north and south *iwans* that served the traditional functions of a *madrasa*, while the lateral *iwans* shrink to the dimensions of mere niches in comparison. As if to compensate for this demotion, they are allotted quite distinctive functions of their own which their architecture expresses. The east *iwan* takes pride of place since it is the one which looks out on to the Haram. Here the *iwan* is merely suggested, not present in full, for there is only the arch of the façade borne on columns with no walls perpendicular to it. It has in fact been transformed into an open loggia offering spectacular views over the Haram. This architectural form, known as *maq'ad* or *tarima*, has a wide distribution in domestic architecture throughout the Near East, for example in medieval Cairo, and may be compared parenthetically with similar forms in contemporary Renaissance architecture. It underlines yet again the deep roots of the *madrasa* in domestic prototypes. But this development, for all its domestic flavour, also had religious implications; for the view from this loggia was over one of the holiest sites in the Islamic world. Architecturally speaking, the departure from the norm of an *iwan* was made with good reason, for the opening out of this area gives ample play to its main feature, a multi-coloured stained glass window. Although the colours of this arcuated window would of course not have been visible externally, its dimensions so greatly exceeded those of the numerous flanking windows that it would have constituted the principal accent of the upper façade. This lavishly fenestrated façade conceals the very different four-*iwan* layout behind it. The familiar schema has been transformed by this unexpected exterior. It

remains only to add that the note of luxury struck by this huge stained glass window is echoed throughout the complex – in the two-tone (*ablaq*) masonry, the polychrome marble flooring of the *iwans* and inner courtyard (a practice frequently encountered in late Mamluk Cairene *madrasas*), the veneered wooden ceilings of the *iwans*, the lead sheeting of the roof, and in its carpets and lamps, whose beauty, in the words of a contemporary historian, was 'unequalled elsewhere'. In short, there is ample evidence that the Ashrafiya was a metropolitan import into the local architecture of Jerusalem.

THE ANATOLIAN MADRASA IN THE SALJUQ AND BEYLIK PERIODS

In the earlier part of this chapter the discussion focused on literary references to the earliest *madrasas*, an emphasis dictated by the lack of surviving structures. It is unlikely that future excavations will substantially illuminate this crucial early period. After all, the written sources indicate clearly enough that the early, pre-Saljuq *madrasas*, in keeping with their private and non-official character, were of a domestic nature. Frequently a house became a *madrasa* without, it seems, any structural alteration, or served impartially as house and *madrasa* by turns. It follows that excavated ground-plans will not be enough in themselves to prove that a given pre-Saljuq structure functioned as a *madrasa*. Even in the Saljuq period itself, two Iranian buildings identified by some as *madrasas* (the ruined structures at Khargird and Rayy) have aroused, as noted earlier, a controversy still not laid to rest. In this situation it seems sensible to accept that the architectural history of the *madrasa* before 530/1136 (the date of the freestanding example at Busra) – or at any rate before 507/1113–4, the date of the *madrasa* beside the Great Mosque of Urfa – is irretrievably lost, no matter how rich the documentation of its character as an institution may be.

Such a conclusion inevitably confers particular evidential value on the earliest considerable group of *madrasas* to survive, namely the examples in Saljuq Anatolia. The word 'considerable' deserves emphasis; fifty Anatolian examples permit a more searching and reliable analysis of trends than do a score of Syrian ones. These Anatolian buildings have been quite un-

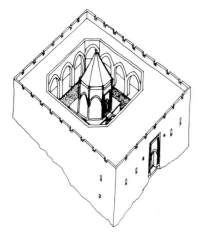

4.86 Kayseri area, Köşk *madrasa*

justifiably neglected in the history of the genre. The extensive account which follows is an attempt to rectify this anomaly. Creswell's obsession with absolute chronology and his bias towards material from Syria, Palestine and Egypt led him to over-estimate the role of this area in the development of the *madrasa* and his views have dominated subsequent discussion. The reasons for the historical significance of the Anatolian *madrasas* as the best available guide to the nature of the building in Saljuq Iran have been touched upon earlier in this chapter, and it is now time to attempt a survey of these monuments.

Thanks to the work of Kuran and Sözen, Anatolian *madrasas* are much better known as a group than any others in the Islamic world. Some eighty of them datable before 1500 survive, and this figure can be supplemented by a further fifty-eight vanished buildings of the same period recorded in the literary sources. In both categories the numerous Ottoman buildings, which form a separate study, are excluded; the grand total of Anatolian *madrasas* surviving or recorded in this period is probably about two hundred. The preponderance of surviving over vanished buildings is highly unusual in the medieval Islamic world and is unlikely to reflect the true state of affairs. But the two sets of figures do complement each other significantly. They confirm what may be deduced from other sources – that building activity was most concentrated in the 13th

century, that is under the Saljuqs of Rum. Forty-one surviving and twenty-seven vanished *madrasas* – that is, almost half of the entire recorded output of Anatolian *madrasas* in the period *c.*493–905/1100–1500 – date from this century. The comparable figures for the 14th century are twenty-two and fifteen, comprising about a quarter of the output of the period as a whole. The Qaramanids were the principal patrons responsible for new *madrasas* in this period. In the 15th century the rate of construction declined still more sharply, by a further 70%. Even the 12th century saw more construction than this, with nine surviving buildings and a further six so far recorded in the literary sources; but of course the decline of Beylik *madrasas* in the 15th century directly mirrors the growth of Ottoman power. Indeed, the earliest Ottoman *madrasa* to survive, that of Sulaiman Pasha at Iznik, predates 760/1359 and was itself 4.116 preceded by a now-vanished *madrasa* at Bursa. With the 15th century, Ottoman *madrasas* began to be erected over much of Anatolia.

The turbulent political history of 12th-century Anatolia is perhaps sufficient explanation for the slow spread of the *madrasa* in this area and period. But with the consolidation of Rum Saljuq power the movement gathered such momentum that it long outlasted the disintegration of the Saljuq state. Clearly it had deep roots in the society which it served.

Not surprisingly, therefore, and in contrast to the situation in Egypt, Palestine and Syria, and for that matter in the Maghrib, these medieval Anatolian *madrasas* were not confined to a few large cities. The surviving examples alone are distributed among thirty-nine cities, towns and villages throughout the length and breadth of the land, while the literary sources add a further dozen localities. In the fullest sense, this was a popular movement. Naturally this did not exclude a concentration of *madrasas* in a few key centres. Konya, as the Saljuq capital, obviously 4.87–4.88, took pride of place, though only seven of its 4.93–4.94, twenty-four *madrasas* have survived. Next 4.80 comes Mardin, the Artuqid capital, where surprisingly enough eleven of the recorded thirteen 4.101 *madrasas* remain, with the Sultan 'Isa *madrasa* at 4.83 their head; similarly, Kayseri retains nine of its 4.85–4.86, eleven recorded *madrasas*. These are without 4.90, 4.97 doubt the three major centres of the time.

However, quite a number of towns had between four and six *madrasa*s erected in this period: Sivas, Sivrihisar, Akşehir, Tire, Aksaray, Erzurum, Diyarbakr and Qaraman. Thus there is ample evidence to indicate that the intensive building activity of a few centres was complemented by provision in depth at a good many more. Finally, seven sites are recorded with two or three *madrasa*s apiece. Such a remarkably even spread of facilities throughout the land may best be explained by the interaction of two complementary trends: a centralised building programme and – though probably to a lesser degree – a popular fashion for the *madrasa* as an institution, or at any rate as a suitable object of modest architectural patronage.

In fact these Anatolian buildings provide the best evidence of the multi-functional nature of the medieval *madrasa*. In so doing they are a reminder that the form of these buildings is not an infallible guide to their function. Many a building now conventionally termed *madrasa/medrese* (and subsumed in the present discussion) was actually intended to serve as a medical school, a mental hospital, an *imaret* or an observatory, and frequently allotted substantial space to a mausoleum, sometimes, indeed – as at the Köşk *madrasa* near Kayseri – giving it pride of place in the centre of the courtyard. The two former functions may be combined in the sense that each is discharged in separate but adjoining premises, as in the Çifte Minare *madrasa* at Kayseri or the Kaika'usiye at Sivas, though the mental hospital (*bimarhane*) of Melike Yildiz Hatun at Amasya is a single self-contained foundation. Nothing in its layout would exclude its identification as a *madrasa*. In the case of long-disaffected, anepigraphic buildings, therefore, a *madrasa*-type should not automatically be taken to signify that the building really was a *madrasa*. Moreover, the curriculum in the Anatolian Saljuq *madrasa* was not confined to the religious sciences but could include such subjects as geometry, astronomy and mathematics. Some *madrasa*s had kitchens to provide the necessary catering facilities for residential staff and students. It is recorded of one Saljuq *madrasa* in Sivas, for example, that it had an endowment which allowed students and teachers alike two meals a day. They were served, so it seems, in porcelain cups.

149 Konya, Qaratai *madrasa*, interior

The rich quantity of Anatolian material available prompts a variety of conclusions. The most important of these is perhaps that no single type of arrangement was dominant. This in turn invites speculation that the evolution of the genre was by no means complete. In some *madrasa*s (Tokat, Karahisar), a whole cluster of rooms of varying shapes and sizes mirror the uncertainties of the architect. In many of these buildings, too, the notional purpose of a *madrasa* – to house students seeking a theological education as a first step to joining the *'ulama'* – obviously comes a poor last to such other functions as providing a place of prayer, an elaborate façade, a mausoleum (or even two, as at the Boyaliköy complex) a minaret, a bath, a fountain or halls for public gatherings. Not surprisingly, the cells are usually tiny, a scant three paces per side. But it is their paucity that is most striking. Even the most splendid of all domed Anatolian Saljuq *madrasa*s, that completed in Konya in 651/1253 by the vizier Jalal al-Din Qaratai and bearing his name, has no

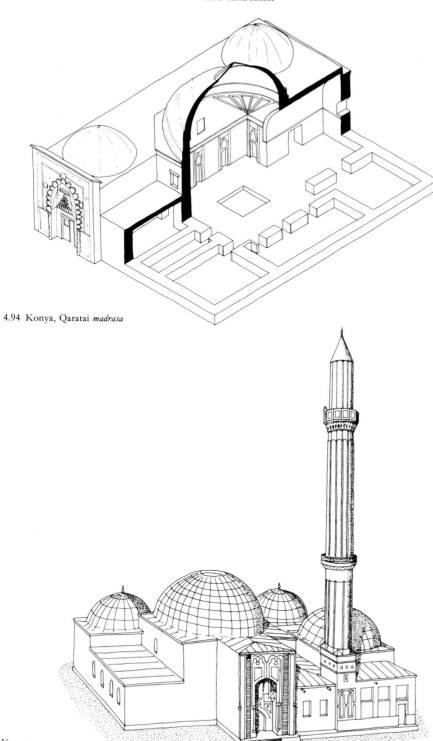

4.94 Konya, Qaratai *madrasa*

4.88 Konya,
Ince Minare *madrasa*

more than a dozen cells. The most capacious *madrasa* of the period, on the other hand – the Çifte Minare in Erzurum, which at 35 m. by 48 m. is the largest Anatolian *madrasa* of the period – still has a mere nineteen cells on each of its two storeys and therefore lags far behind the larger *madrasa*s of the Maghrib or Iraq. A chance reference to the Saljuq *madrasa* at Sivas mentioned above establishes that, at least so far as this particular building was concerned, classes were held on the ground floor in winter and upstairs in the summer. In the 14th century the capacity of the average Anatolian *madrasa* declined still further. Sometimes the building of a *madrasa* seems to have been a move in a power game played between viziers at the highest political level (e.g. at Konya and Sivas). Direct influences from Iran wage a silent, protracted war against locally rooted traditions, such as those involving extensive interlocking vaulted spaces. Certain *madrasa*s are arranged in such an irrational way that the final result smacks of spasmodic accretion rather than planned design (Ince Minare *madrasa*, Konya). This in turn suggests that such ensembles were only incidentally *madrasa*s. In other words, Saljuq Anatolia shows just as clearly as do Syria, Egypt or Iran the growth of the multi-purpose foundation.

Quite apart from such cases, several Anatolian *madrasa*s were built in conjunction with structures serving another purpose altogether. Thus the *madrasa* at Çay bears the same date (677/1278) as the caravansarai which adjoins it.

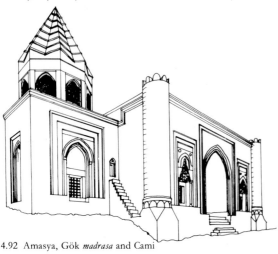

4.92 Amasya, Gök *madrasa* and Cami

Presumably as in the case of similar, though later, joint foundations (those of Amir Mirjan in Baghdad, 756–9/1355-8 and Shah Sultan Husain in Isfahan, 1118–26/1706–15), the revenues of the commercial establishment were intended to finance the running costs of the *madrasa*. It was common enough, too, for a *madrasa* to adjoin a mosque (Zinciriye *madrasa*, Diyarbakr, 595/ 1199; Hajji Kilic *madrasa*, Kayseri, 647/1249–50; Gök *madrasa* and Cami, Amasya). This fact is not necessarily mirrored in the plan of the *madrasa*, for the Khwand Khatun *madrasa*, Kayseri (635/ 1237–8) provides the usual facilities for prayer even though there is a mosque right next door. Perhaps the most diverse group of buildings erected by a single Anatolian patron in one building campaign is the complex of Ibrahim Bey at Qaraman (836/1433), comprising mosque, '*imarat, dar al-qirra*', *madrasa, tabhane* and mausoleum, though the complex of Isma'il Bey at Kastamonu (880/1475) runs it close, comprising as it does a *madrasa*, mosque, tomb, '*imarat*, caravansarai and bath. Such buildings make most sense in an Ottoman context.

Any attempt to characterise the medieval Anatolian *madrasa* must therefore reckon with this very varied background. It is certainly possible to extrapolate a few features which most of these buildings have in common, but even then there remains ample scope for variety. Interior spaces may be domed, vaulted or flat-roofed, façades may be blank or ornate, the surface area may be confined or spacious, there may be one storey or two, half a dozen student cells or six times that number. Moreover, these fluctuations may occur even within a single category of *madrasa*.

Domed Anatolian madrasas

Encompassing and overriding all these no doubt individually significant variants are two broad categories into which the entire body of medieval Anatolian *madrasa*s may be fitted. These are the open type, with a courtyard; and the closed type, with a domed area replacing that courtyard. Of the fifty-three surviving *madrasa*s in good repair, thirty-eight are of the open type and fifteen are domed. The twenty-eight ruined *madrasa*s are deliberately excluded from these calculations because most of them are too fragmentary to be placed with confidence in either

150 Konya, Ince Minare *madrasa*, portal

Anatolia. Nor can regional preferences be invoked, for the type occurs with tolerable consistency throughout the country. An important factor in its genesis may well have been that interchangeability of building types so typical of medieval Islamic architecture. The association of the *madrasa* with burial and worship would make it natural for the forms of mausoleum and mosque to be integrated into the structure of the *madrasa* – as indeed happens – and eventually to exert influence upon its form. Moreover, it can scarcely be coincidence that it is precisely the *madrasa*s of smaller surface area which attest the domed type (Çukur *madrasa*, Tokat and Yaghi- 4.96 Basan *madrasa*, Niksar, both datable to the mid- 4.89 12th century, and the Ertokuş *madrasa*, Atabey, 4.77 dated 621/1224). If very few students were to be accommodated in the building, the need for a substantial courtyard would diminish. In such a situation the building would gain extra dignity and monumentality by the placing of a dome over the central space, while the memory of the courtyard would be retained by means of a skylight and/or a fountain. This ablutions fountain or *shadirvan* readily brings to mind the *impluvium* of the *atrium* in a Roman house, and thus underlines yet again the domestic origins of the *madrasa*. The integrating power of a central dome may also have been a relevant factor in the growing popularity of the domed *madrasa*.

Two further considerations, which are perhaps only at first sight mutually exclusive, may be borne in mind. First, the compact *madrasa* with large central dome and smaller domed or vaulted areas surrounding it cannot fail to recall the standard type of mid-Byzantine church, which was widespread in Anatolia at the time of the Turkish conquest. Nor is this resemblance simply a matter of external silhouette; the rear *iwan* flanked by dome chambers in the domical *madrasa*s of Konya brings to mind a Byzantine church apse flanked by *diaconicon* and *prothesis*. Secondly, when these domed *madrasa*s are seen not simply in their contemporary context but against the later background of Ottoman architecture, especially mosques, their emphasis on an integrated multi-domed and multi-vaulted space (Kirşehir, Caca Bey *madrasa*) 4.99 may be recognised as prophetic. Indeed, some of these domed *madrasa*s, such as the Ince Minareli 4.87–4.88 *madrasa* in Konya (*c.*663/1264–5) or the Taş 150

category. Even so, here too the predominance of the open plan is unmistakable, for of the ruined *madrasa*s whose original layout can indeed be established, eight are open and only two are closed. That the open plan should dominate is only to be expected, given the popularity of this form in non-Anatolian *madrasa*s and the fashion for courtyard houses in the medieval Iranian world which produced the earliest *madrasa*s. The closed, domed *madrasa* – which may have anything from one to four *iwan*s, very occasionally has two storeys (Qaraman, *madrasa* of 4.82 Ibrahim Bey), and may or may not have a portico around the central space – is not so easily explained. Its *raison d'être*, incidentally a more rewarding subject than its architecture, therefore deserves separate consideration.

The most convenient explanations – that the form is dictated by function or by climate – obviously will not do. After all it is the domed, not the open, *madrasa* that is exceptional in

4.74 *madrasa* in Akşehir (648/1250), actually incorporate earlier mosques in their structure. This close link with mosque architecture is not to be seen in the courtyard *madrasa*, which in Anatolia at least developed quite separately. Whatever the origins of the idea, its development was formidably consistent right up to the Ottoman culmination. Just as in the earliest Ottoman mosques, too, the consistent emphasis on vaulting could be seen as an attempt to give the illusion of more ample space in an intrinsically cramped building. The proper weighting to be allotted to each of these various factors is hard to determine, and it is very likely that a complex of motifs generated the domed Anatolian *madrasa*. At all events, its sudden appearance need cause no astonishment.

Anatolian courtyard madrasas

Anatolian courtyard *madrasa*s, like those of domed type, do not readily fall into formal sub-categories, although attempts have been made to analyse the buildings on this basis. The trouble with such an approach is the difficulty of identifying the crucial element and avoiding a purely mechanistic tally of the constituent features of the monument. It may be no more than the whim of the architect that a *madrasa* has one, two, three or four *iwan*s, a large or small courtyard, one or two storeys, multiple domed spaces or none at all. Had the function of the *madrasa* been consistent, these marked variations could well be explained as the outcome of personal preference. But the plain fact is that the workings and functions of these buildings in contemporary society are simply not known in adequate detail. It seems best therefore to note the formal differences and to accept that an explanation of them would still be premature.

This is not to say that all generalisations about these buildings are hazardous. It is clear, for example, that the typical rectangular *madrasa* kept the façade short in relation to the sides. This had the advantage of concentrating student cells on the long sides and separating them physically from the rooms serving other functions. Most cells had a fireplace and a cupboard, but sanitary facilities were communal and there was usually no provision for meals to be cooked on the premises. The extended longitudinal layout encouraged the lavish articulation of the façade,

whether by a porch or applied ornament or both; a long façade treated in the same way would bring in its train severe aesthetic and financial penalties. Equally characteristic is a tripartite division of the building parallel with the major, that is the longitudinal, axis, as in contemporary caravansarais. At the far end of that axis, marking the *qibla* and continuing the major chord first sounded by the portal, is a wide *iwan* or dome chamber serving as the mosque and frequently flanked by a subsidiary vaulted or domed room on either side. Evidently some honorific intent lies behind this placing, though it must be conceded that the mosque was sometimes located elsewhere in the *madrasa* (for example, next to the entrance vestibule as at the Çifte Minare *madrasa*, Erzurum). When the 4.72–4.7 *madrasa* form was used for an observatory (Vacidiye *madrasa*, Kütahya, 714/1314), a small opening in each of the lateral dome chambers served for star-gazing. In a true *madrasa* these two chambers most likely functioned as classrooms and for the library; smaller rooms flanking the entrance perhaps accommodated the professors. In four-*iwan* plans the *qibla iwan* is typically the broadest and the most richly decorated of all, and it has a similar pre-eminence in two-*iwan madrasa*s, in which the *iwan*s, as in Iranian Saljuq buildings of that type, are confined to the longtudinal axis. However, the form of the *iwan* within these buildings – as distinct from their exteriors – does not follow Iranian precedent in that its façade comprises the arch alone without a framing *pishtaq*.

These characteristics adequately define the specifically local quality of the Anatolian courtyard *madrasa*, while the rarity outside Anatolia of the integrated domed *madrasa*, without courtyard, in itself emphasises the Turkish character of this sub-species, sometimes further underlined by vaulting of "Turkish triangle" type (*madrasa* at Çay). Both local varieties share a 4.95 characteristic found only intermittently in *madrasa*s elsewhere: the attention devoted to the exterior walls. This is not simply a question, as so often in Egypt, of exalting the principal façade and neglecting the other perimeter walls, or indeed concealing them within the adjoining mass of buildings. Instead, the architect is at pains to give his building an impressive exterior on all sides. Outer walls are commonly straight

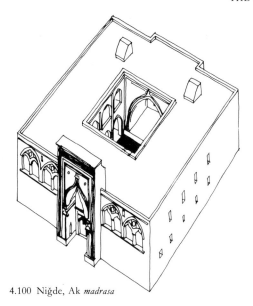

4.100 Niğde, Ak *madrasa*

ceived as public buildings inside and out, and as such – in contradistinction to the Egyptian examples – belong not with houses but with contemporary mosques, mausolea and caravanserais. It is possible to go further than this and to see in the layout of these *madrasa*s evidence

151 Sivas, Gök *madrasa*, main façade

and meet at right angles. High-quality stereotomy ensures that even when they are plain they retain an intrinsic monumentality. Occasionally, as in the Ak *madrasa* in Niğde (812/1409), an arcaded loggia extends across the principal façade on either side of the portal, opening up the entire elevation in very Gothic style. Bastions – square, semi-circular or three-quarters in the round – impart a military air to the building. In many cases this austerity is intensified by the lack of external windows. Above all, the portal, whether or not it is axially placed, is singled out for lavish ornament. It usually projects boldly, and above the *muqarnas* arch over the entrance may tower a pair of minarets. One minaret is readily explained by the simultaneous use of a *madrasa* as a mosque; but two of them have no liturgical justification and may be seen therefore as symbolic 'signs' of the building, an announcement from afar that it serves religious purposes. Hence, no doubt, the huge size of some of these minarets, which are far higher than an audible *adhan* requires (Taş *madrasa*, Akşehir). Hence too the presence of an external *mihrab* on some of these façades (e.g. Ahmediye *madrasa*, Erzurum). At the same time, these monumental exteriors, meant above all to be seen and to be appreciated in the round, underline the emancipation of the *madrasa* from its domestic origins. These are deliberately con-

152 Sivas, Gök *madrasa*, detail of portal sculpture

that Anatolian Saljuq architects were more alive than most of their contemporary colleagues to the scenic dimension of *madrasa* architecture. For this reason, it seems, they took pains to integrate subsidiary structures such as mausolea, fountains or minarets into the design rather than treat them as afterthoughts (Yakutiye *madrasa*, Erzurum; Köşk *madrasa*, Kayseri).

4.76
4.85–4.86

The discussion so far has by implication highlighted the originality of these Anatolian *madrasa*s. The dearth of contemporary comparative material from elsewhere forbids any very positive statement on this score. Even so, one may set against the occasional echo of Syrian *madrasa*s (e.g. in twin domed chambers flanking a portal, as in the Buruciye *madrasa*, Sivas, of 4.81 670/1271–2; or in the tripartite sanctuary of the 4.103, 4. Boyaliköy complex) or of Iranian buildings (e.g. the use of the two-minaret portal or of the four-*iwan* plan), a growing sense of confidence in forging a local style. Imported ideas are rapidly given Anatolian garb, as the fate of Persian elements shows. Minarets become stumpier and stockier than in Iran, with tiers of well-articulated balconies; in four-*iwan* plans, the *iwan*s are diminished and subordinated to the emphasis on continuous arcades surrounding the courtyard, 153 and a pronounced longitudinal axis – at odds with the centralising function of the four-*iwan* plan – makes itself felt. It should also be pointed out that the first four-rite *madrasa* to survive is in all probability not, as is often thought, the

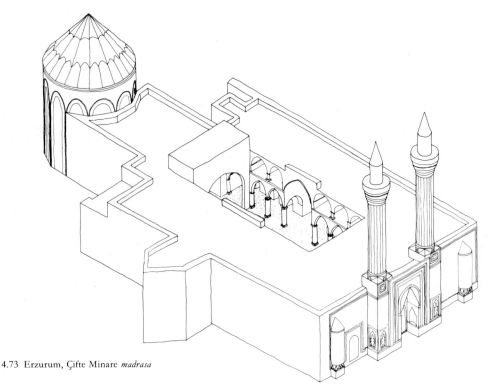

4.73 Erzurum, Çifte Minare *madrasa*

4.29 Mustansiriya in Baghdad but the Mas'udiye in
4.98 Diyarbakr, founded in 590/1194. Such a detail
symbolises the central importance of medieval
Anatolia to an understanding of *madrasa* architecture.

Ottoman *madrasas*

Ottoman *madrasas* inevitably look somewhat
tame when measured against the output of the
preceding centuries, replete as that was with
experiments, false starts and unexpected con-
fluences of building types normally independent
of each other. But what Ottoman *madrasas* lost
in unpredictability, they amply made up for in
symmetry and scale, characteristics hitherto un-
dervalued. Their plans are rational to the last
degree. On the whole, they reject the bastions
which punctuate the exterior walls of their
predecessors, preferring long, uncluttered
façades. This change is symptomatic of the
severity which was to replace the luxuriant
idiom of Saljuq and Beylik architectural
ornament. But it is more than a matter of stylistic preference. The typical Anatolian Saljuq and
even Beylik *madrasa* was a self-contained foundation, even if its *raison d'être* was as often
funerary as educational. Exceptions – such as
4.122 the octagonal Kapi Aghasi *madrasa* at Amasya,
154 dated 894/1489 – are not hard to find, but they
are distinctly recognisable as such. With the
advent of the Ottomans to supreme power, the
joint foundation – typically a mosque-cum-*madrasa*, but frequently a still larger complex –
becomes commonplace. Sometimes several *madrasas* cluster around a mosque. Moreover, such
an ensemble is conceived as an architectural
unity and often executed in a single building

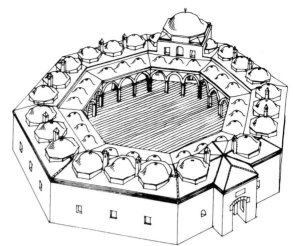

4.122 Amasya, Kapi Aghasi *madrasa*

campaign. No trace remains of the haphazard
agglomeration of individual entities which characterised earlier 'cities of God'.

These changes left their mark on the *madrasa*.
Its function as a place of prayer was now positively subordinated to its role as an educational
institution, and this change is swiftly mirrored
in its architecture. The *iwan* is demoted and by

153 Tokat, Gök *madrasa*, courtyard

154 Amasya, Kapi Aghasi *madrasa*, general view

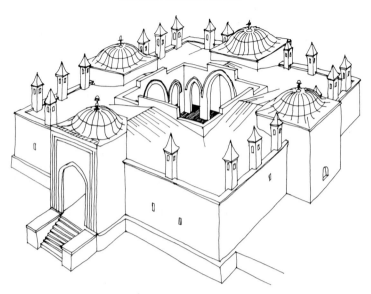

4.124 Merzifon, *madrasa* of Sultan Mehmed II

degrees removed. In its place appears the dominant dome chamber. The Çelebi Mehmet *madrasa*, Merzifon (817/1414), illustrates an intermediate stage of this process. Its compact, square layout focused on a central courtyard is ideally adopted to a cruciform *iwan* plan. But the *iwan*s no longer dominate the arrangement, for behind each of them rises a powerful, four-square domed unit. These chambers, which are of equal size – again the Ottoman urge towards a symmetrically arranged series of domical units makes itself felt – are the largest vaulted space in the building. Their axial location, and their powerful projection externally beyond the curtain walls, underscore their pivotal role. A typically Iranian plan is merging into an embryonically Ottoman one.

The closer relationship between mosque and *madrasa* in this period was to have still more far-reaching results. There was less need to provide ample facilities for prayer, so the *masjid* or sanctuary occupies a smaller proportion of the surface area. Innovations in mosque design are swiftly reflected in the planning of *madrasa*s, for example in the provision of a mediating cloister, each bay domed, between courtyard and cells. Above all, the *madrasa* was now readily conceived as a mosque writ small with proportions reversed. Thus the domed sanctuary

shrinks to a few metres square, although it is symbolically singled out by virtue of its isolation at the far end of the courtyard or even by its projection from the rest of the *madrasa*, as at the *madrasa* of Bayazid II at Edirne and, still earlier, the Murad I complex and the Muradiye and Yeşil *madrasa*s in Bursa. Instead, the courtyard enclosed by cells on three sides takes pride of place. The resultant U (or reversed U) shape soon became standard in the Ottoman *madrasa*. Often a large classroom occupies the centre of the arcade opposite the entrance.

Perhaps the most important change of emphasis in Ottoman *madrasa*s *vis-à-vis* their precedessors lies in the hugely increased numbers of student cells. Plans are blocked out in modular fashion so as to use all available space, including corners and angles (Bursa, complex of Bayazid Yildirim). Inconsistencies are ironed out, and the layouts express a sovereign clarity which evokes the drawing-board rather than the builder on the site. Perhaps as a result, space is used quite prodigally. The cells are now domed, despite their diminutive size, and thus yield all the monumentality and sense of space that they can. The same concern for space and light no doubt explains why they often have two windows apiece. The courtyard has not only a central pool or fountain but is also

216

planted with trees, possibly in an attempt to minimise the sense of regimentation which the plan exudes (*madrasa* of Bayazid II, Istanbul). In their size, their internal logic, their simple square or rectangular silhouettes, these Ottoman *madrasa*s bear the unmistakable imprint of imperial patronage. Their architects had no need to grapple with the intractable sites that had put earlier architects on their mettle. Even if the Ottomans did not have an innate preference for building on unencumbered sites, their gigantic ensembles were, as noted above, prodigal of space and postulated such sites. In their composition these multiple foundations display a growing confidence in the massed disposition of buildings so as to obtain the desired harmony and symmetry. The habit of designing in a vacuum, without constant reference to the particular site in question, would naturally have led to an objective reappraisal of the *madrasa* form. This return to first principles might help to account for the new emphasis on accommodation. At the same time, the rôle of the *madrasa* as one element among several in a composite foundation would probably inhibit an architect from devising any markedly original solution to its functional problems. In its appearance the *madrasa* had to conform to the neighbouring buildings. The larger the complex, the more necessary it would be to take short cuts. That Ottoman architects composed their large ensembles in somewhat modular fashion can scarcely be denied, and what the *madrasa* gained in integration it assuredly lost in individuality. Of the functional efficiency of Ottoman *madrasa*s there is no doubt; yet as a group they do not make a very rewarding study. The reason is not far to seek. By the early 16th century the guidelines for this kind of building had been established, and to ignore them or to do more than tinker with them does not seem to have occurred to Ottoman architects, unless indeed they were actively discouraged from doing so. Whatever the motive behind this lack of change, its effect can be seen in the way that form becomes fossilised. Forms developed in Istanbul were exported far and wide throughout the Ottoman dominions – including the Maghrib, as for example the *madrasa* of ʿUthman Pasha in Tripoli, Libya, 1064/1654. They undergo little change in the process. Sometimes a political or propagandist purpose can be ascribed to these foundations, as in the case of the four *madrasa*s built by Süleyman the Magnificent in Mecca.

The recognition that the form of the Ottoman *madrasa*s gradually stagnated should not blind one to their visual impact. It is a truism that an instinctive feeling for space permeates the buildings of the period, and *madrasa*s are no exception. This explains why they are so often sited so that they can be viewed from all sides, and why the domed *masjid* is set apart from the rest of the building by some device or other. It also explains why in so many *madrasa*s at least half the surface area is wasted – from the narrowly utilitarian point of view – by a vast empty courtyard, why the cells are placed only on the ground floor, and why domed cloisters lead from cells to courtyard. Clearly it was less important to cram the *madrasa* full of students than to ensure that those who lived there had room to breathe (Rüstem Pasha *madrasa*, Istanbul, 957/1550). Consequently, when an Ottoman sultan such as Mehmet Fatih wished to accommodate students on the grand scale, he built no less than sixteen *madrasa*s even though the total number of rooms was only 230. The resultant complex can fairly claim to be the first Turkish university. Architecturally speaking, the culmination of this trend may be seen in the Süleymaniye complex, whose eighteen buildings are conceived as a single entity and, perched on one of the city's highest hills, command a matchless view.

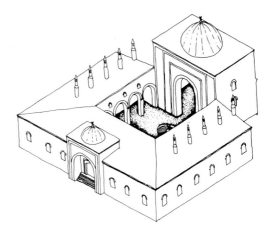

4.120 Bursa, Muradiye *madrasa*

217

SHARED FUNCTIONS OF MOSQUES AND
MADRASAS

The sheer size of these Ottoman *madrasa*s
departs decisively from the Arab tradition. It
finds its natural counterpart, however, in the
later *madrasa*s of the eastern Islamic world. Their
origins pose insoluble problems. In the early
part of this chapter the remarkable dearth of
Iranian *madrasa*s datable before *c.*751/1350 was
emphasised. The Madrasa-yi Imami of 725/1325
and later, discussed above, is one of the few
securely identified Iranian *madrasa*s of this
period to survive. Yet the literary evidence

126, 4.128

function of teaching was frequently discharged
within the mosque. This is not to say, of course,
that many of the Iranian mosques of this period
were *madrasa*s; and even those which might have
been centres of religious instruction could clearly
never have functioned as residential *madrasa*s
because their design did not include cells for that
purpose. Perhaps, then, it is a mistake to assume
that a *madrasa* must always connote a residential
as well as an educational function. Indeed, since
*madrasa*s were apparently built all over the
country in large numbers, the majority of them
might be expected to cater for local students

4.113 Istanbul, *madrasa* of Sultan Bayazid II

makes it clear, as noted earlier in this chapter,
that *madrasa*s were built by the hundred from the
10th century onward. Their absence from the
tally of surviving monuments is all the more
puzzling since representatives of nearly all the
other major building types have survived in
abundance, and since *madrasa*s are plentiful
among the standing monuments of Syria and
Anatolia from the 12th century onwards. This
situation suggests that Iranian *madrasa*s may
indeed have survived – but not under that name.
It is well known that throughout the medieval
period and throughout the Islamic world the

who would not require accommodation within
the building. Only the largest and most prestigious institutions, whose reputation would
attract students from far afield – like the
Nizamiya or the Mustansiriya – would need to
make ample provision for students in residence.

The difficulty, of course, lies in identifying
such 'hidden' *madrasa*s. Inscriptions might
provide the requisite clues; in fact Sauvaget
interpreted the Ardistan *jami'* as a *madrasa* on the
strength of a Qur'anic inscription in the *qibla
iwan* mentioning the ways (*madhahib*) of reaching
God. But this is to go too fast. Rather would it

4.19, 4.29

2.259

be justifiable to infer from that inscription that at least the *qibla iwan* of this mosque may have been used for teaching purposes in the Saljuq period. Such Iranian mosques as have rooms of various kinds on the first floor might be regarded as *prima facie* candidates for residential *madrasa* status in addition to their primary role as communal places of worship; but unfortunately, published plans are almost without exception confined to the ground floor and give no hint as to the disposition of the upper level. The lack of formality which characterised medieval Islamic teaching methods enabled virtually any mosque to perform the teaching and religious functions of a *madrasa*; special lecture rooms were not required. This close functional correspondence between mosque and *madrasa* clearly favoured composite foundations, or at any rate the use of one building for several distinct purposes. Such a concept was of course widespread in other categories of Islamic architecture, and it is one of the leitmotifs of this book. Only when the residential accommodation of students and staff was a prerequisite of the foundation could a mosque of reduced dimensions be unsuitable to serve as a *madrasa*. Mosques with suites of rooms on the first floor, on the other hand, were probably designed to serve simultaneously as residential *madrasa*s. A useful rule of thumb would therefore be that an upper storey of arcades around the courtyard of a medieval Iranian mosque might well connote a composite mosque-*madrasa* foundation – if, that is, those arcades have rooms behind them. Unfortunately no clear epigraphic evidence of this supposed practice has come to light. Nevertheless no better explanation – indeed, no serious explanation – for the presence of first-floor rooms in Iranian mosques seems to have been adduced so far.

THE KHANQAH

Enough has been said to highlight the difficulties of matching the physical and literary evidence about the early history of the *madrasa* in the Iranian world. Before the history of the institution in Iran is investigated in more detail, it will be useful – as a reminder that *madrasa* functions were discharged in buildings that did not bear that name – to review rapidly the history of the *khanqah*, which could be described

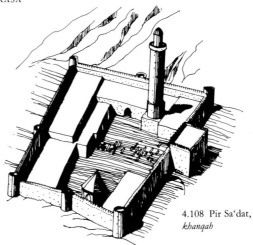

4.108 Pir Saʿdat, *khanqah*

as the sister institution of the *madrasa*. It is merely one of various building types which by virtue both of their function and of their form can be related to the *madrasa*. The term normally denotes a building which houses members of a Muslim mystical order. It implies an institution rather than a particular kind of building. It is a recurrent theme of this book that Islamic architectural terminology is notoriously vague, so it is only to be expected that several other words are used (often impartially) by medieval authors as synonyms for *khanqah*: in the Maghrib, *zawiya*; in Ottoman lands, *tekke* or *dargah*; in Iran, *duwaira*, in India, *jamaʿat khana*; and, quite generally, *ribat*. Sometimes two of these terms are used together in the name of such buildings, such as the *ribat* and *khanqah* of the Eshab-i 4.109 Keyf, Marash (612/1215–6) or the *zawiya* and 4.110 *khanqah* of Sünbül Baba, Tokat (691/1291–2).

The *khanqah* apparently originated in the eastern Iranian world during the 10th century. Its early development was closely associated with the Karramiya sect and through them with Manichaeism. It was Sufism, however, which was permanently to dominate the institution. In its simplest form the *khanqah* was a house where a group of pupils and initiates gathered around a master (*shaikh*), and it had facilities for assembly, prayer and communal living. Though these dervishes often voluntarily observed a specified code of conduct stressing charity and devotion, their *shaikh* was no Muslim equivalent of a medieval Western abbot, nor could the *khanqah* accurately be compared to a monastery or convent – thus *khanqah*s for celibates were exceptional. A common pattern was for dervishes to live in a *khanqah* over the winter months before setting out on their travels again in the spring. Most *khanqah*s would provide free board and lodging for travellers; in some the teaching function bulked large.

The institution flourished under Saljuq rule in the 11th and 12th centuries and benefitted especially from the close association between Sufism, Ash'ari *kalam* and the Shafi'i *madhhab* favoured by the ruling class. *Amir*s, governors and sultans vied with each other to erect *khanqah*s throughout Iraq, Syria, Palestine and then Egypt from the 12th century onwards; in the 1180s Ibn Jubair describes the Syrian *khanqah*s as 'ornamented palaces [. . . since . . .] Sufis are really the kings in these parts'. Similarly, according to Ibn Khallikan, the *amir* Gökböri built at Irbil around 596/1200 'two *khanqah*s for Sufis which housed a large number both of residents and visitors', especially on days when festivals and concerts were held; 'both well endowed to provide all that was needed by those staying there, each of whom had to accept his expenses when he departed'. Egypt's first *khanqah*, made *waqf* in 568/1173, was the Dar Sa'id al-Su'ada, formerly the house of a Fatimid palace eunuch. In Mamluk Egypt, according to Ibn Khaldun, *khanqah*s allowed indigent Sufis 'to follow the rules for acquiring orthodox Sufi ways of behaviour through *dhikr* exercises and supererogatory prayers'; and, when well endowed, 'could furnish livings for poor jurists and Sufis'. The directorships of such *khanqah*s were lucrative posts and were in the gift of the sultans themselves. Elsewhere it was the brethren who often elected the head of the community. Sometimes the office became hereditary, thereby ensuring the continuity of a particular type of teaching or communal life. By degrees a hierarchy of novices, initiates and masters, reminiscent of other corporate bodies like the *sinf* and *futuwwa* organisations, began to operate in *khanqah*s.

After the Mongol invasions (from 616/1219 onwards) the institution spread rapidly – again with official support – to western Anatolia and even to India. The natural Indian propensity to worship a holy man made the *khanqah*, focused on the personality of its *shaikh*, a perfect vehicle for spreading the faith. Particular emphasis was laid on the practice of ascetic exercises, the provision of Sufi training and the ready dispensing of hospitality to travellers. The Chishti and Suhrawardi *tariqa*s dominated this movement, which gradually spread throughout Muslim India and remains vigorous to this day. Further westwards, the later medieval period witnessed a tendency to incorporate a *khanqah* within a much larger complex of buildings – e.g. at Natanz in Iran and several Cairene foundations – and to attach *khanqah*s to the tombs of holy men. Thus centres of pilgrimage developed in which the *khanqah* operated in some sense as a welfare institution (Pir Sa'dat *khanqah* near Baku).

Relatively few medieval *khanqah*s survive; Cairo, with seven dating from the 14th-15th centuries, offers easily the largest number in any one place. Here the *khanqah* of Faraj b. Barquq (803–13/1400–10) with its enormous domes is perhaps the outstanding structure, though that of Baibars al-Jashankir (707–10/1307–10) could apparently house four hundred people. In Syria the most significant survival is the Khanqah fi'l-Farafra at Aleppo (634/1237), a two-storey building with elaborate portal, *iwan* and domed sanctuary, while in Iran the spectacularly tiled portal of an otherwise vanished *khanqah* at Natanz dates to 717/1317. In Central Asia the *khanqah*s of Faizabad near Bukhara (988/1580) and Nadir Divan Beg in Bukhara (1031/1622) comprise a large domed chamber preceded by an *iwan*; their annexes have vanished. Insofar as a standard layout existed, its essentials were a central courtyard flanked by cloisters on to which rows of individual cells opened, with a large hall on the *qibla* side serving for communal assembly and prayer. Further annexes such as mosque, kitchen or *hammam* were optional. In these respects the *khanqah* scarcely differed from the *madrasa*.

IRAQI MADRASAS

The Mustansiriya madrasa, Baghdad

One building from an area hitherto neglected – Iraq – deserves extended discussion at this stage. Already in the late 12th century Ibn Jubair had recorded some thirty *madrasa*s in Baghdad alone, all of them in the eastern sector of the city. They were all eclipsed by the Mustansiriya *madrasa*, also in Baghdad, widely regarded in its own time

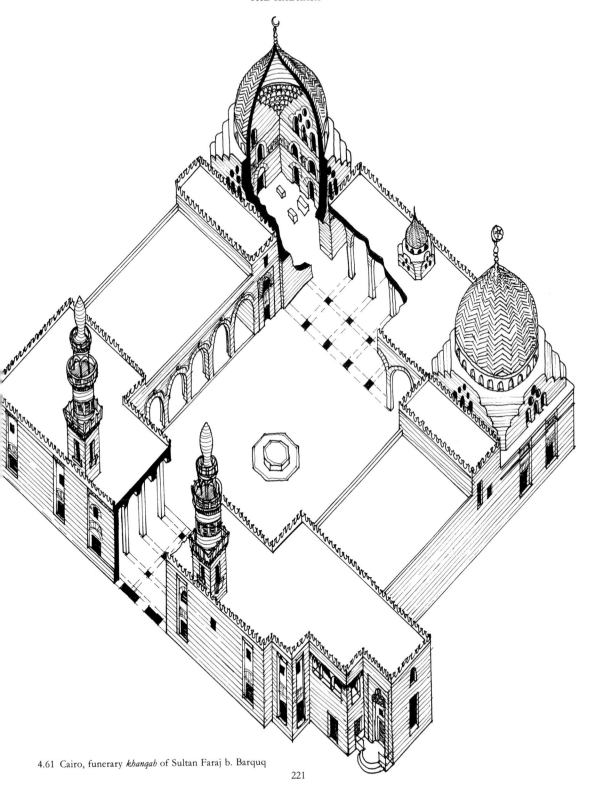

4.61 Cairo, funerary *khanqah* of Sultan Faraj b. Barquq

4.19, 4.29
155 and subsequently as the exemplar of the genre and its fullest, finest expression. Its endowments (*auqaf*), too, exceeded those of other *madrasa*s, being valued at nearly two million gold *dinar*s, and yielding an annual income of 70,000 *dinar*s. The cost of the building itself was 700,000 *dinar*s. To a later age it is the obvious symbol of the rejuvenated late 'Abbasid caliphate and several factors suggest that this symbolism was

claim for all to see. In size alone the building was unprecedented: an oblong of *c.* 105 m. by 44 m. by 49 m. The solemn festivities of its inauguration in 630/1233, after six years of construction, set the seal on its pre-eminent status among the *madrasa*s of the Islamic world. Architecturally speaking, the monument is a triumph of technique. It is built according to a complex system of proportional relationships and modular units.

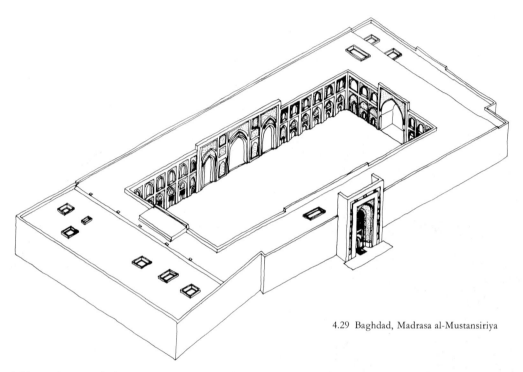

4.29 Baghdad, Madrasa al-Mustansiriya

deliberately intended at the time. The *madrasa* was built in Baghdad, which for six centuries had been the spiritual and intermittently the political centre of the Islamic world. It proclaimed the essential unity of orthodox Islam. Its patron was the caliph himself, who lent his name to the building. It was one of the first *madrasa*s specifically designed to serve each of the four major *madhhab*s, and also contained facilities for the two fundamental ancillary disciplines taught in a *dar al-hadith* and a *dar al-qur'an*. Each *madhhab* had its own place of worship. Thus the building explicitly claimed universal status. The long band of foundation text, inscribed in letters a foot high that unfold in defiance of Islamic custom across its exterior façade, advertises this

Both the ground plan – a modified four-*iwan* layout – and the elevation were based on a grid of ten and thirty Byzantine feet respectively. Thus the unit of measurement (one Byzantine foot = 31.23 cm.) used for Haghia Sophia was still employed seven centuries later in the heart of the Islamic world, an astonishing tribute to the tenacity of Hellenistic influence in Muslim science. The consummate harmony which permeates the monument, and the stately rhythms of the courtyard façades, are therefore based on intricate mathematical calculation. The use of the framed pointed arch as the modular unit for the courtyard façades is visually the most obvious expression of this symmetry. In addition to providing accommodation on two

floors for a large staff and for some three hundred students, the *madrasa* included a celebrated library (as did several Saljuq *madrasa*s in Merv), a kitchen, a *hammam* and a hospital.

Later Iraqi *madrasa*s

The original layout of the Mustansiriya was increasingly obscured in later centuries by numerous modifications, but the study of a closely related local building has clarified most of these problems. The building in question, the so-called "Abbasid palace", is in all probability 4.32–4.33 the Bishiriya *madrasa* of 1255 and seems – to judge by the manifold improvements of detail which it incorporates – to be the work of the same architect as was responsible for the Mustansiriya. The fragmentary state of this later building is all the more regrettable in view of the ambitious scale of what survives, notably a succession of inordinately lofty, narrow, vaulted corridors with elegant built-in ventilation systems. Chief among them is without doubt the spectacular *mabain* – the passage between the courtyard and the cells of the students – a *tour de force* of structural daring and virtuoso decoration. Seldom was the *muqarnas* put to more dramatic use than in this lofty but narrow passage-way, and it transforms a potentially claustrophobic corridor into a spatial unit of illusionistically well-nigh infinite height. Thus the

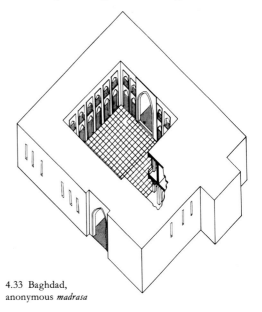

4.33 Baghdad, anonymous *madrasa*

155 Baghdad, Mustansiriya *madrasa*, corridor

223

156 Baghdad, Mirjaniya *madrasa*, courtyard looking north

very disadvantages of this unpromising, gloomy shaft of dead space are triumphantly turned to account. Each of the steeply stilted cells in this aspiring and dynamic creation is lovingly carved with terracotta arabesques of the utmost delicacy. If a mere service space like this

corridor could be so thoroughly metamorphosed into a feast for the eye, it is indeed a pity that so much of the building should have been lost. The corridors of this *madrasa* represent the apogee of late 'Abbasid architecture, both in their advanced and original vaulting technique and in the finesse of their inlaid geometrical terracotta *134* ornament.

It is not surprising that the local impact of the Mustansiriya should have made itself felt very quickly. Indeed, one of the most undeservedly neglected bodies of Islamic architecture is that of the late 'Abbasid school in Iraq in the 13th century, whose vitality survived unimpaired the catastrophe of 656/1258, when the Mongols sacked Baghdad and snuffed out the caliphate. The *khan* and *madrasa* of Mirjan, dated 760/1359 and 758/1357 respectively, are alike of remarkable quality. The latter is especially remarkable for its *133, 156* splendid portal signed by one Ahmad Shah, styled "Golden Pen" (whose activity is also

157 Baghdad, Mirjaniya *madrasa*, prayer hall

158 Yazd, Shamsiya *madrasa*, inscription

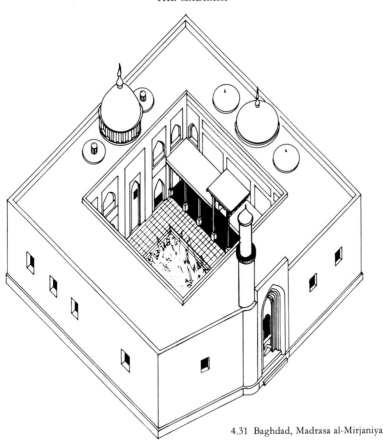

4.31 Baghdad, Madrasa al-Mirjaniya

recorded in metalwork and Qur'anic produc-
123 tion) and for its triple-domed sanctuary. This
5, 4.31 last feature has strong Syrian connections, as
0, 4.30 shown by the Firdaus *madrasa* in Aleppo.

THE IRANIAN MADRASA FROM ILKHANID TO SAFAVID TIMES

14th-century madrasas

The variety of forms attested by the few surviving Ilkhanid *madrasa*s suggests that no one type
predominated in this period. To judge by
Timurid and Safavid buildings, it was the Mad-
4.128 rasa-yi Imami (already discussed) and the custom-built *madrasa* added to the Friday Mosque
4.133 of Isfahan from 768/1366–7 that best expressed
the officially approved layout of such buildings.
The latter is a two-*iwan* courtyard structure
stressing the north-south axis and cramming the
student cells into the two-storeyed lateral wings
of the monument. The main feature of interest
here is a prayer hall set at right angles to the *iwan*

and roofed with a series of transverse vaults.
The *madrasa* of Diya' al-Din in Yazd, otherwise 4.129
known as the Zindan-i Iskandar and datable to
the 14th century, is of substantially lower quality
than the two Isfahani *madrasa*s; indeed, it is
constructed of mud brick. Despite subsequent
modifications, enough survives of the original
layout to suggest that the *iwan*s on two adjoining
sides of the courtyard were complemented by
another pair opposite. Apart from this there is
little observable regularity in the plan: rooms are
indiscriminately oblong or square, broad or
narrow, multi-recessed or with unbroken walls,
and are bundled together with outright careless-
ness. Within a roughly square overall layout,
pride of place is accorded to the huge domed
square mausoleum which takes up most of the
space between the north and west *iwan*s. Here is
the proof that the Anatolian and Syro-Egyptian
type of *madrasa*, with the founder's mausoleum
attached, also flourished in Iran.

the building. Thus there is an unimpeded spatial flow around the courtyard, in the manner of an ambulatory. No parallel for this plan presents itself. Some of the oblong constituent spaces of this ambulatory presumably served for teaching, but the building was clearly a composite foundation, possibly a *khanqah-cum-madrasa*. Both these Yazdi buildings had an upper storey which presumably contained the cells for students.

159 Khargird, Madrasa-yi Ghiyathiya: lecture hall, vaulting

Timurid and Shaibanid madrasas

The Timurid period was unquestionably the golden age of the Iranian *madrasa*. Khurasan and Transoxiana were the forcing-ground for new developments, though competently-designed *madrasa*s were also built in southern Iran, and features from that area are sometimes incorporated into the monuments of the north-east, like the *badgir* at Khargird. The four-*iwan* type predominated and was executed on a scale consistently more spacious than had earlier been the norm anywhere in Islam. This ambitious scale often generated comparably ambitious decoration; the finer *madrasa*s of the period yield nothing in the quality of their ornament to contemporary mosques, and occasionally even strike out in new directions, as in the murals with trees, streams and birds in the *madrasa* of Tuman Agha at Kuhsan (844/1440–1). Such was the prestige acquired by this kind of *madrasa* that it became the model for nearly all the notable *madrasa*s erected in the Iranian world in subsequent centuries. Numerous *madrasa*s in Safavid Isfahan, Shaibanid Bukhara and even Mughal India illustrate this dictum. For that reason such later *madrasa*s will receive very short shrift in this account. Of course variations abound, but the crucial innovation lies in the new-found sense of scale.

159

160

158   The Shamsiya *madrasa* of *c*.766/1365, also in Yazd – indeed, the literary sources record the names of about a score of 14th-century *madrasa*s built in that city – is an incomparably more *soigné*
4.131 variation on the same theme. Here the design is tauter and fully integrated, each half a mirror reflection of the other. The portal *iwan* announces the major axis which continues without interruption until it terminates in the square mausoleum which adjoins the *madrasa* proper but projects well beyond it. Long lateral halls flank the portal *iwan* in a foretaste of Timurid
4.136, 5.120 buildings at Khargird and Gazur Gah. The south *iwan* has lateral doorways giving access to a similar but shorter hall on each side. Broad lateral rooms connect the halls at either end of

This deliberate use of large size had long been known in Iranian mosques, but it was not an obvious corollary of the *madrasa* form. The case of the Ghiyathiya *madrasa* at Khargird (completed in 846/1442) shows how sensitively these large spaces were manipulated. Its square courtyard is related to the shorter and longer perimeter walls in a ratio of 2:3:4. Recent research suggests that such proportional relationships, which extend also to elevations, underlie other Timurid buildings and were far more commonly

4.136

160 Turbat-i Jam, shrine complex, courtyard

used than was previously suspected. Their effect is to humanise the otherwise daunting scale of these large buildings with screen-like façades.

It was in the Timurid period, then, that the consonance between mosque and *madrasa* became so marked that there is little to distinguish them, so far as external and internal façades are concerned. What goes on behind the façades, however, is very different in the two cases. Within the general format of the four-*iwan* plan there was ample room for experiment in the placing of mosques, mausolea, lecture halls and residential accommodation – to mention only the constants of *madrasa* design in this period. The Ghiyathiya *madrasa* at Khargird is a model of how these various functions could interlock with the utmost smoothness: sixteen rooms are distributed in pairs flanking each *iwan* and on two floors, and all the other functional spaces of the building occupy the main axes, corners and entrance complex. A side-effect of the greatly expanded size of these foundations was that room could now be found for a wide range of ancillary units, such as libraries and *khanqah*s for

example, and for differentiated summer and winter chambers. Small domed lecture halls, often disposed as a pair flanking an *iwan*, were popular. The area between the courtyard and the principal façade – that is, the entrance complex – was now developed with great ingenuity, and quickly became a self-contained entity within the *madrasa* proper. Sometimes – as at Ghujduvan, Khargird and in the Ulugh Beg *madrasa* at Bukhara – it contained a mosque, and often a lecture-hall as well. Sometimes both units were mosques (as at Turbat-i Jam) or lecture halls. In other *madrasa*s, such as that of Ulugh Beg at Samarqand, dated 820–3/1417–20, the mosque extended the full length of the *qibla* side opposite the portal *iwan*. By contrast, a trio of *madrasa*s in the Mashhad shrine (Du Dar, Parizad and Bala Sar) have the mosque situated in one of the courtyard *iwan*s – indeed, the Du Dar *madrasa* even has a second mosque in a corner of the building. There was no general rule governing the siting of the mausoleum in these royal Timurid *madrasa*s, but the examples of the Gauhar Shad and Sultan Husain Baiqara

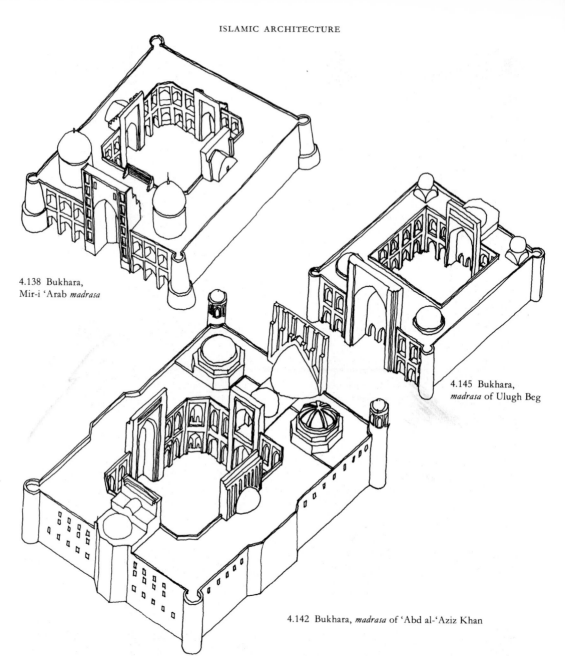

4.138 Bukhara,
Mir-i 'Arab *madrasa*

4.145 Bukhara,
madrasa of Ulugh Beg

4.142 Bukhara, *madrasa* of 'Abd al-'Aziz Khan

*madrasa*s in Herat, and that of Firuzshah at Turbat-i Jam, show that they could be the single dominant feature of the entire complex. Indeed, the fashion of the time firmly favoured the incorporation of mausolea into *madrasa*s, and free-standing mausolea of high quality are exceptional. As a curiosity the siting of a diminutive *madrasa* in the entrance complex of the Ziyarat-gah *jami'* is noteworthy. In smaller *madrasa*s,

such as those of Mashhad, the incorporation of mosques and mausolea seriously over-balanced the ensemble and cut down the space available for student cells. But these cases are somewhat unusual, since the architects had to make do with a site which was already heavily built up and therefore had to sacrifice symmetry to expediency.

The new emphasis on scale implied almost by

4.148

2.294–2.295

4.143, 4

161 Bukhara, *madrasa* of 'Abd al-'Aziz Khan, vaulting

definition a corresponding emphasis on external façades. Minarets are used to mark the corners, e.g. the Ulugh Beg *madrasa* at Samarqand and numerous later examples such as the Mir-i 'Arab *madrasa* at Bukhara, 942/1535–6. The portal is now apt to be recessed and thus streamlined with the curtain walls of the façade rather than projecting from it. The subsidiary lateral and

4.134–4.135

4.137–4.138

162–163

168–169

Bakr complex (967–70/1560–3) outside that city. Sometimes *madrasas* were paired, facing each other across a street – as in a series of *madrasas* in Bukhara, namely those of 'Abdallah Khan (996–8/1588–90) and Madar-i Khan (974/1567), or of Ulugh Beg (820/1417) and 'Abd al-'Aziz Khan (1062/1652).

5.116–5

4.139–4

4.139

4.144–4

4.141–4

As in contemporary Ottoman *madrasas*, the

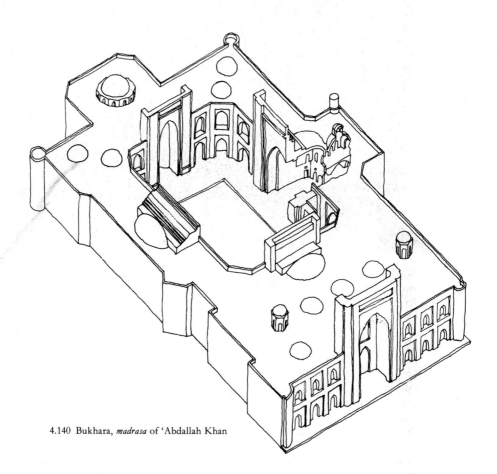

4.140 Bukhara, *madrasa* of 'Abdallah Khan

rear façades are now accorded applied ornament, such as geometric patterns in a combination of glazed and unglazed bricks, or positively articulated by recessed panels and niches. This sensitivity to the setting of the monument made it natural to group such buildings together, notably in the Rigistan at Samarqand (Ulugh Beg, Shir Dar and Tila Kari *madrasas*), the Lab-i Hauz complex at Bukhara or the Char

165

4.134–4.135

increased scale of the structure led to certain simplifications of design. Unbroken exterior walls were one aspect of this; another was the preference for aligning the entrance portal to the *qibla* and thereby ensuring unbroken axial progression. Still another result was the more rational, symmetrical deployment of student cells. The *madrasas* facing the Rigistan illustrate this very clearly, and in addition show how the

127

4.134–4

1 Cairo, *mashhad* of al-Juyushi, detail of stucco *mihrab*

2 Shibam, Yemen, Great Mosque, aerial view

3 Cairo, mosque of al-Aqmar, apigraphic roundel

4 Hisn Kaifa, Turkey, mausoleum of Zainab

5 Antalya, Turkey, Yivli Minare

6 Aleppo, *jami'* and *madrasa* of al-Firdaus, *mihrab*

7 Diyarbakr, Turkey, Great Mosque, courtyard façade

8 Ta'izz, Yemen, Ashrafiya mosque, painted dome

9 Jerusalem, Aqsa Mosque, spandrel with Fatimid mosaics

10 Konya, Qaratai *madrasa*, inscription in tile mosaic

11 Dunaysir, Turkey, Great Mosque, entrance to prayer hall

162 Samarqand, Rigistan, *madrasa* of Ulugh Beg, façade

231

166 typical student cell (*hujra*) was preceded by a diminutive vestibule. Two students occupied each cell; the Ulugh Beg *madrasa* has twenty-eight such cells in the lower storey alone. A new *160* readiness to block out the design in large components seems to be an expression of the same trend. In many *madrasa*s it results in the four

corners assuming a very different configuration of rooms from that which prevails on either side of the four axial *iwan*s. A typical arrangement comprises a series of four intercommunicating cells opening off a narrow corridor leading directly from the bevelled corner of the courtyard to the external minaret (Kukeltash and

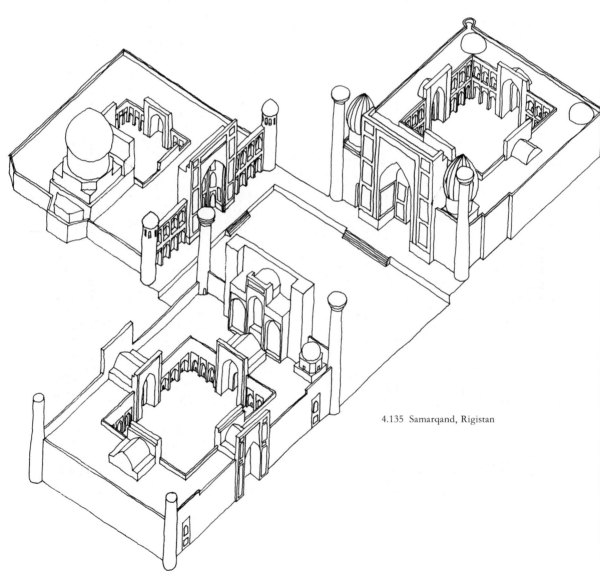

4.135 Samarqand, Rigistan

163 Samarqand, Rigistan, *madrasa* of Ulugh Beg, portal

164 ·Samarqand, Rigistan, *madrasa* of Ulugh Beg, corridor

4.137–4.138 Mir-i ʿArab *madrasa*s, Bukhara). A similar emphasis on the diagonals characterises Safavid caravansarais, yet another reminder of the perennial interchangeability of building types in Iranian architecture.

As in Ottoman times, again, there was a tendency for these very large *madrasa*s, all endowed by royal patrons or high officials of state, to cluster together in the major cities. Thus the original plan conceived by Nizam al-Mulk, whereby *madrasa*s would be built in large

numbers but distributed evenly over a wide geographical area, was reversed. In Iran proper, Qumm, Mashhad and Isfahan account for nearly all the significant post-Ilkhanid *madrasa*s, while similar concentrations may be observed in Sam- 124–1 arqand, Bukhara, Herat and Khiva. The latter 161– city, with its quartet of highly traditional *madrasa*s erected between 1225/1810 and 1328/ 1910 (Pahlawan Mahmud, Allah Quli Khan, Amin Khan and Islam Khwaja) shows how fossilised the Timurid manner had become.

Safavid *madrasa*s

A more appropriate envoi to the Iranian *madrasa*, however, is provided by the buildings of Safavid Isfahan. Several *madrasa*s of medium size were erected there in the course of the 17th century, such as the Madrasa-yi Jadda Kuchik, built in 1058/1648 by the grandmother of Shah ʿAbbas II and with accommodation for sixty-seven students, the Madrasa-yi Sadr, and those of Mullah ʿAbdallah (1088/1677) and Kasangaran (1104/1693). But these are only of secondary interest when set beside the two *madrasa*s which flank the great dome chamber of the Masjid-i Shah, let alone the great Madrasa-yi 2.281–2 Madar-i Shah (1118–26/1706–15). The two 4.149–4 *madrasa*s in the Masjid-i Shah are longitudinally conceived and with their miniature garden courtyards make a delightfully *bijou* impression. They dispense with *iwan*s and with prayer chambers, presumably because both features were readily at hand in the mosque proper. Instead, they exploit the available space to the full for student cells. The Madrasa-yi Madar-i Shah, sited in an originally idyllic environment

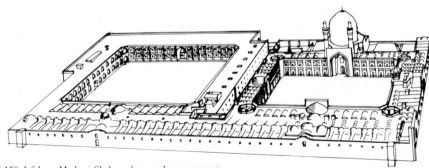

4.150 Isfahan, Madar-i Shah *madrasa* and caravansarai

234

fronting the Chahar Bagh, injects a new dynamism into the traditional four-*iwan* layout by means of a large extra dome chamber in each of the diagonals (possibly to serve as lecture rooms in winter) in addition to those behind the *iwan*s on the major axes. The cells, too, are unusual in their tripartite division: a vestibule and a terminal recess bracket the cell itself. The main prayer chamber here is not easily distingu-ishable from that of the Masjid-i Shah, and the continued intermingling of the two forms in Iran is attested by several joint foundations in Qajar times.

MAGHRIBI MADRASAS: GENERAL BACKGROUND

Although dependence on Andalusia is a constant of Maghribi architecture, little trace of

165 Samarqand, Rigistan, Shir Dar *madrasa*, niche

166 Samarqand, Rigistan, Shir Dar *madrasa*, courtyard

Spanish influence can be detected in the ground plans of the local *madrasa*s. Indeed, since the *madrasa* movement was primarily an eastern Iranian one which by degrees moved westwards, it would be only logical to assume that in this particular genre of building it was atypically the Maghrib that influenced Andalusia. The only surviving physical evidence of the Andalusian *madrasa* would confirm this supposition, if indeed the building in question is a *madrasa* – an identification denied by Makdisi. This is the structure built in Granada by the Nasrid monarch Yusuf I in 750/1349, namely in the golden age of the Marinid *madrasa*. Though largely demolished in the 18th century, the prayer hall was excavated and restored from 1893 onwards; it has nothing to differentiate it from its Marinid contemporaries in Morocco. Of the *madrasa*s built by the Almohad ruler Ya'qub al-Mansur (580–95/1184–99), in Spain as elsewhere in his dominions nothing survives, nor is there any record of further Nasrid *madrasa*s, so the question of reciprocal influences between Andalusia and the Maghrib in this genre cannot be regarded as finally settled. Valuable as this literary evidence is, its very paucity is instructive, for it suggests the virtual absence of one of the major Islamic building types in Muslim Spain. Yet that area was unquestionably the foremost centre of Islamic art west of Egypt. In fact this dearth can easily be explained. By the time that the *madrasa* had established itself in the eastern Islamic world, the great days of the Cordoban caliphate were long over, and the fate of Muslim Spain sealed. The cities of the north, Toledo, and even Cordoba itself had been lost. With the splendid exception of the Alhambra, significantly a secular rather than a religious monument, little architecture of note was erected in the Iberian peninsula in the last three centuries of the Muslim presence there.

Although, as already noted, the *madrasa* genre is first recorded in the eastern Islamic world in the late 9th century, it was not for another hundred and fifty years and more that the full weight of official backing had resulted in *madrasa*s being erected in most major towns of the area. Theoretically the fashion could have spread to the Maghrib around that time. Yet it is doubtful whether the Almoravids had at their

167 Samarqand, Rigistan, Tila Kari *madrasa*, side view

disposal the necessary administrative expertise to launch and execute a programme comparable to that of Nizam al-Mulk. It seems that the Maghrib in any case produced only a tithe of the buildings erected in Iran during the same period, and .in the context of such limited building campaigns *madrasa*s would obviously have claimed less priority than mosques. Moreover, the Almoravids – as their name itself indicates – were noted primarily for building *ribat*s. Not only is there no mention of their building *madrasa*s; it seems, rather, that it was precisely in these *ribat*s that some of the teaching functions later performed by the *madrasa* were carried out. The consonance of plan between the two institutions leaps to the eye. Moreover, the early and marked association of the *madrasa* with the Shafi'i *madhhab*, and to an only slighter lesser extent with the Hanafi and Hanbali *madhhab*s, would perhaps not immediately have struck a chord in the predominantly Maliki Maghrib. Ironically enough, the first recorded *madrasa* (in late 9th-century Nishapur) is in fact Maliki, but in subsequent centuries that *madhhab* noticeably lagged behind the others in the number of *madrasa*s allotted to it. It is perhaps relevant that the religious message preached by Ibn Tumart,

168 Bukhara, *madrasa* of 'Abdallah Khan, portal

169 Bukhara, Mir-i 'Arab *madrasa*, portal

the ideological founder of the Almohad dynasty, was disseminated in mosques rather than in special educational institutions. Hostile as he was to the prevailing orthodoxy, it is not surprising that he did not use the *madrasa* as an instrument for his preaching, since that institution was itself the very emblem of orthodoxy by his time. Finally, one may perhaps pray in aid the well-nigh notorious conservatism of Maghribi society as a reason for the late spread of the *madrasa* movement to this area.

Thus the fashion for building *madrasa*s probably reached the Maghrib late – too late, for example, to make an impact on Andalusia. The references to the late 12th-century *madrasa*s built by the Almohad ruler al-Mansur are somewhat unspecific – indeed the statement of Ibn Sa'id that there was no *madrasa* in 13th-century Spain partially contradicts them – and the first securely dated *madrasa* in the Maghrib, the Shammaya, was built in Tunis by the Hafsid Abu Zakariya

in 647/1249. Within a decade it was followed by the Ma'ridiya *madrasa* built by his widow. Neither has survived and thus the Saffarin *madrasa* in Fez, founded by the Marinid sultan Abu Yusuf in 670/1271, is the earliest Maghribi example to survive. Its location may be seen as prophetic, since for some reason the institution of the *madrasa* took deepest root in Morocco, and specifically in Fez, where most of the round dozen Maghribi *madrasa*s predating 1700 are situated. Moreover, the majority of these *madrasa*s are the work of the sultans of the Marinid dynasty and were erected between 670/1271 and 757/1356. Several Algerian *madrasa*s belong to the same group. This sudden efflorescence of a building type which had hitherto been virtually unknown in the area demands some explanation. Perhaps the answer lies in the fact that the Marinids, unlike their more illustrious predecessors the Almoravids and Almohads, were not swept to power by a wave of religious

4.151

4.153, 4.158

239

fervour. Their uncomfortable consciousness of this deficiency may have led them to make restitution of a kind by providing the patronage for religious buildings. *Madrasa*s fitted the bill admirably. They were much less expensive than mosques, a very relevant factor since the Marinid empire was much smaller than that of their predecessors. Marinid mosques would have suffered by comparison with those of the Almohads; Marinid *madrasa*s, being effectively a new genre, were safer from such unwelcome comparisons. Moreover, they underlined the orthodoxy of their patrons and thus provided a counterweight not only to Shi'ism and to the Almohad movement but also to Sufism, a movement whose popularity was then making spectacular advances. Indeed, a crucial epigraphic document indicates that the Marinid sultans were actuated by motives which had much in common with those of Nizam al-Mulk over two centuries earlier. The Saffarin *madrasa* in Fez (670/1271) mentions in its foundation inscription the need to resurrect the forgotten religious sciences, a clear attack on Almohad heterodoxy:

4.151

> 'Praise be to God, Master of the Two Worlds! Who exalts the status of men of learning, Who recompenses with a generous hand those who devote themselves to acts of piety; Who by means of *madrasa*s revives the vanished traces of *fiqh* and of religion, using as His instrument those of His good servants whom He has specially singled out for His guidance and ennobled by His solicitude and by His care . . . '.

Finally, the desire to make Fez an intellectual centre – the sultans Abu'l-Hasan and Abu 'Inan both prided themselves on being men of learning – may help to explain not only the concentration of *madrasa*s in that city during the Marinid period, but also the endowment of several *madrasa*s with fine libraries in the 13th and 14th centuries (Saffarin, Fez; Bu 'Inaniya, Fez).

4.151, 4.160–4.161

These *madrasa*s all obey a well-defined schema. Their dimensions are smaller than those of any other groups of *madrasa*s elsewhere in the Islamic world, reducing from 35 m. × 36 m. to 14 m. × 14.5 m. Perhaps their exclusive use by a single *madhhab* made larger buildings unnecessary. Around a central courtyard are grouped on the ground floor a mosque, galleries facing each other along the lateral axis, and an entrance vestibule which is frequently open on to the courtyard along its entire length. Unlike the universal practice elsewhere in the Islamic world, the courtyard façades of these various halls are not marked by colonnades or *iwan*s but are fenced off by an unbroken surface of wooden panels. On the first floor, a narrow gallery overlooking the courtyard gives on to the cells in which the students lived; sometimes in the earlier *madrasa*s these cells are also ranged behind the galleries on the ground floor.

174

170

No *madrasa*s with facilities for all four *madhhab*s incorporated into their ground plans are known in the Maghrib. As already noted, one legal school – the Maliki – maintained a virtually unchallenged dominion over the Maghrib throughout the medieval period. Perhaps this exclusiveness, which made it unnecessary for architects to provide separate teaching areas reserved for other *madhhab*s, was the factor which kept the *madrasa*s of this area small.

This diminutive size gives such buildings an essentially human scale which well expresses the informality of teaching in the medieval Islamic world. They are made even more inward-looking and cloistered by the downward pitch of their roofs as seen from the courtyard. Yet the organisation of space within the building is by turns ingenious and dramatic. On the first floor the needs of circulation and accommodation are admirably dovetailed: the corridor which encircles the courtyard and gives access both to individual cells and to the corner staircases is kept so narrow that two people can barely squeeze past each other in it. This frees extra space for accommodation. At the same time it is no mere walkway but has some aesthetic distinction. The openings at regular intervals along its shaded length allow the viewer to catch partial glimpses of a courtyard bathed in sunlight. Most Moroccan *madrasa*s have a central pool with a fountain. Given the somewhat cramped dimensions of these courtyards, the presence of rippling water sets space into motion to a degree that would not be possible in larger expanses. This introduction of nature into the ordered, man-made world of architecture is typically Islamic. These fountains serve a further, and

174

170 Fez, Madrasa al-'Attarin, carved woodwork

buildings – when their names are recorded – should include the sultans themselves (e.g. the Bu 'Inaniya *madrasa*s in Fez, Sale, Meknes and Algiers) and their high officials, and that they should have been lavishly endowed, as their luxurious decoration indicates. 4.160–4.161

More often, however, their names reflect their relative size (*al-Kubra*, 'the greater', or *al-Sughra*, 'the lesser'), their location in a quarter dedicated to a certain trade (*al-'Attarin*, 'the perfumers', as in Fez and Meknes, or *al-Saffarin*, 'the metal-workers'), and occasionally even those who taught there (al-Misbahiya is named after its first professor, Misbah b. 'Abdallah al-Yalsuti), or the subjects in which the *madrasa* specialised (thus the Suba'in *madrasa* derives its name from the study of the *riwaya*, the seven methods of reading the Qur'an). Like so much religious architecture in Islam, these *madrasa*s are often sited in the midst of bazaars – though there seems to be no connection between the presence of a *madrasa* in a particular quarter of the bazaar area and its endowment. Thus, while certain trades or crafts might singly or in concert put up the money for a mosque, the foundation of *madrasa*s seems to have been the result of official patronage. 4.155 4.151 4.152 4.157

That the teaching function of these *madrasa*s was paramount is suggested by the almost total absence of a patron's tomb in them. One may note as exceptions the case of the 18th-century Sulaimaniya *madrasa* in Tunis, founded by one 'Ali Pasha and containing the tomb of his son Sulaiman, and earlier, in the same city, the case of the vizier Ibn Tafrajin who was buried in the *madrasa* he had founded in 765/1364. But this official had significantly spent some time in Egypt, where this practice was widespread.

Such Oriental influences, though rare, are of crucial importance. A later Tunisian *madrasa*, the Muntasiriya (837–40/1433–7), again demonstrates Egyptian influence in the unusual feature of a rectangular bastion or salient placed in the middle of each of the courtyard façades. These projections do duty as portals to significant parts of the building and are thus explicable as interpretations – though in a different idiom – of the *iwan*s in cruciform disposition found in *madrasa*s further east. The lateral lecture halls of the Bu 'Inaniya *madrasa* in Fez also seem to be a local interpretation of the *iwan* scheme. Yet another 4.160–4.161

more directly scenic, function too. For anyone within the halls bordering on the courtyard the view into that courtyard is firmly directed by the fact that the only entrance to these halls is a single arch. On the major axes of the *madrasa* this arch frames the fountain, which thus becomes the centrepiece of a carefully calculated composition.

Most Moroccan *madrasa*s were produced either under the Marinids in the 14th century or under the Sa'dian or Filali sultans in the 17th century. Since these two periods also saw a much greater production of mosques and mausolea than other periods, it is unlikely that the building campaigns in these centuries themselves constitute evidence that a specific penchant for *madrasa*s can be attributed to the patrons of the time. But the political background outlined above provides the missing explanation. Given the role of the *madrasa* in training the politically influential Maliki *'ulama'*, it is not surprising that the patrons of these

derivation from eastern models may be the use of the *madrasa* as one element in a larger complex. A typical example of this fashion is the *madrasa* built in Tlemcen *c*.754/1353 by Sultan Abu 'Inan in association with the mosque, tomb and *zawiya* of Sidi al-Halwi, or the mosque, tomb and *madrasa* of Sidi Ibrahim built in Tlemcen by his successor Abu Hammu II. The Sahrij *madrasa* in Fez (721–3/1321–3) is situated right next to the Mosque of the Andalusians; but, as if this juxtaposition were not enough, it was by 750/1349 given dependencies significantly larger than itself. These included a now-vanished guest-house, the Dar Abi Habasa, with twenty-one rooms, a large ablutions hall and – most important of all – another *madrasa*, that of al-Suba'in, which still survives. This latter phenomenon of paired *madrasa*s linked by a passage cannot but recall the Salihiya complex in Cairo. Also relevant in this connection was the Qadima *madrasa* built by Abu Hammu I in Tlemcen *c*.710/1310 for two pious brothers, for it comprised two halls, each with a house attached. Thus it seems that the principle of separate premises for separate courses was accepted even when there was no question of different *madhhabs* being accommodated within a single building. For all their strong local character, then, these Maghribi *madrasa*s attest the strength of eastern Islamic influences in this genre of building.

In many cases the connection between a mosque and a *madrasa* is so close that the obvious conclusion to draw is that the mosque served *inter alia* as the oratory for the *madrasa* (e.g. the Walad al-Imam mosque, Tlemcen, erected *c*.710/1310 next to the Qadima *madrasa*). Conversely, the oratory of many a Maghribi *madrasa* served as the mosque for the quarter where it was built. Accordingly many of these *madrasa*s have minarets, and one even has a *minbar*, thereby qualifying it to be a *jami'*. It has even been suggested that the *madrasa*, by dint of becoming the most typical and widespread structure of the later medieval Maghrib, began in its turn to influence the layout of the mosque itself, specifically in its preference for square rather than rectangular courtyards, shallow rather than deep prayer halls and monumental portals on the major axis of the building. Something of the same process has been noted in

Mamluk Egypt, where the cruciform plan developed in the *madrasa* was subsequently adopted quite widely for mosques.

MOROCCAN MADRASAS

The type of architecture represented by these *madrasa*s seems to have been unique to the area of Morocco and western Algeria. A few, rather late, *madrasa*s are found sporadically in eastern Algeria and in Tunisia, but they have none of the distinction or individual quality of their counterparts in Morocco, and depend very heavily – as did most Maghribi architecture after the Ottoman conquest – on Turkish models. Perhaps the outstanding feature of these Moroccan *madrasa*s is their lavish decoration. That this was a deliberate emphasis is suggested by the inscription at the Sale *madrasa* dated 742/1341:

> "Look at my wonderful door! Rejoice at how carefully I am put together, at the remarkable nature of my construction and at my marvellous interior! The craftsmen have completed there a piece of artistic workmanship which has the beauty of youth . . ."

This ornament demonstrates that the affinities of such *madrasa*s are far more with secular than with religious architecture, especially in the important role accorded to wood as a structural feature in beams, lintels, brackets, arcades and openwork ceilings. The upper storeys are largely of wood. Occasionally the *madrasa*s have a largely two-dimensional portal, in which the arched entrance itself is dwarfed by an overbearing cantilevered cornice of densely carved woodwork (e.g. *madrasa* at Sale). The Bu 'Inaniya *madrasa* at Fez has a unique clock (*majana* – a kind of clepsydra) consisting of thirteen metal bowls, arranged over its façade, the work of the royal astronomer 'Ali al-Tilimsani. Otherwise most Moroccan *madrasa*s display very little external ornament. Their upper-storey cells, too, are absolutely bare of decoration. Yet their courtyard façades are treated with a fastidious attention to detail more appropriate to filigree jewellery than to architecture. Floors, dadoes and on occasion columns are sheathed in geometrically patterned tiles, the perfect foil for shaded cloisters and running water. Unlike mosques, which typically employ stucco and tilework to the virtual exclusion of other decorative media, these *madrasa*s achieve a harmonious balance of wood, stucco, tilework and sometimes even stained glass, or stone, marble or onyx carving. None of these media is allowed to dominate; all are applied in small, self-contained panels or long narrow bands, with unexpected combinations of disparately proportioned arches, piers and columns ('Attarin *madrasa*, Fez). Contrasts of colour, texture and decorative motifs – floral, geometric and epigraphic – are integral to this type of decorative scheme. The closest parallels lie in domestic architecture, a reminder of the origin of the *madrasa* in the house of the teacher. No other group of *madrasa*s elsewhere in the Islamic world displays a comparable richness of ornament. Perhaps the small size of these buildings recommended such a practice, and made it financially viable.

In contrast to the technicolour splendour of the courtyard façades, the interiors of the halls are more soberly treated, with only a few key areas like the *mihrab* reserved for densely carved stucco-work. Perhaps this simplicity reflects the austerity which had become ingrained in mosque design under the Almohads.

Although the casual visitor to these Moroccan *madrasa*s is apt to believe, after walking around half a dozen of them, that they follow a standard pattern, such an impression is quickly modified on closer examination. Their layouts suggest that while the architects in question had a firm grasp of the essential constituent elements of a *madrasa*, they were unable to impose a preconceived solution on the sites allotted to them. These *madrasa*s are located within an extremely cluttered urban setting and they commonly betray the various shifts of their designers to make the most of a difficult site. In these circumstances it would be idle to expect to find a model which was more or less faithfully copied, or even a consistent, rational development of plan in these *madrasa*s. Even so, all the Moroccan buildings of the genre share an emphasis on interior rather than exterior façades in that they focus on a central courtyard; and their decoration is extraordinarily consistent in medium and ornamental repertoire alike. In these respects, then, it is justifiable to point to their marked generic similarity, which easily asserts itself over such contingent factors as site and size. Moreover, most of the Moroccan *madrasa*s were erected – as noted above – in less than a century, from 670/1271 to 757/1356, a period which also encompasses the surviving work in Algeria and Spain. It is all the less surprising, therefore, that they should exhibit a distinct and well-integrated style. In order to define that style with the necessary precision, perhaps the most fruitful proceeding would be to examine the surviving *madrasa*s with a view to extrapolating from them the essential features which they all, or nearly all, share. Exceptional cases like the Misbahiya *madrasa*, where the modular elements are virtually obscured by the unusual ones, are necessarily excluded. This method will highlight the originality of this school, an originality which easily transcends the inevitable borrowings consequent upon the import of an eastern institution.

Externally, their most striking characteristic

171 Sale, Zawiya al-Nussak, portal

243

is a negative one: they lack a monumental façade allowing the building to proclaim itself from afar. This is no novelty in Islamic architecture, but it is a feature which recurs so consistently in these buildings that it seems justified to regard it as a deliberate principle. The only exception is itself so consistent that it proves the rule: virtually every *madrasa* (and many another building) has an elaborate portal. Sometimes this richness is a matter of decoration alone, but the standard device in this location is a densely carved overhang or hood on brackets, a kind of awning executed in wood. By its marked projection – sometimes as much as two metres – and its commanding height above the bustle of the street, it signals the entrance of the *madrasa* from a distance. The tortuous alleyways of these Moroccan towns would discourage any more marked emphasis on the façade; there is simply no point of vantage from which a general view of the building could be enjoyed. In addition one or two *madrasa*s have a porch in front of the main entrance (e.g. Bu 'Inaniya, Fez, where the vault is crowned by a pyramidal roof). This is more in the nature of the *chahar su* of eastern Islamic bazaars than a monumental enclosed construction like the porch of a medieval parish church, for it is simply a vault or dome spanning the street and supported by the walls which define that street. Most of these *madrasa*s abutted on to the principal streets of the town, streets that were nonetheless so narrow that even a slightly projecting porch would have created an obstacle to traffic. Thus these porches, like the commoner wooden overhangs above the entrance, serve essentially as symbolic markers of the building. Their domes, which may on occasion be flanged internally (Bu 'Inaniya, Meknes) are of course ideally suited to this purpose.

In common with contemporary local domestic architecture, these *madrasa*s very often contain a bent entrance. In part its purpose is identical to that which it serves in private houses, namely to ensure that the interior of the building is sundered from the outside world – a matter of noise as well as proximity and visibility. The length of this bent entrance is perhaps significant, for in the context of a religious building it allows the visitor time to adjust to the different tempo of life within the *madrasa*. It marks a transition from the secular to the spiritual world, and it is fitting that the pace of that transition should be measured. Corridors leading off the entrance passage from left to right respectively give access to the latrine area and a staircase leading to the upper storey ('Attarin and Misbahiya *madrasa*s, Fez), though other locations for the latrines do occur. The standard practice is to provide a series of cubicles around a subsidiary courtyard with a central fountain. This latter feature means that the area can serve for ablutions as well, and it is doubly proper therefore that it should be physically separated from the rest of the *madrasa*.

Several *madrasa*s have minarets (Saffarin, Fez; *madrasa* of Fas al-Jadid; Bu 'Inaniya, Fez) and this may serve as a reminder that the institution often served as an independent place of prayer. Often enough it was located very close to a mosque so that there was no need for a separate minaret. Indeed the interplay between mosque and *madrasa* was close and continuous. Just as the *madrasa* functioned as an oratory, so too did the mosque function as a place of teaching. This is especially relevant when it is remembered that most Moroccan *madrasa*s are in Fez, which boasted in the Qarawiyyin mosque the foremost centre of learning in the western Maghrib. Lectures in the Qarawiyyin would therefore supplement the teaching in the *madrasa*s. Indeed, in some sense the *madrasa*s acted as an overflow facility for the earlier and more prestigious institution. This was clearly part of the function of the Misbahiya *madrasa*, which was situated very close to the Qarawiyyin and whose students, mostly drawn from southern Morocco until recently, were enrolled in studies in the mosque. The Sahrij and Suba'in *madrasa*s illustrate the same phenomenon. Similarly, most Tunisian *madrasa*s are found in Tunis itself, where the students could benefit from the teaching offered in the other great Maghribi university-mosque, the Zaituna. To concentrate the teaching function in a single urban centre in this way obviously made good sense from the economic point of view, and it meant also – since in both cases the centre in question was also the capital city – that the educational activity of mosque and *madrasa* alike would be directly under the eye of the sovereign. Once again, then, the inherently political nature of the *madrasa* asserts itself.

In view of the diminutive size of these Maghribi *madrasa*s *vis-à-vis* equivalent institutions further east in the Islamic world, the emphasis laid on the prayer hall – which functioned concurrently as a lecture-hall, as indeed did many mosques outside the regular hours of

awiyyin mosque, and the new foundation of Fas al-Jadid, which at that time (751/1350) had not yet been given a Friday mosque. Thus the muezzin on the minaret of the Bu 'Inaniya could pass on the *adhan* given in the Qarawiyyin 2.111–2.112 mosque, which was too far away to be audible in

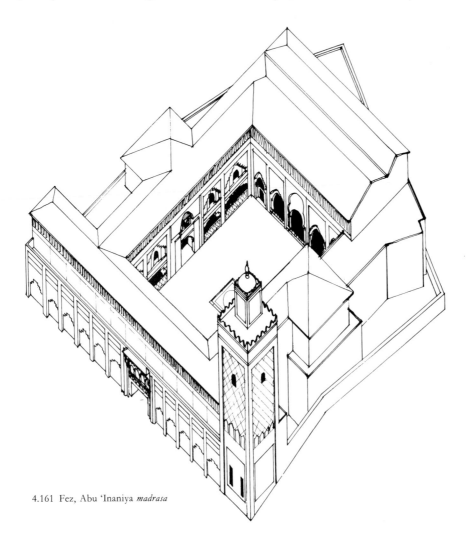

4.161 Fez, Abu 'Inaniya *madrasa*

prayer – is noticeable, and is especially relevant in the context of the preceding remarks. It does seem, in short, that these *madrasa*s functioned quite widely as neighbourhood mosques. The -4.161 case of the Bu 'Inaniya *madrasa* in Fez, though admittedly exceptional, offers supporting evidence for this theory. It is placed midway between the old city, clustered around the Qar-

Fas al-Jadid, and the Friday prayer could accordingly begin there at the ordained hour. The foundation inscription of the Bu 'Inaniya 4.160–4.161 *madrasa* (originally named al-Mutawakkiliya after one of the titles of its founder) specifically states that the building has the advantage of serving as a *jami*'. Built as it was so afer his accession to supreme power, and his bold adoption of the caliphal title *amir al-mu'minin* which no more than one of his predecessors had dared to use (and then only briefly), it could very well have been intended as a celebration of his victory – a practice occasionally recorded of mosques elsewhere in the Islamic world, but never of *madrasa*s. Tradition has it that when he was presented with the bills for the structure, which were enormous for a building of this kind, Abu 'Inan tore them up to symbolise his indifference to the expense, and extemporised a distich of poetry:

"Beauty is cheap, no matter what the cost;
For a thing that enthrals, money's well lost".
This *madrasa* has many of the appurtenances normally reserved for Friday mosques: a *minbar*, a *maqsura*, a mortuary and a Qur'an school, plus the unique external clock, already noted, with a set of songs presumably intended to mark the divisions of the daily prayers. It even has a subsidiary entrance to the rear of the building, as well as an unusual division of the main entrance into two sections, one of which is intended for those with bare feet and is accordingly provided with a threshold of running water. The same idea is applied within the building, for a water-channel runs laterally across the façade of the prayer hall and is crossed by a slab of marble at each side. The building is raised above the level of the bazaar and is reached by a staircase provided with benches; but its roots in everyday life are aptly emphasised by the shops which line its main façade. It is precisely in its flexibility and in its multiple functions that the Bu 'Inaniya *madrasa* approximates most closely not to other *madrasa*s but to the classical type of medieval Friday mosque, as much a community centre as a place of worship.

Although the Bu 'Inaniya *madrasa* is unique in the Maghrib in its comprehensive range of functions, it is typical in that it is a royal foundation. In this particular case the ruler bore not only the expense of building but also financed the provision of water and endowed the salaries of the staff, the board and other expenses of the students, and the upkeep of the building by making over to the institution a formidable list of properties. One of the inscriptions in the *madrasa* says as much: 'Engraved in this marble is that which Abu 'Inan – may God assist him! – has constituted as inalienable goods for the

172 Sale, *madrasa* of Abu'l-Hasan, covered arcade on south side

profit of this *madrasa* so that their revenues may be employed for its upkeep, the salary of the teachers, students and staff of this house . . .'. In the case of the 'Attarin *madrasa* the sovereign personally took part in the laying of the founda-

4.155

173 Marrakesh, Ben Yusuf *madrasa*, *mihrab* in oratory

prominently displayed, identifies the royal patron and lists the *auqaf* of the building. As late as the 17th century a *madrasa* built in Marrakesh by Mulay al-Rashid served as the ceremonial setting in which the letter announcing the sultan's accession to the throne was read out in public. The lavishnss of the royal patronage in these *madrasa*s leaps to the eye, for the interiors make up for their small size by a breathtaking parade of ornament. The cool sheen of tiled *172* floor and dadoes gives way to the lacy filigree of stucco set off by the subtle mellow patina of ancient woodwork. It is like stepping inside a *170* casket of jewels. These seductive interiors, tantalisingly glimpsed *en passant* from the bustle of the surrounding bazaar, contrast most markedly with the ascetic bareness and austerity of the student accommodation tucked out of sight. It seems justifiable to deduce that the sultans deliberately invested in the public part of the *madrasa* at the expense of the private apartments, in an attempt to court public approval.

Various methods are employed to single out the role of the prayer hall in Maghribi *madrasa*s. It was the constant concern of the architects to give this hall pride of place in the overall layout, and the majority of them achieved that aim by means of axiality. Sometimes, as in the Sahrij *4.154* and Bu 'Inaniya *madrasa*s, Fez, the entrance, *4.160–4.161* courtyard and mosque were all disposed on the major chord of the building, and in the former case even the elongated rectangular pool played a spatial role. More often, the exigencies of the site and the predilection for a bent entrance meant that this axial emphasis could assert itself only at the entrance to the courtyard (al-'Ubbad *4.158* *madrasa*, Tlemcen; Misbahiya *madrasa*, Fez). So *4.152* firmly did this axial arrangement establish itself that it was even maintained when it ran counter to the correct orientation of the prayer chamber. Thus in the 'Attarin *madrasa*, Fez, in order to *4.155* mark the *qibla* accurately the *mihrab* has to be placed to the right of the entrance instead of opposite it as the internal logic of the layout demands. The chaotic disposition of the Saffarin *4.151* *madrasa*, Fez, is a textbook example of how an inflexible adherence to the placing of the *mihrab* opposite the main entrance means that orientation and function are at cross purposes. Their conflict dislocates the entire building. Much more adroit than either of these solutions was

tions alongside the *'ulama'* and other men of piety; and a high court official, the *mizwar*, was entrusted with the supervision of building operations. A similar official was appointed to oversee the construction of the Bu 'Inaniya *madrasa*. In other *madrasa*s a white marble slab,

4.152 the device adopted at the Misbahiya *madrasa*, Fez. Here the architect has maintained an axial layout even though the spatial drive of the building is in exactly the opposite direction of the *qibla*. Rather than place the oratory laterally, he has kept it in its traditional place and has also retained the central doorway to it. This has compelled him to omit the *mihrab* altogether, for its proper place would be exactly where the doorway is located. Perhaps this anomaly accounts for the unusually rich decoration accorded to the doorway. In subsequent *madrasas* the *mihrab* regained its role as the pivotal element dictating the entire layout, but this may well be because the lessons of the 4.151, 4.155, 4.152 Saffarin, 'Attarin and Misbahiya *madrasas* had been digested.

173 The oratory is consistently the largest unbroken covered space in the *madrasa* and its impact is intensified by the cramped proportions of all the other rooms. Space is at a premium in these buildings and its generous deployment in these oratories is therefore doubly effective. The prayer hall is sometimes lavishly fenestrated on the *qibla* wall (Bu 'Inaniya *madrasa*, Meknes), a practice which may have been intended to evoke spiritual connotations. Occasionally, too, it echoes both internally and externally the T-shaped disposition which had become canonical for Maghribi mosques (*madrasa* of Fas al-Jadid). The oratory quite often has the same width as the courtyard, which is therefore quite naturally integrated with it, very much in the manner of a mosque. At other times it extends the full width of the nuclear *madrasa*, thereby symbolically embracing the whole life of the institution and serving as the architectural climax of the ensemble. A square plan was however the most 4.156, 4.153 frequent type (Sale; Tashfiniya *madrasa*, Tlemcen). This had the advantage of facilitating a pyramidal roof. In these *madrasas* such roofs are normally reserved for the sanctuaries. Sheathed as they are in green tiles – as are the roofs of the *madrasas* – they blazon forth the colour of the Prophet in a predominantly dun environment. As a further symbol of Islam they 2.33 often bear the *jamur*, a series of superposed balls crowned by a crescent.

The placing of the chambers for students varies quite markedly. In the earlier *madrasas* all the living accommodation was confined to the

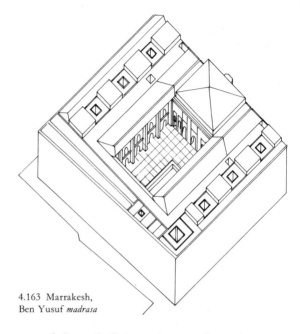

4.163 Marrakesh, Ben Yusuf *madrasa*

ground floor (Saffarin *madrasa*; *madrasa* of Fas 4.151 al-Jadid). In the following decades it continued to be standard practice for the more commodious *madrasas* to provide, in addition to the main accommodation at first-floor level, at least some student accommodation on the ground floor. It is here that the ornate wooden lattice-work screens known as *mashrabiya*s come into their own. Placed between the arcades or other openings of the court, they close off from the public gaze the sections of the *madrasa* which serve for student accommodation. The bleakness of the latter area is therefore masked by a lavish exterior. Symbolically enough it is only the outer, namely courtyard, face of these *mashrabiya*s that is richly carved; the inner face is 170 plain, as perhaps befits the sparse facilities offered to the students. Between these screens and the cells runs a corridor, for all the world like the cloister of some medieval western monastery. These screens continue on the upper storeys, where their principal function is obviously to decorate the interior façade rather than to seal off the student cells. Sometimes the corridors or galleries are located only along the lateral walls of the courtyard ('Attarin *madrasa*, 4.155 Fez; Taza *madrasa*), but they often extend to three sides, especially in the later examples of the genre, and there is even an isolated case of a *madrasa* with student cells arranged unevenly but on all four sides of the ground floor (Suba'in *madrasa*, Fez). The extra height required for a suitably imposing prayer-hall meant that there was frequently no room for student cells above it, and there is even a case of a prayer and assembly hall located on the first floor (Misbahiya, Fez).

Nothing testifies more forcibly to the inadequate publication of these buildings than the widely divergent figures given for the number of student cells which they contain. Often enough these statistics are confused with the number of students which the *madrasa* could accommodate, a figure in itself wide open to discussion. According to some estimates, a typical cell can hold as many as seven or eight students. This is clearly an inaccurate guide for rooms at the smaller end of the scale; indeed, cells measuring no more than 1.50 m. × 2 m. are quite frequently encountered and obviously it would be difficult to accommodate more than one person, or at most two, in such a room. That many cells were intended to house only a single occupant is clearly indicated by the custom that the student 'paid' for his room by buying the key for it from his predecessor. Besides, in many cells the floor space was reserved for living as distinct from sleeping accommodation – a feature which will be discussed in more detail shortly. Within a given *madrasa*, moreover, the size and layout of individual cells will often fluctuate quite markedly. This is especially apt to occur when the *madrasa* has walls built at acute angles because of the spatial constraints of the site. While windowless cells are known, it was standard practice to provide tiny windows, often with metalwork grilles, opening on to the corridor, the main courtyard, a subsidiary courtyard (especially in post-Marinid *madrasa*s), or even – though rarely – on to the street. These remarks should be enough to indicate that generalisations about the nature, size and quantity of student accommodation in these *madrasa*s are somewhat hazardous.

The spartan fittings of these cells reveal that the provision of maximum sleeping space was a priority of the designer. There was no bedding to clutter up valuable space. Students slept under a blanket on a mat. Projecting shelves below the ceiling often function as bunk beds; they are reached by wooden bars mortared diagonally across the corners of the rooms so as to form a simple ladder. Sometimes a small table is provided – the students were, after all, issued with paper, pen and ink. A narrow slot beside the door permitted the daily ration of flat bread to be distributed with maximum speed. Since that ration was fixed at one piece per student, the amount of bread set aside per day for the *madrasa* provides the necessary clue in calculating the maximum occupancy for which the building was designed. This quantity of bread was made

174 Fez, Madrasa al-'Attarin

available daily, according to the requirements of the *waqf* which financed the institution, irrespective of whether the building was fully occupied or not. In practice, therefore, it often happened that at least some students would have extra rations. These would be all the more welcome since the students were perpetually on short commons. Bread was the staple diet, supplemented by such quantities of oil and vegetables – perhaps occasionally meat – as the students could buy from their communal resources. The resultant stew would be cooked over a charcoal brazier in the cell itself – for even the largest of all these *madrasa*s, the Bu 'Inaniya at Fez, has no kitchen. The diet of the students was thus barely above subsistence level, although the ruler would distribute meat and fruit on festival days, and it was traditional practice for the richer citizens occasionally to extend the hospitality of their table to individual students.

4.152   The largest of the medieval *madrasa*s in Morocco is the Misbahiya, for which a tally of 117 rooms has been proposed, with twenty-three on the ground floor alone and the balance in the two upper storeys. A two-storey design is 4.155 commoner, however, and therefore the 'Attarin *madrasa*, in which Bel counted thirty-four cells, 4.160–4.161 or the Bu 'Inaniya *madrasa*, Fez, whose capacity has been estimated at a hundred students, are more representative. These are large numbers for buildings designed on such an intimate scale, especially when it is remembered that the prayer hall of such a *madrasa* could serve as the *masjid* not only for the students and staff but also for the people of the area. It is hard to avoid the conclusion that the students lived a hard life, frequently cold, cramped and underfed.

With the fall of the Marinids the golden age of the Maghribi *madrasa* was over. Not only are there comparatively few surviving *madrasa*s of later date, but the majority of them are either attached to mosques or shrines, and dominated by them, or they are intrinsically of very little interest (Rabat, Ceuta, Tangiers and Ksar el Kebir/Alcazarquivir). Only two deserve closer 4.162–4.163 inspection: the Ben Yusuf or Yusufiya *madrasa* in Marrakesh, dating to 972/1564–5, and the 4.159 Sharratin *madrasa* in Fez, dating to 1081/1670, both royal foundations. Their interest lies in their plans rather than in their decoration or

structural techniques, for in these latter respects they are disappointingly derivative.

Although the Ben Yusuf *madrasa* is tradition- 4.162–4.1 ally believed to have a plan based on that of the Marinid *madrasa* whose site it occupies, it has a *174* degree of integration and symmetry foreign to its predecessors. Externally it forms an almost perfect square but for the projecting polygonal *mihrab*. The internal disposition is admirable in its clarity and economy. Broadly speaking the arrangement is tripartite, with a large porticoed courtyard – containing a substantial pool instead of the usual fountain – acting as the focus of the design, and the student cells relegated to the flanking tracts. The oratory, placed as usual along the main axis, is also divided into three parts, a device already encountered in Marinid *madrasa*s. The arrangement of the cells, however, is novel; for instead of lining a long corridor they are clustered symmetrically in sixes or sevens around a series of seven small courtyards or *duwira*s. These are accessible via a cloister-like corridor which encloses the courtyard on three sides and also leads into the patio for ablutions. A similar arrangement is followed on the first floor, so that the *madrasa* contains about a hundred rooms.

A comparable lucidity of planning informs the Sharratin *madrasa*. Here too the polygonal 4.159 *mihrab* projects forcibly, breaking the even tenor of the perimeter wall. This wall is stepped in three places but is otherwise straight. Exceptionally three separate entrances give access to the corridors which debouch into the courtyard. Each of the three lesser courtyard façades is broken by three bays, and the whole elevation rises to an unprecedented three storeys. Student cells, mostly arranged around somewhat noisome *duwira*s more like pits than courtyards, occupy three of the four sides on the ground floor; traditionally, students from various parts of the country – the Tafilalet, the Rif and eastern Morocco – congregate around the appropriate *duwira* so that each courtyard becomes in some sense a local microcosm. The oratory on the fourth side is similar to that of the Ben Yusuf *madrasa*. Despite the proximity of the building to the Qarawiyyin, the *mihrab* is seriously out of true, facing as it does the north-east. The high walls, cramped courtyard and blank spaces of the building give it a somewhat oppressive atmosphere. Its history does not belie this impression, for the *madrasa* was erected on the site of a Marinid foundation, the Madrasa al-Labbadin, which Mulay al-Rashid had ordered to be demolished because its students had brought women there and given themselves over to debauch. Despite the radial symmetry of its plan, the building falls far below Marinid standards so far as its decoration is concerned. Nevertheless, the large capacity of these two later *madrasa*s and their eminently logical layout put them in a category of their own among Moroccan *madrasa*s, and make them a worthy coda to a distinguished tradition.

V The Mausoleum

Any observant visitor to the Islamic world
cannot fail to be struck by the sheer quantity of
mausolea to be seen in town and country alike.
Their rôle in the architectural environment is
incomparably more important than it is in any
Western country, where monuments to the dead
often take the form of statues. This discrepancy,
therefore, could be laid at the door of the pervasive Islamic distaste for figural sculpture. But to
argue that Muslims raised tombs because they
would not raise statues is to miss the point. The
typical Islamic mausoleum has a social and religious dimension perforce denied to a statue. It is
that dimension above all which explains the
continuing popularity of the mausoleum in the
Islamic world. How, then, did this popularity
come about?

The early stages of the process were remarkably unpropitious. The first generation of
Muslims, taking their cue from Muhammad
himself, set their faces sternly against any ostentation concerned with mourning, death and
burial. Numerous *hadith*s document this repug-
nance, though it must be admitted that the
Qur'an is virtually silent on the matter. Wailing,
the rending of clothes, the sprinkling of ashes or
dust on the body, and a whole range of similar
mourning practices, were explicitly condemned.
When the *littérateur* al-Hamadhani came to draft
his will, he directed 'that no one should loudly
mourn him; that no one should strike his cheeks,
scratch his face; that no door is to be blackened;
no furniture smashed; no plant unrooted and no
buildings destroyed; that he is to be buried in
three white Egyptian pieces of cloth which
should neither be silk nor embroidered nor yet
worked with gold'. Elaborate funeral processions were also discouraged. Instead, the corpse
was to be borne quickly to the grave – for did
not the Prophet himself say that it was good for
the righteous to arrive soon at happiness? The
grave itself was to be level with the ground and
no structure of any kind was to mark it. This
levelling of tombs (*taswiya al-qubur*) symbolised
the equality of all believers in death as in life,
and is of a piece with the ancient Islamic custom

of throwing earth into the grave while quoting
the Qur'an, Sura XX:55: 'From it We created
you, and into it We shall return you, and from
it raise you a second time.' The *hadith*s record
that Muhammad went out of his way to forestall
any attempt to mark his own grave with some
special distinction. Initially his wishes were respected, and he was laid to rest beneath the floor
of one of the rooms in his own house. Thus,
incidentally, was inaugurated the custom of
burial in mosques. It took less than a generation,
however, before the place of his burial was
marked by a special structure, and within some
seventy years of his death his tomb, newly embellished, occupied a much-venerated position
in the magnificent Mosque of the Prophet built 2.65-2.66
by the Umayyad caliph al-Walid I. Whatever the
views of the strictly orthodox, the austerity of
early Islam had been set aside decisively both for
places of burial and for places of worship. Apart
from minor exceptions, there was to be no
looking back.

These remarks should not be taken to mean
that mausolea immediately began to spring up
throughout the Islamic world. Following
perhaps the example of the caliphs themselves,
all but a very few Muslims in the first two
centuries of Islam were buried – there was no
cremation – in simple graves. To that extent the
unyielding hostility of orthodox opinion to
funerary architecture could be said to have
triumphed. As late as the ninth century some
'Abbasid caliphs were still being buried in their
own houses. To be sure, minor infringements of
the traditional simplicity of burial practice
occurred. They included, for example, the use of
a richly-worked silk shroud instead of a plain
white cotton one, or an elaborately carved coffin
made of some exotic and expensive wood
instead of a few planks nailed together. Since the
earth covered shroud and coffin alike, such de-
viations from accepted practice did not flaunt
themselves. Necessarily more public than either
of these was the erection of inscribed funerary
*stele*s over the grave. Just as the grave itself, and
the position of the corpse within it, was oriented
towards Mecca, so too was a typical *stele*, and it
was intended to evoke further religious associa-

175 Samarra, Qubbat al-Sulaibiya

in religious guise. Thus the earliest recorded Islamic mausolea were erected over the graves of noted Companions of the Prophet and, in short order, Shi'ite martyrs and important figures from the Old and New Testaments. None of these seventh- to ninth-century mausolea – which were concentrated in the Levant, Arabia and Egypt – survive, although their memory often persists. The many sites claimed for the head of Husain or of John the Baptist are ample evidence of this. So far as actual buildings are concerned, the earliest surviving Islamic mausoleum is generally agreed to be the Qubbat al-Sulaibiya at Samarra, datable to the mid-ninth century. In comparison with the surviving evidence as to mosques, palaces, baths, *khan*s, reservoirs and other Islamic building types, this is indeed a late beginning. In view of this wealth of earlier architecture to survive, it seems justified to conclude that the absence of contemporary mausolea is not a matter of chance, but reflects their comparative rarity *vis-à-vis* other building types.

175
5.202–

ORIGINS OF THE MAUSOLEUM

Enough has been said to indicate that the concept of a mausoleum was not deeply rooted in early Islamic society. However developed the domestic or even religious architecture of the pre-Islamic Arabs might have been, mausolea played no important rôle in their buildings. What, then, were the origins of the idea, if no indigenous tradition can be identified? The influence of Iran must be ruled out, for the Zoroastrian faith of the Sasanians decreed that corpses should be exposed to scavengers. To inter a body was to violate religious law; deadly contamination would result, and would extend by association to the building which housed the body. The remaining source of inspiration that may be canvassed is also the one most readily to hand from the standpoint of both geography and history. Syria, together with its neighbouring provinces, was saturated with classical and Christian culture, and in that culture mausolea held an honoured place. To this day large numbers of Roman mausolea survive in Syria, and in pre-Islamic times such pagan buildings provided the most obvious models for Byzantine architects charged with erecting Christian memorial structures. The latter, known as

tions. Its formulaic inscription began with the *bismillah*, gave the name, patronymic and date of death of the deceased, and ended with a prayer for God's mercy on the person concerned. Sometimes an apt quotation from the Qur'an was added. Finally, the form of the *stele* was that of a *mihrab*, a detail which facilitated their subsequent re-use as *mihrab*s in many a mosque. Thus minor violations of orthodoxy took on an explicitly religious protective colouring. Later, in similar fashion, the originally heterodox practice of building mausolea was able to profit from the perennial Islamic tradition that any place could serve as a *masjid*. Many an *imamzada* throughout Iran functions as a surrogate mosque to this day. The graves of most of the Umayyad princes were desecrated when the 'Abbasids came to power, a form of revenge that would not have been possible if these graves had not been marked. Presumably, therefore, *stele*s were already in common use by the early 8th century, if not before. Still, expensive shrouds and coffins and inscribed *stele*s were venial sins when set against the gross violation of orthodox practice embodied in a mausoleum.

As so often in the medieval Islamic world, opposition to the dictates of an orthodoxy which was felt to be oppressive manifested itself

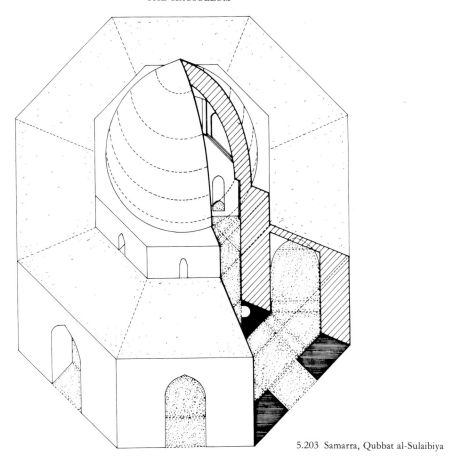

5.203 Samarra, Qubbat al-Sulaibiya

martyria, housed the bodies or relics of saints or Biblical personages, or marked the spot of a theophany or some other significant event in the Old or New Testaments. The forms of these martyria were exceptionally varied – circular, square, cruciform, polygonal, stellar, lobed or multi-foil – but by and large they maintained the relatively modest scale of the classical mausoleum from which they ultimately derived. This was because their prime purpose was not to house a congregation but to commemorate a person or an event, on whose anniversary alone the building would be crowded. Otherwise only pilgrim traffic needed to be catered for, and this was of its nature somewhat spasmodic. The relic cult which swept Byzantine Syria in the fourth century triggered a building boom which changed the face of the country, and whose

impetus was still not entirely exhausted at the time of the Arab invasion. The martyrium was, in short, omnipresent, and it was only natural that the Muslims should derive inspiration from it when, actuated by an obstinately human impulse impervious to theological proscription, they came to build their own funerary structures – or commemorative monuments such as the Dome of the Rock.

2.16–2.17

ISLAMIC TERMINOLOGY FOR THE MAUSOLEUM

As is so often the case in Islamic architecture, the terminology used in medieval sources for the building type under discussion is revealing. The mausoleum is, however, unique in the remarkable number and range of words used in medieval Arabic and, to a much lesser extent,

255

176 Samarqand, Shah-i Zinda (in foreground: tomb of Chujuk Bika)

177 Linjan, shrine of Pir-i Bakran, niche with *muqarnas* hood

Persian sources to denote this kind of monument. Reasons for this are not far to seek. Clearly the utilitarian purpose of a mausoleum – namely, commemoration – by no means exhausted its associations for medieval Muslims. Accordingly, the standard descriptive term *turba*, which evokes nothing but the building itself, is frequently supplemented or replaced by words which evoke something more. It may not be too fanciful to suggest that the word employed may on occasion betray the attitude of the patron or writer to the mausoleum as a genre, and even to its legality. But there are also a number of neutral terms. *Qabr*, for instance, may be regarded as a tolerably exact equivalent of 'tomb' in that it could mean a building as well as a grave; but apart from this ambiguity it has no extra dimension of meaning. Similarly, *marqad*, with its Persian equivalent *khwabgah* ('place of rest' or 'place of sleep'), is, if mildly poetic, essentially bland, while *madfan* ('place of burial') is positively prosaic and quite devoid of symbolic undertones. The very fact that several such humdrum terms are used interchangeably might raise the suspicion that the rôle of the mausoleum in Islamic society was not defined with any precision.

Other terms are substantially more revealing. *Qubba* (Persian *gunbad*) – is an obvious case of *pars pro toto*; the mausoleum is referred to by its most distinguishing feature, the dome. *Qasr*, like its semantic calque in Persian, *kakh*, opens somewhat wider vistas, for it means 'palace' or 'castle'. Such a term evidently presupposes a substantial piece of architecture. When used in an inscription it also implies a degree of pride on the part of the patron, pride that Islamic orthodoxy would regard as improper: with such a word the mausoleum becomes an appurtenance of the life of princes. It must be admittted that this usage is much rarer than terms which evoke religious associations. These are of course at the opposite extreme, and one may account for their popularity by the welcome opportunity of equivocation which they afforded. By the use of such words, then, the builder of a mausoleum might hope to justify the unjustifiable. Several examples might be cited. *Astana* ('threshold') is a term of extreme humility which was especially favoured in the context of Shi'ite shrines. *Mazar* and *ziyarat* are derived from the Arabic root *ziyara* meaning 'to make a pilgrimage', and their use – as at Sar-i Pul in central Afghanistan – is a clear attempt to extenuate on religious grounds the erection of a mausoleum, even though the connection between the deceased and Islamic orthodoxy may be tenuous. The word *mashhad* illustrates a parallel case. It derives from the Arabic verb *shahada*, meaning 'to confess the faith of Islam'; but the associated word *shahid* denotes a martyr for the faith, and thus *mashhad* properly indicates the burial spot of such a martyr. Needless to say, many of those buried in so-called *mashhad*s were never called upon to endure martyrdom. But perhaps the most interesting term in this group is *rauda* (Arabic 'garden'), clearly a symbolic reference to Paradise and thus indirectly an affirmation of the piety of the mausoleum's tenant. In the same spirit tombs may be described as 'illumined' or 'perfumed'.

The conclusion to be drawn from this wide spectrum of terminology is that many Muslims evinced in this way their residual feeling of unease at the erection of a mausoleum. Almost alone among Islamic building types, this genre of building was not fully respectable. At long intervals a wave of fundamentalist feeling might sweep away such buildings, as was the case in Wahhabi territory in 19th-century Arabia. Meanwhile, many a Muslim desirous of building himself a mausoleum would attempt to cloak such culpable egotism by sundry devices. He might embellish the monument with Qur'anic quotations, place a *mihrab* within it to render it a place of prayer, or make provision by means of an endowment for the regular recitation of the Qur'an within its walls. The most popular pal-

5.88–5.89

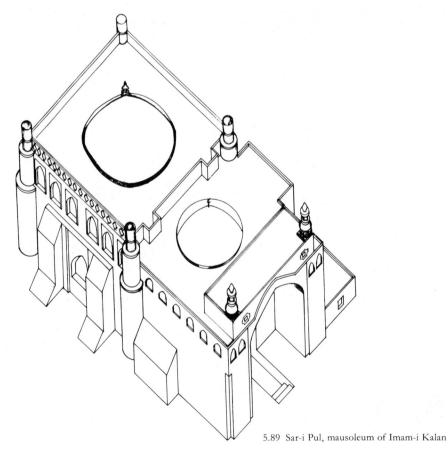

5.89 Sar-i Pul, mausoleum of Imam-i Kalan

178 Bukhara, tomb of Bayan Quli Khan, interior

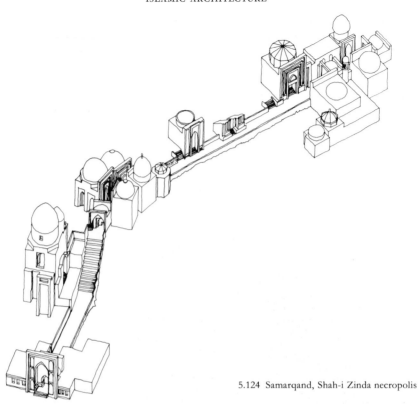

5.124 Samarqand, Shah-i Zinda necropolis

liative was to make the mausoleum part of a joint foundation. By this means it would acquire, by osmosis, the odour of sanctity which properly belonged to the mosque, *madrasa*, *ribat* or other religious building which it adjoined. Such joint foundations are first recorded in sizeable numbers during the Saljuq period. In the course of subsequent centuries the rôle of the mausoleum diminished in direct proportion to the quantity of satellite structures added to such a complex. There was safety in numbers. One mausoleum, be it never so secular, could scarcely arouse the wrath of the pious if the buildings around it were all dedicated to the bodily and spiritual welfare of the Muslim community. Often enough the founder's deed of endowment (*waqf*) specified the scale, appurtenances and details of upkeep envisaged for his mausoleum as well as for the rest of the complex.

2.179–2.180

7.134–7.135

RÔLE OF THE MAUSOLEUM IN ISLAM

The honoured place which the mausoleum enjoyed within the context of multiple foundations indicates clearly enough that its function was not limited simply to a place of burial and commemoration. In fact mausolea occupied a crucial place in medieval Islamic society, often at the level of what might be termed 'folk' or 'popular' religion. This latter aspect was relevant strictly speaking only in the case of the tombs of holy men or of Shi'ite notables, but it was quite common for the identity of the original tenant of a mausoleum to be forgotten and then replaced by a new attribution to a person with some religious associations, even if these were entirely bogus. This readiness to 're-dedicate' secular mausolea is an apt symbol of the aura of sanctity which enveloped mausolea in the Islamic world. Ironically enough, that same aura was of course utterly at variance with the picture painted in the *hadith*s of the Prophet's own forcibly expressed dislike of funerary architecture. It may perhaps be interpreted in a double sense: first, as a popular reaction against an irksome prohibition; and secondly, as a forlorn attempt to honour religious obligations at the very moment of contravening them.

What then, broadly speaking, was the rôle of the mausoleum in medieval Islam? In one respect it was no different from that of funerary architecture in many another culture: it advertised for all to see the importance of the person thus commemorated. There seems to have been no official attempt to restrict the erection of mausolea to people of a given rank, class or status. Anybody who had the will and the money to build one could do so. Nevertheless, a distinction may be drawn between those tombs primarily secular and those primarily religious in intent. As so often in Islam, the dividing line

179 Safid Buland, tomb of Shaikh Fadl

180 Aswan, mausolea

between secular and religious is apt to be blurred; for example, in what category should the tombs of the Prophet's Companions be placed? Again, did the importance of the great Shi'ite shrines reflect the political or the religious standing of the *imam*s? Such questions are not readily answerable; but, in default of clinching contemporary evidence, the practice of subsequent generations may provide, with all due reserve, an adequate rule of thumb. A mausoleum may with some confidence be identified as secular from the outset if it does not subsequently acquire religious associations. The typical secular mausoleum was no more than a memorial. Later generations were indifferent to it; and, as a result, its chances of survival were not good. For a society in which the antiquarian impulse was virtually unknown, there would be little point in maintaining and repairing such monuments. Thus the tomb towers marooned in the wastes of Anatolia and northern Iran are the flotsam and jetsam of history. Occasionally, the names of their founders have survived the *cf.* 5.75–5.77 passage of centuries; more often they are anony-

mous, or bear a purely topographical name, unless indeed they are assimilated – like so many other monuments – into the ever-potent world of myth and legend. Secular mausolea might well evoke a more or less cloudy past; but they were scarcely relevant to the present.

If the identity of secular mausolea on the whole did not long outlive the deaths of their patrons in popular memory, so that these buildings quickly became anachronisms, it fell to mausolea with religious associations to play an active part in medieval Muslim society. Such associations could be very tenuous indeed. The Shah-i Zinda at Samarqand, an early Timurid 5.123 necropolis, consists mostly of mausolea erected 175. for members of the royal house. Yet to view these as a collection of dynastic tombs is to miss much of their significance. The original motive behind this choice of site was the existence there of the (probably bogus) tomb of one Qutham b. al-'Abbas, a Companion of the Prophet. The desire to benefit from the *baraka* ('holiness') exuded by the bones of so early a hero of Islam made people compete for the honour of being

262

181 Uzgend, tomb dated 582/1186–7, detail of portal

buried close to him. Such cases could be multiplied; the key consequence to note is that by extension, the whole group of mausolea came to be venerated, and indeed are visited in a spirit of reverence to this day. The so-called 'Marinid tombs' at Fez exhibit the same process at the opposite end of the Islamic world.

A related but rather different case is presented

180

5.172–5.174

by the Aswan tombs. This is a group of some fifty Fatimid mausolea clustered together in a huge medieval cemetery outside the town. Their presence in such numbers is not easily explained. There is no local tradition associating any of these mausolea with a particularly notable personality, and the texts of the gravestones taken from these buildings preserve a uniformly neutral flavour, recording names and dates but not deeds. The architecture of the mausolea themselves is similarly pared down to essentials. What special concatenation of circumstances, it might be asked, could account for this sudden proliferation, in a provincial Egyptian town, of mausolea erected by or for people bound by no obvious tie of blood or tribal loyalty? The answer may well lie in the location of Aswan on one of the border areas (*thughur*) where Islam faced infidel territory. Similar frontier zones existed in Cilicia, in southern Anatolia; in sub-Saharan Africa; and in Central Asia. It was in these zones that war was constantly waged or brewing, and the simmering unrest of these

borders contrasted strongly with the stability of the Muslim frontier at large. From the *ribat*s established in large quantities in these areas there sallied forth bands of *ghazi*s, warriors for the faith. Those who fell in the task of waging holy war (*jihad*) were assured of Paradise and frequently received honoured burial. Aswan, as the headquarters from which *jihad* against the Nubians was prosecuted, was the obvious place in which to celebrate these martyrs. The choice of the canopy type for these mausolea lends extra support to this interpretation, since there was a strong body of opinion which argued that such mausolea (described in more detail below) did not violate the spirit of Muhammad's interdiction of funerary architecture. The large quantities of anonymous or virtually anonymous mausolea erected in Central Asia, the most extensive frontier of all, during roughly the same period offers yet further corroboration of this theory.

5.64, 5.75–

It seems that in subsequent centuries too the waging of *jihad* was apt to be regarded as at least

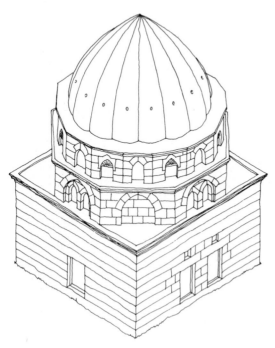

5.205 Damascus, mausoleum in Rukniya *madrasa*

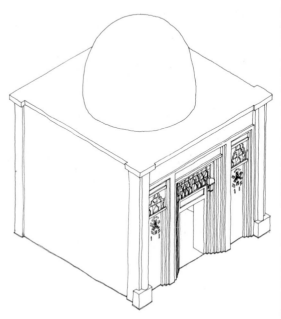

5.106 Takistan, "Pir" mausoleum

182 Samarqand, Shah-i Zinda, tomb of Chujuk Bika, portal

partial justification for building mausolea. This may explain the emphasis on titulature associated with *jihad* in the inscriptions decorating the mausolea of numerous Ayyubid *amir*s in Syria and Palestine. These military leaders refer to themselves as 'wager of holy war' (*mujahid*), 'the support of Islam' (*'adud al-Islam*), 'helper of the fighters for the faith' (*nasir al-mujahidin*), 'the helper of religion' (*mu'in al-din*), 'the sword of Islam' (*saif al-Islam*), 'the one who inhabits a *ribat*' (*al-murabit*), 'the slayer of infidels' (*qatil al-kufar* or *qatil al-mushrikin*), 'the guardian of frontiers' (*al-muthagir*), 'guardian of the frontiers of the Muslims' (*hafiz thughur al-muslimin*), or 'guardian of the lands of God' (*hafiz bilad Allah*). Perhaps these patrons aimed not merely at justifying their mausolea but also at acquiring religious merit for themselves. They might legitimately hope, in short, that their own tombs would exude *baraka*.

The notion that the tomb of a saint, a descendant of an *imam* (*imamzada*), a martyr or a *mujahid* was a source of sanctity had wide repercussions. On occasion there might be an undignified scramble for the right to be buried as close as possible to such a tomb. The most coveted location was at the feet of the venerated person, and the degree of *baraka* received was considered proportionate to the distance from the revered tomb. Thus there occurred a quite remarkable expansion of certain cemeteries, for example that in Baghdad which housed the tomb of the founder of one of the four major law schools, Ahmad ibn Hanbal. A natural corollary of this was the increasingly popular practice of visiting graves, usually on Fridays and on the eve of major festivals. Sometimes commemorative meals were eaten there and prayers were said for the departed, or ex-votos left; the anniversary of the person's death was regarded as a particularly appropriate time for such ceremonies. In addition, such tombs were often a favoured location to say specific prayers, for example the petitions of barren women to have a child. Habits similar to these were of course common among the early Christians, and it is not inconceivable that the Muslims were influenced by such precedents.

In some respects the great Shi'ite sanctuaries, such as Qumm, fit quite naturally into the development described above; in others, they are a special case. To begin with, their size alone sets them apart from all but a very few Sunni mausolea. Moreover, those buried there, being *imam*s, enjoy a status exalted beyond that of any Sunni notable, in that it is much more religious than secular. Nor are they simply mausolea; instead, the normal practice is for the tomb to function as the central point of a number of subsidiary structures. Thus there developed the shrine complex, as at Natanz, Tirmidh or Mashhad, whose functions would include worship, teaching, Qur'anic recitation and secondary burials. Inevitably such a complex would play a more central role in the life of the community than was possible for a Sunni mausoleum. To some extent such buildings could be regarded as surrogate mosques and could be compared, with the due caution which proposed cross-cultural connections invoke, with some of the great pilgrimage centres of the medieval West. They also have obvious points of contact with the larger monastic foundations. Some shrines might operate as a power-house for *jihad*; others might act as the mother-house for the propagation of a particular religious persuasion.

The communal role of the major Shi'ite shrines would come to the fore especially on the occasion of the great festivals of 'Ashura (the 10th of Muharram, the anniversary of the martyrdom of al-Husain) and Ghadir Khumm, when processions, passion plays, recitations and public mourning allowed the whole community to express its grief. The existence of a mourning cult in honour of the mythical Persian hero Siyavush in pre-Islamic Transoxiana may have influenced some of these practices. The fact that they were definitively established under the Buyids, who were so determinedly committed – for their own political ends – to the preservation and revival of the pre-Islamic Persian heritage, is perhaps a pointer in the same direction. This process, then, illustrates yet again the indissoluble connection between religion and politics in Islam. Another facet of that connection is revealed in the periodic sacking and even destruction of shrines as an expression of social or political protest, or of sectarian rivalry. The history of Baghdad in the 10th and 11th centuries, for example, is full of such incidents. Taken as a whole they help to corroborate the suggestion made above that certain mausolea,

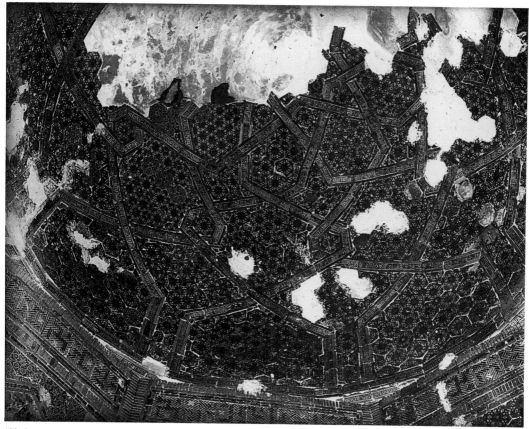

183 Samarqand, Shah-i Zinda, tomb of Shad-i Mulk, interior

whether Sunni or Shi'ite, were the acknowledged focus of particular sections of the community. In the Indo-Pakistan subcontinent certain shrines functioned as a bridge between the Hindu and Muslim communities, for they were venerated by both faiths. A parallel case is offered by the many Muslim sites in the Near East with Biblical connections, such as the shrine of John the Baptist's head in the Damascus *jami'* (one of many putative sites of that relic), and the mosque of Abraham at Hebron. In Iran the tomb of Bibi Shahrbanu near Rayy is only one of several localities revered by Muslims and Zoroastrians alike. In numerous cases the sites of such shrines may have been chosen with a view to exploiting the place's pre-existing sacral associations and overlaying them by those of the new faith. The self-same process is well documented in the case of certain mosques. Thus the site currently occupied by the Great Mosque of Damascus held in the preceding two millennia a shrine to the cult of Hadad, a temple of Jupiter Damascenus and the Church of St John.

The major shrines, then, are only incidentally to be interpreted as mausolea. Far more central to their meaning was the part they played as a focus of Shi'ite or Sunni sympathies or as ambassadors of Islam. A third functional category, however, may be proposed, and it is at least of equal importance. This category comprises shrines whose origins can be traced to a single charismatic personality (quite often a Sufi saint) and which in the course of their evolution came to incorporate the tombs of members of the same family or of his disciples. Such shrines are extremely widespread, being encountered as far west as Morocco (where the tomb of Mulay

267

Idris has grown to dominate an entire town), and as far east as India, where shrines of members of the Chishti family are to be found at Delhi, Ajmir, Fatehpur Sikri and elsewhere. Notable medieval examples in the Iranian world include Ardabil, Bastam, Mahan, Natanz and Tirmidh. Such shrines are neither political nor sectarian in their origins, though sometimes their nature might change over the centuries. They are deeply rooted in their local communities; indeed, they seem to have encouraged and expressed (as did the *marabout*s of Morocco) a popular rather than a strictly orthodox form of Islam. Finally, they were charitable institutions, often richly endowed (presumably with official support) and able to provide, at least on a temporary basis, food and even shelter for the poor.

19, 5.3, 4.37
5.122

FORMS OF ISLAMIC MAUSOLEA:
GENERAL CONSIDERATIONS

So much for the origins of the Islamic mausoleum, the terminology used to describe it, and – more to the point – its religious and secular associations. Before embarking on a brief survey of the major Islamic funerary structures over the centuries, it may be helpful to comment in general terms on the types of forms which found favour over the centuries and to inquire into the reasons for their popularity. One question in particular poses itself: why did Islamic mausolea take the varied forms they did? Such a question

at once generates another: did any of these forms carry with it specific religious, ethnic or other implications? The ineradicable human desire to commemorate the dead is reason enough for the existence of Islamic mausolea, but it does not explain, for example, why they do not take the form of prehistoric European barrows, Indian *stupa*s or Egyptian pyramids, or indeed why Muslim burial itself did not take place in structures comparable to Jewish catacombs or Etruscan hypogea. As noted earlier in this chapter, Christian martyria probably provided the immediate inspiration for Islamic mausolea, but the reasons behind the ready acceptance of this form require further investigation. Islam, after all, did not scruple to reject much of the material culture of Byzantium and of Sasanian Iran. If the martyrium had not fulfilled a recognised need, it too would have been discarded as a source of inspiration.

Reduced to its essentials, the martyrium was a simple square structure with a pitched roof – in other words, a house. The immemorial custom of burying the dead underneath their place of dwelling, which is encountered in a great variety of cultures on a world-wide scale, seems to be at the root of this choice of form. The later history of the mausoleum in the Islamic world offers corroborative evidence on this score. From the 11th century onwards a popular type of mausoleum in the eastern Islamic world, especially in Anatolia and northern Iran, was the so-called tomb tower. This building type reproduced, sometimes with remarkable accuracy of detail, the monumental tent of the Turkic peoples. Still further east, in the Mughal dominions of northern India, the type of building which culminated in the Taj Mahal served its patrons as a pleasure pavilion in their lifetimes and as a tomb after their deaths. These later expressions of the equation between house and tomb help to place the Islamic adoption of the martyrium in its proper perspective. Once that perspective has been established, the varied forms of Islamic funerary architecture fall quite naturally into place. Mausolea may, in short, be expected to exhibit no less varied a range of types than domestic architecture – and the latter category embraces simple hut and royal palace alike.

5.161
5.158

To identify the implications associated with any particular form is a somewhat delicate task.

184 Samarqand, Gur-i Amir

185 Cairo, tomb of Yunus al-Dawadar

mausolea. It would certainly be simplistic to equate square tombs with Sunni reverence for the four *rashidun* (Rightly Guided) caliphs. The forms of garden pavilions and mausolea can be virtually interchangeable, but this does not necessarily invest such mausolea with paradisial associations. It has been argued that the two-tier elevation of certain Anatolian mausolea, with a crypt for inhumation below and an empty chamber above, reflects (though it conflates) successive stages of funerary practice among the nomadic Turkic peoples of Inner Asia. It is equally tempting to interpret in non-Islamic terms the report that in the Gunbad-i Qabus, arguably Iran's finest Islamic mausoleum, the body was not buried but was suspended from the roof. In view of the retrospective emphasis of the cultural milieu which produced this tomb, such a detail inevitably evokes a memory of Zoroastrian burial sites, with their concurrent emphasis on the contamination spread by the corpse and the need to contain that contamination by exposing the body on a *dakhma* or Tower of Silence. It will be apparent that the attempt to read symbolic or religious associations into the forms of Islamic mausolea is full of pitfalls.

There is, however, one exception to this: the connection very generally made in medieval sources between a mausoleum, no matter what its form, and the concept of shade. In early Islamic times, the places where those of high religious status (Companions of the Prophet or members of the *ahl al-bait*) were buried might be marked by a canopy, a tent, or some similar form of covering. The notion embodied here was that of affording shade to the deceased; and this shade was interpreted, following in this the Qur'an, as one of the blessings of Paradise. Thus the original embargo was insensibly infringed, but on impeccably religious grounds. It was only a matter of time before these canopies of cloth found monumental form as open-plan mausolea, a type appropriately termed 'canopy tombs' in Western scholarship. Here again, a way to sidestep the Prophet's strictures was devised, though it smacked of sophistry: a canopy tomb was permissible – so ran the argument – because the earth above the corpse was open to wind and rain.

So much in general terms, then, for the function of the mausoleum in medieval Islamic

It necessarily involves an excursus into the largely uncharted realm of Islamic architectural iconography. The suggestions which follow are, therefore, somewhat hypothetical; many of them will be examined in the requisite detail later in this chapter. Even the affinity between tomb towers and Turkish tents mentioned in passing above cannot be regarded as established fact, not least because the earliest such tombs are found in a resolutely Persian context. Twelve-sided tombs are known in Twelver Shi'ite milieux, but so too are numerous other forms of

society, its basic forms and the complex range of associations which it evoked. It is now time to look more closely at the various regional traditions of funerary architecture which developed over the centuries.

RANGE OF FORMS TAKEN BY MEDIEVAL MAUSOLEA

It would be idle to deny that the forms of medieval Islamic mausolea are varied. Yet it must be conceded that the range of variation is substantially less than that of the mosque or *madrasa*. No doubt this is partially because the absolute size of Islamic mausolea tended to be limited by the traditional fidelity to the domed square plan, which of its nature forbade any extensive expansion laterally. Mausolea with integral courtyards were exceptional. There

186 Marrakesh, tombs of the Sa'dians, interior

270

remained only the option of height. This was frequently taken up, and much of the interest of medieval Islamic mausolea lies in the analysis of how architects responded to this challenge: with double domes, elongated drums, attached minarets, attenuated proportions and numerous other devices. Yet for all the visual, stylistic and art-historical interest of such variations, the fact remains that the essentially conservative nature

mercy on their souls, that are erected over their graves in the cemetery of al-Rabad' in Cordoba. Many were tinged with unorthodoxy, as evidenced by their location beside sacred trees or rocks. They were venerated as the tombs of *marabout*s or local saints, and became centres of pilgrimage where the faithful expected their 5.10 prayers to be answered. The very simplicity of these buildings, and their rough and ready con- 5.5

   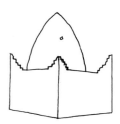

5.5 Maghribi *marabouts*

of the mausoleum genre in most of the Islamic world renders it a somewhat jejune subject for typological analysis. This intrinsic problem is compounded by the extraordinarily uneven spread of mausolea throughout the medieval Islamic world. For large tracts of space and time there is an echoing absence of mausolea, a gap in the record that is highlighted by the very few examples that remain. The medieval Maghrib and Andalusia constitute perhaps the most relevant case in point. In this huge segment of the Muslim world there is virtually not a single 186 mausoleum of note before the Sa'dian tombs 5.9 erected in Marrakesh in the later 16th century; in just the same way, this area produced virtually nothing of note in book painting (as distinct from Qur'an illumination) in the same period. This is not to say that no mausolea were built (an Almohad mausoleum has even been found in Portugal); but the crucial difference between this area and some other parts of the Muslim world was that these mausolea were almost exclusively diminutive and unassuming structures – such as that of the Almoravid Ibn Yasin 5.7–5.8 (d.451/1059) near Rabat. They lacked that di- 5.6 mension of display which characterised the great medieval mausolea of Egypt, Anatolia or Iran. They were in fact the product of local, popular piety, not of exalted patronage – though Ibn Hazm speaks of 'the mausolea of the Banu Marwan [the Umayyad ruling family], God have

struction, militated against their survival; of the thousands of *marabout*s which dot the Maghribi landscape today only a very small proportion could sustain a credible claim to be medieval, though the site itself might well have a history reaching back many centuries. In the few cases where a (late) medieval structure survives, the site is often a cemetery in which several 187 mausolea cluster together, as in the case of Chilla in the suburbs of Rabat, the heavily 5.12 restored so-called 'Tomb of the Sultana' on the 5.13–5.14 outskirts of Tlemcen, or the so-called 'Marinid tombs' on the hill overlooking Fez. It is of course possible that in the great *zawiya*s or shrines of the Maghrib, such as that of Mulay Idris near Meknes or of Shaikh Abu Madyan at 5.11 Tlemcen, the later complex of buildings incorporated some funerary construction commemorating the saint; but if so, the architectural and archaeological record has preserved no trace of it. With these reservations in mind, then, the generalisation made earlier is worth repeating: the Islamic world west of Egypt is effectively a dead letter so far as the history of medieval mausolea is concerned. It is hard to avoid the conclusion that this – like the virtual absence of book painting – has something to do with the dominance of the Maliki *madhhab* in the area, for that law school took a hard line on the breaches of orthodox practice which these particular visual arts entailed. That same orthopraxy has

more notably, Ayyubid Syria are cases in point. Yet the sheer quantity of mausolea produced in these two areas in the 13th century, though very relevant to the social and political history of the period, offer rather less to the historian of architecture and style. They are not part of that recurrent ground swell of change which makes the evolution of a building type such a fascinating study. Unquestionably they mark a significant stage within that evolution; but they do so essentially by means of a single building type. In that sense, they mark time. The evolutionary sequence of Egyptian mausolea in the 13th century produces incomparably more active and varied results than does the same period in Syria. Egypt's role as the senior partner in this relationship relegates the Syrian material to merely provincial status. Nothing could underline that status more inexorably than the spectacle of the dozens of Ayyubid *turba*s of Damascus, Tripoli and Aleppo, virtual carbon copies of each other

5.190, 5.196

187 Rabat, Chilla necropolis

reigned almost uninterruptedly in the Arabian peninsula ever since the coming of Islam, and sufficiently explains why here too the visual arts are confined (and confined even more strictly than in the Muslim West) to religious purposes. The few medieval mausolea or other funerary *188* constructions in the Yemen were for the most part erected within mosques, as in the case of 2.163; 2.156, 2.162 Jibla and Zafar Dhibin. This protective custody successfully discouraged any significant architectural display.

These gaps in the record are in themselves enough to make it impossible to accomplish a truly representative *tour d'horizon* of the medieval Islamic mausoleum. Yet further difficulties lie in wait to discourage such an attempt, difficulties with their source in that conservative attitude mentioned earlier. In certain areas in the central Islamic lands, mausolea were indeed erected in large numbers at specific periods. Saljuq Anatolia and, even

5.14 Tlemcen, "Tomb of the Sultana"

and derived from a model which is itself a simplification of the more unadventurous type of Cairene mausoleum. For this reason they will be mentioned, in due course though only briefly, as an offshoot of that Cairene tradition.

Thus it will be seen that the broad lineaments of medieval Islamic funerary architecture can be grasped even if the discussion is essentially limited to Egypt and Iran. Lest these geographical entities be misunderstood, however, it should be emphasised that – as the foregoing discussion implied – the cultural sway of both these areas was extensive in medieval times and stretched far beyond the modern political borders of these countries. Indeed during the later Middle Ages, Egypt, the Levant and Arabia formed a single political entity under Mamluk domination, and thus the wide catchment area of the house style in mausolea, as in other aspects of architecture, merely reflected political realities. Yet at the same time there can be no doubt that the hub of this empire was Egypt and that in the visual arts the supreme generative force was Cairo, the major Mamluk capital. In the parallel case of Iran, the geographical canvas was still broader, embracing as it did most of Anatolia, Iraq, Caucasia, Central Asia, Afghanistan and the Indian subcontinent in addition to Iran proper. Thus no downgrading of the Anatolian material is implied by treating it as a by-product of the incomparably richer and more varied funerary architecture produced in the rest of the eastern Islamic world. As in the discussion of mosques in Chapter II, the draconian reduction in the quantity of specific monuments presented in this chapter permits a relatively detailed survey of the antecedents and the function of this particular genre of buildings.

THE MAUSOLEUM IN IRAN: GENERAL CONSIDERATIONS

The mausoleum is beyond doubt, with the single exception of the mosque, the most popular building type in the architecture of Islamic Iran. It is rooted in the very fabric of Iranian society and culture, and there must be very few towns in the country without their quota of such buildings. Moreover, hundreds of villages across the length and breadth of Iran with little more than a mosque by way of public

buildings will nevertheless possess their own locally venerated *imamzada*. In all probability this will be a structure of indeterminate age, and the popular identification of its tenant may well rest on nothing more substantial than local tradition. Nevertheless, for the people who visit such shrines on a *ziyarat* or who accomplish other devotions or pious duties there, the genuineness of the popular identification is unchallenged, and thus the place of such a building in the religious life of the people at large is assured. How has this situation come about? The discussion which follows will devote comparatively little attention to the architectural forms taken by medieval Iranian mausolea. After all, the variations in form undergone by this genre of building over the centuries are relatively slight in comparison with, say, the

188 Zafar Dhibin, mausoleum within the mosque

273

mosque or the palace. It will therefore be possible to discuss at some length issues related to the origins, function and religious significance of these monuments, before studying briefly their typology, distribution, location and stylistic development. It goes without saying that a rapid survey such as this can only hint at the complexities of these topics; but such indications will at least serve to flesh out the otherwise uncomfortable austerity of a purely morphological account of medieval Iranian funerary architecture.

Given the obvious dependence of much early Islamic Iranian architecture on the pre-Islamic heritage of Iran, it is worth emphasising that there is no significant tradition of free-standing funerary monuments in pre-Islamic times. The splendid tomb of Cyrus at Pasargadae is the exception that proves the rule. The later Achaemenid monarchs were laid to rest in burial chambers hewn into cliff faces, and such rock tombs seem to have continued for some time after the fall of the dynasty. The burial customs observed in Parthian Iran – to judge by the graphic descriptions of the Greek sources – appear to have ruled out the construction of mausolea. As for the Sasanian kings, while they were not uniformly orthodox proponents of the Zoroastrian faith, the extremely specific provisions in that creed governing the disposal of

corpses, which were thought to pollute the earth by their deadly spiritual infection, would quickly have stifled any tendency to develop a cult of the dead and its associated funerary architecture. Corpses were exposed on raised platforms, or *dakhma*s, preferably in remote locations, and when they had been picked clean by carrion birds and animals the bones were collected and buried in funerary urns or ossuaries. Thus when Islam came to Iran there was no living tradition of mausolea to serve as inspiration for Muslims wishing to erect such buildings.

Funerary practices in Iran cannot be studied in isolation from the rest of the Islamic world. As noted earlier, literary references establish that mausolea were being built widely throughout most of the *dar al-Islam* from the second century of the Hijra onwards. Thus it is entirely possible that Iranian Muslims borrowed the idea from their co-religionists in Egypt, Syria or Iraq, and that the gradual breaches of Islamic orthodoxy in matters of burial were mirrored in Iran. These breaches, fuelled principally by religious particularism and by *jihad*, have been discussed in detail earlier in this chapter. Similarly, the rôle of the classical mausolea of late antiquity, and of the early Christian and Byzantine martyrium, also needs to be reckoned with even in the relatively distant Iranian context.

5.152 Tagisken, ancient Turkic mausolea

Yet there is one further theory that needs to be canvassed in any discussion of the origins of the funerary architecture of medieval Iran. Could it be that the crucial influences were those from the world of the steppe to the north and east of Central Asia? By this reckoning, the nomadic Turkic peoples would have introduced the idea of the mausoleum to the Iranian world, and indeed their geographical proximity to the very area where the earliest Iranian Islamic mausolea are to be found is a powerful argument in favour of this idea. In pre-Islamic times the steppe peoples of Central and Eastern Asia practised quite complex funerary rituals, some of which have survived into modern times. Excavations of the complex of buildings at Tagisken in Central Asia, datable to the 3rd century BC, suggest that the tombs of that time took the form of gigantic *yurt*s executed in durable materials and surrounded by circular walls or set on high plinths. Literary accounts stress the two stages of mourning: exposure of the body in a funerary tent with processions of mourners encircling it (compare the later Muslim *tawwaf*), followed by its inhumation in a funerary mound (*kurgan*). Tomb towers with funerary crypts enclosing the body (sometimes embalmed) and crowned by an empty room have been interpreted as an architectural conflation of these practices. Even the decoration of nomadic tents finds astonishingly close analogies in some Iranian Islamic mausolea. The external elevation of such towers, too, bears an obvious architectural resemblance to the splendid princely tents described in detail by western travellers such as Carpini and Rubruquis, to say nothing of Islamic and Chinese sources. It is at least possible, therefore, that the forms of such tents had an effect on those of early Iranian mausolea. Nevertheless the question remains an open one, for it has to be conceded that the earliest surviving tomb towers were built by princes of Iranian rather than Turkish stock, and in pre-Saljuq times.

Irrespective of how the idea of funerary architecture reached Iran, there can be little doubt that it flourished mightily there. In the 10th and 11th centuries, the period which saw the first great flowering of funerary architecture in Iran, the only area which produced a comparable volume of mausolea was Fatimid Egypt. In the

189 Abarquh, Gunbad-i 'Ali

latter region, it may be noted, the correlation between Shi'ism and funerary buildings is still more explicit than it was in Iran at that time. A likely explanation for this divergence is that Iran was subject to a substantially wider range of influence. Thus there is no parallel in Fatimid Egypt for the Zoroastrian and Turkish elements which enriched the early development of the Iranian mausoleum. It will be convenient to discuss each of these in turn.

Zoroastrian elements

The form of the celebrated 'Tomb of the

5.42–5.44, 5.55

2.225–2.226

189

5.23–5.24, 5.27

194

Samanids' in Bukhara, datable before 331/943, is simply an enriched version of the standard Iranian fire temple (*chahar taq*) of Sasanian times. In its bleak location on a crag outside Abarquh, far removed from the nearest human habitation, the Gunbad-i 'Ali, dated 448/1056, irresistibly recalls some Zoroastrian *dakhma* or Tower of Silence. At the Gunbad-i Qabus (dated 397/1006), which fittingly opens the splendid series of Iranian tomb towers, such Zoroastrian associations – though subtly transmuted into new forms – are again undeniably present. They surface in the use of the Yazdigirdi calendar alongside the Muslim one for the date given in the inscription and – more dramatically – in the method apparently used to dispose of the corpse. According to al-Jannabi, the body of the prince was suspended from the roof in a glass coffin, its head turned towards the single window which faced the rising sun. If this account is to be credited, the careful avoidance of inhumation cannot fail to recall Zoroastrian precepts. In a similar vein, it is tempting to interpret the consistent choice of remote hilltop locations for so many of these early mausolea – e.g. the Gunbad-i 'Ali, Abarquh, or the Samiran mausolea – as a reference to the Zoroastrian *dakhma*. Other equally transitional funerary monuments from this early period have been found at Siraf on the Persian Gulf; these are rock-cut tombs which held corpses rather than ossuaries and thus belong in a syncretist context.

190

Turkish elements

Turkish influence manifests itself slightly later, for example in the Kharraqan tombs of 460/1067 and 486/1093. In this case there is not even a village nearby, and the choice of site, marooned

191

5.25

190 Samiran, anonymous mausoleum

191 Kharraqan, later tower

practice among the pagan nomads of Turkic stock. On the death of a chief or some other notable of the tribe, his body was first exposed for a brief period in his tent, and only then buried or disposed of in some other way. Tomb towers such as Radkan East can be explained as a conflation of these two distinct stages in a single building. From the 13th century onwards, yet another nomadic practice, this time of Mongol origin, infiltrated the Iranian world. This was the custom of keeping secret the burial place of an important leader, and declaring the surrounding area taboo (*qoruq*). An example of this practice is furnished by the burial of the Mongol Ilkhan Hülegü somewhere on the island of Shahi in Lake Urmiya.

Religious and symbolic aspects of the mausoleum

This brief account of the impact exerted by two non-Islamic influences on the development of the mausoleum in Muslim Iran highlights the readiness of Islamic architects in this as in other fields to put old forms to new uses. Often enough these old forms carry some of their familiar associations with them into their new function, and thereby enrich it.

Frequently the very wording of an inscription or a text enforces the interpretation that a given mausoleum also served some other and non-funerary function. Examples of this are *ribat*s, *zawiya*s, funerary *madrasa*s and even funerary mosques, such as the one at Turbat-i Jam. These 2.272 cases show clearly enough how funerary architecture was part of the warp and weft of medieval Iranian society. Such joint – or even multiple – foundations brought the mausoleum into the orbit of society at large and made it natural to extend the functions of a tomb structure beyond simple burial. This did not prevent the secular mausoleum from becoming a symbol of conspicuous consumption. Nevertheless, for patrons desirous of perpetuating their names and at the same time flaunting their piety, or benefitting the local community, or making atonement for their sins by engaging in good works, such joint foundations were ideal. The mausoleum provided, as it were, a stamp of ownership for the entire foundation.

By a natural transition the mausoleum would acquire sanctity from its very surroundings and indeed might become in due time a supplemen-

5.31 in a level plain, may well reflect the popularity of the Kharraqan uplands as a nomadic grazing ground. The very structure of these tombs seems to reproduce in brick features familiar in the perishable materials used in tents: wicker-work creating lattice patterns, and wooden ribs to form a framework for the felt roof. A tower like Radkan East, datable to 602/1206 and again set against the backdrop of limitless open countryside, is an even more explicit rendition in brick of a princely Turkish tent, right down to the conical roof, the plain flat skirts just above ground level, and the bundles of staves set at regular intervals to create the skeleton of the whole structure. Even the woven texture of the outer walls of a *yurt* is reproduced in decorative brickwork. As noted above, the presence of a crypt with a chamber above it in many such tombs has been persuasively explained as a translation into architectural terms of a common

work: Gunbad-i Surkh, 'the red tomb'. Surprisingly few tombs associated with the major political figures of early medieval Iran have survived. Possibly this is because many of them were buried in their palaces or in already existing structures which were not purpose-built mausolea, for example mosques or *madrasa*s. In the 11th and 12th centuries the exception is Sultan Sanjar (d.552/1157), whose great tomb still dominates Merv. In Mongol and Timurid times this picture changes somewhat, but it remains true that most members of the ruling families are not represented by surviving tombs. Time has dealt more kindly with the mausolea of saints, *shaikh*s and *imam*s than with those of political notables. Thus religious associations clearly offer a better guarantee for the survival of a mausoleum than does secular power. Once again, then, the close connection between religion and funerary architecture in the Iranian sphere manifests itself.

5.15–5.
5.21

5.62,
5.65–5.

Given the natural tendency, observable in many cultures throughout the world, to express the multiple associations of death by means of symbols, it would be strange if funerary architecture in medieval Iran did not also avail itself of symbols to evoke resonances or ideas for which words were not the most appropriate means of communication. It was above all by means of symbols, after all, that the heterodox practice of erecting mausolea could claim justification and could allude to the paradise awaiting the virtuous dead. Some of these symbols were common currency in medieval Christendom too: for example, the use of a dome to suggest the heavens, and by extension paradise: or of evergreen trees, which in Iran meant for instance cypress and juniper, to suggest everlasting life. The peacock is another shared symbol of this kind, though its meaning was not the same in Islam as in Christendom. Affronted peacocks flanking a stylised Tree of Life decorate the walls of the first Kharraqan tower. Graves are referred to in deliberately exalted language, being termed for example 'illuminated'. This theme is frequently taken up by the use of tombstones decorated with mosque lamps (a painted mosque lamp is also found in the first Kharraqan tower) and with Qur'anic quotations from *Surat al-nur* precisely in the manner of *mihrab*s. The connection is

5.90

5.94

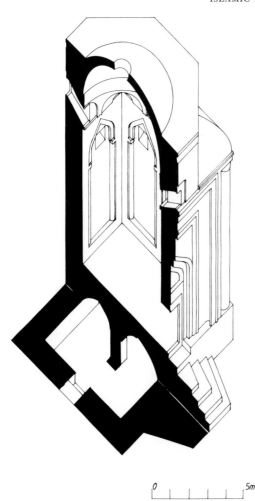

0   5m

5.21 Maragha, Gunbad-i Surkh

5.105–5.106

tary place of worship. It commonly happened that the identity of the original tenant was forgotten, to be replaced by that of a personality more attuned to the requirements of local piety – e.g. the so-called "Pir" mausoleum at Takistan. Often the new identification would gain credence even though an inscription visible to all would tell a very different tale – thus the tower at Lajim, dated 413/1022(?) and commemorating a noble lady of probably Bawandid stock, is now the Imamzada 'Abdallah. At Maragha the memory of an Ahmadili *amir* has suffered the final ignominy, for his tomb (dated 542/1148) is now associated with no one at all and owes its name to the colour of the brick-

often made explicit by placing such tombstones facing the *qibla*, so that they can indeed serve as *mihrab*s. Here again, commemoration of the dead, intrinsically heterodox though it be, is closely bound up with religious observance.

The evidence, sparse though it is, suggests that the aim of the various symbols employed in Iranian funerary architecture was to evoke paradise rather than to express any confessional loyalties. Thus there is a total absence of seven-sided tombs for adherents of the Sevener Shi'a persuasion – as indeed is the case elsewhere in the Islamic world. Even tombs of the Twelver Shi'a very rarely have twelve sides, and the twelve-sided carpet in the shrine of Fatima at Qumm is apparently unique in the way that the form itself is dovetailed with its appropriate setting. At the most obvious level, then, it seems that number symbolism is not a significant feature of Iranian mausolea. The number eight

is – perhaps – an important exception. Octagonal palace kiosks in Safavid Iran and Mughal India, conventionally set within garden precincts amid groves of trees, flower-beds, fountains and water-channels, were sometimes known as *hasht bihisht* ('eight paradises') and it is tempting to suggest that these associations were in some way present in mausolea of similar form, especially when such tombs were placed within a garden setting. In such circumstances the possibility of a delicate allusion to the pleasures of paradise, which included pavilions, shady trees and running water, may well have been intended. If so, such associations were not explicit but seemingly operated at a subliminal level. The evidence for this lies in the inscriptions which so many mausolea bear. These often identify the tenant of the tomb and give its date, with the rest of the space being given over to Qur'anic texts. It is noteworthy that these

7.140–7.141,
7.145

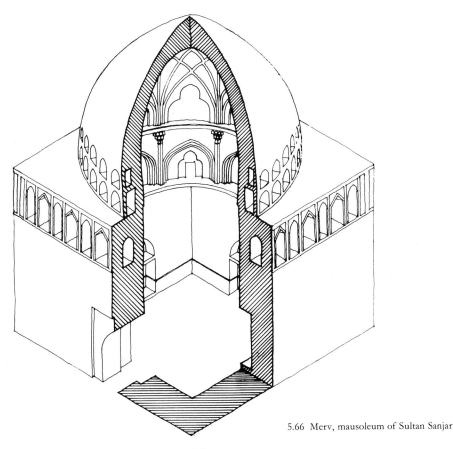

5.66 Merv, mausoleum of Sultan Sanjar

quotations are usually quite unrelated to the themes of death, judgment and paradise. When they do touch on these themes, the commonest quotation seems to be from Sura XXI: 35 – 'every soul must taste of death', or from the almost identical Sura III: 185. There are perhaps no more appropriate quotations than these in the entire Qur'an for a funerary context, but they give little latitude to the theory that mausolea are intended to evoke the blessings which await the elect. Inscriptions, then, shed very little light on the building or on its purpose, aside from its function as a grave marker.

It should be noted parenthetically that the mausoleum was only one of several options open to those who wished to commemorate the dead in some tangible way. These included, as mentioned earlier, *steles* in the form of flat *mihrabs*; elaborately patterned, figured or inscribed shrouds in cotton, linen or even silk; and full-scale representations of rams sculpted in the round. The range and popularity of these memorials, each of them transgressing orthodoxy in some way, indicates clearly enough that the letter of Islamic doctrine was fundamentally at odds with a significant body of popular opinion. Yet in these cases too, either the form of the memorial itself or its inscriptions proclaimed allegiance to Islam.

Enough has been said to show that funerary architecture is a significant factor in our understanding of medieval Iranian society; to indicate how the function of such buildings became gradually more complex than simply to mark a burial; and finally to clarify how this increasing complexity was reflected in a corresponding expansion of the architectural fabric itself. Early mausolea such as the 'Tomb of the Samanids' and the Gunbad-i Qabus were ill-suited for any purpose other than commemorating the dead. At the other extreme, the term 'mausoleum' will scarcely fit the great shrines of Iran, with their symbiotic cluster of secondary buildings around the tomb itself. Yet despite the many morphological changes to which the basic form was subjected over the centuries, and despite the changes of name and purpose which were imposed on individual mausolea, the basic function associated with that form was not misunderstood. Like the minaret, the tomb was instantly recognisable as such. To explain how

5.42–5.44
5.55
5.23–5.24,
5.27

5.1–5.4

this successful integration of form, function and symbol was achieved will involve a brief examination of the architectural forms and styles of funerary buildings in medieval Iran. It will be seen that a significant factor in this success was an innate conservatism which inhibited radical experiment in the architectural form itself. Innovation from outside Iran was exceptional and the adaptation of other established forms to funerary purposes was if anything even rarer. The compass within which formal and stylistic change occurred was therefore limited. Consolidation, not innovation, was the watchword.

THE BASIC TYPES OF MAUSOLEUM IN IRAN

What, then, were these forms? When the well-nigh endless variations are reduced to their essentials, it will be seen that only two basic types bear the architectural history of the Iranian mausoleum. These are the tomb tower and the domed square. Admittedly this excludes combinations of the two, like the mausoleum of Tekesh at Urgench, and one or two types which obstinately refuse to fit into either of these categories, however generously they are interpreted. An example is the *hazira* or funerary compound, of which the Gazur Gah shrine of *c*.828/1425 near Herat is an excellent specimen. Happily such exceptions can be omitted from the present account without seriously impairing its accuracy. A more substantial problem, at first

5.80–5.8
5.84, 5.8

5.120

192 Merv, mausoleum of Sultan Sanjar

193 Bust, Shahzada Sarbaz

sight, is posed by the domed octagon, a very common type indeed. Should it not form a third category on its own? Paradoxical though it may sound, this type should be classed as one of the varieties of the domed square. A brief account of the origins of the domed square, as distinct from those of the tomb tower, will make this clear.

The domed square seems to have a dual ancestry, though intensive research might indicate that these two strands in fact go back to a single source. One element may be the standard Sasanian fire temple or *chahar taq*, its square ground-plan broken by four axial openings and crowned by a dome. The wide diffusion of these buildings throughout Iran at the time of the Islamic conquest makes this architectural type an obvious model for Islamic mausolea of similar plan in Iran. Yet the case is not as straightforward as it might seem. Similar mausolea occur elsewhere in the Islamic world, in contexts where the possibility of Zoroastrian influence does not arise. In such cases, and therefore possibly in the case of Iran as well, the crucial influence appears to have been the other possible ancestor of the Islamic domed square, namely the late antique mausoleum and its

various derivatives – which include pre-Islamic Soghdian ossuaries. Here the transition from the pre-Islamic to the Islamic building was rendered seamless by a continuity of function, whereas the suggested derivation from Zoroastrian *chahar taq*s would involve an abrupt and critical change in function. Moreover, the late antique mausoleum – and the churches, baptisteries and martyria of early Christian and Byzantine date derived from it – was by no means confined, as was the *chahar taq*, to a single architectural expression of the domed centralised form. As it happens, an early and popular expression of this type in Islamic Iranian mausolea was the square; but in time, and by a natural process of development, the notion of a radiating centralised plan found its preferred expression on Iranian soil in the domed octagon. It was the octagon which best combined the requirements of a central focus – usually provided by a sarcophagus – with those of the maximum space for circumambulation (*tawwaf*) and the maximum scope for spatial and other architectural experiments. The square form, by contrast, brought in its train wasted space in the corners and encouraged experiments in decoration rather than

281

form. Whether its gradual replacement by the domed octagon was accelerated by the growing fashion for making mausolea places of pilgrimage and worship is a matter for future research to determine. Symptomatic of this transition 5.42–5.43, 5.48, 5.66, was the increasing rôle played in buildings of 5.78–5.79 square plan by the zone of transition, which was usually octagonal.

The tomb tower

The other major category of mausolea is the 5.19–5.20, 5.22 tomb tower. Its origins are shrouded in uncertainty, though many possibilities might be *cf.* 5.158, 5.52 canvassed: Turkish tents, Sabian temples, Chinese watch-towers and Palmyran tower tombs among them. Cogent arguments can be marshalled against each of these putative models, however, and in the present state of knowledge it seems better to admit ignorance. This course seems especially justified in view of the extremely simple form taken by most of the 5.4, 5.17, 5.22 early examples of this genre: a lofty cylinder with a dome or conical roof. As with the domed square, it was not long before this primitive formula was enriched. In quick succession tomb

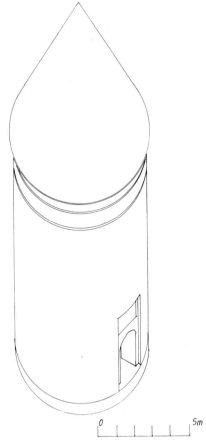

5.22 Radkan West, tomb tower

towers with flanges, engaged columns and 5.28–5.3 corner buttresses were built, while the simple 5.25 cylinder gave way to octagons, hexagons, ten- 5.40–5.4 5.18 and twelve-sided tombs and various kinds of 5.38 stellar elevations. 5.32

Perhaps the most durably popular of these types was the octagon, and this naturally raises the question of how to distinguish an octagonal tomb tower from a domed octagon. While it is true that there are areas of overlap between these two major categories, the case of the octagon is well suited to defining their essential differences. The tomb tower, whatever its ground plan, retains as its major distinguishing feature an emphasis on sheer height, greatly enhanced by the relative constriction of the interior. This results in a ratio of width to height which is usually in the range 1:3.5–1:5.5. Domed squares tend to have far less marked differentials. Thus

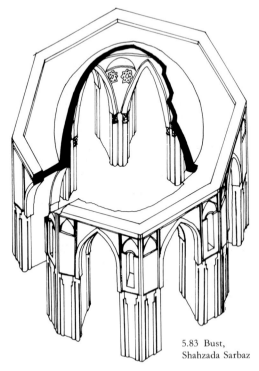

5.83 Bust, Shahzada Sarbaz

282

even the grandest of Saljuq domed square mausolea, the tomb of Sultan Sanjar at Merv (datable soon after 552/1157), has a width to height ratio of approximately 1:2, while its nearest rival in Ilkhanid times, the tomb of Öljeitü in Sultaniya (dedicated 713/1313), which is a gigantic domed octagon some 53 m. high, nevertheless has a width to height ratio of barely 1:2.2. These figures tell their own story. One building type, it seems, is intended to serve primarily as an external marker of a grave, its interior correspondingly neglected; the other is conceived primarily as an interior space, a space to be used regularly, and the exterior is of lesser importance. None of this is to deny that in any given case a patron might as happily choose the tomb tower form as the domed square; but the underlying trend is unmistakable. As the ratio between width and height more closely approaches parity, so does the likelihood increase that the building in question is intended primarily for religious, not secular, purposes, even if – as at Bust in southern Afghanistan – the original purpose cannot be determined.

It is now time to consider briefly the architectural development of the two major building types described above. Their progress was somewhat out of phase. It seems clear that the earliest mausolea in the Iranian world were domed squares, but in the course of the late 10th century they were overtaken in popularity by tomb towers, and it is this form which dominates the Saljuq period. So strong was this preference that examples of virtually all the significant variants in the tomb tower form can be found in the years c.390/1000–c.596/1200. A goodly proportion of these mausolea were built for minor dynasts, *amir*s, *isfahsalar*s and the like. In conformity with the Sunni tenor of the Saljuq centuries, the mausolea of Shi'ite *imam*s scarcely figure among these tomb towers, though several members of the ruling families of the Caspian Shi'ite dynasties built towers for themselves, as at Radkan West.

Pre-eminent among these northern Iranian towers is the Gunbad-i Qabus of 397/1006, a building of uncompromising severity which owes its commanding power to the clean lines that seem to magnify still further its already gigantic size. No subsequent tomb tower approaches the scale of this, the earliest survival of the series. Its circular plan is broken by ten huge, evenly spaced, triangular flanges which break free from the plinth and streak upwards to vanish into the corbelled cornice supporting the conical roof. The single slender arched doorway seems lost in the immensity of unbroken brickwork. Even the site is carefully chosen to accentuate the dwarfing height of the building: the tower rests on a substantial tepe which forms the sole eminence for miles around. Two identical inscription bands girdle the tower, one near the base, the other near the peak of the flanges – illegibly high and thus a symbolic presence only. Most subsequent towers are of high-quality baked brick (e.g. that of Yusuf b. Kuthair at

194 Gunbad-i Qabus

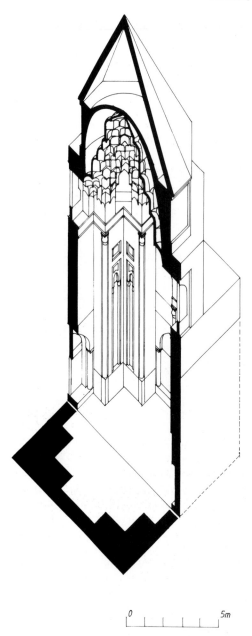

0   5m

5.34 Natanz, mausoleum of Shaikh 'Abd al-Samad

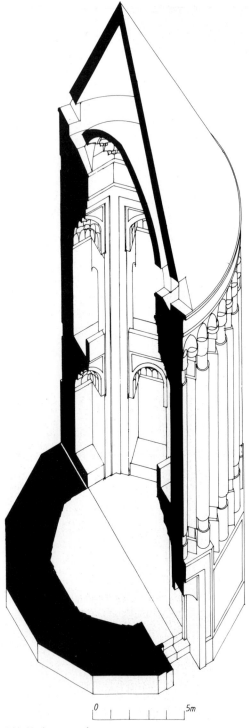

0   5m

5.30 Kashmar, tomb tower

195 Kashmar, tomb, vaulting of interior

196 Qumm, tomb of 'Imad al-Din, interior

285

197 Qumm, tombs in the Bagh-i Sabz

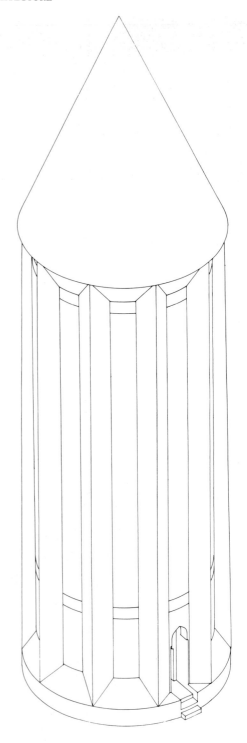

Nakhchivan, 557/1162) enlivened by various decorative bonds – often applied in panels – by inscription bands above the single doorway or below the dome, and occasionally by galleries or elaborate cornices. Polyhedral or candle-snuffer roofs are the norm; these cover much lower inner domes above a cylindrical or polygonal body (Urmiya, 580/1184; Nakhchivan, tomb of Mu'mina Khatun, 582/1186). From the strictly architectural and structural point of view, their elevations are as spartan in their simplicity as their applied ornament is so often lavish. It is this simplicity, this emphasis on a single attenuated shaft constituting the main visual impact of the tower, which by illusionistic means so enhances the impression of loftiness. Even though most of these early towers are only some 15–20 m. high, they seem very much taller than this. A few, such as the so-called tower of Tughrul at Rayy (534/1140) and of course the Gunbad-i Qabus, are even in absolute terms very lofty buildings indeed; yet here too the use of flanges, creating a series of unbroken knife-edge parallel lines running straight from plinth to cornice, makes for an image of propulsion that powerfully fosters the illusion of still greater height. The Ilkhanid period brought nothing substantially new to these developments, though tomb towers do mirror the stylistic tendencies of the time. Accordingly the trend towards attenuated proportions makes itself equally felt in this genre, as the flanged towers of Bastam, Kashmar, Damavand and Varamin (688/1289), or slender octagons and twelve-sided tombs like Darjazin demonstrate. Yet the future was to lie less with these than with a stumpier octagonal mausoleum, whose sixteen-sided drum bore a polyhedral roof. This well-defined three-tier elevation became the norm for the numerous Shi'ite mausolea of Qumm, such

5.24 Gunbad-i Qabus

286

198 Natanz, shrine of 'Abd al-Samad, interior of tomb chamber

demarcation into three tiers, and at ground level was rather more spacious than the typical Saljuq 5.37 tomb tower. *Muqarnas* vaults also became more popular, both for niches (Linjan, *c.*699/1299) 177 and for entire domes (Natanz, 707/1307). A 5.33–5.34, 198 simplified variation of the Qumm type achieved popularity in Mazandaran in the course of the 15th century, but it turned out to be effectively the swan-song of this genre of building. Elsewhere tomb towers are exceedingly rare in Timurid times, and indeed, as noted above, they were never to regain their former popularity.

The domed square

197, 5.37 as the trio of tombs in the Bagh-i Sabz, and thence in subsequent centuries spread throughout the country, though in relatively small numbers. The interior reflected the same clear

The domed square mausoleum and its multiple derivatives had, in contrast, a history of consistent popularity in Iran which extended from at least the early tenth century until modern times and was not, as in the case of tomb towers,

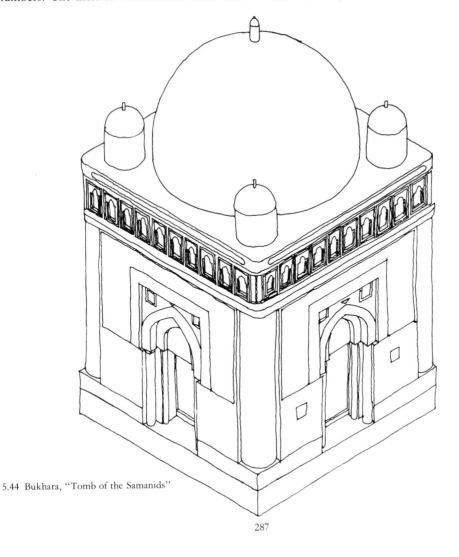

5.44 Bukhara, "Tomb of the Samanids"

199 Bukhara, "Tomb of the Samanids"

generally confined to Northern Iran. In Transoxiana, the 10th century saw the construction
5.47, 5.64 of a whole series of mausolea of domed square

type, often with elaborate brick decoration
('Tomb of the Samanids' in Bukhara; Arab-Ata
mausoleum at Tim; mausolea known as Char   5.57, 5.6
5.79

288

200 Bukhara, "Tomb of the Samanids", detail of gallery

6, 5.70 Jui, Imam-Baba, Kiz-Bibi, Shir Kabir and finally the so-called tomb of Ahmad). The masterpiece of this school is without doubt the 'Tomb of the Samanids', datable before 331/943, possibly the most epoch-making building in *199–201* Iranian Islamic architecture. Yet it looks backward as well as forward. Its domed square form, its arched opening on each side, its lack of directional emphasis and the presence of an upper gallery with corner domes are all features with Sasanian antecedents. It is, in short, a fire temple in Islamic dress. But the Islamic detailing completely transforms the model. Sasanian *chahar taq*s, built of a rough stone which defies applied ornament, rely for their effect on their simple but massive proportions which lend monumentality even to such small buildings. The 'Tomb of the Samanids' retains this monumentality even though every surface but the dome is decorated. It is a triumph of balance. The key to this achievement is the use of baked brick. No earlier Iranian building exploits the decorative potential of the medium, though a Mesopotamian structure of the late 8th century displays sophisticated brick ornament: the palace of Ukhaidir. It is tempting to believe on this evidence that decorative brickwork, like stucco of the Samarra style, was an alien import into north-eastern Iran, especially as a richly ornamented mosque like Hajji Piyada, though later than Ukhaidir, uses stucco instead of brick for decorative purposes. But several factors make this unlikely. Mesopotamia had for centuries been Persian territory and the style developed there may be expected to have been common to Iran proper too. The paucity of standing structures, as distinct from excavated ground plans, which survive from early Islamic Iran indicates (as indeed the literary sources prove) that these survivals give only a very

5.42–5.44,
5.55

2.225–2.226

279

280–282

partial idea of the range of contemporary architecture. Lastly, it is quite unthinkable that so mature a grasp of brick decoration could be achieved in a few years. On the contrary, it argues a long prior period of experiment of which all traces are now lost.

Whatever the source of the new medium, it is used here with splendid assurance. Deep shadow lines are allowed to highlight key elements of the design like the arcaded gallery, *200* the portals and the engaged corner columns. Tripled or quadrupled stretchers alternate with smaller bricks in vertical bond and by their greater mass dominate them. Thus while the effect is that of a woven surface, the horizontal element is stressed, and thus the solidity of the bearing walls is emphasised. To describe the ornament simply as brickwork, however, is mistaken. The mausoleum foreshadows the tendency of medieval architects from Transoxiana to use terracotta moulded into various shapes before firing, for example as joint plugs, or in more complex arabesques (tomb of Bayan Quli Khan, Bukhara, 759/1357–8). The range of *178* the decoration is thus greatly increased, notably by the use of curved shapes. Thick borders of plain brick demarcate the various decorative schemes and obviate confusion.

The mausoleum at Tim, dated 367/977–8, is *5.57, 5.* almost equally prophetic. While the Bukhara *5.79* tomb emphasises the heavy dome, not only by its unalleviated mass but also by the pronounced batter of the bearing walls (a feature shared with the Masjid-i Diggarun, Hazara), the Tim mauso- *2.240* leum hides the dome behind a high *pishtaq* or arched and framed portal. Attention is thereby concentrated on the entrance façade and it almost follows that the other walls should be plain. The truncated rectangular frame of the *pishtaq* bears a monumental inscription, a feature which was to become standard for such buildings. The group of three windows in rectangular frames above the tympanum were not repeated in later structures of this kind; they may echo the gallery of the Bukhara tomb, and more distantly they prefigure the arcade above the entrance arch of the Baghdad Gate at Raqqa; but the motif was experimental only and its lack of obvious function may have caused its omission from subsequent buildings. Inside and out the main decorative accent is provided by

201 Bukhara, "Tomb of the Samanids", interior, zone of transition

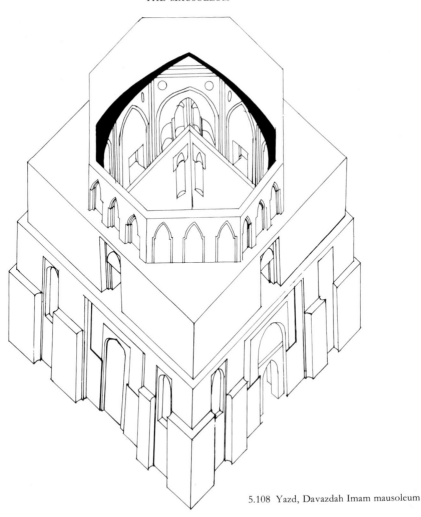

5.108 Yazd, Davazdah Imam mausoleum

double stretchers, a characteristic device of pre-Mongol brickwork in Khurasan and Central Asia. In place of the busy multi-textured surfaces within the Bukhara tomb, and its somewhat compressed zone of transition, the Tim mausoleum exhibits a much smoother interior surface in which a lofty zone of transition is given even greater vertical emphasis by the tri-lobed arch, or squinch, on each side of the octagon. This is the first dated appearance of a motif which came to dominate the architecture of the Isfahan area in the Saljuq period.

The astonishing precision and assurance of the 'Tomb of the Samanids' argues quite a long ancestry, as do the numerous accomplished variations on that theme which were produced within the following century or so. These included an expansion of the gallery area (tombs at Mihna and Turkmenian Sarakhs), an increasing emphasis on the zone of transition (Davazdah Imam mausoleum, Yazd, 429/1037), and the development of the *pishtaq* ('Alambardar mausoleum and that of Baba Luqman in Sarakhs, 757/1356). These features served notice, as it were, that whereas the tomb tower often functioned primarily as a hoarding for elaborate decoration, and was structurally something of a dead end, the domed square and its associated forms, while offering much the same opportunities for decoration, also encouraged spatial experiment, and

5.58, 5.68;
5.59, 5.69

5.107–5.108

5.60, 5.74

291

202 Safid Buland, tomb of Shaikh Fadl, interior

this was to win for them a much more significant rôle in the funerary architecture of Iran. At first such experiment tended to concentrate on a given area rather than affecting the whole of the monument. By degrees, however, a more integrated elevation was devised. A domed square

292

203 Uzgend, tomb of Jalal al-Din Husain

such as Sangbast betrays an intermediate stage in this process. Its tripartite elevation is strongly marked both internally and externally, but it is the interior which claims the lion's share of the decoration – a common feature in domed squares of this period, as at Safid Buland. On the

5.46,
179, 202

293

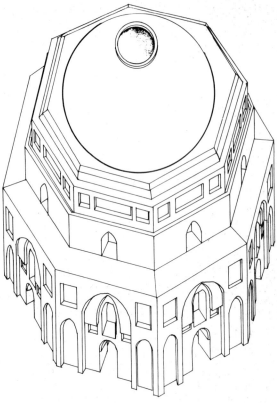

5.102 Kirman, Jabal-i Sang

exterior, base and dome alike were plain and only the now vanished gallery provided some much-needed articulation. The tomb of Sultan Sanjar at Merv, which is probably a little later in date, has the same austerity in the base storey

but its gallery is more ambitious and its dome was covered in blue glazed bricks.

In general, these large Saljuq domed square mausolea owe an obvious debt to the dome chamber which marks the *qibla* of the typical Saljuq mosque. Some, however, develop along markedly different lines. Several approaches may be distinguished. In certain domed squares, such as the Gunbad-i 'Alawiyan at Hamadan or the mausoleum of Muntasir at Astana-Baba and a host of related 11th–12th century tombs in Central Asia (like Yarti Gunbad, the tomb of Muhammad b. Zaid at Merv and above all the tombs at Uzgend, dated or datable 403/1012–3, 547/1152 and 582/1186–7), external applied decoration played as great a rôle as in some contemporary tomb towers. In others, the role of the *pishtaq* took on new significance, as the examples of the Haruniya at Tus and the Baba Luqman tomb at Sarakhs indicate. Yet other mausolea emphasised elaborate external articulation, for example the Davazdah Imam tomb at Yazd, the shrine of Saif al-Din Bakharzi at Bukhara or the Jabal-i Sang at Kirman. Thus the Saljuq heritage to later periods was an exceedingly rich one in this genre.

IRANIAN MAUSOLEA AFTER 1300

Even so, it is interesting to note that whereas Ilkhanid architects had comparatively little to add to the Saljuq achievement in the field of tomb towers, it was a very different story with the domed square and its derivatives, which turned out to offer a much richer vein for experiment. The tomb of Öljeitü at Sultaniya can be

204 Uzgend, tomb associated with Nasr b. 'Ali, squinch

205 Bukhara, complex at Fathabad, shrine of Saif al-Din Bakharzi

206 Kirman, Jabal-i Sang

208 Sultaniya, mausoleum of Öljeitü, tilework in the interior

207 Sultaniya, mausoleum of Öljeitü

seen as the Ilkhanid response to the challenge posed by the great sequence of Saljuq domed square mausolea, as indeed the roughly contemporary tomb of Ghazan seems to have been intended to outdo all previous tomb towers. Öljetiü's tomb solves at a stroke the problems that had beset the architects of earlier domed square mausolea, and the achievement is further enhanced by the sheer scale of the enterprise. To this day the Sultaniya tomb, at 53 m., is the loftiest in Iran. The octagonal plan is carried in elevation to the very base of the dome, which sits snugly within a unique crown of eight minarets, each marking a corner of the octagon. This continuity is reinforced by a rich articulation of the exterior by successive tiers of open or blind arched panels, a scheme which encourages a seamless integration of the gallery with the

5.97 Sultaniya, mausoleum of Öljeitü

295

5.98 Sultaniya, mausoleum of Öljeitü, cutaway view

area below. That gallery is roofed by a matchless array of two dozen vaults sheathed in carved and painted stucco – a miniature museum of contemporary decoration in that medium. Originally the interior was resplendent with glazed tilework employed on a hitherto unprecedented scale. Unfortunately this unique decorative scheme was very soon overlaid by a second and totally different one executed mainly in painted stucco. Yet it is primarily the architecture itself which makes this building a benchmark. Its 5.98 essence is the vast echoing space of the interior, with its billowing niches at ground level and its deep gallery enlarging that space still further. All this is achieved by an unexampled feat of structural engineering whose art is to conceal art. This is reflected in the total absence of corner piers, battered walls, flying buttresses or other shoring-up devices. Every detail conduces to a lightness and poise that strike an exquisite balance with the enormous mass of the whole.

The scale of Öljeitü's mausoleum and the aspiration which it embodied owed much to royal patronage – and significantly enough it was similar patronage which was responsible for its closest contemporary rival, the tomb of 5.104 Rukn-i 'Alam at Multan in Pakistan (c.720/ 1320). Lesser patrons had to content themselves with lesser buildings, as the 14th century mudbrick domed squares of Yazd and Abarquh show clearly enough. Here the plain exterior and the internal sequence of square base, octagonal zone of transition and circular dome base was dictated by an iron convention, but was relieved 209 by rich (and cheap) stencilled internal decoration. This exploited somewhat old-fashioned plaited Kufic inscriptions, and geometric designs reminiscent of manuscript illumination.

Later in the 14th century the centre of gravity in Iranian architecture generally, and thus in mausolea too, began to shift to the north-east. This move found two quite distinct expressions in funerary architecture. One of these, which could be described as sturdily conservative, is exemplified in most of the mausolea of the Shah- 5.124 i Zinda in Samarqand: small and structurally 183, unadventurous domed squares redeemed from 214 banality by their incandescent tiled ornament, often in glazed relief terracotta. As was proper for mausolea jammed close together and facing on to a street, the main decorative and architec-

5.104 Multan, mausoleum known as "Shah Rukn-i 'Alam"

tural accent falls on the portal. The other approach was to seize on a single feature and magnify it to an unprecedented degree. In many mausolea this feature was the *pishtaq* – witness the tomb of Turabek Khanum at Kunya 5.112–5.115 Urgench (c.770/1369), the *mazar* of Khwaja 5.125–5.127 Ahmad Yasavi at Turkistan (799–801/1397–9), the Gunbad-i Manas, c.734/1334 or the *buq'a* at 5.85–5.86 Taybad (848/1444–5) – while in others, such as the tombs at the entrance to the Shah-i Zinda, it was the drum carrying the dome which was greatly elongated. Sometimes a mausoleum exhibited both features, as in the case of the Ishrat Khana at Samarqand. This was the time, too, 5.110–5.111 when the bulbous melon dome established itself in the vocabulary of Iranian Islamic architecture, especially in mausolea. Examples include 184, 215–216 the Gur-i Amir in Samarqand (from 807/1404) 5.118–5.199, and the tomb of Gauhar Shad in Herat (835/ 5.121 1432) – both of them, incidentally, also serving as dynastic mausolea – and the tomb of Khwaja Abu Nasr Parsa at Balkh (c.865/1460). Follow- 5.128

209 Yazd, tomb of Rukn al-Din, interior

210 Samarqand, Shah-i Zinda, tomb of Qadizada Rumi

211 Samarqand, Shah-i Zinda, tomb of Chujuk Bika, interior, dome

212 Samarqand, Shah-i Zinda, tomb of Chujuk Bika, interior

299

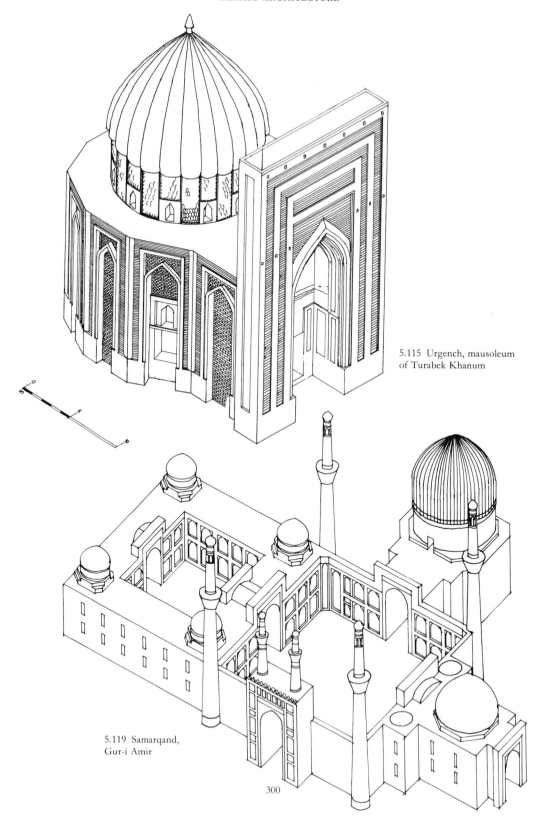

5.115 Urgench, mausoleum
of Turabek Khanum

5.119 Samarqand,
Gur-i Amir

213 Samarqand,
Shah-i Zinda,
tomb of Qutham
b. 'Abbas, interior,
zone of transition

214 Samarqand, Shah-i Zinda, street in the necropolis

5.127 Turkistan,
shrine of Khwaja Ahmad
Yasavi, from N.W.

5.126 Turkistan, shrine of Khwaja Ahmad Yasavi, from S.E.

215 Samarqand, Gur-i Amir, portal

ing the taste of the time, many of these tombs received astonishingly complex non-structural vaults executed in plaster – the so-called 'squinch-net'. This feature effectively disguised the discrepancy between the shallow inner dome and the lofty outer dome which characterised many of these buildings. The bold opening out of the interior space by deep niches scooped out

of the bearing walls in the fashion of Öljeitü's tomb continued apace in many new guises. Finally, the much greater ground surface taken up by the more ambitious Timurid mausolea, notably by such integrated multi-functional structures as the Gur-i Amir or the *mazar* of Khwaja Yasavi, often demanded a free-standing site which made the building visible from all

5.118
5.121
5.125
5.127

302

216 Samarqand, Gur-i Amir, tilework in portal

sides. This fostered a new sensitivity to lateral and rear façades, and resulted in their long plain walls being sheathed in glazed bricks forming geometric or epigraphic designs.

Safavid and later mausolea were something of an anti-climax after the funerary architecture of the medieval period. Secular tombs now gave way definitively to those of saints, and the physical setting of such tombs was often quite grand, comprising secondary buildings, adjoining courtyards and extensive gardens, as for example at Char Bakr near Bukhara or at the Ardabil shrine which comprised not one but several mausolea, the largest being the Jannat-sara. This period saw the major religious shrines of Iran attaining their definitive appearance, more or less in the form they have today. Indeed the enlarging and refurbishing of shrines was the major contribution of the Safavid and later periods to funerary architecture. Mahan and Turbat-i Jam are only two examples among many, and one might also cite the work of Nadir

220, 5.116–5.117 5.3, 5.4

221, 21

217 Turkistan, shrine of Khwaja Ahmad Yasavi, portal

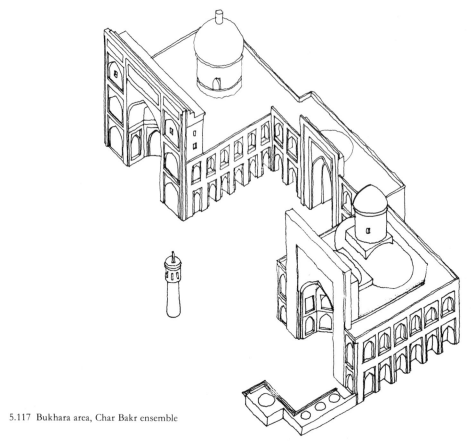

5.117 Bukhara area, Char Bakr ensemble

218 Turkistan, shrine of Khwaja Ahmad Yasavi, side view

Shah, who built on the grand scale at the Mashhad shrine, or the Qajars who were largely 5.1 responsible for the present form of the shrine of Fatima at Qumm. Yet despite this varied and 5.2 abundant building activity on the part of the Safavids in particular, it must be conceded that the end result falls far short of the achievements of earlier periods. However fine the individual contributions to given shrines might be – like the *khiyaban* which Shah 'Abbas added to the shrine of Imam Rida, or the tomb chamber of his general Allahvardi Khan at the same site – they were no substitute for structures like the tombs of Sanjar, Öljeitü and Timur. Indeed, none of the Safavid shahs was laid to rest in a suitably grand purpose-built tomb, and among later rulers the only exception to that rule was Nadir Shah, whose mausoleum in Kalat-i Nadiri 222 is significantly as much Mughal as Iranian in style. The run-of-the-mill Safavid mausoleum – such as the Qadamgah near Nishapur, the tomb

219 Turkistan, shrine of Khwaja Ahmad Yasavi, doors

220 Bukhara area, Char Bakr shrine

221 Mahan, shrine of Ni 'matallah Wali, vaulting

222 Kalat-i Nadiri, tomb of Nadir Shah

of Muhammad Mahruq close by it (1041/1631),
5.92 the tomb of Shaikh Jibra'il in Kalkhuran and the
5.99 mausoleum of Khwaja Rabi'a outside Mashhad
(1031/1622) – are somewhat lesser versions of
their Timurid predecessors. Nor did the post-
Safavid centuries reverse this trend.

Thus the proud tradition of medieval Iranian
funerary architecture suffered a sharp and irre-
versible decline after the advent of the Safavids.
This is a matter for regret, but that regret can be
tempered by the reflection that the Iranian tradition embarked on a new lease of life in Mughal
India, with its matchless series of large free-
standing mausolea in garden settings, and in
Ottoman Iraq, where the Shi'ite shrines of
Najaf, Karbala and Samarra had the golden
domes and the towering *iwan*s of their Iranian
counterparts. In just the same way, centuries
earlier, its influence had made itself felt in the
tomb towers of Saljuq Anatolia, many of them
simple translations into stone of the brick
mausolea of Iran. This overspill of Iranian
modes in funerary architecture affected every
area which geographically adjoined the Iranian
plateau. It might be argued that the radiating
influence of the Iranian mausoleum can be explained by the fact that the territory of medieval
Iran far exceeded that of its modern successor.
Yet such an argument cannot account for the
absolute dominance of Iranian mausolea and
their derivatives in the eastern Islamic world.
The reason for that phenomenon must be
sought in the sheer vitality of the architectural
forms employed and in their astonishing
capacity to renew themselves in fresh guises. In
all of Islam there is no tradition of funerary
monuments which can boast the same longevity,

the same deep-rooted popularity and – in the
medieval period – the same consistently high
level of architectural excellence.

ANATOLIAN MAUSOLEA

The school of funerary architecture which has
the closest relationship to that of Iran while still
preserving some degree of individuality is to be
found, not surprisingly, in neighbouring
Anatolia. It would not be accurate to lump the
Anatolian mausoleum tradition of the 13th century – its most productive period – with that of
Ayyubid Syria mentioned above, or to view this
body of buildings in the same somewhat
negative light. They survive, as do the *madrasa*s
and caravansarais of Saljuq Anatolia, by the
score (a round dozen at Ahlat alone, and even
more in Kayseri); some among them break the
mould (Tokat, tomb of Nur al-Din b. Sentimur)
and are even unique. Nevertheless, these
mausolea too developed out of a richer and
more venerable tradition, that of Saljuq funerary
architecture in Iran, and they scarcely left its
shadow. Particularly striking is the way that the
vast majority of medieval Anatolian mausolea
clung to a single Iranian model, the tomb tower;

5.135–
5.138
5.155,
5.159,
5.140,

5.136 Ahlat,
Ulu Kümbet

223 Tokat, tomb of Nur al-Din b. Sentimur

brick throughout, have elevations of Iranian type and indeed bear the names of craftsmen from Arran, Marand, Maragha and other Iranian cities, the material used throughout is stone, a change that had portentous consequences. In eastern Anatolia the light local tufa is used, and its varying tones (such as ochre, pink, purple and brown) are sometimes exploited for decorative effect, forming random chequered accents as in the tomb of the Amir Saltuq at Erzurum (late 12th century) – an idea later taken 5.132 up in tilework, as in the Green Tomb at Bursa 5.145, 5.151 (816–24/1413–21) – or to enhance a decorative band by executing it in a different colour from that of the surrounding stonework. Further west, marble is encountered on occasion; it is customarily reserved for epigraphic panels or lintels. The difficulty of carving it was such that craftsmen from Syria, with their long tradition of excellence in this technique, sometimes had to be imported. The standard of stereotomy so far as other stone was concerned was no less high; a rubble core was the norm but it was customarily veiled by ashlar masonry. Iran had no comparable tradition of fine stonework, and indeed plastered rubble is often used there for external façades; but in eastern Anatolia – the area which saw the first westward irruption of the Saljuqs – it was the stock-in-trade of the vigorous, productive style of Armenian, and to a lesser extent Georgian, architecture. Not surprisingly, the adoption by the Muslims of the local material also brought with it local ideas.

The Armenian connection

This foreign strain asserts itself even more unmistakably in the elevation and articulation of the Anatolian tomb towers. Many of them are virtually indistinguishable from the top half of 5.153 the standard contemporary Armenian church, with its plain conical roof resting on a high drum articulated by a ring of blind arches. The very different functions of the two building types were, as always, no barrier to Muslim craftsmen in search of inspiration. In these Anatolian tomb towers the more ambitious Iranian types with flanges and engaged columns are all but absent, though the shaft itself takes numerous forms: cylindrical, octagonal and ten- 5.160 or twelve-sided. Specifically Islamic colouring is 5.133 also noticeable; for example, the arch profiles are

their architects were apparently content to render Iranian brick forms into stone with only minor alterations, and even to translate Iranian brick and stucco decoration into stone. For this reason it seems preferable (and justifiable) to deal with the pre-Ottoman Anatolian mausolea somewhat cursorily, and in the context of their Iranian forebears, rather than to attempt to chronicle each minor variant of the standard type.

As noted earlier, most of the Anatolian mausolea of the pre-Ottoman period are tomb towers on the Iranian model, in that they have a cylindrical or polygonal body with a pyramidal or conical roof. Within this basic formula the regional differences are clearly marked and embrace material, articulation, ornament and absolute height. It will be convenient to comment on each of these features in turn.

5.129 With the exception of a few *turba*s in Sivas, Divriği and elsewhere which are executed in

224 Kayseri, Döner Kümbet

5.162, 5.164 often of the characteristically Iranian shouldered
5.160 segmental form, and the *muqarnas* theme is
accorded greater significance than in Armenian
architecture, especially for narrow arched
doorways with a steep stilt, as in many mausolea
at Ahlat. The motif is also often used for both
cornices and plinths, as in the Khwand Khatun
2.179–2.180 mausoleum at Kayseri (635/1237–8), and many
of these mausolea have their simple interiors
furnished with a *mihrab*. Yet it cannot be denied
that the decision to build in stone rather than in
brick inexorably propelled the Anatolian Saljuqs
away from the traditions of Saljuq Iran towards
indigenous Armenian models. Even the elaborate flanged and ribbed roofs for which Iranian
sources could be proposed can also be found
5.154 nearer at hand in earlier Armenian architecture,
while the complex interior articulation of many
Iranian tomb towers finds little echo in Anatolia,
such exceptions as the tomb of the Eşrefoghlu

Süleyman Beg, Beyşehir (701/1301), notwithstanding. By degrees, of course, the Muslim
architects emancipated themselves from
Armenian tutelage. The tomb of Khudavand
Khatun at Niğde of 712/1312 is a broad octagon 5.13♦
so massive as to seem stumpy; such proportions
mark a new departure. So too does the device of
an open arcade placed half-way between the
cornice and the plinth, as on the Bayindir tomb
of 896/1491 at Ahlat. Numerous other such 5.13♦
original developments could be cited. Nevertheless, the tomb tower as a genre never departed
very far from the norm established by the
mausolea of Kayseri and Erzurum, and in such 5.13♦
buildings Armenian influence is strong.

In the decoration of these towers, too, the
pervasive influence of Armenian modes may be
noted. The use of human and animal sculpture,
for example, as at Khachen Dorbatly (714/ 5.16♦
1314) – for all that it may in its new context be
invested with immemorially Turkish beliefs of
an astrological, calendrical, totemistic, funerary
or shamanistic nature – cannot be divorced from
the very similar sculptures adorning the public
external façades of the Armenian churches
which the Muslims saw all around them. The
resemblance extends beyond style to the very
choice of animal – rams, bulls, lions, eagles and
so on – as well as to their location in spandrels,
over doorways, and their use as water-spouts,
gargoyles and corbels. Similarly, the deft juxtaposition of large expanses of smoothly
finished stonework with archivolts, borders or
spandrels crammed with dense, precisely
rendered, geometrically patterned carving finds
numerous Armenian analogues. So too does the
use of twin windows to alleviate the bareness of
a wall, of deeply grooved V-shaped niches with
scalloped heads, and of the continuous patterned rectangular borders enclosing them, as at
the mausoleum of Gevaş (736/1335) beside Lake 5.13♦
Van. Clearly, an extended scholarly assessment
of the interplay of the two cultures in this field
is long overdue.

Yet as in the articulation of these mausolea, so
too in their decoration Muslim craftsmen developed their own style. In the tomb at Niğde
mentioned earlier, the upper third of the
octagon is turned into a sixteen-sided arched
zone, its regular divisions marked by engaged
columns; animal, floral or geometrical carving

fills each blank arch. That same mausoleum has bi-coloured joggled voussoirs of Syrian type. The Döner Kümbet at Kayseri, built for a noble lady called Shahjahan Khatun, also departs from earlier precedent by loading the fields of its external blind arches with dense carving, including a Tree of Life. Yet even this building has large areas of blank space, and thus obeys a different aesthetic from that which generated the all-over patterning of such Iranian tomb towers as Kashmar and Radkan East.

The differences between Anatolian and Iranian tomb towers in the matter of absolute height are readily summarised. Most of the Anatolian buildings vary between 10 m. and 15 m. in height. While there are plenty of Iranian tomb towers in this band – for example, almost all of those built in Mazandaran — the virtual absence of very lofty towers of twice or three times that height is noticeable. Part of the reason lies in a new, specifically Anatolian, development: the

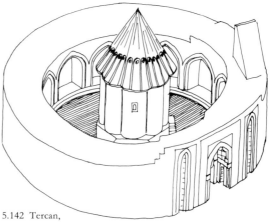

5.142 Tercan,
mausoleum of Mama Khatun

marked emphasis accorded to the crypt in the design of the external elevation. Where many Iranian tomb towers had no crypt at all, or placed it underground, the Anatolian practice was to draw attention to it, even when it was largely underground (as in the case of the Melik Ghazi tomb at Kirşehir), by siting the entrance to the mausoleum well above ground level and providing access to it by a monumental staircase. Sharply chamfered angles created a smooth transition from the square crypt to the octagonal chamber above and thus made an even greater feature of the crypt. The result was a crisply demarcated three-tier elevation in which no one part was so dominant as to eclipse the other two. The almost universal preference for blind arches as the principal decoration of the central shaft would also have discouraged the extreme attenuation of the shaft so often found in Iran. It may be mere coincidence that the preferred proportions of these Anatolian towers corresponded to those observed in the upper half of the typical Armenian church.

These Christian influences are far less marked in the other, though admittedly less popular, types of mausoleum built in pre-Ottoman Turkey. Some of these are unique, notably the Mama Khatun mausoleum at Tercan, datable c.596/1200, which seems to reflect pre-Islamic Turkic funerary architecture in Central Asia. The mausoleum itself has an eight-lobed core which billows out correspondingly into a series of gigantic linked lobes separated by narrow colonnettes. These motifs are taken up into the ribbed conical roof. Even more original,

225 Kirşehir, tomb of Melik Ghazi

5.151 Bursa, Yeşil Türbe

however, is the setting of this mausoleum within a circular precinct furnished inside with thirteen deep bays; the blank exterior wall is broken only by the monumental entrance. Other varieties of mausoleum include the domed square chamber, as in the tomb of Sultan Hamza at Mardin, vaulted rectangular tombs like that of Turumtay at Amasya (677/1278), and tombs consisting of vaulted *iwan*s, of which examples survive in Konya, Akşehir, Boyalıköy and Seyidgazi.

Ottoman mausolea

Ottoman mausolea rejected the Saljuq tradition of the conical roof in favour of a dome, which was sometimes ribbed; but they too are often octagonal, occasionally even hexagonal, in plan. They include one supreme masterpiece, the Green Tomb (Yeşil Türbe) built in Bursa for Sultan Mehmed I by the governor of the city, between 816/1413 and about 827/1424. This octagonal mausoleum, with a high octagonal drum set back from the lower walls, and a saucer dome now restored, attains a monumentality which eclipses that of any of its predecessors in Anatolia. Its great width (21 m.) tends to obscure its even greater height (27 m.), but its dimensions are secondary to the intense chromatic power distilled by its exterior and interior tilework. The deep sea-blue of its walls is perfectly set off by the marble trim of the doorway, cornice, window-frames and archivolts. It is also curiously alive, presumably because the ground colour of turquoise is interspersed with green, ultramarine, black and even white tiles; this technique of subtle colour variations was practised a millennium earlier by Byzantine mosaicists. Overglaze-painted tiles create a radiant *muqarnas* canopy over the doorway; within, a lofty *mihrab* glistening with even more lavishly gilded tiles draws the eye like a magnet. An inner dado of gold-spangled, dark green hexagonal tiles forms a rich and restful backcloth to the lambent light blue of the tiled door frame. This prodigal outpouring of colour climaxed in the brilliant polychromy of the cenotaph of Mehmed I, which bade fair to displace the *mihrab* as the principal focus of attention within the building. The subtlety of these colour harmonies is beyond anything in contemporary Anatolian architecture, and indeed for some it constitutes the pinnacle of achievement for

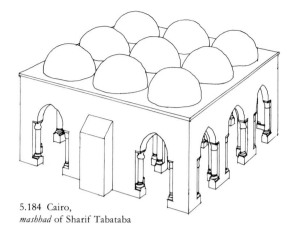

5.184 Cairo, *mashhad* of Sharif Tabataba

tilework in Anatolia. All this was the work of a team of ceramicists from Tabriz led by one Muhammad the Mad, who went on to work for Murad II in Edirne.

Nothing in later Ottoman funerary architecture can match this achievement, and given the unswerving emphasis of successive sultans on architecture which had either a religious or a severely practical purpose, this is not strange. In fact the ancient qualms about building mausolea were revived, and a novel solution was devised: a mausoleum which consisted of an openwork masonry cage and was therefore open to the elements. More popular, however, was the enduringly successful domed square now made as open-plan as possible (perhaps also for religious motives) by means of four axial arches. A popular feature was an arcaded portico marking the main entrance or surrounding the entire mausoleum, a disposition which recalls the tomb of Mama Khatun at Tercan.

MAUSOLEA IN EGYPT AND SYRIA

The Fatimid period

The earliest surviving Egyptian mausolea were not erected in Cairo itself but in Fustat, its predecessor, and the surrounding area. They date from Fatimid times and most of them – with the odd exception, such as the *mashhad* of Sharif Tabataba, *c.*334/943 – fall conveniently into two groups: canopy mausolea, of the kind already discussed in the context of Aswan, erected in clusters outside the city proper, and marked by an extreme simplicity which disdained any applied ornament; and mausolea

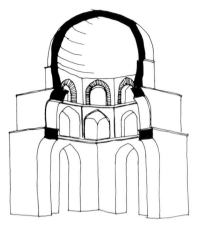

5.166 Cairo, Sab'a Banat, third tomb from E

Aswan. Although none of the Fatimid mausolea in Lower Egypt could be described as major buildings, they number over a score and are thus by far the best-represented building type of the period. At the same time, they could scarcely be called representative of the Fatimid style. Architecturally, many of them could be described with justice as mean; certainly their extremely modest exteriors give no clue of the rich decoration within. Mamluk mausolea go far towards reversing this trend.

The principal mausolea *extra muros* are the four so-called Sab'a Banat, datable *c.*400/1010 and originally a set of presumably seven domed buildings, each comprising three diminishing

5.165

intra muros, still relatively small but now completely roofed over and embellished with carved stucco-work. Neither group seems to reflect high official, let alone royal, patronage, and indeed there is no evidence that any of the Fatimid caliphs was buried in a monumental tomb. Thus there is no hint of what was to come under the Mamluks. Yet it is entirely likely that it was the Shi'ite confession of the regime—a confession not shared by most of the Egyptian population—that provided the initial impetus for the building of mausolea, just as many early mausolea in Iraq and Iran were the product of Shi'ite patronage. In equally striking contrast to the practice in later medieval Egypt and the Levant, these Fatimid mausolea were erected to commemorate either saints or private citizens, women as well as men. The tenants of these mausolea sometimes belonged to wealthy families; others were *ghazi*s or pilgrims, the latter two groups of course best represented at

5.174 Aswan, anonymous mausoleum

226 Cairo, Sab'a Banat

5.170 Qus, mausoleum

226 superposed tiers and measuring approximately 6.5 m.–7 m. square. Built of brick, each has four axial arched entrances; four corresponding openings pierce the next storey, while the third storey has eight windows. Each of these canopy mausolea is set within its own square open enclosure or *hawsh*; in later periods it is known that such enclosures were reserved for family burials.

The walled burial precinct probably predated the earliest Islamic mausolea and found favour in orthodox eyes in many parts of the Islamic world. Its link with the *hazira* compound 5.120 popular in later medieval Iran is patent.

The mausolea at Aswan, which number 5.172–5.174 almost fifty and may be dated for the most part to the 11th century, are of a type closely related to the Sab'a Banat, though most of them clearly belong to a later stage of evolution. This is obvious from the fact that many have reduced the ground-floor openings to a single doorway, adding a *mihrab* in the *qibla* wall, and that most of them bear some kind of decorative articulation: panelled sides, windows with multiple recesses, ribbed domes, often with star-shaped openings, and octagonal drums with concave sides. The latter are corbelled out towards their 5.173 apex, creating a vigorously rhythmic profile of 5.174 truly baroque energy. This evolution can best be plotted in the zones of transition. Most remarkable of all, however, is their varied form, from tiny ($2\frac{1}{2}$ m. per side) open-plan domed squares like the Sab'a Banat type, to groups of three adjoining domed mausolea, all of significantly 5.172 different dimensions. This latter type is also known in Cairo. Rectangular tombs roofed by a single tunnel-vault, or with central domes

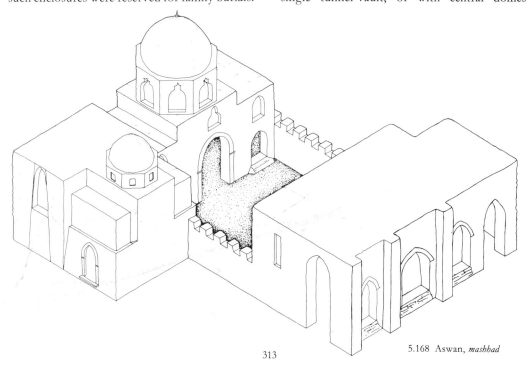

5.168 Aswan, *mashhad*

313

227 Aswan, *mashhad*

228 Cairo, tombs of al-Ja'fari (foreground) and Sayyida 'Atiqa

flanked by tunnel-vaults, sometimes with an adjoining forecourt, are also known. Here then is an authentic survival of popular architecture, far from the great city; and the cheap materials are powerless to quench the verve and vitality of its inspiration. The Fatimid mausoleum at Qus shows that this style was not confined to Aswan, and may indeed give a clue to the otherwise largely vanished medieval architecture of provincial Egypt, a victim in this as in many other respects of the steady impoverishment inflicted by Cairo.

5.169–5.170

In the capital itself a domed square mausoleum on a high two-tier drum – the tomb of Shaikh Yunus – is of a size and complexity beyond the comparable Aswan monuments. Yet it offers little really new. By contrast, the Fatimid *mashhad* is a significant fresh development. Its key feature, whether the scale was small, as at Sayyida Ruqayya (527/1133), or large as at Aswan, is a sanctuary comprising a central domed chamber with a narrow rectangular room on either side; this unit gives on to a portico or courtyard. The mosque (or *zawiya*?) of al-Juyushi (498/1104) is also of this type. At Aswan this courtyard contained tombs and had another three-room unit at its far end. A condensed version of this scheme can be seen in the mausolea of Qasim Abu Tayyib and Umm Kulthum, in which a domed square with two or four axial openings is surrounded on three sides by a tunnel-vaulted ambulatory. The latter detail, which recurs in other Fatimid mausolea, seems to indicate that such tombs, many of them associated with devout proselytisers for the Isma'ili cause, were intended from the outset to serve as places of prayer and pilgrimage, and

5.187

5.171

5.167–

227

5.175

5.185

5.178

5.176 Cairo, *mashhad* of al-Juyushi

314

229 Cairo, aerial view of Mamluk tombs (lower centre: *khanqah* of Faraj b. Barquq; upper centre: Mosque of Sultan Inal; top right: tomb of Qansuh Abu Sa'id; bottom left: tomb of Jani Bay al-Ashrafi)

their frequent location on the presumed sites of 'Alid tombs lends support to this view. Other Fatimid mausolea are domed squares of the simplest kind, sometimes paired (tombs of Muhammad al-Ja'fari and al-Sayyida 'Atiqa).

Despite the rich evidence provided by Fatimid mausolea for the history of funerary architecture in Egypt, none of them has a serious claim to be a monument of the first rank. No trace survives of the 'tombs of the greatest beauty' which the 10th-century geographer (and connoisseur of architecture) al-Muqaddasi admired in the cemeteries of Egypt and which he saw fit to compare with probably the finest mausolea of his time, the lofty Buyid tomb towers at Rayy.

Ayyubid and Mamluk mausolea in Egypt: General considerations

Happily the Ayyubid period has fared better; indeed, it inaugurates important developments in the funerary architecture of Egypt. No longer were mausolea tucked away out of sight in a cemetery *extra muros*, nor were they so diminutive that they made little impact on the urban landscape. Their new high profile, symbolised not just by the more public sites which they occupied but also by the dramatic increase in their absolute size, proclaimed their unprecedented role as instruments of political and religious propaganda. It ensured for them, moreover, a role in the devotional life of the times unmatched by earlier mausolea. They were large enough for scores of Sufis or Qur'an readers to foregather in them. Furthermore, as successive rulers and their *amir*s built conspicuous funerary monuments, the face of the city insensibly changed so that mausolea became the norm and even began to dominate. Not since Pharaonic times had Egypt witnessed such an obsession with the architecture of death. The competition between successive rulers and *amir*s not only sharpened the inventiveness of the architects in their employ, but also created increasing pressure of space on that square mile of the city where most of the important buildings were concentrated – for emulation thrived on proximity. Indeed, some streets – such as Bain al-Qasrain – became showpieces, where a string of public monuments unfolded in close succession.

At first, following the practice elsewhere in the Islamic world, mausolea had been mere adjuncts of buildings with a more unambiguously religious function, such as *madrasa*s or *khanqah*s endowed by sultans or *amir*s. By degrees, however, the mausoleum began to usurp an ever larger share of the foundation – though, as noted above, its greater size permitted it to serve as a setting for devotional activities. It should be noted that this process saw its fullest development in Cairo. In the provincial cities of the Mamluk realm the echoes of Cairene practice were much fainter and the absolute scale of the mausolea was very much smaller.

The scores of mausolea surviving from 13th–15th-century Cairo make a detailed inventory of these monuments impracticable, and indeed the wealth of material positively imposes a highly selective approach. A few key monuments will therefore have to do duty for the entire sequence. At the same time, it should be remembered that a strict morphological division between mosques, *madrasa*s, *khanqah*s and mausolea in later medieval Egypt is liable to be misleading, for all these buildings used the domed chamber as the principal focus of the design. The internal and external elevation of that chamber, moreover, was articulated in much the same way, irrespective of the purpose of the building. Thus to single out the mausoleum in the way demanded by this chapter should not be taken to imply that its architectural expression was unique.

Before examining a few of the key monuments in detail it will be convenient to assess this body of buildings synoptically. Some mausolea were intended straightforwardly as funerary monuments and were therefore erected in the open ground of cemeteries, such as the southern, eastern and western Mamluk cemeteries in the city. Such buildings provide the best available insight into how Mamluk architects grappled with the formal problems presented by free-standing mausolea, and their evidence suggests that a certain austerity was thought appropriate for the lower elevations, in which windows and blank niches with *muqarnas* heads play an important role. Even on such open sites, this relatively simple cubic base is merely a prelude to the much greater elaboration

230 Cairo, tomb of Toghay

reserved for the upper reaches of the mausoleum
(tomb of Toghay). As for most mausolea within
Cairo proper, these were seriously disadvan-
taged by the extremely congested nature of the
city. Although as centralised buildings they
posed no intrinsic problem of orientation, their
integration into complexes incorporating
several religious structures which had to be
aligned to Mecca did present serious problems
in view of this shortage of space. The development of the lower exterior façade, in particular,
was seriously hampered as a result. More significantly, perhaps, the cramped and irregular sites
which were the norm compelled architects to
use every available inch of space, and thus a
mausoleum was often hemmed in by an *ad hoc*
arrangement of corridors, stairways and service
rooms which inevitably reduced its impact as a
separate unit. The street façades of these complexes could cloak these irregularities to some
extent, and in particular disguise the consequences of a *qibla* orientation unsuited to the particular nature of the site; but these façades in
their turn had to accommodate themselves to
the existing environment.

The various shifts to which Cairene architects
resorted in order to make a virtue out of this
necessity lie beyond the scope of this chapter,
involving as they do the careful (and often irregular) placing of ornament, massed fenestration, bent entrances and the like. So far as
mausolea were concerned, the most obvious
solution to the difficulty was to shift the focus of
the building to the drum and the dome, since
these elements thrust themselves out of the ruck
of the surrounding structures. Thus there developed the multi-stage drum carrying a steeply
stilted dome; both features, as it happens, well

illustrated in the mausoleum of Yunus al-Dawadar (784/1382), but both developing independently. Thus the tomb of the Imam al-Shafi'i has an extremely elaborate external zone of transition complete with parapet and crenellations, but a plain dome; while in the case of the mausoleum of Queen Shajar al-Durr a relatively simple two-tier external drum, with three windows forming a trilobed arrangement on each of the main faces of the lower tier, gives no hint of the richly elaborated *muqarnas* zone of transition which corresponds to this area within the mausoleum. Drums were further enriched by means of chamfered angles (often enlivened by cascades of roll mouldings), by shallow relief carving and by diminishing superposed tiers of bull's-eye windows. Sometimes the angles of the drum were stepped to create a more mobile silhouette, as in the tomb of Faraj b. Barquq (801–15/1399–1412).

Conversely, in later Mamluk times the attention of architects shifted to the dome itself, which from being plain (as in the Ayyubid period) by degrees came to acquire buttresses at the collar, or even to be pierced by huge oval depressions containing latticed triangular or round-based windows. Side by side with this unusual type of articulation, which brings to mind the mausolea of Aswan, the dome profile itself became a focus of experiment. Thus within little more than a century the Cairene townscape was embellished by bulbous, stilted, ogee, shouldered and keel-shaped domes among others. Perhaps it was Persian masons that brought to Egypt the idea of the ribbed dome, an idea not intrinsically far-fetched since several earlier Cairene monuments bear unmistakable traces of Saljuq influences. Nevertheless, the steep stilt which local architects gave this form, and which illusionistically magnified its height, has no close parallel in the Iranian world. Perhaps, too, an awareness of the decorated domes of Iran and Transoxiana inspired Egyptians to emulate this achievement in the very different building materials of Egypt. Thus at the end of the Mamluk period, especially in the reign of Qa'it Bay (872–901/1468–96) it became common practice to decorate the entire exterior surface of the dome with geometrical (e.g. herringbone) or floral designs.

So much for the exteriors of these mausolea.

231 Cairo, tomb of Yunus al-Dawadar, interior

Inside, their cynosure was the zone of transition, although the *qibla* wall was designed to monopolise attention in the lower elevation. These two areas complemented each other, in that the former used predominantly architectonic means to heighten the impact of that zone, whereas the means chosen to enrich the *qibla* wall depended principally on costly materials – carved and painted wood (which had to be imported), glass mosaic, coloured marble columns, *ablaq* and intarsia work. Yet the squinch zone, for all its structural function, was scarcely less decorative. In place of the single squinch, often with its interior sub-divided, so familiar in the eastern Islamic world, the Mamluk architect preferred to miniaturise the form, whose distinctive keel-shaped profile he had inherited from the Fatimids, and to manufacture tier upon tier of adjoining squinches which spread across the entire zone and indeed extend its upper and lower borders to a degree unparalleled in Islamic architecture.

Thus a device which was at first exclusively structural took on a supplementary decorative function, until eventually, by a process familiar in monuments across the entire Islamic world, the urge to decorate swamped the frank expression of a structural function. Yet there is little hint of this metamorphosis on the exteriors of such mausolea. It is interesting to observe that Egyptian architects – unlike their Islamic counterparts to both east and west – stopped short at the logical culmination of this process, namely the *muqarnas* vault. The squinch zones of the Ayyubid and Mamluk mausolea, though they are exceptionally broad and indeed resemble a segment cut out of a *muqarnas* vault, are bordered above and below by plain surfaces which present the strongest contrast to the mobile and energetic appearance of the squinch zone itself.

Ayyubid mausolea in Cairo

The marked expansion in the scale, number and importance of mausolea in later medieval Egypt is conveniently epitomised by an outstanding trio of Ayyubid tombs, all of which date from the first half of the 13th century. They are the gigantic mausoleum erected by al-Malik al-Kamil over the grave of the long-dead Imam al-Shafi'i (608/1211), the so-called 'Tomb of the 'Abbasid Caliphs' (perhaps *c.*640/1242–3), and the tomb of al-Malik al-Salih located within his two-*madrasa* complex, and completed in 648/1250. Each of these has an importance which extends beyond its mere architecture: a clear indication of the crucial part which mausolea now played in contemporary society.

The first of them, one of the largest mausolea not only in Cairo – where its only rival is the Qubbat al-Fadawiya of 884–6/1479–82 – but in the entire Muslim world, has preserved its exterior more or less intact, but the interior was subjected to successive major restorations in 885/1480, the 18th century and 1314/1896, and its original aspect is thus hard to recover. Nevertheless, the impact of this vast square interior space, with its diameter of more than 15 m., is scarcely dimmed and must always have been overwhelming. It is indeed an inordinately ambitious undertaking, both spatially and as a *tour de force* of decoration. The brooding presence of the great wooden double dome, which soars to

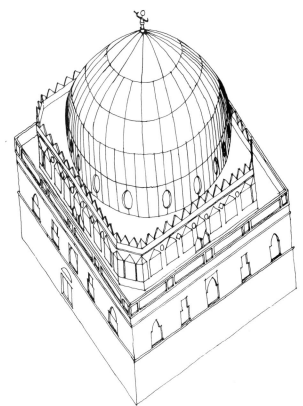

5.182 Cairo, mausoleum of Imam al-Shafi'i

a height of 29 m. (only a little lower than the Dome of the Rock), dominates the whole interior. Yet the upper reaches of this elevation are brought closer to earth, as it were, by the deep massed tiers of *muqarnas* cells, a 15th-century restoration in their present form but probably, to judge by the corresponding articulation of the exterior, reproducing the original arrangement. The *qibla* wall follows Fatimid practice with its triple *mihrab*.

The *raison d'être* of the building allows a fascinating insight into the function of the mausoleum in contemporary society. Ostensibly it honours the founder of one of the four major *madhhab*s or schools of Islamic law, and as such could be seen as a Sunni riposte to the Fatimid propaganda generated in Cairo for most of the previous two centuries. Yet such an interpretation provides only part of the answer. Between 572/1176–7 and 575/1179–80 Saladin had erected a *madrasa* by the grave of al-Shafi'i (who had died in 204/820!), and had replaced the earlier column

319

'Abbasid caliphate in Cairo before 680/1281–2, a date forty years after that of the first inscribed cenotaph and hence, perhaps, of its erection. Cenotaphs, however, could be moved from one building to another, and it is by no means unlikely that the extreme richness of the ornament within this mausoleum could be explained as an act of piety on behalf of the resuscitated caliphate.

Here the squinch zone is not only much narrower in relation to the whole elevation than in the tomb of al-Shafi'i, but is also pierced by four axial trilobed windows, filled with stucco tracery whose interstices glow with stained glass. The field of every niche in the transition zone bears an oval medallion pointed at both ends, and surrounded by further foilate ornament in the corners of the field; in the spandrels the flavour of these designs is that of bookbinding and manuscript illumination. The extrados of every single major arch in that zone, moreover, bears continuous inscriptions, while above the plaited Kufic text at the collar of the dome unfolds one of the supreme masterpieces

232 Cairo, tomb of the 'Abbasid caliphs, niche and window

which had marked that grave by a splendid teak cenotaph. Why should Sultan al-Malik al-Kamil go so much further? The clue may lie in the later burials recorded at the site: those of al-Malik al-Kamil himself; his son; his mother; al-Malik al-'Aziz 'Uthman (the son of Saladin); and of his mother in turn. Thus the building became a dynastic mausoleum too quickly to escape the suspicion that it was built with such an intention from the start. In that event, one may suggest that the royal tomb was justified by its site over the grave of a pillar of orthodoxy.

232 The next great Ayyubid funerary monument in Cairo is much smaller in scale but even more splendid in its decoration. Since it lacks a historical inscription on the fabric itself, the *5.186* original purpose of the building is open to question, though it seems – to judge by its inscribed cenotaphs and *steles* – that it was not used for the burials of princes of the shadow

233 Cairo, tomb of Sultan al-Salih Najm al-Din

4.63 Cairo, Madrasa al-Salihiya, mausoleum

234 Damascus, *madrasa* and mausoleum of 'Izz al-Din

This same motif, but now repeated three-fold, dominates each of the exterior walls below the transition zone; sunburst roundels fill the spandrels of the central arch. No other mausoleum in Cairo makes such concentrated play with the radiating theme, with its ancient inbuilt associations of holiness and power, and it is therefore tempting (if somewhat speculative) to associate this leitmotif with the sacred office held by the 'caliphs' buried within; Creswell has even ventured a comparison with the design of the cloth (*kiswa*) covering the Ka'ba.

Set beside this jewel of funerary architecture, whose influence may be traced in several 13th-century Cairene tombs, the mausoleum of Sultan al-Salih Najm al-Din Ayyub, the last of his line, is an altogether more sober affair; indeed its keynote is austerity, in marked contrast to the two *madrasa*s and minaret of the same complex. Architecturally, it is a reduced and simplified version of the tomb of al-Shafi'i; its principal interest lies rather in the historical circumstances surrounding its erection. The building was raised in eleven months (in 647–8/1249–50) by the Sultan's widow, whose own brief bid for power ended ignominiously with her brutal and sordid murder in the *hammam*. Al-Salih's body was carried to his tomb in a solemn funeral procession and his clothes and weapons were deposited there; in later times, *mamluk*s who had completed their official training swore oaths of allegiance to their master at this spot. This example, then, reveals yet another aspect of the close interplay between political concerns and the cult of funerary architecture.

of Islamic fresco painting, comprising interlaced six-lobed scrolls with foliate interlace in their fields. The range of colours includes dark blue, yellow, dark red and white. Yet even this sumptuous ornament is rivalled by the panels at the centre of each of the four sides of the lower wall. Each panel has a central keel-shaped arch with a radiating design familiar from Fatimid *mihrab*s.

235 Damascus, tomb of Shaikh 'Ali al-Faranthi, zone of transition

236 Aleppo, tomb of Khair Bay (Jami' Shaikh 'Ali Shatila)

Ayyubid mausolea in Syria

No provincial Ayyubid mausolea can rival those of contemporary Cairo in size or splendour, and indeed the domical *turba*s of Tripoli, Aleppo, Damascus and elsewhere cannot readily be isolated from the similar forms used in other types of building. As at Cairo, so too at Damascus there was a marked tendency to concentrate the building of mausolea in certain areas such as the Salihiya quarter and the slopes of the Qasiyun mountain. The material varies according to the region; for example, the prevalence of good building stone in the Aleppo area made it convenient to use stone throughout in the Ayyubid mausolea there, whereas the poorer quality of the stone available in Damascus helps to explain the use of brick for the upper portions of the mausolea there.

The standard ground-plan was square with four narrow axial entrances, which seen from within spread laterally to form broad niches.

Transition zones favoured the squinch, though the corbelled banks of miniature squinches which characterise Cairene architecture find no answering echo in Syria. Two superposed zones were the standard arrangement, and these were mirrored on the exterior by two-tiered drums, octagonal and sixteen-sided respectively, which carried a plain dome (Rukniya *turba*). In the area of Aleppo pyramidal pendentives enjoyed a certain popularity. Similarly, there are in Damascus a few examples of otherwise unusual types, such as *muqarnas* transition zones, ribbed domes and even – in the case of the tomb of Nur al-Din (569/1174) – entire *muqarnas* vaults, some with a rippling exterior silhouette to match. Iraqi monuments, as exemplified by the mausoleum of Muslim b. Quraish at Imam Dur (479/ 1086), which in turn generated the tombs of al-Suhrawardi and Sitt Zubaida, both in Baghdad, as well as numerous other examples in southern Iraq, all of 13th-century date, seem to

237 Damascus, *madrasa* and mausoleum of Nur al-Din, interior of *muqarnas* dome

5.192 Damascus, mausoleum of Nur al-Din, *muqarnas* dome

have been the source of this idea. Such buildings
5.209 are also common in southern Iran.

Most Ayyubid mausolea, however, are of a
marked austerity which precludes any emphasis
on decoration, though both painted and carved
stucco is used inside the buildings. Stone lintels
over the doorways, relieved by segmental arches
above, bear ansate inscriptions detailing the
titles of the tenant of the tomb, the date of death,
and occasionally some appropriate Qur'anic
verses. When studied as a corpus, these inscriptions provide much useful information as to the
religious, political and especially martial aspects
of a society dominated by a military caste. If the
funerary inscriptions are a reliable guide, that
caste was dedicated to the prosecution of *jihad*
against the Crusaders, and to the establishment

of orthodoxy in the *dar al-islam*. In the Mamluk
period, when sea-changes in the political situation had robbed these motives of their urgency,
the number and quality of mausolea in Greater
Syria suffered a marked decline, though there are
some striking examples in Damascus (tomb of
Baibars, in the Zahiriya *madrasa* of 676/1277–8, 4.24
notable for its decoration of glass mosaic) and 4.53–4.
Jerusalem (the Kilaniya, after 753/1352, with its
three-domed façade housing two burial
chambers). The forms of mausolea could also be
used interchangeably for other structures, as
shown by Qa'it Bay's *sabil* in Jerusalem. 5.198–5

Mamluk mausolea in Cairo

Apart from the numerous lesser free-standing
mausolea, like that of Jani Bay al-Ashrafi (831/ 5.179–5

1428), most of the major Mamluk mausolea in Cairo – such as those of al-Nasir Muhammad, Barquq *intra muros*, Faraj b. Barquq, Qa'it Bay and al-Ghuri – are part of some larger complex, usually endowed by the founder and serving some pious function. These other buildings provide a justification for the splendid mausolea which adjoin them – though the mausoleum of Khair Bay (before 910/1505) attached to his palace is the exception that proves the rule.

It must suffice to look at only one of these mausolea in detail, and the tomb of Qala'un has probably the best claim – not indeed as the most typical, but as perhaps the most ambitious (and certainly the most original) of them all. For the purposes of this chapter, the mausoleum has to be wrenched out of its proper context, namely the *maristan*, minaret and *madrasa* of which it

239 Imam Dur, tomb of Muslim b. Quraish, interior

238 Imam Dur, tomb of Muslim b. Quraish

formed part. Nevertheless, because the mausoleum, sandwiched between the minaret and the *madrasa*, had a clear 22 m. of street façade to itself, it does furnish some evidence as to the relative importance which the architect attached to the mausoleum *vis-à-vis* the *madrasa*. It is clear that the mausoleum was given no whit less prominence than the other elements in the ensemble. Given that, once the site had been prepared, the entire complex was built in only thirteen months (683–4/1284–5), and that the mausoleum itself took four months, the

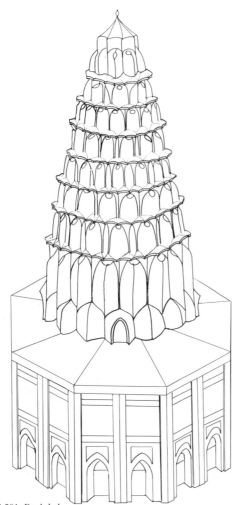

5.201 Baghdad,
mausoleum of Sitt Zubaida

240 Baghdad, tomb known as that of Sitt Zubaida

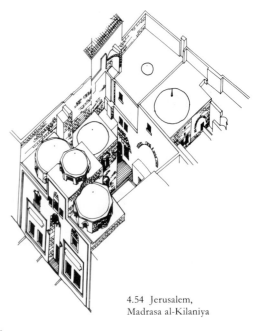

4.54 Jerusalem,
Madrasa al-Kilaniya

quality, quantity, variety and finesse of the decoration are quite breathtaking.

The complex has a plum position on the Bain al-Qasrain, that open-air gallery for connoisseurs of medieval Cairene monuments, and the architect exploits it to the full. A sequence of deeply recessed arched niches reaching to within a couple of metres of the crenellated parapet accentuates the loftiness of the façade. This articulation is as much functional as decorative, for it provides the principal light source for the interior of the mausoleum. The upper parts of these niches contain two-light windows with a central bull's-eye above, a type apparently borrowed from Norman Sicily. This is only one

326

5.207 Imam Dur, tomb of Muslim b. Quraish

5.213 Cairo, funerary complex of Sultan Qala'un

5.180 Cairo,
mausoleum of Jani Bay al-Ashrafi

241 Cairo, funerary complex of Sultan Qala'un, interior of mausoleum

of the many foreign features in this building which here make their first appearance in Egypt. In its own time the ensemble must have been the last word in architectural fashion, but – whether by accident or design – there is also an ecumenical flavour in the range of origins attested in these borrowings. It is as if the entire Mediterranean world had been systematically trawled for ideas so as to make this foundation a monument truly representative of its time. Strictly architectural borrowings include the buttress with a bevelled top, the round horseshoe arch and the horseshoe-shaped *mihrab*, while in the field of decoration the list includes the gilded inscription over the entrance portal, the arcaded *mihrab*, marble mosaic and square or 'seal' Kufic forming rectangles. Spolia include Crusader ironwork used in the windows. Evidently no pains were spared to make this building stand out among contemporary mausolea. The deliberate inclusion of features drawn from a geographically wide catchment area recalls, perhaps only by chance, the Umayyad practice of conscripting craftsmen and materials from many different parts of their domains. It is a practice with clear political implications, although its unifying impact on the visual arts was by no means negligible.

241   In nothing is this more clear than in the interior arrangement. Within an approximate square, a huge open-plan octagon seems to fill up the chamber. Comprising four massive granite piers on the lateral axis and four columns on the *qibla* axis, it supported the original (probably wooden) dome. *Mashrabiya* screens join the outer faces of these piers (which are spolia bearing gilded Corinthian capitals) and create a *maqsura* enclosing the cenotaph of the sultan. These details, when considered in the context of an octagon formed by piers and columns, and of a wooden-roofed ambulatory, cannot help but recall the Dome of the Rock in 2.16– Jerusalem, a city which Qala'un knew well. Even some of the ornamental bands can be seen as a free variation on the themes encountered in that seminal building, while the fastidious quality of the decorative scheme as a whole, especially in its range of materials and its sensitive exploitation of light, bids fair to rival the earlier monument. The light filtered through the windows on the *qibla* wall plays on lavish gilding, mother-of-pearl, stained glass, geometrically patterned window grilles and marble panelling. All these techniques are to be found in the Dome of the Rock, whereas no contemporary building in Egypt employed them all, let alone on the scale of this mausoleum. It remains an open question why Qala'un should have gone to such pains to evoke the most prestigious of all Islamic shrines in his own personal mausoleum; at all events, here is hubris on a grand scale, for the sustained evocation of the Dome of the Rock logically implies an equation between the Rock and the cenotaph of Qala'un himself. Cognate themes, as it happens, can be detected in the metalwork of this same sultan's son.

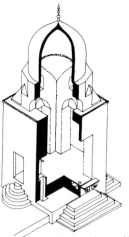

5.199 Jerusalem, *sabil* of Qa'it Bay

VI The Caravansarai

FUNCTION

Put at its simplest, a caravansarai is a building to house a caravan. It is the largest of the standard Islamic building types. Normally it is of square or rectangular plan, with a single projecting monumental entrance piercing high, usually blank, walls that are sometimes provided with airholes near the base. Rounded bastions mark the corners and the centre of the sides. A vaulted vestibule mediates between the entrance and an internal courtyard spacious enough to provide room for up to 400 pack-animals. Upon a raised platform which surrounds this courtyard stand the arcades which articulate the interior façade. Behind them are small cells to lodge the travellers. In two-storied caravansarais, the lower cells are used to store merchandise while the upper cells accommodate travellers. The animals are either stabled in the corners of the building or kept in the courtyard, where they are hobbled, or perhaps tethered to the sides of the platform by iron rings let into the masonry. Water is provided by a well or cistern in the centre of the courtyard. Loading and unloading takes place in the courtyard and is greatly facilitated by the fact that the raised surrounding platform makes it sunken. If stables are provided in the diagonals, a very broad plinth carries the central column supporting the vault; the grooms use this surface to sleep on and to load and unload the animals. This arrangement echoes the relationship between platform and courtyard. In the simplest caravansarais long projecting benches lining the walls perform the same function.

ETYMOLOGY

As usual, the etymology of the words used to describe this kind of building is instructive. These words suggest a wide range of functions, and it is characteristic of Islamic architecture that a simple building type should fulfil multiple functions. Since, however, the same building is sometimes described by two or even more distinct terms (e.g. Khan al-'Arus in Syria is called a *funduq* in its dedicatory inscription), it cannot be assumed that the choice of descriptive term is necessarily significant. *Caravansarai* means a building for a caravan, and caravan in turn derives from *karban*, 'one who protects trade'. A primary meaning of caravan, which has even lingered in English usage, is accordingly that of a body of merchants who have banded together to protect themselves against robbers. The fortified aspect of the caravansarai, and its single entrance framed by bastions, is thus readily explained.

Not all buildings of this type and function, however, are called *caravansarai*s. To this day many of them are described as *rabat*s or *ribat*s. This word comes from the Arabic root *rabata*, meaning *inter alia* to 'tether a horse'. The notion of a brief stopover embodied in the word of course fits a caravansarai to perfection, but *ribat* came to acquire a more specialised meaning. By the 10th century at the latest, it denoted an Islamic *castrum* used as a base from which to prosecute holy war (*jihad*). Most surviving examples of this kind of building are to be found in the Maghrib (e.g. at Munastir, Susa, Tafertast and Tit), and the history of the institution can also be traced in most detail there. Warriors for the faith would congregate in such a camp (often misleadingly translated as 'monastery') for short campaigns against the infidel. Again, fortification would be desirable for a building serving such purposes. *Ribat*s were built throughout the Islamic world, from Spain and the borders of the Sahara to Central Asia. It was in the latter area that they proved most popular, to judge by the literary sources, and some of the fortified structures of the early medieval period which Soviet archaeologists have excavated there may indeed be *ribat*s. As the borders of the Islamic world stabilised, the activity of the warriors for the faith (*ghazi*s) diminished, but the buildings they had used remained. Presumably very little was needed to convert such *ribat*s to peaceful uses. It is perhaps not surprising, therefore, that this word too should come to denote caravansarai.

But the word *ribat* need not necessarily connote exclusively either a frontier building of this kind, or for that matter a caravansarai. It was also used to describe urban structures which served commercial purposes or in which Sufis congregated, as the examples of later medieval

331

242 Ma'arrat al-Nu'man, caravansarai, courtyard

Baghdad demonstrate. A distinct drop in the standing of the urban *ribat* is implied in the statement of the 12th-century geographer Ibn Hauqal that the *ribat*s of Palermo were the resort of the local ne'er-do-wells, who battened on public charity by squatting there.

Perhaps the commonest term for caravansarai in the Arab world is *khan* (*han* in Turkish-speaking areas). The basic meaning of the word in both Arabic and Persian is house. Thus the etymological indications are that at least some early structures which served the needs of travellers were like houses – compare the Arabic word *manzil* meaning both 'house' and 'way-station'. It is an open question whether the

resemblance was a matter of plan type or of the size of the structure. *Sarai* also means house, though the term implies large size and is indeed often used for palaces. Conversely, in the Arab world the word *khan* is often used for small inns situated in or near settlements and offering a wider range of facilities, though less accommodation, than a caravansarai. But it would be mistaken to elevate this comment to the status of a generalisation, for many Syrian *khan*s are as big as Iranian caravansarais and, moreover, are sited in open country.

It is worth emphasising once more that the use of these various terms may imply no more than differences in regional vocabulary rather than connoting distinctive functions or types. The geographer al-Muqaddasi, for example, displays a notable sensitivity to changes of vocabulary from one part of the Islamic world to another. In the particular case under discussion, he uses the terms *funduq, khan, ribat* or *caravansarai* according to the area he is describing. On the other hand, the notion that some ambiguity of function is implied in the use of this varied vocabulary can also be defended. Qasr al-Khara- 7.14 na in Jordan, for example, (before 92/711;

6.4 Susa
(Tunisia), *ribat*

332

243 Aleppo, Khan Utchan, portal

probably Umayyad), is clearly intended as a palace but it also has extensive stables and suites of small rooms. Ribat-i Sharaf in north-eastern Iran combines in two separate sections of one building the functions of palace and caravansarai. In the case of urban caravansarais attempts to define functions are especially hazardous; these buildings deserve separate consideration. It must also be remembered that other types of urban architecture, such as the *khanqah* and the *zawiya*, performed some of the functions of the caravansarai in that they offered selected travellers board and lodging – e.g. the Anatolian foundations of Sünbül Baba, Tokat (691/1291–2) and Eshab-i Keyf, Marash (612/1215–6). In short,

the very varied terminology used of buildings with a hostel function suggests the need for inclusive rather than exclusive definitions. As with other Islamic architectural types, such as the mosque or the minaret, distinctively local expressions of the caravansarai idea abound, but this distinctiveness does not seem to have generated comparably precise descriptive terms.

A sequence of three strongly fortified structures on the outskirts of the village of Darzin, near Kirman in south-eastern Iran, emphasises how thin the dividing line between fort and caravansarai can be. The presence of not one but three such buildings – all roughly contemporary with, and close to, each other – is hard to

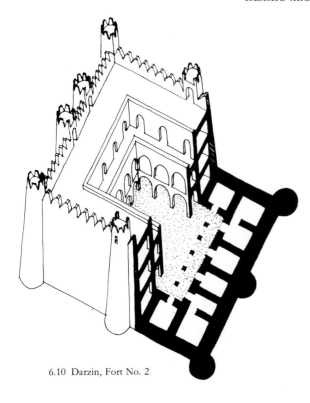

6.10 Darzin, Fort No. 2

explain, irrespective of whether they were erected for defence or trade. Certainly they would have been able to shelter a substantial number of people and animals. A close parallel for these buildings is offered by the equally enigmatic Zindan-i Harun which watches over the road that runs east from Rayy. The construction details at Darzin – ground plan, arrow-slits, entrance gateways and the like – recur in late Sasanian and early Islamic forts, palaces and *khan*s, yet another reminder (if any were needed) of the typically Islamic use of the same form for quite different functions. It is of course quite possible that the monuments at Darzin were intended from the outset to have a double purpose. A comparable uncertainty surrounds 'Atshan, not far from Ukhaidir (perhaps 8th century) – part fort, part stopover.

6.28–6.29, 6.34

7.62–7.63

ARCHITECTURAL ORIGINS

The architectural sources of the various types of medieval caravansarais are virtually impossible to identify with precision. Some, like the forms of Achaemenid and Sasanian post-houses, are

irretrievably lost. Of others, like the Byzantine *pandocheion*, descriptions but few physical remains survive – the earlier Khan al-Zabid in Jordan is perhaps of this period, while in Syria the type is attested at Dair Sim'an and Dair Turmanin. The scattered relics of Roman inns (e.g. Umm al-Walid in Jordan?) give all too little an idea of what standard Roman facilities of this kind offered, although lengthy unbroken lateral spaces for stabling and regular rectangular bastions (as in the two possibly Roman caravansarais in the Tektek area in northern Syria) may have been common features. The loss of nearly all the Roman and Byzantine forerunners is the more regrettable since their function was broadly the same as that of the Islamic caravansarai. Other pre-Islamic buildings which can be linked with the caravansarai, and which do survive at least in part, were founded with rather different purposes in mind. The Roman *castrum* or military camp is a case in point. It is often located far from habitation in difficult or even dangerous terrain. It has a square plan with regular bastions and a single, fortified entrance. Within, the major features of the layout are an open courtyard (like most substantial Near Eastern houses since ancient times) with a central well or cistern, and barracks, including stables on occasion, stacked close against the perimeter walls. The relevance of this design to the Islamic caravansarai is obvious – hence the disputed dating and function of monuments like Qasr al-Khabbaz in Iraq – and may go far to explain the emphasis on fortification in the later genre. Such fortification makes little sense in the absence of a permanent garrison. One may note in passing that the Umayyad desert residences attest to the same process. Indeed the lesser enclosure at Qasr al-Hair East may be an early Islamic caravansarai, and the same identification has been made for the similar but smaller enclosure at Qasr al-Hair West. Presumably the visual impact of fortification was at once desirable and sufficient for caravansarai and palace alike.

7.1–7.
6.38

6.83–6

6.81

It would be unwise, however, to suggest that the influence of the *castrum* spread very far beyond Roman territory in the Near East, and therefore much to the east of Syria and eastern Anatolia. It cannot explain the forms of Iranian caravansarais. For these another source may be

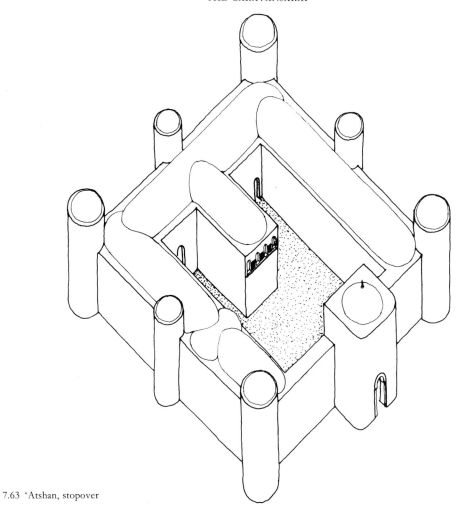

7.63 'Atshan, stopover

canvassed, namely, domestic architecture. As the excavations of Parthian houses in Mesopotamia have shown, for example at Assur and Nippur, domestic architecture in the half-millennium before Islam was essentially inward-looking. Here too attention was focused on the empty central courtyard surrounded by a shaded arcade, behind which the accommodation was neatly tucked away. A particularly significant feature of these houses in the Iranian context is the use of *iwan*s to articulate the courtyard façades. They recur in the earliest Iranian caravansarais. Thus the caravansarai can be regarded as a house writ large, which makes sense because it incorporates many domestic functions. Even the formal façade has its

domestic prototype; pre-Islamic and Islamic houses have high blank walls which give no hint of the internal arrangements. The location of so many caravansarais in the open countryside made a formal symmetrical façade virtually unavoidable – but the frequent lack of articulation in this façade could be interpreted as a survival of a domestic prototype. In caravansarais, too, the courtyard is larger *vis-à-vis* the rest of the building than it would be in a house; but this change is dictated by the need to house many more animals. In general, therefore, domestic architecture can be regarded as a useful clue towards a better understanding of how caravansarais developed. Even so, the great variety of surviving caravansarais suggests that their arch-

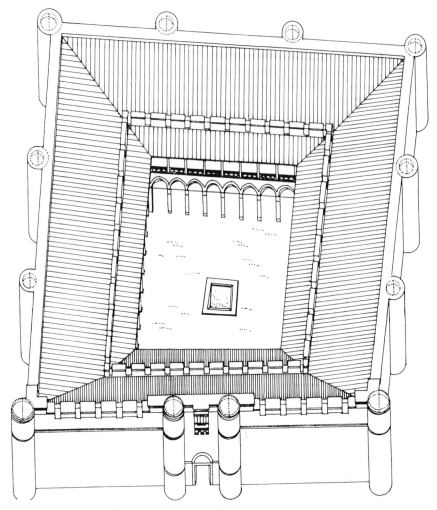

6.84 Qasr al-Hair East, small enclosure (caravansarai?)

itects were able to draw inspiration from several distinct sources.

RURAL AND URBAN CARAVANSARAIS: GENERAL CONSIDERATIONS

Unfortunately, information on urban caravansarais is very scanty. It is of course true that urban caravansarais are likely to present more challenging problems of identification than their counterparts in the countryside. If later Islamic practice is any guide, their functions are likely to have been much wider than those of caravansarais in the open countryside. Lack of space in a dense urban environment would always have imposed limitations of size and therefore accom-modation which did not apply outside towns. Moreover, the concentration of trade in towns naturally gave the buildings associated with trade functions to do with the buying, selling, display and storage of goods which simply did not apply to rural caravansarais. Clearly less protection was needed; fortifications were otiose. Finally, city caravansarais had to be designed so as to accommodate shopkeepers and merchants on a permanent instead of merely a temporary basis. Thus urban caravansarais operated on such a different basis from those in the countryside that direct comparisons between the two types are apt to be misleading. It should therefore be made clear from the outset that the remit of this chapter is to deal principally with rural caravansarais; those in the city are a separate study altogether.

The local variations of the caravansarai may briefly be considered here. In order to avoid comparing essentially dissimilar types of

245 Urfa, Khan Shifta, gateway

244 Cairo, *wakala* of Qa'it Bay at Bab al-Nasr

building, it is desirable to group separately rural caravansarais and those built in cities. Other lines of demarcation could be drawn but this seems to be the most obvious. Within each group further sub-divisions could be proposed, using such criteria as type of building, chronology, size, geographical location, setting, materials used, structural techniques and the range of facilities offered. Space does not permit a full analysis of all these features, but it does seem imperative to identify at least the major schools of caravansarais within the Islamic world and to assess their importance *vis-à-vis* each other. Even this ostensibly simple task is greatly complicated by the fact that the various categories merge and overlap, and correspondingly lose their value as signposting devices.

6.92–6.96,
6.101, 6.104
6.97–6.98,
6.100, 6.124

6.136–6.137

6.141–6.142,
6.146–6.150
Thus Ottoman caravansarais in Syria differ markedly from those of Ottoman Anatolia, while many Iraqi caravansarais of the 19th century have much in common with those of 17th-century Iran. Such examples reveal the pitfalls of relying on dynastic or geographical affiliations in assessing groups of caravansarais. Only a few caravansarai types are so distinctive that they can be assigned with confidence to a particular period and province of the Islamic world. Examples are the axially ordered *han*s of 6.39–6.43,
6.55–6.56 Saljuq Anatolia, with their marked division between open arcaded courtyard and closed 11 three-aisled stables, and those of Ayyubid and 6.70–6.72,
6.74–6.75, Mamluk Syria, square with an open courtyard surrounded by a vaulted walkway (Khan Barur, 6.85 Tektek area).

A further specific difficulty attached to the body of material covered in this chapter is that of distinguishing a caravansarai from such closely related structures as small fortified settlements, guard posts like the chain of structures in Sistan, or watch towers with accommodation

facilities, castles and way-stations. All have an obvious relevance to the architecture of trade. Where structures which are indisputably caravansarais are scarce, such buildings help to fill the gap in current knowledge. It follows that not all the buildings presented here can confidently be claimed as caravansarais. With these reservations in mind, then, one may attempt to trace the development of rural caravansarais.

EARLY MEDIEVAL CARAVANSARAIS IN THE IRANIAN WORLD

The earliest large body of material is from the Iranian world, and dates from the 11th–12th centuries, if not a little earlier. The sheer variety of buildings invites the speculation that as yet no one type had achieved supremacy. In size these structures vary from the diminutive Zindan-i 6.28–6. Harun, a lonely outpost guarding a pass near 6.34 Rayy, where the austere cubical exterior hides a multitude of rooms cunningly packed together, to the huge double-courtyard caravansarais of the north-east, like Akcha Qal'a and Ribat-i 6.26, 6

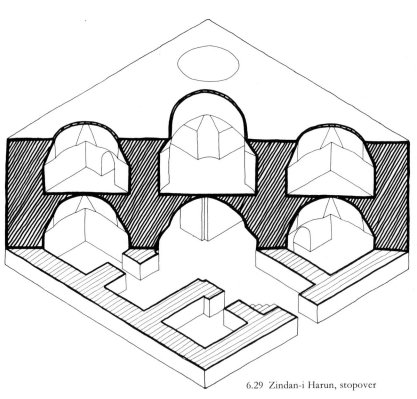

6.29 Zindan-i Harun, stopover

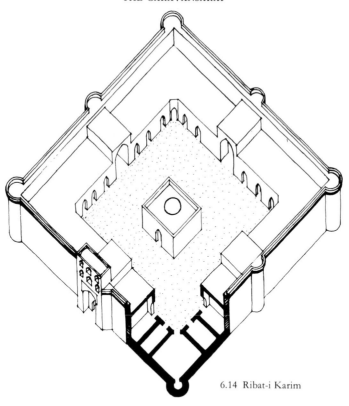

6.14 Ribat-i Karim

Sharaf (completed 549/1154). In north-western Iran, Ribat-i Karim is prophetic of later developments in all its essentials: fortified exterior, single monumental entrance, courtyard, diagonal stables, cellular disposition of rooms around the courtyard, and a central well. Dair-i Gachin and Ribat-i Anushirvan at Ahuvan further enrich this formula, using greater scale to good effect. Ribat-i Turk in central Iran has a military flavour, with a compact, easily defensible layout in which the provision of accommodation is clearly a secondary factor. In Central Asia entirely covered buildings, fortified with continuous fluted bastions and containing quantities of small adjoining cells, were commonplace from the 10th century onwards (Manakeldi caravansarai). It seems idle to look for a thread running through the very varied architecture of travel in the Iranian world before 1200; clearly this was a period of experiment.

The principal significance of the caravansarais built in the Iranian world in the 11th–12th centuries is twofold: first, their mere existence; and

second, their remarkably high quality. These points are worth following up separately. Throughout most of the Islamic world there is an almost total dearth of buildings datable between c.235/850 and c.596/1200 which might have been erected to serve as caravansarais, always excepting the architecture of the hajj. Only in one area is the picture decisively different: Iran and Central Asia. This region preserves perhaps a score of such buildings. True, their size and quality is variable; but the range of the surviving evidence and the numerous indications found in literary sources covering this period both tell the same story. They show clearly enough that the custom of building such monuments was very well established in the Iranian world in the 11th to 12th centuries. Two reason can be proposed for this, one to do with welfare and the other with the Islamic faith.

The notion that it is a duty incumbent upon the virtuous Muslim ruler to build caravansarais for the benefit of the public appears quite early in medieval Islamic thought. One of the earliest examples of the "Mirrors for Princes" literature, a letter of 'Abdallah ibn Tahir to his son, enjoins the recipient to build *ribat*s for the public good, and the same idea is enunciated by Nizam al-Mulk in the *Siyasat Nama* or "Book of Government". Clearly the encouragement of trade is a major factor here; but it is perhaps not the only one. In the 10th century the geographer al-Muqaddasi records that in conversation with his uncle he expressed his own disapproval of the vast sums of money expended by al-Walid I on building the Great Mosque of Damascus, and quotes himself as saying "Had he expended the same on roads, or for caravansarais, or in the

restoration of the frontier fortresses, it would have been more fitting and more excellent of him".

This latter quotation leads to the second reason for the remarkable proliferation of these monuments in this area and period. The word most often used in the sources to describe such buildings – *ribat* – suffers from that fatal imprecision which afflicts architectural terms in Arabic and Persian. Thus al-Narshakhi uses the same word (*ribat*) to describe both a most lavishly endowed foundation of the *amir* Isma'il ibn Saman "by the Samarqand gate inside the city of Bukhara" and for the thousand and more buildings erected by the merchants of Baikand

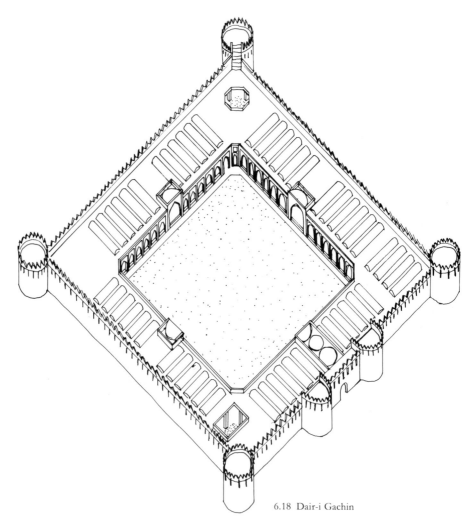

6.18 Dair-i Gachin

in the villages of the area as bases from which to prosecute *jihad*. It is extremely difficult to believe that the buildings of Baikand had much besides their name in common with the *ribat* built by Isma'il, which was clearly a prestigious public structure. But the numbers involved clearly suggest that it was the Baikand type of *ribat* that was the norm. Both al-Istakhri and the author of the *Hudud al-'Alam* corroborate the testimony of al-Narshakhi *vis-à-vis* Baikand, as do recent excavations there, so that there is little justification for dismissing it out of hand. Moreover, al-Muqaddasi gives an even larger figure for the *ribat*s of Mazdakhgan/Mazdakhqan. In his discussion of such *ribat*s, al-Istakhri explains them as caravansarais and says that there is no town, stage or desert in Transoxiana without them. Indeed, he records a statement that in his own time there were over two thousand such buildings in Transoxiana – an obvious underestimate if his own information about Baikand is accurate. Other explanations for the sheer quantity of such buildings in Transoxiana – a quantity apparently not matched in other Islamic lands – emphasise their role in pacifying a dangerously disturbed countryside prone to frequent religious strife, and in protecting the land against nomadic incursions.

In view of the huge numbers of early *ribat*s recorded in the literary texts, it is indeed strange that a settlement east of al-Akhur was called simply al-Ribat; and the *ribat* of that name was described by the geographer al-Muqaddasi, who mentions its three gates, well-built houses, good markets and fine mosques. Such a description is proof positive that at least one meaning of *ribat* connoted a whole settlement rather than a single building. Similarly, the town of Afravah/Faravah nearby, which in the 10th century contained about a thousand families, is described by the geographer Yaqut, writing *c*.617/1220, as a *ribat* built by the 'Abbasid governor 'Abdallah ibn Tahir in the early 9th century.

Such usages are far from exhausting the range of meanings associated with the word *ribat*. In the Transoxanian context of a frontier between the Islamic world and frequently hostile pagan territory, the word connoted the activities not of trade but of the holy war; it was essentially a fort from which *ghazi*s (soldiers of the faith) sallied out against the infidel. Simultaneously it served

as an institution of Muslim learning – an embryonic *madrasa* – and as a mosque. Once Transoxiana had been thoroughly Islamicised and the military function of such buildings had lapsed, their religious aspect became more pronounced. As Professor Frye has noted, the word travelled to the Volga Bulghars and turns up in old Russian chronicles in the form *ropat*, meaning "mosque". The use of these *ribat*s by men bound together by a common religious ideal, who were in addition frequently Sufis, goes far to justify the use of terms like "military monastery" and *khanqah* as glosses on *ribat*.

The most natural way to visualise the hundreds, and probably thousands, of *ribat*s scattered throughout Central Asia in the first few centuries after the Islamic conquest is to relate them to the almost equally numerous fortified residences or *kushk*s of the pre-Islamic nobles of the region. There is certainly a remarkable continuity of architectural forms between a typical *kushk* such as the larger example at Najim Qal'a near Merv or a palace like Varakhsha and a fully-fledged caravansarai like Ribat-i Malik. Although a period of at least three centuries separates them, they share a fortified exterior articulated by serried engaged columns, as well as an interior courtyard surrounded by ranges of rooms. Moreover, while Najim Qal'a looks forward to developed Saljuq caravansarais, it also looks back to such Parthian buildings as Durnali, a border fortress in the Merv oasis dating to the first century B.C. Such connections highlight the origins of the public caravansarai in private palatial architecture. Small wonder, therefore, that the central building of the Kirk-Kiz complex near Termez (Tirmidh), variously dated between the 9th and 12th centuries, should long have been interpreted as a caravansarai – though according to others it could well have been a *khanqah*, an *'imara* or a castle. While some recent scholarship has identified it as a summer palace for the Samanid dynasty, new evidence has disputed this finding; but the crucial point is rather that so many other functions have plausibly been suggested for this building and also for that at Akyr-Tash, among them that of caravansarai. The use of a single architectural form for a wide variety of buildings was of course to remain a standard feature of Islamic architecture.

As in the case of the later Islamic *ribat*s, the

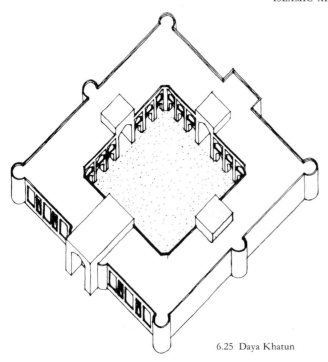

6.25 Daya Khatun

*kushk*s of the local *dihqan*s were concentrated in certain oases. The Merv oasis, for example, contains the sites of Dawali, Eliming Tepe and Kurtly, as well as the two Najim Qal'a structures, besides further residences in the city itself. In the Berkut Qal'a oasis, which measures some 17 km by 2–3 km, over 100 such "castles" have been identified, ranging from full-scale fortified castles a hectare in extent, such as Berkut Qal'a itself, to others barely a hundred metres square. The normal pattern of such buildings comprised high walls of compressed mud surrounding a tower – the residence proper – set on a high mud plinth. Round towers studded the perimeter wall. Apart from the main tower, the interior contained only a few rooms. Clearly a major function of such buildings was to provide a place of refuge, and once again the link with later fortified caravansarais is patent. Interestingly enough, the houses of the peasants themselves were of similar construction though on a smaller scale.

It will be clear from these remarks that the varied material from Central Asia significantly

enriches the profile of the medieval Iranian caravansarai which is gradually emerging. Recent survey work in Iraq and Saudi Arabia has revealed a second body of material directly relevant to the development of the Iranian caravansarai. Over 20 stations of the celebrated Darb Zubaida, the pilgrim road from Baghdad to Mecca lavishly endowed by the spouse of Harun al-Rashid in the early 9th century, have been identified, with their associated hostelries, forts (Ummu Qurun), semi-palatial structures (al-Hamra), corrals and cisterns. It is worth remembering, too, that the Saljuq sultan Malik-shah sponsored a similar chain of way-stations on the route from Iraq to the Holy Cities of Arabia. The degree of overlap, if any, with the Darb Zubaida created nearly three centuries previously has not yet been determined, but the important point in the context of this study is that the very same monarchs who were responsible for the great caravansarais of eastern Iran were also behind the more modest provision of facilities for travellers on the *hajj* routes. It is entirely legitimate, therefore, to look for connections between these two types of building.

One further caveat is required to set a discussion of these early medieval Iranian caravansarais into a proper context. These buildings cannot be understood in isolation, any more than they were built in isolation. Splendid though they were, they would have made little sense as mere vehicles of ostentatious patronage. To function effectively they would have needed other, supporting, buildings along the same route. Very few such buildings survive, or at any rate have been identified, in Iranian Khurasan. Thus the full context of buildings like Ribat-i Mahi and Ribat-i Sharaf (completed 549/1154), remains elusive. It is in this situation that the broadly contemporary caravansarais in Central Asia come into their own. Most of them are to be found in Turkmenistan and Uzbekistan, and thus fall within the borders of medieval Khurasan, a province which embraced parts of the modern territories of Iran, Afghanistan and the ex-Soviet Union. Not only were they built in the same area and period; they also survive in substantially larger numbers, and their origins, thanks to Soviet excavations, are not nearly as cloudy as those of caravansarais elsewhere in the Iranian world. In particular, as noted above, they

342

can be shown to derive at least in part from a popular and distinctive genre of building in pre-Islamic Central Asia: the *kushk* or fortified manor-house. It is precisely the lack of relevant and securely datable domestic architecture in Iran proper that has so far blocked attempts to establish the pre-history of the Iranian caravansarai, though there has been no lack of theories.

What of the nature and quality of these Iranian caravansarais? Significant variations in scale, function and building material forbid any but the blandest generalisations. In both Iran proper and in Central Asia there are numerous structures of this genre in which utility, not quality, was clearly the consideration uppermost in the mind of the builder. It is quite possible that such structures were the norm; Ribat-i Sangi, Ribat-i Sultan, al-'Askar and the many medieval way-stations in Sistan are all examples of this type of building.

Far more interesting, however, from the point of view of architectural history are the major monuments in modern north-eastern Khurasan and Turkmenistan, for which patronage at the highest level can confidently be assumed, if indeed it is not specifically recorded

246 Ribat-i Malik, portal

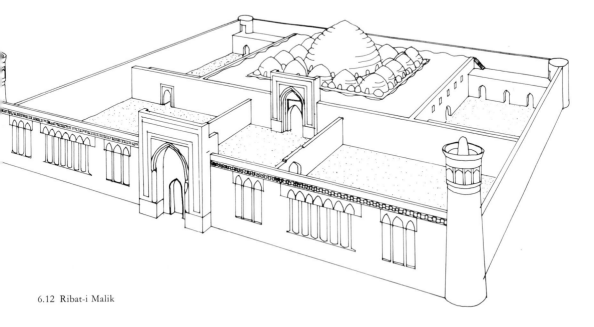

6.12 Ribat-i Malik

247 Ribat-i Sharaf, courtyard

6.21, 6.25
6.11–6.12
6.26, 6.31
6.19–6.20

6.11–6.12

either epigraphically or in the literary sources. Such buildings include Daya Khatun, Ribat-i Malik (470/1078), Ribat-i Mahi, Akcha Qal'a and Ribat-i Sharaf. Some, like the last two, have a double-courtyard plan; others, like Ribat-i Malik, are furnished with an elaborate set of apartments or even a major dome chamber, and thus can scarcely have been intended for daily use by merchants. Such refinements strongly suggest that these buildings had functions which extended well beyond the needs of trade. They could in fact be described more accurately as palaces in the desert – but palaces which doubled as stopovers servicing the caravan trade. Thus one might suggest that the outer courtyard at Ribat-i Sharaf would normally have acted as a caravansarai while the inner courtyard was reserved for the sultan and his retinue, or for other official purposes. The plans of Ribat-i Malik and Akcha Qal'a would also have lent themselves to such an arrangement. The peripatetic life of the sultan in this period would have made some provision of this kind highly desirable. Ribat-i Malik would have offered palatial comfort to travellers of rank plying the road between Bukhara and Samarqand; similarly, Ribat-i Sharaf is strategically sited on the Merv – Nishapur road.

The self-contained nature of these buildings is worthy of comment. The inner courtyard of Ribat-i Sharaf, for example, has its own mosque, stables, luxury accommodation and large *iwan* with a dome chamber behind to serve for official audiences. All this is executed to the highest standard of quality, so that the building has aptly been termed a museum of the decorative (and, one might add, vaulting) techniques known at the time. It is little wonder that when the building was sacked by the Ghuzz nomads it was magnificently refurbished only a few years later, in 549/1154, at the behest of no less a dignitary than the wife of Sultan Sanjar himself

6.19–6.2

247

248

248 Ribat-i Sharaf, interior, detail

246

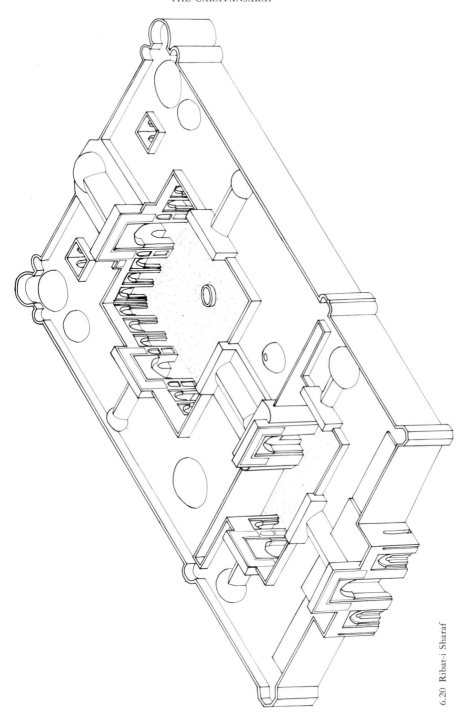

6.20 Ribat-i Sharaf

– clear proof, if any were needed, of royal interest in such buildings. The presence of Ribat-i Mahi and of the ceremonial arch known as Du Baradar as part of the same chain of buildings strongly suggests that this was a royal road. The parallel with the Umayyad desert residences in Syria is a close one and extends even to such minor details as the provision made for passers-by to accomplish their devotions – Ribat-i Sharaf has an exterior *mihrab* for this purpose. These, then, could justly claim to be the major surviving secular buildings of the age. Buildings such as Ribat-i Sipanj show that their influence was still strong in later periods.

SALJUQ CARAVANSARAIS IN ANATOLIA

There is no such pre-history for the sudden surge of caravansarais built in Saljuq Anatolia in the 13th century. These buildings, whose style and layout are remarkably homogeneous, owe little to earlier caravansarais in Iran and no local Byzantine tradition seems to have influenced them. There was, however, a flourishing school of caravansarais centred in Armenia, and while the evidence from the western parts of the area has been destroyed, much still survives in modern Armenia. Not only is the Saljuq tradi-

tion of fine stereotomy and carved stone decoration presaged here; the form of an open courtyard with an adjoining basilical stable is well developed. It seems perverse to ignore a typological parallel which is so conveniently close in time and space. Nor would this be the only area in which Armenian architecture influenced that of the Saljuqs; conical roofs on tall drums, exterior sculpture, stonework in chequerboard patterns and numerous geometrical and floral motifs all come to mind. Even the preponderant use of stone in Anatolian Saljuq architecture, a feature which distinguishes it so markedly from the Byzantine and Iranian buildings which might otherwise have been expected to influence it, is a notable characteristic of Armenian buildings.

Comprising as they do a hundred buildings, these Saljuq caravansarais constitute the largest self-contained group of such buildings in the medieval Islamic world. The large number of examples makes it possible to formulate generalisations about the most popular types of layout, the patronage which generated them, the major road networks which they serviced, and their stylistic features. Without doubt the commonest type of plan was that which comprised

249 Ribat-i Sipanj, main façade

250 Sultan Han, near Kayseri, courtyard with mosque

two distinct adjoining elements, the open arcaded courtyard and the covered hall (*kishlik*). In a few cases these two elements are of equal width, but usually the hall is narrower than the courtyard with its arcades. This hall may feature either parallel tunnel vaults at right angles to the rear wall, or a series of arcades parallel to the rear wall and interrupted by a single central transept at right angles to that wall. Less common were caravansarais consisting only of the hall, without a courtyard; these exhibit much the same variety in articulating that hall as do the caravansarais of which they are a reduced version. Occasionally the hall is conceived horizontally as a continuous series of open vaulted bays with a central lateral entrance (e.g. Şarafşa Han, 634/1236–7). Rarest of all are the caravansarais which dispense with the covered hall altogether and consist solely of an open courtyard, very variable in size, with chambers and stables disposed around it. Many of these plans have a striking similarity to standard types of mosque and thus illustrate yet again the readiness of Islamic architects to find new uses for familiar – one might almost say modular – plans. Thus the plan of the Horozlu Han perpetuates the design of such buildings as the Kucha Mir mosque in Natanz in Central Iran, also of Saljuq date, while the obvious analogy for the Incir Han is the Great Mosque of Damascus. Similarly, the small square pavilion mosques in the courtyards of several larger caravansarais have been explained as small versions of the dome chambers of Saljuq and earlier mosques in Iran, which themselves probably derive from Sasanian palaces or fire temples, whose design is almost indistinguishable from that of the mosques in the caravan-

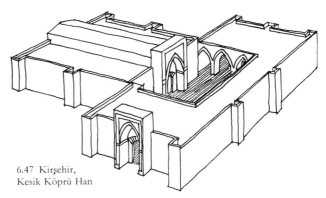

6.47 Kirşehir, Kesik Köprü Han

347

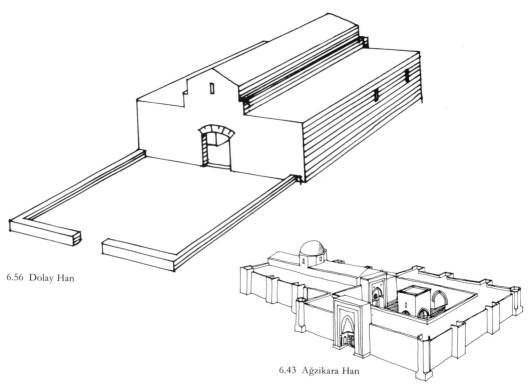

6.56 Dolay Han

6.43 Ağzikara Han

sarais. Thus the wheel has turned full circle: an object lesson in the longevity of architectural forms in the Near East.

The caravansarais of this group were nearly all built in the 13th century, and no less than four of the sultans in this period were responsible for erecting caravansarais. The larger foundations date from the period before the Mongol **6.43** conquest in 641/1243, but many caravansarais were built after this date, when Anatolia had sunk to the status of a Mongol protectorate. This chronological discontinuity between politi-

cal power and artistic activity is equally marked in the case of Saljuq and Mongol Iran. Similarly, the notable dearth of building operations in 12th-century Anatolia, at a time when the Rum Saljuq state (ruled by only two sultans between 510/1116 and 588/1192) was constantly enlarging its power base, finds its analogue in the reigns of the first great Saljuq sultans in Iran.

Enough inscriptions have survived on these buildings to clarify the nature of the patronage which produced them. Among those identified as patrons, the largest group is formed by the

251 Sultan Han near Kayseri, main façade

252 Qaratai Han, portal

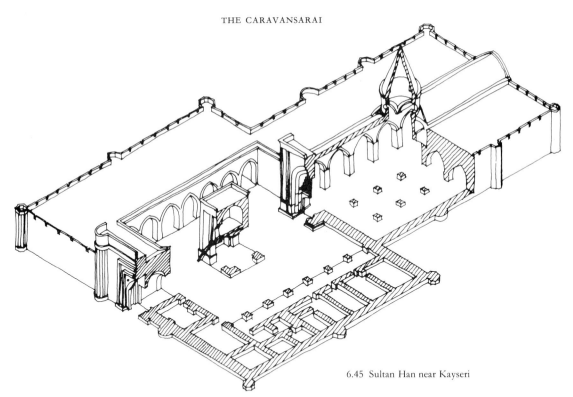

6.45 Sultan Han near Kayseri

6.45 sultans themselves. Patrons within the orbit of the court include the Grand Vizier himself, a 6.47 *sipahsalar*, an *atabeg* and several lesser viziers, *amir*s and high officials. Remarkably enough, the most active patron of all in this field, so far as surviving structures are concerned, was the Sultana Mahperi Khatun, to whom no less than five caravansarais have been attributed. Private 6.42 citizens, both male and female, are recorded, and occasionally their occupation is noted, as in the case of a merchant and of the doctor and arch- 6.41 deacon who built the Hakim Han with its triling-ual inscription in Arabic, Syriac and Armenian. He apparently intended it as a source of income for his son, to whom it was a present; and many lock-up *khan*s in towns were also run at a profit since they figure in the endowments for other charitable buildings.

No detailed study linking the sites of these caravansarais to the major roads which traversed Saljuq Anatolia has yet been pub-lished. It is therefore premature to use these buildings to draw firm conclusions about con-temporary road networks. The most important road of all seems to have been the one between Kayseri and Konya via Aksaray. A score of

*khan*s served this short stretch of some 250 km. From Konya further roads, also well provided with caravansarais, led north-west in the direct-ion of Kutahya and south-west via Beyşehir towards the Aegean ports of Antalya and Alanya. The main north-south artery in the land ran from the Black Sea port of Samsun to Sivas. This traffic would have continued to Kayseri although oddly enough only one Saljuq car-avansarai survives along this stretch of road – and indeed the distribution of Saljuq caravan-sarais in eastern Anatolia is notably sparse. The major road to the south-east from Kayseri took the direction of Elbistan. It is clear that the bulk of trading traffic in Saljuq Anatolia was along the road from Samsun on the Black Sea to Alanya or Antalya on the Aegean, via Sivas, Kayseri and Konya. The most valuable com-modity on this route was apparently slaves. These slaves would change hands in the great marts of the Crimea, which served the catch-ment area of the southern Russian and Uk-rainian steppe, the homeland of the Circassians, Kipchaqs and others who were imported into Egypt to become *mamluk*s. The Rum Saljuqs were the middlemen in this trade. The distribu-

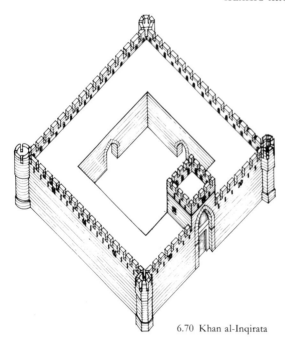

6.70 Khan al-Inqirata

for all the world like the gargoyles of a Gothic cathedral. The portal itself, as if by some magnetic force, attracts all the decoration which most of the building so ostentatiously eschews. It follows the standard format found in other contemporary Anatolian buildings, with a rectangular framework in geometric ornament enclosing a *muqarnas* vault of triangular shape over the entrance itself. This general scheme is usually supplemented by inscriptions and floral motifs. Sometimes the portal is prinked out in two-tone masonry (*ablaq*) and thus attests a Syrian influence which manifests itself in other details too (Zazadin Han, 633–4/1235–7). 6.48 Within, the vaulting is sure, economical, efficient; the stonework has a knife-like precision. The vast vaulted stables again recall some 11 Gothic cathedral (e.g. Sultan Han between 6.39 Konya and Aksaray, begun 626/1228–9). Often these stables have a central lantern whose squinches embody delicate miniature *muqarnas* vaults. As in other decorative details of these caravansarais, such features gain added impact from their designedly bare and severely functional context.

MEDIEVAL SYRIAN CARAVANSARAIS

Contemporary and slightly later work in Syria 6.69–6.8 fell far below this level of achievement. 6.82, Upwards of thirty caravansarais of 12th–14th 6.85–6.8 century date have survived there. They have a strong family resemblance and illustrate a type scarcely encountered in contemporary Anatolia or for that matter in other areas of the Islamic world. Of approximately square form, they have a single entrance – often located off-axis – leading into a spacious open courtyard surrounded by a covered vaulted gallery. Their outer walls are usually devoid of bastions (Khan al-Inqirata 6.69–6.7 is a significant exception) but, as if to compensate for this, they are frequently provided with a guard-room over the entrance, crenellations and continuous machicolation for the delivery of naphtha pots, a kind of medieval Molotov cocktail (Khan al-Sabil). Apart from a room 6.82 beside the entrance, or a pair flanking it, no specific provision is made for private accommodation; moreover, one of these rooms is often a mosque anyway. Thus the quality of the facilities offered in these establishments is appreciably lower than in other groups of Islamic

tion of their caravansarais thus falls into place. So too do the great vaulted dry-docks at Alanya, the so-called Tersane (naval arsenal). They are evidence of a form otherwise known from surviving examples in the Maghrib alone (Mahdiya and Sale). Once built, the caravansarais could serve many purposes, military and civil as well as mercantile. But it seems inherently unlikely that they were built to encourage internal trade or east-west trade, let alone trade with the Byzantines. Hence, presumably, the striking absence of Saljuq caravansarais in western and eastern Anatolia, or to the north and south of the major arterial road. At least some of them were charitable foundations, such as the gener-252, 6.40 ously funded Qaratai Han (628/1230–1) with its substantial complement of permanent staff and an unusually philanthropic endowment which considerably made provision for such little luxuries as leather to repair the shoes of travellers and halva honey for everybody on Fridays.

Stylistically these caravansarais are, as might be expected, the most austere of Anatolian Saljuq buildings. They present a forbiddingly plain exterior façade. The only decoration on the *cf.* 6.138 main curtain walls is the carved animal figures or heads which serve as water-spouts and look

caravansarais. This negative judgement extends also to the standard of their construction. Much of the masonry is rubble and, even where dressed stone is used, the techniques of cutting and coursing alike are slipshod, and much use is made of materials robbed from other buildings. As a result their state of preservation is noticeably inferior to that of their contemporary counterparts in Anatolia. These factors are all the more difficult to explain when it is recalled that the standards of construction in Ayyubid and Mamluk religious buildings are generally much higher, and that the patrons of these Syrian caravansarais, insofar as their names are recorded, were powerful *amir*s – such as treasurers and governor-generals – as well as regents, governors, chief *qadi*s and even the sultan himself. Why, then, should these buildings be so uniformly small, badly built and meanly furnished? According to Sauvaget the reasons for this are to be sought in the absence of deserts in Syria, the comparatively short distances involved, and the presence of many caravansarais close together – at times no more than 14 km apart. Since similar arguments could be deployed in the case of many areas of Anatolia, this reasoning seems defective. It appears, rather, that a local interpretation of the caravansarai form had early on taken root in Syria and maintained itself tenaciously thereafter – a phenomenon which is quite standard in Islamic architecture. It is quite clear, moreover, from a rapid survey of the Syrian architecture built in Ayyubid and Mamluk times under high official patronage, that urban as distinct from rural buildings attracted the lion's share of support. For this reason an urban *ribat* or *khan*, as numerous examples in Jerusalem (such as Ribat Kurt, datable 693/1293–4) and Aleppo (Khan Abrak and *khan* of Khair Bay) attest, was liable to be of higher quality than its rural counterpart (such as Khan al-'Arus, 577/1181–2). Quite apart from this distinction, the tally of Ayyubid and Mamluk architecture in Syria and Palestine makes it clear that religious buildings – mosques, *madrasa*s, *khanqah*s, mausolea – were the most favoured objects of patrons with architectural interests. Purely secular architecture is very much the exception – thus scarcely a single palace of this period survives in the area. Whether the Syrian caravansarais suffered this

comparative neglect for other reasons as well is too complex a question to be discussed in detail here. But one might at least suggest that their intermittently military role as stores for food and munitions, and their function as stations for official couriers (in the *barid* service), weighed at least as much with their patrons – themselves servants of the state – as did their narrowly mercantile *raison d'être*. The state-related functions of these buildings demanded neither great size nor expensive accommodation. It may also be that the volume of internal trade in a country with a long, easily navigable coastline was never on a par with that of more landlocked countries. To take a single example, it seems likely that Syrian caravansarais never serviced the slave trade which was so important in Anatolia. Finally, the comparatively dense settlement of the area was a factor in rendering journeys less dangerous, and thus obviating the necessity for travelling in large bands to gain extra protection. This helps to explain why medieval *khan*s are relatively rare in Palestine (e.g. Khan al-Tujjar and Khan Jubb Yusuf).

The time-span of these Syrian caravansarais extends until the very end of the Mamluk period. In Turkey and Iran, however, very few caravansarais of the 14th and 15th centuries survive and it is only in the 16th century that this situation changes. By that time the entire Islamic world was parcelled out among three super-powers: the Ottoman, Safavid and Mughal states. This situation discouraged the development of local architectural styles and forms, tending rather to impose an oppressive

6.71–6.75

6.91
6.90
6.80

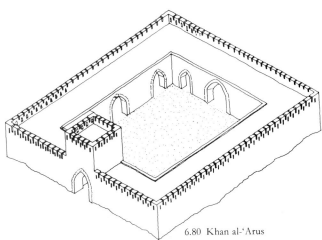

6.80 Khan al-'Arus

351

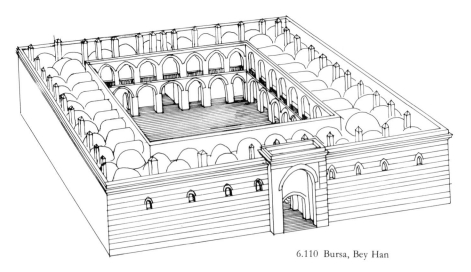

6.110 Bursa, Bey Han

uniformity on areas which had hitherto enjoyed autonomy in this respect. This is of course especially true of the new Ottoman provinces. Thus in caravansarais as in mosques, Turkish forms penetrated Syria, though it is interesting to note the survival of earlier local features in these later Syrian caravansarais.

OTTOMAN CARAVANSARAIS

Syria

Only one group of Ottoman caravansarais outside Anatolia has been studied in detail, and this comprises precisely the eight surviving pilgrim caravansarais in Syria, which mostly date to the 16th and 17th centuries. Since they were planned to accommodate pilgrim traffic, which is of course much heavier than that of normal mercantile caravans, they fall into a class of their own. Built as they were by patrons of high rank – a Grand Vizier, a governor of Damascus and even, in several cases, the sultan himself – as a service to the entire orthodox Islamic world, they serve propagandist as well as functional ends. It comes as no surprise, therefore, that some of them are of surpassing size (rising to 161 m. by 122 m. in the case of the one at Qara Mughurt, possibly 1048/1638) and lavishly equipped with facilities not found in most caravansarais. Many are protected by adjacent purpose-built forts with supplies of food and water; others incorporate large

mosques, probably so that they can serve the local community as well as travellers; yet others have baths. Often they have private chambers for the staff of the building or for travellers of note. In other cases, commodious vaulted niches open off the gallery surrounding the courtyard: each niche can accommodate two people in comfort (Qal'at al-Mudiq). The unchallenged masterpiece of this group, Khan al-Qutaifah, has been described with some justice as a miniature city, with its own water supply, ovens and kitchens providing free meals, mosque, fountains, ingeniously constructed and ventilated latrines, shops, baths and garden in addition to the caravansarai itself. Such facilities may also be found in Ottoman caravansarais not built specifically to service the pilgrim traffic (e.g. the example at Ma'arrat al-Nu'man with its baths and shops). Sometimes a purpose-built Ottoman caravansarai was grafted on to an earlier but still functioning building (Hasya; Khan Shaikhun; Khan Tuman, before 585/1189). Where local models have been used, they are enlarged, improved or liable to unexpected re-interpretations; thus the caravansarai at al-Rastan uses the familiar schema of a courtyard surrounded by vaulted galleries, but for reasons of topography revitalises this somewhat hackneyed design by transforming the square into a narrow elongated rectangle. The most common disposition derives from an Anatolian rather than a Syrian source, and features an open courtyard with an extensive vaulted area at one side. In this vaulted area are platforms (*mastaba*s) with adjoining chimneys; here travellers can cook and sleep. Similarly, the architectural forms and detailing are essentially Ottoman rather than local. It cannot be denied that these foreign influences have produced results which far outstrip the achievements represented by earlier Syrian caravansarais.

Anatolia

Naturally enough, the source of many of the design features of these buildings lies in the caravansarais built by the Ottomans in their political heartland of Anatolia. Unfortunately, the very numerous Anatolian caravansarais of the Ottoman period have not been the subject of detailed study as a group. This is all the more regrettable since they were sometimes, like their Saljuq predecessors, built in a chain (e.g. the Pabsin, Kara, Bas, al-'Aman and Bitlis caravansarais) or, like the examples in Syria, built to serve the *hajj* (e.g. the group comprising Misis, Kurtkulak, Payas, Belen and Karamata). Overall, these Ottoman caravansarais in Anatolia exhibit a very wide variety of layouts. The more popular types include huge barn-like walls roofed by a single tunnel vault (e.g. the so-called Bedesten at Isparta, the Isma'il Bey Han at Kastamonu or the caravansarai by the Kursunlu Cami at Eskişehir). Smaller versions of this type are known in immediately post-Saljuq times (e.g. Pecin). Caravansarais consist-

ing only of a courtyard continued to be built (Kafirbina Han, 948/1541), as did those comprising solely a nave and aisles (Yolcu Han and Pamukcu Han). The former type, already presaged in the Evdir Han of 607–16/1210–20, enjoyed – perhaps because of its simplicity and flexibility – a considerable vogue in Ottoman times. It required little alteration to become the standard model for urban *khan*s whose commercial function was paramount – hence their names, which designate the trade they served (silk, furs, cloth and so on). They are usually of at least two storeys, and occasionally have two or even three courtyards as well (Büyük Valide Han, *c*.1060/1650). Little or no provision was made for animals. The adjoining rooms set against the perimeter walls were used for storage or as shops, and only rarely as stables; the corresponding area on the upper storey, which was laid out in virtually identical fashion, was divided into living accommodation, with windows let into the outer wall (e.g. Bey Han, Bursa). Lavish external fenestration is a feature of urban rather than rural caravansarais of the period; rows of external booths are a frequent feature (Emir Han, Bursa). Imposing portals, tower-like structures at the corners, fountains and sometimes mosques in the centre of the courtyard (the Ipek Han in Bursa has both), and chambers flanking the entrance, for the officials in charge of the building, are all standard features (Kapan and Geyve *han*s, Bursa; and, later in the 15th century, Fidan and Koza *han*s,

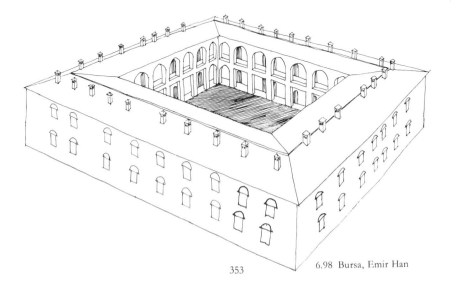

6.98 Bursa, Emir Han

353

Bursa). Such a plan was well suited to urban use, for it could assume a trapezoidal or for that matter any irregularly polygonal form in response to the dictates of an awkward or cramped site (Kürcüler Han, Istanbul, c.871/ 1467). Occasionally, too, the courtyard shrinks to little more than a long corridor (Rüstem Pasha Han, Galata, c.967/1560). Another solution to such problems was to expand the area of the upper storey by using consoles. Galleries surrounding courtyards were frequently domed, as were the rooms behind them; in this feature may be traced the influence of contemporary religious architecture.

URBAN CARAVANSARAIS

Ottoman examples

In many respects these Ottoman urban buildings fit only awkwardly into the category of caravansarai. The vagueness of Islamic terminology in the matter of building types is particularly regrettable in this situation. The clear distinction between the majority of rural and urban caravansarais so far as their function is concerned finds no consistent corresponding reflection in Arabic, Persian or Turkish vocabulary. The same words – notably *caravansarai* and *khan/han* – are used of both types.

Thus the functional distinctions elaborated below have been formulated in the full consciousness that such relatively precise categories were alien to the society which produced these buildings. These distinctions do have a firm factual basis, in that they derive from the architectural layout of urban and rural caravansarais; but unavoidably the evidence is on the whole post-medieval. It may be that from the early Islamic period onwards, urban caravansarais served a greater range of functions than did rural ones and that this imposed rather different priorities on their design. The almost total lack of surviving medieval buildings of this kind in the Islamic world – although presumably they

253 Cairo, Khan al-Khalili, vaulting

did once exist – is a key lacuna in our understanding of the architecture of trade. In medieval Islamic Spain, for instance, it seems that only one relatively well-preserved *funduq* survives – the Corral del Carbon in Granada, perhaps of 14th-century date.

With these reservations in mind, then, it seems justifiable to isolate three basic varieties of urban 'caravansarai': those with an open courtyard and a marked emphasis on the provision of accommodation and stabling; those with an open courtyard, reduced accommodation and stabling but with an emphasis on trading facilities; and finally, those which are entirely roofed. One may note a tendency for the first kind to be situated beside the arterial routes leaving the cities, but in the suburbs rather than the centre. Their ample proportions would naturally cause problems on sites where space was at a premium. Such buildings fall naturally into the category of caravansarai. They are essentially rural *han*s which have as it were strayed into the precincts of a city (e.g. Khan Delaler, Diyarbakr). The third type is also straightforward. Comparatively few examples are known, unless such buildings be assimilated to the commonly encountered category of the covered market, like the Khan al-Khalili (917/1511) in Cairo. They are significantly different, however, in that their dimensions are much more modest and because they do provide limited accommodation for merchants or travellers, though not for their animals. Several examples survive in Damascus; all of these are of Ottoman date. Notable specimens of the genre include the Süleyman Pasha Khan and the Khan al-Tutan; but perhaps the masterpiece among them is the As'ad Pasha Khan of 1166/1753, a model of compact and ingenious planning. Grouped around the large central square with its nine amply fenestrated domes are a series of double inter-communicating rooms; in the upper storey these shrink to single rooms sandwiched between a high parapet and a continuous vaulted gallery. Two-tone marble or stone, lavish intarsia work and stalactite vaulting combine to render this the most resplendent example of its kind. The earliest surviving structure of this type is apparently the Khan Urtma (more properly Khan Mirjan) in Baghdad. As in the Damascus *khan*s just discussed, no provision is made for stables.

254 Damascus, Süleyman Pasha *khan*, interior

It is the middle category of structure, which provided facilities not only for accommodating travellers and their animals but also for trade, that poses the most acute problems of definition. These buildings are typically to be found in the centre of the city rather than its outskirts; but, like the suburban caravansarais, they are often strategically sited, for example at the intersec-

255 Damascus, As'ad Pasha *khan*, interior

tion of main roads. Their plans may even incorporate extra openings in the perimeter wall to facilitate the flow of traffic. The pressure on space in the centre of a city forced the architects of such buildings to resort to numerous expedients not encountered earlier. In some cases only the portal of the building touches the street (Hajji Qasim Aga Khan, Mosul); courtyards occur on the first floor above the stables; rooms are perforce irregular and badly lit. But the distinguishing characteristic of these buildings is that they modify the standard courtyard plan of the rural caravansarai by introducing elements connected with trade, for example long rows of shops, permanent storage space and areas for the manufacture of goods. Nor are these features parasitical; they are organic elements of the design. These modifications necessarily involved a corresponding removal of features catering for caravan traffic, such as stabling facilities. The stables might now be reduced to narrow corridors on the outer flanks

6.102, 6.119 of the long sides of a caravansarai (as at Mardin) or might be partially underground (*khan* of Hasan Pasha, Diyarbakr). The location of several so-called 'caravansarais' on sites adjacent to each other also had clear commercial implications; it presaged the great covered markets of

6.105 Bursa and Istanbul. Many of these caravansarais catered for a single trade or commodity, and this is reflected in such names as Khan al-Sabun ('soap caravansarai') or Khan al-Barud ('gunpowder caravansarai'). A charge was levied for accommodation in these urban *khan*s, though this was usually not done in the case of their rural counterparts. One could term such buildings with equal validity either caravansarais or small markets.

With hindsight it can be seen that the germ of these developments exists in pre-Ottoman

6.106 buildings, for example in the Malatya *han*, or in the Yeni Han between Tokat and Sivas (perhaps *c.*725/1325), in which a road lined with shops is driven through a covered caravansarai, with

6.107 doors at either end. At Ulukişla (1028/1619) a similar device is incorporated into an otherwise Saljuq plan with courtyard and covered hall. The isolated location of such buildings may be the clue to their design, in that hybrid functions can be expected to produce a hybrid plan. Simultaneously, of course, rural caravansarais attuned

256 Fez, Funduq al-Titwaniyin, courtyard

much more directly to the needs of caravan traffic continued to be built in much of Ottoman territory.

Egypt

Egypt and Syria afford some useful parallels for Turkish urban caravansarais. Most of them are also of Ottoman date, though their roots can be traced back into the later Mamluk period (e.g. the Khan al-Manzil, Tripoli; Khan Jaqmaq, 6.96 Damascus). The Ottoman examples, which are especially numerous in Cairo, have close affiliations with contemporary work in Anatolia proper, a reminder of the dominance of an

6.129 Cairo, *wakala* and *rub'* of al-Ghuri

257 Cairo, *wakala*, *sabil* and *sabil kuttab* of Qa'it Bay near al-Azhar

imperial 'house style' in the Ottoman provinces. Unfortunately the earlier history of these buildings is somewhat obscure, for only one pre-Ottoman specimen – the Wakalat al-Ghuri in Cairo, 910/1504–5 – has been the subject of a detailed monographic analysis. As in the case of their contemporary Anatolian counterparts, they demonstrate how uneasily the conflicting roles of market and inn co-existed. Frequently the commercial function dominated, as in the Khan al-Gumruk, built in Urfa in the 17th century. Such dual-purpose buildings are common elsewhere in the Islamic world, though post-medieval examples predominate (Fez, *funduq* of the Titwaniyin; *funduq* in Tripoli, Libya).

6.127–6.129

6.8.

6.1–6.

358

An especially illuminating example of the tendency for one building type to merge with another is provided by the *wakala* of Qa'it Bay near Bab al-Nasr in Cairo (885/1480–1). Its layout has little to distinguish it from a typical *rab'* or tenement block of the kind inhabited by the poorer people of the city, for it has the same open courtyard surrounded by apartments on two storeys, the lower level being reserved for storage space and the upper one for living accommodation. In the case of the *wakala* of Qa'it Bay an extra refinement is introduced, in that the living accommodation in the upper floor was itself of a split-level design which operated in each separate apartment. The higher level in each case had a room with a view over the *qa'a* or reception hall below, which itself had an *iwan* which gave onto the street. A kitchen, latrine and tiny bedroom completed the layout on this lower level. A related and better-preserved *wakala* of Qa'it Bay survives near the Azhar mosque.

The most homogeneous group of *khan*s or *wakala*s in the Arab provinces of the Ottoman empire are perhaps those built in Aleppo, which are mainly of 17th-century date. They include the Khan al-Wazir, the Khan al-Gumruk and the Huppa *khan*. In addition there are the *khans* built for the Frankish factories – each of the European powers represented in the city's trade was allotted such a building by the government. Those of the Venetians, the French and the East India Company survive. The standard layout adopted in most of these Aleppan buildings is that of an open courtyard surrounded on all four sides by a two-storey elevation and with a central fountain or mosque. The lower storey comprises a series of lock-ups for the merchants' goods; the upper storey is for their living quarters, which are provided with balconies overlooking the courtyard. Decoration is sparse but exquisite: delicately carved floral or geometrical designs above, below or around the windows, slender sculpted engaged columns, two-tone masonry, imposing portals. Lighting and ventilation is provided by windows so diminutive that they would look trivial if they were not set in broad shallow bays. Frequently there are two entrances – one lofty enough to allow laden camels through, and a smaller one for humans just beside it.

258 Cairo, *wakala* complex of Qa'it Bay near al-Azhar

The *khan*s at Aleppo are paralleled by those of Damascus, notably the *khan*s of As'ad Pasha and Sulaiman Pasha and the Khan al-Gumruk with its centrepiece of six great domes, and numerous others more widely scattered throughout the Levant: Khan al-Sultan and Khan al-Zait in Jerusalem (the latter featuring a covered courtyard with an oculus), the Khan al-Zait in Gaza, and yet more in Hama, Sidon and Tripoli.

IRANIAN CARAVANSARAIS OF THE ILKHANID PERIOD

Practical and efficiently designed as these *khan*s

are, they cannot rival the broadly contemporary caravansarais of Iran so far as sheer scale and range of facilities are concerned. The grand scale had indeed been characteristic of Iranian caravansarais for centuries. Akcha Qal'a and Ribat-i Sharaf, both of the 12th century, are each large enough to hold two spacious courtyards. In the Mongol period, Sin, Sarcham, Ribat-i Sipanj and the isolated caravansarai between Marand and Julfa – that is, most of the identifiably Il-Khanid caravansarais to have survived into the present century – are characterised by very large open courtyards whose enclosing structures are articulated by *iwan*s. Sin was notable for an elegant and elaborate hexagonal entrance vestibule, while Sarcham and Airandibi on the Marand–Julfa road both had projecting and expensively decorated portals of *pishtaq* type. Corner and lateral bastions were standard features.

266, 249, 6.143

Khan Mirjan, Baghdad

For all that these three major Iranian caravan-

259 Aleppo, Khan al-Sabun, courtyard

sarais of the Ilkhanid period are undeniably of high quality, they must cede pride of place to a fourth building not discussed hitherto. Although it falls outside the modern political boundaries of Iran it has such close political and stylistic links to Iranian work that it has to be considered here. This is the so-called Khan Mirjan, earlier known as Khan Urtma, in

6.132

262–

260 Aleppo, Khan al-Wazir, gateway

Baghdad. It was erected in 760/1359 during the brief but culturally active dominion of the Jala'irid house, one of the minor successor states that disputed control over parts of the crumbling Ilkhanid empire. The sister building of the *khan* is the neighbouring Mirjaniya *madrasa* and it was the founder's intention that the revenues derived from the *khan* should go towards the upkeep of the *madrasa*. This, then, is one of the rare surviving examples of the carefully defined symbiotic relationship between secular and religious buildings which was an ideal of the medieval period. In just the same way the Mongol Ilkhan Ghazan Khan ordered a mosque and *hammam* built in every village of Iran, with the express intention that the *hammam* should generate the revenue needed for the upkeep of the mosque. In later times the huge Safavid complex on the Chahar Bagh in Isfahan, comprising a caravansarai, bazaar and *madrasa*, is a more ambitious expression of the same idea. Surviving medieval examples of such joint, mutually dependent foundations are, however, particularly rare in the eastern Islamic world. Hence the peculiar interest which attaches to the Mirjaniya complex, an interest augmented by the presence on the *khan* (called *tim* here) of one of the longest *waqf* inscriptions to survive from medieval Islamic times.

These two factors are by no means the monument's only legitimate claim to attention. It is of interest too on account of its plan, its vaulting, its decoration and, not least, its function. Each of these features deserves detailed discussion. Yet this *khan* is curiously neglected in view of its pre-eminent status among medieval Islamic buildings; it is on a par with the Mustansiriya *madrasa* and other buildings of that school, which prompted Gertrude Bell to remark that the 'mastery of structural problems shown by the architects of Islam in the thirteenth century is nothing short of amazing . . . the admirable quality of the brick masonry and the feats performed in the vaulting make the half-ruined halls as beautiful as a palace'.

No closely comparable building has survived anywhere in the medieval Islamic world. The nearest counterparts are perhaps the *wakala*s of late Mamluk and Ottoman Cairo, such as the Wakalat al-Ghuri dated 910/1504–5 and the

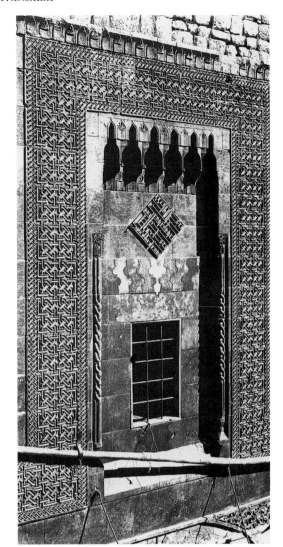

261 Aleppo, Khan al-Sabun, window over entrance

Wakalat Bazar'a, possibly of the 17th century. These, and similar Ottoman buildings in Aleppo, are – like Khan Mirjan – essentially urban institutions and tend towards the warehouse and the shop rather than the fortified refuge for travellers and their animals. The Wakalat Bazar'a, for example, has 25 storage rooms taking up the covered space on the ground floor; the upper storeys contain maisonettes and there is a roof terrace for sleeping in summertime and for keeping animals – a multi-functional concept which applies also to Khan Mirjan.

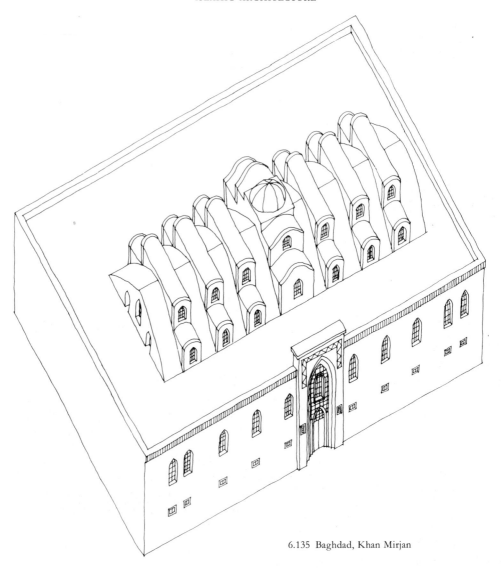

6.135 Baghdad, Khan Mirjan

Most *wakala*s of any size are provided with a courtyard. It is the lack of a courtyard which, when considered in conjunction with the substantial scale of Khan Mirjan, makes this such an unusual building. Reduced to its essentials, the plan comprises a large hall measuring 29.72 × 10.7 m. This hall is completely bare, presumably to allow maximum space for the storage of merchandise. Twenty-two rooms of quite varied dimensions – there are at least ten different room sizes – open off the hall. The largest ones (of which no two have the same

dimensions) are set in the corners, and their entrances bridge the corner itself, being thus effectively bevelled. It is noticeable that, apart from the central chamber on the short north-east side, all the rooms have their entrances placed well off axis. Further minor inconsistencies of planning betray a certain hesitation which sits ill with the effortless technical mastery displayed in the structure and decoration. Exigencies of space or the built-in constraints of the site can scarcely be pleaded as mitigating circumstances since the basic shape of the hall and its

262 Baghdad, Khan Mirjan, corbels for interior gallery

263 Baghdad, Khan Mirjan, main façade

encompassing rooms forms an exact triangle.
Since the hall is nearly three times as long as
it is wide, there is no need for the long axis to
be marked; it is more than sufficient that the
entrance to the central chamber on each short
side should be wider than those which flank it.
The greater size and extra embellishment
accorded to the north-western entrance, and the
presence of the foundation inscription there, is
clear proof that this was the major entrance. The

fourteen shops mentioned in the *waqfiya* are most
likely to have been placed in two symmetrical
groups of seven on either side of this entrance.
This practice is recorded in later Iranian caravansarais such as 'Aliabad.

The upper floor reflects the disposition of the
ground floor with an almost pedantic accuracy.
The total of rooms in the upper storey is 26,
though it is likely that only 23 were intended to
serve as accommodation and that the extra three
were for storage or answered some administrative need. The balcony performs the function of
a cloister in an ordinary caravansarai, but in
another idiom. By allowing easy access from one
room to another it encourages people to mix
more freely and no doubt the bustling activity in
the hall below was something of a draw. The
true glory of the *khan* lies in its vaulting. To a
European eye these vaults can scarcely fail to
suggest a Gothic spirit. The alleged connections
between Islamic architecture – whether in Spain,
Egypt or Iran – and the beginnings of the
Gothic style provided material for a brief,

264 Baghdad, Khan Mirjan, interior

364

265 Baghdad, Khan Mirjan, general view

266 Sin, caravansarai, lateral façade

intense and inconclusive controversy in the 1930s. If the debate is ever re-opened, Khan Mirjan will no doubt be drawn into the argument, as indeed it ought to be. The reasons for this lie only partly in its magnificent series of transverse vaults; they encompass also the treatment of the non-load-bearing walls and the exterior aspect of the building.

Eight great transverse arches vault the hall. Broadest of all are the two central arches; the hierarchy continues with the lesser members, and extends to the treatment of the central spaces in the curtain walls between the transverse ribs. At the exact centre of the hall is a typically Iraqi four-sided vault whose arches break off short to form a flattened central square. This is easily the largest centrepiece of the intervening or membrane vaults. In sum, the careful grading of dimensions and of decorative vaulted centrepieces suggests long familiarity with the concept of continuous transverse vaulting over oblong spaces.

POST-MONGOL CARAVANSARAIS IN IRAN

The few known 15th-century caravansarais maintained the grand scale of their predecessors, though it seems that they were less richly decorated – indeed Ribat-i 'Ishq and Ribat-i Sinchas are of rubble masonry. They are part of a chain of fourteen caravansarais built by the vizier Mir 'Ali Shir between Gurgan and Mashhad in the late 15th century. The same patron was responsible for the splendid Qush Ribat in north-west Afghanistan (912/1506), a building which, in its austerity and its gigantic size, sets the tone for the Safavid caravansarais to follow. These Iranian buildings belong to a world entirely divorced from the court. They are so practical that virtually no extraneous decoration impinges on their starkness. It would have been a waste. The skill they demanded was rather that of construction, a skill deeply embedded in Iranian tradition – vaults, arcades, small-scale domes. They display unfailing taste in the disposition of these elements and their

6.16

combination with the courtyard and *iwan*s so characteristic of public architecture in Iran. A generic similarity in layout did not prevent numerous minor variations; each example displays its own special felicities. Thus the whole aspect of the caravansarai can be changed by the lateral or longitudinal expansion of the courtyard (compare the examples of Chah-i Siyah-i Nau and Jamalabad). The steady procession of identical rooms behind the courtyard façade may be relieved by domed corner chambers (Gaz) or even by small, intimate courtyards (Chah-i Siyah-i Nau). Extra emphasis may be laid on the diagonal axis by deep narrow corridors cutting across the rhythm of individual adjoining cells and allowing extra access to the stabling space along the entire length of the inner perimeter wall (Natanz; for similar stabling see Mahyar, Zur and Gaz among many others). In yet other caravansarais, separate stabling areas are created by the simple expedient of placing a room behind three of the four *iwan*s (Zur, Kuhpaya and Natanz), a device which allows the stabling to be managed with much greater control. Access to these stabling areas may be by passages parallel with the laterally disposed rooms (Mahyar, Kuhpaya) or by bent passages which present a bevelled appearance on the courtyard façade (Jamalabad). The standard accommodation for travellers is a small cell preceded by an open vestibule. Bastions may be solid (Natanz) or, more frequently, hollow, in which case they serve as latrines, following an Islamic tradition going back to the Umayyad 'castles'. Occasionally a bastion may also serve as a lighthouse for the benefit of nocturnal travellers, especially in desert regions where travel by day is counter-indicated (e.g. Gaz). The main façade often accommodates shops; the entrance itself may project powerfully (Gabrabad, Kuhpaya), or be deeply recessed (Mahyar). In either case an *iwan* with a crowning stalactite vault is standard. The principal material used is fired brick, though dressed stone is used as a facing for the base of the building (Gabrabad), and sometimes for the base of the courtyard façade; the foundation itself is usually of rubble masonry. The range of plans is very wide indeed. It includes, for example, octagonal examples like Dihbid and Aminabad; in the latter case the octagonal form

permeates the building, since it is also used for the platform in the courtyard. Caravansarais in the mountains comprise nothing more than long, narrow covered halls, or are composed of a central covered hall enclosed by stables (Shibli caravansarai). There are even circular examples (*ribat*s of Zain al-Din and Ziza). It is the cruciform type, however, with four *iwan*s grouped symmetrically around an open courtyard and linked by a two-storey range of buildings, that is virtually ubiquitous (e.g. Bisutun). Symmetry is the keynote, so much so that, apart from the area of the entrance portal, the plan of many caravansarais can be reconstituted on the basis of a single quadrant. The almost identical function of these caravansarais is perhaps sufficient explanation of this uniformity. If a caravansarai were built as part of a chain of such structures and were intended for a given size of caravan, the implication would be that the next building in the chain would cater for the same

267 Za'faraniya, caravansarai, vaulted passage

size of caravan. Thus little purpose would be served by major changes in layout. Such changes would be produced only in response to unusual geographical environments, to routes that took in towns and villages as well as open country, or to less frequented routes plied by correspondingly smaller caravans. Certain sections of a route might attract much heavier traffic – for example if they served local as well as long-distance travellers – and might therefore require larger caravansarais.

The basic similarity of caravansarai plans in the Safavid period could be interpreted as a sign of a practice apparently not followed in other areas of Safavid architecture: the use of an official blueprint, as in Ottoman provincial mosques. If, as popular tradition has it, Shah 'Abbas I (995–1037/1587–1628) built most of them, the existence of some central office which co-ordinated the work and in which standard types of caravansarai were evolved seems quite possible. Such central control would also help to explain their marked lack of decoration. A single caravansarai put up by a wealthy individual would be more likely to bear expensive ornament, thereby calling attention to the munificence of the private patron, than a caravansarai conceived as one link in an extensive chain put up by the monarch to facilitate trade, pilgrimage and other types of travel which benefitted the country at large. The concern of Shah 'Abbas to foster trade and communications also led to the construction of the 'Stone Carpet', the great causeway through the Caspian marshes.

LATER IRAQI CARAVANSARAIS

The clarity, symmetry and generous scale of Safavid caravansarais established a tradition which continued into modern times in Iraq and Iran. Those in Iraq, which date largely from the 18th and 19th centuries, are rather less well-known than their Iranian counterparts and are therefore the focus of the present discussion. They are normally of rectangular shape and have a single courtyard surrounded by living accommodation and stables, the latter either unfolding continuously around the courtyard (Khan Mashahida) or broken by axial *iwan*s (Khan 6.137 Jitan). Their long sides rarely measure more than 50 m. but a few caravansarais, like Khan Asad and the *khan* at Mahmudiya nearby, or the Banu Sa'd *khan*, are appreciably larger. Khan Asad, for example, measures some 74 m. by 92 m. and has correspondingly deeper wings which permit a triple row of niched cells for housing travellers without having to cut down on stabling space. Raised platforms in the corners of the buildings permit the grooms to sleep close to their charges. Along heavily travelled roads the traditional solution of

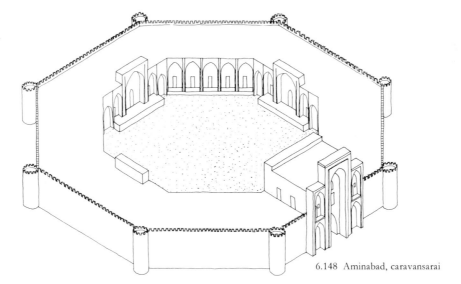

6.148 Aminabad, caravansarai

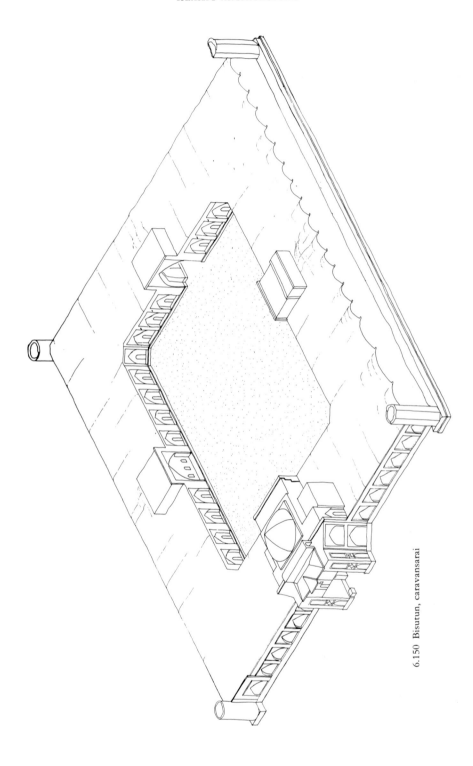

6.150 Bisutun, caravansarai

268 Sangbast, caravansarai

building extra-large caravansarais was rejected in favour of building several smaller hostelries in the same place. The addition of *suq*s and tea- or coffee-houses, plus starkly functional *khan*s that were little more than walled enclosures to contain camel caravans, combined in such cases to create a settlement entirely devoted to servic- ing the flood of traffic along that road. In such a development may be recognised the increasing importance of commercial motives, which in time came to diminish the rôle of the traditional *waqf* system.

There was nothing new about the bastioned, crenellated and generally fortified appearance of the Iraqi caravansarais. Similarly, their heavy emphasis on the portal is easily paralleled in earlier buildings, although the expression of this emphasis is sometimes new. Thus at Khan Jitan the portal is flush with the entire wall in which it is set, while in other examples the projecting portal is flanked by bevelled niches (*khan*s of Mashahida and Haswa). Commodious rooms for privileged travellers may be placed con- veniently flanking the entrance itself (*khan*s of

Jitan and Passingan in Iran). In some cases the portal complex becomes almost a separate building in its own right, sundered by unbroken walls from the rest of the caravansarai, as at Aminabad in Iran or at Khan Bi'r al-Nus, which features a splendid domed chamber in the shape of a saltire cross immediately within the portal. A set of long, narrow, domed chambers set side by side perpendicular to the principal façade flank this central chamber.

Other distinctive features of these later Iraqi caravansarais are the provision of *mihrab*s, raised platforms for sleeping, cisterns and latrines in the courtyard (*khan*s of Nasriya, Haswa, Mash- ahida and Mahauwil); latrines are also regularly provided in the corner towers (Khan Jitan and Khan Mashadida). In the latter building the corner towers each accommodate domed chambers and niches, perhaps in an attempt to avoid having a useless mass of masonry there, a feature which is a minor defect in the caravan- sarais of Bi'r al-Nus and Nasriya and of the Asad *khan*. The bevelled exterior corners of some Iraqi caravansarais seem to have been intended to overcome this difficulty (e.g. Khan Mahauwil and Khan Musalla); in other cases the bevel is deliberately emphasised so that it becomes a major articulating feature of the exterior (Khan Haswa).

The preference for building several discrete structures in the same area rather than con- centrating facilities within a single building did not prevent the construction of one or two monster caravansarais. The most extreme example is perhaps the complex of Khan Hamat, no doubt a product of accretion over many years rather than of a single building campaign. It has

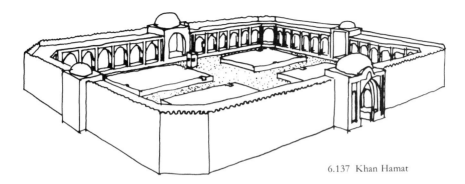

6.137 Khan Hamat

269 Bisutun, caravansarai, entrance complex from courtyard

a total of five courtyards and is in fact two separate but adjoining buildings, one of two and the other of three courtyards, whose asymmetrical layout was dictated by the inconvenient presence of a graveyard to the north. The outer courtyards are little more than enclosures for camel caravans; the inner courtyards, on the other hand, are surrounded by ample living accommodation and contain *mihrab*s, sleeping platforms, cisterns or fountains and latrines. The same marked division between spartan and ample facilities can be seen in Khan Musalla, where the double function is unmistakably and logically expressed in a two-courtyard design measuring some 88 m by 146 m. The caravansarai of Sa'dabad on the Isfahan-Teheran road shows that this ancient type, known at least as early as the Saljuq period, continued in use in Iran. Most of the other features of the Iraqi caravansarais discussed above could equally well be illustrated from Iranian examples, which, although much more numerous, are still known only rather inadequately. If recent survey work in Azerbaijan and in southern Khurasan is any guide, the number of surviving caravansarais in Iran of Safavid and later date is likely to exceed three figures by a comfortable margin.

FUNCTION OF CARAVANSARAIS

So much, then, for the major variants in the caravansarai type across the Islamic world. It may now be useful to consider more generally the function of these buildings. Fundamentally, of course, they were built to provide secure if spartan accommodation for man and beast. This simple formula, however, lent itself to numerous adaptations dictated by the needs of those who used the system. Some caravansarais, for example, served the requirements of the

barid. This ancient Near Eastern institution, recorded at least as early as the Achaemenid period (6th–4th centuries B.C.), flourished under the Sasanians and maintained its importance in medieval Islamic times. The Mongols operated a similar system called the *yam*. The most detailed study of the *barid* is the one which Sauvaget carried out in the context of Mamluk Syria, but the earlier history of the institution in Islamic times is tolerably clear. It functioned primarily as an express carrier service for state documents and messages. Already in Achaemenid times a message could travel the 1600 miles from Susa to Sardis, that is from southwest Iran virtually to the Aegean, in ten days. Changes of horses were kept in perpetual readiness at the stopovers designated for the *barid* service. The *barid* was also an obvious means of transmitting military and, for that matter, civil intelligence. In sparsely populated areas, in desert or mountainous terrain, or in stretches that were otherwise unsafe, it seems that the *barid* made use of caravansarais whose principal function was to serve private, not official, traffic.

Systems of communication in the Mongol empire

It is regrettably true that the tally of surviving caravansarais in Iran is much more modest in Ilkhanid than in Saljuq times. This is strange. After all, substantially more buildings have survived from the later period, and therefore one would expect to find proportionately more caravansarais among them. The apparent dearth of examples is all the harder to explain in view of the abundant literary evidence which bears on the matter. For the first time since Herodotus, with his exact account of the functioning of the Royal Road, the literary sources preserve a description of the scope and functioning of a state-organised communications network. There is a certain irony in the reflection that this network is a creation of Mongol rule. After all, for centuries after their conquests the Mongols were a byword for wanton destructiveness, and the trauma they inflicted on the Muslim psyche was never entirely forgotten. Their energy in setting up and maintaining a secure system of communications nevertheless exceeds anything recorded for the Saljuq period. Saljuq sources mention the efforts of Malikshah to restore and extend the pilgrim route between Mesopotamia and the Holy Places, or the chain of caravan-sarais and watchtowers built by Qawurt in the Kirman region. Such initiatives, though impressive in themselves, were no substitute for transcontinental arteries of the kind maintained by the Achaemenids and Mongols. Under both these states, if contemporary sources can be believed, travel was remarkably safe. Their determined maintenance of law and order may have made it unnecessary for either of them to have built massive, strongly fortified caravan-sarais. Thus the Pax Achaemenica and the Pax Mongolica respectively may be a strong contributory factor to the dearth of surviving caravan-sarais in these periods. It can surely be no accident that the two states which seem to have created the most impressive networks of communication were also the two largest empires in Iranian history. The Achaemenid empire stretched from India to Libya, from Central Asia to Greece, while at its furthest extent the Mongol state controlled much of the Eurasian land mass from Korea to East Germany. This is the largest continuous tract of territory ever ruled by a single power and in that sense can claim to be the largest empire in the history of the world.

The evidence bearing on the safety of travel in the Mongol empire is abundant and, what is more, disinterested. It comes largely from the reports of the Catholic friars who made the prodigious journey from Rome to Karakorum and back, and lived to tell the tale. Ordericus of Pordenone, William of Rubruck, John de Plano Carpini and others were enabled to complete their embassies to the Great Khan only because travel was safe. The classic account of how the system of royal couriers worked is that given by Marco Polo. It specifically mentions the immense geographical range of the network, and incidentally suggests how little things had changed since Achaemenid times.

'The messengers of the emperor in travelling from Cambaluc, be the road whichsoever they will, find at every twenty-five miles of the journey a station which they call *Yamb*, or, as we should say, the "Horse-Post-House". And at each of those stations used by the messengers, there is a large and handsome building for them to put up at, in which they find all the rooms furnished with fine beds and all other necessary articles in rich silk, and where they are provided with everything they can want. If even a king were to arrive at one of these he would find himself well lodged. At some of these stations, moreover, there shall be posted some four hundred horses standing ready for the use of the messengers; at others there shall be two hundred, according to the requirements, and to what the emperor has established in each case. At every twenty-five miles, as I said, or anyhow at every thirty miles, you find one of these stations, on all the principal highways leading to the different provincial governments; and the same is the case throughout all the chief provinces subject to the Great Khan.'

This detailed account raises a number of interesting points. The first is that, as in the time of Herodotus, the service described here was not set up with the needs of the travelling public in mind. It is explicitly depicted as a facility for government use, and therefore its couriers are messengers employed by the state. The reference to hundreds of horses standing ready for use emphasises this exclusiveness. While Marco Polo does not state that ordinary merchants are forbidden to use post-stations, the implication is that such use, if it were permitted at all, would be exceptional. Postal relay inspectors were charged with the oversight of the service and their duties included preventing its unauthorised use, for example to transport private goods, an offence repeatedly committed by Tibetan monks among others. These minor violations are, of course, a far cry from the regular use of such facilities by caravans. Besides, a station that had permanent stabling for up to four hundred horses would be ill-suited to accommodate in addition the large numbers of beasts accompanying a caravan.

Secondly, the distances between stages – twenty-five or even thirty miles – would be far greater than the average caravan could cover and these intervals would therefore be quite unsuitable to the needs of caravan traffic. Rather does such spacing suggest the maximum distance which a courier on a fast mount could cover at speed. Greater intervals would entail a slower average speed and the danger of riding the horse to death. Herodotus' account of the Achaemenid Royal Road yields about 15 miles as the length of an average stage. Since speed was of the essence in both the Achaemenid and the Mongol service, the much greater distance per stage covered by the Mongol couriers suggests that circumstances were somehow different in the later period. It is possible that the terrain in much of the Mongol empire, being steppe, was easier than that of the notoriously difficult Royal Road. A more likely explanation, however, is that the horses used were different and that the Mongols used the wiry ponies for which they were celebrated – animals whose powers of endurance were legendary.

The standard stage of twenty-five to thirty-miles was, according to Marco Polo, increased to thirty-five and, in some case, over forty miles in uninhabited countryside. Yet here too the same richly appointed and provisioned staging posts were set up. The Ramusio edition of Marco Polo adds that 'the Khan sends people to live at these places, and till the soil and serve the posts, so that they grow into good-sized villages'. Perhaps such resettlement, like the running of the post-stations themselves, was delegated by the central government to local authorities such as prefects, district magistrates or provincial bureaux.

These *yam*s are described as 'large and handsome', with 'fine beds' and silken articles in every room, so luxurious in fact that they are suitable for a king. These details suggest a level of comfort well above that of almost all the earlier caravansarais known in Iran, and therefore might be taken to imply a different kind of building. If such a description can be legitimately applied to a caravansarai, however, the apparently exceptional mantle of ornament which bedecks the portal of the Airandibi caravansarai near Marand would be explained. Indeed, it might have been less unusual, in its time than seems the case to a modern observer.

Mention of Ilkhanid caravansarais in Iran serves as a reminder that Marco Polo is describing the situation in Mongol China. Is it significant that he makes no reference to it in his account of Iran? Admittedly he spent much longer in China and knew it much better, and this is reflected in the short shrift that he gives Iran in his *Travels* in comparison to his very lengthy and detailed account of China. For the

time being the question must remain unanswered.

MOTIVES FOR TRAVEL

While the bulk of caravan traffic was no doubt mercantile, many private citizens travelled for other reasons – though only rarely for pleasure. Craftsmen were frequently on the move in search of commissions, and their inscriptions on the objects they made, from buildings to astrolabes, document their wanderings. The wandering scholar was just as familiar a figure of medieval Islamic as of medieval European society. Students often travelled great distances to study with many different masters. It was a common practice to make a living by sitting at the feet of a renowned scholar, recording his material and then, armed with his personal authorisation (*ijaza*), teaching that same material elsewhere. This was in fact a standard way of disseminating knowledge throughout the Islamic world. The emphasis laid on oral teaching and learning made it incumbent upon younger scholars at least to travel widely. Established scholars, too, commonly moved from court to court, or from one institution of learning to another, in search of better jobs.

Others travelled so to speak professionally, and wrote accounts of their journeys. Thus there grew up a rich geographical literature, intended at once for those who wished to follow the same route and for the armchair traveller, hungry for information about exotic climes. These travel writers came from all over the Muslim world. Ibn Battuta was a native of Tangiers, Ibn Jubair and al-Idrisi were Spaniards, al-Muqaddasi hailed from Jerusalem while Yaqut apparently came from Anatolia. Most of the travel writers were Iranian: al-Istakhri, al-Jaihani, Ibn Khurdadhbih, Hamdallah Mustaufi and Nasir-i Khusrau among others. Some of the books produced by such writers are encyclopaedic gazetteers; others are little more than timetables, detailing the length of the stages of the journey, noting the presence of caravansarais (*ribat*s) and commenting on any hazards of travel. The tradition of composing such guides lasted into modern times; one may cite a Turkish guidebook to one of the pilgrimage routes (*Kitab Manasik al-Hajj*) dated 1093/1682 and the guide-cum-gazetteer entitled *Matla' al-Shams*

270 Gaz, caravansarai, courtyard

composed by Sani' al-Daula in 1299/1882; this also covers a pilgrimage route, namely that between Teheran and Mashhad. Such books might well be written at the behest of official patrons, for the state would benefit directly from accurate, up-to-date information about the state of the roads. Revenue collection, official visits and the constant round of military activity were among the elements of state business that benefited from the guidebooks of the travellers.

The pilgrim traffic, although concentrated within a limited period of the year, also benefited appreciably from the provision of caravansarais. Many pilgrims came by sea, but the geography of the Islamic world dictated that the majority of them should travel by land. Naturally the huge pilgrim caravans departing from Cairo and Damascus could not possibly be accommodated in normal caravansarais. Usually, therefore, the members of these caravans camped in the open air. A chain of Ottoman caravansarais, however, was constructed in Syria in the 17th century precisely for pilgrim traffic, and served other travellers for the remainder of the year. Perhaps the most celebrated work of this kind was the so-called *Darb Zubaida*, which served the pilgrim traffic from Iraq and cut across north-eastern Arabia. Sponsored by the wife of Harun al-Rashid, it was provided with regular cisterns and *ribat*s and was even paved for long stretches. It was completed soon after *c.*184/800 and remained in use for centuries. Similarly, the Buyid ruler 'Adud al-Daula provided for the construction of reservoirs and cisterns and for the storage of provisions at the stations on the roads leading to the Holy Cities. As the distance from Mecca in-

creased, so did the quantities of pilgrims thronging any given road diminish, and to that extent ordinary caravansarais could handle the pilgrim traffic more successfully.

Al-Bundari's obituary of the Saljuq Sultan Malikshah (died 485/1092) puts such constructions within the much wider context of the building activities of a ruler dedicated, it seems, to the public weal:

> 'he cared for buildings and lavished expenditure on them. He dug rivers and strengthened city walls and constructed *ribat*s in the desert and bridges for travellers. And among the beautiful buildings he erected were the establishments (*masani'a*) he constructed on the road to Mecca and the way stations (*manazil*) for it.'

In much the same way, 'Adud al-Daula is said to have ordered the building of 3000 mosques and inns in the later 10th century, presumably in Western Iran for the most part; but such figures have a somewhat legendary flavour. The caravansarais themselves were only one aspect of a series of measures designed to facilitate travel.

Nasir-i Khusrau, writing in the early 11th century, reports that there was a dome with a tank of water every 12 to 18 km. on the shortest road through the desert of Eastern Iran. By Lake Van he found the path indicated by posts driven into the soil. These served as guides in snowy or foggy weather. Similar posts marked the road through the salt marshes of North Africa, while Mamluk roads made of flat basalt stones can still be seen in parts of southern Jordan.

Such considerations applied with diminished force the closer the pilgrim came to Mecca. Possibly in order to avoid bottlenecks, a large number of routes to Mecca were devised within Arabia itself, and to a lesser extent in the neighbouring countries. The major arterial roads ran from Kufa (27 days to Mecca), Damascus (30 days to Medina) and Cairo (35 days to Mecca). It is noteworthy that the routes from Cairo and Damascus, though close and parallel to each other, did not meet until shortly before Mecca. A network of branch roads opened off the various stages of these arterial routes. Each was furnished with at least some caravansarais, though if the practice of the last century is any guide, such buildings would have been devoid alike of monumentality, decoration and even

1, 6.104

36–6.37

comfort – little more than bare walls, courtyards and roofs.

While the building of chains of caravansarais makes most sense in the context of long-distance trade, individual buildings could service a local, short-haul trade in staples or heavy goods. It might plausibly be suggested, in fact, that some caravansarais were specifically built for such purposes, and were perhaps financed by local patrons. Changes in trading patterns might also generate new buildings. The traffic in slaves between the Crimea and Egypt, a traffic which the political system had kept insignificant before the advent of the Ayyubids in 566/1171, may well be one such example. The quantities of caravansarais built by Shah 'Abbas may be another. The emphasis which that monarch laid on trade, especially on trade with powers other than the Ottoman empire, implied significant capital expenditure on roads, caravansarais and other facilities intended to encourage trade.

Finally, the role of other, more imponderable, motives might be examined. Caravansarais were a prime expression of the fulfilment of a duty incumbent upon all Muslim rulers: to build widely for the public good. In that sense it could be classed with more modest forms of welfare activity, like planting a tree, digging a well, or putting up a fountain. But unlike these acts of piety, the building of a chain of caravansarais was a demonstration of government power and resolve. It had a certain symbolic, not to say propaganda, value, as did Roman roads or the telegraph system in British India. It rendered hitherto impassable areas traversable, and in so doing blazed a trail for soldiers, administrators, merchants, pilgrims and indeed for the community at large. It was only incidentally, however, that such projects – aimed as they were at providing basic facilities for the maximum number of travellers – produced public architecture of quality. The enormous geographical area of the 'Abbasid empire at its height suggests that the *ribat*s of 9th- to 11th-century itineraries were very simple buildings indeed – hence it is not surprising that they have mostly vanished without trace. Not all the patronage from which travellers benefited was extended by the ruler or his high officials and this too might explain the provision of simple rather than complex buildings. One wealthy Persian landowner in

the 10th century maintained hostels on his estates for the use of travellers, and endowed these establishments with a hundred or more cows, whose milk was freely offered to travellers. In Khuzistan their needs were met in a rather more cumbersome way: buckets of water, which often had to be fetched from a distance, were placed along the road at intervals of a parasang (about 6 km.), as al-Muqaddasi reports.

The provision of caravansarais varied dramatically from one part of the Muslim world to another. Even if there is no need to take absolutely literally the report of al-Qalqashandi that before the Ayyubids came to Egypt in the later 12th century the country had no hostels or inns, it is nonetheless clear that facilities were much more lavishly provided in the eastern than in the western Islamic world. The need for such facilities is highlighted by the account which al-Muqaddasi gives of the predatory Qufs tribe which infested Luristan. Wild of face and hard of heart, they 'are not satisfied with money, but slaughter anyone on whom they lay hands in the style wherein people put snakes to death. They hold the man's head down on a slab of stone, and hurl stones at it till it is crushed'. In Arabia the Bedouin were equally feared, and many non-pilgrims sought safety in numbers by joining one of the great *hajj* caravans.

CARAVAN TRAVEL

In conclusion, it may be appropriate to discuss briefly what might be termed the mechanics of caravan travel. It was standard practice among travellers to ride rather than to go on foot. Shelter had to be provided, therefore, for horses, mules, donkeys and camels; ample fodder and water was required; means had to be found to stop these animals from straying or being stolen. Hence the presence of corrals adjoining many caravansarais. Many of these animals would be carrying merchandise, and this, like fodder, would demand storage space. Thus the determinants of a caravansarai were as much accommodation for animals, fodder and merchandise as for people. As far as possible the roof was kept flat, and therefore provided ample sleeping space. This function of the roof helps to explain the ready access to it, often by multiple staircases.

Most larger caravansarais had at least one

271 Incir Han, general view

resident porter whose services were paid for by the institution or charity which had funded the caravansarai. He would maintain order and be responsible for security. At night this consisted of closing the portal by heavy wooden doors and iron chains. In small caravansarais the facilities would be too primitive to require supervision; the animals would be tethered outside. In such a situation the responsibility for security would rest on the official leader of the caravan, whose authority (conferred upon him by the travellers themselves) was absolute and who often had a small team of helpers including scouts, a scribe, a crier and an *imam*, for the route would have to be patrolled, transactions authenticated, the day's orders broadcast and prayers led – if they were not curtailed, anticipated or postponed, as Islamic tradition permitted.

The substantial number of people and animals involved in a typical caravan kept down the distances covered in an average day. Even so, it was rare for a caravan to log less than 30 km. in a day. Much information about the mechanics of caravan travel comes from 19th-century travellers, and can therefore be applied only with reserve to the medieval period; but in many respects the situation probably changed very little over the centuries. Travel was seasonal; winter and high summer were avoided if at all possible. Journeys, following the Qur'anic injunction, customarily began on Fridays. On the first day the travellers would cover only a few miles. This would suffice to bring the caravan well outside the orbit of the city or other starting place, and at the same time would allow

friends and relatives to accompany the travellers for the traditional first stage. Late-comers could also profit from this arrangement to join the caravan before serious travelling started. The day's journey would be in two parts. The first would begin at dead of night, some time after 3 a.m., and would end around 10 a.m. The caravan would rest while the sun was at its fiercest and would take the road again some time after 2 p.m., continuing until 6 p.m. or even 8 p.m. Thus a day's journey would range from about nine to thirteen hours. This substantial variation shows how misleading it is to compute the average distance covered per day. The situation is complicated still further by other factors. A mule, for example, travels almost 40% faster than a camel. A camel with a load of about 250 kilos can go at about 30 km. a day; if this load is halved, the distance travelled in the same period can reach about 40 km. If the terrain were very difficult, short stages were covered. Alternatively, in areas where water was scarce or robbers were numerous, the daily stage might reach 60 km. Caravans in Central Asia are recorded as travelling at a trot, the animals being led by two or three cameleers; distances of up to 120 km. per day can thus be achieved. Conversely, prolonged halts of several days at a time may be made. Finally, the size of the caravan is itself a decisive factor in calculating the average distance covered. Caravans of some 400–600 animals, divided into files of 50 roped together, were standard. The pilgrim caravans were on another scale altogether, numbering up to 40,000 people at a time with 25,000–30,000 camels. They would travel from about 3 p.m. to about 7 a.m., with torches to light the way once the sun had gone down. Even for these very slow caravans a steady pace was maintained; thus the fate of the straggler, as graphically described in literature and painting, was death at the hands of robbers or of nature itself. Finally one may mention as a curiosity the so-called 'corpse caravans', which bore the bodies of pious Shi'ites for burial in Najaf and Karbala, the holy cities of Iraq. Their stench kept them away from all settlements and also prevented them from using caravansarais.

VII The Palace

PROBLEMS OF CLASSIFICATION

The Islamic palace is a genre of building which perhaps of its very nature obstinately refuses to fit into a convenient typology. The refractory quality of the material is enough to explain why there has still been no serious overall study of this genre of Islamic building. There are in fact further difficulties in the way of such a synthesis.

One such difficulty is the very patchy survival of medieval palaces. Huge tracts of time and space yield scarcely a single example: Egypt until the Mamluk period; Syria from 'Abbasid to Ottoman times inclusive; medieval Iran before the 12th century; Anatolia between 648/1250 and 957/1550; the Maghrib outside the period 287–493/900–1100. If it be argued that this gap may be filled by literary sources, which often describe palaces in detail, the answer must be that such accounts are intrinsically more likely to be exaggerated than descriptions of lesser, non-royal buildings. Indeed, the danger that the medieval author is simply repeating a *topos* must be borne in mind. Moreover, no matter how highly coloured and apparently circumstantial such descriptions might seem, they are virtually never precise enough to permit a convincing reconstruction of the vanished building. Palaces, in short, invite hyperbole. This is exemplified often enough in their names; Ibn Khaldun mentions 'the seven Arabian castles named after the planets and their influences', while the palaces of Safavid Isfahan bore names redolent of nightingales, mulberries and love. Such romance is itself at odds with the notion of permanence. Even when a palace is described in the literary sources, the language, while flowery, is apt to be too vague to be useful. Thus Ibn Bibi, describing the construction of Qubadabad, erected by the Rum Saljuq sultan 'Ala' al-Din Kayqubad I, says that 'its delightful beauty put the palaces of Sadir and Khawarnaq into the shade . . . its vaulted domes challenged the *muqarnas* of the highest heaven. For envy of its turquoise and azure ornament, the face of the turquoise Heaven became as blue as indigo and as yellow as saffron'. Yet amidst such hyperbole some useful information lies embedded: 'the Sultan drew out the image of that palace accord-

ing to his own conception, freehand, and stipulated the site of every single room . . . (it had) heart-delighting belvederes (and was) continually ventilated by a delicious breeze'. Nevertheless, such descriptions – for all their length – are generally too unspecific to be helpful and thus the literary sources often do not fill the gaps left by the random nature of the survivals – all of which discourages a coherent account of this building type.

A second and related difficulty is still harder to overcome. This is the absolute rarity of Islamic palaces, a great pity in view of their importance as the acme of secular architecture. Even the surviving examples are relatively isolated in their own time. Only very occasionally – in Umayyad Syria or Safavid Isfahan – do enough palatial buildings cluster in one place at one time to allow generalisations. In the two examples just cited, the differences between one group and the other could scarcely be more marked, which is a salutary warning of the many intermediate, and for that matter entirely unrelated, kinds of Islamic palaces that once existed. Nothing reliable can be deduced from this paucity of material as to the evolution of the Islamic palace over a millennium. There can be no assurance that the palaces which do survive are on the whole typical of the area and period in which they were produced.

These are not the only obstacles to a better understanding of the medieval Islamic palace. It seems to have been the rule that the precautions taken to ensure that mosques, *madrasa*s, caravan-sarais and other public buildings should be solidly built were by no means regularly observed in the construction of palaces. After all, there was no religious justification for building them, nor did they promote the common weal. Many palaces, it seems, were run up at lightning speed in cheap and even shoddy materials. Outward appearance counted for more than durability. The idea that a palace should be the royal seat of a dynasty for the indefinite future – an idea that in the West produced the Louvre or Buckingham Palace – seems never to have caught on in the Islamic world. As a result, the norm was for a ruler quickly to erect his own palace in the early part of his reign on a site of his own choosing. It was the exception rather than the rule for a monarch to inhabit the palace of one of his predecessors. Sometimes these palaces were so jerry-built that they scarcely endured for the lifetime of their patrons. Nor was it rare for a ruler enthusiastically to demolish the palaces of his predecessors in order either to assert his own importance or to re-use whatever valuable materials had thus been acquired. This combination of expensive external decoration and cheap 'basic architecture' may be seen at its most poignant and 7.201–7.202 flamboyant at the Alhambra. There it has – against all expectation – survived, and survived triumphantly. Nevertheless, it is the exception that proves the rule.

Mention of the Alhambra raises a final difficulty which bedevils the study of Islamic palaces: the difficulty of distinguishing the original appearance of the building beneath a crust of later accretions. Very few Islamic palaces have been examined in the requisite detail, but those that have – for example the Alhambra or the Topkapi Saray in Istanbul – 7.224 indicate that successive monarchs had no hesitation in refurbishing the building on a substantial scale. These buildings, however, seem to constitute exceptions to the run of Islamic palaces by virtue of the fact that they have not been left to decay, but have been continuously inhabited, and it is this that has necessitated their restoration. Such repeated restoration, incidentally, is a reminder that the original construction was flimsy rather than solid. The obvious question which arises in such cases is why the two examples quoted are both sited in areas which border on Europe. Thus the influence of European palaces, with their tradition of continuous use by one monarch after another, cannot be ruled out, even if this influence operated at a relatively abstract level, being

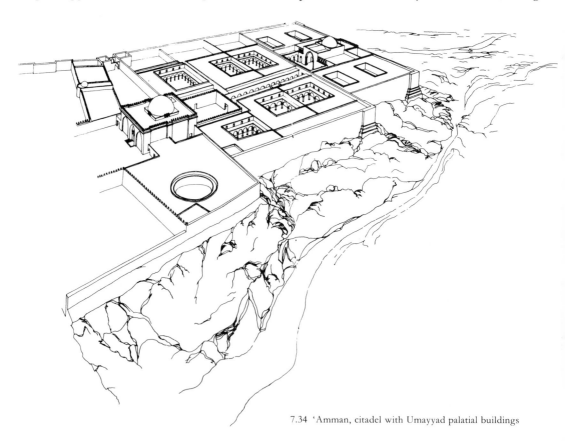

7.34 'Amman, citadel with Umayyad palatial buildings

7.36 'Amman, ceremonial building, reconstruction without dome, interior

confined to an idea and not linked to a particular European building. Nevertheless, it would seem more promising to seek the explanation for this constant upkeep over the centuries in the exceptionally favourable nature of the site itself. The abrupt massif on which the Alhambra is built, dominating the city of Granada and its water supply, was the obvious place to build a palace. Similarly the Topkapi Saray occupied a prime, indeed unique, site on the furthest promontory of the Golden Horn, cut off by wall and water from the rest of the city and thus permitting maximum isolation and privacy for the royal living quarters. It may be significant that when these topographical advantages were not to be had, the question of re-using the site – even when it had been extensively exploited – did not usually arise. Thus 'Abd al-Rahman III, the Umayyad caliph of Cordoba, built Madinat al-Zahra as a palatial complex on a hillside a few miles outside the city, but one of his successors, al-Mansur, chose to build a similar and also fabulously expensive complex, Madinat al-Zahira, elsewhere on the outskirts of Cordoba. Such a procedure means that if the building is eventually excavated, it will yield information

clearly applicable to a single period, as has also been the case with the palaces of Samarra.

So much for at least some of the difficulties that beset any attempt to develop a synoptic picture of medieval Islamic palaces. These difficulties, however, need not render any such attempt otiose. It will simply be necessary to discard the concept of a single prototypical palace against which to measure the random examples that survive. Rather is it important to remember that palaces could service a wide range of royal and courtly activities, and that it was therefore the specific nature of the activity which determined the choice of palace type. It follows that the range of buildings was correspondingly wide. Indeed, some of them, notably citadels and castles, overlap with other types of architecture which are outside the remit of this book.

'TYPES' OF PALACE

At its broadest, the palace was not a single building but an entire complex, which might measure as much as a mile along its principal axis and over half a mile along the secondary axis. Such an ensemble would be designed to

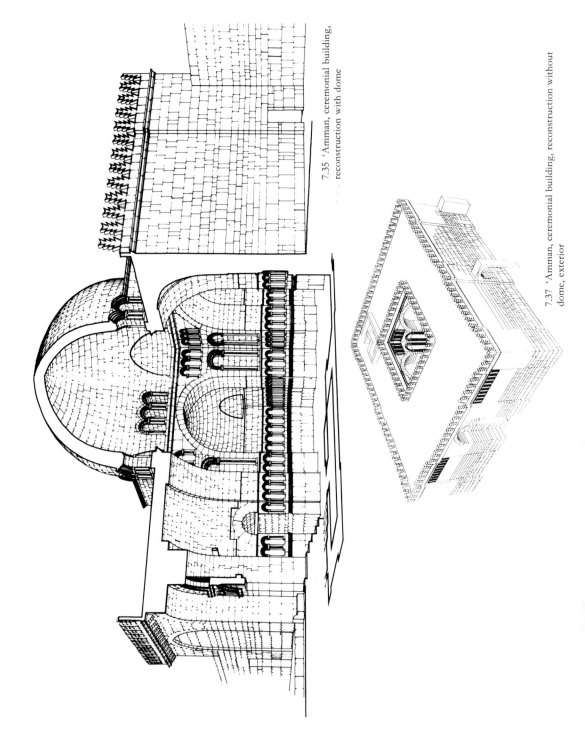

7.35 'Amman, ceremonial building, reconstruction with dome

7.37 'Amman, ceremonial building, reconstruction without dome, exterior

meet all the private and official requirements of the court. Accordingly, its ample private quarters for the monarch, his family and his retinue would be supplemented by facilities for his bodyguard, including barracks, arsenal and stables, and for his officials, whose various *diwan*s would be located within the palace walls. Equally official in its import would be the public audience hall (*diwan al-'amm*) and its private counterpart (*diwan al-khass*). Gardens and fountains encompassed these various buildings, while a strongly fortified entrance complex would monitor access to the whole. Since the palatial precinct would include a mosque, a bath, and often enough a cemetery, it is clear that the intention behind such foundations was to render them independent of life outside their walls. Once again, the Alhambra or the Topkapi Saray are good examples of this type, even if their deliberately asymmetrical layout minimises the absolutism implicit in such an arrangement. That absolutism can be quite explicit, as in palaces such as the Jausaq al-Khaqani and Balkuwara, both at Samarra. The Umayyad palatial compounds at 'Amman and Jerusalem (the latter as yet imperfectly understood) illustrate an intermediate stage between these two polarities.

At its most simple, on the other hand, the palace could shrink to a single building, such as the Safavid pavilion known as Hasht Bihisht, or the Saljuq kiosk at Konya. Even in this, its most reduced, form the palace maintained a division between the monarch's public and private life. An open space at ground level, relatively accessible to all, catered for public receptions. The upper part of the building was reserved for the private use of the monarch. Naturally enough, the external environment of such diminutive structures was more important than it was for much larger ensembles: hence their frequent location in garden settings. Nor was it rare for a number of such buildings, as at Edirne and Isfahan, to cluster in an extended, deliberately idyllic landscape, perhaps intended to evoke paradise. It may even be that in their negation of solidity, their pierced walls and general lightness of design, they incorporate the essence of the *qusur* or pavilions under which the blessed recline in paradise. Some evocative lines by the Sicilian poet Ibn Hamdis conjure up such palatial architecture:

7.43 Khirbat al-Mafjar, fountain

'. . . expert armourers
    Garnish with gilt hoods
        the gates: and an invert
    terrace of stalacitites
        glows in a submarine recess.'

The various vanished Umayyad palaces whose shared characteristic was a "dome of heaven" (*qubbat al-khadra*) may also have been so laid out as to suggest paradise, an association no doubt strengthened by their lush gardens and fountains. The forecourt of Khirbat al-Mafjar may serve as an indication of such lost gardens. The kiosk, though it was indeed the most popular kind of isolated palatial structure, was not the only one. The Umayyad hunting lodges of Qusair 'Amra and Hammam al-Sarakh in the Jordanian desert were presumably intended to serve as temporary retreats for the prince and a select few of his companions. As befits bases for hunting, their keynote is simplicity rather than luxury, and a similar economy no doubt dictated the combination of several functions within a confined space – retiral rooms, audience-chamber and bath.

Numerous intermediate types of palace could of course be identified, but for the purposes of introducing the genre it must suffice to define its extremes. Shortage of material forbids a discussion of each possible category of palace that might be proposed, and for this reason the range of types discussed below is deliberately generalised. Inevitably this procedure does violence to the innate variety of Islamic palaces, but it has the compensating advantage of highlighting the common features within each category. With that caveat registered, it will be convenient to put down as a marker that most of the buildings mentioned in the ensuing discussion fall under one of the following four headings: the palace as country villa, the palace as a combined administrative centre and 'machine for living', the palace (often fortified) as royal residence with little emphasis on other functions, and finally the palace as a modest temporary retreat. The distinctions between the various types will on occasion break down but

this should not compromise their general validity. The discussion which follows will not be organised according to these functional divisions but will be based on largely regional and chronological differences. Nevertheless, it is as well to identify the major types at the outset.

EXOTICA

Islamic palaces were not complete without their fair share of exotica. The Tulunid palace in 9th-century Cairo, for instance, had a quicksilver pond, 50 cubits square, which was accounted a marvel. Massive silver pillars stood at its corners. Attached to these were silver cords with silver rings, and these were fastened to a floating leather mattress filled with air. On this the ruler slept. The device presented a marvellous sight on a moonlit night when the moonbeams mingled with the sparkling quicksilver. In 305/917 the 'Abbasid caliph in Baghdad showed the Greek ambassador a lake of tin more resplendent than polished silver; it measured 30 by 20 metres and had four beautiful pleasure-boats covered with gold-embroidered Egyptian linen.

That large expanses of water were a regular feature of these royal palaces is revealed both by detailed accounts of lakes and their uses, as in the cases of Sabra/al-Mansuriya and the Qal'a of 7.184 the Banu Hammad, and by chance anecdotes, 7.179 such as one recording the caliph's displeasure when in 423/1032 the Sultan with three of his courtiers rowed in a boat in the garden of the caliph's palace in Baghdad and relaxed under a tree with music and wine.

Water was of course prized for its cooling properties; but various other methods of mitigating excessive heat were known. Tradition had it that in summer the kings of pre-Islamic Iran had taken their siesta in a room with double walls, the intervening space being filled with ice, and the Umayyads were thought to have done likewise. Another method was to keep a felt awning constantly wetted, and this was done in Shiraz and Baghdad in Buyid times, while *sirdab*s or underground rooms for use in summer – an idea possibly borrowed from the Uighurs of Central Asia, who are reported to have used this device in the 10th century – are known at Khirbat al-Mafjar and at Samarra. 7.44

No doubt the caliphal palaces were sometimes

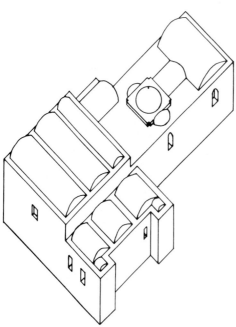

7.32 Hammam al-Sarakh

272 Shahr-i Sabz, Aq Saray, main portal, detail

rivalled by those of high officials. Thus Ibn Muqla, the vizier of no less than three caliphs, built (according to Ibn al-Jauzi) a magnificent palace on the most valuable land in Baghdad. On the advice of his astrologers he laid its foundations after sunset. Its finest part was its garden, where palms alone were conspicuous by their absence. It had a menagerie too in which all kinds of birds were kept, as well as gazelles, wild cows, wild asses and ostriches.

Indeed, many a palace had a zoo attached to it. The Tulunid prince Khumarawaih, a noted lover of nature, furnished each cage with a water-basin. It is recorded that in the year 300/912 exotic creatures were sent to the menagerie at the caliphal palace in Baghdad from all over the world, though the account of a combat between lions and elephants staged by the caliph al-Mu'tazz suggests that an interest in natural history was not the only motive in making these collections.

THE UMAYYAD PRINCELY RESIDENCES IN SYRIA, c.700–c.750

This is not the place to rehearse in detail the tired controversy about the exact function of the Umayyad desert residences. Various theories as to their *raison d'être* have circulated over the last half-century and the vagaries of fashion have in turn brought each to the fore. Yet the fact that no one theory has commanded anything approaching universal support is perhaps a warning that the various explanations have been couched in unnecessarily exclusive terms. Espousal of one theory need not entail the total rejection of another. Indeed, the popularity and the sheer multitude of these buildings suggest that they catered successfully for many different needs. On the most practical level they provided a place to live in the country. Such a *pied-à-terre* might be desirable in time of pestilence; the plague repeatedly ravaged Syria in later Umayyad times. It might also satisfy an atavistic craving for the desert on the part of those Arabs whose roots were not in the mercantile urban oligarchy of the Hijaz. Even those Arabs whose origins and loyalties predisposed them towards urban life recognised the distinctive advantages of the desert as a place to hunt, to toughen body and spirit, and to acquire a better knowledge of Arabic, spoken in its "purest" form by the

Bedouin. From an economic standpoint, such a residence might become the natural nerve-centre of extensive agricultural exploitation, whether the material cultivated was grain, oil, fodder for animals or some other kind of cash crop. Such a farm or estate would require the construction of new facilities for irrigation or the maintenance of extant installations: dams, aqueducts, sluices, underground channels or retaining walls. In most cases, it seems, the Arab magnates took care to settle in places where such facilities were already available, though they frequently repaired or extended them. Politically, these residences had much to recommend them. They dispersed the princes of the royal house, and often wealthy and influential notables as well, over the Syrian countryside, thereby lessening the dangers of faction bred by a concentration of the royal family in the capital. Looking after their estates gave these princes a stake in the continued prosperity of Syria. The wide dispersal of such residences, too, could not fail to strengthen the dynasty's hold on the land, keeping in good repair their relationship with the Bedouin tribes in the desert. The more magnificent such residences were, the more directly they transmitted the message of Umayyad power and wealth. Finally, there is the dimension of security to be considered, although the term 'castle' with its attendant Western concepts of massive fortifications is a gross misnomer for such structures. The term often used for these Umayyad buildings in the Arabic sources is *qasr*, a word used into modern times to denote a walled compound into which animals could be driven at night and which also housed members of a family or clan. Its modicum of defensive strength was quite adequate for the purposes of desert society in which siege warfare was virtually unknown. Its permanence – in contradistinction to tents or other temporary structures – was enough to guarantee its importance.

These remarks highlight the range of functions which could be discharged by the Umayyad desert residences. It is noticeable that these buildings are readily explicable within the context of their times without recourse to the notions of self-conscious display which are normally inseparable from the concept of a palace. That does not mean, of course, that splendour was of little account to the Umayyad

273 Shahr-i Sabz, Aq Saray, main portal, upper part

patrons of such structures. It is, however, a salutary reminder that such splendour may well have been incidental to the true function of these buildings. The admittedly compelling personality of al-Walid II, and his association with the two grandest of Umayyad palaces, namely Khirbat al-Mafjar and Mshatta, is liable to distort the overall picture of Umayyad palatial architecture, which was by and large much more simple and sober than those two dominating and eccentric masterpieces would suggest.

Much more typical of the genre was the *qasr* at Jabal Sais or Usais, probably the work of al-Walid I: this is a good example of the modular nature of Umayyad palaces. It is a square enclosure measuring, like Qasr Kharana, some 35 m. per side; other residences, such as Qastal or Khirbat al-Minya, were 70 m. or – like Mshatta – 140 m. per side, and in all these cases the dimen-

sion is a multiple of the Roman foot. Corner bastions and semi-circular towers placed at intervals along the sides, together with the single fortified entrance, give an embattled air to the building. Internally the main feature is a courtyard with a surrounding portico, which gives access to a double range of small cell-like rooms disposed on two storeys along the inner walls of the building. Above the entrance is a larger room, perhaps the royal audience-chamber, sometimes marked externally by twin windows which may have had an official function connected with the *adventus* ceremony borrowed from the world of late antiquity, and the *bit hilani*. The kinship of such a building with the better style of Roman domestic architecture leaps to the eye: the avoidance of external display, the use of a large central courtyard to bring air, light and space to the rest of the

385

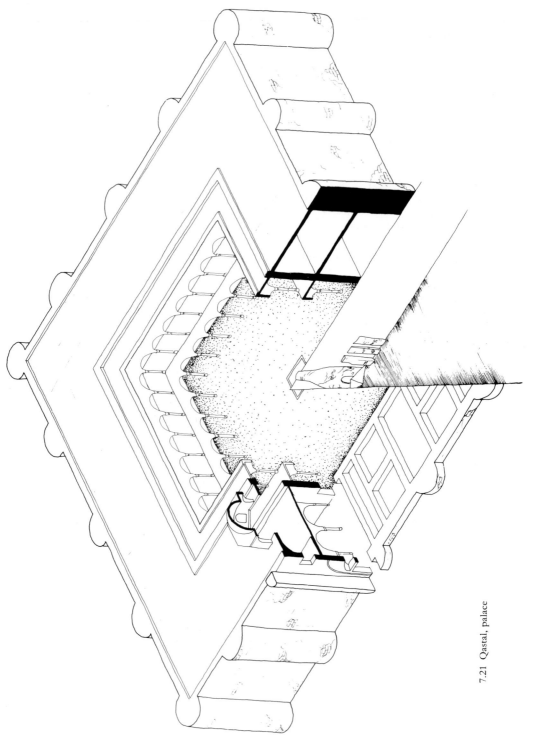

7.21 Qastal, palace

building, and the disposition of living quarters and other rooms around that courtyard. A further Roman element in the plan is the external fortification, especially the salient buttresses flanking the main entrance; these features derive not from domestic but from military architecture, presumably the frontier forts which helped to protect the Roman Provincia Arabia from incursions by the nomadic Arabs.

The Umayyad patrons clung to this model with remarkable fidelity in building their residences. Its versatility was quickly apparent, for it could operate, it seems, with equal success on both a diminutive and a gigantic scale. At Qasr al-Tuba, for example, two identical palaces were built side by side. If extra functions were required, they might be incorporated within the plan, as in the palace structure at Khirbat at Mafjar, where provision is made for a private mosque, shower room and underground retiral room (*sirdab*); or, if something grand was required – as in the combined bath and audience hall at Khirbat al-Mafjar – an extra, independent structure could be added to the nuclear plan. Such refinements apart, the most striking aspect of these palaces to a modern eye is the low

premium which they apparently placed on personal comfort. The owner alone might expect to enjoy reasonably spacious quarters, and then perhaps only in the relatively public section of the palace, namely the audience hall. It must be admitted at the outset that such a conclusion can only be provisional, for, apart from Qasr Kharana, not one of these buildings has kept its upper floor intact. Such reconstructions of these upper floors as have been made on the basis of excavations, however, do not include substantial private chambers. If the prince were accompanied by a sizeable retinue, many of them would have had to fend for themselves outside the residence, presumably pitching tents. It is well to remember that probably none of these 'palaces' were ever intended to serve as the permanent home of the patron in question. The semi-nomadic lifestyle of several later Umayyad caliphs is well known. Thus these residences are perhaps best explained as the final incarnation of the pre-Islamic *hira* or *badiya*, an encampment for short-term use which might include a permanent building as its central feature. Other details point to the spartan character of these residences. Rooms flush with

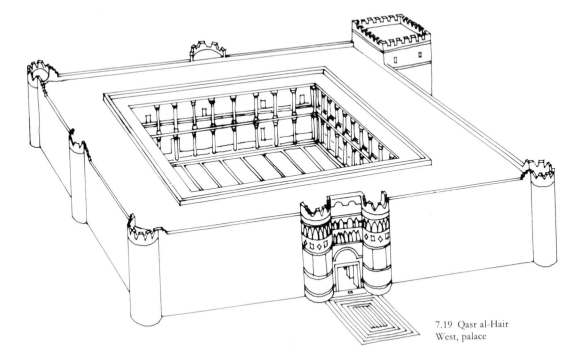

7.19 Qasr al-Hair West, palace

387

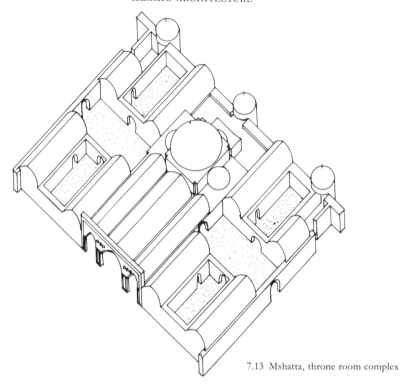

7.13 Mshatta, throne room complex

274 Mshatta, façade, detail

275 Mshatta, royal quarters

the outer walls lack windows and must have been plunged in a permanent penumbra, cold and poorly ventilated since access to the court-yard was possible only via another similar room. There is no sign of any built-in furniture. No provision was made for running water in any of the individual rooms. Access to many rooms was only through other rooms, with consequent loss of privacy. Latrines were few and often awkwardly placed. 'Palace', then, seems a curious misnomer for such residences and the presence of lavish ornament in certain areas of 7.12 these buildings – especially those sections 7.42 intended for public use – was an inadequate substitute for comfort and convenience. In these latter respects the Umayyad desert residences fall far behind the typical Roman or Byzantine villa of the immediately preceding centuries, such as the governor's residence at Dura 7.23 Europos on the Euphrates. It is noteworthy, however, that the Umayyad patrons in general favoured sturdy construction. Accordingly a good many of these structures have survived in an adequate state of preservation. The abund-ance of good building stone in Syria, coupled

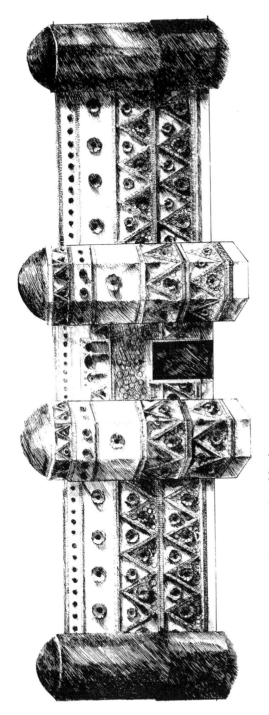

7.12 Mshatta, palace, proposed reconstruction of façade

with a long tradition of stone-masonry, made it natural to build most of these residences in stone, though occasional concessions were made to Persian practice, resulting in mud-brick walls, as at Qasr al-Hair West, or vaults in baked brick, as at Mshatta.

The degree to which such palaces resembled a medieval Western manor house – and almost contemporary versions of such structures are known, such as Charlemagne's foundation at Ingelheim – or a late antique villa remains obscure. Excavations, understandably, have tended to concentrate on the principal structure of the site, to the detriment of its immediate environment. Nevertheless, the archaeological evidence that has emerged over the past fifty years decisively contradicts the earlier popular image of Umayyad palaces marooned in a hostile landscape. It was the rule rather than the exception for the palace to be embowered in lush gardens irrigated by various types of hydraulic devices. Fountains and pools were also part of the ambience, while at Qasr al-Hair East there was even, it seems, a *paradeisos* or game park – a facility for which both occidental and oriental origins have been proposed. Lest it be assumed that this garden setting placed the Umayyad residences in a man-made oasis, it should be pointed out that the irrigation schemes developed, say, at Khirbat al-Mafjar with its aqueduct, and the two sites known as Qasr al-Hair, with a massive dam and a 30 km. underground canal respectively, imply substantial investment for agricultural purposes. Olive trees were certainly cultivated – the discovery of an oil press at Qasr al-Hair East provides the necessary evidence – and the animals used by the court would also have created a continuing need for fodder, best met perhaps by growing the necessary crops on the spot. This implies irrigation.

The fall of the Umayyads in 132/750 finished this almost frenzied building activity for ever. Indeed a reaction had set in a few years earlier, possibly as a response to the wildly extravagant building projects of al-Walid II. At all events, his successor, Yazid III, pledged in his coronation oath not to lay brick on brick or stone on stone, or to dig canals; and the caliph Hisham, who had ruled a few years earlier, was chided for spending too much time in laying out gardens

and digging canals. Ample archaeological evidence has been adduced to prove that Qasr al-Hair East, which with Rusafa lies nearer to Iraq than any other extant Umayyad palace, was re-used in early 'Abbasid times, and several palaces at Raqqa datable to c.184/800 testify to the strength of the 'Abbasid presence there. Nevertheless, the implacable hostility of the Bedouin in Syria, who cherished the memory of the golden days they had enjoyed under the Umayyads, would have made it a dangerous undertaking for 'Abbasid notables or their sympathisers to take over these Umayyad buildings *en masse*. They were therefore consigned to the slow destruction of the centuries.

ADMINISTRATIVE AND RESIDENTIAL PALACES IN 'ABBASID IRAQ

The next group of Islamic palaces is as neatly defined in time and space as are the Umayyad residences. In the palaces of early 'Abbasid Iraq, erected between c.143/760 and c.246/860, the most obvious change *vis-à-vis* their Umayyad forerunners is a marked increase in size. Two principal reasons could be adduced for this: local tradition and greater absolutism. The Sasanian monarchs had had their capital, Ctesiphon, near Baghdad rather than in Iran proper, and its palace was and remained a byword for imperial splendour throughout the Middle Ages. Its principal relic, the great *iwan* known as the Arch of Khusrau (Taq-i Kisra), was a constant challenge to Muslim architects by virtue of its size and boldness; indeed, it became a literary *topos*. An attempt on the part of the caliph al-Mansur to demolish it so as to re-use its bricks for his own building projects ended in humiliating

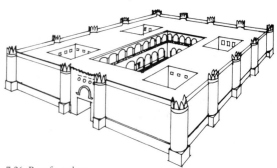

7.26 Rusafa, palace

276 Ctesipon, palace

failure, and of course added extra glamour to the great arch. In much the same way al-Mas'udi records 'it is said that certain kings sought to demolish the pyramids; but found that the combined budgets of Egypt and her neighbours were inadequate for the commission'. Perhaps here too is a *topos*. At all events, to this day its vault has the widest span of any pre-modern brick building. Moreover, the palace at Ctesiphon, like that at Qasr-i Shirin, merely continued a tradition of huge palaces which was deeply rooted in Mesopotamia. This had found expression in Parthian times at Nippur, Warka and Hatra, and before that in the huge complexes of the Babylonians and Assyrians at Babylon, Khorsabad, Nineveh and elsewhere.

The Dar al-Imara *at Kufa*

It is therefore entirely in keeping that the earliest palace in Iraq should have relatively little in common with comparable early Islamic buildings in Syria. This is the *dar al-imara* ('house of government') in Kufa. Erected in 17/638 – a remarkably early date, only a year after the conquest of Iraq and six years after the death of the Prophet – by the successful general Sa'd b. Abi'l-Waqqas, the caliphal vice-gerent in Iraq, it was much rebuilt in the succeeding cen-

turies. It was sited next to the mosque because a burglary had caused the caliph 'Umar to recommend such a location as a safety precaution. In just the same way the communal treasury (*bait al-mal*) was located within the *jami'* in early Islamic times, in the belief that the wealth of the community could have no better protection than the community itself. The mosque at Bardha'a, just south of the Caucasus, had a treasury like that which still survives in the Damascus mosque; it rested on nine columns, and another such domed treasury was to be found in the mosque of 'Amr at Fustat. In later 9th-century Fustat, too, Ibn Tulun built a mosque which had a door leading directly to the neighbouring *dar*, and similar combinations were to be found not only elsewhere in Mesopotamia, as at Wasit and Abu Dulaf, but throughout the length and breadth of the Islamic world, from Cordoba in Spain to Merv in Central Asia.

The *dar al-imara* at Kufa belongs by virtue of its size and its layout squarely within the local Mesopotamian tradition. Its focus was a courtyard – often referred to as a Court of Honour in modern scholarship, though without good reason – which was broken by an *iwan* on each side. The south *iwan* led to a triple-naved basili-

7.13 cal hall (a formula which recurs at Mshatta a century later) ending in a square chamber which was probably domed. This was, in fact, a thoroughly Sasanian plan complete with royal appurtenances. The caliph 'Umar was not slow to recognise an implied bid for power here; incensed, he ordered the building to be burned to the ground.

Consideration of the Kufa palace leads naturally to the other factor which dictated the development of early 'Abbasid palaces: the growing absolutism of the caliph. The seeds of this process can be detected in the later Umayyad period, when the caliphs began to adopt some of the institutions of oriental monarchy, such as the chamberlain, eunuchs and a police system. The trend is still more obvious in late Umayyad architecture, especially in such large self-contained foundations as 7.42, 7.11 Khirbat al-Mafjar and Mshatta. Here facilities are provided for screening visitors at the entrance to the palace, and the royal quarters are physically removed from the public sections of the residence. At Mshatta, indeed, the gulf between ruler and ruled is as wide as it well could be, given the dimensions of the building; for the royal niche in the audience chamber abuts on the back wall of the palace, and thus at the furthest possible remove from the entrance. 7.44–7.45 The bath hall at Khirbat al-Mafjar takes up the same idea.

The 'Abbasid caliphs, then, simply continued and intensified an already extant emphasis on royal aloofness. The relative accessibility of the ruler, a factor on which Mu'awiya I had prided himself and which was a concession to the fierce and jealous egalitarianism of Bedouin tribal society, was now a thing of the past. The caliph hedged himself around with bodyguards, courtiers and officials, while an elaborate royal ceremonial – which owed much to east and west alike – governed his dealings with his subjects. The vizier, the executioner, the spymaster and the *harim* all made their appearance in early 'Abbasid times, if not before. It was only natural that the architectural environment of this increasingly formal court should emphasise the god-like status which the caliph was by implication claiming for himself. A big palace was an obvious necessity to this end. Only size would allow the architect to manipulate axiality adequately and thus to orchestrate the effects of suspense, surprise and sheer magnificence required to exalt the caliph beyond the level of mere man. Ibn Khaldun summarised this development with typical acuteness:

'While the State keeps (its) primitive nomad character, its head, true to his nomad ways, is free from arrogance, close to his people, easily accessible. But as his power takes root and his magnificence begins to discriminate him, he requires the means of conferring with his

277 Ukhaidir, aerial view

generals and advisers apart from his people and the rank and file of his attendants; he looks for maximum seclusion in which to deal with confidential affairs. Accordingly he introduces a system of permits at the door, which keeps out even members of his retinue and administration if they are such as he prefers not to trust; and he appoints an usher to operate the system. As . . . the head of the State gradually assumes the strange and peculiar role of monarch . . . - he . . . seeks continuously to preserve himself from scenes that may provoke his displeasure and expose his subjects to punishment. He nominates a second usher, more intimate than the first . . the 'Abbasid caliphs, as their annals record, had at their gates two establishments, one for their special officials, one for the general public. Then a third usher comes, more personal than either of his predecessors, his presence necessary to meet attempts on the head of the State'.

Baghdad

By far the most striking expression of the new order was Baghdad, its custom-built capital. 7.61, 7 Founded in 145/762 by the caliph al-Mansur, it was intended from the first to be much more than the capital city of the new dynasty. It broke with all Islamic precedent by being built as a series of concentric circles, a concept found in Mesopotamia as far back as Assyrian times and echoed in Parthian Hatra, while Achaemenid Hamadan, with its sevenfold walls (though perhaps their number and material are literary embellishments) and the Sasanian cities of Shiz, Darabgird and Firuzabad attest the type in Iran. The latter parallel is particularly significant, since this was the Sasanian capital, and its name of Ardashir Khurra ('Glory of Ardashir') gives felicitous verbal expression to an idea visually latent in both foundations – that the city itself is a giant nimbus of power encircling the ruler. Baghdad, like Firuzabad, had four gates; but while at Firuzabad each one was orientated towards one of the cardinal points of the compass, at Baghdad the orientation of the four equidistant city gates is dictated by the fact that the Kufa Gate, to which palace and mosque are both aligned, faces Mecca. Thus the supremacy of Islam complements the implied political statement. It is at least tenable to interpret this arrangement as a claim to world domination, or at any rate as an attempt to present Baghdad as the *omphalos* of the world. These wider horizons explain, too, why astrologers were employed; one of them, it is recorded, 'looked into the horoscope of the city which was for Jupiter in Sagittarius'. In the context of the present chapter, however, Baghdad is relevant on quite another count: it is the ultimate expression in Islamic architecture of the subordination of public to private architecture. This is a city so planned that its focal point is the royal palace. Moreover, the physical presence of that palace extends far beyond its walls to dominate the great empty heart of Baghdad – for an empty circular precinct, perhaps as much as two kilometres across, enclosed the palace and the much smaller mosque adjoining it. Tents for the royal bodyguard were occasionally pitched in this area. Living quarters for the citizens were ranged in radial symmetry in adjoining segments, each walled off from the next, along the outer circumference of this precinct. Only the passageways linking the precinct to the four gates drove through this solidly crammed residential area. The caliph, therefore, was as surfeited with space as his subjects were starved of it. In this way the design of the city was itself a metaphor of caliphal power.

Thus the city plan conveyed remoteness, self-sufficiency and an iron authority. Its credibility, of course, depended on the people of Baghdad living where they were supposed to live. When they stopped doing so, and took to making their homes outside the Round City, the majesty of the caliphal office dissipated and its unique prestige plummeted. Despite later attempts to ape Baghdad – for instance the Fatimid foundation of Sabra/al-Mansuriya in Tunisia or Dailamite Isfahan – no later Islamic city was able to exercise its peculiar spell, a compound of total political ascendancy and the indefinable mystique exercised by a felicitous symbol.

It is crucial for a proper understanding of Baghdad to realise that the principal focus of the Round City was not the mosque but the royal palace next to it. The palace took precedence quite simply by virtue of its much greater size: its dimensions are four times those of the mosque. This imbalance had occurred, it is true, with the very same dimensions in earlier buildings at Merv and Wasit, but was a reversal of earlier practice, for instance in Damascus, and was also an aberration when compared with the norm in later periods. It would be hard to find a more obvious way of asserting the dominance of the secular over the religious arm in the caliphal office at this time, although the close juxtaposition of the two meant that each reinforced the other to the greater glory of the caliph.

The form of this palace and of its analogues is notable for its imaginative re-working of Sasanian themes. This is exactly what might be expected in a building erected so close to the Sasanian capital Ctesiphon and in obvious emulation of it. The traditional interpretation of the literary evidence – though it is one which has recently been challenged – asserts that the palace was square and consisted of a central domed chamber from which four *iwan*s opened out on the same axes as the city gates. Each led to a square courtyard. The corner blocks were presumably used for living space. Here, then, are all the components of Sasanian palatial architecture – dome, *iwan*, courtyard – but they are integrated with a new economy and power. The leisurely processional quality which somewhat loosely controls the vast bulk of a Sasanian palace like Qasr-i Shirin has no place here. Now,

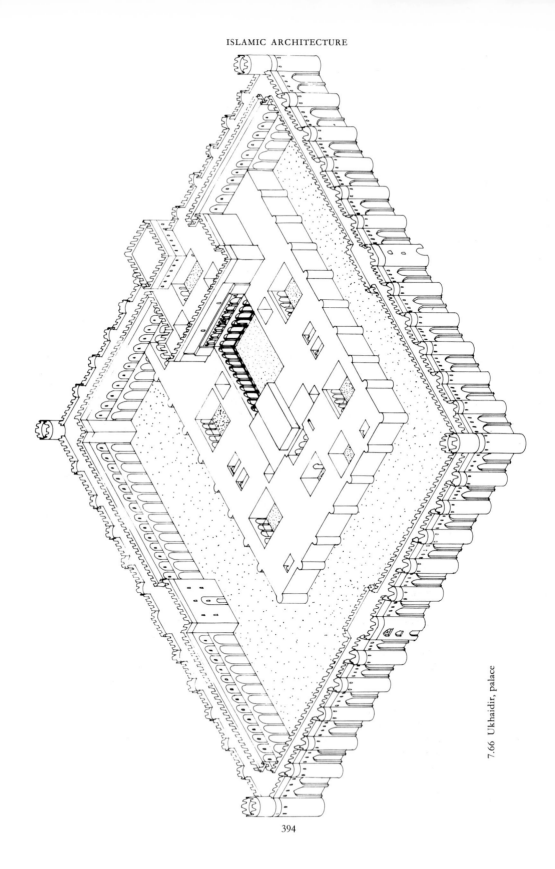

7.66 Ukhaidir, palace

too, the horizon of the ensemble has broadened very considerably, for the palace must be assessed against the backdrop of the city which encompasses it. In Herzfeld's convincing reconstruction, axiality drives home this message since the four gates of the city are aligned with the four *iwan*s in cruciform disposition which radiate from the central dome chamber. The principal lines of the Round City therefore converge on the throne room, a detail which lays bare the megalomania of the entire conception. Its dome, 'to which the stars confide their secrets', as a poet said, was a lineal descendant of Nero's Domus Aurea.

It is a striking testimony to the deeply-ingrained belief in the sacrosanct status of the caliphal office that an alternative architectural language was so quickly found to express that status. In the royal palaces of Samarra – which gave the cue for lesser but still ambitious buildings erected by those of wealth and rank – there is no attempt to impose the ruler's will on an entire city. Instead, almost by sleight of hand, the ruler inflates his palace to urban size. The implications are far-reaching. They speak of withdrawal into an aristocratic seclusion into which the common man could not penetrate. At least in Baghdad the private palace adjoined the public mosque; it was visible to all at any time and expressed by its sheer closeness to that mosque the ruler's commitment to the public and sacred aspects of his office. The caliphs at Samarra were no longer powerful enough to dictate the form of an entire city with a palace as its fulcrum, but they yielded nothing to al-Mansur in personal pride. Immured within their colossal palaces, accountable to no-one and independent of the outside world for their daily needs, their lifestyle expressed in the most extreme form the ancient Near Eastern concept of the king as god, even though such a belief was utterly incompatible with Islam.

Ukhaidir

Shortage of space will necessarily limit the discussion of these later 'Abbasid palaces to four examples: three at Samarra, in all probability royal buildings, and one which may be royal, that of Ukhaidir. The latter is generally regarded as the earliest of this quartet, though its commonly accepted date is of 159/775–6 is far

from being finally established. It is also typologically and geographically distinct from them; above all, it forms a natural continuation from Umayyad palaces by virtue of its size, general type, remote location, and anonymity. It will therefore be convenient to begin with this building. For all that Ukhaidir has been intensively analysed by competent scholars, it must be remembered that modern views of the palace (the word may safely be used here) depend very heavily on work done before the First World War and lightly revised by Creswell some twenty years later. Knowledge of early Islamic palatial architecture was then still at a fairly primitive stage, and a serious full-length attempt to re-assess Ukhaidir in the light of excavations of the last half-century in Syria and Iraq is now long overdue. Such an attempt might very well entail a revised dating and an explanation of the prodigal waste of space in the building.

The resemblances of Ukhaidir to late Umayyad palaces are unmistakable. What gives the building its extra spice of interest is the way that these Syrian Umayyad features are overlaid by others which are less readily identified. Some seem to be rooted in native Mesopotamian traditions, for example the *bit hilani* derived from Syro-Hittite temple architecture. Others, like the system of rooms (*bait*s) grouped around a courtyard, or the sequence of courtyard, *iwan* and dome or audience chamber, have a decidedly Persian flavour, which is echoed in other early Islamic palaces in Iraq, e.g. Tulul al-Sha'iba and Uskaf Bani Junaid. With this medley of conflicting influences at work, it is easy to overlook the common-sense approach – that Ukhaidir was built as a 'machine for living'; in other words, that it answered the specific needs of a high-ranking wealthy Muslim with a well-developed taste for solitary but luxurious living. Even after Finster and Schmidt's recent excavations of Tulul al-Ukhaidir in the immediate vicinity of the palace, the milieu within which Ukhaidir functioned has still not been fully explained. Enough survives to show that, like many an Umayyad residence, this palace was intended to be self-supporting, and may indeed have been an agricultural centre. Aerial photographs reveal traces of underground water-channels and a good three dozen fields of various sizes. The palace itself is set within a much larger trapezoidal enclosure which had at least ten chambers adjoining the inner face of its western wall. This enclosure was divided into two unequal parts by a wall which joined the south-western corner of the palace proper to the southern wall of the outer enclosure. Creswell interprets this outer enclosure as a combined corral and pasturing ground, but the chambers along the west wall indicate that it was something more than this. Excavations will perhaps cast further light on this problem, and may reveal whether the outer enclosure was formerly much more extensive to the north, as the plan seems to imply.

278   The palace proper is a fortified rectangle measuring 175 m. by 169 m. within which is placed another fortified rectangle. This lesser rectangle, whose dimensions are 112 m. by 82 m., contains virtually all the living quarters of the building. Thus the space between the enclosures is empty, but for a small square annexe (an afterthought) to the east. The obvious question that presents itself is why the architect adopted a plan which wasted so much space. Military security is emphatically not the answer, since the inner palace abuts directly on to the outer fortified wall, and thus has no *cordon sanitaire* on that side. Moreover, the breadth of this empty area is different on all three sides, a detail which would be hard to justify from a military standpoint. The analogy with the keep of a medieval western castle, though tempting, is therefore not tenable.

277   It must be admitted, then, that the outer fortified enclosure remains a riddle so long as a functional explanation for it has to be found *à tout prix*. Yet if it is recalled that this double enclosure is not encountered in any of the Umayyad residences, and if the example of Baghdad is borne in mind, it will not be hard to account for this feature as an attempt to translate the despotism of Baghdad into the architectural language of the Umayyad residences. Once this crucial change – it would be wrong to call it a development – has been noticed, other details fall quite naturally into place. The empty space can be seen to correspond, though admittedly on a much smaller scale, to the precinct which girdled the caliphal palace at Baghdad. The same 7.61, 7. idea, incidentally, is repeated – though on a smaller scale – in the vaulted corridor which entirely seals off the central ceremonial complex. The Round City is similarly the source for the huge gateway block which far outstrips any comparable Umayyad structure. As at Baghdad, too, and in striking contrast to most Umayyad residences, the fortifications are real, not sham, including ample towers, buttresses and portcullises and two vaulted *chemins de ronde*, both liberally furnished with loopholes.

In other respects Ukhaidir can be seen to reject the Umayyad model and to presage future developments in Islamic palaces. The relative clarity of design which marked the Umayyad palaces has gone. It is true that the sequence of rooms can be identified and that once the principal elements of the plan are recognised it is possible to make sense of the design; but that should not be so difficult a task as it is. The principle on which the whole palace is designed

278 Ukhaidir, east façade

279 Ukhaidir, vault

is one of continuous and often unexpected interaction between closed and open spaces, small intimate chambers and long corridors. A significant problem is that the building comprises dozens of separate elements which require a strongly defined symmetry if they are to mesh successfully. Such symmetry reigns only intermittently; it is most effective in the central section, which occupies some two-thirds of the ensemble. For that reason it will take pride of place in this account.

The central ceremonial complex is flanked by four broadly similar units probably intended as living quarters. Each of these comprises a central courtyard, which extends the full width of the unit, and *iwan*s to north and south, each flanked by rooms: a version, in short, of the *bait* system already familiar from Umayyad palaces. 7.10–7.11, 7.48 Each of the four courtyards gives access to a long corridor which entirely surrounds and thus isolates the whole of the central ceremonial complex. The parallel to Mshatta, with its 7.11

397

central tract cut off from the side tracts where most of the living quarters were probably sited, is striking. That parallel extends still further, and may be seen at its closest in the section immediately within the entrance. A vestibule with the first surviving fluted dome in Iraq gives way to a great vaulted hall with laterally placed arched recesses. This replaces the more humble courtyard at Mshatta, but it is flanked by similar rooms and probably this unit had the same function of housing guards and screening visitors. Like Mshatta, too, it had a mosque to the right of the entrance, and this mosque in approved Umayyad fashion was accessible from outside the inner enclosure by a postern gate. Finally, the building has the same uncompromising axiality as Mshatta, in that an undeviating line runs from north to south right through the centre of the building, to end in a modest *iwan* abutting on the rear wall. This then corresponds to the spinal column of the palace, and along that axis are to be sought the major ceremonial stages at Ukhaidir. It must be conceded, however, that the purpose of the areas placed further back in this central unit has yet to be satisfactorily explained.

At the core of the palace is the so-called 'court of honour', entered from the great hall. Here a curious discrepancy makes itself felt. At its south side is a high *iwan* towering over the bays which flank it — a true Persian *pishtaq*, the earliest surviving example in Islamic architecture. This was the place of public audience. Four rooms, whose decoration bespeaks some official function, open off its sides, while along the principal axis it led directly into a square room used for private audience. The vault between the two spaces, being of the same type and height and almost continuous, expressed this link. The whole southern façade of the court of honour, then, was single-storeyed, though its *pishtaq*, redolent of Ctesiphon, proclaimed its ceremonial importance. The northern façade, on the other hand, had no less than three storeys and was magnificently decked out with crenellations and multiple recessed blank arches – though admittedly it lacked a pronounced central feature of any kind. Yet this splendid pile could not compete in functional significance with the façade opposite. Moreover, the axial emphasis of the palace would naturally favour the

276,
7.51–7.52

southern rather than the northern façade. Architectural splendour and ceremonial significance are therefore at cross purposes rather than mutually supportive.

The overall impression generated by Ukhaidir is one of gloomy magnificence, and depends much more on architecture than on decoration. This austerity is broken only intermittently by panels of decorative brickwork and by the ingeniously varied brick vaulting systems. Structural strength, often forbiddingly displayed, was the keynote, and was exemplified in the choice of masonry for the lower walls. It has resulted in Ukhaidir surviving in a relatively good state of preservation, whereas the palaces of Samarra – 'vast improvisations', as they have been called, in which mud brick was the preferred material – have largely disappeared.

279

Samarra: introduction

Aerial photographs have revealed that Samarra was virtually a city of palaces; Istabulat, al-Huwaisilat, Ashnas, al-Quwair, Qasr al-Jiss, Zanqur and many more. Only a fraction of these have been excavated and even fewer have been published. Of these the most significant are the Jausaq al-Khaqani (probably from 221/836 onwards), Balkuwara (probably 235–45/849–60) and Qasr al-'Ashiq (probably late 9th century), and it is this trio of buildings which will be discussed below. Their context is the rapid decline in caliphal authority which made the caliphs unable to control their Turkish troops and, after numerous bloody clashes between these troops and the people of Baghdad, constrained them to leave that city and build themselves a new capital in Samarra. No expense was spared; workmen and materials were gathered in prodigious quantities from all over the Near East, and the work proceeded at well-nigh breakneck speed. It was the use of mud brick as the basic means of construction that made such speed possible – and which also dictated the need for a decorative facing that would decently veil its crudity. Christian churches were ransacked for precious materials and the palaces must have made a fine show with their ornament in glass mosaic, marble paving, fresco, gilt bronze, mother-of-pearl, lustre tiles, lapis lazuli, millefiore glass, carved and inlaid ivory, ebony and other rare woods. Virtually nothing has

7.70
7.72
7.69

7.76–7.7
7.74–7.7
7.73

280 Samarra, stucco, Style 1

survived of all this; it seems all too likely that the buildings of Samarra, once deserted by their tenants, were systematically despoiled of building material or ornament which could be used elsewhere. The stucco decoration could not be so removed and was therefore left undisturbed. It would be wrong, however, to accord it pre-eminence in the decorative scheme of these buildings just because it is the only type of ornament that has survived in quantity.

The Jausaq al-Khaqani

The earliest, and easily the largest, of these royal palaces is that of the caliph al-Mu'tasim, known as the Jausaq al-Khaqani after the Central Asian official (or conceivably architect) entrusted with its erection, one Khaqan Urtugh Abu'l-Fath ibn Khaqan. As its principal excavator, Ernst Herzfeld, remarked, it would have taken twenty years to uncover its 432 acres, even allowing for the fact that 71 acres of this was taken up by

7.76–7.77

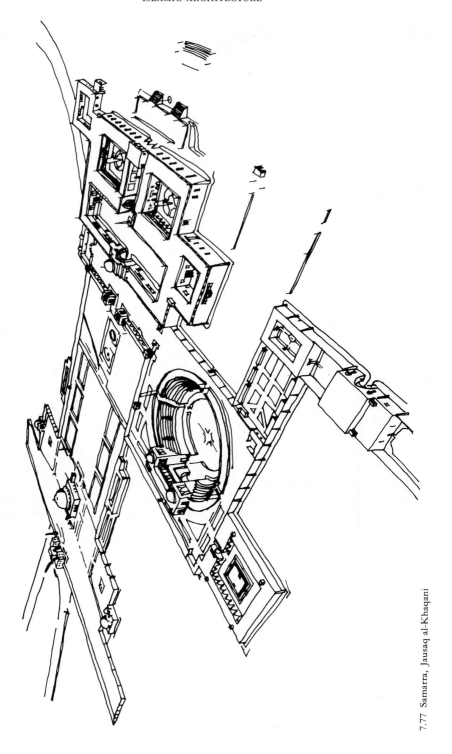

7.77 Samarra, Jausaq al-Khaqani

281 Samarra, stucco, Style 2

gardens and their associated buildings. Thus our knowledge of it can only be partial.

Gargantuan size is in fact the key to this palace. Herzfeld's plan reveals to the full how powerless the architect was to create an integrated design on this scale. Instead, the building is an amalgam of individually fine elements whose full effect is ruined by inept juxtapositions, awkward bridging passages, divergent axes and inadequate communications. Some parts of the palace are uncomfortably cramped, others un-

necessarily sprawling; some lie open to all, others – like the north wall of the *harim*, or the treasury – are strongly fortified even though they are placed within the perimeter wall of the entire palace. The whole complex smacks of second thoughts, even to the haphazard placing of three diminutive mosques scattered here and there on the huge parade ground hard by the barracks. Possibly the outer sections to north and south were added later, a theory made more likely by the violent swerves of orientation in these areas as compared to the central tract. Gigantism stands exposed in all its intellectual emptiness in the endless ramifications of this building.

What, then, of the kernel of the palace, a densely designed tract some 200 m. square? Evidence that this was indeed more carefully designed than the outlying sectors is provided by its well-calculated riparian site. A steep ridge set several hundred metres back from the Tigris gave an ideal emplacement for what was apparently the sole entrance to the palace, the Bab al-'Amma. Gardens fringed the low-lying banks of the river, giving way to a great square basin from which a ramp or a great flight of steps 60 m. across ascended the 17 m. to the gateway. These initial flourishes betray a fine sense of theatre; they are also firmly within a tradition of Near Eastern palaces that reaches back to Persepolis and beyond.

The Bab al-'Amma ('Gate of the People') is the only substantial part of the palace to survive and has for that reason attracted perhaps undue attention. It too is an ancient idea in Islamic dress; its forerunners include Roman city gates and Parthian palace façades. Two counterparts of roughly contemporary date are recorded in the literary sources. According to al-Ya'qubi, al-Mutawakkil built his palace with three huge gates "through which a rider could pass lance in hand"; this was known as the Hira style. Similarly, the façade of Ibn Tulun's palace in Fustat had three doors side by side; only on grand festive occasions were these flung open. The high central *iwan* of the Bab al-'Amma served as an audience hall every Monday and Thursday, while the diminutive flanking *iwan*s probably held the requisite bodyguards. Like the barracks to the north, which housed 3,000 troops, and the provision of only one formal entrance in a palace of this magnitude, they betray an obsession with security which is typical of Samarra. The existence of an upper storey here suggests that there was a window of appearances (a *bit hilani*?). The main *iwan* had a painted stucco dado with a triangle and rosette design reminiscent of Mshatta. Themes of power, royal accessibility and luxurious living were therefore neatly amalgamated in this commandingly sited gateway.

A series of six transverse chambers, each opening into the next, and flanked on each side

by a long corridor, leads by way of two courtyards into the area of the throne room. To the north of this principal axis clustered the private apartments of the caliph, comprising three courtyards each surrounded by rooms; to the south stretched the *harim*, vast and rambling but well provided with water and drains. Underground corridors linked the two blocks, and indeed honeycombed the whole palace. They were typical of this period and were perhaps a response both to the sheer complexity of these buildings and to the familiar obsession with secrecy and security. The relatively great distances involved explain why the medieval sources so often describe important personages riding donkeys or other animals through such tunnels.

At the heart of this gateway block lies the throne room, and this too, like the processional approach and the triple-*iwan* entrance, can claim no special originality. It is cruciform, with a domed square chamber at the centre and a triple-aisled basilical hall forming each arm. It is a plan which owes much to the fourth- and fifth-century experiments of Christian architects seeking to combine longitudinal and centralising emphases. The martyrium of Qal'at Sim'an (St Simeon) near Aleppo offers perhaps the nearest analogy. Closer at hand still are the throne-room at Mshatta – where a single basilical hall gives on to a triconch rather than a domed square – and the palaces at Merv and Baghdad, with their strong Sasanian connections, already discussed above. Clearly this was a plan which could have drawn on a wide range of sources.

This compact ceremonial and living unit commands admiration for its economy and efficiency. Though twice the size of Mshatta, it is recognisably of the same mould. Yet the buildings which hem it in on all sides rob this unit of its full force and indeed dwarf it. This is a textbook case of the tail wagging the dog.

These 'subsidiary buildings' include – to the north – a great *sirdab* or underground room with fountains and canals intended as a cool refuge from the oppressive summer heat; a treasury almost three times as large as the royal unit; and barracks. To the east, there opens up the so-called Grand Esplanade, measuring 180 m. by 350 m., a largely open space partly paved in

282 Samarra, stucco, Style 3

marble and provided with gardens and water channels. This terminates in a small *sirdab* surrounded by stables so as to form a square. A further courtyard gives on to a huge transverse yard, some 530 m. long, which served for polo. At the centre of its east side is a grandstand which would allow spectators to view races in the area still further east; remains of a clover-leaf race-track have been found. A game preserve (*hair*) also occupied part of this tract. If the mere enumeration of these numerous features – which by no means exhaust the tally that could be drawn up – is bewildering, their effect on a visitor must have been a great deal more so. The complexity of the plan is self-defeating. To be understood, the building must be examined *seriatim*. Only along the main west-east axis is there a reasonably clear path through the building, and that stretches almost 1½ km. Along the opposite axis no single direction or path is maintained for long. Individually the components of the palace are well planned; together, they make up a warren which is all but impassable. This warren of rooms large and small which characterised the palaces of Samarra left its mark elsewhere in the Islamic world. The palace of 'Adud al-Daula in Shiraz had 360 rooms so that he could use a different room every day of the lunar year. This may be a *topos*, however, since Ibn Khurdadhbih retails a similar story about the Pharos of Alexandria. Nasir-i Khusrau notes that the Fatimid palaces consisted of large and small buildings interconnected with underground passages.

Balkuwara

The next palace, Balkuwara, datable between 235/849 and 245/860, marks a return to the clarity of planning which characterised so much late Umayyad and very early 'Abbasid architecture. Its colossal size is enough to identify it as typically Samarran; but that size is kept under

7.74

403

iron control, with the result that the various parts of the palace are rationally related. This is beyond doubt the most satisfying building of the whole series and the most consummate re-working of the ideas expressed on a diminishing scale at Ukhaidir and Mshatta. The concept of the Islamic palace as a luxuriously refurbished Roman camp could be carried no further, and indeed future palaces in the Islamic world developed along significantly different lines, as if there were an instinctive realisation that the last word had been said in this idiom.

No detailed ground plan of the Balkuwara site in its entirety has been published, and the description given by Herzfeld, on which all subsequent comments on the building are grounded, does not tally with his measurements, as indeed his general plan of Samarra and the aerial photograph of the site confirm. In particular the relationship of the palace proper to its surrounding enclosure, and the proportions observed in that relationship, remain uncertain. Nevertheless, the difficulties of maintaining exact proportional relationships in a complex of this size must be borne in mind, and credit should perhaps go more to the intention than to the execution of the whole. Herzfeld's measurements will therefore be quoted without further qualification.

Balkuwara, then, is a *castrum* within a *castrum*. Both *castra* are fortified by regularly spaced semi-circular towers. The outer *castrum* measures $1\frac{1}{4}$ km. per side and is so placed that its south-west side hugs the cliff above the Tigris. Each of the three landward sides is pierced by a single gate. From these gates run two great *cardines* which divide the outer *castrum* into four unequal quadrants. Only the western and northern quadrants seem to have been built up, the latter to the extent of having a secondary central arterial way running parallel with the river. These areas, however, have not been excavated. Straddling the two riparian quadrants was the smaller *castrum*, the palace proper. Its principal entrance coincided with the intersection of the two *cardines*, a thoroughly Roman piece of planning, while the far side facing the river backed onto the outer *castrum* wall. This arrangement has an obvious kinship with Ukhaidir.

In its basic outlines the palace is a rectangle of

460 m. by 575 m., though a rectangle that is slightly stepped at the halfway mark. Just as in the outer *castrum*, this area is subdivided into four unequal quadrants, though this time not by streets. On the longitudinal axis the spine of the building is formed by three courts in succession, each with a monumental salient gateway, leading eventually to a huge cruciform throne room flanked by deep *iwan*s on the main axis. This in turn gives way to yet another court, outside the palace proper, sloping gently down to the water's edge. On the lateral axis the division is created by a fortified wall which separates the second from the third court. Even within the palace proper, therefore – as at the Jausaq al-Khaqani – some sections were walled off from others for greater privacy or security. That half of the palace which is closest to the river is relatively full of buildings; the other half is relatively empty. Such contrasts are typical of 'Abbasid palatial architecture.

Although the image of quadrants has been used to describe the palace, and could also be used of the roughly contemporary palace at al-Istabulat nearby, its essential affinity with other early Islamic architecture is highlighted if the complex is analysed in rather different terms. The emptiness of the northern and eastern quadrants emphasises the T-shape of the remainder. It is precisely this T-shape, comprising the central nave and the *qibla* aisle, which singles

283 Samarra, Jausaq al-Khaqani, Bab al-'Amma

out the most significant area of the great Friday mosques of Arab plan. In view of this convergence it is hard not to attribute a ceremonial rôle to this T-shape. Alternatively the plan could be read as a series of three adjoining longitudinal strips, a layout which at once recalls Mshatta. The successive subdivision already noted at Balkuwara simply reinforces this resemblance. Although the presence of an extra courtyard leading to the river technically creates a cruciform arrangement, the effect is a secondary one since that courtyard is outside the walled enclosure. The very fact that several geometric patterns can be traced in this ensemble – even though it may seem that they are mutually exclusive – warrants the conclusion that the architect 'thought big', simplifying the several components of the design into blocks which would be variously arranged. Textual evidence adduced by Herzfeld indicates that such palaces were actually conceived in pictorial terms in the medieval Islamic world. Al-Mas'udi tells how the example of one of the kings of Hira was followed by the caliph al-Mutawakkil and contemporary men of rank. This pre-Islamic monarch was so obsessed with all things military that he built himself a palace of warlike form: 'the *hiri* (from Hira) with two sleeves'. This had a throne-room complex where the ruler, as breastplate of the state, held audience; to its right and left hung the 'sleeves' which accommodated his retinue. To the right clothes were stored, to the left beverages. An open piazza served both the throne-room complex, to which a triple gate gave access, and the 'sleeves'. The same image of a body dressed in a short tunic or *qamis* seems to underlie al-Maqrizi's description of the ninth-century palace of Ibn Tulun in Fustat. The connections between architecture and textiles in the medieval Islamic world are legion and constitute a fertile field for future research.

The throne room and its immediate precinct are a miracle of precisely synchronised and graded emphases. From the river and from the innermost courtyard the approach is equally imposing: a deep central *iwan* flanked by two shallow ones. Opening from the square and probably domed central chamber along the cardinal points are four halls. Tucked away snugly within the arms of the cross are four little courtyards, each surrounded by eight rooms, while the lateral arms end in T-shaped halls entered by a triple arch facing a courtyard. Maximum security is ensured by walling off the central tract from those to either side. A sequence of *bait*s occupies the north-west side of this central tract; perhaps this area was intended for the royal *harim*.

The two side tracts are laid out rather differently in obedience to their basic functions. The south-east tract comprises a series of discrete but adjoining living units, the norm being a courtyard with sixteen to twenty-one rooms grouped around it, often with a single T-shaped reception room and occasionally with two such rooms. Here presumably were housed the courtiers attendant on al-Mu'tazz. The living units (*bait*s) are joined to form bigger entities of two, three or four *bait*s; the passages between these islands are veritable streets, as much as 250 m. long. To the north-west the density of occupation falls off dramatically. At the far end of the tract, and running alongside its entire length, is a rectangular plaza probably used for polo. A smaller plaza adjoining it has shops lining its north-west side, presumably the bazaar, while the southern corner contains *bait*s possibly intended for the royal bodyguard. No trace of a mosque was found in the royal precinct or its flanking dependencies, but two small mosques, whose immediate environment is a matter for speculation, were located on either side of the second court.

This summary description still leaves much of the palace unexplained, but now it is at least possible to take stock of the conception as a whole and to identify its important characteristics. Hierarchy is the leitmotif of the ensemble. This idea is expressed spatially, visually, in the lie of the land and in the choice of materials. In each case much is made of the force of contrast. It will be worth examining in some detail how this is done.

Balkuwara is more than a little reminiscent of Baghdad in its resolute direction of space. No less than three huge and empty courtyards create a swelling prelude to the imperial theme of the throne-room itself. Seen from the outer entrance, each is smaller than the last. Massive gate complexes on the chord of the throne-room usher the way into each of these courtyards, and an axial path runs through the centre of each courtyard on the long side. Thus empty space is used to induce a sense of awe in the visitor, and to put him in a suitably chastened frame of mind for his encounter with the caliph. It is integral to this spatial approach that deep *iwan*s should lead into the throne room off the long axis but not on the transverse one, since there is no formal processional way on that axis.

The visual hierarchy of Balkuwara is of course closely related to the spatial hierarchy. Here again empty space has as great a part to play as densely utilised space. Lack of excavation of the side tracts forbids any definite conclusion as to their appearance, but the indications are that these spaces did contain accommodation. The central tract, however, is dominated by the three empty courtyards. From the outermost court, with its relatively simple gateway block, and with no other feature of note, the way leads into the middle court with its central pool and elaborate gates at each end. This courtyard must have looked substantially more impressive than the first. The third courtyard not only had a central pool but was surrounded on three sides by a portico with chambers behind it, while the fourth side was monopolised by a great triple *iwan*, its central arch raised well above the flanking ones. Behind this would be visible the great dome over the throne-room proper, the logical culmination of the central tract. On either side of the third courtyard was closely packed living accommodation. Visually, then, the contrast would highlight the spacious layout of the royal quarters as against the crowding to which all others were subject.

The lie of the land is in turn intimately connected with the establishment of a visual and spatial hierarchy. Careful landscaping and judicious artificial terracing made of an inherently felicitous site one that was probably unsurpassed in the city. The ground level rose by stages – stages which approximated to the progressively closer approach to the throne-room – so that each courtyard was higher than the previous one. At the climactic and therefore

7.75 highest point of the ensemble, the throne-room itself, the floor was at the height of the roof of the side tracts. This arrangement expressed in a new way the age-old Near Eastern notion of the king literally standing on his subjects, and also

rang the changes on the idea of the royal palace built on a high platform. It also permitted an 7.56 unequalled view along the major axes of the palace: the 500-metre vista of the processional way to the north-east, the garden, pleasure pavilions, harbour and river to the south-west, while along the transverse axis on both sides there unfolded the panorama of the entire 'Abbasid city. Perhaps it was the same desire for spacious views that induced the roughly contemporary Tulunid ruler Khumarawaih to have a watch-tower built high up on the Muqattam hills overlooking Cairo; it had four bow windows, one for each point of the compass.

Finally, the choice of materials reflected the hierarchy already well established by other means. The humblest construction material of all, stamped earth or *pisé*, sufficed for the outer *castrum*, to be replaced by mud brick for the two outer courtyards and eventually by baked brick for the innermost courtyard and the throne room. It is entirely likely that the quality of decoration varied accordingly and also followed a crescendo of magnificence. Unfortunately the lack of a final excavation report – and there is little doubt that Herzfeld's projected volume on the architecture of Samarra would have been the crowning achievement of his career – means that the location and nature of the various types of decoration which were found were never specified in the requisite detail.

For all its complex splendour, Balkuwara sounds a warning note as a specimen of 'Abbasid palatial architecture. It brings to mind the meditations of the great 14th-century Maghribi historian Ibn Khaldun on the rise and fall of dynasties. In particular it seems to correspond to that moment when 'the monarch . . . - imposes the belief that contact with himself involves the violation of an awful veil and the transgression of the code of etiquette, and thus hopes to avoid intercourse with society. As he persists in this practice it gradually lays hold on him till self-seclusion is one of his essential characteristics. This normally happens when a State is almost at the end of its career. It is a symptom of senility and exhaustion of power'.

Qasr al-Jiss

The Jausaq al-Khaqani was built in the early years of Samarra, and Balkuwara in its middle

284 Samarra, Qasr al-'Ashiq

period; Qasr al-'Ashiq and Qasr al-Jiss are from the final years of the city's history as the caliphal capital, and probably date to *c.*264–8/877–82. Both are foundations of the caliph al-Mu'tamid, and both are much smaller than the earlier palaces discussed above. Qasr al-Jiss is built of brick, despite its name ('Plaster Castle'), and comprises a square with a central throne room preceded in turn by a transversely placed hall and an *iwan* on each of the main axes. These *iwan*s face courtyards closed at the far end by three adjoining longitudinal halls and finally a transverse hall. The latter projects beyond the walls of the palace. The four quadrants placed between the arms of this cruciform design are filled with a tightly-crammed sequence of rooms and courtyards, linked by the long corridors so typical of 'Abbasid palaces. Since the south-east and north-west quadrants are virtually mirror images of each other, it is perhaps legitimate to assume that a similar diagonal reciprocity ruled the other two quadrants. Externally a novel arrangement is adopted: a series of free-standing rectangular piers follows the line of the curtain wall and presumably supported vaults. Stepped square towers mark the corners. It is curious that this extremely concise epitome of some of the most characteristic Samarran features did not recommend itself to later architects.

Qasr al-'Ashiq

Qasr al-'Ashiq proves that right to the very end the architects of Samarra were developing palatial architecture along unexpected lines. All the more credit for this should go to its architect, one 'Ali ibn Yahya ibn Abi Mansur,

because he was a seasoned veteran who had been employed in his office by three previous caliphs. For this reason it is not surprising that many of its features are familiar from earlier buildings. The palace proper measures some 140 m. by 93 m., thereby conforming to the 3:2 ratio so widespread in the buildings of Samarra. It is set within an outer enclosure of some 230 m. by 180 m., a disposition which recalls Balkuwara, as does the internal division of the palace into three tracts following the longitudinal axis. Large areas of the palace remain unexcavated, and some aspects of its surviving architecture, such as the huge vaulted undercrofts, have not yet been analysed in print. Any general assessment of Qasr al-'Ashiq, therefore, would be somewhat premature.

Certain features, however, do stand out. In place of the frankly fortified air of other Samarran palaces, it puts equal if not greater emphasis on external decoration. Lobed blind arcades enclosing trilobed niches – an imaginative reworking, perhaps, of a theme with all the authority of Ctesiphon behind it – occupy the spaces between the salient rounded buttresses, and formerly took up two storeys. This decoration, like the ground plan, employed proportional ratios in its layout. A gigantic entrance block comprising five vaulted halls, of which the central one is the widest, projects 16 m. from the main body of the palace. It may have been linked by drawbridge to a complementary structure on the opposite side of the ditch. The effect of this gateway is greatly enhanced because it takes up almost half of the north side, and is its most notable feature. It is as if the Bab al-'Amma had been spirited away from its original context to become effectively the principal entrance to the throne room. That sense – so dear to Samarran architects – of the measured unfolding of huge empty spaces to act as a curtain-raiser to the throne chamber itself, has gone. Visually illimitable vistas have been telescoped to create a more intimate, even domestic scale. Lest this be misunderstood, it is as well to remember that Qasr al-'Ashiq is larger than any single Umayyad palatial building except Mshatta.

Mention of Mshatta prompts the recognition that the contrast between empty side tracts and obviously royal central tract is in essence an Umayyad idea. Yet the analogy cannot be pushed very far. Firstly, the central tract is twice as broad as each of the side tracts, not the same size. Secondly, royal functions do intrude into the east tract at least, which contains a *sirdab* and a belvedere resting on vaulted substructures, providing a memorable view of the entire extent of the ancient city from north to south. Finally, and most significant of all, the official reception rooms are in the centre of the royal tract, not at its far end. Their idiom is mixed. A broad and very deep *iwan* flanked by lesser arches invites access to the audience chamber in an authentically Persian fashion. It leads to a group of three adjoining square rooms transversely placed, with a courtyard behind – all very much on the model of the Sasanian palace of Firuzabad. Yet these Persian forms are subsumed into the characteristically Arab unit of the T-shape, whose royal and liturgical associations have already been mentioned. Moreover, this official ensemble is flanked on the long axis by empty courtyards, which would thus serve to focus attention on the central structure. Even when space was relatively short, then, the architect was concerned to exploit to the full contrasts between open and closed areas.

Perched on a plateau some 30 m. above the river, on the largely virgin land of the west bank, Qasr al-'Ashiq strikes the visitor as the private eyrie of a wealthy prince rather than the urban headquarters of a powerful administrator. To that extent it is much more Umayyad than 'Abbasid, and indeed the future was to lie with this concept of a palace rather than any other. A few 'palace-cities' were indeed built, notably the Alhambra and the Topkapi Saray, but they generally lacked the sense of relentless organisation which stamped the palaces of Samarra. Nevertheless, the unique glamour which attached to 'Abbasid court life, to say nothing of the aura of religious sanctity and political authority which clung to that dynasty, ensured that the influence of Samarra would radiate widely through the Islamic world. The numerous imitations of Samarran pottery, stucco and architectural features from Egypt to Central Asia sufficiently attest to this influence.

MEDIEVAL PALACES IN THE IRANIAN WORLD

The Dar al-Imara *of Abu Muslim at Merv*

Pitifully few palaces survive from the medieval Iranian world. Literary sources preserve the

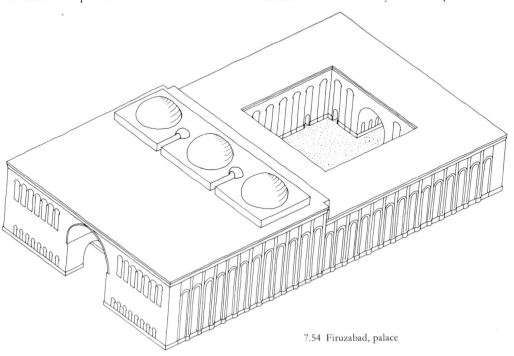

7.54 Firuzabad, palace

7.95 memory of a *dar al-imara* constructed at Merv in 129/747 by Abu Muslim, at the very place and time that the 'Abbasid revolution which he had so long fomented finally exploded. It would be hard to find clearer evidence than this of the propaganda dimension of certain architectural types. In the case of Merv the form of the palace is as significant as its nature and its timing, for it echoes – if indeed it does not ape – the great

1–7.52 palace of Ctesiphon, the very exemplar of the oriental palace. It employs – to judge by Creswell's lucid diagram – the same sequence of courtyard, *iwan* and dome chamber, but goes a crucial step further. In place of the single axis found at Ctesiphon the same sequence is repeated in four-fold symmetry, one group for each of the four points of the compass. A single great domed hall at the centre of this cruciform plan acts as the focal point for each combination of courtyard and *iwan*. The cosmic implications of such a building are evident, and descend

7.46, perhaps from the palace of Khusrau II, the
7.49 fabled Taq-i Taqdis, with its revolving dome. It
1, 7.67 is the message of al-Mansur's Baghdad expressed on a smaller scale and in a different but still Persian idiom. A century before, the long arm of the caliph 'Umar had ensured the swift destruction of an unacceptably grand palace erected at Kufa – and thus in the orbit of Ctesiphon – by the successful general Sa'd b. Abi Waqqas. Now the enfeebled Umayyad caliph, beset by faction, was powerless to take similar action as history repeated itself. Abu Muslim's *dar al-imara* was an apt symbol of the vaulting ambition of the 'Abbasid revolutionaries.

Kirk-Kiz

Gratifying corroboration of Creswell's analysis of the *dar al-imara* of Abu Muslim is provided by an unexpected survival from early medieval Tirmidh (Termez): the so-called Kirk-Kiz, dated variously between the 9th and 12th centuries. A connection with the Samanid dynasty, which is rendered architecturally and historically plausible by the form of the building and by its location in Tirmidh, a major centre of Samanid power for almost three centuries, is still further justified by the name traditionally given to the suburb in which the building stands – *Shahr-i Saman*, the city of Saman. Historical sources confirm that the Samanids did indeed maintain an exten-

sive palatial complex outside the city. This may well be part of it, though a later date is tenable.

An inescapable weakness of Creswell's reconstruction of the *dar al-imara* of Abu Muslim is the emptiness of large tracts of the building, an emptiness which is hard to credit, and yet which is imposed on the suggested reconstruction by the sparseness of the medieval accounts. Kirk-Kiz fleshes out the bare bones of the literary description of Abu Muslim's *dar* and establishes that the earlier building was itself in the tradition of the Central Asian *kushk* as revealed, say, by excavations in Khwarizm. One major difference between the two structures as currently known must be faced at this stage. Abu Muslim's *dar* is a building directed outwards; its *iwan*s along the cardinal axes invite visitors. Kirk-Kiz, by contrast, turns resolutely inwards. It is more a private than a public building. Whether this distinction is more apparent than real cannot readily be decided in the present state of knowledge. Its 8-bay mosque(?) and its plainly multifunctional spatial diversity seem to rule out a military post or a *khanqah*, but scholars still disagree on whether it was a caravansarai (admittedly a luxury one) or a palace.

7.86–7.87;
7.92–7.94,
7.110

Externally the building gives little away. Its façades are essentially blank. Apart from massive (though hollow) corner towers the main device employed to articulate the façades is a plethora of narrow windows, mere slits in the *cf.* 7.14 wall, and superposed arcades of blind niches above the four axial entrance archways. The latter have obvious links with Samanid mausolea such as that at Bukhara, while the other ar-5.42–5.44 ticulating devices recall pre-Islamic palaces in the area, such as Varakhsha. Such decorative 7.91 touches do not, however, offset the somewhat uninviting, even forbidding, impression which the exterior makes. The interior, by contrast, could scarcely be more different. In place of long expanses of virtually blank wall – the external dimensions are 53.8 m. per side – is a labyrinth of passages, halls, cubicles and vestibules. Narrow corridors cordon off the ground floor into four quadrants. Three of these are treated in a broadly similar way, with five rooms fitted into a rectangular space at right angles to each other. The remaining quadrant has two such rooms but the rest of the space is taken up by an 8-bay hall. According to one reconstruction, this was roofed with eight domes; according to another, eight cross-vaults. The kinship to early mosques in this area, such as the Nuh Gunbad/Hajji Piyada mosque at Balkh, makes it more tempting to regard this as a mosque than as a reception hall or *mihman sarai*. At the centre of the plan is an open area 11.5 m square, presumably a courtyard since no evidence of a dome was found here. To this extent the design develops that of the pre-Islamic *kushk*, or for that matter the *dar* of Abu Muslim, where the plan pivots on a central domed chamber. Four *iwan*s open from the four sides of this diminutive courtyard and in turn each *iwan* opens into a double vaulted vestibule which leads to one of the four entrances. Thus the familiar schema of the 4-*iwan* plan is adapted to new purposes, with the emphasis placed on the areas between the *iwan*s rather than on the *iwan*s themselves. Internal light and ventilation is provided by means of multiple loopholes as on the outer façade. The dim lighting that resulted would have emphasised the impression of a maze and the disorientation of the casual visitor would have been completed by the constant changes of

height, width and direction built into the plan. The obvious contemporary parallel in this respect is Ukhaidir; there too it is the vaulting which provides the finishing touch of self-conscious virtuosity. Virtually every available space at Kirk-Kiz is vaulted in one of a dozen and more techniques. The preponderant use of mud brick is no deterrent to this technical mastery. Presumably the upper storey, of which enough remains to indicate that it mirrored the lower one, provided yet further variations. The well-preserved upper storey of the somewhat later Zindan-i Harun near Teheran, a pocket-sized replica of the Kirk-Kiz, certainly suggests that there would have been no falling off in the standard of the upper storey. For all its complexity, however, and despite its fifty rooms, the Kirk-Kiz palace makes better sense as a seasonal retreat for a ruler anxious to preserve his privacy than as the permanent residence of a ruler with all the concomitant apparatus of court and government, like the broadly contemporary *ordu* of the Uighur Moyuncur Qaghan at Tuva to the

285 Lashkar-i Bazar area, arch at Bust

north-east, datable *c.* 132/750, itself curiously reminiscent of some Umayyad *qasr.*

OTHER EARLY IRANIAN PALACES

Subsequent palaces described in the written sources do not so readily lend themselves to analysis as does the palace of Abu Muslim. Too often the crucial dimensions are lacking or the description is only partial. This is not simply the fault of the chronicler. It seems likely that the palace at Merv was a special case because of the energetic economy of its plan, which lent itself to precise description. Sprawling residential ensembles loosely scattered over a wide area were apparently nearer the norm, to judge by the descriptions of various 9th–11th century palaces at Baghdad and elsewhere. Thus the palace of 'Adud al-Daula in late 10th-century Shiraz, as noted above, had a room for each day of the year. Again, cosmic implications may be read into this. Naturally it had its high spots – a storied library over which Ibn al-Bawwab, the premier calligrapher of the age, presided, and a set of apartments executed in the "Chinese" style – but there is no hint of the singleness of purpose and the political ambition which brought the Merv palace into being. Nevertheless the lack of surviving structures forbids any dogmatic assertion about the nature of the vanished palaces of the Saffarids, Samanids, Buyids and other, lesser, Iranian dynasties which preceded the Saljuqs. It is particularly disappointing that otherwise fruitful excavations at the Samanid capitals of Afrasiyab and Nishapur have yielded no palaces; a richly decorated residence in Afrasiyab produced two chambers with stucco ornament but with a room size of 6.5 m. by 12 m. the monument was obviously not of royal status. Much the same can be said for some of the residential units along the Darb Zubaida.

The Saljuq palace at Merv

It is only from the 11th and 12th centuries – conventionally if somewhat inaccurately termed the Saljuq period – that enough palaces survive to give some idea of contemporary trends in this genre. The lack of palaces in Iran proper is to some extent made good by two in Central Asian republics (at Merv and Tirmidh) and two in Afghanistan (Ghazni and Lashkar-i Bazar). The Arg or Shahriyar palace at Merv, attributed by its excavators to the 11th–12th century, is set inside a separately fortified enclave within the Saljuq royal precinct at Merv, the so-called Sultan Qal'a, a vast area of some four square kilometres in extent which was further protected by a ditch and a wall some 15 m. high. No civilian could enter this precinct without special permission. Near the palace proper were barracks and a library. The palace itself is curiously asymmetrical given its adoption of the traditional 4-*iwan* plan and its almost square layout (*c.* 45 m. by 39 m., with a courtyard of 16 m. per side). Though apparently entered from the east, its throne *iwan* lay to the north and thus off axis. The whole bears a more than fleeting resemblance to the contemporary and not far distant Ribat-i Sharaf in its ability to extract the maximum spatial interest from a severely restricted surface area. This is done in both buildings by continually changing the sizes of the rooms, their axial emphasis, their vaulting and the location of their doorways. While there is relatively easy access from one room to another behind the courtyard façade, that façade is almost entirely shut off from the rest of the building apart from its four *iwan*s. This substantially strengthens the unity and continuity of the façade. It also drives home the contrast between the dim, almost labyrinthine succession of small adjoining rooms – some fifty of them in all, since this was a two-storey building – and the very different architecture of the courtyard, flooded with light and with a continually changing movement of shadow playing across its highly mobile surfaces. This undulating series of pilasters and multi-recessed niches continues a fashion established a century and more previously in the Friday mosque of Isfahan. For all the high quality of its detail in planning and execution, however, the Saljuq palace of Merv is domestic rather than grand – a far cry indeed from the splendours of Samarra. Though the term 'palace' has been used of other Saljuq and earlier buildings surveyed or excavated in the Merv oasis, such as the forbiddingly plain cubic structure east of Giyaur Qal'a, their diminutive size excludes such an identification. Presumably these are the seats of the *dihqan*s, the local landed gentry. Possibly the residence attached to the Ghaznavid citadel of Khulbuk, the former capital of Khuttal, is indeed a palace; but details of this discovery are not to hand.

Tirmidh

The other early medieval Central Asian palace to survive is in Tirmidh (Termez) on the Oxus. Built in the 11th century and restored at some time before 523/1129–30 in the reign of the Ghaznavid sultan Bahramshah, it too forms part of an extensive walled precinct which already held the remains of a much smaller palace as well as living and industrial quarters. The main palace, measuring approximately 80 m. by 94 m. and commonly called the Regent's Palace, is rectangular, with an imposing salient portal giving on to a large central courtyard surrounded by chambers, apparently not yet fully excavated, furnished with a central square pool and closed at the end by an audience chamber whose layout recalls much earlier models such as the Sasanian palace at Tepe Hisar near Damghan. A five-arched portico mediates between the courtyard and the audience hall; the central arch has a broader span and was presumably higher. This is a development of a scheme already familiar at Ukhaidir and foreshadowed at Mshatta. Behind this façade lay a very broad central nave carried on cylindrical piers set so close to the walls that only narrow corridors of space were left in between. A gallery ran around the three sides of this hall; presumably the ruler's throne was set against the back wall. A discreet postern door gave egress from this part of the palace. It is, however, by virtue of its decoration that the palace at Tirmidh is most remarkable. In addition to ceilings painted with floral designs and inscriptions, and to walls covered with networks of *girikh* designs in carved stucco – which, following such precedents as the Na'in mosque, spread impartially over niches, dadoes, vaults, columns, over curvilinear as over flat surfaces – the designs featured heraldic and fantastic, perhaps demonic, creatures in the same medium. These are treated in a style closely related to contemporary textiles. Their purpose may be apotropaic. The animals are rendered ornamental not only by a confident abstraction and symmetry of form but also by the treatment of their bodies as fields for ornamental devices – stars, roundels and triangular groupings of dots. Birds,

mounted figures, rosettes and other symbolic motifs, some in glazed tilework, and insets of stained glass completed this unusually rich and original decorative ensemble. As at Samarra, and as at Kirk-Kiz nearby, the building material was mud brick, though baked brick was used for the floors. Yet while Kirk-Kiz looks back to the specifically local tradition of the fortified *kushk* or manor house, the Regent's Palace evokes a more spacious and open arch-

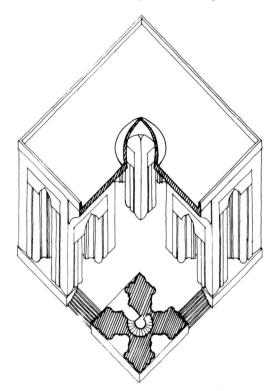

7.109 Qal'a-yi Dukhtar, pavilion

itectural tradition whose ultimate source is Ctesiphon. Just as this tradition was to count far more in later Islamic palaces than was the memory of the Khwarizmian *kushk*, so too was the lavish decoration of the Regent's Palace more in tune with later Islamic taste than were the spatial intricacies of Kirk-Kirz – though the 15th-century Tash Ribat in Kyrgyzstan, variously identified as a palace and a caravansarai, perpetuates the type.

Lashkar-i Bazar

Perhaps the most faithful evocation of the Samarran spirit in later architecture is to be found at Lashkar-i Bazar on the River Helmand in south-west Afghanistan, datable between the 10th and 12th centuries. This was still a time when memories of Samarra might not have been entirely dispelled. Here, too, it is a case not of one palace but of several, strung out at irregular intervals along the river bank and sundered from their parent city. It is a vast enclosed ensemble measuring some 7 km. by 2 km. These palaces also had huge forecourts and were sited within even larger walled enclosures; and their material was the mud brick so widely used at Samarra. Finally, the architects at Lashkar-i Bazar seem to have been as alert as their counterparts in Samarra to the topographical or landscape potential of the palaces they designed, and the river is thus frequently a vital component of their layouts. The riparian Central Palace, set in gardens, is a good example; its residential upper floor would have yielded splendid views, as would the adjoining earlier *kushk*.

The so-called 'Southern Palace' at Lashkar-i Bazar is the most thoroughly excavated and therefore best known of these buildings. Though its core measures only some 170 m. on its longer axis, the precinct – which includes a Friday mosque – is roughly twice that size. In turn, and maintaining the same axis, it gives on to a street some 500 m. long, lined with a hundred shops, which leads to the city of Bust. This is a faithful echo of the gigantism and axiality of Samarra. The palace itself, which was enlarged to the west and north-east after being sacked in 545/1150, is girdled by a wall heavily buttressed to east and west; the cliff-like river bank affords sufficient protection to the north, and, as at Samarra, was no doubt an integral element in the landscaping of the site. To the south, the multi-niched entrance façade in two storeys immediately recalls al-'Ashiq and thus, by implication, Ctesiphon itself. It is broken by a deeply recessed central *iwan* which leads into a four-*iwan* courtyard, presumably intended as a vestibule. This forecourt is the nerve centre of the densely built-up southern section of the palace, which may well have housed the royal bodyguard.

The principal feature of the whole palace, however, is the vast courtyard (*c.* 50 m. by 60 m.) at its centre. This is articulated in traditional Iranian style by four *iwan*s, with halls or cruciform rooms between them, which would presumably have been used by the functionaries of the court. At the far end of this courtyard is the principal *iwan* – broader, deeper and higher than the others – which led into a square throne-room equipped with its own little oratory. Rectangular halls of unknown function flanked this area and the corners were taken up by diminutive courtyards with a four-*iwan* plan and rooms in the corners. If, as seems possible, these were living quarters for the *harim*, this would be a translation into an Iranian idiom of the arrangement expressed through the *bait* system at Mshatta. Such planning illustrates the longevity of facets of court life and ceremonial first developed in the Umayyad period.

Hygiene and sanitation were, however, of far superior quality. A canal was cut from the river and the water was raised to supply a reservoir, whence it was diverted through the palace to ensure that each block of living quarters had its own running water, baths and latrines. In addition three pools were run off the canal. Two of these pools were covered with kiosks as at Khirbat al-Mafjar. This lavish display of water in a desert zone also has its Umayyad antecedents. Decorative brick and stucco prinked out the walls, but the principal discovery was of frescoes of forty-four Turkish bodyguards on the side walls of the throne room, doubtless an allusion to the custom of Sultan Mahmud of Ghazna, who on ceremonial occasions enthroned himself – presumably in the open air – in the presence of four thousand such bodyguards. The court historian, al-Juzjani, boasts that these palaces were without equal in the world. One may doubt whether he was acquainted with the splendours of Samarra, Cairo or Cordoba; but in its verdant prime, nestled like many an Umayyad residence within a fertile irrigated countryside, and with an elephant park nearby to evoke the wider world under Ghaznavid sway, Lashkar-i Bazar must have been a gladsome sight.

Ghazna

The natural pendant to this grandiose conception of palatial life is the palace of Mas'ud III (reigned 492–507/1099–1114) at Ghazna, a pocket-sized rendering of many of the same ideas. The excavations here lasted for only two seasons, which was not long enough to enable the form of this palace to be reconstituted with adequate assurance. The ensemble is set on a platform and is of pronounced trapezoid form, its walls measuring between 158 m. and 127 m. This walled enclosure is furnished with rounded corner towers and a half-rounded bastion on the side opposite the entrance; it seems likely that two of the other sides were similarly equipped. The main façade was presumably different. Its arrangement cannot be reconstructed with certainty, but it seems as if a long open corridor which ran the whole length of the façade separated the main body of the palace from a narrow strip some thirty metres to the north of it. Yet this narrow strip, whose succession of deep niches was plausibly identified by the excavators as the shops of a bazaar, continues the line of the lateral fortified wall of the palace proper, even to the extent of having a rounded tower at the corner. Such a tower makes no sense in a bazaar but is readily understood if the bazaar were intended to function visually as part of the palace. To that extent, it represents an advance on the more expansive but also more loosely organised arrangement at Lashkar-i Bazar. The main façade of the palace seems to have had salient rectangular towers somewhat 6.19–6.20 like Ribat-i Sharaf; it is quite possible that the north façade of the bazaar was blank because it was, so far as the shops were concerned, a back wall. They naturally faced the entrance of the palace.

The palace itself testifies to the remarkable authority exercised by Umayyad architectural types on later buildings. Neither the passing of the centuries nor geographical remoteness dimmed the prestige of these early buildings. Making allowances for the reduced scale and the essentially Iranian idiom, the palace of Ghazna is none the less a very direct descendant of 7.11, 7.13 Mshatta. Its proportions may be rather skewed, its bazaar may be a footling concession to the practicalities of court life, its façade may well have been unworthy of its interior. The mud brick of Iran, not the stone of Syria, was its building material. Yet the basic ceremonial sequence of vestibule, huge court (some 50 m. by 32 m.), ante-room and throne-hall is exactly

that of Mshatta. As if to drive home the resemblance, the reconstitution of the side tracts here too presents formidable difficulties. That to the east is still unexcavated; that to the west is only partially so, though two courtyards have been revealed. The courtyard appears to have four *iwan*s linked by a succession of arched niches; a mosque whose correct orientation was slightly at odds with the rest of the building was fitted into the north-west corner just off the courtyard.

If the conception of the palace as a whole has no special surprise in store, its decoration was not only rich but also, in one significant regard, totally unexpected. In addition to terracotta ornament of the kind found at Lashkar-i Bazar, the court façade had a unique marble dado, whose slabs bore not only floral and animal motifs but also a continuous inscription in Persian verse. This was, it seems, a custom-made poem designed to glorify Mas'ud III. It extolled the deeds of his forebears by way of preamble to a panegyric directed at him alone; this section of the poem seems, appropriately enough, to have been located in the immediate neighbourhood of the *iwan* leading to the throne room. Its location at waist level suggests that the poem was intended to be read by those at court. As such it represents a new aspect of the familiar use of epigraphy as an agent of royal glorification.

Herat

Aufi's detailed description of the long-since vanished palace of the Saljuq princeling Tughanshah at Herat fleshes out the scanty information yielded by the palaces at Ghazna and Lashkar-i Bazar. As was so often in the case in medieval Islamic palaces, expanses of water were crucial to the total effect. Accordingly the palace was located beside a lake, and the richly decorated *iwan* on the shore itself presumably combined business with pleasure. Artificial terracing is mentioned, and this too was no doubt carried out with the wider landscape setting in mind. Other *iwan*s and residential wings suggest that this was more a city-palace than just a luxuriously appointed but temporary stopover. The decoration is singled out for praise, and included sculptures, frescoes and even royal portraits in medallions, the latter reserved for the princely quarters. All in all this foundation

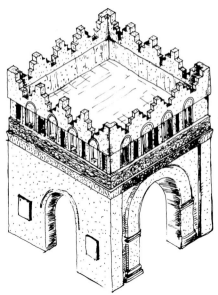

7.58 Qal'a-yi Zahhak, Parthian (?) pavilion

seems remarkably prophetic of the Ilkhanid structures at Takht-i Sulaiman, to say nothing of its kinship with Qubadabad and Kayqubadiye. If such were the residence of a minor prince, the total disappearance of all the palaces built by the Saljuq sultans themselves is all the more grievous. Such chance and tantalising survivals as the 12th-century pavilion at Qal'a-yi Dukhtar, a remote mountain-top eyrie in central Azerbaijan – which recalls, though in a different stylistic idiom, the still more splendid Parthian pavilion of Qal'a-yi Zahhak in the same area – show that the nature of at least some of this princely architecture could not be deduced from other contemporary buildings.

ROYAL RESIDENCES IN THE 13TH CENTURY

The destruction of the Saljuq capitals of Rayy and Hamadan, and the disappearance of the royal palaces at Isfahan and Merv, mean that the two Ghaznavid buildings must do duty for contemporary structures further west in the Iranian world. The tale is taken up in the 13th century by a series of very different buildings in Anatolia – such as Qubadabad, Kayqubadiye and Diyarbakr – as well as by three isolated palaces in Syria, Iraq and Iran: Qasr al-Banat at Raqqa, the Qara Saray of Mosul and the kiosk of the Mongol Ilkhan Abaqa at Takht-i Sulaiman.

In all of these buildings a marked change of emphasis is detectable. Perhaps under the influence of a semi-nomadic way of life, perhaps because the idea of a self-contained palace-city had lost its appeal, perhaps as a result of a new taste for informality – whatever the reason, the scale of these palaces diminishes. They remain multi-functional, but the several functions to be met accommodate themselves quite naturally in discrete structures located in somewhat random fashion. The flavour is domestic rather than imperial. No attempt is made to subordinate the constituent buildings of a palace to a master plan. These palaces seek to charm rather than to coerce. It may well be argued that these changes of emphasis in some measure reflected the self-image of these later medieval rulers. Gone were the pretensions to universal power which underlay the Samarra palaces. With them had gone the need to make the palace a suitable expression of that power. Now it could be a place in which to enjoy a sybaritic and above all more personal and private life-style. The rulers of Anatolia and the Jazira were minor dynasts, not caliphs, and their residences reflected that fact.

ANATOLIAN PALACES

The richest material for the 13th century comes from Anatolia. An unequalled picture of Saljuq court life has been drawn by the chronicler Ibn Bibi. His richly circumstantial account of the major Saljuq sultans fleshes out the otherwise enigmatic evidence of standing and excavated structures. In his pages may be traced the transition of the Saljuq monarchs from a nomadic to a settled way of life. At first they seem to have used tents, probably *yurt*s, as indeed the Timurid princes were to do a couple of centuries later. The connotations of primitive, cheap and makeshift accommodation which the word 'tent' naturally evokes in a Western mind would be quite inappropriate in this context. Some tents might take a month to put up and might hold several thousand people; the very pegs with which they were anchored were on occasion made of gold. Eventually these tents might achieve monumental form as free-standing pavilions loosely grouped within an encircling wall. Such pavilions or kiosks would be suitable for a variety of functions. They could serve as private apartments for the ruler and his *harim*, as council halls, kitchens, repositories for the sultan's clothes, presents and plate, as armouries or food stores, or for the royal silk workshop. The palace grounds would also have buildings for riding schools and quarters for the hunt. Gardens with pools and fountains would create a continuous backdrop to these varied buildings and foster an atmosphere of privileged ease. Sometimes such a pleasure garden might have a prospect over water; thus Ibn Battuta landing at Alanya/Ala'iya in 733/1333 was received by the *amir* in his garden 'seated by the sea-shore with his hair dyed black'. In most cases space was rarely a problem, since many of these palaces were intended as occasional winter or summer residences deliberately removed from the major centres of population. In this seasonal division may be recognised the influence of immemorial Turkish nomadic custom, with the regular removal from *yaylaq* (summer pastures) to *qishlaq* (winter quarters).

The kiosks of Anatolia

Within the capitals, however, as at Konya, Sivas, Alanya (if the fresco paintings in the south-east tower are any guide) and Diyarbakr, the royal palace – following virtually immutable Islamic norms – was located safely within the citadel. Sometimes extra precautions were taken, especially in the case of isolated structures in the open countryside. Thus the Haidar Bey kiosk at Argincik near Kayseri, datable to *c*.648/1250, has a defensive tower which juts out boldly from the main body of the building but which contrives also to contain the entrance hall, and a staircase which turns it into a watch-tower. The door is in the lee of the building and is thus well protected. Indeed, for all its diminutive scale (17 m. by 22 m.) the building is more of a fortress than a palace, an impression which the stark austerity of its exterior does nothing to dispel – even though the interior arrangement, with rooms ranged on the long sides of a central vaulted hall, makes ample concessions to domesticity. Barrel-vaulted ceilings and slit windows leave the interior cool and dark. From the lack of decoration it is perhaps permissible to conclude that this was never intended as the royal residence itself.

A second residence of the period, also in the Kayseri area and also constructed of fine cut stone, is the kiosk of Hizr Ilyas at Erkilet formerly furnished with an inscription dated 639/1241. It certainly deserves the name 'kiosk' rather better, for it calls to mind a varied series of early Islamic buildings in Central Asia, for example from the Merv region, which share its characteristics of lavish external buttressing and an internal subdivision into small vaulted chambers. The core of the structure is an S-shaped corridor variously vaulted along its length; this gives access to a couple of vaulted rooms and a lavishly appointed mosque. Here too a staircase leads up to the terrace, and the watch-tower function which this suggests is confirmed by the location of this pavilion atop a hill dominating the plain for miles around. A white marble porch with geometric ornament in the best style of contemporary caravansarais is an eye-catching centrepiece in the dark stone façade.

Other examples of the kiosk form known from this period include a remarkable specimen of lateral thinking on the part of the sultan 'Ala' al-Din Kayqubad, who converted a staircase tower at the Roman theatre of Aspendos into a pavilion and decked it out with figural tiles. He seems to have done something of the same sort at Alanya. The same monarch, if we may believe Ibn Bibi, himself sketched the plan for his palace at Qubadabad discussed below. The finest of all these kiosks, though, was appropriately enough the example at Konya, attributed by some to the sultan Qilich Arslan IV (655–65/1257–67) though the traditional attribution is to Qilich Arslan II (551–88/1156–92) with extensive restorations by 'Ala' al-Din Kayqubad. It might have been this work which inspired the latter's activities at Aspendos, since the Konya kiosk – now demolished but still reasonably preserved a century ago – was originally a tower of the city wall. A distinctively palatial character was conferred on this essentially military building by raising a tall brick superstructure, supported on *muqarnas* brackets, on the tower proper and furnishing this with balconies. It is a new variation on the familiar theme of a 'suspended' mosque (such as that of al-Salih Tala'i' in Cairo) or a typical medieval Anatolian mausoleum with its raised upper chamber. The upper storey comprised a large vaulted hall, a true *mafraj* by virtue

Margin references: 7.120, 7.119, 7.86-7, 7.92-7, 7.110, 7.116, 2.99, 5.156

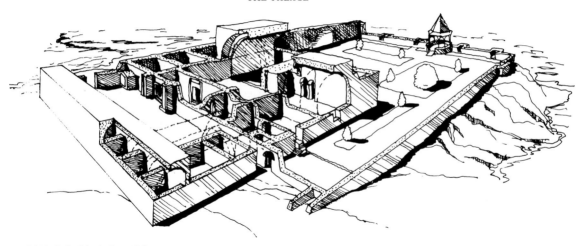

7.118 Qubadabad, Great Palace

of its excellent ventilation and windows offering a fair prospect of the town and countryside below. The tilework was of many different kinds – monochrome and polychrome, with epigraphic and abstract designs and even scenes of falconers in the *mina'i* technique – while other decoration included stone sculptures of lions, stucco carvings of other animals and of dragon-slaying warriors, a painted ceiling and finally much decorative brickwork in an Iranian style. Together all this must have made a most sumptuous impression. Yet this refurbished tower was only a fraction of the original Saljuq palace, which stretched, as a group of loosely linked buildings, from the city walls to the 'Ala' al-Din mosque. Some elements of this ensemble were clearly of outstanding interest. In the time of the Rum Saljuq sultan Qilich Arslan II (569/1173–4), for example, the citadel of Konya had an *iwan* that supposedly rivalled the Iwan-i Kisra. It seems likely that these buildings were conceived as individual entities rather than as parts of some greater whole. Both Umayyad and 'Abbasid models have therefore been replaced by an entirely different concept of palatial architecture.

Diyarbakr

Whether this was equally the case in other urban palaces of the period is not clear. The full extent of the Artuqid palace in the citadel at Diyarbakr has been revealed only partially by excavation, but its remains are evidence of a very different architectural tradition. They comprise a cruciform arrangement of four *iwan*s of unequal depth, focusing not on a courtyard but on a fountain in a pool, presumably set beneath a dome with a skylight in the fashion of later mosques at Bursa. That association of fountains and pools with palaces was to recur frequently throughout the Islamic world in subsequent centuries, though it was of course known before. Just as tell-tale a feature as the four-*iwan* plan, with its Iranian associations, is the decoration used in the pool: glass mosaics and inlaid marble of various colours forming geometric patterns. Both techniques point to Syrian influence. Among other decoration found here, a square tile depicting a black double-headed eagle under a blue glaze is of outstanding interest and quality and fits neatly into the development of Anatolian tilework further west. Altogether, then, this Jaziran monument draws impartially from Iranian, Syrian and Antolian sources, an apt symbol of the hybrid culture of its patron dynasty.

The palaces of Sultan 'Ala' al-Din Kayqubad

Two foundations of 'Ala' al-Din Kayqubad, both named after him as were others of his buildings, take up the theme of palaces by the shore, as does a third structure known from literary sources. According to Evliya Chelebi, the sultan suffered from gout, and because the warm waters of Ilgin near Konya gave him relief he had a domed glass pavilion built over the pool. This was fed by water pouring from the

286 Mosul, Qara Saray

7.104,
7.111–7.112

7.104

250

2.225–2.226;
cf. 5.51, 7.46,
7.49

mouths of two lions. It was a pleasant but fragile conceit, now totally vanished. Happily the more substantial royal palace of Kayqubadiye near Kayseri is better preserved. It comprises a trio of pavilions set by a lake and built *c.* 621/1224. The best-preserved pavilion, a square of 6 m. per side with austere external stone carving in geometrical patterns, is a square broken by four arches on the main axes and is thus identical in form to the *masjid* of contemporary caravansarais, which itself may ultimately derive from the Sasanian *chahar taq*. Such continuity testifies yet again to the readiness with which Islamic architects used a single form for multiple purposes. The diminutive scale of this pavilion suggests that Kayqubadiye functioned more as a temporary resting place than as a palace. Another pavilion here comprised three parallel vaults behind a platform projecting into the lake and used as a quay, a feature presumably required for boating excursions, regattas and other water sports. A third pavilion, which included a large hall and a kitchen, yielded glazed wall tiles.

7.112

7.111

7.113

Its sister foundation, Qubadabad, was altogether more ambitious, for it was nothing less than a royal town of which some sixteen elements have been excavated. These include, besides the statutory walls, a *paradeisos* and a dockyard. All was built rapidly by fiat in 633/1235–6. Pride of place, however, must go to the Great Palace – though for a structure measuring 50 m. by 35 m., this is a curious misnomer. The size nevertheless gives a clue to the essentially domestic and intimate nature of the building. Hence, for example, the lack of any processional approach. A forecourt with rooms asymmetrically disposed along two of its sides leads via a gateway (itself off-axis) to the palace proper. A vestibule then gives indirect access to a large rectangular hall with a deep *iwan*, doubtless used by the enthroned monarch, at its far end. Various intercommunicating rooms open off from these elements. For all the clarity of the exterior design, the interior is hard to fathom, not least in its persistent disregard of symmetry and axiality. It is very likely, however, that the prodigal splendour of the decoration in its pristine state would have swamped all such reservations. No Islamic palace of any period can rival the tilework of Qubadabad. It covered the walls up to a height of two metres, using both

7.117–7.118

square and cross-and-star types. Monochrome, lustre and polychrome underglaze tiles all occur in huge quantities, and there were also stucco figures. The subject-matter of this decoration is a topic in itself; it must suffice to draw attention to its predominantly figural character. Thus the Qubadabad tiles offer an unrivalled insight into royal iconography as well as animal, magical and zodiacal themes in this period. Not for the last time the contrast between expensive decoration and cheap building material is striking.

In the Lesser Palace, which is perched on a hilltop with a fine view over Lake Beyşehir, the accent is paradoxically not on decoration but on an unfailing symmetry. Neat, compact, its two halves exact mirror-images of each other, this palace resembles no other building of the period and thus emphasises the yawning gaps in current knowledge of medieval Anatolian palaces. The single entrance is centrally placed and marks the chord of the whole building. An oblong narrow vestibule flanked by corner rooms leads to a continuous rectangular hall, itself flanked by an unequal trio of rooms on each side and extending unbroken to the back wall. Presumably at the far end the ruler sat enthroned. Somewhat out of character with this interpretation of the building as a palace are the splayed windows, which suggest rather a fortified watch-post, as does the hilltop location. The excavations do not yield conclusive evidence either way.

7.114

LATER MEDIEVAL PALACES IN SYRIA AND IRAQ

Qasr al-Banat

The very fact that the thirteenth-century palaces in eastern Syria, Iraq and Iran are each the only surviving examples in their respective areas is warning enough not to generalise from their evidence. At best Qasr al-Banat in Raqqa and the Qara Saray in Mosul might be examined together, since – though now in different countries – they are little more than a hundred miles apart. The unfinished state of the excavations at Qasr al-Banat inhibits speculation somewhat, but the main outlines of the plan are not in doubt: a central courtyard is articulated in Iranian fashion by four (not strictly axial) *iwan*s, the rear one leading to the principal room in the building.

Quantities of rooms, some domed, are crammed into the interstices of the outer rectangle. A massive four-storeyed tower dominated the east side, with another tower to the southwest. These bore *muqarnas* motifs in stucco, and stucco carving occurs sparingly elsewhere in the monument, whose material is baked brick. Qasr al-Banat, it must be emphasised, is essentially an urban building, being sited close to the eastern gate of the city, and presumably space was at a premium. In such circumstances the four-*iwan* plan comes into its own; its central courtyard puts air and space within easy reach of every part of the building and yet wastes none of the available surface area. The emphasis on brick and stucco attests to the influence of Iraq if not Iran, as indeed the location of Raqqa on the Euphrates makes plausible.

Apart from Qasr al-Banat, the best-preserved medieval palace in Syria is so small that it scarcely deserves so resounding a title. Built by the Ayyubid sultan al-Malik al-'Aziz Muhammad, it is perched atop the great fortified *tell* of Aleppo. It dates to 630/1233, and replaces an earlier structure of his predecessor, al-Zahir Ghazi, comprising an inner courtyard and a garden. The later palace, which adjoins a similarly rebuilt arsenal, contains a reception hall with an octagonal central pool. It is focused on a deep *iwan* with a *muqarnas* hood at the back. The best-preserved element in the ensemble is the portal, which also has a *muqarnas* hood and is decked out in *ablaq* masonry. Similar 'palaces' are to be found in other Syrian castles of the period, such as Sahyun and Qal'at Najm, and also in the Jazira, as at Mardin.

The Qara Saray, Mosul

The Qara Saray in Mosul is yet another medieval palace in which a prospect over water is an intrinsic element of the whole plan. The details of this plan are, however, lost beyond recall, though it seems likely that its founder, Badr al-Din Lu'lu', erected it over the remains of an earlier Zangid palace in the very year (631/1234) that the caliph formally recognised him as ruler of Mosul. Thus, as so often in the Islamic world, the building of a palace served as a symbol of the new order. When the building was recorded earlier this century little enough remained, but the imposing scale of the undertaking was still plain to see: the riparian façade, nestling in the lee of the citadel, stretched a full 120 metres. That façade, rearing high above the river, was punctuated by doorways and windows, and fragmentary supports for their associated balconies have survived. Like the Dux Ripae at Dura Europos a millennium earlier, Badr al-Din could escape from the noisy bustle and confined spaces of the city and instead take solace in the extensive uncluttered prospect afforded by the river, with the ruins of Nineveh directly opposite as a bonus. Contemporary fashion in Iraq favoured the use of long horizontal inscriptions to decorate lengthy plain façades, and Badr al-Din was quick to exploit this idea for his own ends. In effect he transformed the riverine façade of his palace into a vast hoarding, which proclaimed to all the world the sounding brass of his official titles. Good quality cut stone – a commodity hard to come by in the Mosul area – provided an appropriate and durable surface for this roll-call of honorifics. Most of the building material, however, was of rubble masonry, its ugliness masked inside and out by a plaster coat.

It is impossible to interpret with any certainty the elevation which survived into this century. Its layout is simple: three narrow adjoining rooms at right angles to the façade. Clearly it had two storeys, the upper one apparently carried on a *muqarnas* vault. Of the three rooms which survive, that to the south-east is a later construction, and is therefore omitted from the discussion which follows, while the largest room – to the north-east – has barely retained some of its foundations. To interpret what is now the central room as an area of special importance is therefore not justified. Nor is there sufficient basis for an otherwise tempting recon-

287 Sinjar, niche

struction of these remains as a three-*iwan* plan. Indeed, since the central room of the ruin is smaller than its neighbours, such a reconstruction is virtually excluded. A far more likely arrangement is a whole suite of rooms along the river-front, of which the present 'central' room is a chance survival. How such a putative suite fitted into the layout of the palace as a whole must remain a mystery; after all, the surviving remains account for no more than a fifth of the palace frontage – less than a tenth if the later room is discounted.

A curious clue is at hand to facilitate a reconstruction of the 'central' room. From the scattered indications provided by fragmentary walls and foundations, Herzfeld computed its depth as 10 m. Its width of 6.7 m. yielded a ratio of 3:2 – the common module in medieval Iraqi architecture from 'Abbasid times onwards. Was it closed to the south-west, making it simply a room? Or was it open, and therefore an *iwan*, with all the ceremonial implications of that form? This is where the decoration of the chamber comes into play. Immediately above the door lintel at the back of the room is a continuous frieze of miniature trilobed arches, each containing a nimbed figure – an idea which recalls the ceremonial niche with royal *mamluks* found at Sinjar. Since the short side contains twenty such figures, the long sides would have held thirty. A closed room would therefore have held a hundred such figures, an *iwan* only eighty. A similar computation can be made for the frieze of carved partridges at Khirbat al-Mafjar. The decoration of the Jausaq al-Khaqani consistently uses units in multiples of a hundred and Herzfeld reports that the notion of this number as an aesthetic ideal has survived in Iraq into modern times. It seems marginally more likely, therefore, that the room was closed and was thus not of any special significance.

The rest of the decoration, all of it in painted stucco, provides no grounds for disputing this conclusion. In conformity with Jaziran taste in the late Saljuq period, it makes free play of figural themes – heraldic-looking birds with outstretched wings, parrots and animal heads as well as the frieze of mannikins. Yet the subordination of these motifs to the decorative scheme as a whole is vividly epitomised by the location of the birds (probably eagles) with outstretched wings. They fill to a nicety the spandrels of the dwarf arcade and invite the suspicion that they are there simply because they do fill it so well. The exigencies of design explain the presence of these mannikins and eagles almost as well as the needs of royal iconography, and the fact that this frieze accounts for no more than a fifth of the decora-

tive band to which it belongs actually downplays the royal theme. But the theme of royal glorification is taken up in a thoroughly explicit manner by means of epigraphy. Pride of place goes to a highly sculptural *naskhi* inscription, twice as high as the figural band, which vaunts the titles of Badr al-Din. The same theme is taken up by the inscription in the slightly smaller arched band above, and yet again by the other two *naskhi* inscriptions, which are on a more diminutive scale. An equally small Qur'anic inscription in Kufic is quite swamped by the insistent secularity of the epigraphy as a whole. The Qara Saray is too isolated a survival from its own period and region to give any clue as to whether this secular emphasis was anything out of the ordinary.

LATER MEDIEVAL PALACES IN THE IRANIAN WORLD

Takht-i Sulaiman

A similar dearth of evidence characterises the Iranian world under Mongol domination. Apart from scantily published remains at Baku and at Saray Berke, the capital of the Golden Horde, it seems that all that survives is the Ilkhanid palace at Saturiq, the modern Takht-i Sulaiman, on a site known in Sasanian times as Shiz and venerated as the site of one of the most sacred fires of Zoroastrian Iran, Atur Gushnasp. It is a place of dramatic and awe-inspiring beauty. Located in the uplands of Kurdistan, far from major centres of population, Takht-i Sulaiman is a natural sanctuary: an extinct volcano rearing its crest far over the surrounding plains and 220 m. above sea level, its flat crown containing a central crater transformed by a perpetual spring into a wide lake. The site is virtually inaccessible in winter-time. Here the pagan Ilkhan Abaqa built himself a summer palace in the 670s/1270s. Thus the *yaylaq*, or tended summer pastures of nomadic tradition, took on monumental form. It may even be that some of the major buildings of this Ilkhanid complex – notably the two large octagons – were translations into permanent materials of features already long familiar in Mongol encampments. Yet the re-use of many of the surviving Sasanian structures ensured that this Mongol palace would not depart too radically from traditional

421

forms. To some extent the densely built-up Sasanian complex, though partially ruined, inhibited the Ilkhanid architects, and this was only to be expected. Their response to the associated problems of design was both ingenious and bold. Where the Sasanian site had clustered in the northern sector of the fortified hilltop, they moved the centre of gravity southwards. This had the effect of making the lake not an appendage but the focus of attention. Despite this significant change of emphasis, the principal axis of the Sasanian complex was respected; only now it was extended to run diametrically through the middle of the lake and to connect up with a new south gate driven through the exterior ring of fortifications. This south gate had a purely notional and visual pendant to the north, where the main Sasanian gate was blocked and remodelled as an *iwan* facing the lake. Thus the only way into the site was now from the south. This major alteration in the access to the site could not fail to divert attention from the Sasanian structures, which were now automatically relegated to the background, and conversely bring the new Ilkhanid complex into the limelight.

What form, then, did these Ilkhanid buildings take? It is probable that the lake was a somewhat inhibiting, if not indeed downright disruptive, feature. After all, at its narrowest it measured some 75 metres, while its greatest length exceeded 160 metres; to incorporate such a vast irregular mass into a harmoniously planned structure was no easy feat. The solution adopted was to make a virtue of necessity by treating the lake as the pool in the courtyard of a typical four-*iwan* structure. This involved the creation of a courtyard on a scale to match the lake itself. Thereafter, the required buildings could be erected – admittedly in a rather straggling sequence – within the framework of a familiar building type. Apparently the courtyard was defined by a continuous arcaded façade, again a familiar feature. The result of all this is one of the largest four-*iwan* plans in Persian architecture (*c.* 120 m. by *c.* 148 m.), and beyond doubt the most aberrant. Three of the four *iwan*s are clustered at the northern end of the complex, forming a virtually self-contained annexe and probably destined for the ruler's quarters. At the centre of the north side the core of the Sasanian building – a *chahar taq* set within an enclosing wall – was retained, and presumably served as an audience hall. The *iwan* to the south of it now had a much more significant role to play, since it was both the major approach to that domed chamber and, at the same time, on the traditionally major axis in the newly devised four-*iwan* plan. Accordingly its breadth was more than doubled, to 17 m., and it was furnished with a centrally placed monumental staircase leading to the domed chamber. For all this undoubted distinction bestowed upon the north *iwan*, its dominant status was at least challenged if not usurped by the west *iwan*, which has been persuasively identified with the ceremonial *iwan* of Khusrau II. Here the original dimensions, at least so far as length and breadth were concern-

288 Shahr-i Sabz, Aq Saray, main portal

ed, were respected; but the *iwan* was embellished with an unusually fine *muqarnas* vault and the arrangements behind the *iwan* itself were new. Traces of a preliminary Mongol building campaign can be detected, but are largely overlaid by the remains of a much more ambitious scheme which can be dated mostly to the years 669–72/1270–4 by inscriptions on individual tiles. The rear of the *iwan* opened into a transverse hall presumably roofed by a flat ceiling on wooden pillars. At either side of this hall, which perhaps served as a chamber for private audience, was a domed octagon. The analogy to the entrance complex of the typical Timurid *madrasa* is striking, and invites the speculation that this spatial arrangement was already known in the religious and public architecture of earlier centuries; yet paired tents

7.129

13 Chisht, Afghanistan, mausolea

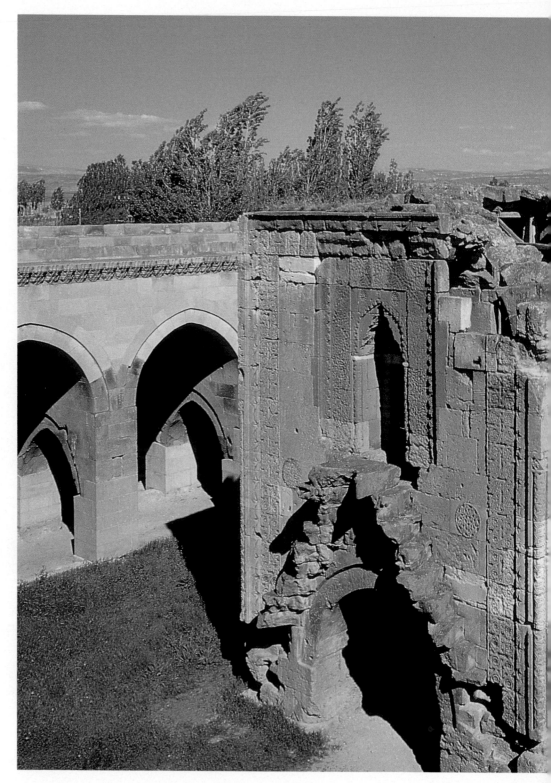

14 Sultan Han, Turkey, courtyard of caravansarai

15 Tinmal, Morocco, Great Mosque, arcades

16 Cairo, mausoleum of Imam al-Shafi'i before restoration

17 Dunaysir, Turkey, Great Mosque, interior

18 San'a', Yemen, Great Mosque, interior

19 Natanz, Iran, minaret and tomb of 'Abd al-Samad

20 Ardistan, Iran, Friday Mosque, interior of dome chamber

22 Isfahan, Friday Mosque, detail of *mihrab*

23 Tlemcen, Algeria, Great Mosque, cupola

of centralised plan with an awning between them seem also to have been known in the princely tentage of medieval Eurasian nomads. The north octagon is provided with eight deep niches, one serving to communicate with the adjoining hall and another containing a door to the exterior. This, when taken in conjunction with the unbroken line of high benches in the other niches, suggests that the north octagon might have been a banqueting hall and that the eastern door made it possible for food to be brought there by the quickest route. The south octagon, though essentially similar, has minor divergences from its sister building which hint at a different purpose. Three of its niches are raised higher than the others, with wider openings; four of the others were much more enclosed, being separated from the central space by walls and doors, a detail which suggests that they might have been used as sleeping chambers. The eighth niche opened directly into the transverse hall.

The complex formed by the west *iwan* and the custom-built structures behind it was rounded off by an imaginative re-use of the surviving Sasanian fabric. On the south side of this *iwan* an upper storey was constructed over the Sasanian vaults. Access to it was by way of a spiral staircase reached from the courtyard. The staircase led to a loggia open on two sides and commanding a splendid prospect over the lake and the surrounding countryside.

The structures lying due south of this, the principal complex of the Ilkhanid site, are still relatively little known. Yet they would assuredly repay closer examination, especially since medieval palace architecture in the Iranian world is virtually *terra incognita*. Most of them are set serially along the west side of the courtyard. They include a duodecagon, rather smaller than the two octagons just discussed; an abbreviated four-*iwan* structure with a central dome; and another four-*iwan* building conceived on a more generous scale, with the *iwans* developed at greater depth and an open central courtyard. Further west of this row of buildings is a four-arched pavilion within an enclosing wall – not unlike the structure to the north tentatively identified here as the public audience hall – and a very similar structure on the east side, where one might have expected an *iwan* instead. Finally, neatly tucked away between the

north and west *iwan* lies yet another four-*iwan* building whose north *iwan* projects powerfully on the exterior. It will be seen, then, that the entire palace can be seen as a set of variations on a very few models: four great *iwans*, four four-*iwan* plans, three square kiosks, three rectangular halls and three polygonal centralised structures. It is this very interchangeability which makes it so hard to match form with function.

Takht-i Sulaiman has yielded a plethora of decoration. Patterned floors, some paved with greenish marble; glazed dadoes of star and cross tiles; rectangular and polygonal tiles with figural motifs (often in lustre or *lajvardina* technique and in high relief) including scenes from epic and lyric poems, Chinese themes like the dragon and the phoenix, and lengthy inscriptions from the *Shahnama*; stucco *muqarnas* vaults, some containing carvings of animal motifs – all these indicate that no expense was spared. Kilns have been found on the site, which shows that much of this decoration was produced locally. The range of architectural decoration is so varied that it entails a complete revision of current understanding of the history of glazed tilework in Iran. Similarly, the lucky find of a stucco plaque incised with a geometrical *aide mémoire* for the construction of a *muqarnas* vault has shed unexpected light on the early history of this technique and has proved how far advanced it was by this time. Finally, the strength of Chinese influence in the decoration of this palace imposes a substantial revision in the hitherto accepted chronology of such influences in Iranian painting. All in all, then, Takht-i Sulaiman illuminates what was earlier a somewhat obscure and apparently empty period in Iranian art.

The *Ak Saray, Shahr-i Sabz*

The next substantial surviving royal palace from the Iranian world dates from a full century later. It was founded in 782/1380 at an astrologically propitious time by Timur, close to his birthplace, in Kesh – the modern Shahr-i Sabz – and is known honorifically as the Ak Saray, 'White Palace'. Like some gigantic Ozymandias, a solitary *iwan* rears its vast and trunkless mass from out of the surrounding desolation. Indeed, one of its now vanished Persian inscriptions proclaimed 'Let him who doubts our power and munificence look upon our buildings'. Its colossal proportions – a span of some 22 m. and a height, even in ruin, of over 30 m. – make it the largest Islamic *iwan* to survive. Yet despite limited excavations on the site, and much research by Soviet scholars, no comprehensive plan of the ensemble has been published. Hence the major problem of how to dovetail this massive fragment with the literary accounts, which in this case are almost embarrassingly copious. Two of them are sufficiently early and specific to be of critical importance: those of the Castilian envoy Ruy Gonzales de Clavijo, who visited the palace in 806/1404 when workmen were still busy on it, and of Babur, himself a descendant of Timur, who wrote a little over a century later. These accounts neither agree with each other very satisfactorily nor do they present an unambiguous picture of where the present-day ruins fit within the whole palace precinct. Slight but crucial variants in these texts can be used to justify widely divergent interpretations.

Basically two possibilities present themselves. The first, which is that favoured by modern Soviet scholarship, is that the present *pishtaq* is the portal *iwan* of the entire palace; the second, that this *pishtaq* – far from being merely the portal – was the centrepiece of the palace, both figuratively and literally, in that it had major constructions in front of it and behind it. In favour of the first interpretation is Clavijo's opening reference to the building: 'this palace had a long entrance and a very high gateway'. Nevertheless, he makes no further mention of that gateway, but instead describes at enthusiastic length a second 'very broad and lofty doorway' which is 'ornamented with gold and blue patterns on glazed tiles, richly and beautifully worked', and bears at its crown the emblem of the lion and the sun. Unless one is to assume that this latter gateway was still more magnificent than the surviving *iwan*, the natural conclusion to draw is that Clavijo's detailed description *272–273,* refers to this surviving *iwan*, especially as his *288–290* account tallies with the decoration it still bears. It is at this stage that Babur's somewhat gnomic reference to the building can be made to shed some light on the problem. It appears to support the second interpretation, for significantly it makes no mention of an entrance portal and describes the function of the great *iwan* as holding Timur's own court – in other words,

the place of public audience. His description strongly implies that there was only one great *iwan*. Babur notes that it was flanked on each side by a lesser *iwan* for his *beg*s or courtiers. This triple-*iwan* format of course already had a distinguished history in Persian architecture. From Ctesiphon onwards such a central *iwan* was *7.51–7* normally located well within the body of the palace. The surpassing size of the *iwan* – of which Babur says 'there is not in the world any *taq* that can be compared with the large one, which is said to exceed even the Taq-i Kisra' (i.e. Ctesiphon) – makes it more suitable to act as the cynosure of the palace than as its entrance; otherwise the rest of the palace would be an anticlimax. In a very similar way, the Ilkhanid mosque of 'Ali Shah in Tabriz, which was also *2.278* compared in its time to the Taq-i Kisra, had its immense *iwan* at the far end of the main courtyard. All in all, then, the weight of tradition can be seen to favour an interpretation which would make the surviving *iwan* the central feature of the palace precinct. To what extent can its surroundings be reconstructed on that basis?

Visitors to the palace, it seems, were channelled through the lofty entrance – presumably the centrepiece of an extended façade articulated by niches occupied by attendants. It seems to have been the only formal means of access to the precinct as a whole. They were then screened by having to pass through a long narrow corridor flanked by guardrooms. This debouched into a large paved courtyard, apparently some 90 m. in width and of four-*iwan* plan, and provided with a large central pool. At the end there reared the stately mass of the main *iwan* with a flanking *iwan* for lesser officials set back a little on each side. Here Timur kept his state. On the central axis of the *iwan*, and directly behind it, lay a square and no doubt domed chamber presumably reserved for purposes of private audience, as dictated by immemorial custom. It seems to have been the most richly decorated element in the whole palace. Beside and behind this reception hall was a farrago of lesser apartments disposed in up to six storeys; they included the *harim* and a banqueting chamber opening into the great orchard with fountains and water-channels. A notable feature of the *iwan* is the provision of multiple rooms and staircases within its mass, which makes it a fully functioning component of the ensemble rather than just an impressive façade.

Clavijo's account insists on the splendid decoration which embellished this palace throughout. Happily the surviving *iwan* bears out his remarks; and indeed, many would regard the tilework at Shahr-i Sabz as the high-water mark of the use of colour in Iranian architecture. The range of patterns is nothing short of astonish-

base of one of the cylindrical corner buttresses, symbolically supporting it, reads 'the Sultan is a shadow' instead of the complete phrase found elsewhere on the building: 'the Sultan is the shadow of God on earth'. Perhaps, however, the inscription continued further (though asymmetrically) along the now-vanished façade.

Many other passages in Clavijo's account

289 Shahr-i Sabz, Aq Saray, main portal, rear view

ing, and most of the techniques of glazed ornament known at that time are represented. It seems, moreover, that the rear face of the *iwan* was also meant to be covered in tilework. The effect of this technicolor splendour was actually enhanced by the decision to orientate the building towards the Timurid capital, Samarqand, and thus to the north, for this meant that much of the tilework is cast into shade, which allows one to appreciate subtleties of palette which bright sunlight would destroy. In striking contrast to the endless pains lavished on this decoration is a careless mistake, potentially lethal to its author, whereby the huge Kufic inscription in mint condition which girds the

make it clear that the palace at Shahr-i Sabz broke right out of the mould of contemporary Timurid palaces. Court life had a markedly *al fresco* quality which is exquisitely captured in contemporary manuscript painting. Huge tents complete with architectural features like buttresses, domes, crenellations and gates – all rendered in precious but perishable materials – were pitched within walled gardens. Open-plan garden pavilions characterised by radial symmetry and trabeate construction abounded. Some were even set on high plinths and surrounded by water. This interplay of tents, pavilions, gardens and water has an illustrious ancestry in the Iranian world, for it stretches back all the way to Achaemenid Pasargadae in the sixth century BC.

The palace of the Shirvanshahs in Baku

The one other major remaining palace from the late medieval Iranian world is a very chance survival indeed, for it is located on the periphery of that area rather than in one of its major centres and is not associated with any key political figure. It is the palace of the Shirvanshahs in Baku, which dates principally to the early 15th century, though its core is some two hundred years earlier. Its importance, however, lies less in its rarity than in the fact that, unlike nearly all the palaces discussed so far, it represents the standard type of royal residence found throughout the Middle East among the minor powers which flourished alongside or at the expense of major dynasties such as those of the 'Abbasids and Saljuqs. For such a residence, the term 'palace' is quite inadequate. Security mattered more than luxurious living. Accordingly the favoured site for such foundations was the highest spot in the town, a spot which was often already fortified. Within this castle lay not only the ruler's palace but also his treasury, the seat of his administration and his arsenal. It was obviously desirable for such a site to be well-watered and well-provisioned, and thus as self-sufficient as possible.

The ensemble at Baku fulfils most of these requirements, yet is at the same time part and parcel of the whole urban fabric, set amidst the busy thoroughfares of the town. Indeed, a public alley bisects the entire palace complex. None the less, it seems likely that much of the ensemble was originally walled, even though the present fortifications date mainly from the nineteenth century. The site itself, at the summit of an outcrop dominating the western section of the city and commanding spacious views of the town and of the Caspian Sea, is well chosen. Four public gateways set at irregular intervals along the perimeter walls give access to the palace buildings, while internal communications are assured by a veritable warren of corridors and staircases.

The royal precinct is divided into three separate sectors, each at a lower level than the one before, and it is hard to avoid drawing the conclusion that these different levels are intended to represent descending levels of importance, though the constant switching to and fro of levels also had the result of cramming maximum variety into the available space. At the highest point, appropriately enough, is the palace proper. Its exterior is frankly unpromising, for it comprises two unequal, barrack-like buildings set at right angles to each other and both fronting on to a courtyard. This courtyard somewhat mitigates the severity of the surrounding architecture, for most of it was flagged and it was enlivened with a pool, a fountain and probably flower-beds. The larger of the two palace buildings has two storeys which share a near-identical plan: each has twenty-five rooms, with some half-dozen internal staircases linking them. Since virtually no two rooms on a given floor share the same plan, and since the irregular stepping of the rectangular plan itself discourages a symmetrical organisation of space, it is hard to interpret the layout with any confidence. Both the main block and its annexe contain a domed vestibule to mark the entrance; in the larger building this is contained within an austere salient *iwan* of towering proportions, while in the smaller structure a modest staircase heralds the entrance proper. The *iwan* leads straight into a huge domed octagon which creates a well of space extending to the full height of the building. Here, if anywhere, was the place for public business to be transacted.

If the palace proper is strangely forbidding, with the bare mass of its exterior walls relieved only by a few square cavities functioning as windows, the structure to its north-west is an outright enigma. Known as the *diwan-khana* and significantly located at the same level as the palace, it comprises a square courtyard surrounded by arcades on three sides which create a continuous cloister. In the centre of the courtyard, and again surrounded by arcades on three sides, though this time they are set on a high plinth, rises a domed octagon. On the fourth side, which faces a gate leading into the palace courtyard, is a triple-vaulted narthex; the western vault with its splendid *muqarnas* is part of a monumental *iwan*. Architecturally, this *iwan*, for all its slender grace and fastidious stone-carving, is purposeless. The only entrance to the octagon lies to the south, while there is no corresponding entrance to the courtyard itself on the axis of the *iwan*. Tacked on to the elegant arcade which girdles the octagon, grossly over-balancing that arcade and threatening by its huge dimensions to dwarf the dome itself, it is a classic example of the lofty *iwan* as a white elephant, an architectural cliché removed from its normal context and thereby robbed of significance.

Several interpretations as to the function of the *diwan-khana* have been aired. It could have functioned as a place for the administration of justice, or as a reception hall for embassies or councils, or as a mausoleum. Its Qur'anic inscription, a very rare quotation from the *sura* of Jonah, could fit with either the first or the last possibility. Yet the lack of funerary inscriptions in a building of this quality and degree of finish is hard to explain away. It is true that the only close architectural parallel for the building is in fact a mausoleum in Tercan, in eastern Anatolia, datable *c.*596/1200. But there the inscriptions identify the building as a tomb; the surrounding niches number twelve, not twenty-five; and several of those niches contain sarcophagi, whereas the *diwan-khana* has none. Moreover, while the crypt here would indeed be a standard feature in a mausoleum, the presence of a second and larger underground complex beneath the courtyard itself is hard to explain as an adjunct of a funerary building. Finally, the presence of two other mausolea nearby – the *turba* of Sa'id Yahya Bakuvi outside the southern wall of the place and, more to the point, the spacious dynastic mausoleum of the Shirvanshahs in the second level of the ensemble, which would render a second collective tomb redundant – together with the lack of epigraphic evidence for the funerary role of the *diwan-khana*, makes it perhaps preferable to opt for the theory that the building, as its name hints, was intended for the administration of justice. In that case the arcades around the courtyard would have held petitioners, the domed octagon would have been the court-room and the underground chambers could have served as cells.

The middle level of the palace contains an irregular two-domed mosque whose minaret is dated 845/1441, and, placed at an obtuse angle to it, the rectangular family mausoleum of the Shirvanshahs, dated 838/1435. The dog-leg of empty space in front of these buildings is turned into an

290 Shahr-i Sabz, Aq Saray, main portal, detail

irregular four-*iwan* courtyard by the addition of an eastern *iwan* which backs on to the enclosing wall and thus leads nowhere, and of the *iwan* which gives access to this second level. This ham-fisted arrangement is a backhanded tribute to the innate adaptability of the cruciform *iwan* scheme, used here at the uttermost confines of the Iranian world.

The lowest level of the palace precinct is taken up by a commodious *hammam*, with an adjoining cistern provided with vertical ventilation shafts and fed by underground channels linked to another cistern some distance away – an engineering achievement that excited the admiration of medieval travellers. All these buildings are executed in stone, cut and sculpted with knife-edge precision. This makes the technical perfection of the stone-work the principal ornament of the architecture, while throwing into relief the voluptuous quality of the dense floral decoration placed so parsimoniously at a few key locations on these façades. A much lower standard of masonry, however, characterises the 15th-century summer residence of the Shirvanshahs at Nardaran near Baku, a square domed pavilion with deep axial bays and vaulted corner chambers set in gardens with a pool and fountains. Such a structure is simply a lesser but more permanent version of the stately pleasure domes which grace contemporary miniature paintings.

SAFAVID PALACES: GENERAL CONSIDERATIONS

It is only as late as the Safavid period that, for the first time since the century of the Umayyads, palaces survive in sufficient quantity and in a sufficiently good state of preservation to shed some light on the contemporary conventions governing this genre of building. Moreover, standing monuments can be supplemented by a still greater number of now vanished palaces which were recorded by European travellers in detailed engravings – e.g. at Ashraf, and in Isfahan the 'Ayina Khana, the Bagh-i Zirishk, Asadabad, Sar Pushida and the Talar-i Tawila. These Safavid palaces also make it possible to weigh the hyperbolic literary accounts – so often dismissed as mere bombast – against actual buildings, and it is intriguing to note that many of these palaces do in fact embody some element of extravagance or excess. In the Chihil Sutun it is the marked disparity between the apparently featherweight façade and the lowering mass of what lies behind. In the 'Ali Qapu this contrast of solids and voids is experienced directly, not *seriatim*, for the veranda is sandwiched between the solid blocks of the ground floor and the second storey; yet there, too, the quirk of fantasy which contrives to transport this designed emptiness halfway up the façade has something slightly mannered about it. And who would expect behind the unpromising façade of the Hasht Bihisht a vast billowing *muqarnas* dome, which reduces the exterior to little more than a shell and effectively turns the building inside out? In the Khaju bridge the centrepiece is not some spectacular hydraulic device but rather a compact two-storeyed octagonal kiosk, wafted as if by magic into the heart of an already hybrid structure, part thoroughfare and part dam. In each of these cases the architect confounds the reasonable expectations of the visitor, and indeed there may be a touch of mischief in this high-handed manipulation of familiar forms.

No account of Safavid palaces would be complete without an examination of the en-vironment in which they were set. Indeed, the open plan which was adopted for so many of them would have made little sense had they been built right alongside the busy world of streets and bazaars. The underlying intention is rather that the entire precinct should function as an extended palace, of which actual buildings are merely one component part. In some cases it is the buildings that dominate; in others, the gardens. This was by no means a new idea in Iran; the palaces of the Achaemenids at Pasargadae, the Sasanians at Qasr-i Shirin, the Samanids at Bukhara, the Buyids at Shiraz, the Saljuqs at Isfahan and the Mongols at Ujan – to cite merely a few examples which have not been discussed earlier in this chapter – exploited various combinations of pavilions, belvederes, terraces, water, flower-beds and both fruit-bearing and umbrageous trees. Since gardens are of their very nature much more vulnerable than buildings to the ravages of time, it is not surprising that none of these medieval and pre-medieval examples survive. Yet to analyse the buildings themselves without reference to their wider setting would be seriously to misrepresent them; a warning that should be heeded in the case of almost every single palace described in this chapter, but is especially relevant in 17th-century Iran. The great gardens of Safavid Isfahan, especially the Chahar Bagh and the Hazar Jarib, entranced all the European travellers who saw them: 'gardens' (as Sir Thomas Herbert said) 'which for grandeur and fragour no city in Asia outvies . . . so sweet and verdant that you may call it another paradise'; while he sums up the Hazar Jarib as 'a compendium of sense-ravishing delights'.

These gardens varied so substantially in scale, in layout and in overall effect that to generalise about them would be perilous. *Grosso modo*, however, two major types may be distinguished on the basis of recent research: the extensive walled garden – the so-called *chahar bagh* – containing plots of trees, canals and pools embowering a palatial building which is little more than incidental to the whole; and the much smaller garden which is itself contained within the palace and thus in a sense incidental to it. The carefully calculated asymmetries and informality of later European gardens held, it seems, little charm for Persian taste, and the large tracts of land which were essential to the *chahar bagh* concept were usually subdivided according to principles of radial symmetry or the equipoise of large masses. Where virtually unlimited space was available – as at Ashraf and even Isfahan in its Safavid expansion – several walled gardens, each very differently organised, might be scattered as it were at random over a large surface area. The buildings in such gardens would resemble jewels in elaborate settings – strategically located, for example, at the end of a long vista like the four-fold pavilion in the Bagh-i Chashma at Ashraf, or perhaps placed at the dead centre of the garden and surrounded by an ornamental lake, as is depicted in a garden carpet made in 1041/1632, probably in Kirman, and now in the Jaipur museum. The other end of the scale, where nature was subordinated to man-made structures, is illustrated by the royal precinct directly west of the *maidan* at Isfahan. Here a vast area is subdivided into dozens of enclosures. These are for the most part square, rectangular or octagonal, criss-crossed by inter-communicating passageways; open and covered

spaces are interwoven. The garden element may shrink to a well of open space in the centre of a large multi-domed area; or it may expand right up to the perimeter walls of a courtyard. These various devices make it impossible to obtain an overall impression of the area. Instead, each separate enclosure preserves its own particular character. The cumulative effect was thus not of a single garden but of many small patches of water, of colour, of greenery serving to enhance the varied architectural forms around them.

Apart from the palaces in Qazvin, Ashraf and Isfahan, which will be examined shortly, other and more utilitarian monuments designed for the ruler – probably Shah 'Abbas I – and his entourage have survived. Chief among these is a quartet of structures lining the road from Isfahan to Ashraf, and found respectively at Dumbi, Chaharabad, Safid Ab and 'Abbasabad or Siyah Kuh. They are mentioned here less for their intrinsic importance than because of the light they shed on court life, for from Saljuq times onwards it was customary for the court to be peripatetic, and this created a need for stopovers along the most frequently travelled routes. In the pre-Safavid period an excellent example of such a site is Ribat-i Sharaf, begun in 508/1114–5 and probably built for Sultan Sanjar. Here the double courtyard plan allows the building to cater both for the general public and for the royal retinue. Unfortunately, while the *ribat* of Akcha-Qal'a in Turkmenistan appears to offer a contemporary parallel, in later centuries the type does not recur. The Safavid monuments under discussion suggest that the division between public and royal use formalised itself over the centuries to the point that separate structures intended exclusively for royal use began to be erected. Notable features of this quartet of related buildings include their substantial size (the double courtyard layout at Safid Ab measures some 86 m. by 47 m.), the novel use of *iwan*s on the long axis only, rather than in cruciform disposition as is standard practice in such large courtyard buildings, and of long transversely vaulted halls accessible by side openings in the *iwan*s. The presence of blank walls or long, narrow, rectangular halls on one or more sides of the courtyard is equally aberrant. Aside from their obvious function as rest-stations punctuating the long road to the

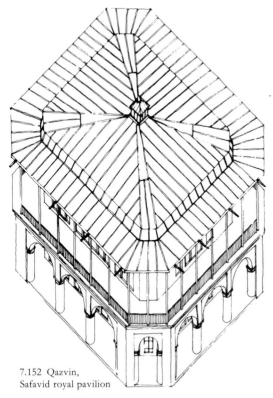

7.152 Qazvin,
Safavid royal pavilion

Caspian, they may well have served as hunting lodges, while the local term used nowadays of the establishment at 'Abbasabad/Siyah Kuh – *harim sara* or 'ladies' quarters' – may accurately reflect its original function. The lack of architectural or applied ornament in these foundations, however, drives home their primarily utilitarian character.

Safavid palaces outside Isfahan

The principal interest of the Safavid palaces outside Isfahan lies in the pointers they offer towards their more splendid and famous successors. Only the palaces at Na'in develop an independent idiom in architecture and ornament. The pavilion at Qazvin, for example, reveals some of the most daring features of the 'Ali Qapu and the Hasht Bihisht, yet only at an embryonic stage. Here, for example, is the airy loggia of the 'Ali Qapu; yet its wooden columns are placed at uneven intervals and encircle the whole upper floor. The impact made in the 'Ali

7.151–7.152

7.133, 7.144

291 Na'in, palace, vaulting

Qapu by the forest of uprights hemmed in by solid masonry – an immediate visual image of liberation – is here too dispersed to be effective. Similarly, while the octagonal plan (really more of a square with bevelled corners) with corner rooms and a central vault, raised podium, axial *iwan*s and ring of outer columns, seems a natural predecessor of the Hasht Bihisht, the interior arrangement adopted at Qazvin, with its two storeys throughout the elevation, relegates the vault of the ground floor to very modest proportions. At the Hasht Bihisht, by contrast, the central part of the building consists of a single spacious room crowned by a gigantic *muqarnas* dome. Similarly, the principle of radial symmetry developed with such finished assurance at the Hasht Bihisht occurs about half a century earlier in the Bagh-i Chashma built at Ashraf on the Caspian shore by Shah 'Abbas. Here too the pavilion is at the far end of an extensive garden project, but the cruciform plan is much looser, for in place of the integration of levels and spaces in the Hasht Bihisht, it resolves itself into four separate chambers in two storeys grouped around a central pool fed by outlets linked to the gardens. Externally the elevation is a massive cube lavishly but repetitively articulated by both open and blind niches. The kiosk by the pool in the garden of Bairamabad near Kirman, datable to the early 17th century, takes the form of a powerfully buttressed *iwan* shorn of its vault, but the starkness of the elevation is somewhat redeemed by its colourful tilework.

7.140–7

7.145

7.150

Palace at Na'in

The major palace at Na'in mentioned above, and datable *c*.967/1560, stands somewhat apart from the mainstream of Safavid palaces. This applies in equal measure to its location, its plan, and its decoration. Na'in, a small town some 100 km. east of Isfahan, never housed the Safavid court, nor was it a major provincial centre like Kirman, Mashhad or Ardabil. Since there appears to be no record of who commissioned the building, its contemporary context remains obscure. The original plan, though overlaid by later additions, is clear enough in its essentials. It comprises an oblong courtyard with a deeply sunken pool; each of its long sides has two *iwan*s while the short sides are broken by doorways and windows. The elevation is two-storeyed

292 Isfahan, Hasht Bihisht, entrance façade

throughout; one of the upper rooms has niches whose silhouettes simulate pottery shapes as in the 'Ali Qapu. The main *iwan* bears a complex net vault, its interstices crammed with thinly incised plaster whose figural designs draw freely on the repertory of contemporary miniature painting, such as scenes of hunting, polo, feasting and enthronements, even to the extent of depicting scenes from the works of Nizami and Jami and with quotations from Hafiz.

Interesting as these various provincial palaces are, there can be no doubt that pride of place in this genre rightfully belongs to the three major palaces that survive from 17th-century Isfahan: the 'Ali Qapu, the Chihil Sutun and the Hasht Bihisht.

'Ali Qapu

The importance of the 'Ali Qapu – 'high gate' or rather 'Sublime Porte' – leaps to the eye by virtue of its site alone. Alone among these buildings it is not a private retreat tucked away in secluded gardens, but a palace with a public face, as is symbolised by its site fronting on the main square of the city. The 'Ali Qapu, says Herbert, 'juts out in the street further than the other buildings . . . her greatest gallantry being in the outward trim . . . within, the rooms are arched and enlightened with trellises, embossed above and painted with red, white, blue and gold'. Its many small rooms admirably answered the needs of office-space for the royal administration, without in any way detracting from the high profile of the open multi-columned loggia on the third floor, an ideal vantage point from which to enjoy the constantly changing spectacles, by turns solemn and festive, enacted in the *maidan* below. Here the shah could see and be seen. Appropriately enough, the rear façade of the building – irreverently termed a bootbox by Robert Byron – had no such central feature, presenting merely a seemingly endless succession of blank niches and windows in five storeys; for the back of the building faces the private gardens of the shah. Under Shah 'Abbas I the 'Ali Qapu was a much more modest building than it now is; its modular nature facilitated subsequent major additions. As with so many of these palaces, pools and fountains invade the precincts of the building itself; here they occur at both ground-floor and third-floor level. Rooms for the administration of justice, for public and private receptions and for music – the last doubling as a vast display cabinet for part of the royal ceramics collection, complete with custom-made plaster niches to house the pieces – indicate merely some of the functions discharged within the 'Ali Qapu. Nevertheless there is a labyrinth of smaller rooms with interconnecting passages and staircases; presumably many of these were for members of the shah's family, *harim* or retinue. The courtly subject-matter of their paintings makes it unlikely that all these rooms were simply offices. Externally the decoration is architectonic rather than applied, with much emphasis on lattice-work, blind niches and arched openings. There is a notable absence of costly and labour-intensive ornament.

Chihil Sutun

7.143, 7.146   The Chihil Sutun at first sight resembles the loggia of the 'Ali Qapu brought back down to earth. Here again water is an integral part of the

7.142   design, for a huge rectangular pool is placed directly in front of the building and on the main axis; indeed, the name Chihil Sutun ('Forty Columns') could be interpreted as a picturesque play on the idea that the many-columned façade is reflected in the water. Here again the arch-

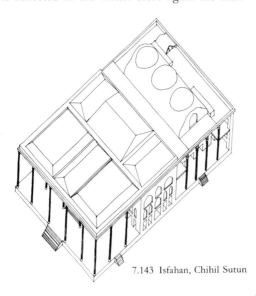

7.143 Isfahan, Chihil Sutun

itects – for the building was not erected in a single campaign but in three – play fast and loose with some of the most time-honoured conventions of Persian architecture. Moreover, it would be hard to find a clearer proof of the modular nature of Islamic architecture in Iran, of its deep-rooted conservatism and of its readiness to transform familiar elements by giving them unfamiliar contexts. In its original form the palace consisted of an oblong hall roofed by 7.146 three adjoining domes. Lateral rooms opened behind and in front of the outer domes, while the central dome was preceded by an *iwan* and had a similar space behind it. Such an idea had a pedigree as ancient as Sasanian Firuzabad. Yet 7.53–7.54 the broad lateral *iwan* leading to each of the flanking domes is a most unexpected detail. It introduces the idea of access from the sides and thus makes the building much more centralised. In the second campaign a large open space with a central pond was placed directly in front of the entrance *iwan*; longitudinal halls flanked this space, which operated like a traditional *iwan*. Finally a portico or *talar* of twenty columns carrying a pitched roof was tacked on to the 7.143 already enlarged building; in its centre was another pond, complete with fountain. Obviously the nature of the building was fundamentally altered by each of these additions. Its core remains the triple-domed oblong hall, to which the *talar*, the broad space behind it and finally the *iwan* proper all lead. Yet these curtain-raising devices occupy more space than the *raison d'être* of the building itself. Each successive addition, too, was higher than the last, with the result that the *talar* dwarfs the building to which it is a mere preliminary. Yet the versatility of each of these various sections of the building is well illustrated by their use in isolation in other contemporary palaces: the *talar* in the Asadabad palace, the broad *iwan* in the palace within the Bagh-i Zirishk, and the oblong triple-vaulted hall (admittedly in modified form) in the Talar Ashraf of *c*.1102/1690. The smaller niches on both the interior and the exterior walls bear paintings of courtiers, pages and maidens, while elaborate scenes of feasting and battle take up 293 the larger wall surfaces. Carved stone column-bases with caryatids and lions, gaily patterned curtains and awnings, the gilding and marquetry work of the ceilings, *muqarnas* capitals and of course carpets by the score all made their distinctive contribution to the glamour of the whole. The fitful illumination of countless torches and the constant murmur of running water provided a congenial backdrop to the nocturnal scenes of feasting courtiers, music-making and dancing girls enacted in this sumptuous setting.

Hasht Bihisht

With the Hasht Bihisht of 1080/1669 the long succession of Safavid palaces approaches its end. Into a bevelled rectangle of *c.* 27 m. by 30 m., with a maximum height of about 16 m., is crammed a remarkable variety of spaces large and small, open and closed – and all with no sense of crowding. Quite the contrary. The central domed hall with its octagonal pool and fountain is easily accessible, via axial *iwan*s, from each of the major points of the compass. The four corner piers which support the great *muqarnas* dome contain rooms on two floors linked by staircases; vaulting is used throughout to increase the illusion of space. Originally the surfaces sparkled with gilding, paintwork and tiles. The twisting passages and staircases and the abrupt turns tend to disorientate the casual visitor and make the individual rooms as private as the main hall is public. Yielding at every turn extensive prospects over the surrounding gardens, the palace is well named Eight Paradises. Even the normally prosaic traveller Chardin, who lived in Isfahan for many years and had an eye for architecture, waxed lyrical about this building: 'I cannot stop myself from saying that when one walks in this place expressly made for the delights of love and one sees all these rooms and riches one's heart is so affected that to speak frankly one always leaves with regret'.

Safavid Palaces: Conclusions

In summary, it will be seen that these palaces were never intended to outlast the centuries or even to impress by their size and grandeur. Instead, they make a positive feature of their apparent frailness. Obviously solid bearing walls are minimised or disguised; their surfaces tend to be pierced by large windows, niches, wooden grilles or loggias while the interior walls are encrusted with yet more niches, sus-

293 Isfahan, Chihil Sutun, fresco of a royal audience

pended ceilings and stalactite vaults. The structural role accorded to wood in these buildings is a new departure for official architecture in Iran, and may betray the origins of these structures in vernacular buildings, though many of their features hark back to pre-Islamic palaces.

It will be clear from this necessarily sketchy account of Safavid palace architecture that in 17th-century Iran there seems to have been no exact equivalent of the great palaces of the rest of the Islamic world, or for that matter of contemporary Europe. Indeed, 'palace' is to some extent a misnomer for the buildings under discussion. They were put up quickly and quite cheaply. It seems probable that the gardens in which they were set represented a much greater capital outlay than the buildings themselves. None of the latter were conceived as permanent homes for the monarch. Hence the temporary, even makeshift, air which clings to them. Kiosks, pavilions, gazebos, summer-houses, reception halls – none of these add up to a permanent royal residence. They are, so to speak, a translation of the tented Turco-Mongol culture into more durable materials. Nor was this concept of palace life confined to the Safavid shahs. To the east and the west alike, the same period saw very similar ideas find local expression in the Topkapi Saray in Ottoman Istanbul and in the Mughal palaces of Agra, Delhi and Lahore. In all these cases the earlier emphasis on a single major building is replaced by a more sensitive awareness of the wider garden setting, with the consequence that the multiple functions of a large palace complex are decentralised to a wide range of much smaller purpose-built structures.

MEDIEVAL PALACES IN EGYPT

Egypt and the Levant offer only very sparse material for the history of medieval Islamic palaces. This state of affairs is especially frustrating in the case of Tulunid and Fatimid Egypt, since the palaces erected in Fustat/Cairo by the rulers of these dynasties were a byword for sybaritic refinement, symbolised by the pond of quicksilver in the palace of Khumarawaih. That gardens were part of these splendours may be inferred from the reference to a menagerie of exotic animals housed in that same palace. Sometimes, however, the literary information on these gardens is more specific.

The Tulunid prince Khumarawaih laid out a splendid garden on his father's parade-ground. It had rare grafts, such as almonds grown on an apricot trunk; roses galore; and lotuses of red, blue and yellow. The layout of the garden created patterns of pictures and letters, and it was the task of the gardener to ensure that no one leaf overlapped another. Ponds, wells, fountains and pavilions were scattered broadcast throughout the garden. A little later, one of the Fatimid caliphs covered the paths of his own garden with Mesopotamian mats, and in obedience to a similar taste the palm-trunks were sheathed in gilded metal plates. A similar device had been recorded in the courts of pre-Islamic Iran, where plane-trees had been entirely

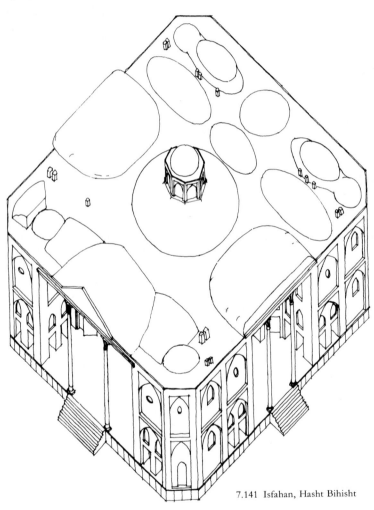

7.141 Isfahan, Hasht Bihisht

wrapped in silver leaf. The caliphal court at Baghdad went one better than this: in the midst of a round pond of clear water, so al-Khatib al-Baghdadi relates, was a tree of eighteen branches, most of silver but some of gold. Its multi-coloured leaves trembled in the breeze just like real ones, while numerous varieties of birds fashioned from silver sang from its branches. When the Byzantine ambassador saw this in 305/917 he was apparently amazed, though it is well known that similar devices were to be seen in the court at Constantinople – including gilded (and presumably life-size) lions beside the royal throne which could open their mouths, roar and strike the ground with their tails.

The very term 'palace' becomes strangely ambiguous in Fatimid times; Nasir-i Khusrau in 438/1047 describes something much more like a miniature city – as one might expect of a complex which was the political and administrative heart of Cairo – consisting of ten major units connected by underground passages, which also embraced kiosks, kitchens, reception rooms, banqueting halls and chambers bulging with precious garments. Gilded marble cloisters enclosed gardens with artificial trees (recalling the Dar al-Shajara at Baghdad) and clockwork singing birds. There was even a great golden filigree screen behind which the caliph could watch court festivals.

The plethora of textual details available about the appurtenances of this palace-city is matched by the scarcity of data on the architecture itself. The sole clue available is provided by the late 10th-century palace of Sayyidat al-Mulk. This featured a courtyard with four *iwan*s, three of them provided with a *shadirwan* or water-channel at the rear, which presumably met at a fountain in the centre of the courtyard. A colonnaded portico to the north gave access to a deep narrow hall. Most of the later medieval palaces in Cairo took the traditional local form of a *qa'a*, a long hall with an *iwan* at each end and a sunken area (*durqa'a*) in the middle. One such structure, perhaps the Dar al-Qutbiya, has recently been uncovered in the courtyard of the Qala'un *madrasa*. A similar building type, somewhat modified so as to resemble a four-*iwan* plan with a wooden-domed central area and shortened arms, can be recognised in the now destroyed

294 Cairo, palace of Yashbak, vaulting

palace of the Ayyubid sultan al-Salih on Roda Island, built in 638/1241 and probably, if the Crusader-style doorway there was any guide, built at least in part by captured Christians. This *qa'a*, which adjoined the Nilometer, was reached by switchback corridors and was hemmed in by other, somewhat haphazard, structures.

The sheer shortage of building space in later medieval Cairo – apart from the privileged site of the Citadel, a special case to be discussed shortly – made palaces of extensive surface area an unrealistic prospect. For this reason alone the *qa'a* remained assured of popularity, for it could readily be transported to the first floor, sometimes accessible by an external stair, as in the palace of Bashtak (738/1337 or 740/1339), where the private rooms in the storey above display richly painted and carved wooden ceilings. Thus the tradition of a multi-storey urban palace insensibly developed. A good example of this is the palace of Muhibb al-Din (713/1313?), similar to the more famous *qa'a* of

435

7.169, 7.171 'Uthman Katkhuda, a building some 15 m. high with a fountain in the wall of one *iwan* feeding a pool in the domed *durqa'a*. The roughly con-
7.159 temporary palace of Alin Aq had the *qa'a* placed above the stables which occupied the ground floor; its severe and forbidding exterior gave it a quasi-military aspect. Some of these palaces of
7.153–7.156 *qa'a* type, such as those of Manjak al-Silahdar (747–8/1346–7), Amir Taz (753/1352) or Amir
294, 7.158 Yashbak (originally built for Qusun and dating from *c.* 738/1337) also had monumental porches on their street façades. Of the palace built by the
7.164 Amir Mama'i in 901/1496 only the graceful open loggia (*maq'ad*) of its façade, now known as the Bait al-Qadi, and its adjoining *muqarnas* porch, remains; this fragment boasts splendid woodwork and *ablaq* while its architecture has much in common with Persian palaces. A related
7.166–7.167 *maq'ad* graces the palace of Qa'it Bay (890/1485);
295 the same ruler built a further *maq'ad* near his mosque. A provincial echo of such buildings may be noted in the sole surviving Mamluk

palace of Jerusalem, that of Sitt Tunshuq (*c.* 790/
7.123, 7.126 1388) with its first-floor stone-vaulted *qa'a* above the ground-floor stables, twenty-five additional rooms reached by four staircases, and an unusually elaborate cinquefoil arched portal, 296 itself only one element in a highly developed street façade. The Matbakh al-'Ajami in Aleppo, 7.125 also immured in a densely built-up area, attests an equally ingenious use of space.

Yet for the most part such buildings are at once too small and too plain to fit comfortably into the category of 'palace' as developed in this chapter. Much grander in conception and execu- tion was the Qasr al-Ablaq built in 713–5/1313– 7.162, 7.16 15 by Sultan al-Nasir Muhammad in the Cairo citadel, possibly a free copy of the similarly named palace of Baibars at Damascus; it fell victim to an explosion in 1241/1824. This too was a complex of structures rather than a single building. It included a huge *qa'a* with a wooden dome and, far more spectacular, a porch or *iwan* resting on a massive platform carried on corbels

295 Cairo, Sikkat al-Mardani or house of Qa'it Bay

and comprising a veritable forest of columns. These allowed the occupants (who included the weavers of the *kiswa* produced annually to drape the Ka'ba) the most extensive view in Cairo; the Mamluk palaces in Damascus and Aleppo were also sited with such panoramas in mind. Palaces in citadels were also of course a standard feature of medieval Islamic architecture; those of Aleppo and Diyarbakr, both furnished with *shadirwan*s to bring nature within the palace itself, are typical examples. At Qasr al-Ablaq the porch proper led to a square open-plan chamber whose wooden *muqarnas* dome was carried entirely on gigantic columned arcades. At the far end of the room was the royal throne. Mosaic, stained glass, mother-of-pearl, lapis lazuli and marble paving supplemented the two-tone masonry which gave the palace its name. Nearby was al-Nasir's Great Iwan which served as a hall of justice. The symbiosis of royal residence, court of law and high place was already a familiar combination, and continued to have numerous echoes in later Islamic palaces.

PALACES IN THE MAGHRIB

A steady succession of examples documents the history of the palace in the western Islamic world from the 9th century onwards. Yet here too there is the same lack of consistency as can be noted further east. The conclusion is unavoidable: there simply is no standard type of palace anywhere in the Islamic world. Once again, then, the only practical approach is to examine each of the sites in turn. It will be convenient to deal with the Maghrib first before examining the evidence from Andalusia.

The earliest relevant palatial monument to survive in the Maghrib already betrays the dependence of this area on ideas worked out in the Islamic heartlands. It is situated in Tahart, a town somewhat preposterously dubbed 'the Balkh of the West' in its own time, which functioned as the capital of a tiny Kharijite kingdom ruled by the Rustamid *amir*s in western Algeria in the 9th century. The Qasba of Tahart was, it seems, their palace. It was thoroughly reworked a thousand years later, but enough of its original form survives to indicate that it was a free reinterpretation of the standard Umayyad palace type in Syria. Its rectangular fortified enclosure was entered by a single gate, whose vestibule

was flanked by benches, and a range of rooms abutting on the perimeter wall surrounded the courtyard. Ramps or staircases at the corners led to the upper floor. Even the dimensions (some 66 m. by 35 m.) recall Syrian models, in which 35 m. was the smallest unit for overall planning purposes.

Sadrata

Even more remote than Tahart was the Ibadite capital of Sadrata, some 800 km. south of Algiers, which flourished briefly in the 10th and 11th centuries. Unfortunately, the site has had a particularly chequered history in the last hundred years, with at least eight separate excavation campaigns whose findings were for the most part lost without being recorded. This makes it hard to put the very fragmentary finds into context and, for the purposes of this chapter, to determine whether the two buildings described as 'palaces' do indeed merit that term. Of one, situated at the eastern outskirts of the town, too little was excavated to permit a clear picture of the architecture to emerge: merely

296 Jerusalem, palace of Sitt Tunshuq

part of a court with a blank wall to the east concealing a pair of rooms and to the north a transversely vaulted hall. The principal interest of the building lay in its abundant carved stucco decoration. The information available on the other palace, the so-called Mahkama at the northern edge of the town, is still more fragmentary; but before the excavations were prematurely broken off they had disclosed a complex of thirty-four rooms with a central court articulated by two porticos and lavishly decorated with carved stucco using floral and geometric motifs and inscriptions. The rooms are often much longer than they are wide. In the most splendidly decorated chamber of all, a bed constructed of plaster-coated rubble occupied each of the extremities of the T-shaped plan. One room had quite elaborate squinch decoration, which featured lobed niches joined by a row of blank arcades, the whole executed in carved stucco in a style which owes much to both Cordoba and Samarra. It may be relevant to recall that it was precisely at Samarra, and for that matter Nishapur as well, that many private houses displayed large-scale stucco panelling of a similar kind.

7.178

cf. 280–282

Ashir

In the Maghrib the earliest palace whose remains are sufficiently well preserved to merit that name is at Ashir, some 100 km. due south of Algiers. A town was founded here by Ziri b. Manad, a vassal of the Fatimid caliph al-Qa'im, in 324/ 935–6. The latter sent him for this purpose, besides quantities of iron and other materials, an architect more accomplished than any in Ifriqiya. Al-Qa'im's seat at this time was the coastal town of Mahdiya, where the remains of an early 10th-century palace have been found. Although no more than the gate complex survives (with some fine geometrically patterned mosaic floors), its remarkable similarity to the comparable feature at Ashir suggests that the same man built both palaces; the one at Ashir, as befitted the lesser status of its patron, was the smaller of the two. It is a curious blend of Syrian and Mesopotamian ideas, with other elements whose ancestry is not easily traced. The dimensions – 72 m. by 40 m. – are, as at Tahart, based on the multiples favoured in the Umayyad residences. From the same source, too, may

7.172

7.174

ultimately derive the boldly salient entrance with its echoes of Roman triumphal arches, though these had already been subsumed and given distinctively Muslim expression in the entrance to the Great Mosque at Mahdiya, built less than a generation earlier. This re-use in a secular context of an architectural form employed in the same period and area for religious purposes is a reminder of the easy interchangeability of forms in Islamic architecture. Finally, the square or rectangular buttressing of the exterior wall is a feature often encountered in the Roman *castra* of the Near East, and subsequently in a string of Byzantine fortresses in North Africa, which may indeed have provided the immediate inspiration. Numerous Islamic citadels in Spain perpetuated the type for centuries. The gate complex, with its guard-rooms flanking the entrance passageway, is again easily paralleled in Umayyad Syria. Not so, however, the bent entrance which confronts the visitor who has fairly entered the palace. Here the closest medieval analogies are in the 'Abbasid architecture of Mesopotamia, for example the *dar al-imara* at Kufa, and the city gates of Baghdad, though it may be even more significant that such bent entrances are to this day the standard means of maintaining privacy in Maghribi vernacular architecture.

2.137–2.13[?] *46*

7.15, 2.45

Internally, the palace at Ashir is subdivided into three adjoining rectangular tracts. The central tract, moving from south to north, comprises the entrance complex, an open courtyard of 22.5 m. by 23.6 m., and an oblong transverse hall leading into a large rectangular chamber, whose massive stepped projection from the north wall suitably reinforces its dominant position in the building. This was beyond reasonable doubt the audience-hall of the prince. To either side of the central tract, and separated from it by a line of three long and narrow chambers accessible only from the courtyard, were a pair of courtyards with surrounding chambers: the Maghribi version of the *bait* system. The side tracts are mirror images of each other, though in each tract the southern *bait* is marginally better appointed.

This symmetrical tripartite subdivision cannot fail to recall Mshatta, and is indeed the closest known analogy to that building. Perhaps the most significant difference is that, for all its

7.11

three-tract form, Ashir is essentially an expansion of the central tract at Mshatta rather than a reduced version of the entire building. At Mshatta the four *bait*s clustered around the triconch hall at the far end of the palace are conventionally (and plausibly) explained as accommodation for the caliph's four legal wives. The comparable provision at Ashir has expanded to such a degree that it accounts for most of the building's surface area. It seems unlikely that the *amir*'s wives would have rated accommodation on so lavish a scale; perhaps, therefore, these four self-contained units were intended for members of his family or for the highest officers of state. The term 'lavish', incidentally, cannot be applied with justice to the

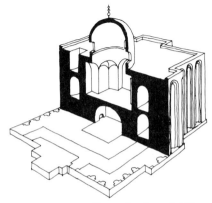

7.177 Qal'a of the Banu Hammad, palace of al-Manar

surviving decoration. Finely dressed stone blocks embellish the exterior façade, but the excavations disclosed so little in the way of decoration that the original aspect of the palace must have been quite severe. Even the main courtyard had plain walls (like Mshatta?) apart from a salient arcade along its southern face. The key to the ensemble is the treatment of the audience hall. Very much in the manner of Mshatta, it is approached by a triple opening in the north façade of the courtyard, which leads into a barrel-vaulted transverse anteroom with the audience-hall itself directly behind it on the central axis. This reversed T-shape arrangement is found at the palaces of Kufa and Ukhaidir and — perhaps more significantly still — in the domestic architecture of Fustat. As for the audience-hall itself, its greater width *vis-à-vis* its

length makes a dome less likely than a semi-dome – a solution for which the analogy of Mshatta, with its similar triconch throne-room, can be cited as supporting evidence. Thus across great gulfs of space and time the tenacious vitality of forms developed and refined in Umayyad Syria makes itself felt once more.

These Syrian influences might well have reached Ashir through the agency of earlier Aghlabid palaces, of which the most substantial surviving example is that of Raqqada, outside Qairawan, begun in 263/876. Here the multi-towered square enceinte perpetuates the modes of Umayyad Syria, while its division into two roughly equal sections, one apparently reserved for the densely packed living quarters of the royal retinue and the other designed for use by the ruler himself, can be seen as a development of ideas expressed as Mshatta. The sector tentatively identified as 'royal' – the incomplete state of the excavations renders any definite statement inappropriate – has a bent entrance of standard Maghribi type leading to a porticoed courtyard with suites of rooms along the back walls and a central pool. At its far end is a tripartite basilical hall with an apse, presumably the throne room, with a suite of three adjoining deep and narrow rooms on each side. Here again Syrian influence is patent.

The Qal'a of the Banu Hammad

Some of the themes enunciated at Ashir resurface at the Qal'a of the Banu Hammad, in northeastern Algeria, whose palaces probably date from the period when the city was the *de facto* capital of Ifriqiya, namely the later 11th–early 12th century. Crowning some of the ridges of this steeply contoured site, they include the Qasr al-Salam/Qasr al-Sham (with some fine *muqarnas* fragments) and the Qasr al-Kawkab; but it is two other palaces in a much better state of preservation that make it possible to form some impression of the distinctive architecture of this Berber capital. The Qasr al-Manar, perched on a cliff and incorporated into the external fortified wall of the city, offers a curious combination of a domed reception hall and a vaulted basement which served as a store-room or dungeon. Access to the reception hall on the upper floor is by a ramp, very much in the manner of the Almohad minarets. This gives on to an extensive roof-top terrace with dramatic views to the distant hills. The cubic mass of the building is somewhat lightened by the lofty cannular arched niches which articulate its exterior walls, a motif repeated in the somewhat similar two-storeyed Burj al-'Arif near Mahdiya, whose external Kufic inscription suggests an 11th-century date. The luxurious appointments of the Qasr al-Manar have all vanished save a few marble columns and interlaced bands of inscription in the oratory, but their memory was celebrated by the poet Ibn Hammad:

> Shall I ever see again the arcades of al-Manar,
> Their flower-beds thickly bordered with blossoms?
> Surely its domes, as they rear above its horizon,
> Are stars shining in the house of Aquarius?

Far more about Hammadid palatial architecture can be deduced from the vast congeries of disparate structures which go to make up the principal royal residence sited suitably enough at the centre of the city, the Qasr al-Mulk or 7.179 Qasr al-Bahr ('Lake Palace'). The reason for the latter name is the substantial artificial lake, measuring some 45 m. by 64 m., to the east of the palace proper; it was used for naval tournaments. A similar feature graced the contemporary Hammadid palace at Bougie, and the earlier 7.186 Aghlabid palace at Raqqada near Qairawan. As with the much later Mongol palace at Takht-i 7.128 Sulaiman in Iran, it was no easy task to incorporate this broad expanse of water into a rational overall design, and indeed no attempt was made to dovetail the sprawling asymmetrical houses, store-rooms, cisterns, gardens and open spaces – which make up most of the surface area of the palace – with the relatively organised spatial units at the southern extremity of the site. These unfold in orderly sequence. A monumental domed portal, boldly salient from a mobile multi-niched façade, announced the principal axis, an axis immediately denied by a series of transversal halls and dog-leg passages which eventually debouched on to the lake itself, whose encircling arcades invite a comparison with the courtyard standard in Islamic palatial architecture. To the west the view was closed by three domed chambers, the largest centrally placed and leading, again by a bent

entrance (as at Ashir), to a smaller inner court- 7.172 yard with a *hammam* in one corner.

To the north of this complex lay another, presumably royal, palace with transverse vestibule, courtyard and salient domed complex, the whole flanked by lateral tracts of chambers – a disposition immediately recalling Mshatta. 7.11 This is in no sense an isolated instance of Umayyad influence on Maghribi architecture, a theme already explored in the context of Ashir and one which resurfaces at the 10th-century Fatimid *qasr* of Ajdabiya in Libya. It would 7.190 repay thorough study. A related intrusion of eastern influences into Maghribi palaces is provided by the constructions of the Aghlabid monarch al-Mansur, who like his 'Abbasid namesake built a round city with four gates: Sabra/al-Mansuriya in the suburbs of Qairawan, 7.68 erected *c.* 335/947. The excavations there have yielded a palace whose walls were decorated with glazed tilework; one part of it comprised a wide vestibule, courtyard and deep *iwan*, with 7.184 two adjoining rooms, a somewhat prosaic corrective to the enthusiasm of the literary sources describing palaces which bore such evocative names as the Camphor Room, the Myrtle

7.188 Palermo, Ziza palace

Chamber, the Jewel of the Diadem and the Silver Stone; but two others known as the Iwan and Khawarnaq are redolent of pre-Islamic associations from the Sasanian east. Excavations and aerial photographs of Sabra/al-Mansuriya have brought to light a huge circular enclosure containing round and rectangular basins. Clearly, vast sheets of expensively created water were an important factor in defining the princely life-style followed here and evoked by the early Fatimid court poet 'Ali b. Muhammad al-Iyadi, whose description of a palace is worth quoting *in extenso* in Jonathan Bloom's translation:

> Now that glory has become great and the great one rules over the stars, a porticoed pavilion spreads.
>
> He built a dome for the dominion in the midst of a garden which is a delight to the eye.
>
> In well-laid-out squares, whose courtyards are green, whose birds are eloquent.
>
> Surrounding an enormous palace among palaces, as if you could see the very sea gushing in its corners.
>
> It has a pool for water filling its vast space across which eyes race and flit.
>
> The rivulets which gush into it lie like polished swords on the ground.
>
> In the midst of its waters an audience hall stands like Khawarnaq amidst the Euphrates' flood.
>
> As if the purity of its waters – and its beauty – were as smooth as glass of azure hue.
>
> If night unrolls the figure of its stars over it, you would see blacks burned by fire.
>
> And if the sun grazes it, it appears like a beautiful bejewelled sword on the diadem of al-Mu'izz.
>
> The secluded balconies around it were virgins wearing girdled gowns.
>
> The foam dissolves on the face of its waters as does the rain on parched soil.

Palaces in Sicily

The continuation of the palatial style found at Ashir and the Qal'a of the Banu Hammad may most conveniently be traced in the following century in Sicily, where the Norman kings delighted in palaces that were at least as much Islamic as Western. The major buildings are all to be found in Palermo, and should be assessed

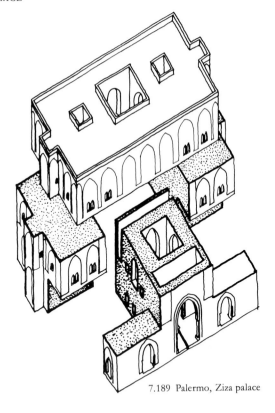

7.189 Palermo, Ziza palace

in the wider context of a huge park, now largely vanished, which gave them a suitably luxurious setting. They include the Cuba, Ziza, Cubola, Favara and the larger royal palace whose sole 7.185 remaining tower, the Torre Pisano/Torre di Santa Ninfa, complete with *muqarnas* work and superposed vaulted rooms enclosed by corridors, bears a striking resemblance to the Manar tower 7.176–7.177 at the Qal'a of the Banu Hammad. The Cubola is a delightful open-plan, domed pavilion, probably erected to cover a fountain, in the gardens of the Cuba; of the Favara only a ruined 7.185 wall with blind arcades survives. Thus interest centres on the Cuba and the Ziza. Both are lofty, compact, oblong buildings with forbidding cliff-like façades; a distinctly military air is conferred on them by lateral towers and by later battlements. At the Cuba (dated 576/1180 by an 7.182–7.183 Arabic inscription in the name of William II) there are also matching salients at the centre of the front and rear façades, exactly as at the two major palaces at the Qal'a of the Banu Hammad, 7.173, 7.179 an analogy strengthened by the consistent emphasis on serried blind arches of varied dimensions as a means of articulation, and by the side rooms which flank the domed central hall. This, with its three fountains along the northwest/south-east axis, mosaics and *muqarnas* work, provided a *mise-en-scène* of fitting luxury for official receptions. The Ziza palace (from *al-'aziza*, 'the splendid') was completed in 576/ 1180. Though only slightly larger than the Cuba (32 m. by 23 m. as against 30 m. by 18 m.) it displays very much more spatial complexity in its interior arrangements, with a cramped mezzanine floor on the wings serving to highlight the more ample disposition of the central chambers on the ground floor and the first floor. An oblong vestibule of the type familiar from Zirid and Hammadid palaces leads to a great central archway so deep as to serve as an *iwan*; this towers to the full height of the mezzanine floor. Its ornament in mosaic and in *muqarnas* canopies on all three sides matches this bold architectural statement. This central hall with its multiple niches is separated by a double lateral corridor from a suite of three interconnecting rooms which take up the full length of each short side; these dispositions again have North African origins. The mosaics, with roundel designs of affronted archers and peacocks on either side of a date palm, seem to mirror in a more durable medium the textiles which might once have graced the walls of these Norman palaces. The topmost floor echoes the spatial and decorative arrangement of the ground-floor centrepiece, but on a reduced scale. Water played a key rôle in this palace, for a hidden conduit brought a stream which flowed over a patterned ramp at the back of the main *iwan* to form successive square pools along the central axis of the hall and was thence channelled into a large open reservoir right in front of the palace. This had a central island apparently garnished with a pleasure pavilion on the model of Qairawan and Raqqada.

7.187–7.189

7.172, 7.179, 7.174

7.188

Later Maghribi palaces

Nothing in later Maghribi palatial architecture rivals these Sicilian buildings. The remains of an extensive 14th-century royal villa at Tlemcen revealed luxurious fittings but the architecture itself was not excavated in sufficient detail. As for the 17th–18th century palaces in Tunis (Dar

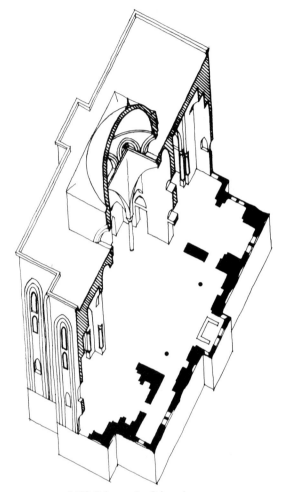

7.183 Palermo, La Cuba palace

al-Bay, Dar Hasan and the Bardo), and their equivalents in Constantine (palaces of Ahmad Bay and Bay Hajj Salah) and in Algiers (Bardo and Bakri palaces; Dar 'Aziza Bay), they are essentially an amalgam of Turkish and Andalusian features. But with their loose groupings of open patios surrounded by public rooms, their elaborate portals and vestibules, first-floor galleries and *mirador*s – and above all their decoration in marble, tile, glass, wood and stucco promiscuously assembled from various Islamic and European sources – they exude an undeniable charm.

PALACES IN SPAIN

Spain is unique in the Islamic world in that it has

preserved palaces of the first importance from both ends of the medieval historical spectrum, namely Madinat al-Zahra and the Alhambra. In addition it has two major palaces from the intervening years – the Aljaferia at Zaragoza and the Alcazar of Seville – which, while much altered under Christian rule, nevertheless retain enough of their Islamic structure and decoration to rate at least a brief mention here.

The earliest Islamic palace in Spain was probably the country villa erected by 'Abd al-Rahman I in the later 8th century two miles outside Cordoba – the administrative centre being his *dar al-imara* in the city itself – and named Munyat al-Rusafa after the favourite Syrian town of his caliphal grandfather. He stocked its garden with Syrian plants, including a palm tree to which he penned a nostalgic ode. In Cordoba itself the major palace of this period bore the name Damascus. This psychological dependence on Syria was to remain an abiding characteristic of Muslim Spain.

Madinat al-Zahra

Madinat al-Zahra was founded by the dazzlingly successful 'Abd al-Rahman III in 324/936, shortly after he had assumed the symbolic title of caliph. It may therefore be taken to express his imperial aspirations. Named after his favourite wife and sited, following the example set by his distant ancestor, a few miles from the crowded bustle of Cordoba, Madinat al-Zahra offered the closest analogy in Western Islam to the palace-city of Samarra. Its open-plan palaces, 4,313 marble columns (meticulously itemized by Ibn Idhari), fountains of gilt bronze and green marble, the latter with twelve bejewelled golden aquamaniles in the form of animals and birds, ebony doors, marble Roman Venus, spacious gardens and matchless views – for this is a steeply terraced site – were justly celebrated. Indeed, seven centuries later the Maghribi historian al-Maqqari could write that one of the four things in which Cordoba surpassed the capitals of the world was precisely Madinat al-Zahra. Nevertheless, modern excavations – even though these are still very incomplete – suggest that the Islamic sources exaggerate in stating that a court of 25,000 lived and worked here. The lie of the land was utilised to drive home social divisions: the highest terrace was reserved

for the palace and its attendant structures, a series of loosely connected units each with its own patio; the second was given over to gardens and a game preserve; and the third was taken up by the mosque and the private houses of the citizens. Ramparts divided these various levels, and within the palace level long corridors reminiscent of Samarra and presumably intended for servants and for easy communications, but also to ensure privacy, sundered the various units. No doubt the palace and the city proper grew apace in the later 10th century, since Madinat al-Zahra became the favoured residence of successive caliphs; but its glory was short-lived, for the city was thoroughly sacked in the Berber revolt of 400/1010, and work there had in any case ceased by 371/981 with the creation of a new capital, Madinat al-Zahira, under the usurper al-Mansur. Of this nothing remains, but part of another foundation of al-Mansur near Cordoba, al-'Amiriya, survives. Here, a huge arcaded courtyard, measuring at its greatest extent some 50 m. by 30 m., and an adjacent domestic unit with some two dozen rooms have been excavated.

According to the Islamic literary sources, the chief marvel of Madinat al-Zahra was the *dar al-khulafa* ('Chamber of the Caliphs') or *majlis al-dhahabi* ('Golden Reception Hall') whose ceilings and walls were partly of gold and partly of translucent or multi-coloured marble blocks. A magnificent pearl, the size of a pigeon's egg – the gift of the Byzantine emperor Leo – was suspended from the ceiling's central dome with its mosaics in silver and gold, apparently over the green marble fountain mentioned earlier, which was also of Byzantine origin. The hangings of the chamber were of gold and silver brocade; eight gold and ebony doors flanked by piers of crystal and coloured marble led into the hall on each side. In front of this hall, and at a slightly lower level, was set a domed pavilion containing a pool of quicksilver. There was much more to this choice of materials than a love of display; for nearly all the substances described were not only rare and costly but also sensitive to the play of light, so much so that when the sun's rays entered this hall they had a blinding effect. Similarly, when at the caliph's command the quicksilver pond was stirred, flashes of light shot forth until the room itself seemed to revolve around a central axis in obedience to the course of the sun. This conceit, known to the Roman and Sasanian emperors centuries before, was exploited by them by means of clockwork contraptions and not only illusionistically; it was to be attempted by means of the *muqarnas* dome in the Alhambra, as several of the poetic inscriptions there testify. The total disappearance of these splendours at Madinat al-Zahra, as elsewhere (such expensive fittings were the first targets of looters and insurgents), makes it mandatory to examine the literary evidence with particular attention, for this kind of effect was not attempted in religious architecture, where the desire for magnificence found markedly different visual expression. In just the same way, al-Khatib al-Baghdadi's account of a Byzantine embassy to the 'Abbasid caliph al-Muqtadir in 305/917, or the descriptions of Fatimid palaces and treasures given by Nasir-i Khusrau and al-Maqrizi, or the magical lighting effects of the Dhu'l-Nunid palace at Toledo recorded by al-Maqqari, flesh out the skeletal physical remains of these palaces with a wealth of unexpected and exotic detail.

It is not possible to establish beyond doubt the exact location of the storied *dar al-khulafa* or *majlis al-dhahabi* in the jumble of buildings uncovered since 1911. It seems tolerably assured, though the excavation has yet to begin. Thus for the purpose of the present account attention must focus on two units which have been very thoroughly examined and in part restored: the *majlis al-gharbi* and, directly to the south of it, the so-called *dar al-mulk*, itself also a *majlis* or reception hall. Of the former, only the piers and columns are left, but this makes the general arrangement clear: a triple-naved basilical plan with a massive central dome and a lateral communicating chamber to east and west, the whole knitted together by an open vestibule giving on to a sanded courtyard with peripheral rooms for visitors. It is an early version of an architectural type which recurs at Malaga (where the division into naves is replaced by a single oblong room, and there is only a single lateral room to the west, but the transverse vestibule fronting a courtyard remains) and in the Room of the Ambassadors in the Alcazar of Seville. The square, open-plan 11th-century pavilion in the

7.200; cf. 7.194

7.207

7.213

297 Madinat al-Zahra, Dar al-Mulk, audience hall

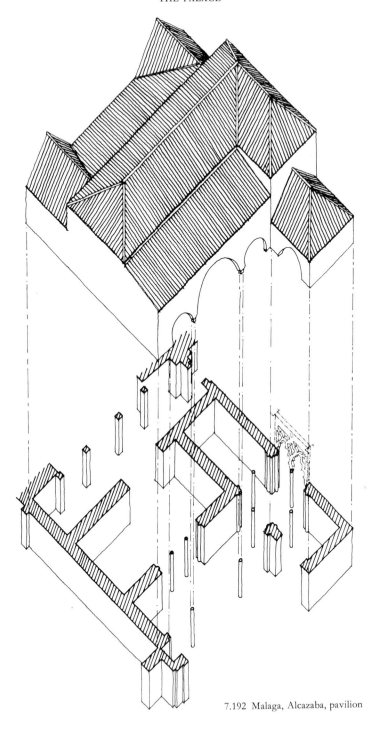

7.192 Malaga, Alcazaba, pavilion

7.191 Alcazaba of Malaga survives in much better
7.192 condition, with a pitched wooden and tiled roof
7.193 covering an elegant system of interlacing lobed
arches and carved voussoirs, both details very
much in the tradition of the Great Mosque at
Cordoba. Even so, enough survives of the *majlis
al-gharbi* to indicate that its decoration was sufficiently rich in the dense and frozen arabesque
style of the period. At the end of the central aisle
stood a throne, saluted by visitors even when
empty.

297, 7.207   Much more can be deduced from the lovingly
restored *dar al-mulk*, dated by inscriptions to
342–5/953–7. Its layout is much the same as that
of the *majlis al-gharbi*, though here the central
triple-aisled basilical unit – which was roofed
with a coffered wooden ceiling – is more definitively separated from the lateral flanking
chambers, both of which end in a second domed
room intended for guests. The main hall also
served the needs of official business; here the
council of viziers met. The arcaded vestibule
seems even more open by virtue of the contrast-
275 ing blankness of its flanking walls, a feature
7.11 familiar from Mshatta. This vestibule gives on
to an intimate courtyard furnished with a deep
pool, and the prospect is closed at the end of the
axis by a domed pavilion. The complex also
included an extensive walled terrace, *hammam*
and latrines. The principal decoration of the
majlis proper was by means of thin, carved stone
plaques, and its lavishness sufficiently explains
why the excavators dubbed this *el salon rico*. The
copious inscriptions recovered here include the
names of no less than twelve of the participating
craftsmen. A typologically related reception
7.208 hall, the *dar al-jund*, has also been excavated.

Castillejo of Murcia

Given the addiction to horticulture which
characterised the Muslims of Spain, it is not
surprising that even the palaces tucked away in
forbidding citadels should be set off by gardens.
The pavilion at Malaga already cited is one
7.206 example; another is the Castillejo of Murcia,
conventionally attributed to Ibn Mardanish and
the period 541–66/1146–71. Here the palace is
actually at the foot of the citadel, but as if to
disguise this vulnerability the exterior walls
positively bristle with square and rectangular
towers. Once inside there unfolds a suite of

spacious rooms leading to an inner rectangular
courtyard, presumably laid out as a garden since
its axial paths quarter the space, with inviting
recesses at the end of the longer arms, recesses
preceded by isolated square pavilions – a
foretaste of the Court of the Lions in the 7.205
Alhambra, but also an idea already developed in
part for the royal reception rooms at the Qal'a of
the Banu Hammad, and found slightly later at 7.179
the Ziza in Palermo. The theme of a cruciform 7.187
garden courtyard was taken up in the same
century at the Almoravid palace of Marrakesh.

Palace of Zaragoza

There remain for discussion the palaces of Zaragoza and Seville, both woefully denatured
under Christian rule. Islamic elements are more
readily recognisable in the former than in the
latter. The Aljaferia of Zaragoza takes its name
from its builder, Abu Ja'far Ahmad b. Sulaiman
(441–75/1049–83) of the Banu Hud, one of the
many minor princelings (*muluk al-tawa'if*) who
disputed the control of Muslim Spain between
themselves and thus prepared the way for the
Christian Reconquista. Ignoring for the
purposes of this analysis the modifications made
under Christian rule, the palace presents itself as
a trapezoidal and heavily fortified citadel 7.209
broadly reminiscent of an Umayyad *qasr*, though
the modest single entrance tucked away in the 7.196
north-east corner is atypical. The interior is
divided into three long strips, of which the 7.210
central one, significantly the most symmetrical,
contains the royal apartments. These are 7.211
grouped at either end of the long courtyard,
which is bisected by a water-channel feeding a
pool in front of each set of apartments. This
latter detail is Andalusian, but the rest of the
arrangement cannot fail to recall the tradition
inaugurated by Mshatta. Both suites are trans- 7.11
versally grouped; the major ensemble is to the
north, where projecting wings enclose three
sides of the pool. Immediately behind that pool
lies a transverse vestibule which gives on to the
throne-room by a central triple arcade, reminiscent of the *dar al-mulk* at Madinat al-Zahra. An 7.207
octagonal two-storied oratory occupies the 7.212
eastern nook of the northern vestibule.

So far as the layout of this palace is concerned,
there is little to lift it above the ruck of the many
other Spanish and Maghribi palaces which

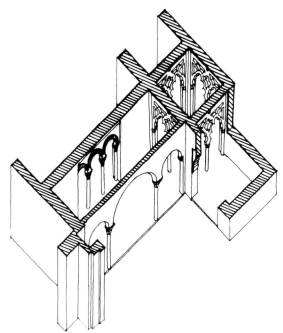

7.193 Malaga, Alcazaba, pavilion

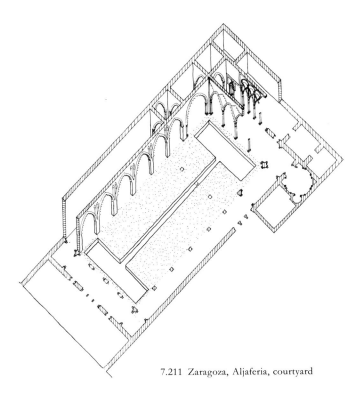

7.211 Zaragoza, Aljaferia, courtyard

447

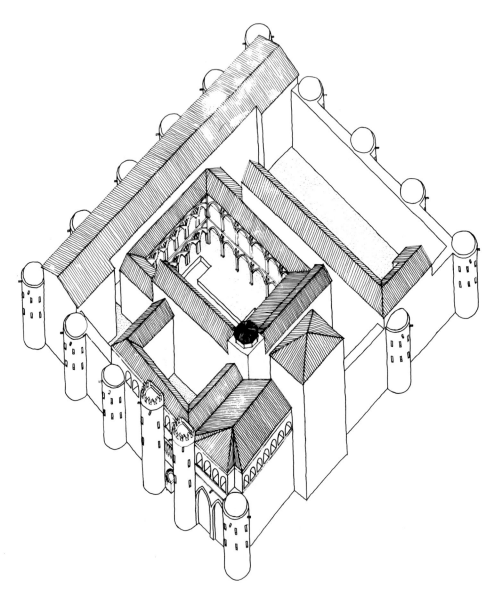

7.210 Zaragoza, Aljaferia

7.212 Zaragoza, Aljaferia, mosque

derive more or less directly from Umayyad Syria. The special glamour of the Aljaferia resides rather in its spectacular rococo decoration, which constitutes a *ne plus ultra* in the metamorphosis of architecture into decoration, of vegetal into abstract ornament, and of the lobed arch into a quasi-vegetal form. Thus a similar way of seeing can be recognised in architecture and applied ornament alike. The architectural mode selected is quintessentially Andalusian: the system of multiple interlaced arches, a motif complex enough in all conscience when employed with arches of horseshoe profile, but when – as here – it is used in conjunction with wide-spanned lambrequin arches, the effect is one of overwhelming richness, which only the most severe discipline can rescue from confusion. These complexities, already announced in the long arcades of the courtyard, take on a new intensity in the north portico and

the hall behind, and – as is entirely fitting – reach a crescendo in the oratory, whose diminutive size is thus illusionistically expanded. The densely drilled carving adds its own sense of riotous organic growth to this spectacular *trompe l'oeil*. In the arcades of the south portico, too, the theme of the lambrequin arch as a sculptural motif threatens to break the confines of the arch frame. There was no further to go along this road.

The Alcazar of Seville

The earliest part of the Alcazar of Seville dates from the 12th century and is the only section of this otherwise Mudejar building that comes within the purview of this chapter. It is the so-called courtyard of Yeso at the centre of the palace, and its sunken pool and low hedges give it a peaceful, intimate atmosphere. Each of the short sides of the rectangular courtyard is domi-

298 Granada, Alhambra, Court of the Lions

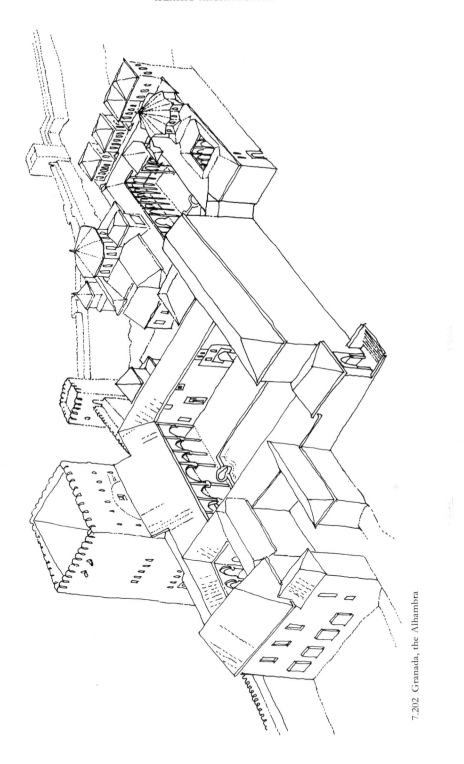

7.202 Granada, the Alhambra

nated by a huge central arch of lambrequin profile, whose low springing is carried on massive stumpy piers. This is the authentic idiom of the *sahn* of the Seville *jami'*, itself also of Almohad date: the epitome of muscular strength. Yet the three lesser arches on either side of this cavernous opening are so slender as to seem inadequate to bear the apparently continuous wall surface above them, even though on closer inspection this proves to be latticed with an openwork lozenge screen. Similar contrasts enliven the nearby and closely contemporary Giralda minaret. Whether the rest of the Alcazar, which dates largely from the rebuilding begun under Pedro the Cruel in 765/1364 and continued by later monarchs, perpetuates the spirit of the lost Almohad palace is open to question. A tolerably reliable impression of a large-scale royal Muslim residence in later medieval Spain can be gained only from the Alhambra, and even there the evidence can be challenged on many points.

96, 3.50

The Alhambra

7.201–7.202 The Alhambra, the most fully preserved medieval Islamic palace to survive and the undisputed masterpiece of western Islamic art, is situated on a high plateau – the Sabika – measuring 740 m. by 220 m. (an area of thirty-five acres) and located outside the city of Granada in southeastern Spain. The setting is typical of Islamic citadels, though its verdant location against the backdrop of the Sierra Nevada is exceptionally beautiful: Moorish poets called the Alhambra 'a pearl set in emeralds'. The name of the site is probably a corruption of *qal'at al-hamra'* – 'the red castle' – from the colour of the multi-towered enclosing wall.

The earliest Islamic structure on this natural citadel was the 9th-century Alcazaba, which itself overlay Iberian and Roman remains, and was originally girdled by a wall with twenty-four towers. This lone fort was enlarged in the mid-11th century by the palace of Jehoseph bar Najralla, the Jewish vizier of the then ruler of Granada, a palace now lost but minutely described in contemporary panegyric poetry (notably by the Jewish bard Ibn Gabirol), which emphasises the Solomonic associations of its architecture. These associations were deliberately heightened and exploited in subsequent buildings.

The Alhambra is in fact a palimpsest of successive royal residences. In its final form it could be described as a Moorish acropolis, or as a self-contained royal city which functioned as a seat of government, like Madinat al-Zahra or the Almohad *qasaba* of Marrakesh. But it is equally an array of villas set amidst gardens and parks, many of them stocked with animals – in short, a vast *paradeisos*. As such, it fits into a late antique tradition widespread throughout the Mediterranean world, in which palaces were a casually composed aggregate of individual, carefully designed parts (e.g. Piazza Armerina or Hadrian's palace at Tivoli). The Topkapi Saray in Istanbul, the earlier Saray at Edirne, of which only tantalising fragments were recorded before its destruction, and the 18th-century palace of Ishak Pasha at Doğubayazit, are late examples of the genre.

7.181, 7
7.224–7
7.223
7.221,

Serious work on the Alhambra in its present form began with Muhammad I, who from 635/1238 built the aqueduct which supplies the site with water from the River Darro. The enclosing walls are largely due to his son Muhammad II, and are datable between 671/1273 and 702/1303. Later work is well documented by inscriptions. From 733/1333 Yusuf I expanded, decorated and fortified the Alhambra on an heroic scale, thereby setting the tone for its later buildings. Thus to him are due the huge Torre de las Damas, the Court of the Myrtles, and the Gate of Justice (748/1347–8), a feature with ancient associations in the Islamic world. But the principal patron was Muhummad V, who in his second reign especially (763–93/1361–91) built such masterpieces as the Court of the Lions (begun 779/1377). The years after the Christian reconquest in 897/1492 saw much refashioning of the buildings in various European styles, and even more neglect. Brand new palaces and churches were also erected. Serious restoration and conservation of the Islamic structures, however, has continued virtually unabated since 1828.

The Alhambra has a triple layout, which from west to east comprises citadel, palace complex and residential annexe. The Alcazaba is a fortified keep independent on the rest of the site, with its own gateway opening on to the exterior world. The annexe, known as the Alhambra Alta or 'Upper Alhambra', is largely destroyed but traces of important towers, gateways and of another citadel remain. The rambling core of the Alhambra is its group of palaces, which themselves follow a tripartite layout. The first element clusters around the Mexuar (*mashwar*), a public reception hall or tribunal, and comprises *inter alia* guardrooms or barracks, stables and an oratory. The second, the *diwan*, features accommodation for court officials arranged around a great court of honour, the Court of the Myrtles, which in turn leads to a vast audience chamber (the Hall of the Ambassadors) enclosed in a bastion. The third component is the *harim*, whose focus is the Court of the Lions and which comprises the private domestic quarters of the Sultan himself, complete with two large chambers – the Hall of the Two Sisters and that of the Abencerrajes – smaller rooms, a modest oratory and gardens, notably the Partal. The relationship between these two great courts recalls that of the public *atrium* and the private *tablinum* in Roman houses. The *harim* in turn led to the royal funerary precinct (*rauda*), and to the Great Mosque. A similar tripartite disposition occurs in palaces in Tunisia and Morocco (e.g. the Badi' palace in Marrakesh [986–1002/1578–94]) and in the Alcazar of Seville (decorated in 765/1364 by artists from Granada at the behest of King Pedro the Cruel), while the size of the *harim* quarters in the royal palace at Fez, as recorded in 1031/1622, suggests that the entire complex yielded little in scale to the Alhambra.

Despite its tripartite layout, the Alhambra carefully avoids symmetry. Instead, it exploits contrasts of closed and open, occupied and empty spaces, light and darkness, private and public functions, massive towers and insubstantial colonnades. Unexpected views abound, often opening from belvederes placed to catch the breeze, and the perspectives change constantly. Its keynote is surprise. Even the two big courtyards which form the hub of the whole design are set at right angles to each other. The buildings which cluster around them seem the result of organic growth, not planning. Bent entrances are a standard feature. The discrete, additive nature of the buildings, their continually changing axes and the rectangular form which transcends their varieties of shape and ornament all mean that the eye is invited to wander freely, but within well-defined boundaries. Despite its spectacular views, the Alhambra is an essentially inward-looking creation, emphasising seclusion and privacy. Seen as a whole, it is a labyrinth; but its constituent parts are coherent and well-ordered.

Space permits only a brief discussion of the major buildings. The Court of the Myrtles takes its name from the low hedges flanking the central pool which dominates the marble-paved courtyard and which reflects the huge mass of the tower to the north. Thus the great size of the courtyard – 36.6 m. by 23.5 m. – is magnified illusionistically. Galleries carried on columns of alabaster and jasper embellish its long sides.

Its natural pendant is the Court of the Lions, named for its central fountain with an alabaster basin carried by twelve marble lions, which probably come from the 11th-century palace. They represent a late but self-conscious reminiscence of the 'brazen sea' carried by twelve oxen in Solomon's temple (I Kings 7.23–6) and may also have zodiacal significance. They function as aquamaniles, spouting water into a marble canal linked to watercourses in adjoining chambers. The courtyard itself (28.5 m. by 15.7 m.) is divided by two water-channels in cruciform disposition, and the four quarters thus created – perhaps a cosmological reference – were, it seems, originally planted with orange trees. An ethereal arcade of 124 slender columns of white marble, subtly placed in staccato and syncopated rhythms, carries a low gallery. Gabled porticoes with filigree ornament project from the arcade on the cardinal axes, a Moorish version of the classical four-*iwan* plan of eastern Islam. The massed volumes of the roofs offer a vigorous contrast to the fragile beauty of the court below.

299 Granada, Alhambra, Court of the Lions, north façade

7.205 Granada, the Alhambra, Court of the Lions

Several large halls functionally related to the two major courts are grouped around them. The *300* Hall of the Abencerrajes is a perfect square, lit by latticed windows and with a pendent *muqarnas* or stalactite ceiling whose cells seem to explode like comets outwards and downwards but also serve to trap and filter light. The Hall of the Ambassadors, a subtly illuminated throne-room, occupies most of the Torre de Comares (al-Qamariya) and is notable for its cedarwood ceiling, some seventy-five feet high, with inlaid work in white, blue and gold forming crowns, circles and stars to imitate the seven heavens of the Qur'an. Finally, the Hall of *7.204* the Two Sisters has arguably the finest *muqarnas* dome in the Islamic world, a technical *tour de force* comprising a lacy, insubstantial mass of over 5,000 individual cells which appear to be in continuous motion and – to judge by the poetic inscriptions in the chamber – are intended to evoke the revolving heavens. It is a theme bequeathed to Islamic architecture from Nero's *7.46,* Domus Aurea and Khusrau II's Taq-i Taqdis. *7.49*

The many poetic inscriptions in the Alhambra address the visitor directly and purport to express the thoughts of the buildings themselves: 'Nothing can match this work . . .' (the Tower of the Captives); 'Incomparable is this basin. Allah, the exalted One, desired that it should surpass everything in wonderful beauty' (Fountain of the Court of the Lions); and 'I am a garden full of beauty, clad with every ornament . . . The stars would gladly descend from their zones of light, and wish they lived in this hall instead of in heaven' (Hall of the Two Sisters). Such verses, many of them by the Grenadine poet Ibn Zamrak, are typical of the self-conscious, literary and somewhat precious flavour of the Alhambra. They extol the princely patron in language echoing with Qur'anic and cosmological resonances.

But the site, besides being a fortress and a monument to the Islamic faith – not least to its last great victory on Spanish soil, the Battle of Algeciras in 770/1369 – is a celebration of water and fertility. Water, whether in static pools or dynamic fountains and canals, is as integral to the buildings as the brick and stone of which

300 Granada, Alhambra, Hall of the Abencerrajes, *muqarnas*

301 Granada, Generalife, garden

they are constructed. It serves obvious practical and aesthetic functions, but also psychological ones, for it fosters a sense of peace and spiritual tranquillity. Indeed, the Qur'an describes paradise as 'a garden flowing with streams'. This atmosphere is best savoured in the Generalife (probably *c*.719/1319), a summer villa outside the Alhambra proper but really an extension of it, and a chance survival of the many such villas which once graced the hillsides of Cordoba and Granada. Typically, its gardens are far more extensive than its buildings – though these included baths and a whole group of palaces – and are integral to the overall conception. Along the whole length of the principal garden runs a canal flanked by a series of fountains whose quiet plashing adds the dimension of pleasurable sound to the visual opulence of the garden. Shaded parterres, clipped hedges, pavilions, reflecting pools, sunken flower-beds and a network of intersecting alleys are girdled by an enclosing wall. Together these elements create the sense of a jewelled private world removed from the pressures of daily life, a true *hortus*

conclusus and thus an image of paradise. The many pavilions, too, readily evoke the buildings of paradise described in the Qur'an. In the midst of this seclusion, remote perspectives of the distant plain and mountains may suddenly unfold. Some faint echo of such splendours, as retailed by Frankish travellers and Crusaders, might have inspired the potent Western medieval legends of the magic gardens of Klingsor and Armida.

The spatial ingenuity, airy vistas, modulations of light and sensitivity to colour which characterise the Alhambra gardens typify the architecture of the palace too. Externally, at roof level, continually varied vistas are revealed, as in the intersecting angles of the glazed tile roofs – a study in solid geometry – or in the domes of the baths with their multiple skylights in stellar shape. Evidence that the architects delighted in contrasts is legion; thus the austere exteriors give no clue to the opulence within, ponderous ceilings are miraculously borne on latticed walls, massive piers alternate with matchstick columns, and tiled dadoes give way to panels of filigree stucco in subtly changing tonal harmonies further enlivened by the play of light. It is a paradox, indeed a minor miracle, that a palace of such fragility should be the almost unique survivor of the storied tradition of medieval Muslim royal residences.

A few decorative motifs are used consistently, on many scales, and with an exquisite sensitivity to nuance. They include elaborate, stilted, round-headed arches and *muqarnas* for domes, capitals and the intrados of arches. Similarly, doorways, windows, *mirador*s and other openings are so placed as to mark the different levels of the building and to maintain its essentially human scale – for the constituents of the Alhambra are those of the typical Maghribi house writ large. *Cuerda seca* and mosaic tilework are used extensively for floors and dadoes. They employ a modest palette of white, ochre, brownish violet, green and occasionally light blue. Stucco in varied rectangular panels, much of it moulded and painted in red, blue and yellow-gold, fills the area above this, while wood is often used for the ceilings, which often display decoratively interlaced beams (*artesonados*). Other materials include carved stone (for doorways), polished marble (for columns and sometimes floors), engraved or pierced bronze plating (for doors) and stained-glass windows set in lead frames or in plaster grilles.

Apart from the scenes of hunting, courtly life and fighting painted by Christian artists in the Hall of Justice, the human figure is absent from the decorative repertoire, though it seems to have featured significantly in frescoes now lost. Instead, the standard themes of Islamic ornament are deployed in such density as to deserve the hackneyed term *horror vacui*. They comprise geometric patterns, often interlace designs on multiple levels; floral motifs, with particular emphasis on the pine-cone, the palmette and the palm leaf; and epigraphy. Here a cursive script of great plasticity is prominent. It is most often used for a single phrase set in a heraldic cartouche and repeating, in the rhythm of a chant, the talismanic motto 'There is no victor except God'. It is a peculiarly appropriate sentiment for this monument to a doomed civilisation.

In architecture and decoration alike, the Alhambra offers little that was not explicit or implicit in earlier Moorish and Maghribi art. To that extent its art is stagnant if not decadent. But in its poised and lyrical classicism, its consciously antiquarian quality with numerous Graeco-Roman reminiscences, it encapsulates the many centuries of Moorish art and brings that art to its final flowering. In that sense it is an extended elegy. Washington Irving captured this spirit intuitively in his meditations on the building, and his work ensured that to this day the Alhambra would evoke such associations in a Western mind.

TOPKAPI SARAY, ISTANBUL

It is a tribute to the tenacious grip of tradition in Islamic palatial architecture that the last great palace to be considered in this chapter, the Topkapi Saray or Seraglio in Istanbul, whose chronology straddles the later Middle Ages and the early modern period, should reflect its remote Roman and Byzantine forebears as faithfully as does the somewhat earlier Alhambra at the other extremity of the Mediterranean world. This continuity is all the more remarkable given that the Ottoman palace was only beginning to take shape at a time when the career of the Alhambra was all but over. Its history is essentially one of slow, organic growth, and this piecemeal evolution excluded any coherent overall plan. The massive scale of the enterprise, the monument's generally excellent state of preservation (despite much destruction and rebuilding over the centuries) and the ample textual documentation for the way that it functioned make it appropriate to present an unusually detailed account of the site. Though late in time, this is nevertheless the Islamic palace *par excellence*.

Within a year of the capture of Constantinople in 857/1453, Mehmed the Conqueror had completed the so-called Eski Saray ('Old Palace'), probably a conglomeration of flimsy wooden structures. Soon afterwards, however, he began work on his Yeni Saray ('New Palace'), which in approved Turkic fashion comprised summer quarters – a series of pavilions by the seashore, essentially a nomadic encampment rendered into more durable material – and a separate winter residence further up the hill. This, the core of the future Seraglio, was dubbed Topkapi ('Gun Gate') *pars pro toto* after

7.224–7.225

a minor palace of that name built by Ahmed II centuries later and burned in 1280/1863; and the name stuck. So did the concept of the palace as a succession of discrete buildings devoid of axial order.

The site was indeed peerless, and had in fact been chosen by the Byzantine emperors a millennium previously for their own palace. This peninsula, strategically located between the Golden Horn and the Sea of Marmara, perfectly answered the potentially conflicting needs of privacy and defence. Its roughly triangular shape was fortified on two sides with walls lapped by the sea itself, while its landward flank was closed off by a third massive wall. Behind

by any study focused on the ground-plan and architecture alone. This idea was not new in Islamic palatial architecture, but the absence of any one focal building is striking. Indeed, it is the consistent modesty of the individual buildings, for the most part single-storeyed, that lends the ensemble its distinctive character. This simplicity is only partially to be attributed to the need to cater for the very varied needs of the population of the 'city': ten mosques, fourteen baths, five schools, twelve libraries and so on. Buildings on the scale of the great Ottoman mosques would have been absurdly out of place. Yet there would certainly have been room for throne-rooms and audience-chambers more in

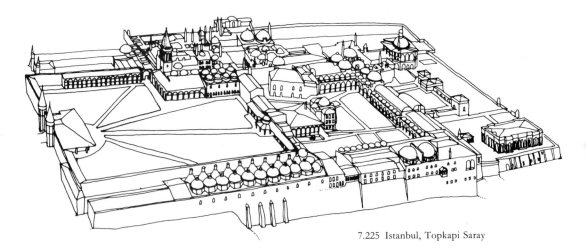

7.225 Istanbul, Topkapi Saray

that latter wall there unfolded a succession of five courtyards – not three or four, as might appear from most published plans and statements – constituting *in toto* a miniature city of some 5,000 souls accommodated in about 350 rooms. The heart of this 'city' lay in the second, third and fourth courts, in which were concentrated the working and living quarters of this huge population. Yet the sheer scale of the enterprise can be deceptive, for most of the 700,000 square metres of the palace was taken up by parks, parade grounds, tree-lined paths, gardens both practical and decorative, pools and fountains. The landscape setting – often enlivened by terracing to accommodate the steep slope of the site – was thus every whit as important as the buildings themselves, a fact obscured

keeping with earlier Islamic tradition and the power of the Ottoman sultans. Of course, splendour was not absent; but its favoured expression seems to have been less the buildings themselves than the objects which they housed, such as porcelain, silk hangings, fine manuscripts, bejewelled weapons, carpets and the like. The detailed inventories regularly drawn up at the behest of the Ottoman sultans flesh out the · starkness which characterises much of the palace today. Even so, visually speaking, the Topkapi Saray is a surprisingly low-key monument for the palace and administrative headquarters of the most powerful ruler in the 16th-century world.

This judgement is borne out by the fact that the Çinili Kiosk, which by general consent is the 7.228–7.

masterpiece among the buildings on the site, is a mere pleasure pavilion, whose location just within the outermost walls of the compound debars it from playing any significant official role. Begun in 869/1465 and finished in 877/1472, its thoroughly Persian flavour, though masked at first sight by the screen of stone columns added in 996/1588, is mirrored by the hyperbole of the Persian verses inscribed over the portal:

> This pavilion, which is as lofty as the heavens, was so constructed that its great height would seem to stretch a hand up to the Gemini themselves. Its most worthless part would adorn the most precious item in Saturn's crown. Its emerald cupola sparkles like the heavens and is honoured with inscriptions from the stars. Its floor of turquoise with its varied flowers . . . reminds one of the eternal vineyards of Paradise.

After such a fanfare, the building itself cannot fail to be an anticlimax. It has two storeys, not ten, the upper one reserved for the sultan and the lower one for his attendants. The cruciform plan with *iwan*s centrally placed on three of the four sides finds its natural analogue in the Safavid palaces of Isfahan, and thus sheds indirect light on the vanished pavilions of the Timurid age, an age evoked also in the net vaults of the interior and the tile-mosaic decoration, the last major use of this technique in the Ottoman period. Yet this building is much more than pastiche, for it turns its steep hillside location to advantage by means of an ingeniously planned basement complete with servants' quarters, kitchens and icehouse, and accessible by a double staircase, with stepped sills for access through the windows from outside. Extensive views to the parkland beyond are the reward for this resourceful response to the challenges of the site.

While it is usual to describe the Topkapi Saray as a succession of courtyards, that is only partly accurate, for the mass of structures which fills the most densely occupied part of the site lies outside, and to the north-west of, this sequence and straddles the second and third courtyards.

The first court is entered by the Imperial Gate, the Bab-i Humayun built by Mehmed the Conqueror in 883/1478. It is essentially a triumphal arch incorporated into the outermost wall of the palace. Behind it lies a dome; on either side are guard-rooms. It is the familiar formula of the Bab al-'Amma at Samarra, a fitting prologue to what follows. The huge courtyard now entered – it is some 300 metres long – was largely given over to military purposes, and was indeed known as the Court of the Janissaries. Its extensive flat and open spaces were well-suited for ceremonial parades and exercises, while the buildings along the perimeter included hospitals, barracks, a mint and armoury, stables, storerooms, and law courts. The latter theme is echoed by the 'Hangman's Fountain' (Cellat Çeşmesi) and the executioner's block, the well-named 'stone of warning' just in front of the gateway to the second court, and placed – *pour encourager les autres*? – directly in the way of bureaucrats bound on official business.

The Middle Gate, otherwise known as Bab al-Salam ('Gate of Peace'), led into the second court, which only the sultan himself could enter on horseback, a distant echo of 'Abbasid etiquette at Baghdad. Here the emphasis was squarely on administration, for on the north-west wing lay the Council Chamber (*divan*), where the viziers assembled to transact official business, watched from above by the sultan, concealed behind a balcony with a grille. Next to the *divan* was the Inner Treasury, while behind it was a high tower which served as a vantage point from which to observe what was going on in the two main courtyards. Tree-lined paths led from the gate to the three main wings of the courtyard. The south-east wing was given over to the main kitchen range, comprising ten two-domed units. It is recorded that in 940/1534 fifty cooks and hundreds of more menial servants laboured here. The north-east wing was reserved for the quarters of the Chief Eunuch and of the White Eunuchs; these served to divide the second court from the third. A continuous arcaded portico conferred a certain symmetry on this congeries of buildings. It was in front of the gateway to the third courtyard – the Bab al-Sa'adat ('Gate of Felicity') – that the janissaries were paid, and in this courtyard, too, sessions were held for petitions to be submitted and complaints heard. Thus in some sense this area could be regarded as an equivalent to the space in front of the royal tent in time of war.

The Gate of Felicity, which in its original

283

40. 7.146

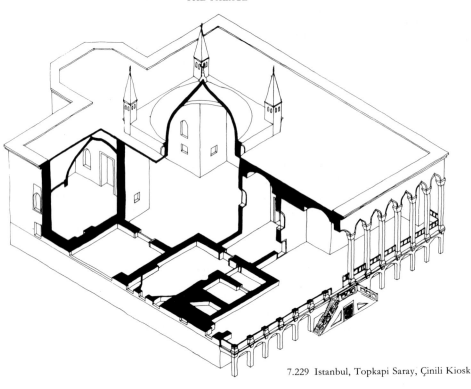

7.229 Istanbul, Topkapi Saray, Çinili Kiosk

form was probably domed, had perhaps the best claim to be the focal building of the palace, especially if it is viewed as a unit with the reception hall (Arz Odasi), also probably domed, which lay immediately behind it and dates to 993/1585. Once again, the combination has venerable associations in Islamic palatial architecture. It was at this gate that the sultan celebrated his coronation and certain religious holidays, while in the hall behind, which – significantly – *cf. 7.146* was reached by a flight of steps, foreign ambassadors were received. The domestic flavour of both structures, their relative lack of pomp and circumstance, is striking. The projecting roof of the gateway is little more than a permanent awning, an obvious translation of a tented form into permanent materials, while the exterior of the Arz Odasi is essentially a wide-eaved continuous veranda. All this is a far cry from the imperial vocabulary of *iwan*s and domes wielded by earlier Islamic autocrats. Similar ideas are encountered elsewhere in Ottoman palatial arch- *7.222* itecture, for instance in the Köprülü Yalisi at Anadolu Hisar nearby.

Behind the Arz Odasi, and isolated in the

centre of the courtyard, is the library of Ahmet III. The other three sides of the courtyard were reserved for the pages of the Privy Chamber, the Treasury, the Commissariat or Pantry and the Campaign or Expeditionary Force. These were preceded by a sequence of domed arcades of the type familiar in Ottoman mosques and *külliye*s, which lent this courtyard the same uniform appearance as its predecessor. This court, then, was essentially the preserve of the palace school, though it also had a music conservatory and a chamber which contained luxury items. Its northern corner held a pavilion housing the staff and seal of the Prophet Muhammad, relics brought by Selim I as booty from his Egyptian campaign. At the eastern corner of the courtyard is one of the oldest buildings in the Seraglio, the 'kiosk' – a name covering a multitude of building types – erected by Mehmed the Conqueror around 872/1468. This is a suite of five roughly square rooms, two of them domed, backing into the outer wall of the palace, the whole knitted together by a shallow portico and with an adjoining *hammam*. The main attraction of this rather unpromising assembly of spaces lies in the superb view over the Sea of Marmara. Similar arrangements were of course standard in the Alhambra.

To the north-west of the second and third courts, divided from them by the so-called 'Golden Road' and constituting a world apart, is the *harim*. In the late 16th century it had 44 courts and over 200 rooms, and was thus a palace within a palace. Its confused architecture – a confusion compounded by the provision of extra storeys in response to the sloping lie of the land – may well have been deliberate. It is certainly an apt visual equivalent for an obsessively closed world pullulating with intrigue. This private world was sub-divided according to a daunting range of functions, with separate suites for the Queen Mother (the Valide Sultan), the Black Eunuchs, the sultan and his ladies, and of course the slaves. Here too was the notorious Cage (*kafes*) in which the younger brothers of the sultan lived out lives of precarious luxury in the shadow of the bowstring. Pre-eminent

among the splendours of this hothouse of oppressive luxury is the bedchamber of Murad III (986/1578), a well-nigh blasphemous evocation of a mosque complete with dome on pendentives, the *Ayat al-Kursi* around the walls and a fireplace reminiscent of contemporary *mihrab*s. Next to it is the domed Throne Room Within; a new version, therefore, of the old theme of the throne room with the royal quarters adjoining it.

The atmosphere of the fourth court was much lighter. Its tone was set by an agreeable ambience of pools, fountains, gardens and kiosks with carefully engineered views over the Golden Horn, the harbour, the Sea of Marmara, the Bosphorus and beyond to the shores of Asia. The ambience here was intimate rather than official; indeed, the atmosphere was in some respects strangely prophetic of the contrived casualness of the 18th-century English landscaped garden, with its strategically placed gazebos and summer-houses. Set pieces like the

302 Istanbul, Topkapi Saray, Baghdad Kiosk

tulip garden (Lale Bahcesi) and the marble terrace (Mermer Set) struck the appropriate note of quiet luxury. Amidst this generally relaxed atmosphere, it is nevertheless significant that the two major structures – for all that they are kiosks and thus avowedly pleasure-oriented buildings – are victory monuments, erected in rapid succession to celebrate the Ottoman capture of Erivan in 1045/1635 (Revan Kiosk) and Baghdad in 1048/1638 (Baghdad Kiosk). Sited in close proximity to each other, they follow the same general layout: a domed octagon set on a high podium (perhaps rostrum would be a more appropriate word in the circumstances), and furnished with a minaret-like tower, possibly itself a reference to victory. Presumably these kiosks were intended to function as a pair. As befits the greater victory which it celebrates, the Baghdad Kiosk is much the larger of the two, and has a decidedly theatrical air with its sweeping eaves, its outer ring of twenty-two columns, its adjoining pool and

fountain and its view over the Bosphorus. Iznik tiles in profusion cover its inner and outer walls, and here too the majestic *Ayat al-Kursi* is inscribed around the inner chamber. The versatility of the kiosk form is underlined by the totally different rectangular form and lavish external arcading of the Mecidiye Kiosk and that of Mustafa Pasha. The only other major structure in this courtyard is the rhomboidal Circumcision Room (Sünnet Odasi) of 1051/1641, essentially a richly decorated interior, which is linked to the Baghdad Kiosk by an observation terrace.

The hand of man lay much more lightly on the fifth court, later turned into the Gülhane Park. Entered by the so-called Third Gate (Ücüncü Kapi) it served the court as a hunting and sports ground, but also contained extensive gardens with flowers, fruit and vegetables. And on that homely note one may fittingly close this survey of Islamic palaces: places to live in as well as to look at.

COMPOSITE CATALOGUE
OF
LINE DRAWINGS

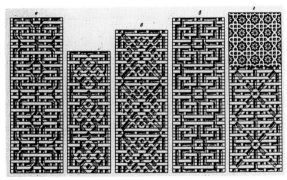

2.1

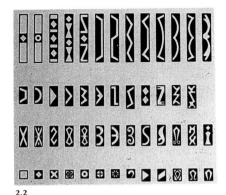

2.2

2.3

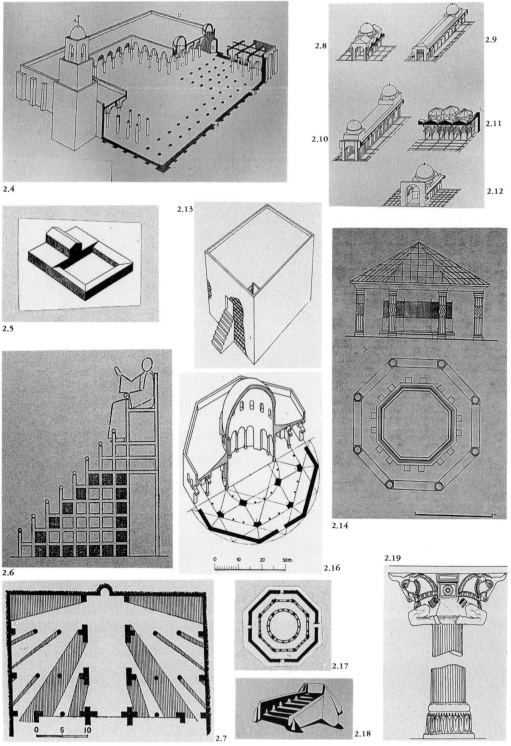

2.4

2.8

2.9

2.10

2.11

2.12

2.5

2.13

2.14

2.6

2.16

2.7

2.17

2.18

2.19

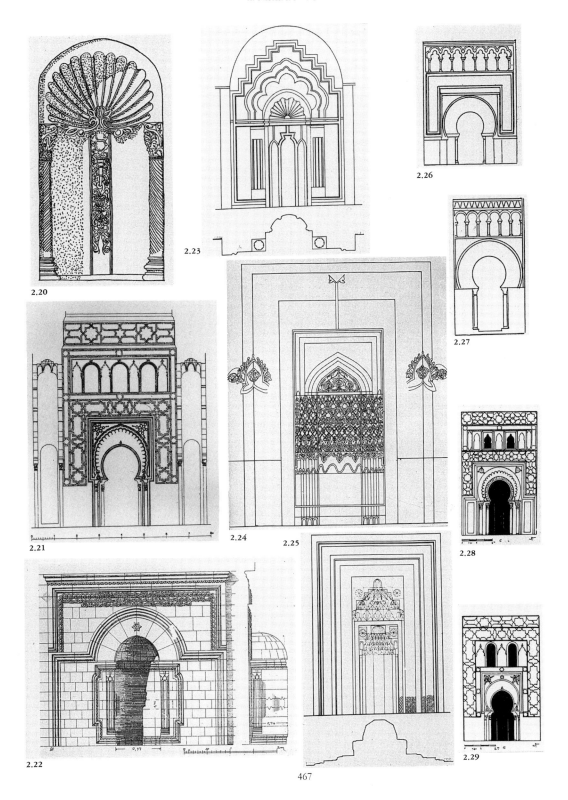

2.20

2.23

2.26

2.27

2.21

2.24

2.25

2.28

2.22

2.29

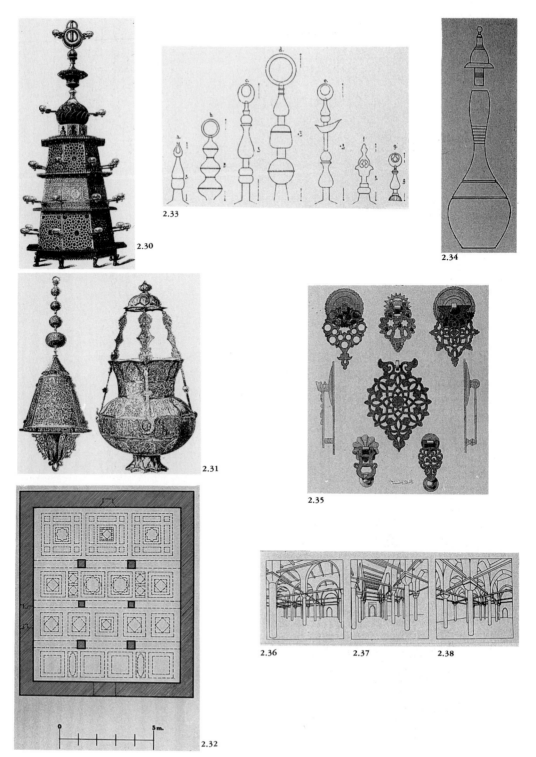

2.30

2.33

2.34

2.31

2.35

2.32

2.36   2.37   2.38

468

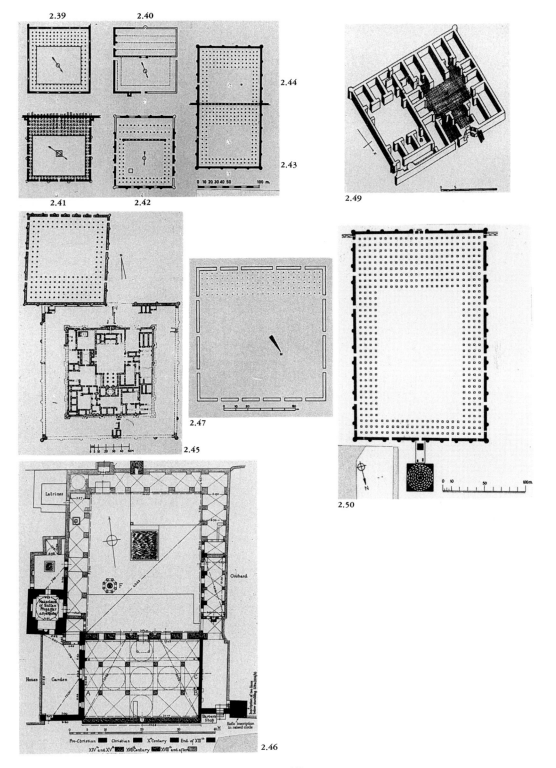

2.39

2.40

2.44

2.43

2.41

2.42

2.49

2.45

2.47

2.50

2.46

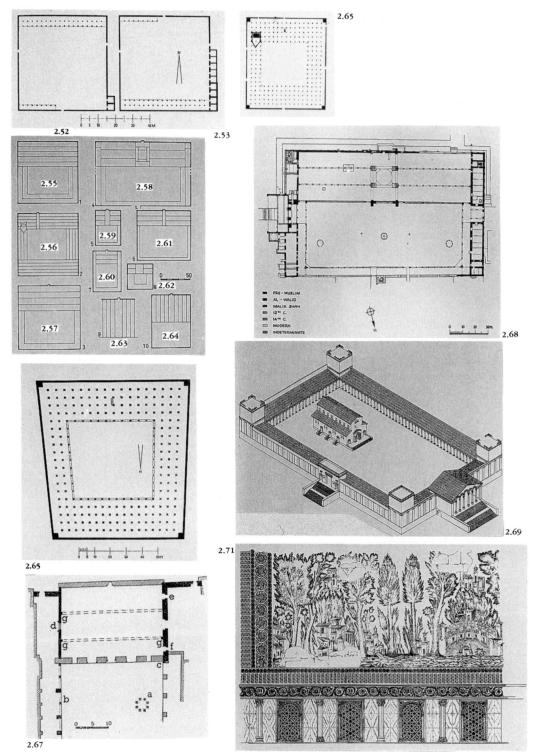

2.52

2.53

2.65

2.55

2.58

2.56

2.59

2.61

2.60

2.62

2.57

2.63

2.64

2.68

PRE - MUSLIM
AL - WALID
MALIK SHAH
12ᵀᴴ C.
14ᵀᴴ C.
MODERN
INDETERMINATE

2.69

2.65

2.67

2.71

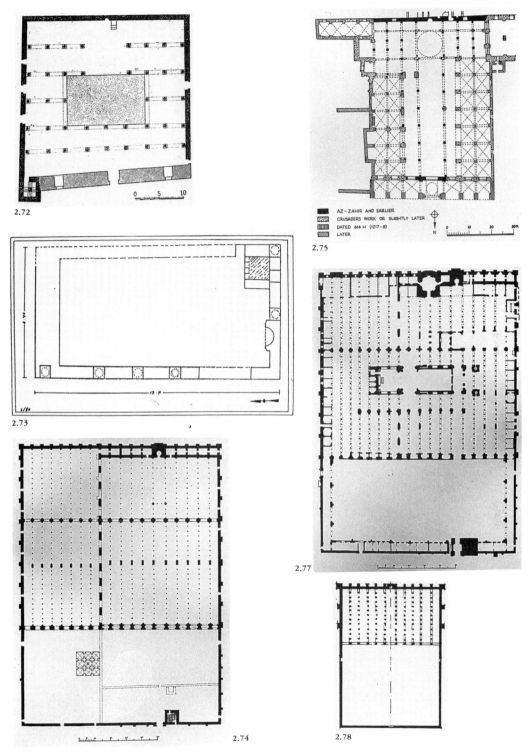

2.72

0   5   10

2.73

2.74

AZ-ZAHIR AND EARLIER.
CRUSADERS WORK OR SLIGHTLY LATER
DATED 614 H (1217-8)
LATER

N

0   10   20   30m.

2.75

2.77

2.78

471

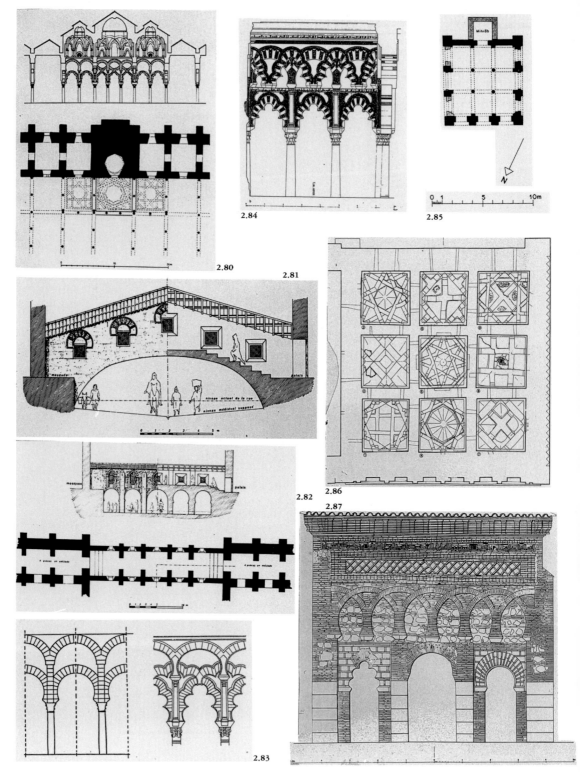

2.80

2.81

2.84

2.85

2.82

2.86

2.87

2.83

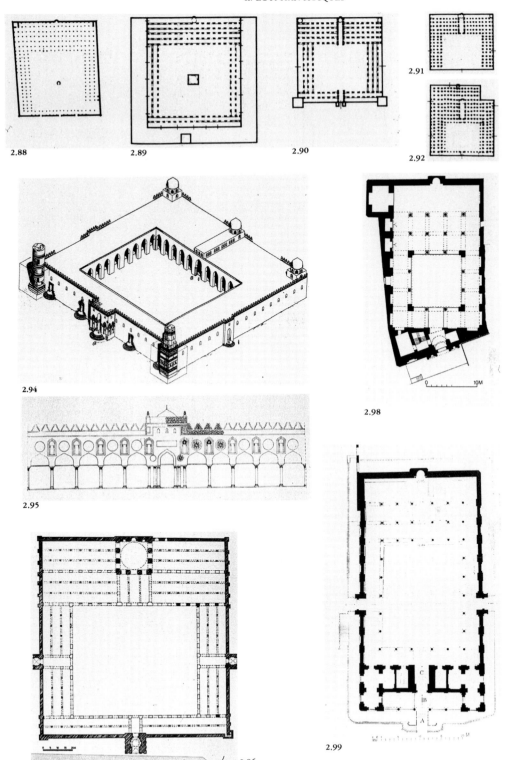

2.88

2.89

2.90

2.91

2.92

2.94

2.95

2.96

2.98

2.99

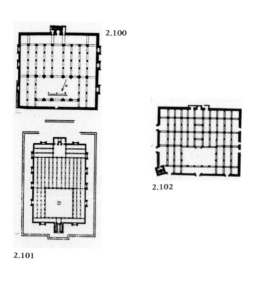

2.100

2.102

2.101

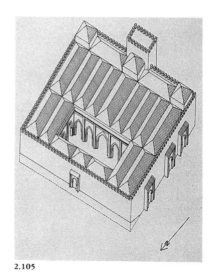

2.105

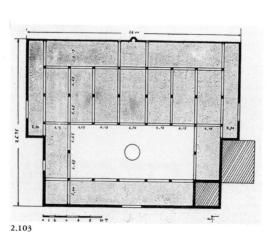

2.103

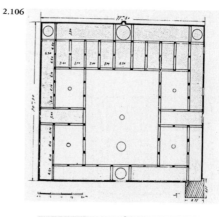

2.106

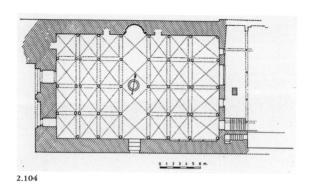

2.104

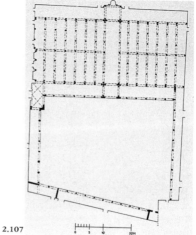

2.107

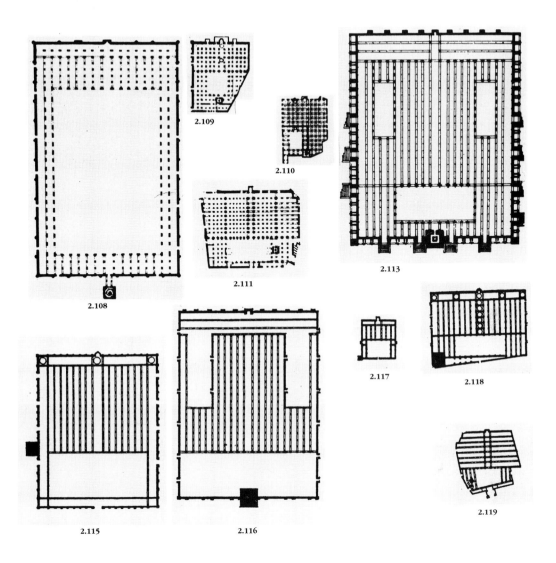

2.108

2.109

2.110

2.111

2.113

2.115

2.116

2.117

2.118

2.119

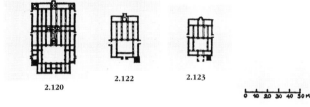

2.120

2.122

2.123

0 10 20 30 40 50 M.

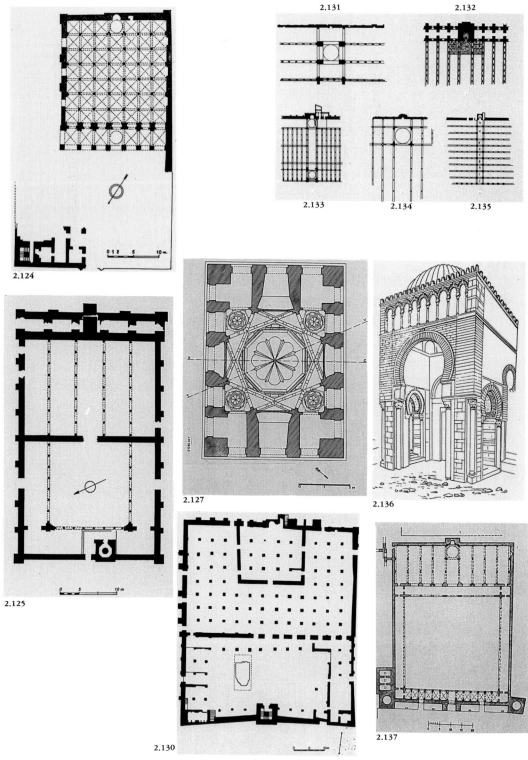

2.124

2.125

2.131

2.132

2.133

2.134

2.135

2.127

2.136

2.130

2.137

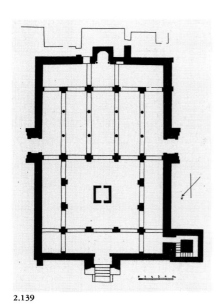

2.139

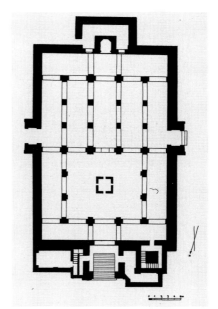

2.140

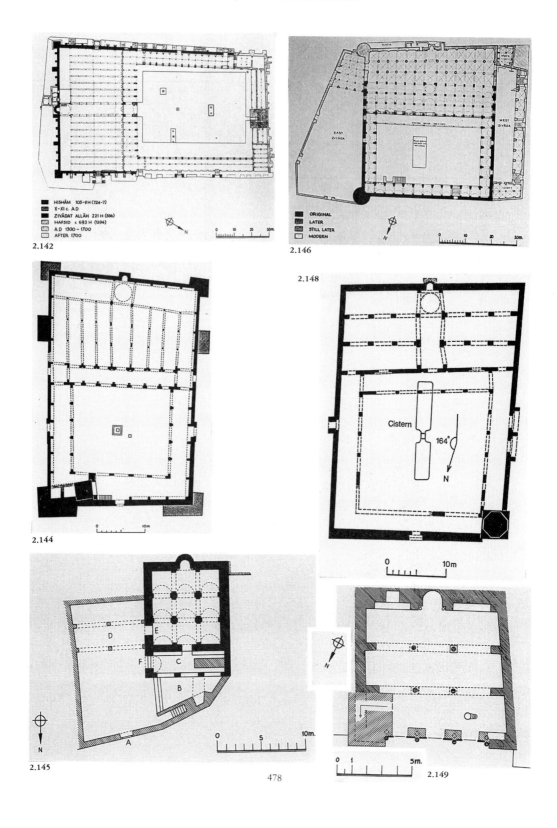

2.142

HISHĀM 105-9 H (724-7)
X-XI c. A.D.
ZIYĀDAT ALLĀH 221 H (836)
HAFSID c 693 H (1294)
A.D. 1300 - 1700
AFTER 1700

N

0   10   20   30m.

2.146

ORIGINAL
LATER
STILL LATER
MODERN

N

0   10   20   30m.

2.148

2.144

0   10m

Cistern   164°   N

0   10m

2.145

D   E
F   C
B
A

N

0   5   10m.

2.149

Cistern

0   1   5m.

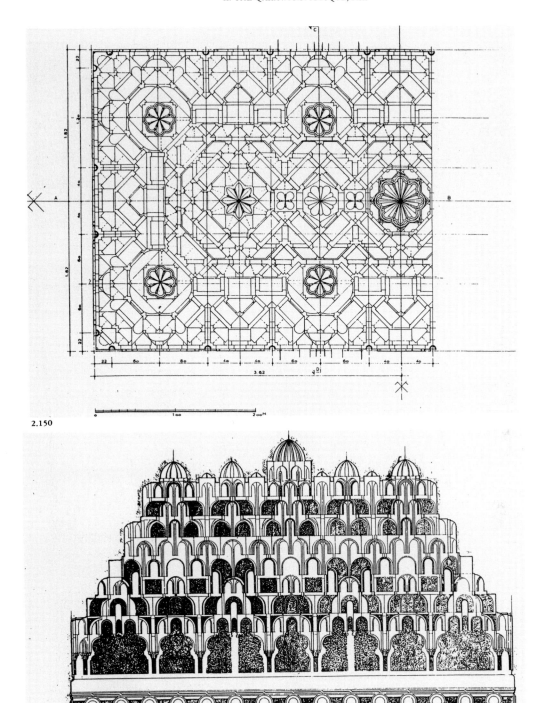

2.150

2.151

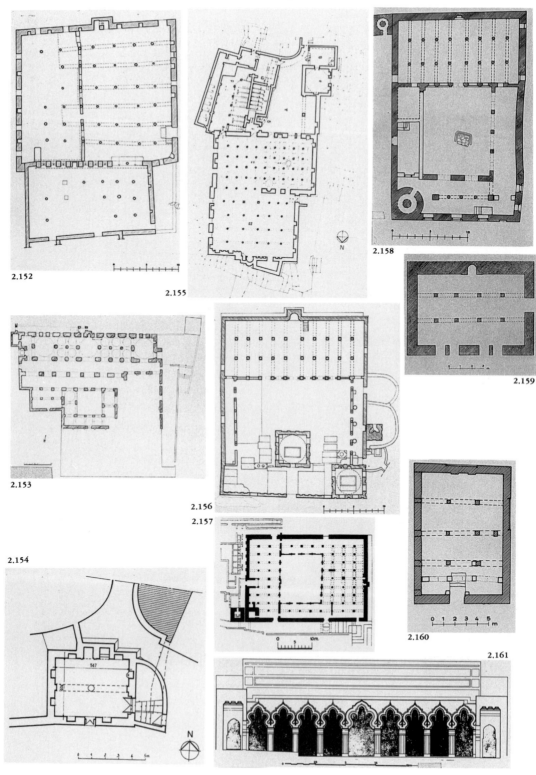

2.152

2.155

2.158

2.153

2.159

2.154

2.156
2.157

2.160

2.161

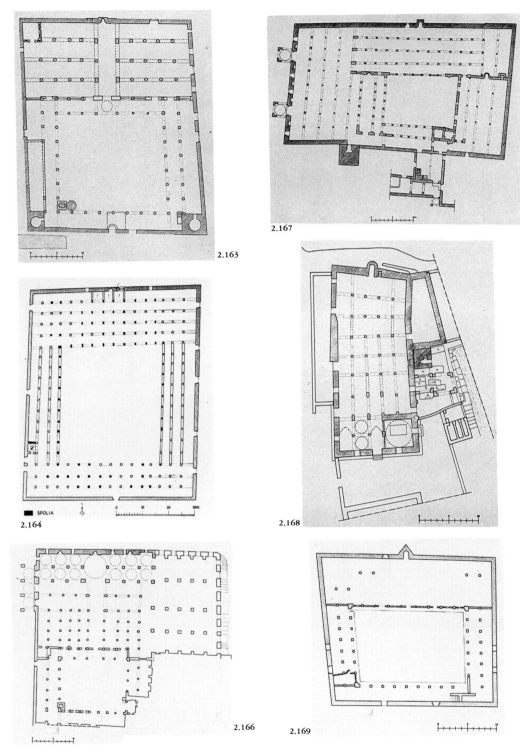

2.163

2.167

2.164

2.168

SPOLIA

2.166

2.169

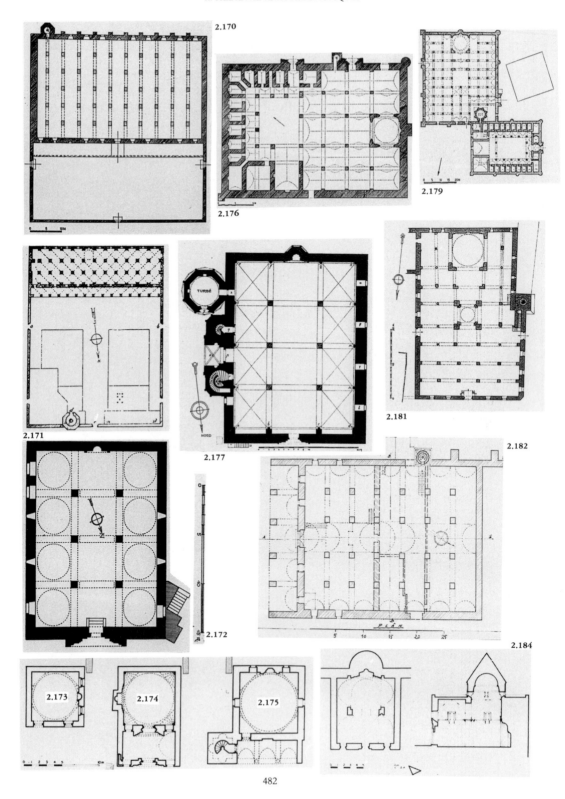

2.170

2.176

2.179

2.171

2.177

2.181

2.182

2.172

2.184

2.173

2.174

2.175

482

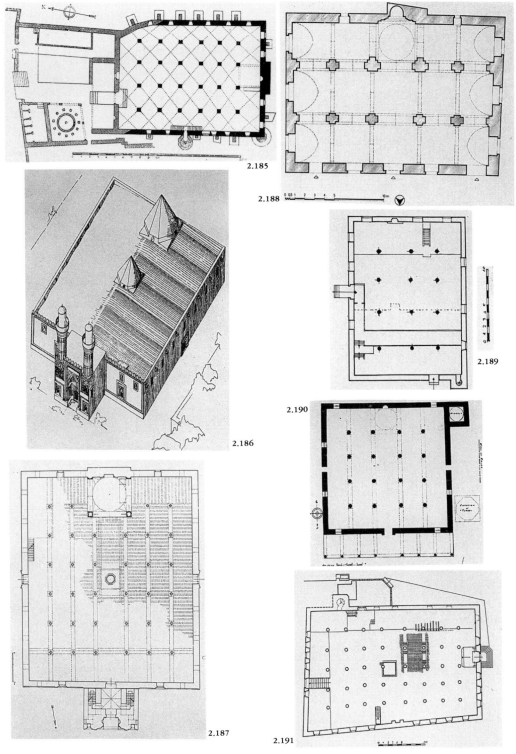

2.185

2.188

2.186

2.189

2.190

2.187

2.191

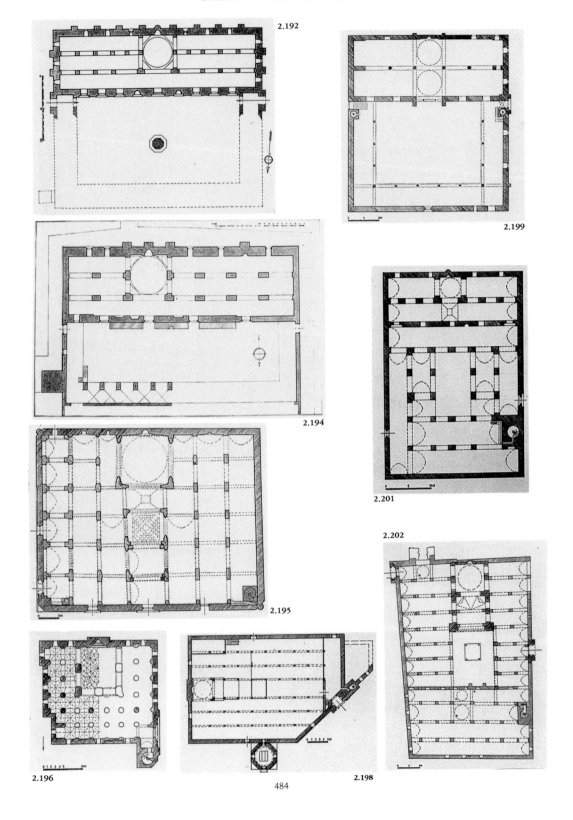

484

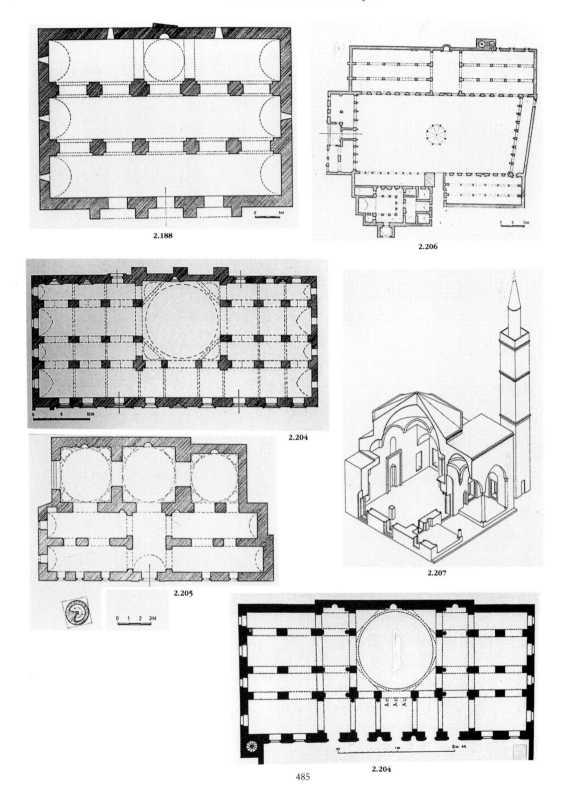

2.188

2.206

2.204

2.205

2.207

2.204

485

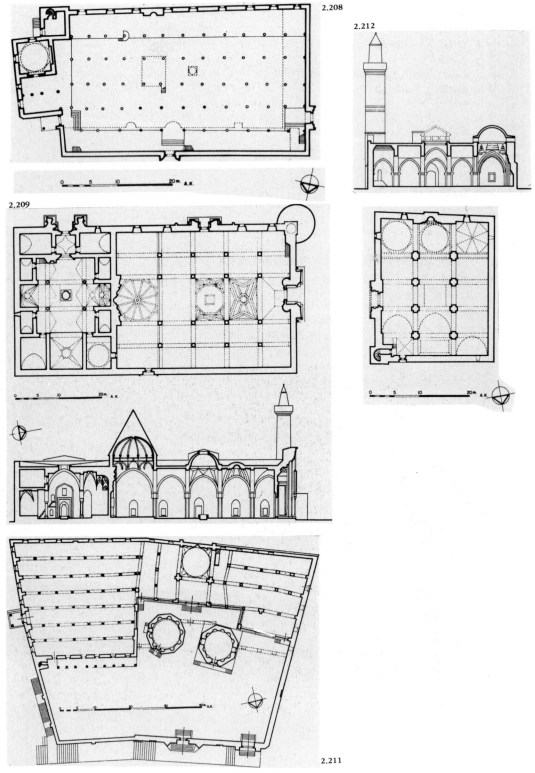

2.208

2.212

2.209

2.211

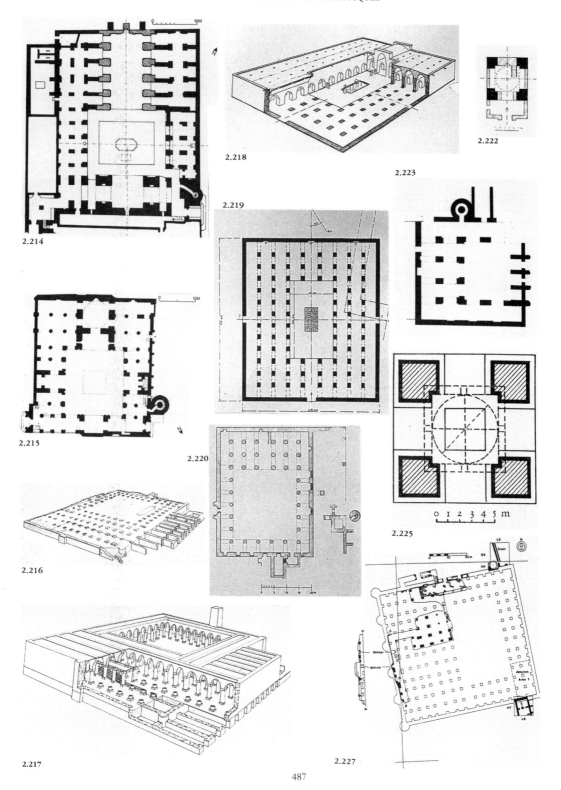

2.214

2.215

2.216

2.217

2.218

2.219

2.220

2.222

2.223

2.225

2.227

487

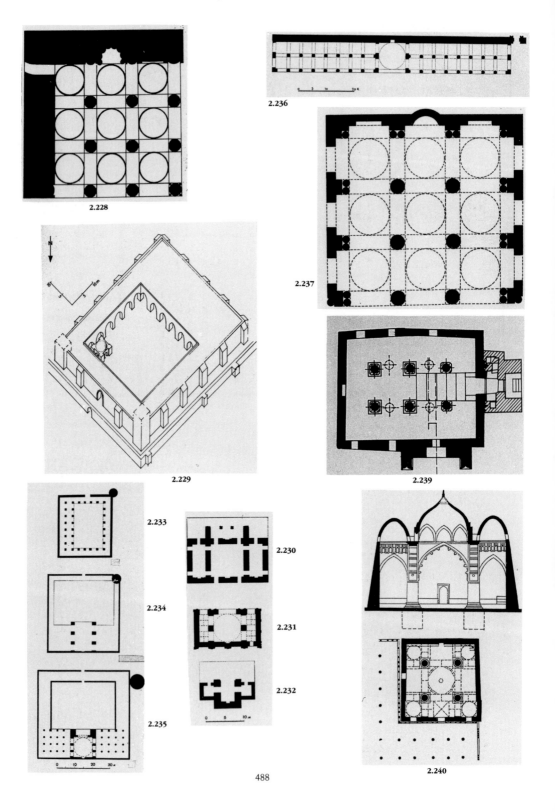

2.228

2.236

2.237

2.229

2.239

2.233

2.230

2.234

2.231

2.232

2.235

2.240

488

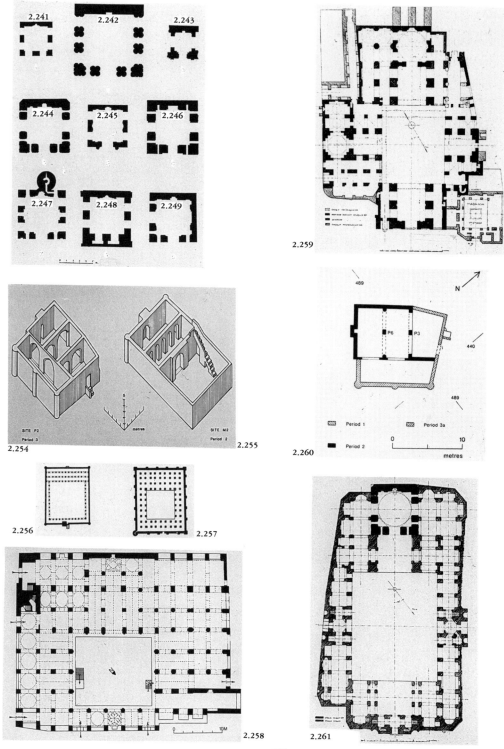

2.241
2.242
2.243
2.244
2.245
2.246
2.247
2.248
2.249

2.254
2.255

SITE P2
Period 3

SITE M2
Period 2

metres

2.256
2.257

2.258

2.259

489

N

P6
P3

440

489

Period 1
Period 2
Period 3a

0
10

metres

2.260

2.261

489

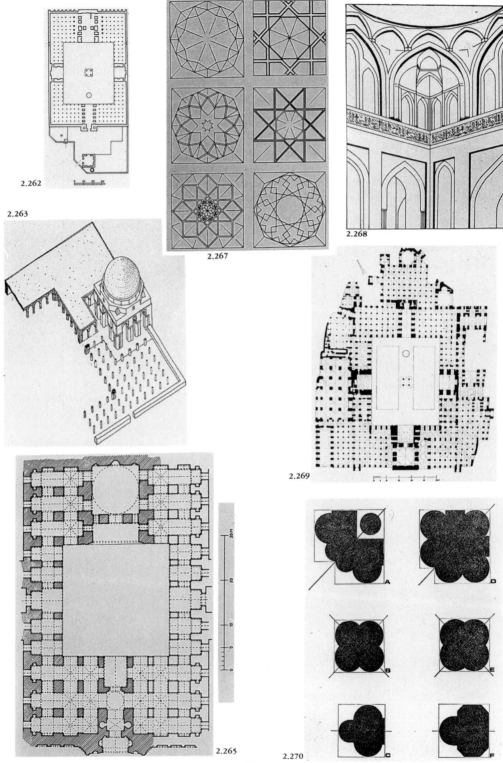

2.262

2.263

2.267

2.268

2.269

2.265

2.270

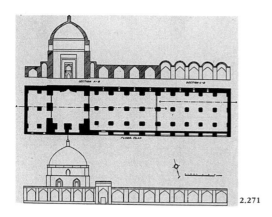

2.271

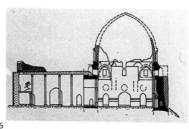

2.276

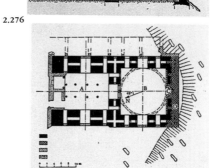

2.277

2.272

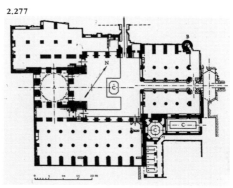

2.274

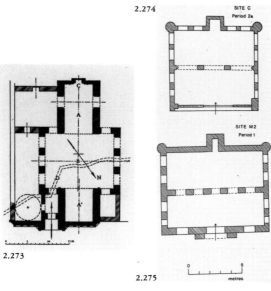

2.273

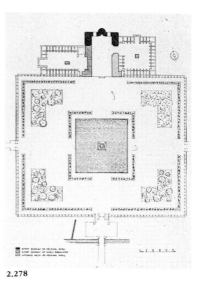

2.275

2.278

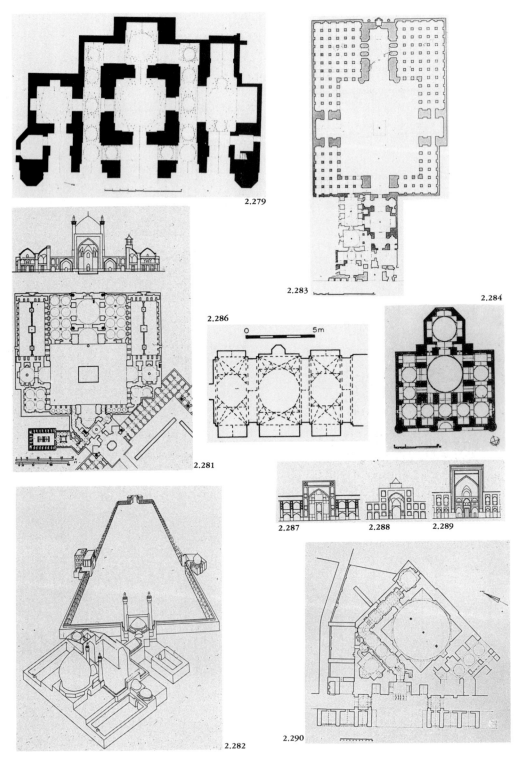

2.279

2.283

2.284

2.286

2.281

2.287   2.288   2.289

2.282

2.290

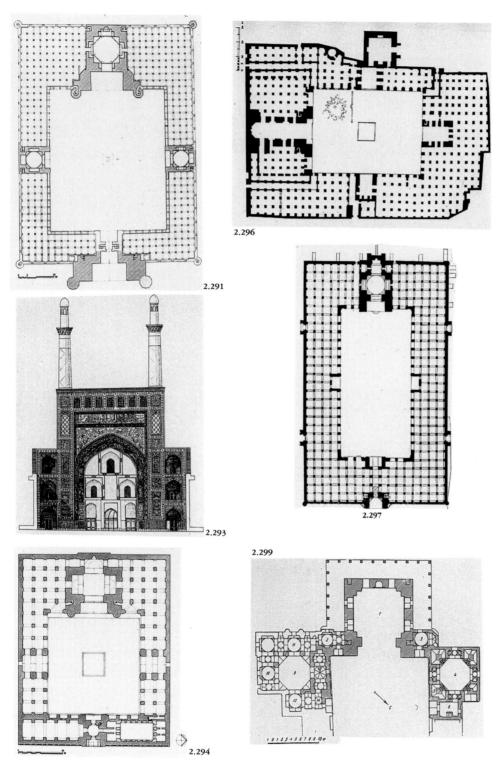

2.291

2.296

2.293

2.297

2.294

2.299

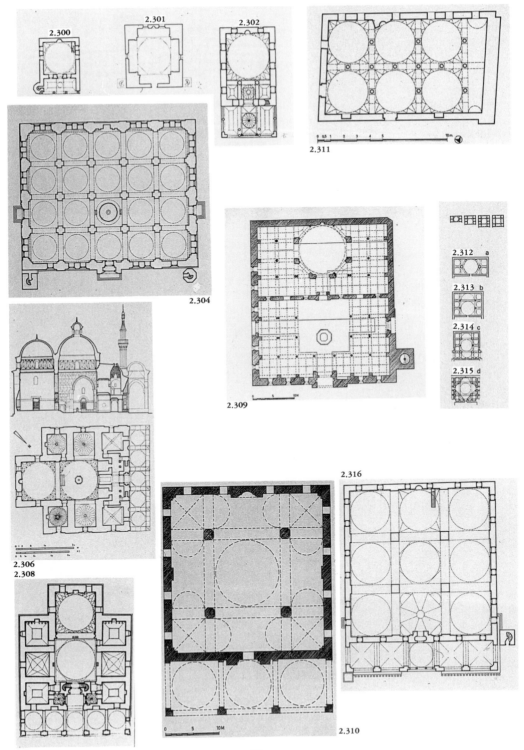

2.300

2.301

2.302

2.311

2.304

2.309

2.312 a

2.313 b

2.314 c

2.315 d

2.306
2.308

2.316

2.310

494

2.317

2.318

2.319

2.320

2.321

2.322

2.323

2.324

2.325

2.326

2.327

2.328

2.329

2.330

2.331

2.332

2.333

2.334

2.335

2.336

2.337

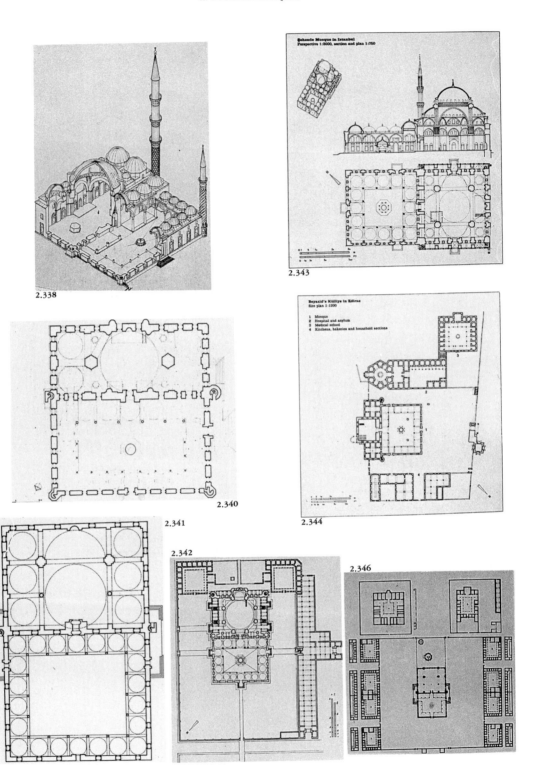

2.338

Şehzade Mosque in Istanbul
Perspective 1:2000, section and plan 1:750

2.343

Beyazid's Külliye in Edirne
Site plan 1:1200

1 Mosque
2 Hospital and asylum
3 Medical school
4 Kitchens, bakeries and household sections

2.344

2.340

2.341

2.342

2.346

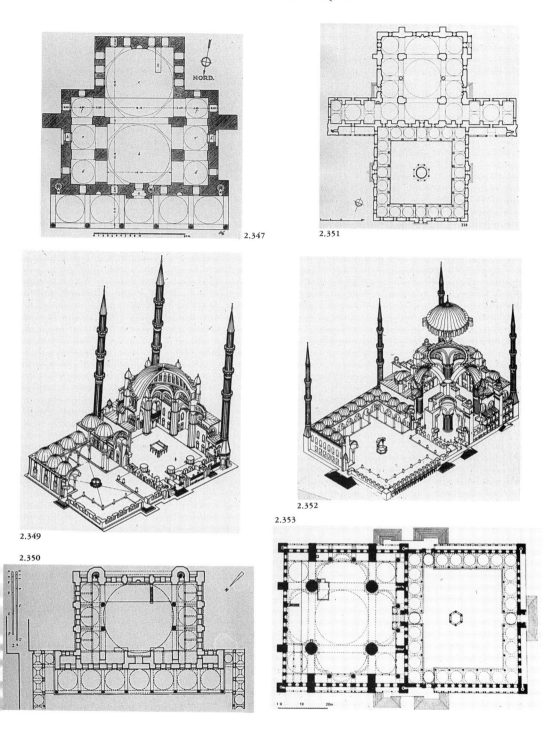

2.347

2.351

2.349

2.350

2.352

2.353

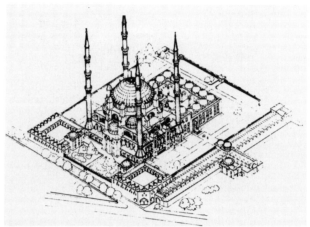

2.354

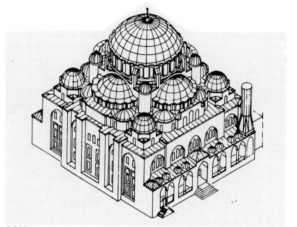

2.355

2.356

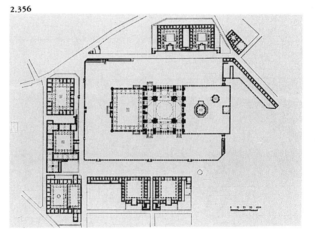

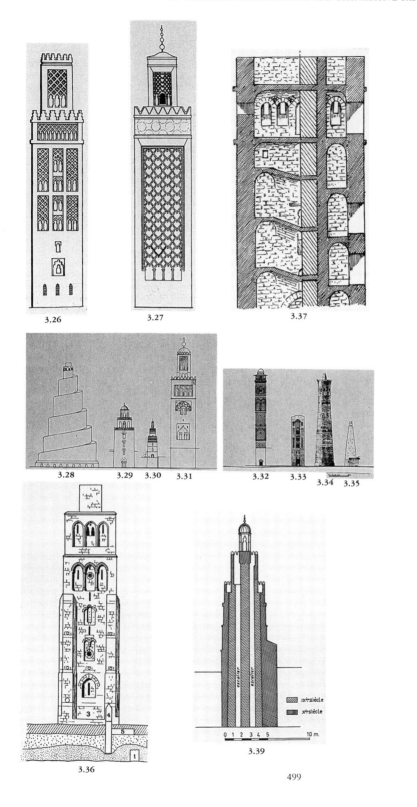

3.26   3.27   3.37

3.28   3.29   3.30   3.31   3.32   3.33   3.34   3.35

3.36   3.39

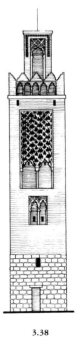

3.38

3.40

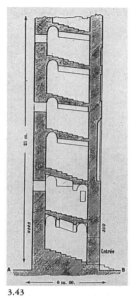

3.43

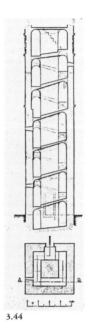

3.44

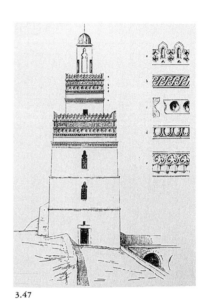

3.47

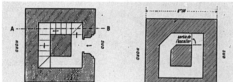

3.41

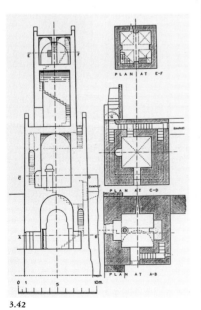

3.42

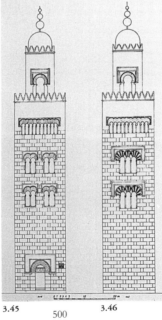

3.45

3.46

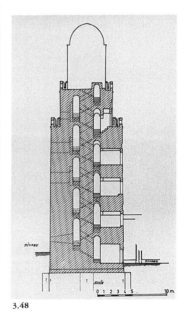

3.48

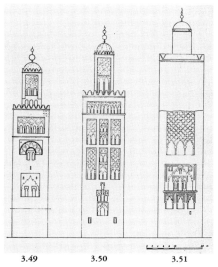

3.49   3.50   3.51

3.56

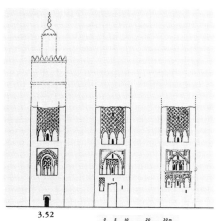

3.52

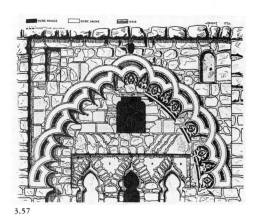

3.57

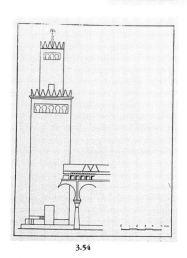

3.54

3.58

501

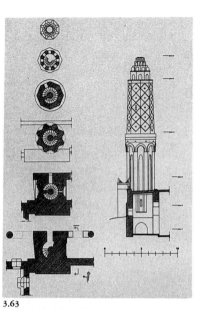

3.63

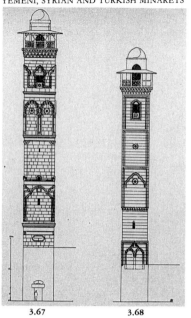

3.67   3.68

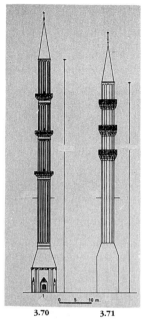

3.70   3.71

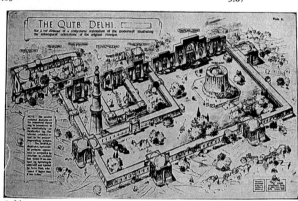

3.64

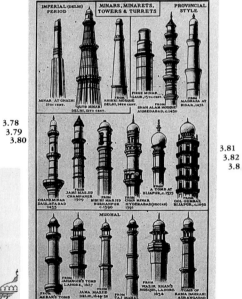

3.72 3.73 3.74 3.75 3.76 3.77

3.78
3.79
3.80

3.81
3.82
3.8

3.84 3.85 3.86 3.87 3.88 3.89

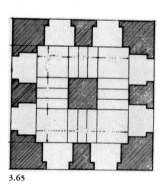

3.65

3.66   3.69

502

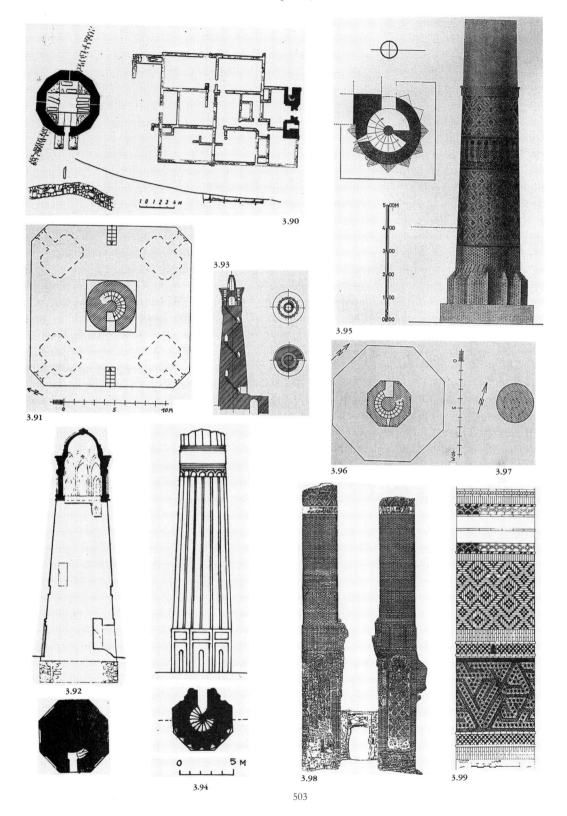

3.90

3.91

3.93

3.95

3.96

3.97

3.92

3.94

3.98

3.99

3.102

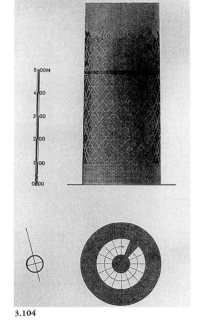

3.104

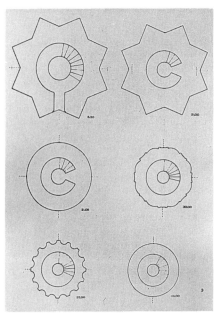

3.103

504

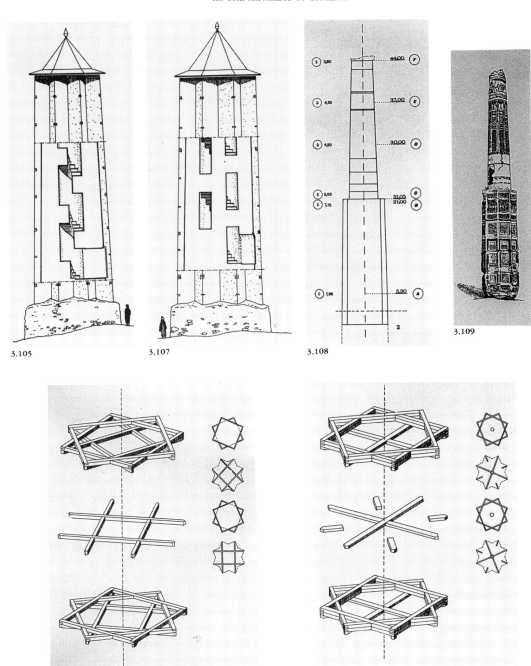

3.105

3.107

3.108

3.109

3.106

3.110

3.112

3.115

3.119

3.121

3.113

3.116 3.117 3.118

3.120

3.122

3.123

3.114

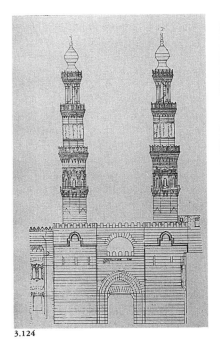

3.124

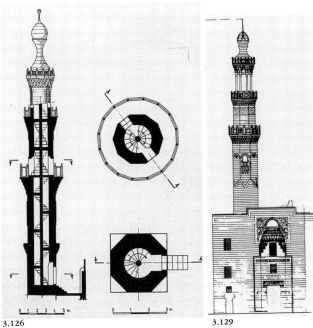

3.126

3.129

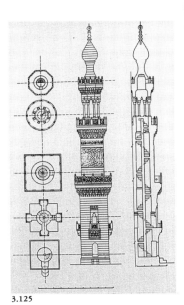

3.125

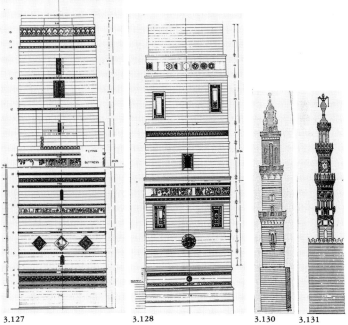

3.127

3.128

3.130

3.131

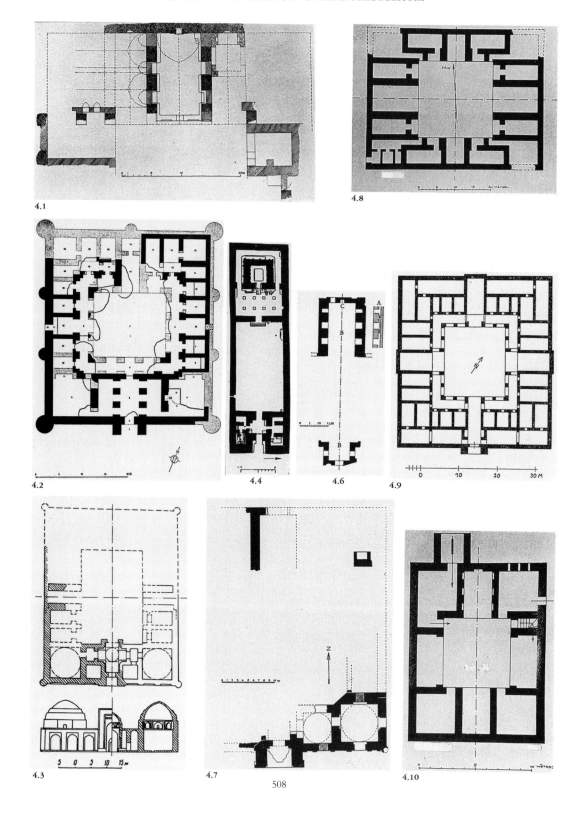

4.1

4.8

4.2

4.4

4.6

4.9

4.3

4.7

4.10

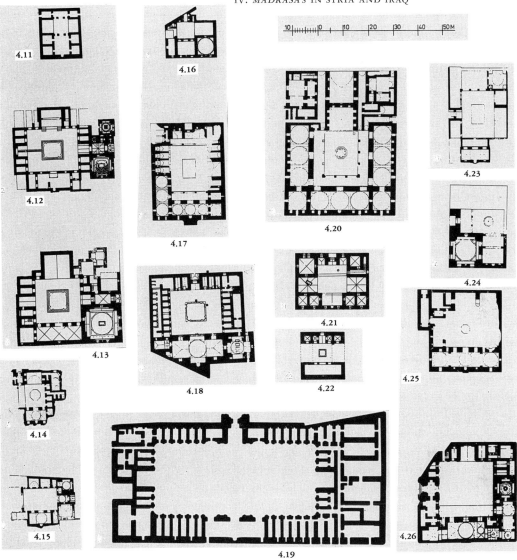

4.11

4.16

4.12

4.17

4.20

4.23

4.24

4.13

4.18

4.21

4.22

4.25

4.14

4.15

4.19

4.26

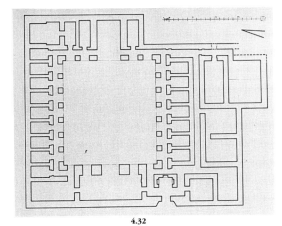

4.32

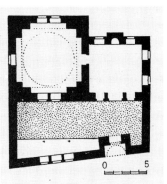

4.34

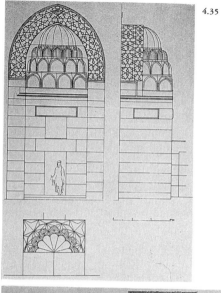

4.35

4.38

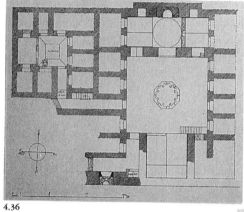

4.36

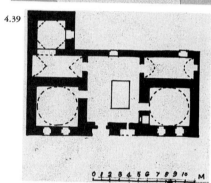

4.39

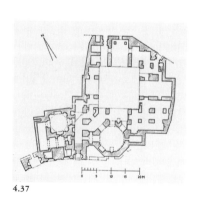

4.37

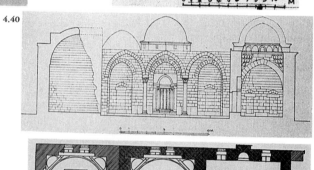

4.40

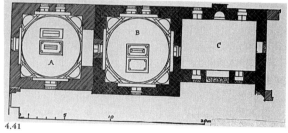

4.41

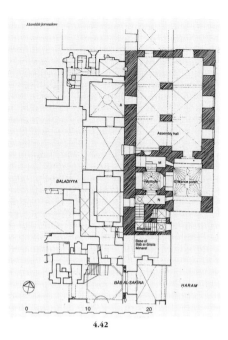

4.42

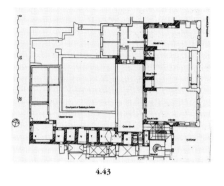

4.43

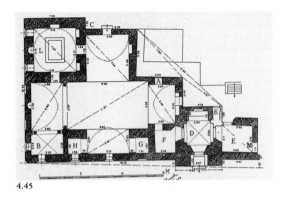

4.45

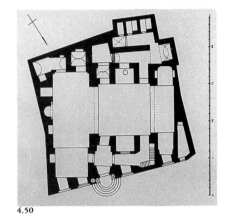

4.50

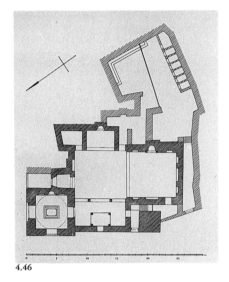

4.46

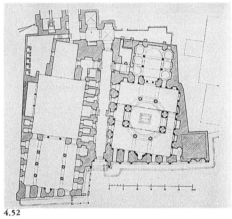

4.52

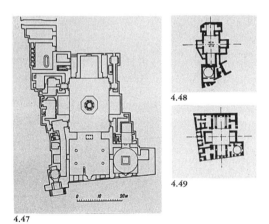

4.47

4.48

4.49

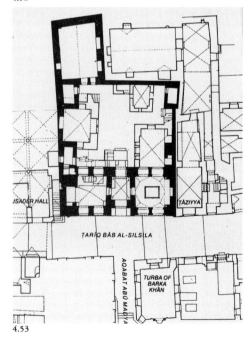

4.53

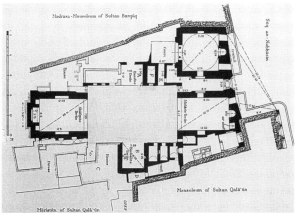

4.55

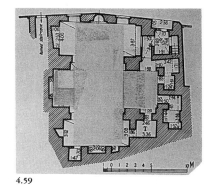

4.59

4.56

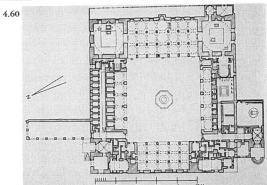

4.60

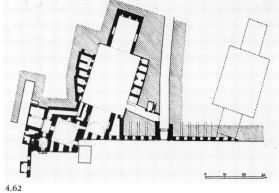

4.62

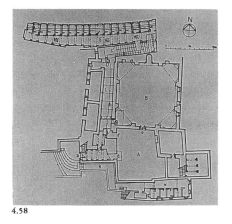

4.58

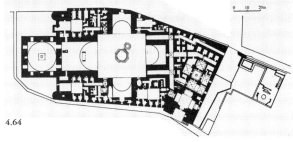

4.64

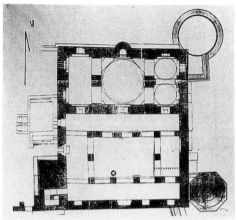

4.66

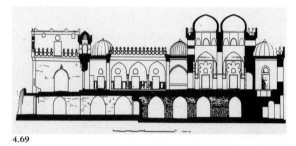

4.69

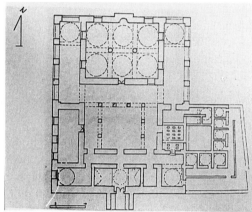

4.67

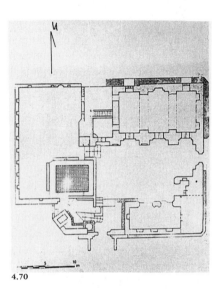

4.70

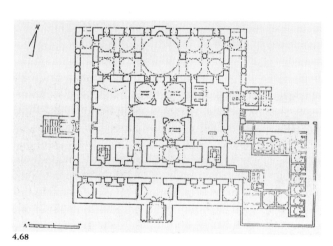

4.68

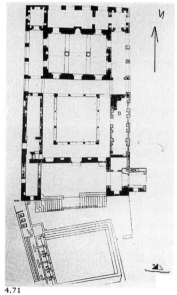

4.71

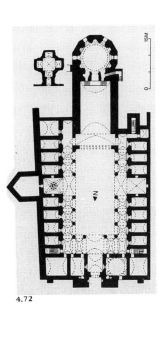

4.72

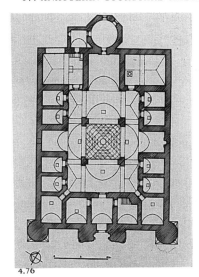

4.76

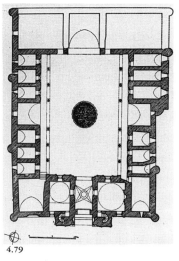

4.79

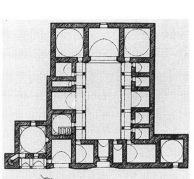

4.74

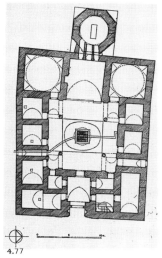

4.77

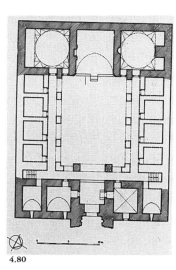

4.80

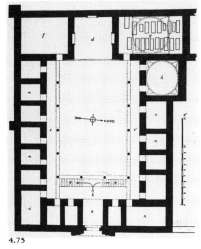

4.75

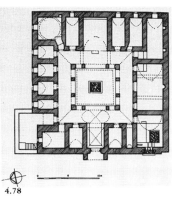

4.78

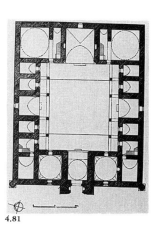

4.81

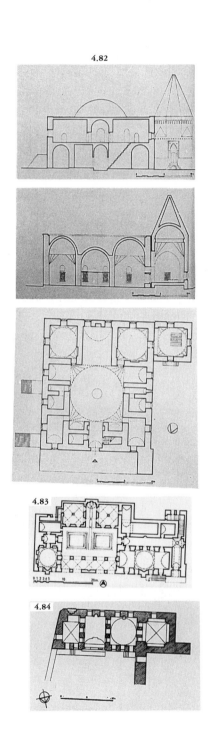

4.82

4.83

4.84

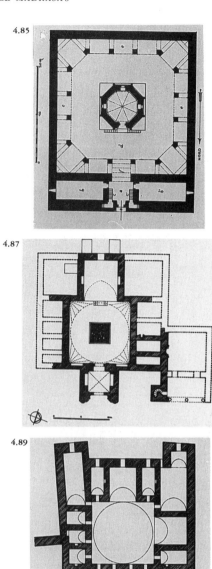

4.85

4.87

4.89

516

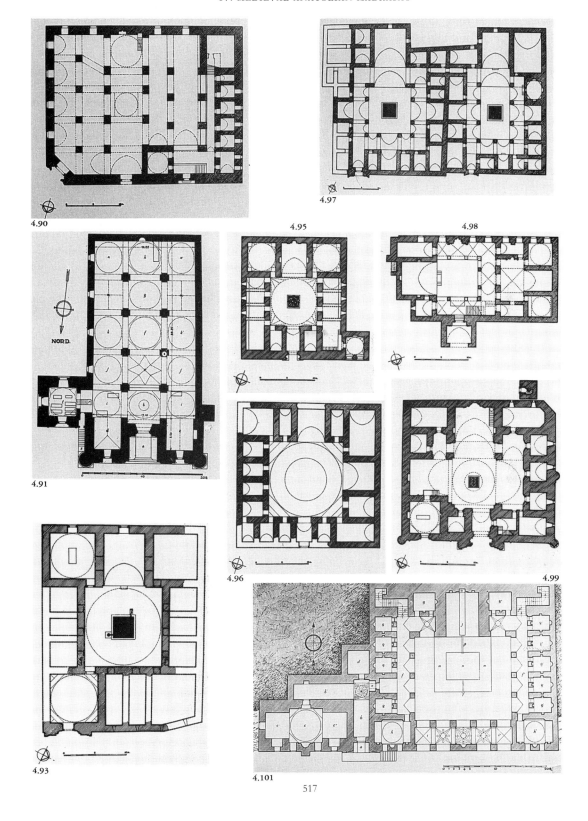

4.90

4.91

4.93

4.95

4.96

4.97

4.98

4.99

4.101

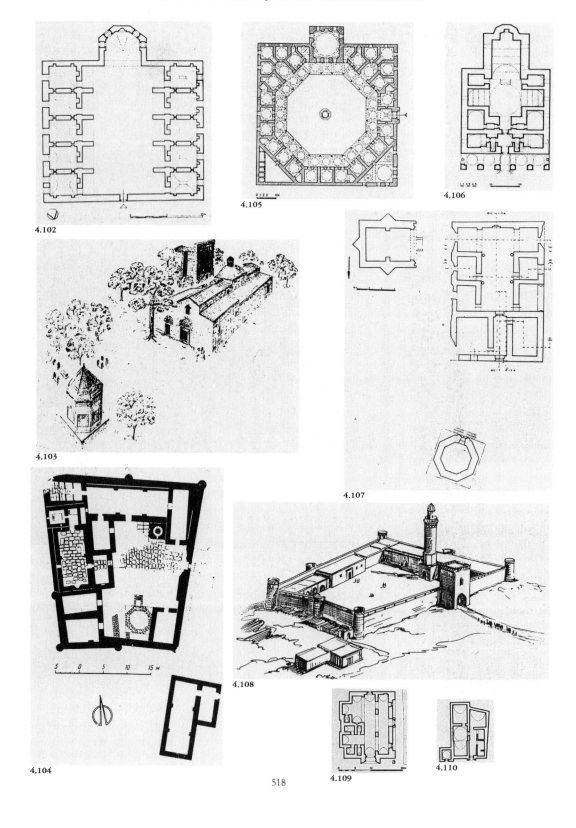

4.102

4.105

4.106

4.103

4.107

4.104

4.108

4.109

4.110

518

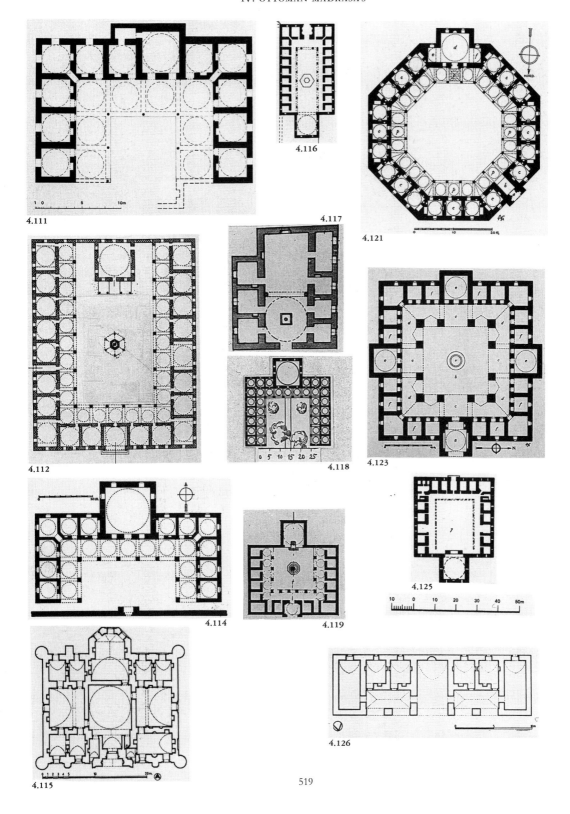

4.111

4.116

4.117

4.121

4.112

4.118

4.123

4.114

4.119

4.125

4.115

4.126

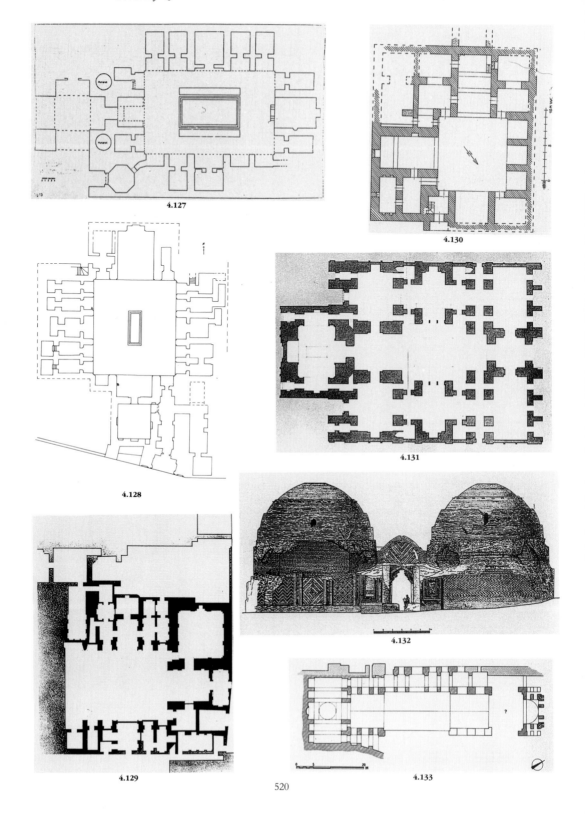

4.127

4.130

4.128

4.131

4.132

4.129

4.133

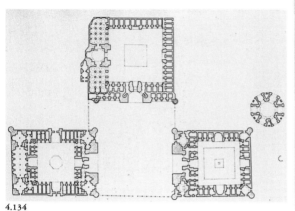

4.134

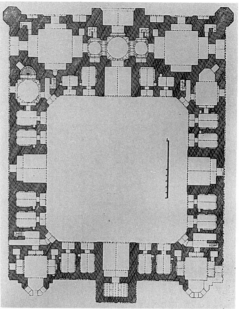

4.136

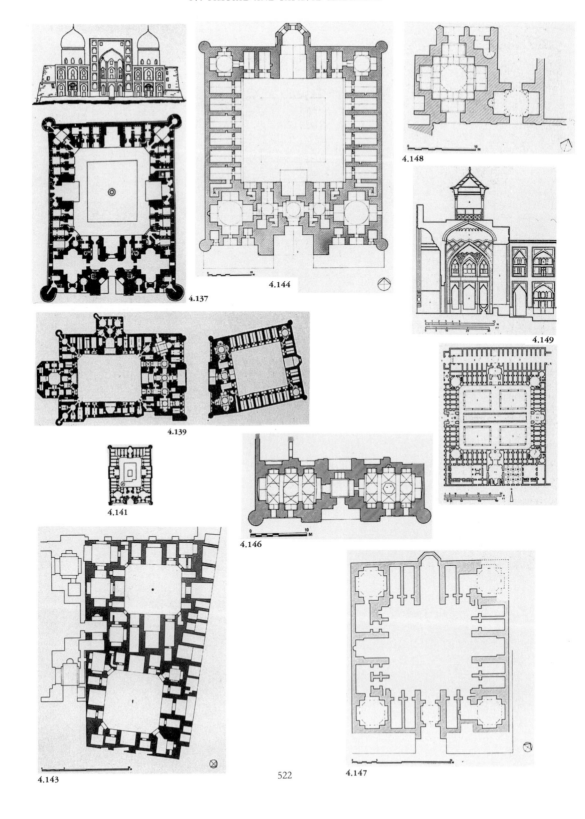

4.137

4.144

4.148

4.149

4.139

4.141

4.146

4.143

4.147

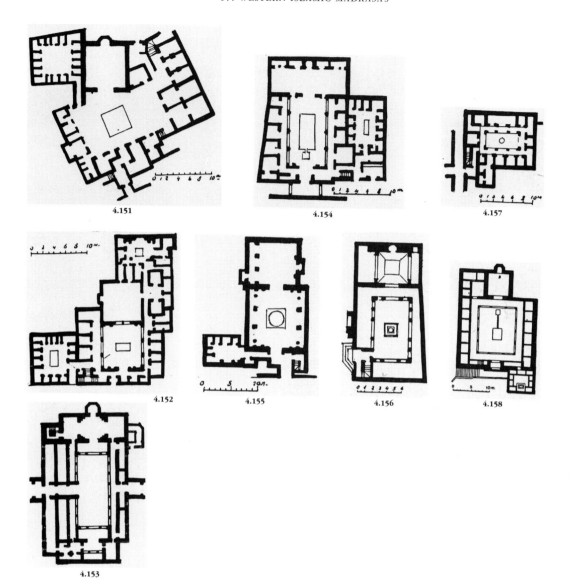

4.151

4.154

4.157

4.152

4.155

4.156

4.158

4.153

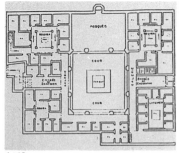

4.159

4.162

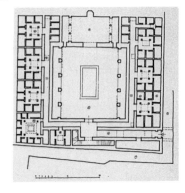

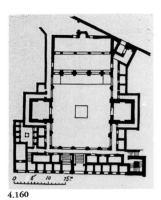

4.160

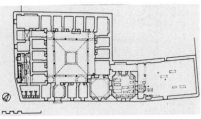

4.164

4.165

524

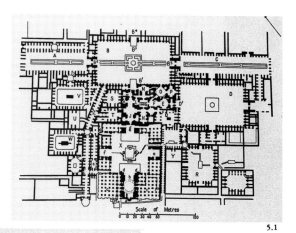

5.1

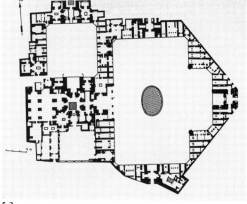

5.2

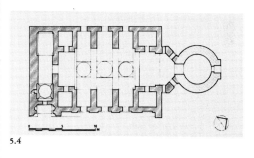

5.4

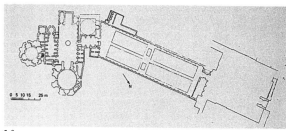

5.3

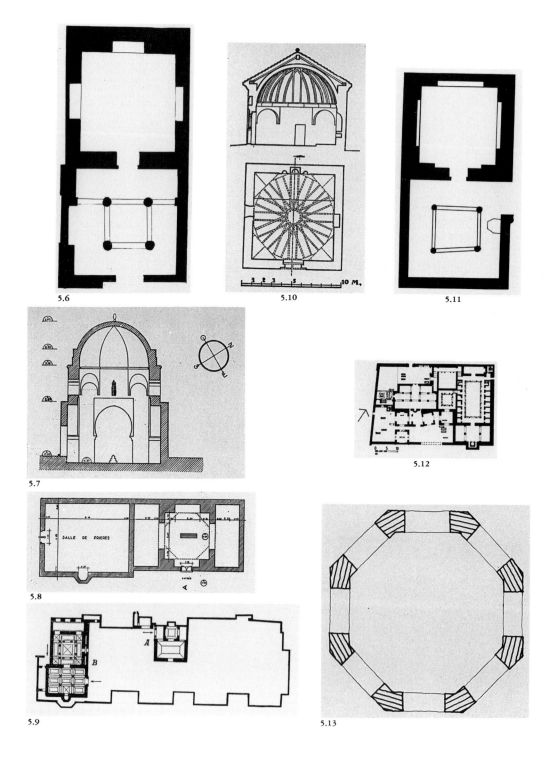

5.6

5.10

5.11

5.7

5.12

5.8

5.9

5.13

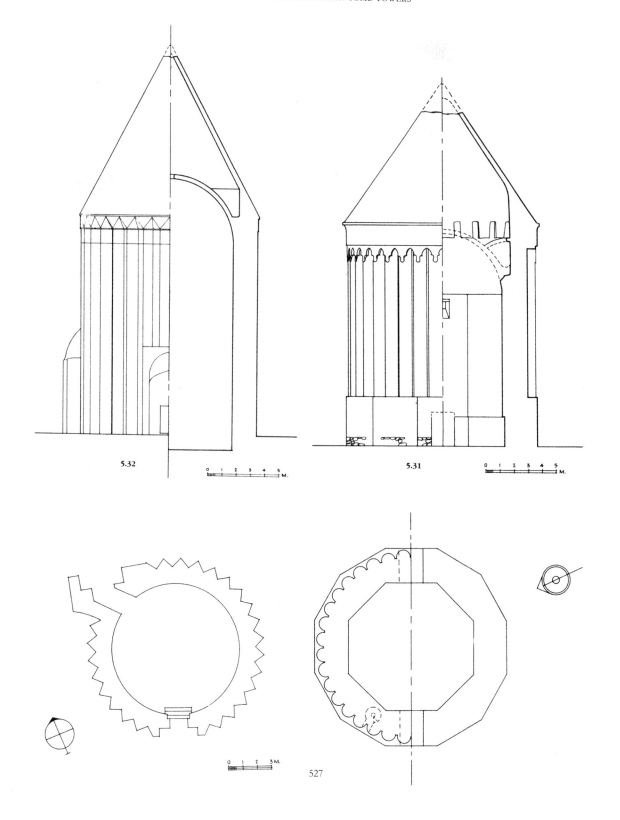

5.32

0 1 2 3 4 5 M.

5.31

0 1 2 3 4 5 M.

0 1 2 3 M.

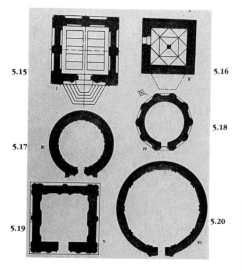

5.15

5.16

5.17

5.18

5.19

5.20

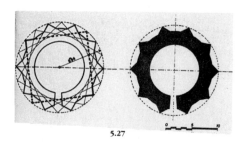

5.27

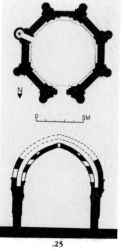

.25

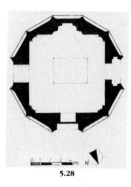

5.28

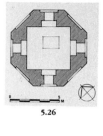

5.26

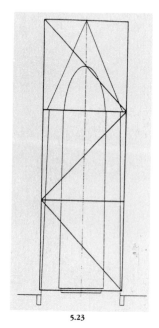

5.23

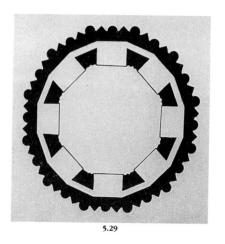

5.29

Scale : 1:100

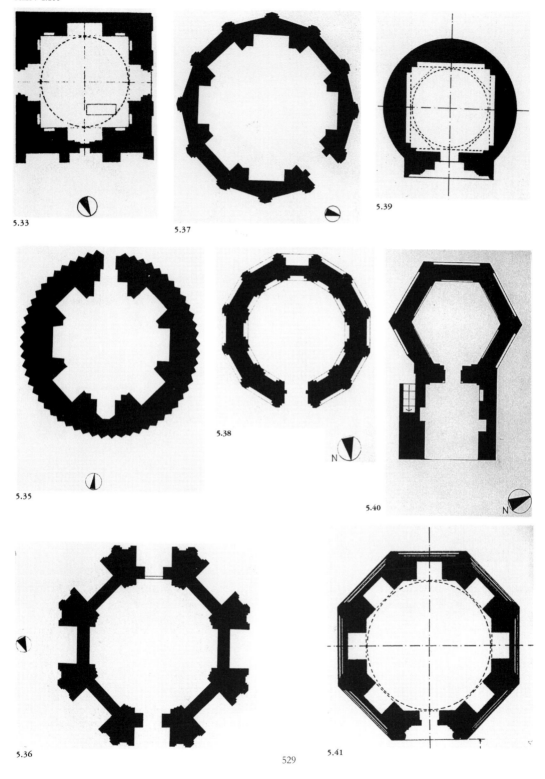

5.33

5.37

5.39

5.35

5.38

5.40

5.36

5.41

529

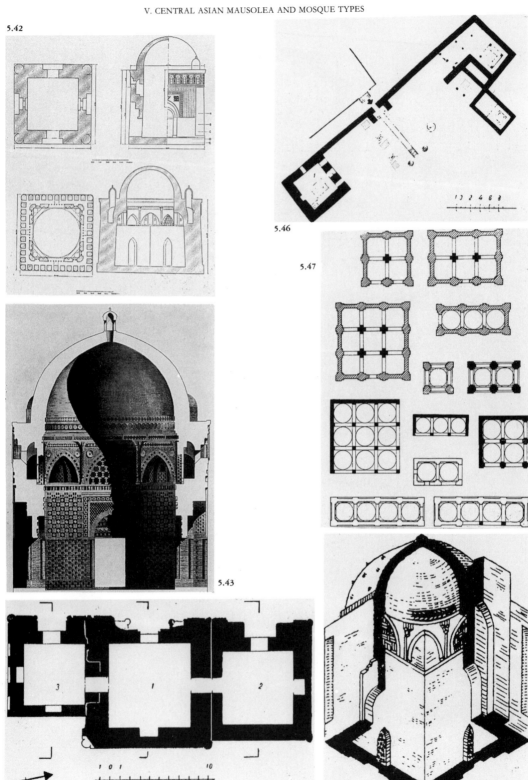

5.42

5.46

5.47

5.43

5.45

5.48

5.49   5.50   5.51   5.52   5.53   5.54

5.55   5.56   5.57   5.58

5.59   5.60   5.61   5.62

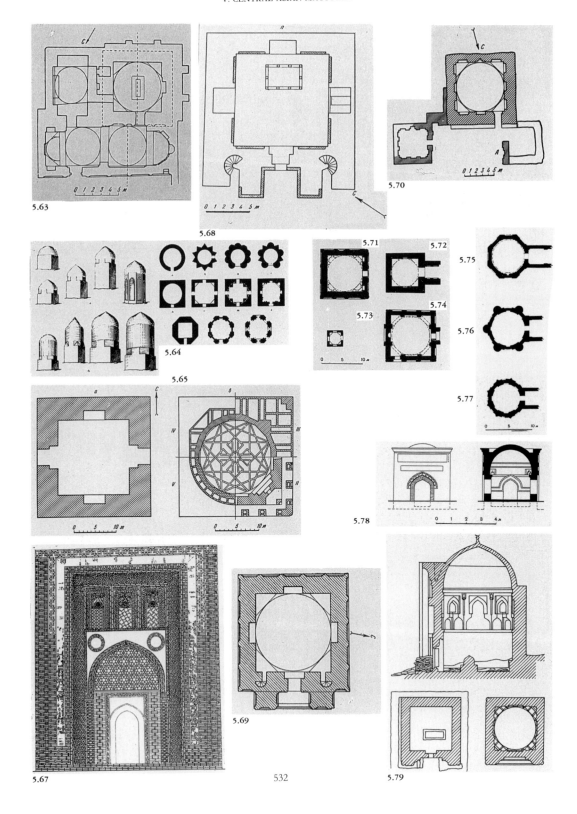

5.63

5.68

5.70

5.64

5.65

5.71

5.72

5.73

5.74

5.75

5.76

5.77

5.78

5.67

5.69

5.79

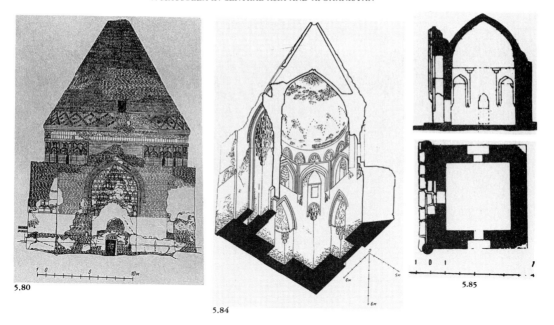

5.80

5.84

5.85

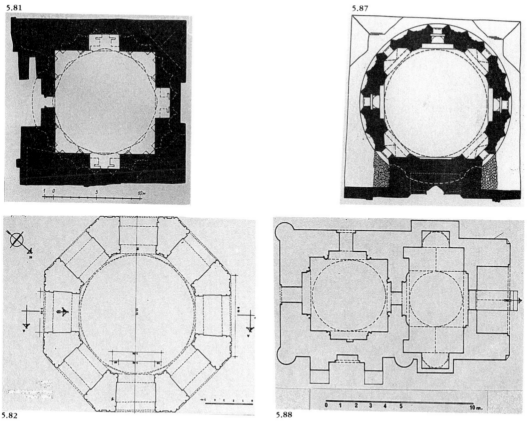

5.81

5.87

5.82

5.88

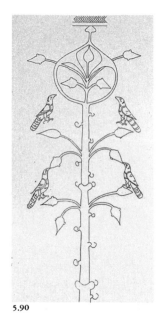

5.90

5.93

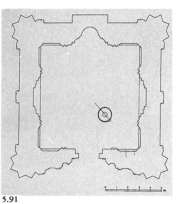

5.91

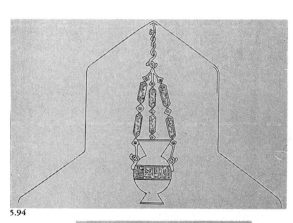

5.94

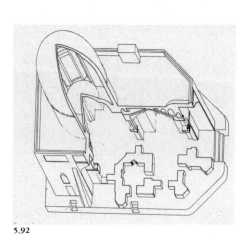

5.92

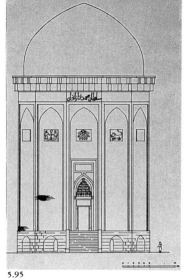

5.95

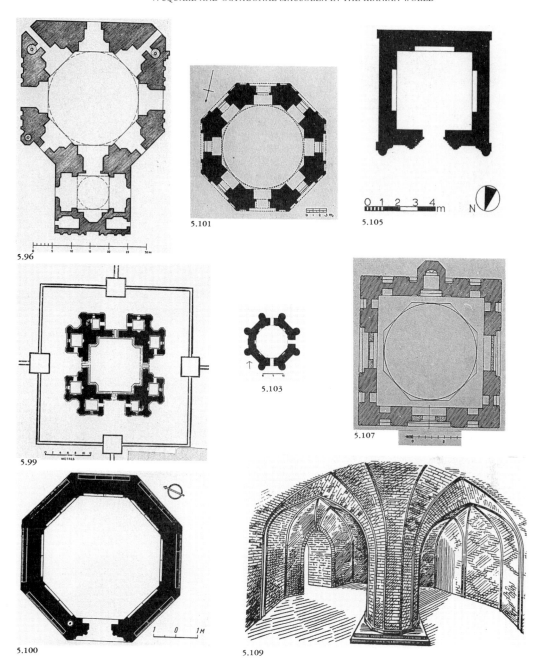

5.96

5.101

5.105

5.99

5.103

5.107

5.100

5.109

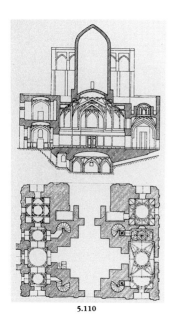

5.110

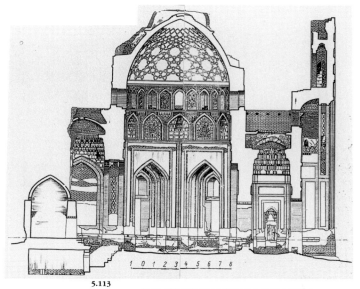

5.113

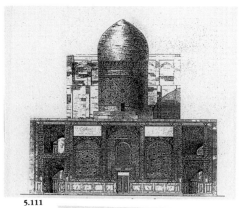

5.111

5.114

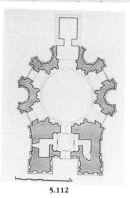

5.112

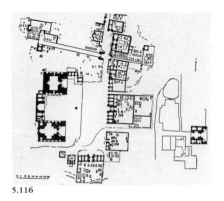

5.116

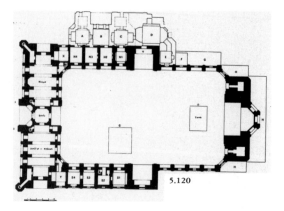

5.120

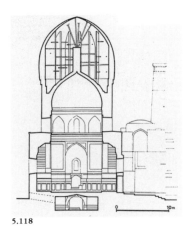

5.118

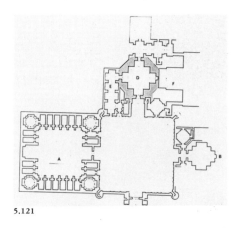

5.121

5.122

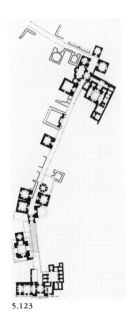

5.123

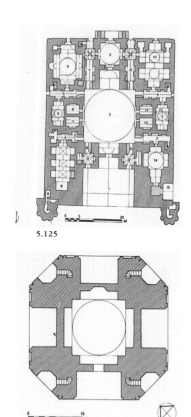

5.125

5.128

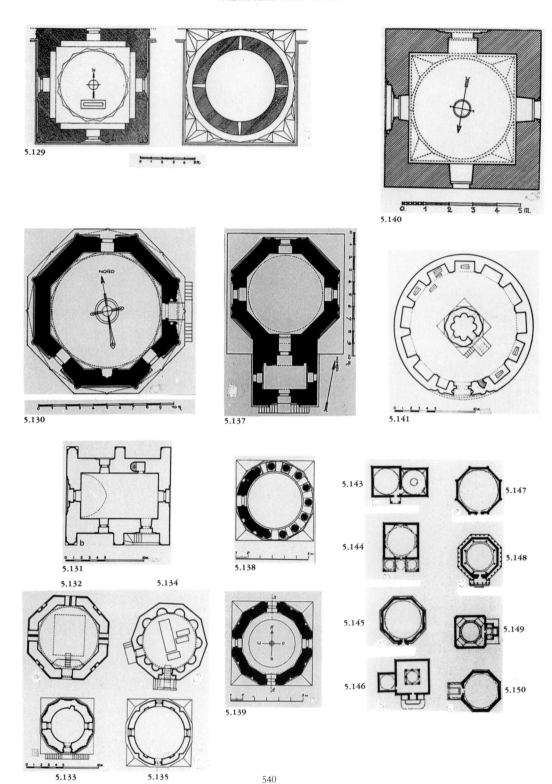

5.129

5.140

5.130

5.137

5.141

5.131

5.132   5.134

5.138

5.143

5.147

5.144

5.148

5.145

5.149

5.146

5.150

5.133   5.135

5.139

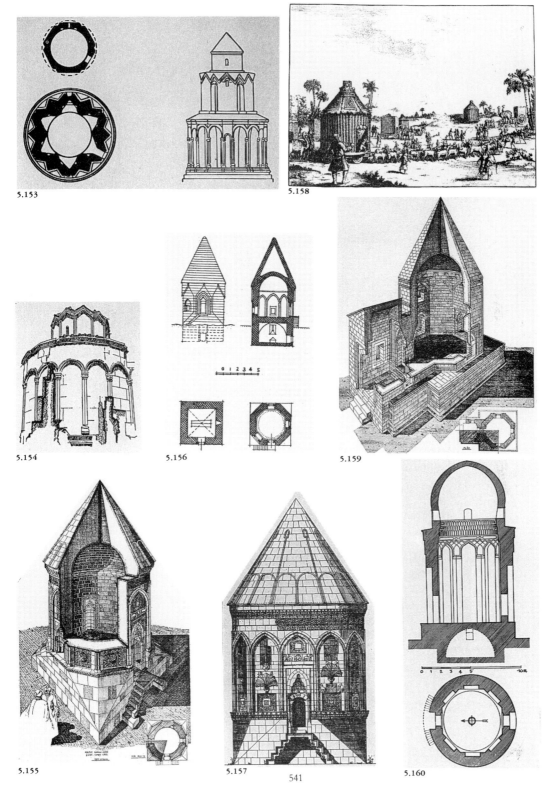

5.153

5.158

5.154

5.156

5.159

5.155

5.157

5.160

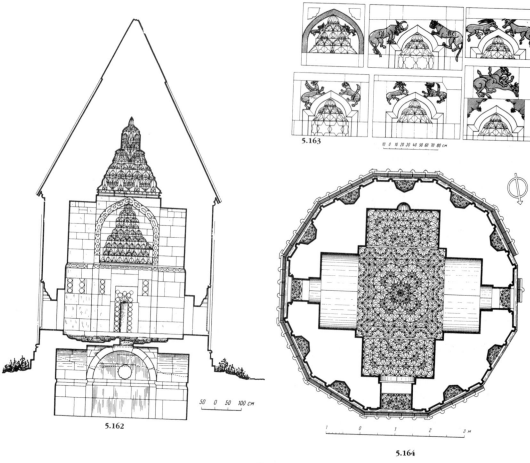

5.163

5.162

5.164

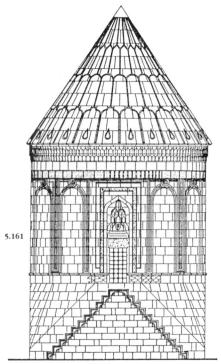

5.161

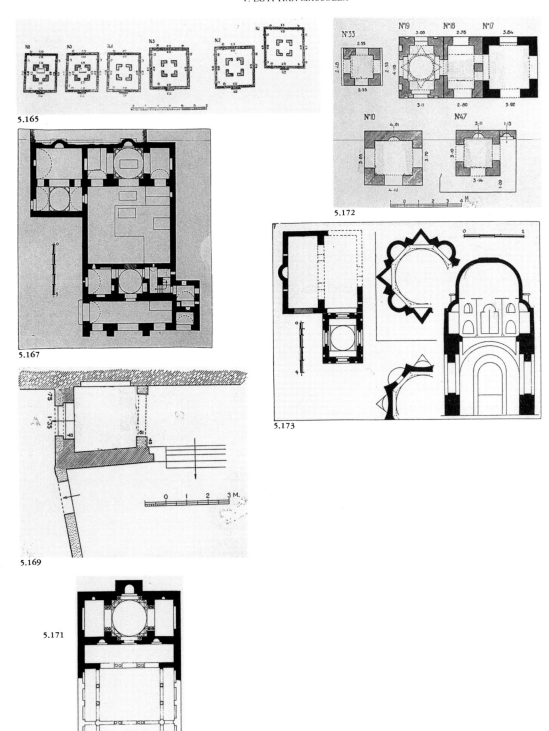

5.165

5.172

5.167

5.173

5.169

5.171

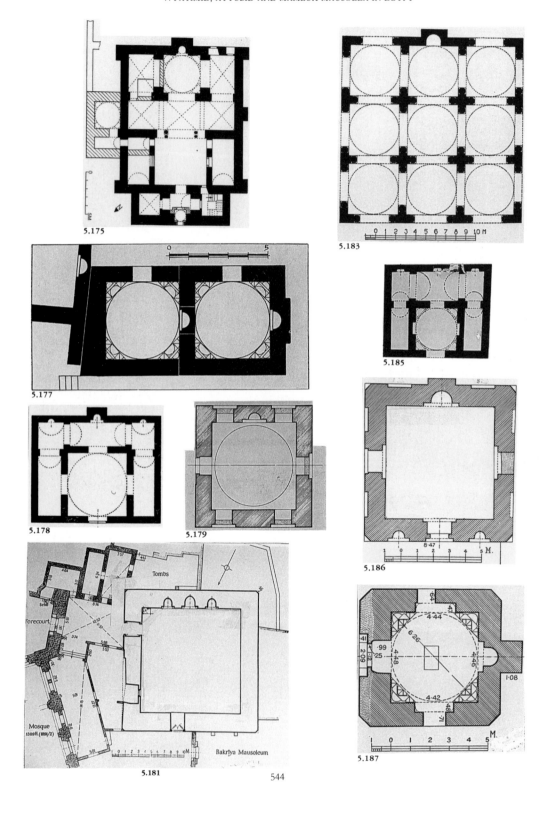

5.175

5.183

5.177

5.185

5.178

5.179

5.186

5.181

Tombs

Forecourt

Mosque
1309H (1891/2)

Bakrīya Mausoleum

5.187

544

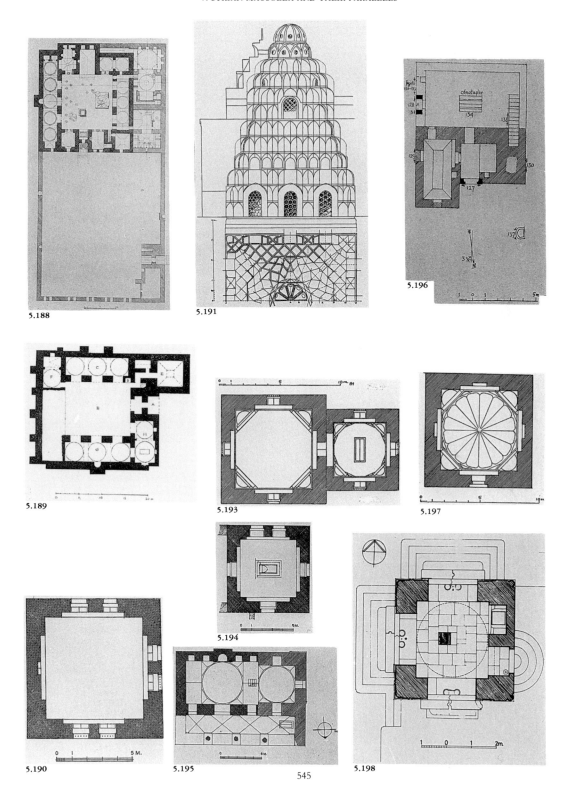

5.188

5.191

5.196

5.189

5.193

5.197

5.194

5.190

5.195

5.198

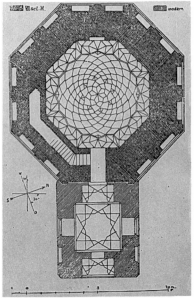

5.200

5.206

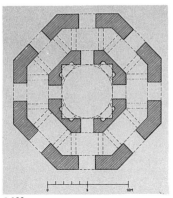

5.202

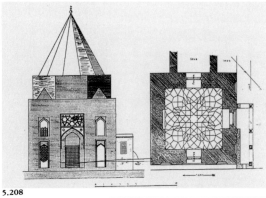

5.208

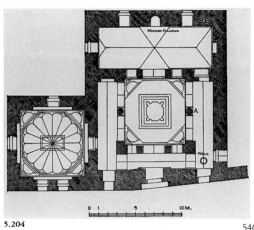

5.204

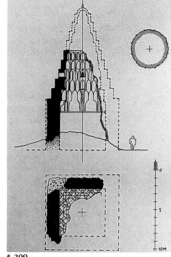

5.209

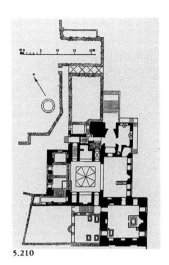

5.210

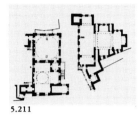

5.211

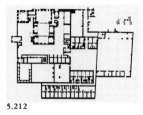

5.212

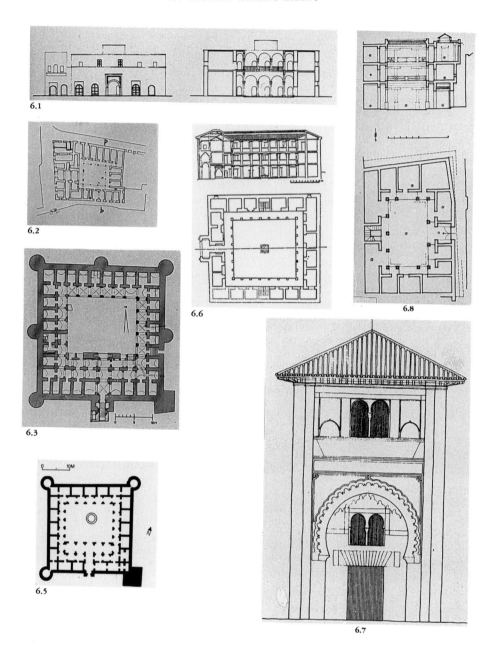

6.1

6.2

6.3

6.5

6.6

6.8

6.7

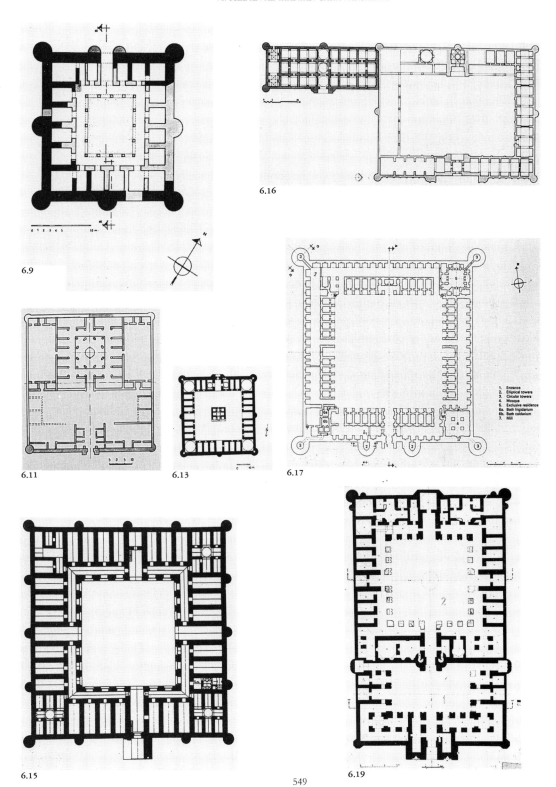

6.9

6.16

6.11

6.13

6.17

6.15

6.19

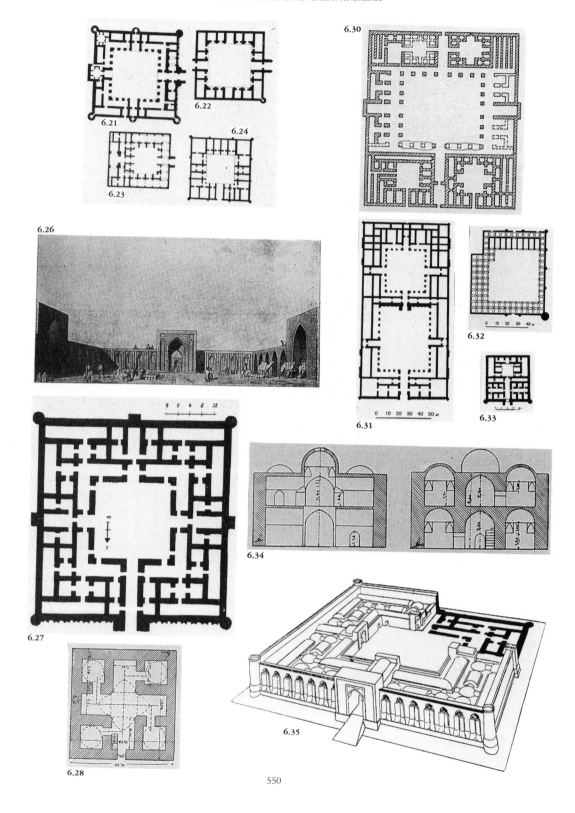

6.21

6.22

6.23

6.24

6.26

6.27

6.28

6.30

6.31

6.32

6.33

6.34

6.35

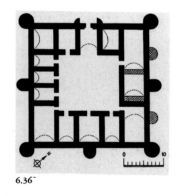

6.36

6.37

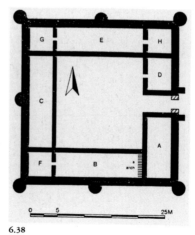

6.38

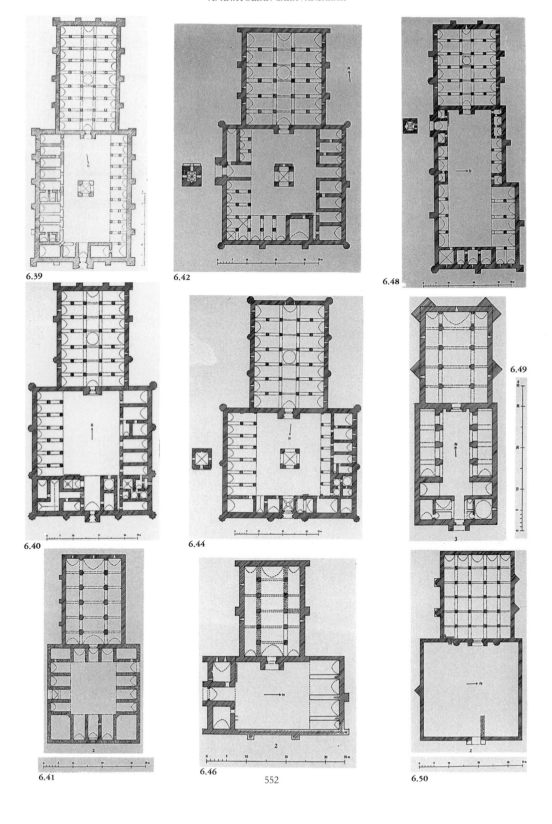

6.39

6.42

6.48

6.40

6.44

6.49

3

6.41

2

6.46

2

552

6.50

2

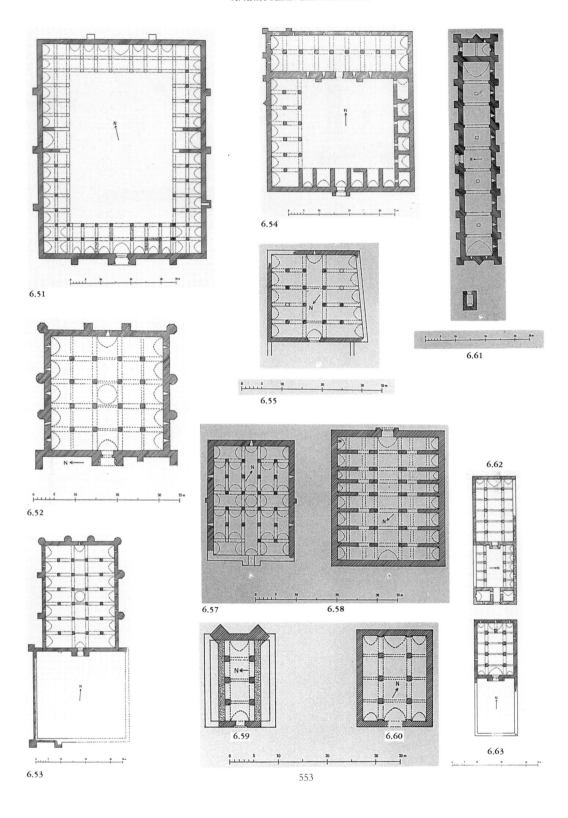

6.51

6.52

6.53

6.54

6.55

6.57

6.58

6.59

6.60

6.61

6.62

6.63

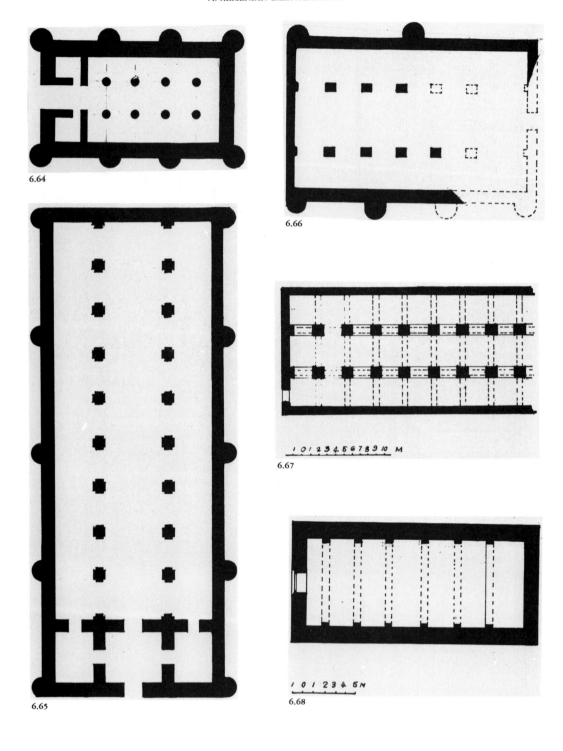

6.64

6.66

6.65

6.67

6.68

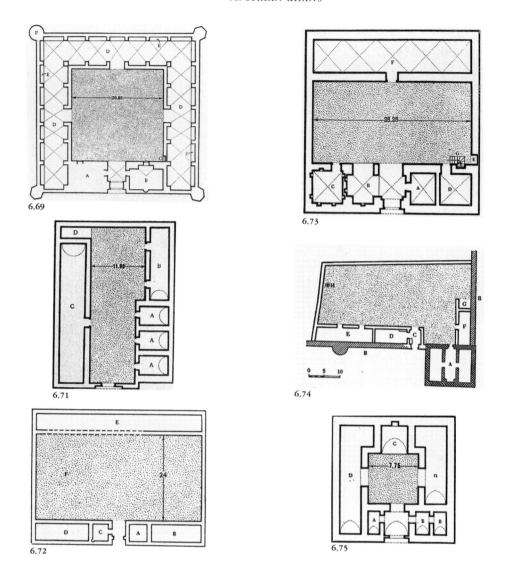

6.69

6.71

6.72

6.73

6.74

6.75

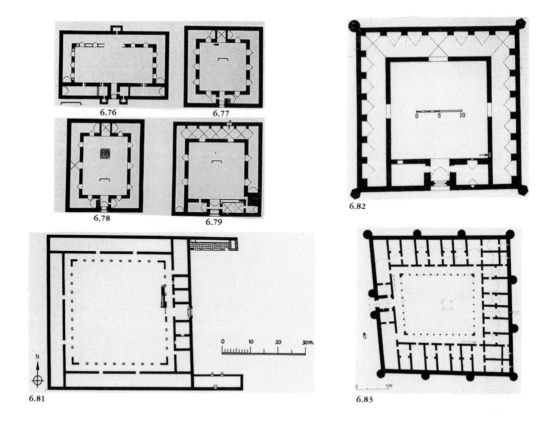

6.76

6.77

6.78

6.79

6.82

6.81

6.83

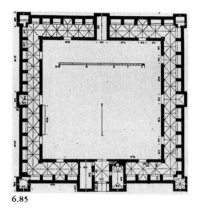

6.85

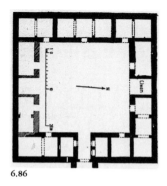

6.86

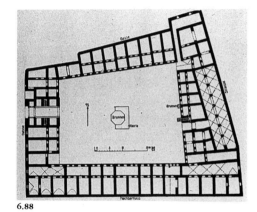

6.88

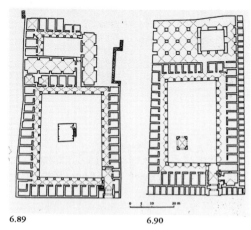

6.89   6.90

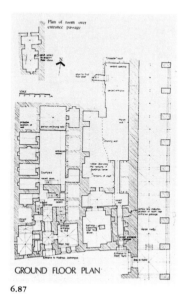

GROUND FLOOR PLAN

6.87

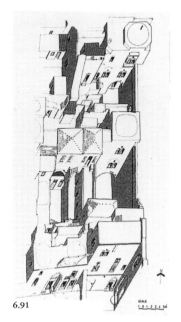

6.91

557

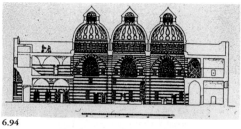

6.94

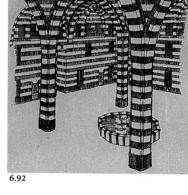

6.92

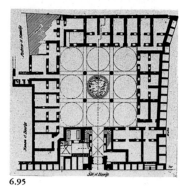

6.95

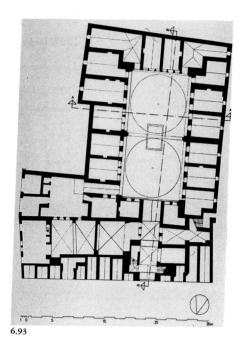

6.93

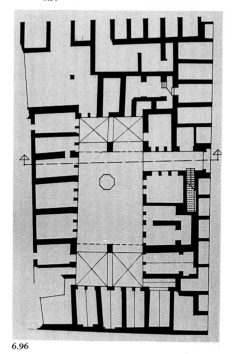

6.96

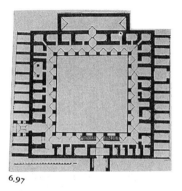

6.97

6.102

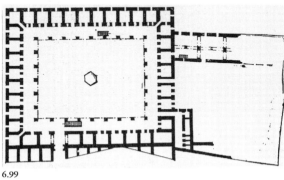

6.99

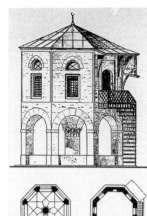

6.103

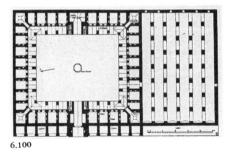

6.100

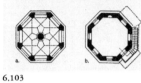

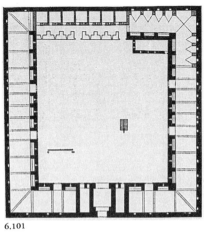

6.101

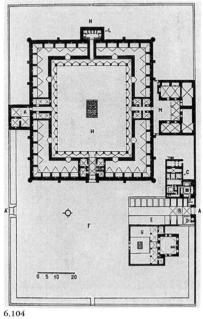

6.104

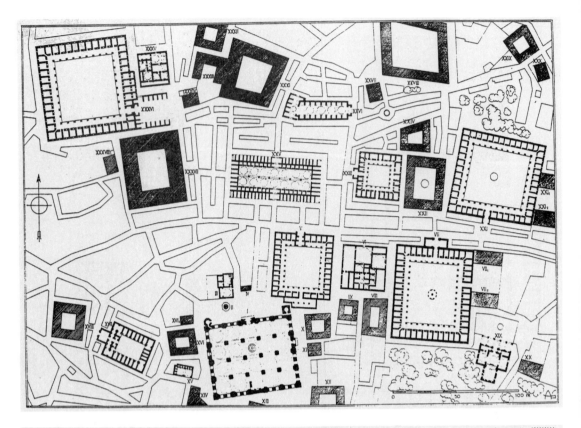

I. Grande Mosquée. - II. Şadırvan. - III. Şengül hamamı. - IV. Muvakkithane. - V. Emir hanı. - VI. Orhan hamamı. - VII. Koza hanı. - VIII. Zeytin hanı. - IX. Küçük zeytin hanı. - X. Medrese. - XI. Mekteb. - XII. Medrese. - XIII. Mısrî tekkesi. - XIV. Mısrî mezarlığı. - XV. Latrines publiques. - XVI. Vaiziye medresesi. - XVI₃. Müftülük. - XVII. Kapan hanı. - XVIII. Doğan gözü hanı. - XIX. Orhan camii. - XX. Imaret ambarı. - XXI. Fidan hanı. - XXII. Yeni harir hanı. - XXIII. Geyve hanı. - XXIV. Sandıkçılar hanı. - XXV. Bedesten. - XXVI. Sipahiler çarşısı. - XXVII. Ertuğrul camii. - XXVIII. Eski Yeni han. - XXIX. Medrese. - XXX. Yiğit cedid camii. - XXXI. Karaca bey hanı. - XXXII. Kuşbazlar hanı. - XXXIII. Ivaz paşa medresesi. - XXXIV. Ivaz paşa camii. - XXXV. Meyhaneli hamamı. - XXXVI. Pirinç hanı. - XXXVII. Eski harir hanı (Arabacılar). - XXXVIII. Sağrıcı Songur camii.

6.105

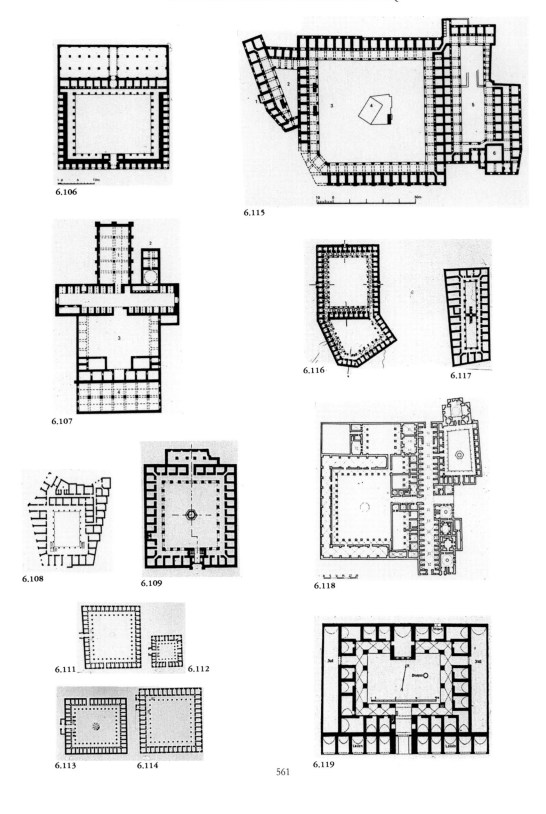

6.106

6.115

6.107

6.116

6.117

6.108

6.109

6.118

6.111

6.112

6.113

6.114

6.119

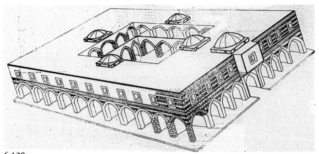

6.120

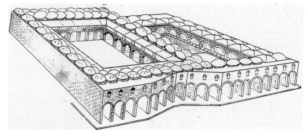

6.121

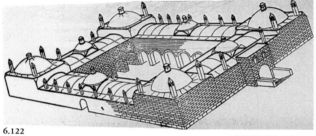

6.122

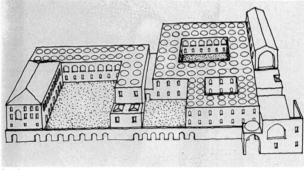

6.123

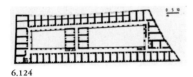

6.124

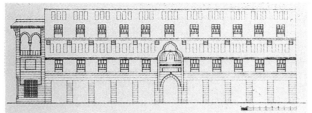

6.125

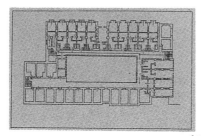

6.126

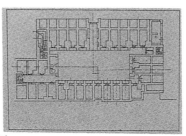

6.130

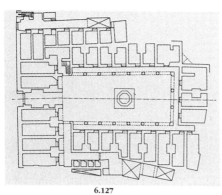

6.127

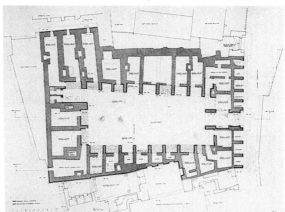

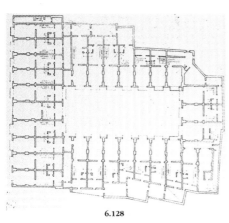

6.128

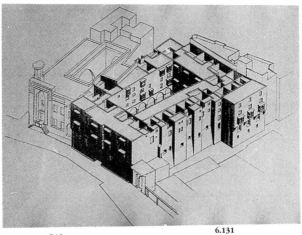

6.131

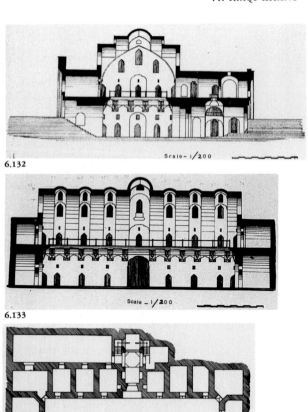

6.132

Scale – 1/200

6.133

Scale – 1/200

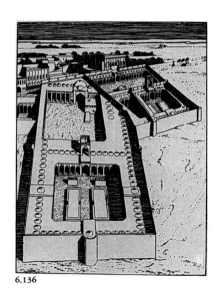

6.136

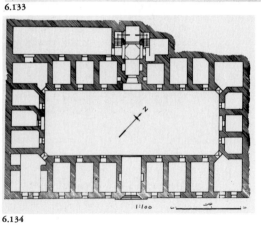

6.134

1:100

6.138

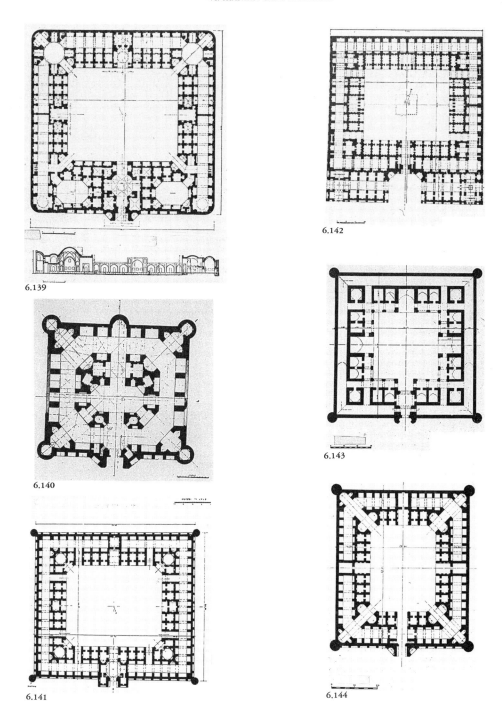

6.139

6.140

6.141

6.142

6.143

6.144

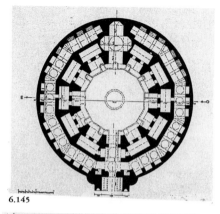

6.145

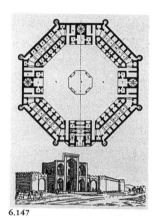

6.147

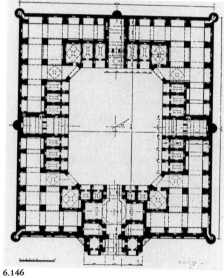

6.146

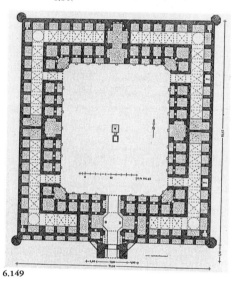

6.149

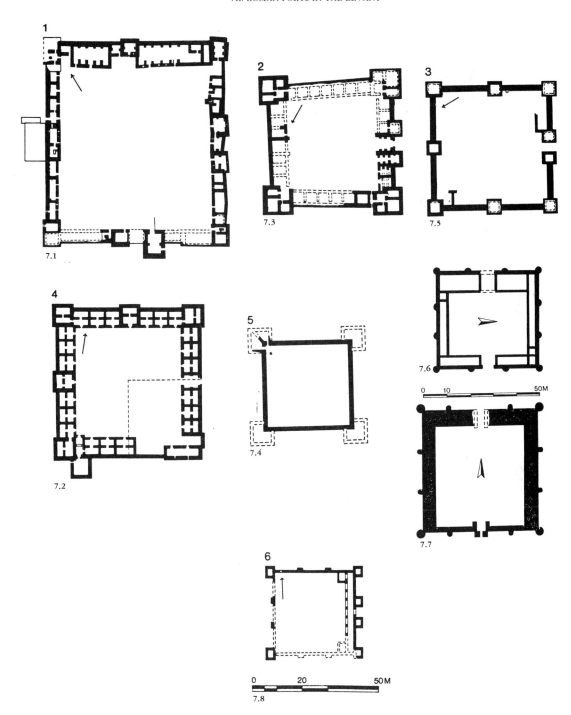

7.1

7.2

7.3

7.4

7.5

7.6

7.7

7.8

0   10   50M

0   20   50M

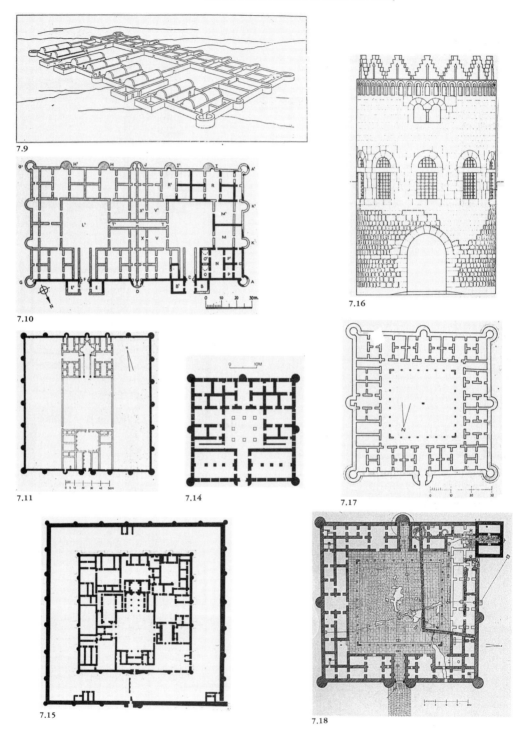

7.9

7.10

7.16

7.11

7.14

7.17

7.15

7.18

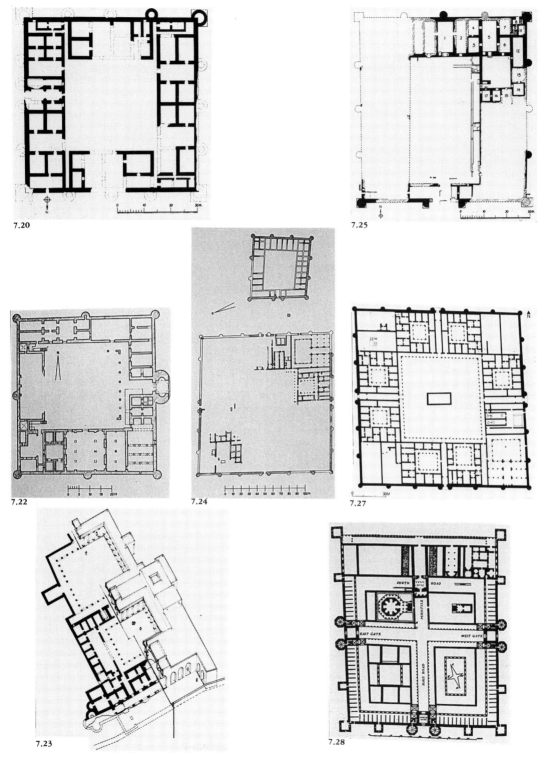

7.20

7.25

7.22

7.24

7.27

7.23

7.28

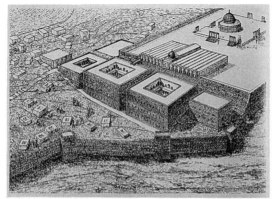

7.29

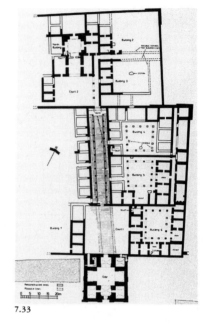

7.33

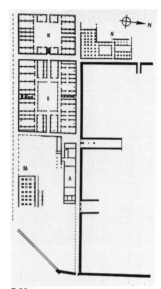

7.30

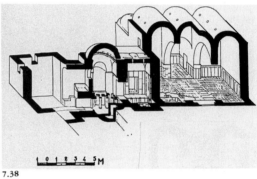

7.38

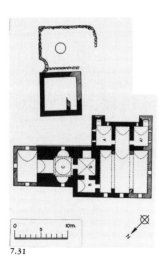

7.31

7.39

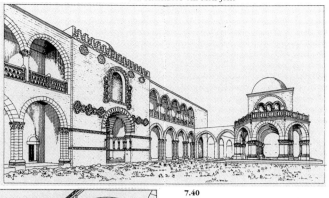

7.40

7.41

7.42

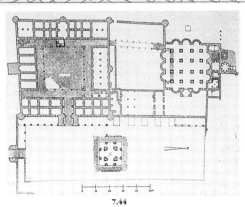

7.44

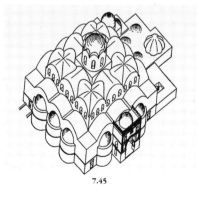

7.45

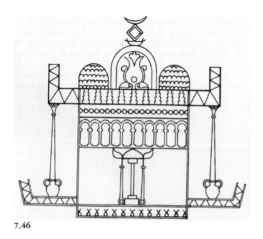

7.46

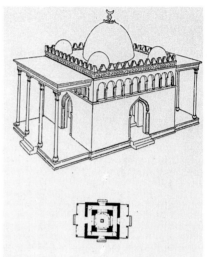

7.49

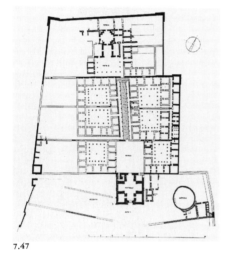

7.47

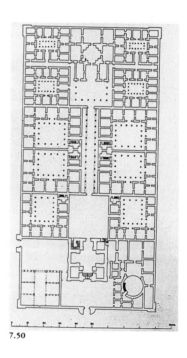

7.50

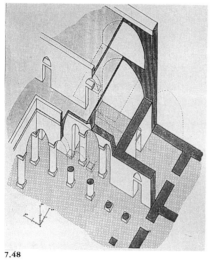

7.48

572

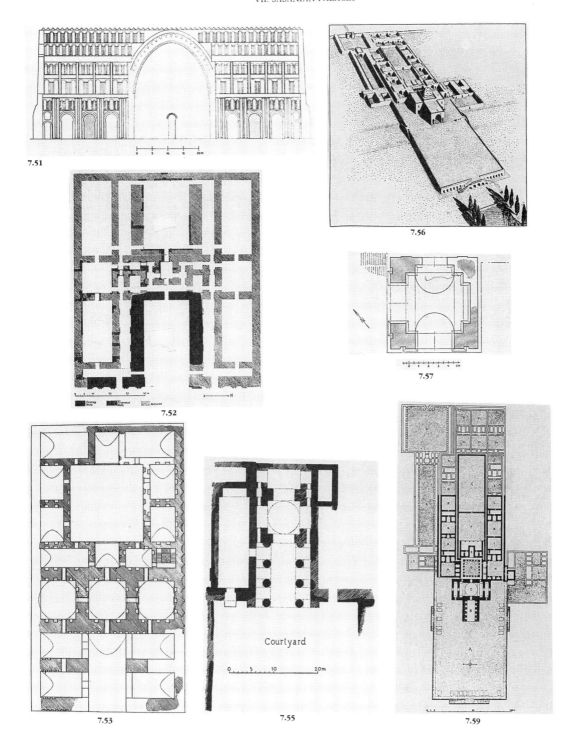

7.51

7.56

7.52

7.57

7.53

Courtyard

0   5   10   20m

7.55

7.59

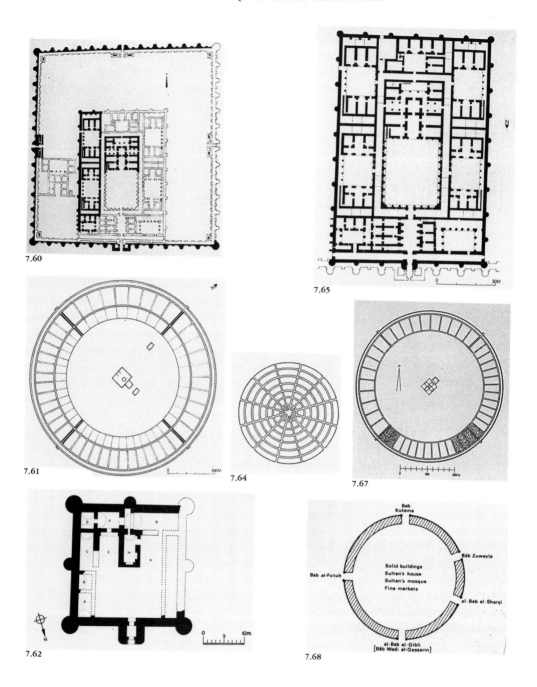

7.60

7.65

7.61

7.64

7.67

7.62

7.68

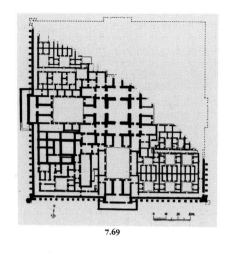

7.69

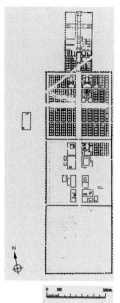

7.72

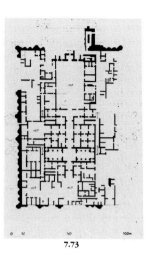

7.73

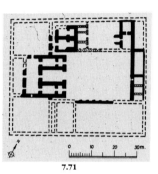

7.71

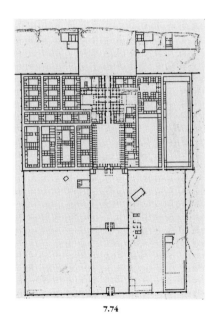

7.74

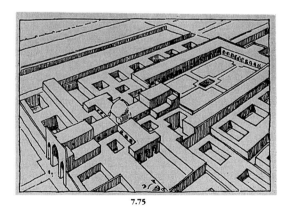

7.75

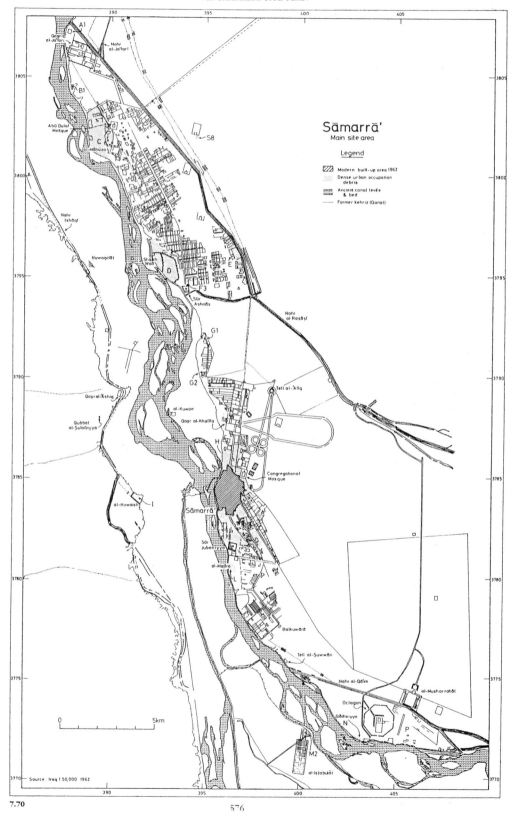

Sāmarrā'
Main site area

Legend

Modern built-up area 1962
Dense urban occupation debris
Ancient canal levée & bed
Former kehrīz (Qanal)

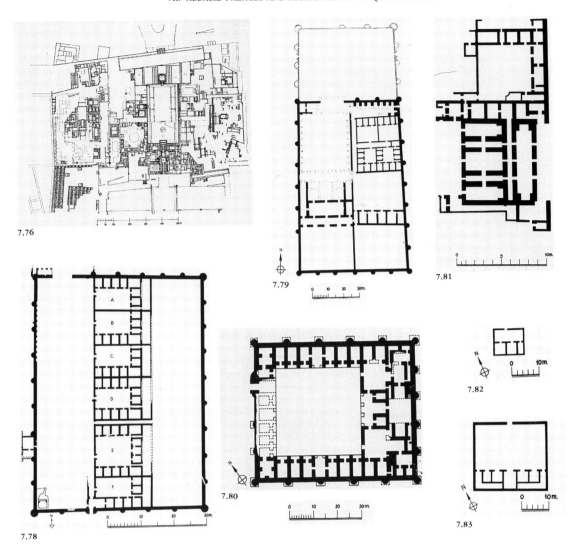

7.76

7.79

7.81

7.78

7.80

7.82

7.83

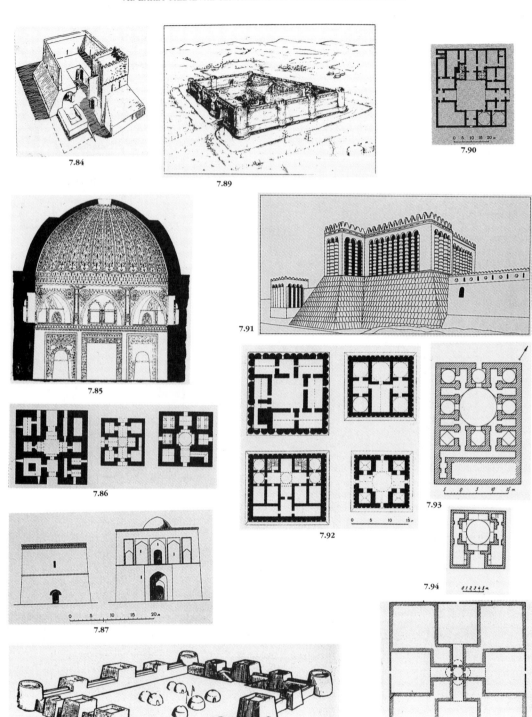

7.84

7.89

7.90

7.85

7.91

7.86

7.92

7.93

7.87

7.94

7.88

7.95

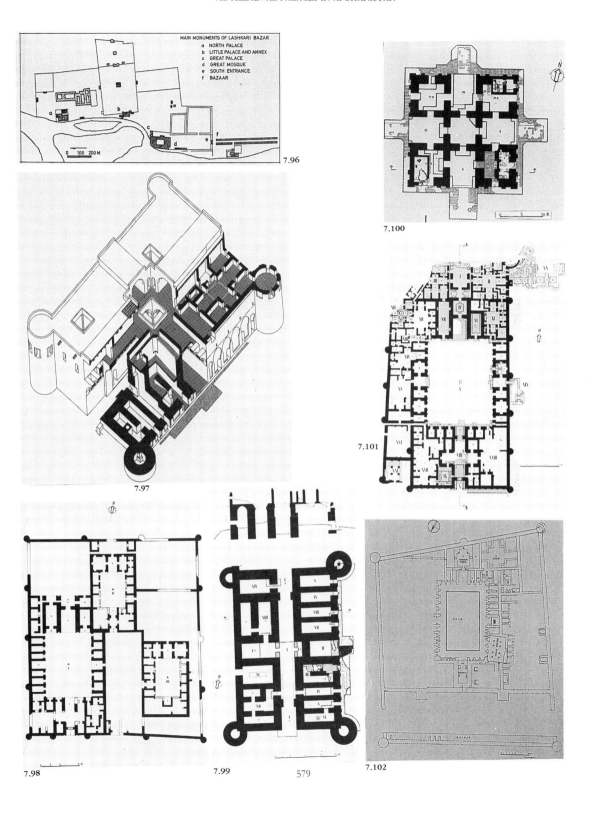

7.96

7.97

7.100

7.101

7.98

7.99

7.102

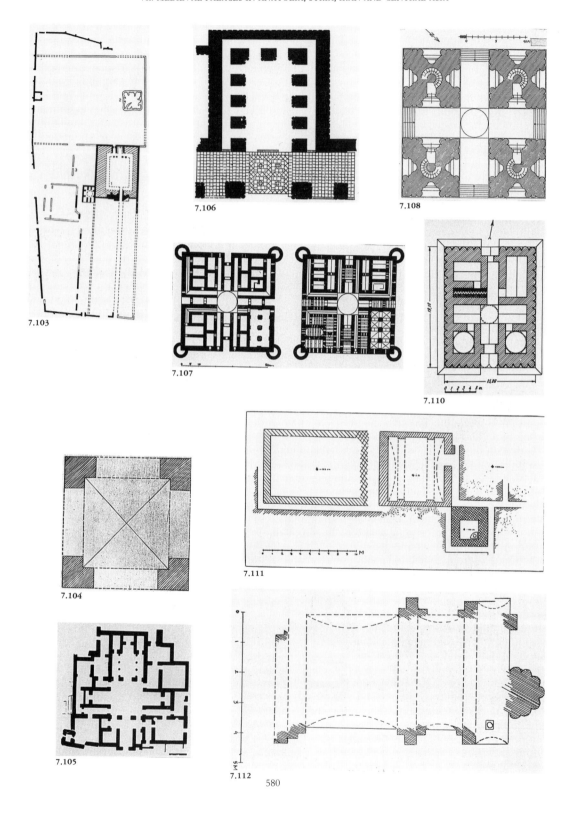

7.103

7.106

7.108

7.107

7.110

7.104

7.111

7.105

7.112

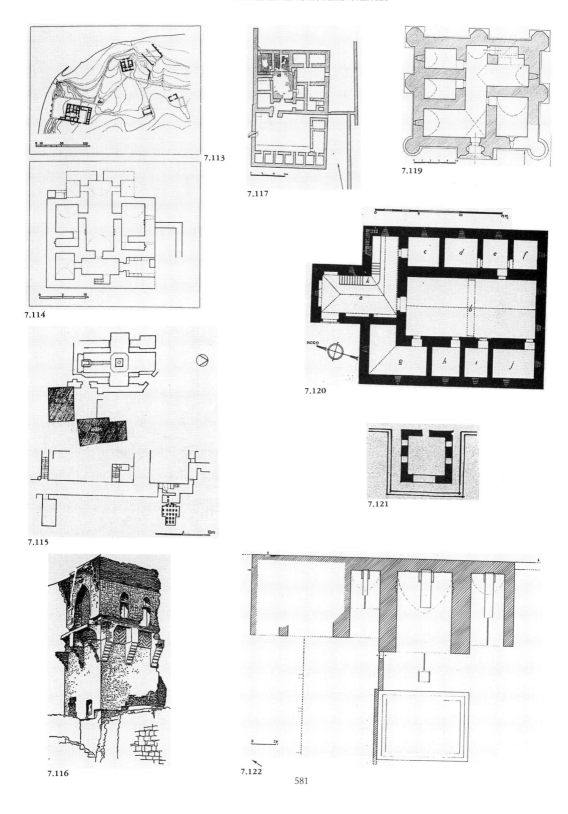

7.113

7.114

7.115

7.116

7.117

7.119

7.120

7.121

7.122

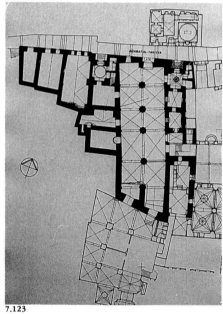

7.123

7.124

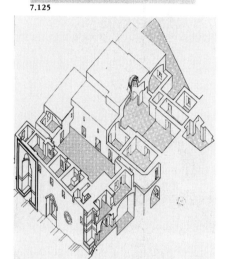

7.125

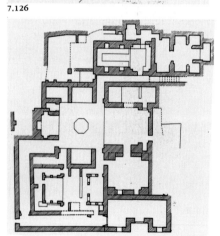

7.126

7.127

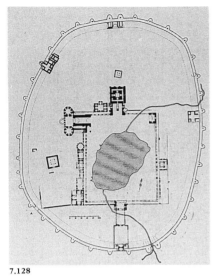

7.128

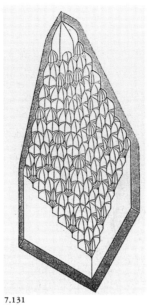

7.131

7.132

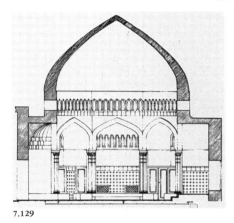

7.129

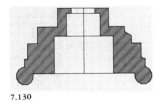

7.130

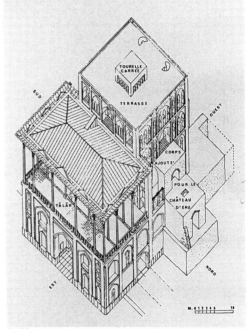

7.133

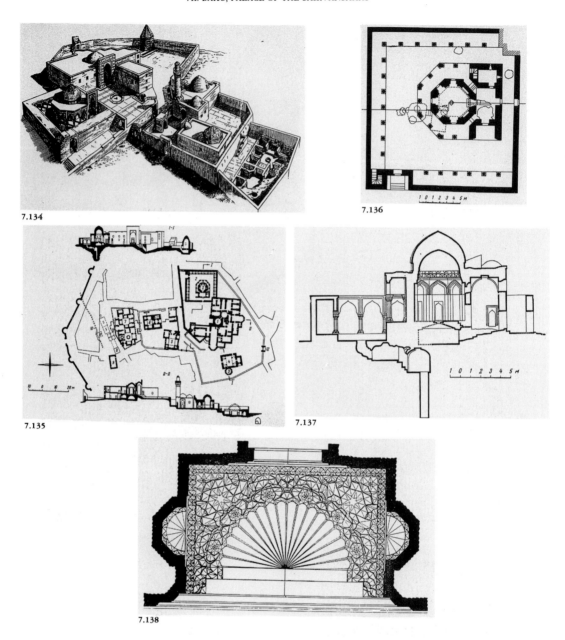

7.134

7.136

7.135

7.137

7.138

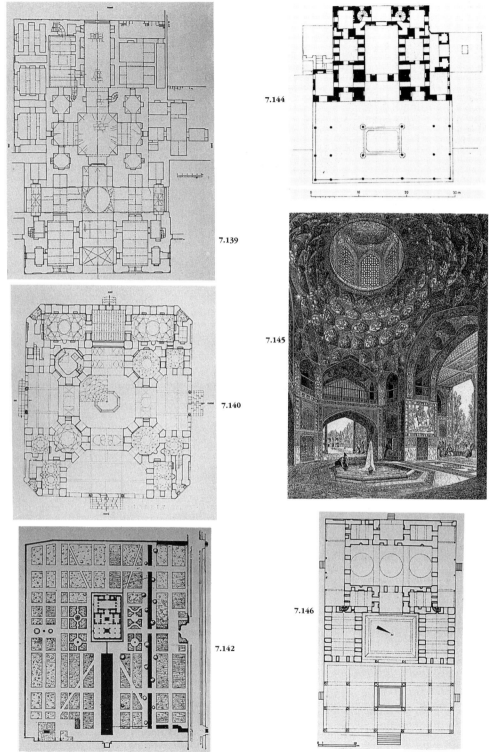

7.139

7.140

7.142

7.144

7.145

7.146

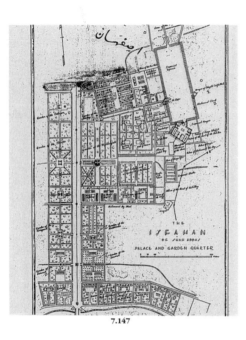

7.147

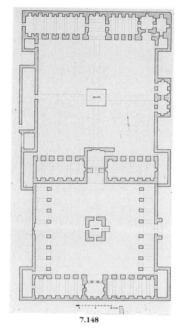

7.148

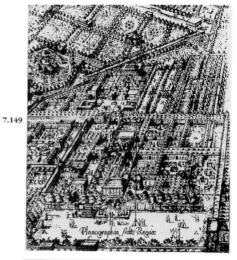

7.149

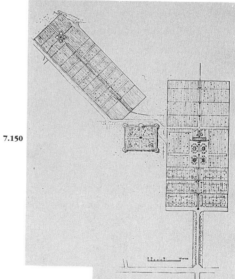

7.150

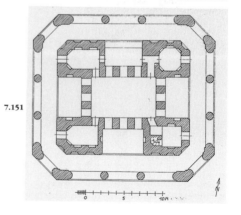

7.151

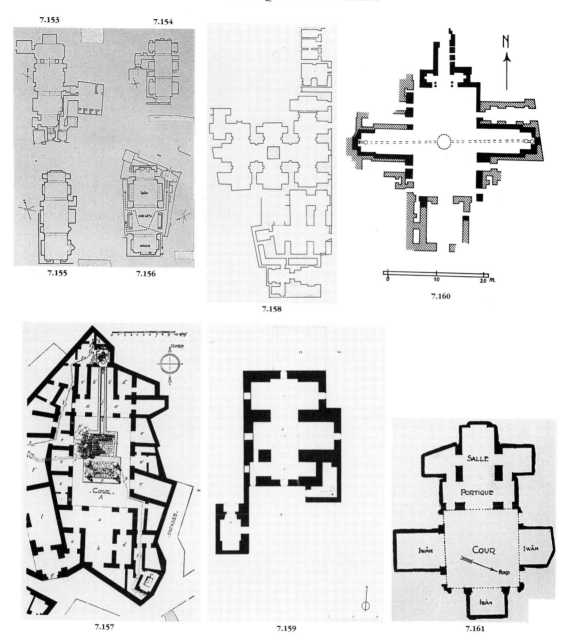

7.153 7.154

7.155 7.156

7.158

7.160

7.157

7.159

7.161

587

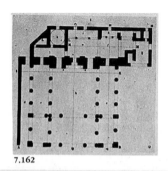

7.162

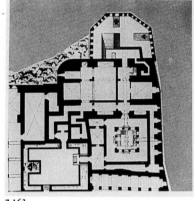
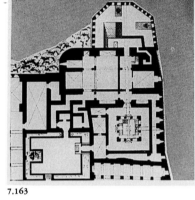

7.163

7.165

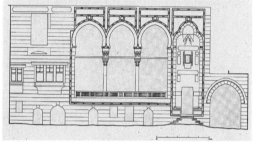

7.166

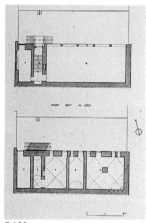

7.164

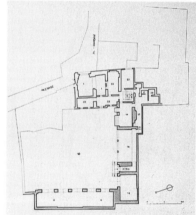

7.167

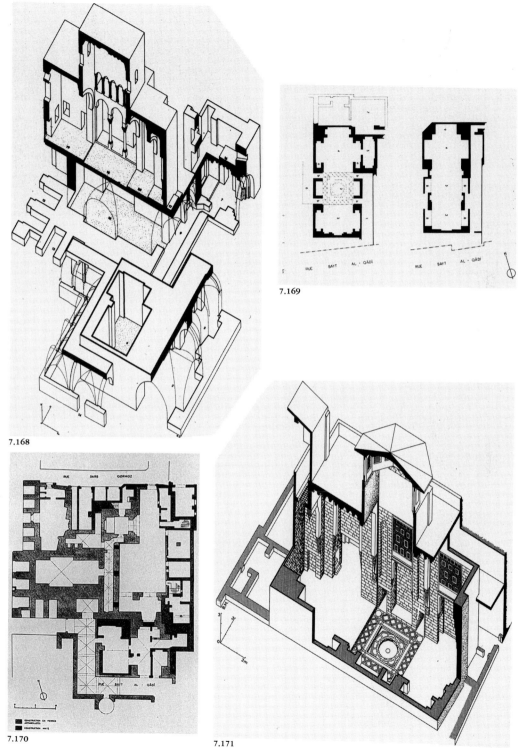

7.168

7.169

7.170

7.171

589

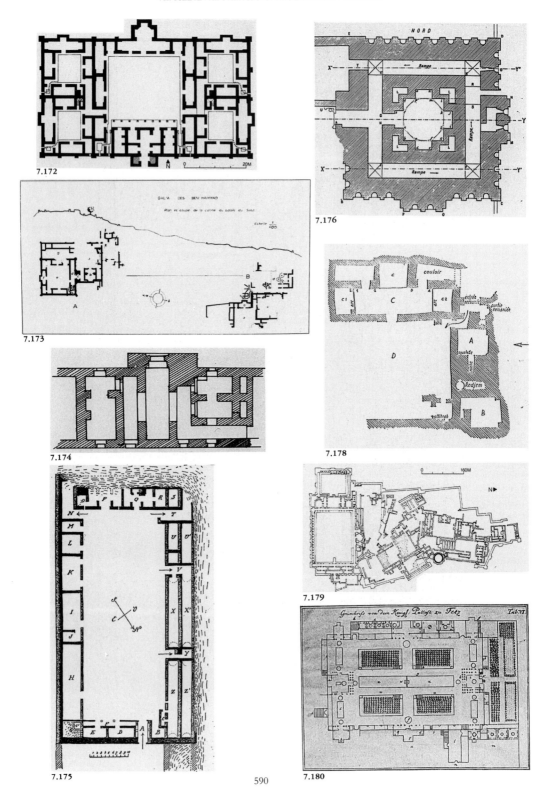

7.172

7.173

7.174

7.175

7.176

7.178

7.179

7.180

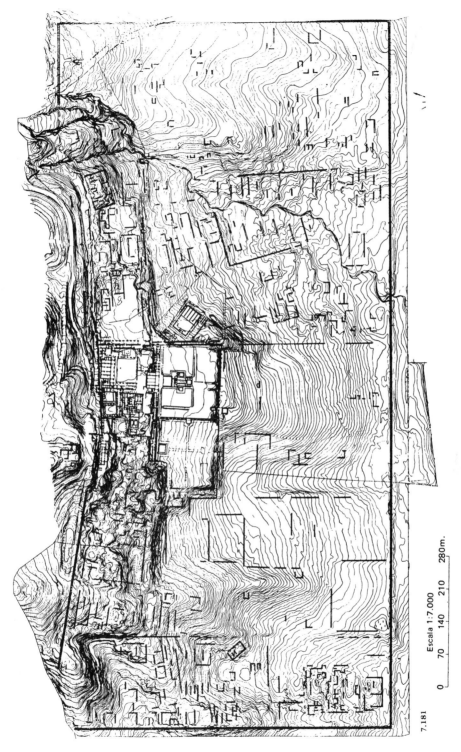

Escala 1:7.000

0   70   140   210   280m.

7.181

7.182

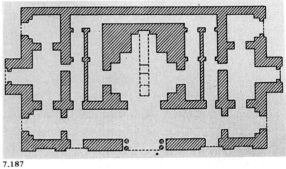

7.187

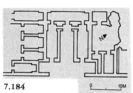
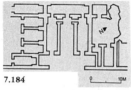

7.184

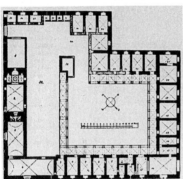

7.185

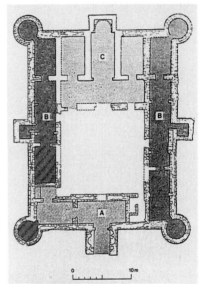

7.190

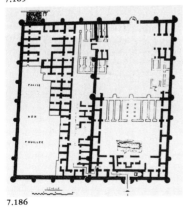

7.186

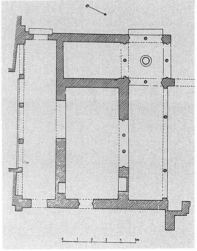

7.191

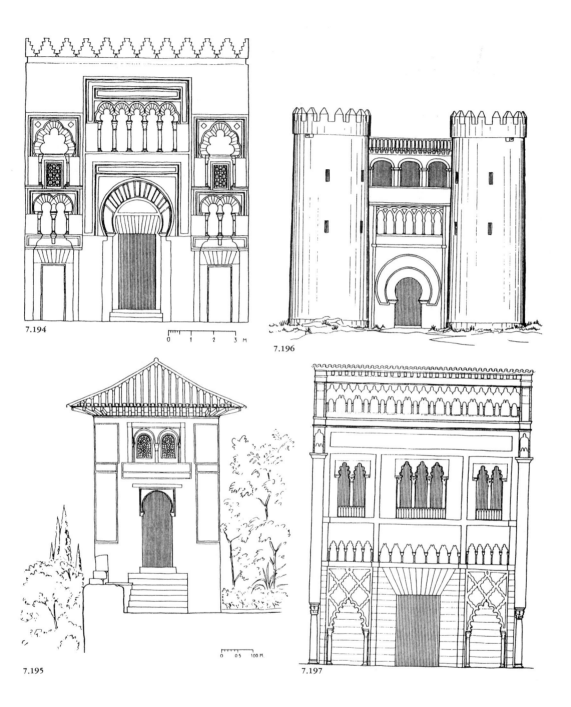

7.194

7.195

7.196

7.197

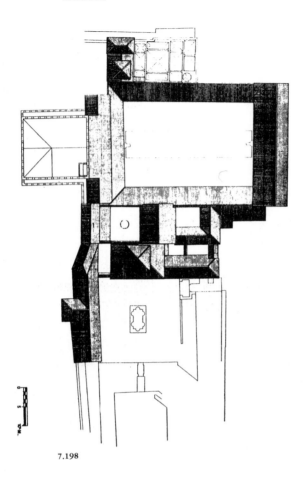

7.198

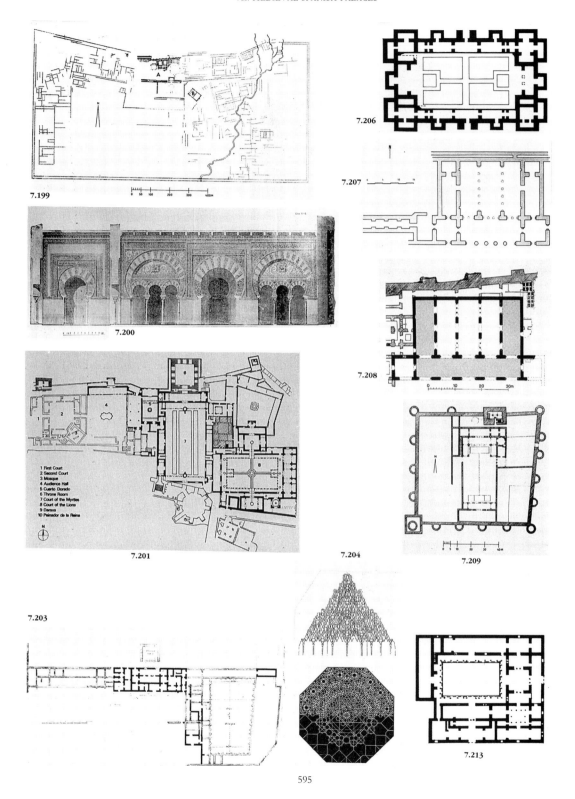

7.199

7.200

7.201

1 First Court
2 Second Court
3 Mosque
4 Audience Hall
5 Cuarto Dorado
6 Throne Room
7 Court of the Myrtles
8 Court of the Lions
9 Daraxa
10 Peinador de la Reina

7.203

7.206

7.207

7.208

7.204

7.209

7.213

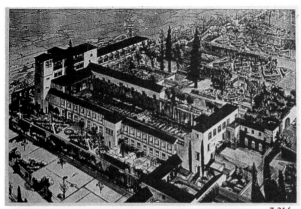

7.214

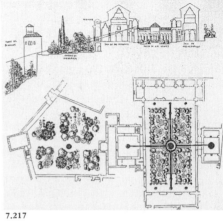

7.217

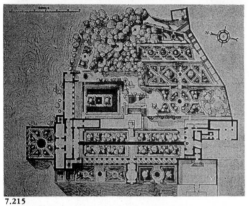

7.215

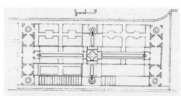

7.218

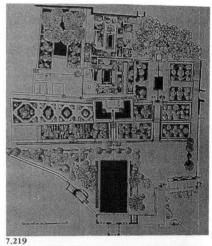

7.219

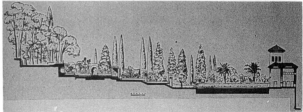

7.216

7.220

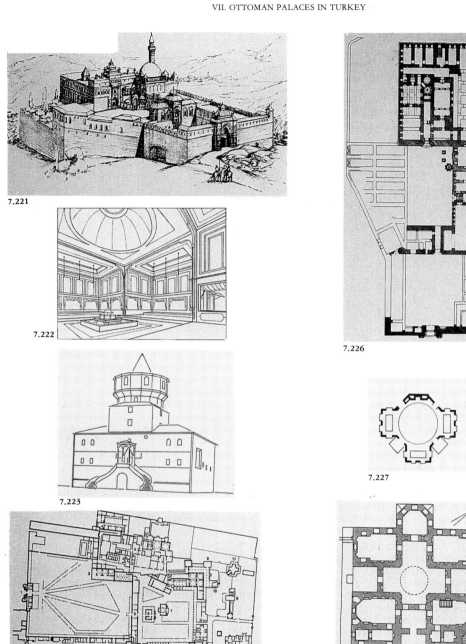

7.221

7.222

7.223

7.224

7.226

7.227

7.228

Glossary of Islamic Terms

ablaq: two-tone masonry (lit. "piebald")

adhan: call to prayer

ahl al-bait: the family of the Prophet

ʿalam/ʿalama: finial; flag; signpost; boundary marker; minaret

amir al-muʾminin: Commander of the Faithful (title of the caliph)

amir: commander

ʿanaza: spear (of the Prophet, and symbolic of his authority)

aqsa: furthest

asas: place of watching; minaret

astana: threshold; shrine

atabeg: guardian of a prince; often a governor

ʿaziza, al-: The Splendid

badgir: wind tower

badiya: nomadic encampment

bagh: garden

bait al-mal: treasury

bait: house; living unit consisting of a self-contained suite of apartments

baraka: spiritual power which emanates from a holy person or object, and which is a source of blessing

barid: postal service

bayʿa: oath of allegiance

bazar: market

bedesten: covered market, often domed

beg/bey/bay/bek: commander, lord

bimarhane: mental hospital

bismillah: in the name of God (the opening of the invocation "In the name of God, the Merciful, the Compassionate")

bit al-hilani: fenestrated gatehouse

cami: Friday Mosque

caravansarai: lodging place for travellers or merchants

chahar bagh: garden divided into four quadrants

chahar su: domed intersection of two bazars

chhatri: kiosk or miniature pavilion, often on a roof

daʿi: missionary

dakhma: Tower of Silence: flat-roofed tower used to expose corpses

dar al-hadith: foundation for the teaching of Islamic traditions

dar al-hikma: House of Wisdom

(specifically the research institute and translation bureau founded by the ʿAbbasids)

dar al-huffaz: foundation for the recitation of the Qurʾan

dar al-imara: seat of authority; usually governor's palace

dar: palace; house

dargah: shrine or mausoleum; portal; dervish lodge

dhikr: repetition of pious formulae (lit. "reminding oneself"); by extension, prayer; dervish ceremony

dihqan: landowner

dikka/dakka: platform used by supplementary prayer leaders

dinar: gold coin

diwan al-ʿamm: public audience

diwan al-khass: private audience

diwan: government office or ministry; royal reception chamber

durqaʿa: sunken area at the centre of a long hall

duwaira: shrine or mausoleum

duwira: small courtyard

faqih: specialist in religious law

fathnama: declaration of victory

fiqh: jurisprudence; the science of Islamic religious law

funduq: warehouse or inn

futuwwa: order of chivalry; organisation of young men, often with Sufi or professional associations

ghazi: fighter for the faith, often on the frontiers of Islam

girikh: geometrical knotted ornament

guldasta: roof kiosk for the call to prayer (lit. "bunch of flowers")

gunbad: dome

hadith: collective body of traditions relating to Muhammad and his Companions

haidar: lion (also used of ʿAli)

hair: game preserve

hajj: the Pilgrimage to Mecca

hammam: public baths

han: lodging place for travellers or merchants

haram: sanctuary (lit. "forbidden", i.e. sacred or private)

harim sara: palatial women's quarters

harim: women's quarters

hasht bihisht: lit. "Eight Paradises"; a name often given to octagonal pavilions

haush: unroofed funerary enclosure

hazira: unroofed funerary enclosure, especially in the Iranian world

hijra: Muhammad's emigration from Mecca to Medina in September 622; this marked the beginning of the Muslim calendar

hira: encampment for short-term use

hisba: craft or market law

hujra: chamber, cell

ʿid: festival

ʿidgah: open-air place for communal extraordinary prayer, often outside a settlement

ijaza: authorisation, licence

imam: spiritual leader; prayer leader; leader of the Shiʿite community

imamzada: Shiʿite shrine

imaret: hospice; public kitchen providing food for the needy

isfahsalar: military commander-in-chief

iwan: vaulted or flat-roofed hall, open at one end

jamaʿat khana: dervish convent; place of prayer in a *madrasa*

jamiʿ: Friday Mosque

jamur: finial

jihad: holy war

kakh: palace; castle

kalam: Muslim scholastic theology; more generally, rational argument

karban: one who protects trade

khalqa: circle, for example of students

khan: lodging place for travellers or merchants

khanqah: residential Sufi convent, often with an additional funerary function

khatib: preacher and prayer leader

khiyaban: avenue

khutba: Friday sermon (originally with a strong political dimension); address; bidding prayer

khwabgah: mausoleum (lit. "place of sleep")

kilim: floor covering in flat tapestry weave

kishlik: covered hall

kiswa: covering (in later times

598

usually of black cloth) sent annually by the caliph for the Ka'ba

külliye: foundation comprising multiple buildings centred on a mosque but with a strong educational and welfare bent – typically Ottoman

kurgan: funerary mound

kushk: pavilion; residence, often fortified

kuttab: schools for teaching the Qur'an

lajvardina: pottery with a cobalt blue glaze and enamelling

mabain: corridor, cloister

mabkhara: finial crowning a minaret, in the shape of a censer

madfan: tomb

madhhab: school of Islamic law

madina: city

mafraj: reception room, often commanding a view

maidan: public square; ceremonial open space

majana: clepsydra

majlis: reception hall

majma': large assembly hall

malqaf: airshaft or wind-catcher

malwiya: helicoidal tower

mamluk: slave; but the term is often used of manumitted slaves too

manar/manara: minaret

manzil: house; way-station

maq'ad: loggia, often on the second storey

maqsura: enclosure near the *mihrab* for the protection of the caliph or his representative; screen enclosing the grave proper in a mausoleum

marabut: local saint; by extension, the mausoleum of such a person

maristan: infirmary

masani'a: way-stations

mashhad: mausoleum (of a martyr)

mashrabiya: window-grille or screen of turned wood

mashwar: public reception hall or tribunal

masjid: mosque (lit. "place of prostration"); usually without a *minbar*

mastaba: bench or platform, usually made of stone

mazar: mausoleum (lit. "place of visitation")

mi'dhana: minaret

mi'raj: the Ascension of the Prophet to Heaven

mihman sarai: guest quarters; hotel

mihrab: arch or arcuated niche, flat or concave, which indicates the direction of Mecca (the *qibla*)

mil: tower, sometimes used for signals

mina'i: pottery in which colours are applied both under and over the glaze

minbar: pulpit, to be found in mosques used for Friday prayer

mizwar: high court official

mu'adhdhin: the man who makes the call to prayer (muezzin)

mudarrisun: lecturers

mughatta: the sanctuary or covered part of the mosque

mujahid: fighter of the holy war

muluk al-tawa'if: the Party Kings (rulers of minor Spanish principalities after the break-up of the Cordovan caliphate)

munazara: disputation

muqarnas: honeycomb or stalactite vaulting made up of individual cells or small niches; often used as a bridging element

murabit: fighter for the faith

musalla: open-air place of communal prayer, usually outside a settlement; oratory; prayer rug

mutawadda': washroom

muthaghir: a fighter on the Muslim frontier

nar: fire

naskhi: cursive script used as a scribal hand

nur: light

pishtaq: lofty arch framing an *iwan*; hence, monumental portal

qa'a: central reception hall of Egyptian palaces, with a covered central space and one, two or four *iwan*s

qabr: grave

qadi: Muslim judge, especially on points of religious law

qamis: short tunic

qandil: lamp

qasaba: citadel; capital; metropolis

qasr: palace; residence; fort; *château*

qibla: direction of prayer, i.e. to the Black Stone in the Ka'ba in Mecca

qishlaq: winter quarters (often for an army)

qubba: dome; mausoleum

qubbat al-khadra': Dome of Heaven

qubbat al-mazalim: Dome of Justice

qulla: finial of a minaret, resembling the upper part of a water-container

qurra: Qur'an reciter

rab'/rub': tenement block

rabata: to tether one's horse

rabita: hermitage

rashidun: rightly guided (usually referring to the first four caliphs)

rauda: garden; funerary garden; mausoleum

ribat: fortified religious outpost on the Muslim frontier; caravansarai; royal stopover

riwaq: portico or cloisters around a courtyard; tent-flap

riwaya: inter alia, the seven methods of reading the Qur'an

sabat: vaulted passage

sabil kuttab: foundation combining a Qur'an school with a unit for distributing free water

sabil: a public fountain giving free water

saha: terrace

sahaba: Companions of the Prophet

sahn: courtyard

sajada: to prostrate oneself; prayer rug

salat: prayer, especially at the five canonical times of day

sara'i: palace

sauma'a: minaret; cell

shadirvan: fountain for ritual ablutions, usually in the courtyard of a religious building

shahada: creed, profession of faith

shaikh: leader, whether tribal or religious (e.g. Sufi); title of respect

sinf: organisation of workers into guilds

sipahsalar: commander-in-chief

sirdab: underground room for summer use; basement

suq: market, usually subdivided according to trades

sura: chapter of the Qur'an

tadris: explanation and commentary

tafsir: Qur'anic commentary

talar: open columned hall, veranda, portico

tanur: oven

taq: arch

tarima: open loggia

tariqa: Sufi brotherhood

tawwaf: ritual circumambulation

tekke: dervish lodge

tim: covered market

turba/turbe: mausoleum (lit. "dust")

ulama': scholars; clerics; the learned class

ulu cami: Great Mosque, Friday Mosque

wakala: urban caravansarai, market and warehouse

waqf: land or property charitably endowed in perpetuity for the benefit of a pious institution, and yielding an income

waqfiya: legally attested deed of endowment

wudu': partial ritual ablution

yaylaq: summer pastures

yurt: circular tent

zawiya: small residential building for Sufis, also discharging a teaching and at times funerary function

zilu: flatweave floor covering

ziyada: enclosed extension to a mosque

ziyarat: mausoleum (lit. "visitation")

zulla: shaded area in a mosque; hence, sanctuary

Select Bibliography

ABBREVIATIONS

AADAI   *Archaologischer Anzeiger des Deutschen Archäologis-chen Instituts*
AeI   *Athar-é Iran*
AI   *Ars Islamica*
AIEO   *Annales de l'Institut d'Etudes Orientales, Université d'Alger*
AION   *Annali dell'Istituto (Universitario) Orientale di Napoli*
AM   *Archives Marocaines*
AO   *Ars Orientalis*
BEO   *Bulletin d'Etudes Orientales*
BIFAO   *Bulletin de l'Institut Français d'Archéologie Orientale*
BM   *Baghdader Mitteilungen*
BSOAS   *Bulletin of the School of Oriental and African Studies*
BSOS   *Bulletin of the School of Oriental Studies*
CAJ   *Central Asiatic Journal*
DI   *Der Islam*
EI   *Encyclopaedia of Islam*
EW   *East and West*
IA   *Islamic Art*
IC   *Islamic Culture*
IJMES   *International Journal of Middle East Studies*
JA   *Journal Asiatique*
JAOS   *Journal of the American Oriental Society*
KdO   *Kunst des Orients*
MIFAO   *Mémoires de l'Institut Français d'Archéologie Orientale*
MM   *Madrider Mitteilungen*
RA   *Revue Africaine*
REI   *Revue des Etudes Islamiques*
SI   *Studia Islamica*
STY   *Sanat Tarihi Yilliği*
ZDMG   *Zeitschrift der Deutschen Morgenländischen Gesellschaft*

REFERENCE WORKS

(a) *Bibliographies, reference handbooks and encyclopaedias*

Arnold, Sir T.W., *et al.*, *The Encyclopaedia of Islam* (first edition, 1913–38)

Bacharach, J. *A Near East Studies Handbook* (Seattle, 1986)

Bosworth, C.E. *The Islamic Dynasties* (Edinburgh, 1967)

Creswell, K.A.C. *A Bibliography of the Architecture, Arts and Crafts of Islam* (Cairo, 1961; *First Supplement*, Cairo, 1973; *Second Supplement*, Cairo, 1984)

Gibb, H.A.R., *et al.*, *The Encyclopaedia of Islam*, second edition, 1954–

Pearson, J.D. (with J.Ashton) *Index Islamicus, 1906–1955: A Catalogue of Articles on Islamic Subjects in Periodicals and Other Collective Publications* (Cambridge, 1958); various *Supplements* covering 1956–1980 and 1660–1905 (Cambridge and London, 1962–89)

(b) *Journals of Islamic Art*

Art and Archaeology Research Papers, 1–20 (1972–1980)
Ars Islamica, 1–16 (1934–51)
Ars Orientalis, 1–22 (1954–92)
Athar-é Iran, 1–4 (1936–49)
Islamic Art, 1–4 (1981–91)
Kunst des Orients, 1–12 (1954–79)
Muqarnas, 1–10 (1981–92)

(c) *Monographs and multi-author works on history and religion*

Andrae, T. *Muhammad, the Man and his Faith* (London, 1936)

Bosworth, C.E. and Schacht, J. *The Legacy of Islam* (Oxford, 1974)

Cahen, C. *Pre-Ottoman Turkey*, tr. J.Jones-Williams (London, 1968)

Gibb, H.A.R. *Muhammedanism* (New York, 1962)

Hawting, G.R. *The First Dynasty of Islam. The Umayyad Caliphate AD 661–750* (London and Sydney, 1986)

Hitti, P.K. *History of the Arabs* (London, 1943)

Hodgson, M. *The Venture of Islam*, 3 vols. (Chicago, 1974)

Holt, P.M. *The Age of the Crusades. The Near East from the eleventh century to 1517* (London and New York, 1986)

Hourani, A.H. *A History of the Arab Peoples* (Cambridge, Mass., 1991)

Inalcik, H. *The Ottoman Empire. The Classical Age, 1300–1600*, tr. N.Itzkowitz and C.Imber (New York, 1973)

Irwin, R. *The Middle East in the middle ages. The early Mamluk Sultanate 1250–1382* (London and Sydney, 1986)

Julien, C.-A. *History of North Africa From the Arab Conquest to 1830*, tr. J.Petrie (London, 1970)

Kennedy, H.N. *The Prophet and the Age of the Caliphates. The Islamic Near East from the sixth to the eleventh century* (London and New York, 1986)

Lewis, B. *The Arabs in history* (London, 1958)

idem (ed.) *The World of Islam: Faith, People, Culture* (London, 1976)

idem, et al., (eds.) *The Cambridge History of Islam*, 2 vols. (Cambridge, 1970)

Morgan, D.O. *Medieval Persia 1040–1797* (London and New York, 1988)

The Cambridge History of Iran 1–7 (Cambridge, 1968–91)

Watt, W.M. *Muhammad, Prophet and Statesman* (London, 1961)

GENERAL WORKS ON ISLAMIC ARCHITECTURE

Note: many of the books in the following list should be consulted not only for general information but also to supplement the titles given in the more specialised bibliographies which refer to Chapters 2 to 7. They will therefore not be cited in those bibliographies.

Allen, T. *Five Essays on Islamic Art* (Sevastopol, 1988)

Creswell, K.A.C. *Early Muslim Architecture. II. Early 'Abbasids, Umayyads of Cordova, Aghlabids, Tulunids and Samanids, A.D. 751–905* (Oxford, 1940)

idem, Early Muslim Architecture. Umayyads. A.D. 622–750, 2 vols. (Oxford, 1969)

idem, rev. J.W.Allan. *A Short Account of Early Muslim Architecture* (Aldershot, 1989)

Ettinghausen, R. and Grabar, O. *The Art and Architecture of Islam, 650–1250* (Harmondsworth and New York, 1987)

Franz, H.-G. *Palast, Moschee und Wüstenschloss* (Graz, 1984)

idem, Von Baghdad bis Córdoba: Ausbreitung und Entfaltung der islamischen Kunst, 850–1050 (Graz, 1984)

Golvin, L. *Essai sur l'architecture religieuse musulmane*, I–IV, (Paris, 1970–6)

Grabar, O. *The Formation of Islamic Art* (New Haven, 1973, repr. 1987)

Grube, E.J. *The World of Islam* (Feltham and New York, 1967)

Hoag, J.D. *Islamic Architecture* (New York, 1977)

Jairazbhoy, R.A. *An Outline of Islamic Architecture* (Bombay, 1972)

Kuban, D. *Muslim Religious Architecture*, 2 vols. (Leiden, 1974–85)

Mayer, L.A. *Islamic Architects and their Works* (Geneva, 1956)

Michell, G. (ed.) *Architecture of the Islamic World* (London, 1978)

Monneret de Villard, U. *Introduzione allo studio dell'archeologia islamica, le origini e il periodo omayyade* (Venice, 1966)

Otto-Dorn, K. *L'art de l'Islam*, tr. J.-B.Simon (Paris, 1967)

Richmond, E.T. *Moslem Architecture, 623 to 1516. Some causes and consequences* (London, 1926)

Spuler, B. and Sourdel-Thomine, J. *Die Kunst des Islam* (Berlin, 1973)

GENERAL WORKS ON BUILDING TECHNIQUES AND DECORATION

Dimand, M. "Studies in Islamic Ornament, I. Some Aspects of Omaiyad and Early Abbasid Ornament", *AI* IV (1937), 293–337

Dodd, E.C. and Khairallah, S. *The Image of the Word*, 2 vols. (Beirut, 1981)

Ecochard, M. *Filiation des monuments grecs, byzantins et islamiques* (Paris, 1977)

El-Said, I. and Parman, A., *Geometric Concepts in Islamic Art* (London, 1976)

Ettinghausen, R. "The 'Beveled Style' in the Post-Samarra Period", in G.C.Miles (ed.), *Archaeologia Orientalia In Memoriam Ernst Herzfeld* (Locust Valley, 1952), 72–83

idem, "Islamische Architekturornamente", *Du* XXXVI (1976), 20–62

Flury, S. *Die Ornamente der Hakim und Ashar Moschee* (Heidelberg, 1912)

Giménez, F.H. "Die Elle in der arabischen Geschichtsschreibung über die Hauptmoschee von Córdoba", *MM* (1960), 182–224

Godard, A. "Voûtes iraniennes", *AeI* IV/2 (1949), 187–360

Gye, D. "Arches and Domes in Iranian Islamic Buildings: an Engineer's Perspective", *Iran* XXVI (1988), 129–44

Herzfeld, E. *Der Wandschmuck der Bauten von Samarra und ihre Ornamentik* (Berlin, 1923)

idem, "Arabesque", *EI* (1st ed.), I, 363–7

Hillenbrand, R. "The use of glazed tilework in Iranian Islamic architecture", *Akten des VII. Internationalen Kongresses für Iranische Kunst und Archäologie. München 7.–10. September 1976* (Berlin, 1979), 545–54

Hinz, W. *Islamische Masse und Gewichte umgerechnet ins metrische System* (Leiden, 1955)

Kühnel, E., tr. R.Ettinghausen, *The Arabesque* (Graz, 1977)

Maldonado, B.P. *El Arte Hispanomusulmán en su Decoración Geometrica (Una teoria para un estilo)* (Madrid, 1975)

Meinecke, M. *Fayencedekorationen seldschukischer Sakralbauten in Kleinasien*, 2 vols. (Tübingen, 1976)

idem, "Zur Entwicklung des islamischen Architekturdekors im Mittelalter", *DI* 47 (1971), 200–35

Rempel', L.I. *Arkhitekturnyi Ornament Uzbekistana* (Tashkent, 1961)

Rosintal, J. *Pendentifs, trompes et stalactites dans l'architecture orientale* (Paris, 1928)

Schneider, G. *Geometrische Bauornamente der Seldschuken in Kleinasien* (Wiesbaden, 1980)

Wilber, D.N. "The development of mosaic faïence in Islamic architecture in Iran", *AI* VI (1939), 16–47

Wulff, H. *The Traditional Crafts of Persia* (Cambridge, Mass., 1966)

REGIONAL STUDIES

Allen, T. *A Classical Revival in Islamic Architecture* (Wiesbaden, 1986)

Aslanapa, O. *Turkish Art and Architecture*, tr. A.Mill (London, 1971)

Bourouiba, R. *L'art religieux musulman en Algérie* (Algiers, 1973)

Bretanitsky, L.S. *Zodchestvo Azerbaidzhana XII–XV v.v., i ego mesto v arkhitekture perednego vostoka* (Moscow, 1966)

Briggs, M.S. *Muhammadan Architecture in Egypt and Palestine* (Oxford, 1934)

Burckhardt, T. *Moorish Culture in Spain* (London, 1972)

Burgoyne, M.H. *Mamluk Jerusalem. An Architectural Study* (London, 1987)

Cohn-Wiener, E. *Turan. Islamische Baukunst in Mittelasien* (Berlin, 1930)

Creswell, K.A.C. *The Muslim Architecture of Egypt. I. Ikhshids and Fatimids, A.D. 937–1171. II. Ayyubids and Early Bahrite Mamluks, A.D. 1171–1326* (Oxford, 1952–60)

Diez, E. *Churasanische Baudenkmäler* (Berlin, 1918)

idem, Persien. Islamische Baukunst in Churasan (Darmstadt, 1923)

Finster, B. and Schmidt, J. *Sasanidische und frühislamische Ruinen im Iraq, Baghdader Mitteilungen* 8 (1976)

Gabriel, A. *Une Capitale turque Brousse, Bursa*, 2 vols. (Paris, 1958)

idem, Monuments turcs d'Anatolie, 2 vols. (Paris, 1934)

idem and J.Sauvaget, *Voyages archeologiques dans la Turquie Orientale*, 2 vols. (Paris, 1940)

Golombek, L. and Wilber, D. *The Islamic Architecture of Iran and Turan in the Timurid Period*, 2 vols. (Princeton, 1988)

Gomez-Moreno, M. *El arte árabe hasta los Almohades; arte mozárabe (Ars Hispaniae, III)* (Madrid, 1951)

Goodwin, G. *A History of Ottoman Architecture* (London, 1971)

Hill, D., Golvin, L. and Hillenbrand, R. *Islamic architecture in North Africa* (London, 1976)

Hill, D. and Grabar, O. *Islamic Architecture and its Decoration 800–1500*, 2nd ed. (London, 1967)

Janabi, T. al- *Studies in the medieval architecture of Iraq* (Baghdad, 1982)

Lézine, A. *Architecture de l'Ifriqiya. Recherches sur les monuments aghlabides* (Paris, 1966)

Marçais, G. *L'architecture musulmane d'Occident: Tunisie, Algérie, Maroc, Espagne et Sicile* (Paris, 1955)

Meinecke, M. *Die mamlukische Architektur in Ägypten und Syrien (648/1250 bis 923/1517)* (Glückstadt, 1992)

Ögel, S. *Der Kuppelraum in der türkischen Architektur* (Istanbul, 1972)

O'Kane, B. *The Timurid Architecture of Khurasan* (Costa Mesa, 1987)

Pope, A.U. *Persian Architecture* (London and New York, 1965)

idem and P.Ackerman (eds.), *A Survey of Persian Art from Prehistoric Times to the Present*, 6 vols. (London and New York, 1938–9)

Preusser, C. *Nordmesopotamische Baudenkmäler altchristlicher und islamischer Zeit* (Leipzig, 1911)

Pugachenkova, G.A. *Puti razvitiya arkhitekturi Iuzhnogo Turkmenistana pori rabovladeniya feodalizma*, in *Trudi Iuzhno-Turkmenistanskoi Arkheologicheskoi Ekspeditsii* VI (Moscow, 1958)

eadem and L.I.Rempel', *Istoriya Iskusstvo Uzbekistana* (Moscow, 1965)

Riefstahl, R.M. and Wittek, P., *Turkish Architecture in Southwestern Anatolia* (Cambridge, Mass., 1931)

Rogers, J.M. "al-Kahira", *EI* (2nd ed.), IV, 424–41

Sarre, F. *Denkmäler persischer Baukunst* (Berlin, 1901–10)

idem and Herzfeld, E. *Archäologische Reise im Euphrat- und Tigris-Gebiet*, 4 vols. (Berlin, 1911–20)

Sauvaget, J. *Alep. Essai sur le développement d'une grande ville syrienne, des origines au milieu du XIXe siècle* (Paris, 1941)

Serjeant, R.B. and Lewcock, R. (eds.), *San'a'. An Arabian Islamic City* (London, 1983)

Torres Balbás, L. *Arte Almohad, Nazrí, Mudéjar (Ars Hispaniae* IV) (Madrid, 1949)

idem, Artes almoravide y almohade (Madrid, 1955)

Useinov, M., Bretanitsky, L.S. and Salamzade, A. *Istoriya arkhitekturi Azerbaidhzana* (Moscow, 1963)

Wilber, D.N. *The Architecture of Islamic Iran. The Il-Khanid Period* (Princeton, 1955)

THE MOSQUE

Akkush, M. *Contribution à une étude des origines de l'architecture musulmane. La Grande Mosquée de Medine (al-Haram al-Madani)*, *Mélanges Maspéro* III (1940), 377–410

Basset, R. and Terrasse, H. *Sanctuaires et forteresses almohades* (Paris, 1932)

Becker, C.H. "Die Kanzel im Kultus des alten Islam", *Orientalische Studien (Theodor Nöldeke Festschrift)* (Gieszen, 1906), 331–51

Diez, E. *Masdjid. III. Architecture*, in *EI* (1st ed.), 378–89

Dietrich, A. "Die Moscheen von Gurgan zur Omaijadenzeit", *DI* XL (1964), 1–17

Egli, E. *Sinan, der Baumeister osmanischer Glanzzeit* (Zurich, 1954)

Ewert, C. and Wisshak, J.-P. *Forschungen zur almohadischen Moschee. Lieferung 1: Vorstufen. Hierarchische Gliederungen westislamischer Betsäle des 8. bis 11. Jahrhunderts: Die Hauptmoscheen von Qairawan und Córdoba und ihr Bannkreis* (Mainz, 1981)

Finster, B. *Islamische Bau- und Kunstdenkmäler im Yemen, Archaologische Berichte aus dem Yemen* I (1982), 223–75

eadem, "Die Freitagsmoschee von San'a'. I", *BM* IX (1978), 92–133

eadem and Schmidt, J., "Die Freitagsmoschee von San'a'. II", *BM* X (1979), 179–92

Gabriel, A. *Les mosquées de Constantinople*, in *Syria* VII (1926), 353–419

Galdieri, E. *Isfahan: Masǧid-i Ǧum'a*, 3 vols. (Rome, 1972–84)

Godard, A. "Les anciennes mosquées de l'Iran", in *AéI* I/1 (1936), 187–210; continued in *Arts Asiatiques* III (1956), 48–63 and 83–8

idem, "Historique du Masdjid-é Djum'a d'Isfahan", in *AéI* I/2 (1936), 213–82

Golvin, L. *La Mosquée. Ses origines. Sa morphologie. Ses diverses fonctions. Son rôle dans la vie musulmane, plus spécialement en Afrique du Nord* (Algiers, 1960)

Grabar, O. "La Grande Mosquée de Damas et les origines architecturales de la mosquée", *Synthronon. Art et Archéologie de la fin de l'Antiquité et du Moyen Age. Receuil d'Etudes* (Paris, 1968), 107–14

idem, "The Architecture of the Middle Eastern City from Past to Present: The Case of the Mosque", *Middle Eastern Cities*, ed. I.M.Lapidus (Berkeley and Los Angeles, 1969), 26–46

idem, The Great Mosque of Isfahan (London and New York, 1990)

Gurlitt, C. *Die Baukunst Konstantinopels*, 3 vols. (Berlin, 1907–12)

Hautecoeur, L.Y. and Wiet, G. *Les Mosquées du Caire*, 2 vols. (Paris, 1932–4)

Hillenbrand, R. "Saljuq dome chambers in North-west Iran", *Iran* XIV (1976), 93–102

Kühnel, E. *Die Moschee. Bedeutung, Einrichtung und kunsthistorische Entwicklung der islamischen Kultstätte* (Berlin, 1949)

Kuran, A. *The Mosque in Early Ottoman Architecture* (Chicago and London, 1968)

idem, "Thirteenth and fourteenth century mosques in Turkey", *Archaeology* XXIV/3 (1971), 234–54

Lambert, E. "La synagogue de Dura-Europos et les origines de la mosquée", *Semitica* III (1950), 67–72

idem, "Les origines de la mosquée et l'architecture religieuse des Omeyyades", *Studia Islamica* vi (1956), 5–18

Lewcock, R.B. and Smith, G.R. "Three Medieval Mosques in the Yemen", *Oriental Art* N.S. XX (1974), 75–86, 192–203

Marçais, G. "L'église et la mosquée", in *L'Islam et l'Occident. Cahiers du Sud* (Marseilles, 1947), 174–84

Maslow, B. *Les mosquées de Fès* (Paris, 1937)

Miles, G.C. "Mihrab and 'Anazah: A Study in Early Islamic Iconography", in G.C.Miles (ed.), *Archaeologia Orientalia in Memoriam Ernst Herzfeld* (Locust Valley, 1952), 156–71

Pauty, E. "L'évolution du dispositif en T dans les mosquées à portiques", *BEO* II (1932), 91–124

Sauvaget, J. *La mosquée omeyyade de Medine* (Paris, 1947)

idem, "Observations sur quelques mosquées seldjoukides", *AIEO* IV (1938), 81–120

Sebag, P. *La Grande Mosquée de Kairouan* (Zurich, 1963)

Serjeant, R.B. "Mihrab", *BSOAS* XXII (1959), 439–52

Smith, M.B. *Material for a Corpus of Early Iranian Islamic Architecture. I–III, AI II* (1935), 153–71; IV (1937), 1–40; and VI (1939), 1–10

Sourdel-Thomine, J. "Inscriptions seljoukides et salles à coupoles de Qazwin en Iran", *REI* XLII (1974), 3–43

eadem, "La mosquée et la madrasa. Types monumentaux caractéristiques de l'art islamique médiéval", *Cahiers de civilisation médiévale, Xe–XIIe siècles, Université de Poitiers, Centre d'Etudes Supérieures de Civilisation Médiévale* XIII/2 (1970), 97–115

Stern, H."Les origines de l'architecture de la mosquée omeyyade", *Syria* XXVIII (1951), 269–79

Strika, V. "Caratteri della moschea irachena dalle origini al X secolo", *Accademia Nazionale dei Lincei, Rendiconti della Classe di Scienze morali, storiche e filologiche, Serie VIII*, Vol. XXVIII (1973), 1–46

Torres Balbás, L. "Origen de las disposiciones arquitectónicas de las mezquitas", *Al-Andalus* XVII (1952), 388–99

idem, La mezquita de Córdoba (Madrid, 1965)

Vogt-Göknil, U. *Die Moschee. Grundformen sakraler Baukunst* (Zürich, 1978)

eadem, Türkische Moscheen (Zürich, 1953)

Mohammed, G.R. *The minaret and its relationship to the mosque in early Islam*, 2 vols. (unpublished Ph.D. thesis, University of Edinburgh, 1964)

O'Kane, B. "Salǧuq minarets: some new data", *Annales Islamologiques* XX (1984), 85–101

Schacht, J. "Ein archaischer Minaret-Typ in Ägypten und Anatolien", *AI* 5 (1938), 46–54

idem, "Sur la diffusion des formes d'architecture religieuse musulmane à travers le Sahara", *Travaux de l'Institut de Recherches Sahariennes* 11 (1954), 11–27

idem, "Further Notes on the Staircase Minaret", *AO* 4 (1961), 137–41

Sourdel-Thomine, J. "Deux minarets d'époque seljoukide en Afghanistan", *Syria* XXX (1952), 108–36

Smith, M.B. "The Manars of Isfahan", *AeI* I/2 (1936), 313–58

Thiersch, H. *Pharos: Antike, Islam und Occident* (Leipzig and Berlin, 1909)

van Berchem, M. "Die Inschriften", in E.Diez, *Churasanische Baudenkmäler* (Berlin, 1918), 109–16

Whitehouse, D. "Staircase Minarets on the Persian Gulf", *Iran* X (1972), 155–8

THE MINARET

Adle, C. and Melikian-Chirvani, A.S. "Les monuments du XIe siècle du Damqan", *Studia Iranica* I (1972), 229–97

Behrens-Abouseif, D. *The minarets of Cairo* (Cairo, 1985)

Bloom, J.M. *Minaret. Symbol of Islam (Oxford Studies in Islamic Art VII)* (Oxford, 1989)

idem, "Five Fatimid Minarets in Upper Egypt", *Journal of the Society of Architectural Historians* XLIII/2 (1984), 162–7

Creswell, K.A.C. "The evolution of the Minaret, with special reference to Egypt", *The Burlington Magazine* XLVIII (1926), 134–40, 252–8 and 290–8

Diez, E. "Manara", *Encyclopaedia of Islam* (1st ed.), III, 227–31

Doutté, E. "Les minarets et l'appel à la prière", *Revue Africaine* 43 (1899), 339–49

Gimenez, F. Hernandez. *El alminar de 'Abd al-Rahman III en el mezquita mayor de Córdoba. Genesis y repercusiones* (Granada, 1975)

Gottheil, R.J.H. "The Origins and History of the Minaret", *JAOS* 30 (1909–10), 132–54

Hassid, S. *The Sultan's turrets, a study of the origin and evolution of the minaret in Cairo* (Cairo, 1939)

Husain, A.B.M. *The Manara in Indo-Muslim Architecture* (Dacca, 1970)

Hutt, A.M. "The Central Asian origin of the eastern minaret form", *Asian Affairs*, N.S. VIII/2 (1977), 157–62

idem, The development of the minaret under the Saljuqs, 2 vols. (unpublished M.Phil. thesis, University of London, 1974)

Lammens, H. "Phares, minarets, clochers et mosquées: leur origine, leur architecture", *Revue des Questions Historiques* N.S. XLVI (1911), 5–27

Lézine, A. "Le Minaret de la Qal'a des Banu Hammad", *Bulletin d'Archéologie Algérienne* 2 (1966–7), 261–70

Maricq, A. and Wiet, G. *Le Minaret de Djam (Mémoires de la Délégation Archéologique Française en Afghanistan 16)* (Paris, 1959)

THE MADRASA

Blair, S.S. "The Madrasa at Zuzan: Islamic Architecture in Eastern Iran on the Eve of the Mongol Invasions", *Muqarnas* 3 (1985), 75–91

Brandenburg, D. *Die Madrasa. Ursprung, Entwicklung, Ausbreitung und künstlerische Gestaltung der islamischen Moschee-Hochschule* (Graz, 1978)

Bulliet, R.W. *The patricians of Nishapur* (Cambridge, Mass., 1972)

Casimir, M.J. and Glatzer, B. "Šah-i Mašhad, a Recently Discovered Madrasah of the Ghurid Period in Gargistan (Afghanistan)", *EW* N.S. XXI (1971), 53–68

Chabbi, J. "Khankah", *EI* (2nd ed.), IV, 1025–7

Creswell, K.A.C. "The origin of the cruciform plan of Cairene madrasas", *BIFAO* XXI (1922), 1–54 (summarised and revised in his *MAE* II, 104–33; cf. the review by E.Herzfeld, *Deutsche Literaturzeitung* 1926 (No. 9), cols. 417–23)

Erdmann, K. "Vorosmanische Medresen und Imarets vom Medresentyp", *Studies in Islamic Art and Architecture in honour of Professor K.A.C.Creswell* (Cairo, 1965), 49–62

Godard, A. "L'origine de la madrasa, de la mosquée et du caravansérail à quatre iwans", *AI* XV–XVI (1951), 1–9

Halm, H. "Die Anfänge der Madrasa", *ZDMG*, Suppl.III/I, XIX, Deutscher Orientalistentag (1977), 438–48

Herzfeld, E. "Damascus: Studies in architecture. II', *AI* X (1943), 13–30

Kuran, A. *Anadolu medreseleri* (Ankara, 1969)

Makdisi, G. *The rise of colleges. Institutions of learning in Islam and the West* (Edinburgh, 1981)

idem, "The madrasa as a charitable trust and the university as a corporation in the Middle Ages", *Correspondance d'orient*, II, *Actes du Ve Congrès International d'Arabisants et d'Islamisants* (Brussels, 1970), 329–37

idem, "Madrasa and university in the Middle Ages", *SI* XXXII (1970), 255–64 *idem*, "Muslim institutions of learning in eleventh-century Baghdad", *BSOAS* XXIV (1961), 1–56

idem, "The Madrasa in Spain: some remarks", *Revue de l'Occident Musulman et de la Méditerranée. Mélanges Le Tourneau* (1970), 153–8

Massignon, L. " Les Medresehs de Bagdad", *BIFAO* VII (1909), 77–86

Meinecke, M., *et al.*, *Die Restaurierung der Madrasa des Amirs Sabiq ad-Din Mitqal al-Anuki und die Sanierung des Darb Qirmiz in Kairo* (Mainz, 1980)

O'Kane, B. "The Madrasa al-Ghiyasiyya at Khargird", *Iran* XIV (1976), 79–92

Pedersen, J. "Some aspects of the history of the madrasa", *IC* III (1929), 525–37

Péretie, A. "Medersas de Fez", *AM* XVIII (1912), 257–372

Sayili, A. "Higher education in medieval Islam: the Madrasa", *Annales de l'Université d'Ankara* II (1947–8), 30–69

Schmid, H. *Die Madrasa des Kalifen al-Mustansir in Baghdad. Eine baugeschichtliche Untersuchung der ersten universalen Rechtshochschule des Islam* (Mainz, 1980)

idem, "Die Madrasa al-Mustansiriyya in Baghdad", *Architectura* IX (1979), 93–112

Sourdel D. "Réflexions sur la diffusion de la madrasa en Orient", *REI* XLIV (1976), 165–84

Sourdel-Thomine, J. "Locaux d'enseignement et madrasas dans l'Islam médiéval", *REI* XLIV (1976), 285–97

Sözen, M. *Anadolu medreseleri. Selcuklular ve Beylikler devri.* 2 vols. (Istanbul, 1970)

Talas, A. *La Madrasa Nizamiyya et son histoire* (Paris, 1939)

Terrasse, C. *Médersas du Maroc* (Paris, 1927)

Tibawi, A.L. "Origin and character of al-Madrasah", *BSOAS* XXV (1962), 225–38

Tritton, A.S. *Materials on Muslim education in the Middle Ages* (London, 1957)

THE MAUSOLEUM

Adle, C. and Melikian-Chirvani, A.S. "Les monuments du XIe siècle du Damqan", *Studia Iranica* I/2 (1972), 229–97

Allen, T. "The tombs of the 'Abbasid caliphs in Baghdad", *BSOAS* XLVI (1983), 421–31

Azarpay, G. "The Islamic Tomb Tower: A Note on Its Genesis and Significance", *Essays in Islamic Art and Architecture In Honor of Katharina Otto-Dorn*, ed. A.Daneshvari (Malibu, 1981), 9–12

Bartol'd, V.V. "The burial rites of the Turks and the Mongols", tr. J.M.Rogers, *CAJ* XIV/1–3 (1970), 195–222

Bates, Ü.Ü. "An introduction to the study of the Anatolian türbe and its inscriptions as historical documents", *STY* IV (1971), 73–84

Berchem, M. van, in Diez, E., *Churasanische Baudenkmäler* (Berlin, 1918), 87–116

Blair, S.S. *The Ilkhanid Shrine Complex at Natanz, Iran* (Cambridge, 1986)

Cauvet, Commandant "Les marabouts. Petits monuments funéraires et votifs du Nord de l'Afrique", *RA* 64 (1923), 274–329, 448–522

Daneshvari, A. *Medieval Iranian Tomb Towers* (Lexington, 1986)

Diez, E. "Kubba", *EI* (1st ed.), Supplement, 127–34

Esin, E. ""Al-Qubbah al-Turkiyya". An essay on the origins of the architectonic form of the Islamic Turkish funerary monument", *Atti del Terzo Congresso di Studi Arabi e Islamici, Ravello* (Naples, 1967), 281–309

Godard, A. *Les monuments de Maragha. Publications de la Société des Etudes Iraniennes et de l'Art Persan*, 9 (Paris, 1934)

Goldziher, I., *Muslim Studies*, 2 vols., ed. S.M.Stern, tr. C.N.Barber and S.M.Stern (London, 1967–71)

Golombek, L. *The Timurid Shrine at Gazur Gah* (Toronto, 1969)

eadem, "The cult of saints and shrine architecture in the fourteenth century", *Near Eastern Numismatics, Iconography, Epigraphy and History. Studies in Honor of George C.Miles*, ed. D.K.Kouymjian (Beirut, 1974), 419–30

Grabar, A. *Martyrium* (Paris, 1946)

Grabar, O. "The earliest Islamic commemorative structures, notes and documents", *AO* VI (1966), 1–46

Granquist, H. *Muslim death and burial. Arab customs and traditions studied in a village in Jordan* (Helsinki, 1965)

Grütter, I. "Arabische Bestattungsbräuche in frühislamischer Zeit", *DI* 31 (1954), 147–73 and 32 (1955), 79–104

Hillenbrand, R. "The development of Saljuq mausolea in Iran", *The Art of Iran and Anatolia from the 11th to the 13th Century A.D. (Colloquies on Art & Archaeology in Asia No. 4)*, ed. W.Watson (London, 1974), 40–59

Ibrahim, L.A. *Mamluk monuments of Cairo (Quaderni dell'Istituto Italiano di Cultura per la R.A.E.)* (Cairo, 1976)

Jaworski, J. "Quelques remarques sur les coutûmes funéraires turques d'après les sources chinoises", *Rocznik Orientalistyczny* IV (1926), 255–61

Katanoff, N.T. "Ueber die Bestattungsgebräuche bei den Turkstämmen Central- und Ostasiens", *Keleti Szemle* I (1900), 100–13, 225–33 and 277–86

Kessler, C. "Funerary architecture within the city", *Colloque international sur l'histoirre du Caire* (Cairo, 1972), 257–67

Kriss, R. and Kriss-Heinrich, H. *Volksglaube im Bereich des Islam, I: Wallfahrtswesen und Heiligenverehrung* (Wiesbaden, 1960)

Nemtseva, N.B. "Istoki kompozitsii i etapy formirovaniya ansamblaya Shakhi-Zinda ("The origins and architectural development of the Shah-Zinde")", tr., with additions, by J.M.Rogers and A.Yasin, *Iran* XV (1977), 51–73

Ragib, Y. "Les premiers monuments funéraires de l'Islam", *Annales Islamologiques* IX (1970), 21–36

Rempel, L.I. "The Mausoleum of Ismail the Samanid", *Bulletin of the American Institute for Persian Art and Archaeology* IV (1936), 198–208

Roux, J.P. *La mort chez les peuples altaiques anciens et médiévaux* (Paris, 1963)

Sauvaget, J. *et al.*, *Les Monuments Ayyoubides de Damas* I–IV (Paris, 1938–50)

Strika, V. "The turbah of Zumurrud Khatun in Baghdad. Some aspects of the funerary ideology in Islamic art", *AION* N.S.38 (1978), 283–96

Stronach, D.B. and Cuyler Young, T. "Three Seljuq Tomb Towers", *Iran* IV (1966), 1–20

Sümer, F. "The Seljuk turbehs and the tradition of embalming", *Atti del Secondo Congresso Internazionale di Arte Turca* (Naples, 1965), 245–8

Tritton, A.S. "Muslim Funeral Customs", *BSOS* IX (1937–9), 653–61

Will, E. "La tour funéraire de la Syrie et les monuments apparentés", *Syria* XXVI (1949), 258–312

Williams, C. "The Cult of 'Alid Saints in the Fatimid Monuments of Cairo. Part II: The Mausolea", *Muqarnas* 3 (1985), 39–60

THE CARAVANSARAI

Aalund, F. "Proposal for the restoration and rehabilitation of Wakalat Bazar'a", in M.Meinecke, *Die Restaurierung der Madrasa des Amirs Sabiq ad-Din Mitqal al-Anuki und die Sanierung des Darb Qirmiz in Kairo* (Mainz, 1980), 119–39
Brice, W.C. "Caravan traffic across Asia", *Antiquity* XXVIII (1954), 78–84
Chabbi, J. "La fonction du ribat à Baghdad du Ve siècle au début du VIIe siècle", *REI* 42 (1974), 101–21
Elisséeff, N. "Khan", *EI* (2nd ed.), IV, 1010–7
Erdmann, K. *Das anatolische Karavansary des 13. Jahrhunderts*, 3 vols. (Berlin, 1961–76; last vol. with H.Erdmann)
Godard, A. "Robat Sharaf", *AeI* IV/1 (1949), 7–68
Kiani, Y. *Iranian Caravansarais With Particular Reference To The Safavid Period* (Tokyo, 1978)
Kiani, M.Y. *Robat-e Sharaf* (Teheran, 1982)
Kleiss, W. and Kiani, M.Y. *Iranian Caravansarais*, 2 vols. (Teheran, 1983–9)
Lézine, A. *Le Ribat de Sousse* (Tunis, 1956)
Marçais, G. "Note sur les ribats en Berbérie", *Mélanges René Basset* II (1925), 395–430
Marçais, G. "Ribat", *EI* (1st ed.), III, 1150–3
Müller, K. *Die Karawanserai im Vorderen Orient* (Berlin, 1920)
Nemtseva, N.B. "Rabat-i Malik", in L.I.Rempel' (ed.), *Khudozhestvennaya Kul'tura Srednei Azii IX–XIII Vekov* (Tashkent, 1982), 112–42
Orhonlu, C. "Karwan", *EI* (2nd ed.), IV, 676–9
al-Rashid, S.A. *Darb Zubaydah* (Riyadh, 1980)
idem, al-Rabadhah (Riyadh, 1986)
Raymond, A. *Artisans et commerçants au Caire au XVIIIe siècle*, 2 vols. (Damascus, 1974)
Sauvaget, J. "Inventaire des monuments musulmanes de la ville d'Alep", *REI* (1931), 59–114
idem, "Les caravansérails syriens du Hadjdj de Constantinople", *AI* IV (1937), 98–121
idem, "Caravansérails syriens du Moyen Age", *AI* VI (1939), 46–55 and VII (1940), 1–19
idem, La Poste aux Chevaux au Temps des Mamelouks (Paris, 1941)
Scharabi, M. "Drei traditionelle Handelsanlagen in Kairo: Wakalat al-Bazara, Wakalat Du l-Fiqar und Wakalat al-Qutn", *Mitteilungen des Deutschen Archäologischen Instituts, Abteilung Kairo* 34 (1978), 127–64
Siroux, M. *Caravansérails d'Iran MIFAO LXXXI* (Cairo, 1949)
idem, Anciennes Voies et Monuments Routiers de la Région d'Ispahan (Cairo, 1971)
idem, "Caravansérails seldjoucides iraniens", *The Art of Iran and Anatolia from the 11th to the 13th Century A.D. (Colloquies on Art & Archaeology in Asia No. 4)*, ed. W.Watson (London, 1974), 134–49
Sprenger, A. *Die Post- und Reiserouten des Orients* (repr. Amsterdam, 1962)
Taeschner, F. *Das anatolische Wegenetz* (Leipzig, 1924–6)
idem, "Die Entwicklung des Wegenetzes", *Anadolu Arastirmalari* I/1 (1959), 169–93

Yetkin, S.Y. *L'architecture turque en Turquie* (Paris, 1962), 46–62, 153–8

THE PALACE

N.B. Vol. 23 of the journal *Ars Orientalis* is devoted to the theme of the palace in the Islamic world.

Bargebuhr, F.P. *The Alhambra: A Cycle of Studies on the Eleventh Century in Moorish Spain* (Berlin, 1968)
Behrens-Abouseif, D. "The Citadel of Cairo: Stage for Mamluk Ceremonial", *Annales Islamologiques* 24 (1988), 25–79
Bell, G.L:. *Palace and Mosque at Ukhaidir. A Study in Early Muhammadan Architecture* (Oxford, 1914)
Bombaci, A. and Scerrato, U. "Introduction to the excavations at Ghazni", *EW* N.S. 10 (1959), 3–55
Caskel, W. "al-Uhaidir", *DI* XXXIX (1964), 28–37
Davis, F. *The Palace of Topkapi in Istanbul* (New York, 1970)
Dickie, J. "The Hispano-Arab Garden. Its Philosophy and Function", *BSOAS* 31 (1986), 237–48
Eldem, S.H. *Köşkler ve Kasirlar. Kiosks and Pavilions* (Istanbul, 1969)
Ettinghausen, R. *From Byzantium to Sasanian Iran and the Islamic World* (Leiden, 1972)
Ewert, C. *Spanisch-islamische Systeme sich kreuzender Bögen. II. Die Aljafería in Zaragoza* 3 vols. (Berlin, 1978–80)
Garcin, J.-C.; Maury, B.; Revault, J.; and Zakariya, M., *Palais et Maisons du Caire. I—Epoque Mamelouke (XIIIe–XVIe siècles)* (Paris, 1982)
Golvin, L. *Recherches archeologiques à la Qal'a des Banu Hammad* (Paris, 1965)
Grabar, O. "al-Mushatta, Baghdad and Wasit", *The World of Islam. Studies in Honor of P.K.Hitti,* ed. R.B.Winder (London, 1959), 99–108
idem, et al., City in the Desert: Qasr al-Hayr East (Cambridge, 1978)
idem, The Alhambra (London, 1977)
Hamilton, R.W. *Khirbat al-Mafjar* (Oxford, 1959)
Herzfeld, E. "Die Genesis der islamischen Kunst und das Mshatta-Problem", *DI* I (1910), 27–63, 105–44
idem, Erster vorläufiger Bericht über die Grabungen in Samarra (Berlin, 1912)
Hillenbrand, R. *"La dolce vita* in early Islamic Syria: the evidence of later Umayyad palaces", *Art History* 5/1 (1982), 1–35
idem,"Islamic Art at the Crossroads: East versus West at Mshatta", *Essays in Islamic Art and Architecture in Honor of Katharina Otto-Dorn,* ed. A.Daneshvari (Malibu, 1981), 63–86
Jaussen, J.A. and Savignac, R. *Les Châteaux arabes de Qeseir 'Amra, Haraneh et Tuba* (Paris, 1922)
Lehrmann, J. *Earthly Paradise. Garden and Courtyard in Islam* (London, 1980)
Lézine, A. "Les salles nobles des palais mamelouks", *Annales Islamologiques* 10 (1972), 63–148
MacDougall, E.B. and Ettinghausen, R., eds. *The Islamic Garden* (Washington, 1976)
Marçais, G. "Dar", *EI* (2nd ed.), II, 113–5
idem, "Salle, Antisalle. Recherches sur l'évolution d'un thème de l'architecture domestique en pays d'Islam", *AIEO* X (1952), 274–301

Naumann, R. *Die Ruinen von Tacht-e Suleiman und Zendan-i Suleiman und Umgebung* (Berlin, 1977)

Necipoğlu, G. *Architecture, Ceremonial and Power. The Topkapi Palace in the Fifteenth and Sixteenth Centuries* (Cambridge, Mass. and London, 1991)

Northedge, A. "Planning Samarra: A Report for 1983-4", *Iraq* 47 (1985), 109-28

idem, and Falkner, R. "The 1986 Survey Season at Samarra", *Iraq* 49 (1987), 143-73

Otto-Dorn, K. "Bericht über die Grabung in Kobadabad 1966", *AADAI* (1969), 438-506

Pauty, E. *Les palais et les maisons d'époque musulmane, au Caire* (Cairo, 1932)

Prieto-Moreno, F. *Los jardines de Granada* (Madrid, 1973)

Reuther, O. *Ocheidir* (Leipzig, 1912)

Revault, J. and Maury, B. *Palais et maisons du Caire du XIVe au XVIIIe siecle, MIFAO* 96 (Cairo, 1975)

Revault, J. *Palais et demeures de Tunis (XVIe et XVIIe siècles)* (Paris, 1967)

Rogers, J.M. (ed.) *Topkapi Saray. The Architecture* (London, 1988)

idem, "Samarra: A Study in Medieval Town Planning", *The Islamic City*, eds. A.H.Hourani and S.M.Stern (Oxford, 1970), 119-55

Sarre, F. *Der Kiosk von Konia* (Berlin, 1936)

Sauvaget, J. "Observations sur les monuments omeyyades", *JA* 228 (1939), 1-53

idem, "Châteaux omeyyades de Syrie", *REI* XXXIX (1967), 1-42

Schlumberger, D. *et al.*, *Lashkari Bazar. Une résidence royale ghaznévide et ghoride (Mémoires de la Délégation Archéologique Française en Afghanistan*, 18) (Paris, 1978)

Staacke, U. *Un palazzo normanno a Palermo. La Zisa. La cultura musulmana negli edifici dei Re* (Palermo, 1991)

Stern, H. "Notes sur l'architecture des châteaux omeyyades", *AI* XI-XII (1946-8), 72-97

Trümpelmann, L. *Mschatta* (Tübingen, 1962)

Torres Balbás, L. *La mezquita de Córdoba y las ruinas de Madinat al-Zahra* (Madrid, 1952)

Wendell, C. "Baghdad: *imago mundi*, and other foundation-lore", *IJMES* 2 (1971), 99-128

Zander, G., ed. *Travaux de restauration de monuments historiques en Iran* (Rome, 1968)

Zbiss, S.M. "Mahdia et Sabra-Mansouriya: nouveaux documents d'art fatimite d'Occident", *JA* 244 (1956), 79-93

Sources of the Line Drawings accompanying the text

These drawings, almost all of them three-dimensional, were the work of the following, many of whom put in hour upon hour of devoted work to finish a single drawing to their own high standards, and to all of whom I am very grateful; without their willingness to walk the extra mile, the book would have been much the poorer:

A.Almagro Gorbea *et al.*: 734-7.35

A.Antar: 2.66, 2.128, 2.129, 2.213, 2.224, 2.264, 3.38, 3.55, 3.94, 4.28, 4.31, 4.33, 4.54, 4.61, 4.63, 4.65, 4.108, 4.161, 4.163, 5.83, 5.89, 5.98, 5.102, 5.108, 5.151, 5.176, 5.180, 5.207, 5.213, 6.18, 6.20, 6.70, 6.129, 7.13, 7.32, 7.63, 7.118, 7.212

V.Bernie: 7.12

R.Bishop: 2.251

C.Burns: 2.70, 6.135

J.Cooper: 2.285, 5.203, 6.84

C.Dawson: 2.138, 2.253, 4.44, 4.51, 5.199

M.Day: 2.48, 2.51, 2.54, 2.76, 2.112, 2.143, 2.147, 2.162, 2.165, 2.178, 2.180, 2.200, 2.203, 2.226, 2.252, 2.266, 2.348, 3.1-3.25, 3.59-3.62, 3.100-3.101, 4.5, 4.30, 4.86, 4.92, 4.100, 4.122, 4.124, 4.150, 5.5, 5.119, 5.136, 5.142, 5.152, 5.166, 5.170, 5.174, 5.184, 5.192, 6.12, 6.43, 6.47, 6.56, 6.98, 6.110, 6.137, 7.26, 7.77, 7.177, 7.205

G.Esposito: 7.189

S.Fraser: 2.121, 6.80

D.H.Gye: 6.20

F.Hayati: 2.114, 2.126, 2.141, 3.111, 4.27, 5.14, 5.66, 5.182, 6.10, 6.14, 6.25, 6.29, 7.14, 7.63, 7.109, 7.143, 7.152, 7.183, 7.188, 7.192, 7.193, 7.210, 7.211

S.Keenan: 2.221, 5.66, 5.97, 5.126, 5.201

A.Northedge: 7.36-7.37

A.Reid: 2.15, 2.97, 4.88, 4.113, 5.127, 6.4, 7.19

M.Sharif: 7.58

S.Shaw: 2.183, 2.210, 2.250, 2.305, 2.307, 2.339, 2.345, 4.57, 4.94, 4.120, 5.168, 6.29, 6.148, 6.150, 7.21, 7.229

J.Sherring: 2.238, 2.292, 2.298, 4.29, 4.135, 4.138, 4.140, 4.142, 4.145, 5.106, 5.117, 5.124, 5.205, 6.45, 7.43

H.Strange: 2.193, 2.197, 2.280, 2.295, 4.73, 7.54

A.Thomson: 2.79, 2.93, 5.21, 5.22, 5.24, 5.30, 5.34, 5.44, 5.104, 6.20, 7.66, 7.202, 7.225

R.S.Wilson: 5.115

Sources of the Line Drawings at the back of the book

The list of sources which follows is as full as is practicable, given that there are almost a thousand drawings at the back of the book. In the case of drawings reproduced from articles, to save space the names of the relevant journals alone are provided, in preference to citing author, article, volume number, date and page.

Actes de la Ve Congrès International d'Arabisants et d'Islamisants (Brussels, 1970)

Afghanistan

Afghanistan Journal

Akten des VII. Internationalen Kongresses für Iranische Kunst und Archäologie. München 7.–10. September 1976 (Berlin, 1979)

Akurgal, E., ed., *The Art and Architecture of Turkey* (Oxford , 1980)

Albaum, L.I., and Brentjes, B., *Herren der Steppe* (Berlin, 1976)

Almagro Gorbea, A., *El Palacio Omeya de Amman. I. La Arquitectura* (Madrid, 1983)

Almagro, M., Caballero, L., Zozaya, J., and Almagro, A., *Qusayr ʿAmra: Residencia y baños omeyas en el desierto de Jordánia* (Madrid, 1975)

Annales Islamologiques

Annual of the Department of Antiquities

anon., *Mission Archéologique Française en République Arabe du Yemen. Cinq Années de Recherches 1978–1982. Exposition* (n.p., n.d.)

Archaeology

Archäologische Mitteilungen aus Iran

Archäologischer Anzeiger

Arik, M.O., *Bitlis Yapilarinda Selcuklu Rönesansi* (Ankara, 1971)

Arkhitekturnoe Nasledstvo

Ars Islamica

Ars Orientalis

Art and Archaeology Research Papers

Arts Asiatiques

Aslanapa, O., *Türk Sanati. II. Anadolu Selcuklularindan Beylikler devrinin sonuna kadar* (Istanbul, 1973)

Aslanapa, O., *Turkish Art and Architecture* (London, 1971)

Aslanapa, O., ed., *Yuzyillar boyunca Türk sanati* (Istanbul, 1977)

Atasoy, N., *Ibrahim Pasha Sarayi* (Istanbul, 1972)

Athar-é Iran

Atil, E., *Turkish Art* (Washington, D.C. and New York, 1980)

Atlal

Bachmann, W., *Kirchen und Moscheen in Armenien und Kurdistan* (Leipzig, 1913)

Basset, R., and Terrasse, H., *Sanctuaires et forteresses almohades* (Paris, 1932)

Bastan Chenassi va Honar-e Iran

Behrens-Abouseif, D., *The Minarets of Cairo* (Cairo, 1985)

Belenizki, A.M., *Mittelasien. Kunst der Soghden* (Leipzig, 1980)

Belleten

Ben-Dov, M., *In the Shadow of the Temple. The Discovery of Ancient Jerusalem* (Jerusalem, 1985)

Benachenhou, A., *La dynastie almoravide et son art* (Algiers, 1974)

Bianca, S., *Architektur und Lebensform im islamischen Stadtwesen* (Zurich, 1975)

Borouiba, R., *L'art religieux musulman en Algérie* (Algiers, 1973)

Brandenburg, D, and Brusehoff, K., *Die Seldschuken. Baukunst des Islam in Persien und Turkmenien* (Graz, 1980)

Brandenburg, D., *Die Madrasa. Ursprung, Entwicklung, Ausbreitung und künstlerische Gestaltung der islamischen Moschee-Hochschule* (Graz, 1978)

Bretanitski, L.S., *Zodchestvo Azerbaidhzana XII-XV v.v., i ego mesto v arkhitekture perednego vostoka* (Moscow, 1966)

Briggs, M.S., *Muhammadan Architecture in Egypt and Palestine* (Oxford, 1924)

Brown, P., *Indian Architecture. The Islamic Period* (Bombay, 1942)

Budge, E.A.W., *Cook's Handbook for Egypt and the Sudan* (London, 1905)

Bulatov, M.S., *Mavzolei Samanidov–Zhemchuzhina Arkhitekturi Srednei Azii* (Tashkent, 1976)

Bulletin de l'Institut Français d'Archéologie Orientale

Bulletin des Etudes Orientales

Bulletin of the American Institute for Iranian Art and Archaeology

Bulletin of the School of Oriental and African Studies

Burckhardt, T., *Moorish Culture in Spain* (London, 1972)

Burgoyne, M.H., *Mamluk Jerusalem. An Architectural Study* (London, 1987)

Cahiers de la Délégation Archéologique Française en Iran

Caillé, J., *La mosquée de Hassan à Rabat*, 2 vols. (Paris, 1954)

Castejón, R., *Medina Azahara* (Leon, 1985)

Cezar, M., *Anadolu Oncesi. Türklerde Şehir ve Mimarlik* (Istanbul, 1977)

Creswell, K.A.C., *Early Muslim Architecture I* (Oxford, repr.1969) and II (Oxford, 1940)

Creswell, K.A.C., rev. J.W.Allan, *A Short Account of Early Muslim Architecture* (Aldershot, 1989)

Creswell, K.A.C., *The Muslim Architecture of Egypt I-II* (Oxford, 1952, 1959)

Damaszener Mitteilungen

De Beylié, L., *La Kalaa des Beni Hammad, une capitale berbère de l'Afrique du Nord au XIe siècle* (Paris, 1909)

Der Nersessian, S., *The Armenians* (London, 1969)

Diez, E., *Churasanische Baudenkmäler* (Berlin, 1918)

Diez, E., *Die Kunst der islamischen Völker* (Berlin, 1917)

East and West

Ecochard, M., *Filiation de monuments grecs, byzantins et islamiques. Une question de géométrie* (Paris, 1977)

Erdmann, K., *Das anatolische Karavansaray des 13. Jahrhunderts* , 2 vols. (Berlin, 1961)

Ettinghausen, R., ed., *Aus der Welt der islamischen Kunst. Festschrift für Ernst Kühnel zum 75. Geburtstag am 26.10.1957* (Berlin, 1959)

Ewert, C., *Spanisch-Islamische Systeme sich kreuzender Bögen. III. Die Aljafería in Zaragoza* (Berlin, 1978)

Ewert, C. and Wisshak, J.-P., *Forschungen zur almohadischen Moschee. I: Vorstufen* (Mainz, 1981)

Ezerskoi, N.A., principal ed., *Istoriya Iskusstva Narodov SSSR. Tom 2. Iskusstvo IV–XIII Vekov* (Moscow, 1973)

Fernández-Puertas, A., *La Fachada del Palacio de Comares. I. Situación, Función y Génesis* (Granada, 1980)

Foroughi, M., *et al., Masterpieces of Iranian Architecture* (Tehran, n.d. - c.1977)

Franz Pascha, J., *Die Baukunst des Islam* (Darmstadt, 1887)

Franz, H.G., *Palast, Moschee und Wüstenschloss. Das Werden der islamischen Kunst 7.–9. Jahrhundert* (Graz, 1984)

Franz, H.G., *Von Baghdad bis Córdoba. Ausbreitung und Entfaltung der islamischen Kunst 850-1050* (Graz, 1984)

Gabriel, A., *Monuments Turcs d'Anatolie* (Paris, 1931–4)

Gabriel, A., *Une capitale turque, Brousse, Bursa* , 2 vols. (Paris, 1958)

Gabriel, A., *Voyages Archéologiques dans la Turquie Orientale* (Paris, 1940)

Galdieri, E., *A few conservation problems concerning several Islamic monuments in Ghazni (Afghanistan). Technical report and notes on a plan of action* (Rome, 1978)

Galdieri, E., *Isfahan: Masǧid-i Ǧumʿa,* 2 vols. (Rome, 1972–3)

Garcin, J.-C., Maury, B., Revault, J. and Zakariya, M., *Palais et maisons du Caire. I - Epoque Mamelouke (XIIIe–XVIe siécles)* (Paris, 1982)

Gayet, A., *L'Art arabe* (Paris, 1893)

Gink, K., Turanszky, I., *Aserbaidschan. Paläste, Türme, Moscheen* (Hanau, 1980)

Glück, H., and Diez, E., *Die Kunst des Islam* (Berlin, 1925)

Godard, A., *The Art of Iran* (London, 1965)

Golombek, L. and Wilber, D.N., *The Timurid Architecture of Iran and Turan* (Princeton, 1988)

Golombek, *The Timurid Shrine at Gazur Gah* (Toronto, 1969)

Golvin, L. and Fromont, M.-C., *Thula. Architecture et urbanisme d'une cité de haute montagne en République Arabe du Yemen* (Paris, 1984)

Golvin, L., *Essai sur l'architecture religieuse musulmane, I-II* (Paris, 1970–1)

Golvin, L., *La Mosquée* (Algiers, 1960)

Golvin, L., *Recherches archéologiques à la Qalʿa des Banu Hammad* (Paris, 1965)

Gómez Moreno, M., *El arte árabe español hasta los Almohades: Arte Mozárabe (Ars Hispaniae,* III) (Madrid, 1951)

Goodwin, G., *A history of Ottoman architecture* (London, 1971)

Grabar, O., *The Alhambra* (London, 1978)

Grabar, O., *The Formation of Islamic Art* (New Haven, repr. 1987)

Hamilton, R.W., *Khirbat al Mafjar. An Arabian Mansion in the Jordan Valley* (Oxford, 1959)

Hamilton, R.W., *Walid and his Friends* (Oxford, 1988)

Harb, U., *Ilkhanidische Stalaktitengewölbe. Beiträge zu Entwurf und Bautechnik* (Berlin, 1978)

Herzfeld, E.E., *Erster vorläufiger Bericht über die Ausgrabungen von Samarra* (Berlin, 1912)

Herzfeld, E.E., *Matériaux pour un Corpus Inscriptionum Arabicarum. Deuxiéme Partie: Syrie du Nord. Inscriptions et Monuments d'Alep* (Paris, 1954)

Hillenbrand, R., *The Tomb Towers of Iran to 1550* (unpublished D.Phil. thesis, University of Oxford, 1974)

Hoag, J.D., *Islamic Architecture* (New York, 1977)

Hutt, A., Petherbridge, G., and Whitehouse, D., *Islamic Art and Architecture in Libya* (London, 1976)

Hutt, A.M., *The Development of the Minaret in Iran under the Saljuqs* (unpublished M.Phil. thesis, University of London, 1974)

Iran

Iraq

Israel Exploration Journal

Janabi, T. al-, *Studies in medieval Iraqi architecture* (Baghdad, 1982)

Journal of the Royal Asiatic Society

Kiani, M.Y., ed., *Iranian Architecture of the Islamic Period* (Tehran, 1987)

Kiani, M.Y. *Robat-e Sharaf* (Tehran, 1982)

Kuban, D., *Muslim Religious Arcitecture. Part I. The Mosque and its early Development* (Leiden, 1974)

Kühnel, E., *Die Moschee* (Berlin, 1949)

Kühnel, E., *Maurische Kunst* (Berlin, 1924)

Kunst des Orients

Kuran, A., *Anadolu Medreseleri* (Ankara, 1969)

Kuran, A., *The Mosque in Early Ottoman Architecture* (Chicago and London, 1968)

Lamʿi Mustafa, S., *Al-turath al-miʿmari fi Misr* (Beirut, 1975)

Leacroft, H. and R., *The Buildings of Early Islam* (Reading, Mass., 1976)

Les Annales Archéologiques Arabes Syriennes

Les Annales Archéologiques de la Syrie

Levant

Lezine, A., *Deux Villes d'Ifriqiya: Sousse, Tunis. Etudes d'archéologie, d'urbanisme, de démographie* (Paris, 1971)

Libya Antiqua

MacDougall, E.B. and Ettinghausen, R., eds., *The Islamic Garden* (Washington, D.C., 1976)

Madrider Mitteilungen

Marçais, G., and Golvin, L., *La Grande Mosquée de Sfax* (Tunis, 1960)

Marçais, G., *L'Architecture musulmane d'Occident: Tunisie, Algérie, Maroc, Espagne et Sicile* (Paris, 1955)

Masson, M., and Pugachenkova, G.A., *Gumbez Manasa* (Moscow, 1950)

Mélanges d'Histoire et d'Archéologie de l'Occident Musulman (Algiers, 1957)

Mémoires présentés par divers savants à l'Académie des

Inscriptions et Belles -Lettres

Meunié, J., Terrasse, H. and Deverdun, G., *Nouvelles recherches archéologiques à Marrakech* (Paris, 1957)

Michell, G., ed., *Architecture of the Islamic World. Its history and social meaning* (London, 1978)

Mitteilungen des Deutschen Archäologischen Instituts, Istanbuler Abteilung (= Istanbuler Mitteilungen)

Müller, K., *Die Karawanserai im Vorderen Orient* (Berlin, 1920)

Muqarnas

Musil, A., *Qusejr ʿAmra* (Vienna, 1907)

Mustafavi, M.T., *Persian Architecture at a Glance* (Teheran, 1967)

Naumann, R., *Tacht-e Sulaiman* (Munich, 1976)

Nemtseva, N.B. and Shvab, Y.Z., *Ansambl' Shakh-i Zinda* (Tashkent, 1979)

O'Kane, B. *Timurid Architecture in Khurasan* (Costa Mesa, Ca., 1987)

Ögel, S., *Der Kuppelraum in der türkischen Architektur* (Istanbul, 1972)

Önge, Y., Ateş, I., and Bayram, S., eds., *Divriği Ulu Camii ve Darüşşifasi* (Ankara, 1978)

Oriental Art

Otto-Dorn, K., *L'Art de l'Islam* (Paris, 1967)

Pander, K., *Sowjetischer Orient. Kunst und Kultur, Geschichte und Gegenwart der Völker Mittelasiens* (Cologne, 1982)

Pilyavskii, V.I., *Kunya-Urgench* (Leningrad, 1974)

Pope, A.U. and Ackerman, P., eds., *A Survey of Persian Art from Prehistoric Times to the Present* (London, 1938)

Prochaska, B., *Architecture in Islamic Societies* (Zurich, 1985)

Pugachenkova, G.A. (Pugatschenkowa), *Termes. Schahr-i Sabz. Chiwa* (Berlin, 1981)

Pugachenkova, G.A. and Rempel', L.I., *Istoriya iskusstv Uzbekistana s drevneyshikh vremen so seredini devyatnadtsatogo veka* (Moscow, 1965)

Pugachenkova, G.A., *Iskusstvo Turkmenistana* (Moscow, 1967)

Pugachenkova, G.A., *Pamyatniki Iskusstva Sovetskogo Soyuza Srednyaya Aziya Spravochnik - Putevoditel'* (Moscow, 1983)

Pugachenkova, G.A., *Puti Razvitiya Arkhitekturi Iuzhnogo Turkmenistana Pori Rabovladeniya Feodalizma (Trudi Iuzhno-Turkmenistanskoi Arkheologicheskoi Ekspeditsiy, VI)* (Moscow, 1958)

Pugachenkova, G.A. and Rempel', L.I. *Vydaiushchiesia pamyatniki arkhitekturi Uzbekistana* (Tashkent, 1958)

Rashid, S. al-, *Darb Zubaydah* (Riyadh, 1980)

Rempel', L.I., *Khudozhestvennaya Kul'tura Srednei Azii. IX–XIII veka* (Tashkent, 1983)

Renz, A., *Geschichte und Stätten des Islam* (Munich, 1977)

Revue Afrique

Revue des Etudes Islamiques

Revue Tunisienne

Rice, D.T., *Islamic Art* (London, 1965)

Rivista degli Studi Orientali

Rogers, J.M., *The Spread of Islam* (Oxford, 1976)

Rölöve ve Restorasyon Dergisi

Salam-Liebich, H., *L'art islamique. Bassin méditerranéen* (Paris, 1983)

Sanat Tarihi Yilliği

Sarre, F., and Herzfeld, E., *Archäologische Reise im Euphrat- und Tigris-Gebiet*, 4 vols. (Berlin, 1911–20)

Sauvaget, J., *La Mosquée Omeyyade de Médine* (Paris, 1947)

Sauvaget, J., *La Poste aux Chevaux dans l'Empire des Mamelouks* (Paris, 1941)

Schlumberger, D., *Lashkari Bazar. Une résidence royale ghaznévide et ghoride* (Paris, 1978)

Schmidt, H., *Die Madrasa des Kalifen al-Mustansir in Baghdad . Eine baugeschichtliche Untersuchung der ersten universalen Rechtshochschule des Islam* (Mainz, 1980)

Seher-Thoss, S.P., *Design and Color in Islamic Architecture* (Washington, D.C., 1968)

Shiha, M.A., *Madkhal ila al-ʿimara wa'l-funun al-islamiya fi'l-jumhuriya al-yamaniya* (Cairo, 1408/1987)

Shokoohy, M., *Studies in the Early Mediaeval Architecture of Iran and Afghanistan* (unpublished Ph.D. thesis, Heriot-Watt University and the Edinburgh College of Art, 1978)

Siroux, M., *Anciennes voies et monuments routiers de la région d'Ispahan, suivie de plusieurs autres édifices de cette province* (Cairo, 1971)

Siroux, M., *Caravansérails d'Iran et petites constructions routières* (Cairo, 1949)

SKH. Sergej Chmelnizkij (Berlin, 1985)

Society for Libyan Studies

Sourdel, D., and Sourdel-Thomine, J., *La civilisation de l'Islam classique* (Paris, 1968)

Sözen, M., *Anadolu Medreseleri. Selcuklular ve Beylikler Devri* Istanbul, 1970)

Sözen, M., *Diyarbakir'da Türk Mimarisi* (Istanbul, 1971)

Spuler, B., and Sourdel-Thomine, J., *Die Kunst des Islam* (Berlin, 1973)

Stewart, D., *Early Islam* (Weert, 1967)

Studia Iranica

Syria

Terrasse, C., *Médersas du Maroc* (Paris, 1928)

Terrasse, H., *La Grande Mosquée de Taza* (Paris, 1943)

Terrasse, H., *La Mosquée al-Qaraouiyin à Fes* (Paris, 1968)

Torres Balbás, L., *Arte Almohade. Arte Nazarí. Arte Mudéjar (Ars Hispaniae, IV)* (Madrid, 1949)

Türk Arkeoloji Dergisi

Türk Etnografya Dergisi

Ünal, R.H., *Les monuments islamiques anciens de la ville d'Erzerum et de sa région* (Paris, 1968)

Ünsal, B., *Turkish Islamic Architecture in Seljuk and Ottoman Times 1071–1923* (London, 1959)

Useinov, M., Bretanitski, L.S. and Salamzade, A., *Istoriya arkhitektury Azerbaidzhana* (Moscow, 1963)

Velázquez Bosco, R., *Excavaciones en Medina Azahara* (Madrid, 1923)

Vogt-Göknil, U., *Die Moschee. Grundformen sakraler Baukunst* (Zurich, 1978)

Vogt-Göknil, U., *Living Architecture: Ottoman* (New York, 1966)

Voronina, V.L., *Kair* (Leningrad, 1974)

Welch, A., *Shah ʿAbbas and the Arts of Isfahan* (New York, 1973)

Whitehouse, D., *Siraf III. The Congregational Mosque and other mosques from the ninth to the twelfth centuries* (London, 1980)

Wilber, D.N., *Persian Gardens and Garden Pavilions* (Rutland, Vt., 1962)

Wilber, D.N., *The Architecture of Islamic Iran. The Il Khanid Period* (Princeton, 1955)

World Archaeology

Wulzinger, K., and Watzinger, C., *Damaskus. Die islamische Stadt* (Berlin and Leipzig, 1924)

Zander, G., *Travaux de restauration de monuments historiques en Iran* (Rome, 1968)

Zeitschrift für Bauwesen

The small scale of the drawings at the back of the book precludes desirable standards of sharpness in repro-

duction. They are there for reference purposes only. Nevertheless, it has been an enrichment of the book to have had access to this material, and I am grateful to the original copyright holders.

I should also like to thank Drs. D.Fairchild Ruggles, Mehrdad Shokoohy and Yasser Tabbaa for their help in procuring illustrations.

Index of Individual Monuments

NOTE: In this index, the pages on which half-tone plates are to be found are given in **bold** numbers; the pages on which line drawings are to be found are given in *italic* numbers. Turkish names are given in their modern form, but the undotted i is not used. Names of places and monuments from the former Soviet Union are rendered, in the interests of easy recognition, following Russian transcription, with the exception of those already well established in English usage.

Abarqūh, Friday Mosque, 110
   Gunbad-i ʿAlī, **275**, 276
   Niẓāmīya, 155
ʿAbbāsābād, stopover, 429–30
ʿAbdallāhbād, mosque, 104
Abū Dulaf, Great Mosque, *475*
   minaret, 144–5, **146**
   palatial suite, 49, 391, *469*
Abū Muslim, *dār, see* Marv, *dār al-imāra* of Abū Muslim
Abyāna, Friday Mosque, **101**
   minbar, 40
Adzhina Tepe, 175
Afrāsiyāb, palatial house, *578*
Afūshta, mosque, 121
Afyon Karahisar, Great Mosque, 95, *483*
Agadez (Niger), minaret, *131*, 142
Āgra, palaces, 433
   Sikandra, tomb of Akbar, minaret, *502*
   Tāj Maḥal, 7, 21, 161
   tomb of Iʿtimād al-Daula, 161
Aḥmad, tomb of, Central Asia, 289
Aḥmadābād, Jāmiʿ Masjid, minaret, 160
   Shāh ʿĀlam mosque, minaret, *502*
Ahūvān, Ribāṭ-i Anūshirvān, *549*
Airandībī caravansarai, 360, 372
Airtam (Buddhist site), 175
ʿĀ'isha Bībī, mausoleum, *531*
Ajdābiya, mosque, 86, *478*
   qaṣr, 440, *592*
Ajmīr, Chishtī shrine, 268
Ak Beshim, Buddhist temple, 175, *175, 508*
Akcha Qalʿa, caravansarai, 338, 344, 360, 429, *550*
Akhkend, caravansarai, *554*
Akşehir, Ferruh Shah mosque, *482*
   īwān tomb, 311
   Taş *madrasa,* 211–3, *515*
   Taş *madrasa,* minaret, 163
Akyr-Tash, near Dzhambul, caravansarai, 341, *550*

ʿAlāʾiya, Saljūq palace, 416
   Tershane, 350
ʿĀlambardār, mausoleum, 291, *531, 532*
Alanya *see* ʿAlāʾiya
Aleppo (Ḥalab), al-Firdaus, *jāmiʿ* and *madrasa,* **187**, 187–9, *188*, 225, *509*
   citadel, palace of al-Malik al-ʿAzīz Muḥammad, 419, 437, *582*
   citadel, palace of al-Ẓāhir Ghāzī, 419
   Great Mosque, **25**, 68, **137**
   Great Mosque, minaret, *131*, 137, 140, *499, 502*
   Great Mosque, Umayyad state, *470*
   Huppa *khān,* 359
   Khān Abrak, 351, *557*
   Khān al-Barūd, 356
   Khān al-Gumruk, 359
   Khān al-Ṣābūn, 356, **360–361**
   Khān al-Wazīr, 359, **360**, *557*
   Khān Utchān, **333**
   khān of Khair Bāy, 351, *557*
   Khānqāh fi'l-Farāfra, 220, *510*
   Madrasa al-Anṣārīya, 203
   Madrasa al-Ḥalawīya, 191
   Madrasa al-Kāmilīya, 189, *509*
   Madrasa al-Saffāḥīya, 203
   Madrasa al-Sharafīya, **188**, 189, *509*
   Madrasa al-Sulṭānīya, 188, *189*, 190, *509*
   Madrasa al-Taruntaʾīya, 203
   Madrasa al-Ẓāhirīya, 187–8, *509*, *510*
   Madrasa Khān al-Tutun, 187
   madrasa of Maʿrūf Shādbakht, 187, 192, *509*
   Mamlūk palace, 437
   Maqām Ibrāhīm, *miḥrāb,* 467
   Mashhad al-Dikka, 545
   Mashhad al-Ḥusain, 545
   Matbakh al-ʿAjami, 436, *582*
   Shādbakhtīya *madrasa, see* Aleppo, *madrasa* of Maʿrūf Shādbakht
   tomb of Khair Bay, **322**

Turbat ʿAlī al-Ḥarawī, *545*
Turbat Umm Malik al-Afḍal, *545*
Alexandria (al-Iskandariya), the Pharos, 132, 138, 167–8, 403, *506*
Algiers (al-Jazāʾir), Bakrī palace, 442
   Bardo palace, 442
   Bū (= Abū) ʿInānīya *madrasa,* 241
   Dar ʿAzīza Bay, 442
   Friday Mosque, 87, *474*
   Jāmiʿ al-Sammāk, minaret, *131*
Alhambra *see* Granada, Alhambra
ʿAliābād, caravansarai, 364
Almohad mausoleum in Portugal (Mertola), 271
ʿAman, al-, caravansarai, 353
Amasya, Gök *madrasa* and Cami, 116, 210, *210, 517*
   Kapi Aghasi *madrasa,* 215, *215, 519*
   mausoleum of Turumtay, 311, *540*
   mosque of Sulṭān Bāyazīd, 117, *118, 495, 497*
   Sulṭān Bāyazīd *madrasa,* *519*
Aminabad, caravansarai, 366, *367*, 369, *566*
ʿAmmān, ceremonial building, *379, 380*
   citadel with Umayyad palatial buildings, *378, 570*
   palace, *380*, 381, *572*
Anau, mosque, **111**, 113, *493*
Ānī, Shepherd's Chapel, *541*
Ankara, Akhi Elvand mosque, 98, *483*
Antalya, Yivli Minare mosque, 98, *494*
   Yivli Minare mosque, minaret, **163**, 164, *502*
Aqṣā, al-, *see* Jerusalem, Aqṣā mosque
arcades in a hypostyle mosque: converging in both directions, *468*
   parallel to the *qibla* wall, *468*
   perpendicular to the *qibla* wall, *468*

Arch of Khusrau *see* Ctesiphon, Ṭāq-i Kisrā
Ardabīl, Friday Mosque, 104, *491*
  shrine of Shaikh Ṣafī, 106, 268, 303, *525*
  shrine of Shaikh Ṣafī, Jannat Sarā, 303
Ardistān, Friday Mosque, **18, 103**, 178, 218, *489*
  Masjid-i Imām Ḥasan, 105, 154
Argincik, Ḥaidar Bey kiosk, 416
Aruch, caravansarai, *554*
Ashīr, palace, 438–41, *590*
Ashraf, Bāgh-i Chashma, 429–30
  gardens, 429
  palace, 428–9
Ashtarjān, Friday Mosque, **105–106**, 107, 155–6
'Askar, al-, caravansarai, 343, *550*
Asnaf, Masjid al-'Abbās, 91–2, **92–93**
  schema of ceiling, *468*
Aspendos, Roman theatre, 416
  Saljūq pavilion, 416
Assūr, Parthian house, 335
Astāna-Bābā, mausoleum of al-Muntaṣir, 294
Aswān, *mashhad,* **313, 314**, *543*
  mausolea, **262**, 264, 311–3, *312*, 318, *543*
  minaret, 165
Atabey, Ertokuş *madrasa,* 211, *515*
'Aṭshān, stopover, 144, *335*, 344, *574*
Aurangābād, tomb of Rabī'a Daurānī, *502*
Āva, Shī'ite *madrasa,* 177
Azhar, al-, *see* Cairo, mosque of al-Azhar
Azīrān, mosque, 107
Baghdād, Bishiriya *madrasa, see* Baghdād, so-called "'Abbāsid palace"
  caliphal palace, 21, 83, 393, 395, 402
  city gates, 438
  Dār al-Shajara, 435
  early medieval palaces, 411
  Friday Mosque, first state ("A" - 192/807), *469*
  Friday Mosque, second state ("B" - 260/873), *469*
  Jāmi' al-Khāṣṣakī, *miḥrāb, 467*
  Khān Mirjān, 210, 224, 355, 360–5, *362*, **363–365**, *564*
  Khān Urtma *see* Baghdad, Khān Mirjān
  Mirjāniya *madrasa,* 28, **29, 174, 184**, 210, **224**, 224, *225*, 361, *509*

Mustanṣirīya *madrasa,* 14, 215, 218, 220, *222*, **223**, 223–4, 361, *509*
Niẓāmīya *madrasa,* 175, 218
Round City, 19, 83, 144, 392–3, 395–6, 409, *574*
Round City, Kūfa Gate, 393
Saljūq *madrasa,* 174
so-called "'Abbāsid palace", **185**, *223*, 223, *509*
tomb attributed to Sitt Zubaida, 323, **326**, *326*, *546*
tomb of Aḥmad b. Ḥanbal, 266
tomb of al-Suhrawardī, 323
Baiburt, Ulu Cami, minaret, 163
Bairam 'Alī, ossuary, *531*
Bairamābād, kiosk, 430
Bajistān, mosque, 110
Bākū, palace of the Shīrvānshāhs, 426–7, *584*
Bākū, palace of the Shīrvānshāhs, *dīwān khāna,* 426–7, *584*
  palace of the Shīrvānshāhs, dynastic mausoleum, 427, *584*
  turba of Sa'īd Yaḥyā Bākūvī, 427
Ba'labbak, mosque, 77
Bālis area, staging post, *555*
Balkh, Masjid-i Nuh Gunbad or Ḥājjī Piyāda, 78, *78*, 104, 290, 410, *488*
  mausoleum of Khwāja Abū Naṣr Parsa, 158, 297, *539*
  Naubahār, 175
  Saljūq *madrasa,* 175
Bāmiyān, house, 175, *508*
Banū Sa'd, *khān,* 367
Bardha'a, mosque, 391
Barsiyān, Friday Mosque, 103, *105*, *489*
Bās, caravansarai, 353
Bāshān, mosque, 103, *488*
Baṣra mosque, minaret, 134
  first mosque, 67
Basṭām, flanged tomb tower, 286
  Friday Mosque, minaret, 152
  shrine, 106, 268
Bāyazīd II, mosque of, *see* Istanbul, mosque of Sulṭān Bāyazīd II
Belen, caravansarai, 353
Berkut Qal'a, castle and donjon, 342, *578*
Berlin, pavilion on bronze salver, *531*, *572*
Beyşehir, Eşrefoghlu Süleyman Bey Cami, **95**
  tomb, 308
Bīdakhavīd, shrine of Shaikh 'Alī Binyamān, *miḥrāb,* **21**
Bīdar, *madrasa,* minaret, *502*
Bījāpūr, Gol Gumbaz, minaret, *502*
  Jum'a Masjid, minaret, *131*, 161
  tomb, minaret, *502*

Bilecik, Orhan Ghāzī mosque, 116, *494, 495*
Birge, Friday Mosque, 98, *483*
Birrābād, mosque, 104
Bīshāpūr, mosque, 101
Bīsutūn, caravansarai, 366, *368*, **370**, *566*
Bitlis, caravansarai, 353
  Great Mosque, 116, *483, 485*
  Ihlasiye *madrasa, 519*
Bône (al-'Annāba), mosque of Sīdī Bū Marwān, *476*
Bougie (Bijāya), Ḥammādid palace, 440
Boyaliköy, complex (*khānqāh* and mausoleum), 208, 214, *518*
  īwān tomb, 311
Bukhārā, *khānqāh* of Nādir Dīvān Beg, 220
  Kukeltash *madrasa,* 232, 234
  Lab-i Ḥauḍ complex, 230
  Madār-i Khān *madrasa,* 230, *522*
  madrasa of 'Abd al-'Azīz Khān, **179, 228, 229, 230**, *522*
  madrasa of 'Abdallāh Khān, 230, *230*, **238**, *522*
  madrasa of Ulugh Beg, 227, *228*, 230, *522*
  Maghak-i 'Aṭṭārī mosque, *488*
  Masjid-i Kalyān, 108, **109**, 112, *493*
  Masjid-i Kalyān, minaret, 148, **150–151**, *499, 503*
  Mīr-i 'Arab *madrasa,* **228**, 230, **239**, *522*
  Sāmānid palace, 428
  shrine of Saif al-Dīn Bākharzī, **294**
  "Tomb of the Sāmānids", 14, 153, 275–6, 280, *287*, 288–91, **288–290**, 409, *530, 531*
  tomb of Bayān Qulī Khān, **259**, 290
Burhānpūr, Bībī ki Masjid, minaret, 159, *502*
Burj al-'Arif, near Mahdīya, 440
Bursa area, mosque and *madrasa* of Murād I, 216
  'Alā' al-Dīn mosque, 116, *117*, *494, 495*
  Bey Han, *352*, 353, *561*
  complex of Bāyazīd Yildirim, *madrasa,* 216, *519*
  early Ottoman *madrasa,* 207
  Emir Han, 353, *353*, *559*
  Fidan Han, 353, *560, 561*
  Geyve Han, 353, *560, 561*
  Great Mosque, 117, *494, 495*
  Great Mosque, minaret, *130*
  Hudavendigar mosque, 163
  Ipek Han, 353, *559*
  Kapan Han, 353, *560*
  Koza Han, 353, *560, 561*

madrasa in Yeşil Külliye, 216, *519*

madrasa of Lala Salin Pasha, *519*

market and caravansarai area, *560*

mausoleum of Bāyazīd Yildirim, *540*

mosque and *madrasa* of Murād I, *518*

mosque of Bāyazīd Yildirim, 117, *494*

mosque of Murād I, minaret, *131*

mosques, 417

Muradiye *madrasa*, 216, *217*, *519*

Pirinc Han, *560*, *561*

tomb of Murād II, *540*

Yeşil Cami, 117, *118*, *163*, *494*

Yeşil Türbe (Green Tomb), 307, *310*, 310–11, *540*

Burujird, Friday Mosque, 102, *102*, 152, *489*

Buṣrā, bishop's palace, 45
cathedral, 45
madrasa of Abū Muḥammad Gümüshtegin, 183, 186–8, 206, *509*

mosque of al-Khiḍr, 138

Umayyad mosque (Mosque of 'Umar), 68, 137, *470*, *471*

Bust, ceremonial arch, **410**
tomb of Shaikh Sarbāz, *282*, 283, *533*

Büyük Valide Han *see* Istanbul, Büyük Valide Han

Cairo (Fusṭāṭ), mosque of 'Amr, 59, 66, 74, 129–30, 134, 137, 139, 391, *473*

mosque of 'Amr, minaret, *506*

mosque of Ibn Ṭūlūn, *75*, 76–7, 83, **147**, 391, *473*

mosque of Ibn Ṭūlūn, minaret, *131*, 145–6, **147**, *506*

Cairo (al-Qāhira), aerial view of Mamlūk tombs, **315**

anonymous *qāʿa*, *587*

Bāb Zuwaila, minarets, 171, *507*

Bait al-Qāḍī, 436

Dār al-Quṭbiya, 435

Dar Saʿīd al-Suʿāda, 220

dome finials, *468*

door-knockers, *468*

Fāṭimid palaces, 403, 435

funerary complex (mosque, *madrasa* and mausoleum) of Sultān Ḥasan, 99, *195*, 196, **195–196**, 197, *513*

funerary complex (mosque, *madrasa* and mausoleum) of Sultān Ḥasan, minaret, *130*, 171, *506*

funerary complex of al-Ghūrī, 171, 199

funerary complex of Qāʾit Bāy, 171, 196, **198–199**, 202, 325, *547*

funerary complex of Sultān Īnāl, 197, *547*

funerary *khānqāh* of Baibars al-Jāshankir, 220, *512*

funerary *khānqāh* of Sultān Faraj b. Barqūq, 196, 220, **315**, 318, 325, *507*, *513*

funerary *khānqāh* of Sultān Faraj b. Barqūq, minaret, *507*

funerary *madrasa* and *khānqāh* of Barsbāy, 835/1432, **7**

funerary *madrasa* of al-Malik al-Nāṣir Muḥammad, 197, *513*

funerary *madrasa* of Amīr Sarghitmish, 199

funerary *madrasa* of Amīr Sunqur Saʿdī, 202

funerary *madrasa* of Salār and Sanjar al-Jāwilī, 200–1, *201*, *513*

funerary *madrasa* of Sultān Qalāʾūn, 50, **194**, 195–6, **329**, 435, *506*, *512*

funerary *madrasa* of Sultān Shaʿbān, 196, 200

funerary *madrasa* of Zain al-Dīn Yūsuf, 199, *512*

Great Īwān of al-Nāṣir, 437

house no. VI at Fusṭāṭ, *587*

Iskandar Pasha mosque, minaret, *506*

Khān al-Khalīlī, **354**, 355

Madrasa al-Ghannāmiya, 199

Madrasa al-Mithqālīya, 199, *200*, 202, 205, *512*

Madrasa al-Ṣāliḥīya, 171, 192, 195, 242, 319, 322, *513*

Madrasa al-Ṣāliḥīya, mausoleum, *see* Cairo, mausoleum of Sultān al-Malik al-Ṣāliḥ Najm al-Dīn Ayyūb

Madrasa al-Ẓāhiriya, 193

madrasa of al-Ṣāliḥ, *see* Cairo, Madrasa al-Ṣāliḥīya

madrasa of Aqbugha, 197

madrasa of Barsbāy, 828/1425, **197**

madrasa of Īl-Malak al-Jukundār, 200, *513*

madrasa of Īlgay Yūsufī, 199, *512*

madrasa of Jauhar, 197

madrasa of Khwand al-Baraka *see* Cairo, funerary *madrasa* of Sultan Shaʿbān

madrasa of Qāḍī 'Abd al-Bāsiṭ, *zuraya*, *468*

madrasa of Qāʾit Bāy at Qalʿat al-Kabsh, **191**

madrasa of Ṭaibars, 197

madrasa of Tatar al-Ḥijāziya, 199, *512*

Maqʿad Māmāʾī, *588*

mashhad (or mosque, or *zāwiya*) of al-Juyūshī, 100, 168, 314, *314*, *544*

mashhad of Sharif Ṭabāṭabāʾ, 78, 311, *311*, *544*

mausoleum of Abu'l-Ghaḍanfar, 168, 170

mausoleum of al-Nāṣir Muḥammad, 325

mausoleum of al-Sayyida 'Ātiqa, 314, **314**, 316, *544*

mausoleum of Barqūq *intra muros*, 325

mausoleum of Imām al-Shāfiʿī, 200, 318, *319*, 319–20, *544*

mausoleum of Jānī Bāy al-Ashrafī, **315**, 324, *328*, *544*

mausoleum of Khair Bāy, 325

mausoleum of Muḥammad al-Jaʿfarī, 314, **314**, 316, *544*

mausoleum of Qānsūh Abū Saʿīd, **315**

mausoleum of Qāsim Abū Ṭayyib, 314, *544*

mausoleum of Queen Shajar al-Durr, 318

mausoleum of Sayyida Ruqayya, 314, *543*

mausoleum of Shaikh Yūnus, 314, *544*

mausoleum of Sultān al-Malik al-Ṣāliḥ Najm al-Dīn Ayyūb, 319, **320**, *321*, *513*

mausoleum of Sultān Qalāʾūn, 325–7, *327*, 329–30

mausoleum of the 'Abbāsid caliphs, 319, **320**, *544*

mausoleum of Ṭughāy, **11**, **317**

mausoleum of Umm Kulthūm, 314, *544*

mausoleum of Yūnus al-Dawadār, **269**, 318

mausoleum *see also* Cairo, funerary complex, funerary *khānqāh* and funerary *madrasa*

minaret finial, *468*

minaret of Amīr Sarghitmish, *507*

minaret of Aqbugha, *506*

minaret of Aqsunqur, 171

minaret of Bashtāk, 168, 171

minaret of Ghānim al-Bahlawān, **168**

mosque lamps (polycandelon), *468*

mosque of al-Aqmar, 99, **124**, 126, *473*

mosque of al-Ashraf Barsbāy, minaret, *506*

mosque of al-Azhar, 52, 54, 59–60, 77, 79, 83, 176–7, 359

mosque of al-Azhar, extension, *473*

mosque of al-Azhar, minaret of al-Ghūrī, 171, *506*

mosque of al-Azhar, minaret of Qā'it Bāy, *506, 507*

mosque of al-Azhar, original state, *473*

mosque of al-Azhar, sanctuary façade, *473*

mosque of al-Ḥākim, 52, 74, 77, 83, **167**, *473*

mosque of al-Ḥākim, northern minaret, 166, *507*

mosque of al-Ḥākim, western minaret, 166, *506, 507*

mosque of al-Mu'ayyad, **99**

mosque of al-Nāṣir Muḥammad in the citadel, 100

mosque of al-Nāṣir Muḥammad in the citadel, minarets, 171

mosque of al-Ṣāliḥ Ṭalā'i', 21, 416, *473*

mosque of Baibars, **48**, *50*, 50, 52, 99–100, *473*

mosque of Jamāl al-Dīn al-Ustadār, 197

mosque of Muḥammad ʿAlī, minaret, *130*

mosque of Muḥammad Bāy Abu'l-Dhahab, minaret, *507*

mosque of Qā'it Bāy, minaret, *507*

mosque of Qalā'ūn in the citadel, minaret, *506*

mosque of Qānī Bāy, minaret, 171

mosque of Sulṭān Īnāl, **315**

mosque, *madrasa* and *khānqāh* of Sulṭān Barqūq, 196–7, *221*, *512*

mosque, *madrasa* and mausoleum of Qānṣūh al-Ghūrī, 325, *547*

Mughalbāy Ṭāz mosque, minaret, **169–170**

Nilometer, 435

palace of Ālīn Āq, 436, *587*

palace of Bashtāk, 435, *589*

palace of Qā'it Bāy, 436, *588*

palace of Sayyidat al-Mulk, 435, *587*

palace of Yashbak, **435**, 436, *587*

qā'a of ʿUthmān Katkhudā, 436, *589*

qā'a of Aḥmad Kuhya, *587*

qā'a of Amīr Ṭāz, 436

qā'a of Manjak al-Silāḥdār, 436

qā'a of Muḥibb al-Dīn Yaḥyā, 435, *587*

qā'a of Shākir al-Ghannām, *587*

qā'a of Ṭashtīmūr, *587*

Qaṣr al-Ablaq, 436–7, *588*

Qubbat al-Fadāwiya, 319

Roda Island, palace of Sulṭān al-Ṣāliḥ, 435, *588*

Sab'a Banāt, *312*, **312**, 313, *543*

Sikkat al-Mardānī, **436**

the citadel, 435

Ṭūlūnid palace, 382

wakāla and *rub'* of al-Ghūrī, *357*, 358, 361, *563*

wakāla and *rub'* of Qā'it Bāy near Bāb al-Naṣr, **337**, 359, *563*

wakāla, sabīl and *sabīl kuttāb* of Qā'it Bāy near al-Azhar, **358–359**

Wakālat Bazar'a, 361, *563*

Çardak Han, 552

Çay, *madrasa* of Yūsuf b. Ya'qūb, 210, 212, *517*

Central Asian mausolea, typical plans and elevations, *532*

Ceuta (Sabta), *madrasa*, 250

Chāh-i Siyāh-i Nau, caravansarai, 366, *565*

Chahār Dih, *madrasa*, 182, *520*

Chahārābād, stopover, 429

Champaner, Jāmi' Masjid, minaret, *502*

Char Bakr (Bukhārā area), shrine, 230, 303, *304*, **305**, *538*

Char Jui mausoleum, 288–9

Chasum, Friday Mosque, 114

Chihilburj area, mosque, *488*

Chotski, tower, 147

Chugudur-Bābā, mausoleum, *532*

Constantine (Qusṭanṭīna), palace of Aḥmad Bāy, 442

palace of Bāy Ḥajj Salāḥ, 442

Cordoba (Qurṭuba) area, al-ʿĀmirīya, 443

Damascus palace, 443

dār al-imāra, 443

Great Mosque, 24, 74, **77,79,** 87, **88**, *89*, 140, 391, 438, 446, *470, 471*

Great Mosque, arcade, *472*

Great Mosque, arch systems, *472*

Great Mosque, axial nave, *476*

Great Mosque, façade, **83, 84,** *593*

Great Mosque, *maqṣūra*, 466

Great Mosque, *miḥrāb* and *maqṣūra*, *472*

Great Mosque, *miḥrāb*, *467*

Great Mosque, minaret, 138, 140, *500*

Great Mosque, original state, *471*

Great Mosque, *sābāṭ* of ʿAbdallāh, 49, *472*

Great Mosque, *sābāṭ* of al-Ḥakam II, 49, *472*

Great Mosque, scheme of development to end of 10th century, *471*

Ctesiphon (al-Madā'in), Ṭāq-i Kisrā, 102, 107, 390–1, **391**, 398, 407, 409, 412–3, 417, 424, *573*

Dāhistān (Mashhad al-Miṣrīyān), caravansarai, *550*

mausoleum No. 1, *532*

mausoleum No. 2, *532*

mausoleum No. 3, *532*

mosque, *488*

namāzgāh mosque, *488*

Dair al-Kahf, fort, *567*

Dair Sim'ān, 334

Dair Turmanīn, 334

Dair-i Gachīn, caravansarai, 339, *340, 549*

Damascus (Dimashq), Amjadiya *turba*, 190

church of St John the Baptist, 69, 267

Dār al-Ḥadīth al-Ashrafīya, 191

dār al-ḥadīth of Nūr al-Dīn, 187–8, *509*

Farrūkhshāhīya mausoleum, 190, *545*

funerary *madrasa* of Shaikh Ḥasan Rā'ī al-Himma, 202, *510*

Great Mosque, 14, 22, 26, 38, 46, **51**, 51–2, 61–2, **69**, *70*, 71–3, 77, 81, 83, 98, 133, 137, 140, 267, 340, 347, 391, *470*

Great Mosque, axial nave, 51–2, *466, 476*

Great Mosque, decoration of west *riwāq*, *470*

Great Mosque, Manārat al-ʿArūs, 133

Great Mosque, *maqṣūra*, 466

Great Mosque, vanished minaret, 137–9

inner *temenos*, *470*

Khān al-Gumruk, 359

Khān al-Tutan, 355

Khān As'ad Pasha, **355**, 359, *558*

Khān Jaqmaq, 356, *558*

Khān Süleyman Pasha, **355**, 359, *558*

Madrasa al-ʿĀdilīya, *186, 187*, 190, *509*

Madrasa al-Atābakīya, 190, *509*

Madrasa al-Farrūkhshāhīya, 190

Madrasa al-Jaqmaqīya, 202

Madrasa al-Māridānīya, 191, *509*

Madrasa al-Murshidīya, 191

Madrasa al-Nūrīya al-Kubrā (funerary *madrasa* of Nūr al-Dīn), 187–8, **323**, *324, 509, 545*

Madrasa al-Qiliḥīya, 191

Madrasa al-Rashidīya, 202

Madrasa al-Ruknīya, 190, *546*
Madrasa al-Ṣāḥibīya, 190, *509*
Madrasa al-Sayyida, 202
Madrasa al-Ẓāhirīya, 202, *509*
Madrasa al-Ẓāhirīya, mausoleum
    of Baibars, 324
madrasa and mausoleum of 'Izz al-
    Dīn, 190, **322**
Mamlūk palace, 437
mausoleum of Nūr al-Dīn *see*
    Damascus, Madrasa
    al-Nūrīya al-Kubrā
mausoleum of Shaikh Nahlawī,
    202
mosque of Sīdī Shu'aib, 202
Qaṣr al-Ablaq (palace of Baibars),
    436
Ṣāliḥīya, Madrasa al-Jaharkasīya,
    190, *510*
Ṣāliḥīya, mausoleum of Abū
    Jarash ('Abdallāh al-Raqqī),
    545
Shiblīya mausoleum, *545*
temple of Hadad, 69, 267
temple of Jupiter Damascenus,
    69, 267
tomb of Shaikh 'Alī al-Faranthī,
    322
turba in Madrasa al-Ruknīya, *264*,
    323
Turbat al-Najmīya, *545*
Turuzīya mosque, 202
Umayyad palace, 393
Damāvand, Imāmzāda 'Abdallāh,
    286, *529*
Dāmghān area, Tepe Ḥiṣār, palace,
    412, *573*
    Tarī Khāna mosque, **34**, 46, 77,
      101–2, *102, 487*
    Tarī Khāna mosque, minaret, 148
Dandānqān, mosque, 103
Danistama, *madrasa* (?), 180, *508*
Daqūq *see* Tā'ūq
Darjazin, Imāmzāda Hūd, 286, *529*
Darzīn, Fort No. 2, 333–4, *334, 549*
    forts, 333–4
Dashtī, mosque, 107
Daulatābād, Chand Minār, *502*
Daurān, Friday Mosque, **13**
Dayā Khātūn, caravansarai, *342*,
    344, *550*
Delhi (Dihlī), Begampūrī mosque,
    159
    Chishtī shrine, 268
    Jum'a Masjid, 159
    Jum'a Masjid, minaret, *131*, 159,
      502
    Khirkī mosque, minaret, 159, *502*
    mausoleum of Adham Khān, 161
    mausoleum of Humāyūn, 161
    palaces, 433
    Quṭb Minār complex, 158–9, *502*

Quṭb Minār, 129, *130*, 158–9
Quwwat al-Islām mosque, 158
Dhamār, Friday Mosque, 91, *481*
Dhibīn, mosque, 91–2, *481*
Dhū Ashrāq, mosque, 91, **92**, *480*
Dhu'l-Kifl, minaret, 153, *503*
Dihbīd, caravansarai, 366
Dimetoka, mosque of Chelebi
    Sulṭān Mehmed, 117, *494*
Divriği, castle mosque, **9**, 95, *482*
    Friday Mosque and hospital,
      14,**17, 95,** *96*, 97, 99, 163,
      486
    Friday Mosque and hospital,
      miḥrāb, *467*
    turba, 307
Diyarbakr, Artuqid palace, 415–7,
    437, *581*
    Great Mosque, 52, 92, **94**, *485*
    Khān Delaler, 355, *559*
    Khān Ḥasan Pasha, 356
    madrasa of 'Alī Pasha, *518*
    madrasa of Muṣliḥ al-Dīn Lārī,
      519
    Mas'ūdīya *madrasa*, *215*, *517*
    mosque of Bahrām Pasha,
      shadirvan, *466*
    Nebi mosque, 116, *485*
    Zinciriye *madrasa*, 210, *515*
Doğubayazit, Isḥāq Pasha palace,
    452, *597*
Dokuzum Derbent Han, *553*
Dolay Han, near Kayseri, 348, *553*
Dome of the Rock *see* Jerusalem,
    Dome of the Rock
Domus Aurea *see* Rome, Domus
    Aurea
Dū Baradār, ceremonial arch, 346
Dumbī, stopover, 429
Dunaysir, Great Mosque, 92, **94**, 99,
    484
    minaret, 163, *502*
Dura Europos, palace of the Dux
    Ripae, 388, *569*
Durnali, fortress, 341
Edirne, Eski (Ulu) Cami, 117, *494*
    Jahān-Numa Kasiri, *597*
    külliye of Sulṭān Bāyazīd II, 122,
      123, 496
    madrasa of Sulṭān Bāyazīd II, 216
    mosque of Sulṭān Bāyazīd II, *495*
    Rüstem Pasha caravansarai, *559*,
      562
    sarai, 452
    Selimiye complex, *496, 498*
    Selimiye mosque, 122, *495, 497*
    Selimiye mosque, minaret, *502*
    Üç Şerefeli mosque, 118, *119*,
      494, 495, 496
Elbistan, mosque, 161
Ereğli, Ulu Cami, minaret, 163
Erkilet, kiosk of Hizr Ilyas, 416,

581
Ertokuş Han, *552*
Erzurum, Ahmediye *madrasa*, 213
    Çifte Minareli *madrasa*, 162, 210,
      212, *214, 515*
    Great Mosque, 97, 116, *484*
    mausoleum of Amīr Saltuq, 307,
      540
    mosque in citadel, *482*
    Rüstem Pasha caravansarai, *562*
    Yakutiye *madrasa*, *515*
    Yakutiye *madrasa*, minaret, 163,
      214
Eski Hisar, fort, *567*
Eski Malaṭyā, caravansarai, *561*
Eskişehir, caravansarai by Kurşunlu
    Cami, 353
Evdir Han, 353, *553*
Fahrāj, Friday Mosque, *76*, 77, *487*
Fā'iẓābād, near Bukhārā, *khānqāh*,
    220
Farūmād, Friday Mosque, 104, *491*
Fās al-Jadīd, Great Mosque,
    minaret, 141, *499*
    Jāmi' Ḥamrā', 245, *475*
    madrasa, 244, 248
Fās, Bū (Abū) 'Inānīya *madrasa*,
    240–2, 244–5, *245*, 246–7, 250,
    524
    Dār Abī Habasa, 242
    Funduq al-Titwanīyin, **356**, 358,
      548
    ḥarīm in royal palace, *590*
    Madrasa al-'Aṭṭārin, **241**, 243–4,
      246–8, **249**, 250, *523*
    Madrasa al-Labbādīn, 251
    Madrasa al-Miṣbāḥīya, 241,
      243–4, 247–50, *523*
    Madrasa al-Mutawakkilīya (= Bū
      'Inānīya), 245
    Madrasa al-Ṣaffārīn, 239–41, 244,
      247–8, *523*
    Madrasa al-Ṣahrīj, 242, 244, 247,
      523
    Madrasa al-Sharrāṭīn, 250, *524*
    Madrasa al-Suba'īn, 241–2, 244,
      249, *523*
    Marīnid tombs, 263, 271
    Mosque of the Andalusians
      (Jāmi' al-Andalus), 242, *475*
    Qarawiyīn mosque, 52, 60, **67**,
      86, 244–5, 250, *475*
    Qarawiyīn mosque, axial nave,
      476
    Qarawiyīn mosque, *muqarnas*
      vault, 479
    royal palace, 453
Fatih mosque *see* Istanbul, complex
    of Mehmed II Fatih
Fātiḥpūr Sikrī, Chishtī shrine, 268
Fazzān, *minbar, 466*
Fez *see* Fās

Fezzan *see* Fazzān
Firdaus, Friday Mosque, 104
Fīrūzābād, palace, 144, 408, *408*, 432, *573*
Fūdīna, mausoleum of Isḥāq ʿAṭā, *530*
Fusṭāṭ *see also* Cairo
palace of Ibn Ṭūlūn, 402, 405
palace of Khumārawaih, 434
Gabrābād, caravansarai, 366
Gaur, Chota Sona Masjid, 161
Fīrūz Minār, *502*
Gaz, caravansarai, 366, *373*, *565*
mosque, 107
Gaza (Ghazza), Khān al-Zait, 359
Gazūr Gāh, Harāt area, shrine of ʿAbdallāh al-Anṣārī, 226, 280, *538*
Gebze, mosque, 163
Gevaş, mausoleum, 308, *540*
Ghalvār, Masjid-i Ḥauḍ-i Karbās, *492*
Ghardāya, Great Mosque, minaret, *131*, 142, *499*
Ghazna, minaret of Bahrāmshāh, 147, 153, 158, *505*
minaret of Masʿūd III, 147, 153, **157**, 158, *502*, *504*, *505*
palace of Masʿūd III, 411, 413–4, *579*
Ghujduvān, *madrasa*, 227, *522*
Granada (Gharnāṭa) area, Rābita de San Sebastian, *526*
Alcazaba, 452
Alhambra (*al-ḥamrāʾ*), 7, 10, 21, 28, 237, 378–9, 381, 408, 443–4, *451*, 461, *594*, *595*, *596*
Alhambra Alta ("Upper Alhambra"), 452
Alhambra, Court of the Lions, 446, *450*, 452, 453, 454, *454*
Alhambra, Court of the Myrtles, 452–3
Alhambra, *dīwān*, 453
Alhambra, Gate of Justice, 452
Alhambra, Great Mosque, 453
Alhambra, Hall of Justice, 457
Alhambra, "Hall of the Abencerrajes", 453–4, **455**
Alhambra, Hall of the Ambassadors, 453–4
Alhambra, Hall of the Two Sisters (Torre de las Damas), 452–4, *595*
Alhambra, Mexuar, 453
Alhambra, the Partal, 453, *593*, *596*
Alhambra, Torre de Comares (al-Qamarīya), 454
Alhambra, Tower of the Captives, 454
Corral del Carbon, 355, *548*

Generalife, 456, **456**, *596*
minaret of San Juan de los Reyes, *500*
the Alhambra, *ḥammām* area, *596*
Gulpāyagān, Friday Mosque, 103, 178, *489*
minaret, 153, 156
Gunābād, Friday Mosque, 104
Gunbad-i Manas *see* Manas
Gunbad-i Qābūs, 28, 269, 276, 280, 283, **283**, 286, *286*, *528*
scheme of proportions, *528*
Gūr-i Amīr *see* Samarqand, Gūr-i Amīr
Gurgān, Imāmzādā Nūr, *528*
Güroymak, near Bitlis, tomb tower, *542*
Gwalior (Gwāliyār), mausoleum of Muḥammad Chaus, 161
Hafshūya, mosque, 107
Ḥaidar Bey kiosk, near Kayseri, *581*
Ḥaidarīya, Imāmzāda Kamāl al-Dīn, *529*
Ḥair, al-, staging post, *555*
Ḥājji Piyāda *see* Balkh, Masjid-i Nuh Gunbad or Ḥājji Piyāda
Ḥākim, al-, *see* Cairo, mosque of al-Ḥākim
Ḥakīm Han, 349, *552*
Ḥamā, Great Mosque, **55**, 83
Great Mosque, minaret, **148**
Great Mosque, *minbar*, **35**
Great Mosque, modern state, *469*
Great Mosque, Umayyad state, *470*
Hamadān, Gunbad-i ʿAlawīyān, 294, *534*
Saljūq *madrasa*, 174
Ḥammām al-Sarākh, hunting lodge, 381, *382*, *570*
Hamrāʾ, al- *see* Granada, Alhambra
Darb Zubaida, residential unit, 342, 411, *577*
Harāt, complex of Gauhar Shād, 109
Friday Mosque of Gauhar Shād, 157
Friday Mosque, 104, **105**, 110–11, *493*
madrasa of Gauhar Shād, 157, 227–8
madrasa of Sulṭān Ḥusain Bāiqarā, 227–8
mausoleum of Gauhar Shād, 297
Saljūq *madrasa*, 175
Saljūq palace, 414–5
Harput, Great Mosque, 97, *484*
Ḥarrān, Great Mosque, 77, *469*, *470*
Hasht Bihisht *see* Iṣfahān, Hasht Bihisht
Haswa, caravansarai, 369
Ḥasyā, caravansarai, 352

Hatra (al-Ḥaḍr), Parthian city plan, 393
Parthian palace, 391
Hazāra, Masjid-i Diggarān, 104, 290, *488*
Hebron (al-Khalīl), Mosque of Abraham, 267
Herat *see* Harāt
Ḥiṣn Kaifā, mausoleum of Zainab, *541*
Rizq mosque, minaret, 163
Horozlu Han, 347, *553*
Hurmuzfarra, caravansarai, *550*
Ḥūth, Masjid al-Saumiʿa, 91, *481*
Hyderabad (Ḥaidarābād) (Deccan), Char Mīnār, *130*, *502*
Friday Mosque, 161
Ibb, Great Mosque, 91, **92**, *481*
Ilgin, glass pavilion, 417
Imām Dūr, mausoleum of Muslim b. Quraish, 323, **325**, *330*, *546*
Imām-Bābā mausoleum, 289
Incesu, Kara Mustafa Pasha caravansarai, *562*
Incir Han, **19**, 347, *375*, *553*
Irbil, minaret, *152*, **153**
Iṣfahān area, Rahrūn minaret, 152
Iṣfahān, ʿAlī Qāpū, 428, 430–2, *583*, *585*
ʿAyīna Khāna, 428
Asadābād, palace, 428
Bāgh-i Zirishk, palace, 428, 432
Chahār Bāgh, 235, 361, 428
Chihil Dukhtarān minaret, 153, **155**
Chihil Sutūn, 428, 431–2, *432*, **433**, *585*
Dū Minār Dardasht, 156
Friday Mosque, 21, 50, 83, 103, *104*, 107, 110, 411, *489*, *490*
Friday Mosque, Būyid piers, *490*
Friday Mosque, *maqṣūra*, *466*
Friday Mosque, Ṣuffa-yi ʿUmar (*madrasa?*), 107, 179, 225, *520*
Friday Mosque, vaults, *490*
Hasht Bihisht, 381, 428, 430, **431**, 433, *434*, *585*
Hazār Jarīb, 428
Khājū bridge, 428
Madār-i Shāh *madrasa* and caravansarai, 210, 234, *234*, *522*
Madrasa-yi Imāmī, *178*, 218, 225, *520*
Madrasa-yi Jadda Kuchik, 234
Madrasa-yi Kasangarān, 234
Madrasa-yi Mullā ʿAbdallāh, 234
Madrasa-yi Ṣadr, 234
maidān, 112, 114, *492*
Manār-i Bāgh-i Qūshkhāna, 156
Manār-i Khwāja ʿĀlam, 156–7
Manār-i Sarabān, *131*, 152, **154**,

156, *503*
Masjid-i ʿAlī Qulī Aghā, 114
Masjid-i ʿAlī, 112, 154
Masjid-i Ḥākim, 114
Masjid-i Shāh (now Masjid-i Imām), 24, 234–5, *492*
Masjid-i Shaikh Luṭfallāh, 112, *492*
palace precinct, *586*
Saljūq *madrasa*, 174–5
Saljūq palace, 415
Saljūq palace, 428
Sar Pūshida, palace, 428
Ṭālār Ashraf, 432
Ṭālār-i Ṭawīla, 428
Isna, Jāmiʿ al-ʿAmrī, minaret, 165, *506*
Isparta, *bedesten*, 353
Iṣṭakhr, mosque, 77, 101, *487*
Istanbul, Anadolu Hisari, Köprülü Yalisi, 460, *595*
Büyük Valide Han, 353
Büyük Yeni Han, *562*
complex of Mehmed II Fatih, 122, 217, *496*
Eski Saray ("Old Palace"), 457
Haghia Sophia, 36, 118, 122–3, 222
Ḥasan Pasha Han, *561*
Ibrāhīm Pasha Saray, *562*
Kürkçüler Han, 354, *561*
madrasa of Sulṭān Bāyazīd II, 217, *218, 518*
madrasa of Rüstem Pasha, 217, *518*
mausoleum of Barbaros, *540*
mausoleum of Maḥmūd Pasha, *540*
mausoleum of Sulṭān Selim II, *540*
mausoleum of Süleyman the Magnificent, *540*
Mihrimah mosque, **121**, *495, 497*
mosque of Ahmed Pasha, 121
mosque of ʿAtiq ʿAlī, *495*
mosque of Mehmed II Fatih, 120, *494, 496*
mosque of Murād Pasha, *495*
mosque of Qara Ahmed, *495*
mosque of Rüstem Pasha, *495*
mosque of Shamsī Pasha, *495*
mosque of Sokollu Mehmed Pasha, *495*
mosque of Sulṭān Ahmed, 122, *495, 497*
mosque of Sulṭān Bāyazīd II, **120**, 122, *494, 497*
mosque of Zul (= Dhu'l-) Maḥmūd, *495*
Rüstem Pasha Han, Galata, 354, *561*
Şehzade mosque, **120**, 121–2,

494, 495, 496, 498
Selimiye mosque, **120**, *495*
Selimiye mosque, minaret, 164
Süleymaniye complex, 121,**122**, 122–3, 217, *498*
Süleymaniye mosque, minaret, 165, *502*
Takkeci Ibrāhīm Aga, 121
Topkapi Saray, 378–9, 381, 408, 433, 452, 457, *458*, 458–62, *597*
Arz Odasi, 460
Bāb al-Saʿādat (Gate of Felicity), 459
Baghdād Kiosk, 462
bedchamber of Murād III, 461
Campaign or Expeditionary Force quarters, 460
Çinili Kiosk, 458, *460, 597*
Circumcision Room (Sunnet Odasi), 462
Commissariat or Pantry, 460
Council Chamber (*divan*), 459
Court of the Janissaries, 459
Golden Road, 461
Gülhane Park, 462
Hangman's Fountain (Cellat Çeşmesi), 459
Imperial Gate (Bāb-i Humāyūn), 459
Inner Treasury, 459
kiosk of Mehmed the Conqueror, 460
kiosk of Mustafa Pasha, 462
Library of Ahmed III, 460
Marble Terrace (Mermer Set), 462
Mecidiye kiosk, 462
Middle Gate (Bāb al-Salām, Gate of Peace), 459
Privy Chamber, 460
quarters for slaves, 461
Revan Kiosk, 462, *597*
royal quarters, 461
suite of the Black Eunuchs, 461
suite of the Queen Mother (Valide Sultan), 461
The Cage (Kafes), 461
the Throne Room Within, 461
Third Gate (Üçüncü Kapi), 462
Topkapi (Gun Gate), 457–8
Treasury, 460
tulip garden (Lale Bahcesi), 462
Valide Han, *561*
Yeni Saray ("New Palace"), 457
Īwān-i Karkha, Imāmzāda Ṭūʾīl, *546*
Īwān-i Kisrā *see* Ctesiphon, Ṭāq-i Kisrā
Iznik, Haci Özbek mosque, *495*
mausoleum of Khair al-Dīn

Pasha, *540*
Süleyman Pasha *madrasa*, 207, *519*
Yeşil Cami, 116, *116*, 163, *494, 495*
Jabal Sais, palace, *see* Usais, palace
Jajarm, Friday Mosque, 111
Jām, minaret, *130, 132*, 154–6, 158, **159–160**, 182–3
Jamālābād, caravansarai, 366
Janad, al-, minaret, *131*
mosque, 91
Jar Kurgan, minaret, 148, 158, 164, *503*
Jarash, Umayyad mosque, 68, *471*
Jausaq al-Khaqānī *see* Sāmarrāʾ, Jausaq al-Khaqānī
Jayy (Iṣfahān), round city, *574*
Jerusalem (al-Quds), Aqṣā mosque, 20, **25**, *47*, 63, *71*, 71–3, 77, 79, 205, *470, 471*
Aqṣā mosque, axial nave, *476*
Aqṣā mosque, *maqṣūra*, *466*
Aqṣā mosque, *minbar*, **35, 37**
Dome of the Rock, 4, 7, 14–15, 19–21, 23, 26, 48, 72–3, 93, 131, 201, 204–5, 255, 319, 330, *466*
Ḥaram al-Sharīf, 21
Holy Sepulchre, 14, 72, 167
hypothetical Umayyad palatial complex, *570*
Khān al-Sulṭān, 359
Khān al-Zait, 359
Madrasa al-Ashrafīya, 21, **25**, *203*, 204–6, **204–205**, *510, 511*
Madrasa al-Baladīya, 204–5
Madrasa al-Dawadārīya, 203
Madrasa al-Isʿardīya, **203**
Madrasa al-Jauharīya, 203, 205, *557*
Madrasa al-Khātūnīya, 203
Madrasa al-Kīlānīya, 14, 324, *326, 512*
Madrasa al-Muzhirīya, 203–4
Madrasa al-Rasāsīya, 203
Madrasa al-Tankizīya, 204
Madrasa al-Tāshtīmūrīya, 203
Madrasa al-ʿUthmānīya, 204
Ribāṭ Kurt, 351, *557*
sabīl of Qāʾit Bāy, 324, *330, 545*
Temple of Solomon, 72, 453
Umayyad palace, 381
Madrasa al-Salāmīya, 203
palace of Sitt Ṭunshuq, 436, **437**, *582*
Jibla, funerary mosque of Arwa bint Aḥmad, 91, 272, *481*
Kaʿba *see* Makka, Kaʿba
Kafirbina Han, 353
Kāj, mosque, 107
Kalai-Kafirmigan (Buddhist site), 175

Kalāt-i Nādirī, mausoleum of Nādir Shāh, 305, **306**
Kalkhūrān, mausoleum of Shaikh Jibrīl, 306, *534*
Kara *see* Qara
Karabaghlar *see* Qarābaghlar
Karahisar, Saljūq *madrasa*, 208
Karamata *see* Qaramata
Karatai *see* Qaratā'i
Karbalā', shrine (al-Mashhad al-Ḥusainī), 306
minaret, *131*
Kargi Han, *553*
Kāshān, Friday Mosque, 110
Masjid-i Vazīr, 114
minarets, 152
Shī'ite *madrasa*, 177
Kashmār, flanged mausoleum, *284*, **285**, 286, 309, *528*
Kastamonu, complex of Ismā'īl Bey, 210, 353
Kayqubadiye, palace, 415, 418, *580*
Kayseri area, Köşk *madrasa*, *207*, 208, 214, *516*
Çifte Minare *madrasa*, 208, *517*
Döner Kümbet, **308**, 309, *540*, *541*
Great Mosque, 97, 116, *482*
Hajji Kiliç mosque and *madrasa*, 210, *482*
Han Cami, *81*, *482*
Khwand Khātūn complex, 97, *98*, 210, 308, *482*
Külük Cami *madrasa*, *517*
mausoleum of 'Alī b. Ja'far, *540*, *541*
Khachen Dorbatly, mausoleum, 308, *542*
sculpture, 308, *542*
Khairpūr, mosque of Abū Amjad, 159
Khān al-'Arūs, 331, 351, *351*, *556*
Khān al-Barūd *see* Aleppo, Khān al-Barūd
Khān al-Inqirata, 350, *350*, *555*
Khān al-Quṭaifa, 352, *559*
Khān al-Sabīl, 350, *556*
Khān al-Tujjār, 351
Khān al-Zabīd, 334
Khān Asad, 367, 369
Khān Barūr (Tektek area), 338, *557*
Khān Bi'r al-Nus, 369
Khān Ḥamāt, 369–70, *564*
Khān Jitan, 367, 369
Khān Jubb Yūsuf, 351
Khān Mashāhida, 367, 369, *369*
Khān Muṣallā, 369–70
Khān Shaikhūn, 352
Khān Ṭūmān, 352, *556*
Khān, al-, near Mauṣil, *564*
Khargird, Madrasa al-Ghiyāthīya, **226**, 226–7, *521*

Niẓāmīya *madrasa* (?), 180–1, 206, *508*
Kharraqān mausolea, 276
mausoleum of 1067, 278
mausoleum of 1067, frescoes, 278, *534*
tower of 1086, **277**, *528*
Khirbat al-Khān, fort, *567*
Khirbat al-Mafjar, 381–2, 385, 387, 390, 392, 421, *571*
bath hall, 16, *571*
fountain, *381*, 413, *571*
Khirbat al-Minya, 385, *569*
Khīva, *madrasa* of Allāh Qulī Khān, 234
madrasa of Amīn Khān, 234
madrasa of Islām Khwāja, 234
madrasa of Pahlavān Maḥmūd, 234
Masjid-i Jāmi', minaret, *130*
Khulbuk, royal residence in citadel, 411
Khusraugird, minaret, 147, 152–4, *503*
Khūy, tower of skulls, 160
Khwāja Mashhad (Sayot, Tājikistān), *madrasa*, 174, 183, *520*
Kilij *see* Qilij
Kirāt, minaret, 153, 155–6
Kirk-Kiz near Tirmidh, 341, 409–10, *580*
Kirmān, Jabal-i Sang, 294, *294*, **295**, *535*
Masjid-i Malik, minaret, 148, *504*
Kirşehir, Caca Bey *madrasa*, 211, *517*
Kesik Köprü Han, *347*, *552*
mausoleum of Melik Ghāzī, 309, **309**, *541*
Kiz-Bībī mausoleum, 289
Kocamustafapasha, mosque of Ramazan Efendi, 121
Konya, 'Alā' al-Dīn mosque, 61, **65**, 94, **95**, 99, 162–3, 417, *486*
citadel *īwān*, 417
Hajjī Ferruh mosque, *482*
Hoca Ḥasan mosque, *482*
Hoca Ḥasan mosque, minaret, 164
Ince Minare *madrasa*, *209*, 210, **211**, *516*
Ince Minare *madrasa*, minaret, 163
īwān mausoleum, 311
mausoleum of Qilij Arslan II, *540*
Meram mosque, 98
Qaratā'i *madrasa* **208**, *209*, *517*
Ṣāḥib 'Aṭā' mosque **99**, 162, *483*
Saljūq kiosk, 381, 416, *581*
Sirçali *madrasa*, *515*
Sirçali mosque, minaret, 164

Zemburi mosque, minaret, 164
Ksar el Kebir/Alcazarquivir *see* Qaṣr al-Kabir
Kuba (Buddhist site), 175
Kūfa, first mosque, 67
Great Mosque and *dār al-imāra*, *468*
Great Mosque, 38, **43**, 62, 68, *469*, *470*
palace (*dār al-imāra*), 391–2, 438–9, *467*
palace of Sa'd b. Abī Waqqāṣ, 409
Kūhpaya, caravansarai, 366, *566*
Kūhsan, *madrasa* of Tūmān Āghā, 226
Kunya Urgench *see* Urgench
Kurtkulak, caravansarai, 353
Kuru Han, *553*
Kuruçeşme Han, *553*
Kütahya, Vacidiye *madrasa*, 212
Lahore (Lāhaur) area, Shāhdāra, tomb of Jahāngīr, minaret, 161, *502*
Bādshāhī mosque, 159
mosque of Wazīr Khān, 159
mosque of Wazīr Khān, minaret, *502*
palaces, 433
Lajīm, Imāmzāda 'Abdallāh, 278
Lashkar-i Bāzār, Central Palace, 413, *579*
Friday Mosque, 413, *488*
Northern Palace, *579*
palaces, 411, 413–4
pavilion, 413, *579*
site plan, *579*
Southern palace, 413, *579*
Lednice, minaret, *130*
Linjān, shrine of Pīr-i Bakrān, 106, **257**, 287
Luxor, mosque of Abu'l-Ḥajj, minaret, **165**, 166
Ma'arrat al-Nu'mān, caravansarai, **332**, 352
Great Mosque, **56**
Great Mosque, fountain, *55*
Great Mosque, minaret, 140, *502*
Shāfi'ite *madrasa*, 187, 189, *509*
Madīna, House of the Prophet, first state, 22, 33, *39*, 39–40, 42, 45–6, 63, 68, 73, 83, 138, *470*
House of the Prophet, second state, 73, *470*
Mosque of the Prophet, *madrasa*, 204
Mosque of the Prophet, Umayyad state, 53, 63, 71, *72*, 73, 253, *470*
Mosque of the Prophet, Umayyad state, minarets, 137, 139
Umayyad *minbar*, 466

Madīnat al-Zāhira, 379, 443
Madīnat al-Zahrā', 379, 443–6, 452, 591
   dār al-jund, 446, *595*
   dār al-khulafā' (Chamber of the Caliphs), 443–4
   dār al-mulk (El Salon Rico), **444**, 446, *595*
   Friday Mosque, minaret, 139, *501*
   Great Mosque, *125, 476*
   majlis al-dhahabī (Golden Reception Hall), 443–4
   majlis al-gharbī, 444, 446, *595*
   site layout, *595*
Madīnat Sulṭān, mosque, 86, *478*
Māhān, shrine of Niʿmatallāh Walī, 268, 303, **305**
Mahauwil, *khān*, 369
Mahdīya, Great Mosque, 78, *79, 80*, *438, 476*
   naval arsenal, 350
   palace of Abu'l-Qāsim al-Qā'im (?), *438, 590*
Mahjam, al-, minaret, 92
Maḥmūdīya, *khān*, 367
Mahyār, caravansarai, 366, *565*
Maibūd, Friday Mosque, 110
Makka, al-Ḥaram, *madrasa*, 204
   minaret, *130*
Makka, Ottoman *madrasa*s, 217
Makka, the Kaʿba, 21, 31, 40, 322, 437
   reconstruction of original form, *466*
Malaga, Alcazaba, 444–6, *445, 447, 592*
Malatya, Great Mosque, 97, *484*
   Great Mosque, *qibla īwān*, *96*
Malatya, *khān*, 356
Manakeldi, caravansarai, 339, *550*
Manākhir, al-, staging post, *555*
Manārat Mujda *see* Mujda, minaret
Manas (Kyrgyzstan), mausoleum, 297, *533, 536*
Manisa, Great Mosque, 98, *494*
Manṣūra mosque *see* Tilimsān area, Manṣūra mosque
*marabūṭ*s, 271, *271*
Marāgha, Gunbad-i Ghaffārīya, *528*
   Gunbad-i Surkh, 278, *278, 528*
   Gunbad-i Surkh, crypt, *528*
   Joi Burj, *528*
   Round Tower, *528*
Marand, Friday Mosque, *489*
Marash, *ribāṭ* and *khānqāh* of Eshab-i Keyf, 219, 333, *518*
Mardin, Firdaus palace, 419, *581*
   Great Mosque, 93, *484*
   Great Mosque, minaret, **162**, 163
   khān, 356, *559, 561*
   mausoleum of Sulṭān Ḥamza, 311

Sulṭān ʿĪsā *madrasa*, 207, *516*
Sulṭān Qāsim *madrasa*, *517*
Maʾrib, Masjid Sulaimān b. Dāʾūd, 91, *480*
Marrakesh *see* Marrākush
Marrākush, Almohad *qaṣaba*, 452
   Badīʿ palace, 453
   Ben Yūsuf *madrasa* **247**, 248, 250, *524*
   first Kutubīya mosque, *miḥrāb, 467*
   Kutubīya mosque, **86**, *475*
   Kutubīya mosque, minaret, **141**, *142, 499, 501*
   madrasa of Mūlāy Ismāʿīl, 247
   mosque of Ben Ṣāliḥ, *474*
   mosque of the Qaṣba, 88, *474*
   Qubbat al-Barudiyīn, **27–28**, 55, *56, 57, 476*
   second Kutubīya mosque, 86, 89
   second Kutubīya mosque, *miḥrāb, 467*
   tombs of the Saʿadians, **270**, 271, *526*
Marv area, Ḥaram kiosk, *578*
   palatial houses, *578*
   Sulṭān Qalʿa kiosk, *580*
   dār al-imāra of Abū Muslim, 19, 391, 393, 402, 408–11, *578*
   Giyaur Qalʿa, 411
   kiosk, 416, *578*
   mausoleum of Muḥammad b. Zaid, 294, *465, 532*
   mausoleum of Sulṭān Sanjar, 278, *279*, **280**, 283, 294, 305, *531, 532*
   mausoleum of Sulṭān Sanjar, brickwork, *465*
   mosque, 391, 393
   Saljūq *madrasa*s, 174–5, 223
   Saljūq palace (Arg or Shahrīyār), 411, 415, *578*
   Shīr Kabir, *mazār*, 289, *531, 532*
   Sulṭān Qalʿa, 411
Mashhad area, mausoleum of Khwāja Rabīʿa, 306, *535*
   Masjid-i Shāh, 111–2, *114, 492*
   Masjid-i Shāh, minarets, *114*, 156–7
   mosque of Gauhar Shād, 107, 157, *492*
   shrine of Imām Riḍāʾ, 21, 106, 158, 179, 266, 305, *492, 525*
   shrine of Imām Riḍāʾ, Bālā Sar *madrasa*, 227–8, *522*
   shrine of Imām Riḍāʾ, Du Dar *madrasa*, 227–8, *522*
   shrine of Imām Riḍāʾ, *khiyābān* of Shāh ʿAbbās, 305
   shrine of Imām Riḍāʾ, Parizād *madrasa*, 227–8, *522*
   shrine of Imām Riḍāʾ, tomb

chamber of Allāhvardī Khān, 305
Mashhad-i Miṣrīyān, 103; *see also* Dāhistān
Masjid-i Shāh *see* Iṣfahān, Masjid-i Shāh
Mauṣil, al-, al-Ḥājjī Qāsim Āghā Khān, 356
   Jāmiʿ al-Nūrī (Nūrī mosque), **45**
   Jāmiʿ al-Nūrī, minaret, *131*, 153
   mausoleum of ʿAun al-Dīn, 546
   Qarā Sarāy, 415, *418*, 419–21
   Zangid palace, 419
mausoleum types from Transoxiana, *530*
Mayyāfāriqīn, Great Mosque, 92, 99, *485*
Mazdakhgān/Mazdakhqān, *ribāṭ*s, 341
Mecca *see* Makka
Medina *see* Madina
Meknes *see* Miknās
Merv *see* Marv
Merzifon, Çelebi Mehmed *madrasa* (*madrasa* of Sulṭān Mehmed II), 216, *216*, *519*
Mihna, mausoleum of Abū Saʿīd, 291, *531, 532*
Miknās, Bū (Abū) ʿInānīya *madrasa*, 241, 244, 248
   Madrasa al-ʿAṭṭarin, 241
Mīl-i Nādirī, 154
Mīl-i Qāsimābād, 154
Mīl-i Rādkān, tomb tower, 277, 309, *527*
Miletus, Ilyas Bey mosque, 163
Minya Konka, tower, 147
Miṣbāhīya *madrasa see* Fās, Madrasa al-Miṣbāhīya
Misiṣ, caravansarai, 353
Miskina, minaret, 148, **149**
Monastir *see* Munastir
Mosque of the Prophet *see* Madina, Mosque of the Prophet
mosque types from Transoxiana, *530*
   transept, schema, *466*
   typical, cutaway schema, *466*
Mosul *see* Mauṣil, al-
Moyunçur Qaghān, fortified residence, *578*
Mshattā as a source for later palaces, 397–8, 402, 404–5, 407, 412–4, 439–40, 446
   palace, 16, 45, 385, **388**, *388, 389*, 390, 392, 407, 413, 438–9, *568*
Mughayir, fort, *567*
Muḥammadīya, Masjid-i Sar-i Kūcha, **62**, *63*
Mujda, minaret, **145**
Mukhaṭaṭ al-Ḥajj, fort, *567*

Mūlāy Idrīs (Miknās area), shrine, 267–8, 271
Multān, mausoleum attributed to Shāh Rukn-i ʿĀlam, 297, *297*, *535*
Munastir, *ribāṭ*, 331, *548*
Munyat al-Ruṣāfa, villa, 443
Murcia, Castillejo, 446, *595*
Nāʾin, Friday Mosque, 77, 102, 412, *489*
Friday Mosque, minaret, 148
palaces, **430**, 430–1
Naisar, fire temple, 36, *36*, *487*, *531*
Najaf, shrine, 306
Najīm Qalʿa, near Marv, 341
Nakhchivān, mausoleum of Muʾmina Khātūn, 286, *528*, *535*
mausoleum of Yūsuf b. Kuthair, 283, 286, *534*, *535*
mosque, 105, 154
Nardārān, palace of the Shīrvānshāhs, 427–8, *583*
Naṣrīya, *khān*, 369
Naṭanz, caravansarai, 366, *565*
Masjid-i Kūcha Mīr, 104, 347
shrine and *khānqāh* of ʿAbd al-Ṣamad, 106, 156, 220, 266, 268, *284*, 287, **287**, *510*, *529*
Nerkiyi Dzhrapi, caravansarai, *554*
Nigār, Friday Mosque, minaret, 153, *503*
Niğde, Ak Madrasa, 213, *213*
mausoleum of Khudāvand Khātūn, 308, *540*
mosque of ʿAlāʾ al-Dīn, 95, 116, *116*, 162–3, *486*
mosque of ʿAla' al-Dīn, *miḥrāb*, 467
mosque of Sunqur Beg, *100*, *482*
Niksar, Friday Mosque, 95, *483*
madrasa of Yaghi-Basan, 211, *516*
Nippūr, Parthian house, 335
Parthian palace, 391
Nīrīz, Friday Mosque, 102, *487*
Nisā, *namāzgāh* mosque, *488*
Nīshāpūr area, mausoleum of Muḥammad Mahrūq, 306
area, Qadamgāh mausoleum, 305
Friday Mosque, 110
Madrasa al-Saʿīdī/Saʿdiya, 174
Madrasa al-Sulṭānīya, 174
Madrasa-yi Ibn Fūrak, 174
Madrasa-yi Miyān-i Dāhīya, 173, 237
Niẓāmīya *madrasa*, 173
private houses, 438
Ode-Mergen, caravansarai, *550*
Öljeitü, tomb of *see* Sulṭānīya, mausoleum of Öljeitü
Öresin Han, *553*

Pabsin, caravansarai, 353
Palermo, Great Mosque, 36
La Cuba, 441–2, *442*, *592*
La Cubola, 441
La Favara, 441, *592*
La Ziza, *440*, *441*, 441–2, 446, *592*
Torre Pisano/Torre di Santa Ninfa, 441
ʾPamukcu Han, 353
Parthian tower tombs, 282
Pasargadae (Madār-i Sulaimān), gardens, 426
madrasa, 182, *508*
palaces, 428
tomb of Cyrus, 274
Passingān, caravansarai, 369
pavilion on bronze salver in Berlin, *531*
Payas, Sokollu Mehmed Pasha Han, 353, *561*
Peçin, caravansarai, 353
Persepolis, *apadāna*, capital, 466
palaces, 402
Piazza Armerina, 452
Pīr Saʿdat (Bākū area), *khānqāh*, 219, 220, *518*
Qairawān, first mosque, 66
Great Mosque, 20, **41**, 46, 48, **49**, 50, *54*, **58**, 61, 74, 77, 81, *478*
Great Mosque, axial nave, *476*
Great Mosque, Bāb Lālla Raiḥāna, *476*
Great Mosque, entrance, *467*
Great Mosque, *maqṣūra*, *466*
Great Mosque, minaret, *131*, 138–9, **139**, 167, *499*, *500*
mosque of Muḥammad b. Khairūn, 78, 83, **84**, *478*
mosque of Sīdī ʿUqba *see* Qairawān, Great Mosque
pleasure pavilion, 442
Qalʿa of the Banū Ḥammād, 382, 439–41, 446, *590*
Great Mosque, *476*
minaret, 140, *499*, *500*
palace of al-Manār/Qaṣr al-Manār, *439*, 439–41, *590*
palace of Qaṣr al-Salām/Qaṣr al-Shām, 439, *590*
Qaṣr al-Kaukab, 439
Qaṣr al-Mulk/Qaṣr al-Baḥr, 440
site plan, *591*
Qalʿa-yi Ḍaḥḥāk, Parthian pavilion (?), 415, *415*, *573*
Qalʿa-yi Dukhtar, Abaghlū area, pavilion, *412*, 415, *580*
Qalʿat al-Muḍīq, caravansarai, 352, *559*
Qalʿat Najm, palace, 419
Qalʿat Simʿān, *martyrium*, 402

Qara Mughurt, caravansarai, 352
Qara, caravansarai, 353
Qarabaghlar, funerary complex, 155, *503*
Qaraman, complex of Ibrāhīm Beg, 210–11, *516*
Qaramata, caravansarai, 353
Qaratāʾi Han **348**, 350, *552*
Qarawiyīn *see* Fās, Qarawiyīn mosque
Qaryatain, al-, area, "The Cistern" staging post, 555
Qaṣr al-Azraq, fort, *567*
Qaṣr al-Banāt, tower, 138
Qaṣr al-Ḥair al-Gharbī *see* Qaṣr al-Ḥair West
Qaṣr al-Ḥair East, large enclosure, 390, *569*
Qaṣr al-Ḥair East, mosque, 77
Qaṣr al-Ḥair East, *paradeisos*, 390
Qaṣr al-Ḥair East, site plan, *569*
Qaṣr al-Ḥair East, small enclosure (caravansarai?), 334, *336*, *556*
Qaṣr al-Ḥair West, *khān*, 334, *556*
Qaṣr al-Ḥair West, palace, 138, *387*, 390, *568*
Qaṣr al-Kabīr, *madrasa*, 250
Qaṣr al-Khabbāz, caravansarai (?), 334, *551*
Qaṣr al-Quwaira, fort, *567*
Qaṣr al-Ṭūba, palace, 387, *568*
Qaṣr Bashīr, fort, *567*
Qaṣr Kharāna, palace, 332, 385, 387, *568*
Qaṣr-i Shīrīn, ʿImārat-i Khusrau, 391, 393, 428, *573*
Qastal, al-, palace, 385, *386*, *569*
Qazvīn, Friday Mosque, 152, 178
Ḥaidarīya, mosque (?), *489*
Ṣafavid palace, 429, 429–30, *586*
Shāhzāda Ḥusain, 158
Qubādābād, Great Palace, 415–6, *417*, 418, *581*
Lesser Palace, 418, *581*
palaces, 417–8, *581*
Qumm, 12th-century Shīʿite *madrasa*, 177
Imāmzāda ʿImād al-Dīn, *529*
Shāhzāda Ibrāhīm, *529*
shrine of Fāṭima, 106, 158, 279, 305, *525*
tomb towers in the Bāgh-i Sabz **286**, 287
Qurva, Friday Mosque, 101, *101*, *489*
Qūṣ, mausoleum, *313*, 313–4, *543*
Quṣair ʿAmra, hunting lodge, 381, *570*
Quṣair, al-, caravansarai, *556*
Qūsh Ribāṭ, 365, *549*
Quṭaifa, al-, area, "At the Fork"

staging post, *555*
Quṭaifa, al-, caravansarai, *556*
Rabaṭ area, mausoleum of ʿAbdallāh
　b. Yāsīn, 271, *526*
　madrasa, 250
　mosque of al-Ḥassān, 89, *90, 140,*
　475
　mosque of al-Ḥassān, minaret,
　130, 140, **141**
　Shālla necropolis, 271, **272**, *526*
Radāʿ, Madrasa al-ʿĀmiriya **192**,
　193, *514*
　mosque, 91
Rādkān East *see* Mīl-i Rādkān
Rādkān West, tomb tower, *282*
Ramla, White Mosque, minaret, **27**,
　499
Raqqa area, *khān*, *557*
Raqqa, Baghdād Gate, 290
　Great Mosque, *469*
　Palace B, *577*
　Palace D, *577*
　Palace G, *577*
　palaces, 390
　Qaṣr al-Banāt, 415, 418–9, *580*
Raqqāda, palace, 439–40, 442
　Qaṣr al-Ṣaḥn, *592*
Rastan, al-, caravansarai, 352
Rauḍa, mosque, 91
Rayy area, tomb of Bībī Shahrbanū,
　267
　Būyid tomb towers, 316
　excavated *madrasa* (?), 180–1, 206,
　508
　Saljūq *madrasa*, 175
　Shiʿite *madrasa*, 177
　tower of Ṭughrul, 286
Ribāṭ-i Anūshirvān, Ahūvān, 339
Ribāṭ-i ʿIshq, 365
Ribāṭ-i Karim, 339, *339, 549*
Ribāṭ-i Māhī, 342, 344, 346
Ribāṭ-i Malik, 341, *343,* **343**, 344,
　549
Ribāṭ-i Sangī, 343
Ribāṭ-i Sharaf, 183, 333, 338–9, 342,
　344, 344–6, *345*, 360, 411, 414,
　429, *549*
Ribāṭ-i Sinchās, 365
Ribāṭ-i Sipanj, **346**, 360
Ribāṭ-i Sulṭān, 343
Ribāṭ-i Turk, 339
Ribāṭ-i Zīza, 566
Riḍāʾiya, Friday Mosque, 103, *489,*
　491
　Sa Gunbad, 286, *529*
Rome, Domus Aurea, 395, 454
Rubruquis' description of Mongol
　tents: 18th-century drawing,
　541
Ruṣāfa, mosque, diagram showing
　visibility of *miḥrāb*, 466
Ruṣāfa, palace, 390, *390, 569*

Ruṣāfa, Umayyad mosque, *470*
Rushkhvār, Friday Mosque, 110
Ṣaʿda, funerary mosque of the Imām
　al-Hādī Yaḥyā, 91
　Masjid ʿUlayyān, *166*
　Masjid al-Shamrī, *166*
　mosque, 91
Saʿdābād, caravansarai, 370
Sabian temple, *531*
Ṣabra/al-Manṣūriya, 382, *592*
　Camphor Room, 440
　Khawarnaq, 441
　Myrtle Room, 440–1
　round city, 393, 440, *574*
　The Īwān, 441
　The Jewel of the Diadem, 441
　The Silver Stone, 441
Sabzavār, Shiʿite *madrasa*, 177
Sadrāta, Maḥkāma, 438
　palaces, 437–8
　palatial house, *590*
Safīd Āb, palace, *586*
Safīd Buland, mausoleum of Shāh
　Faḍl, 261, **292**, 293, *530*
Ṣāhyūn, palace, 419
Sale (Shāla), *madrasa* of
　Abuʾl-Ḥasan, 242–3, 246, **246**,
　248, *523, 524*
　madrasa of Bū (Abū) ʿInān, 241
　naval arsenal, 350
　Zāwiya al-Nussāk, **243**
Ṣāliḥ Ṭalāʾiʿ, al-, mosque of *see*
　Cairo, mosque of al-Ṣāliḥ
　Ṭalāʾiʿ
Saljūq transition zone of standard
　type, *490*
Samarqand, Gūr-i Amīr, **268**, 297,
　300, **302–303**, 305, *538*
　Ishrat Khāna, 297, *537*
　madrasa of Ibrāhīm I, 174,
　508
　mausoleum of Quthām b. ʿAbbās,
　301
　mosque of Bībī Khānum, **107**,
　108, *108*, **109–110**, 110, 114,
　493
　Qarakhānid mosque, 76
　Rigistān, 108, 230, *232, 521*
　Rigistān, *madrasa* of Ulugh Beg,
　176, 227, 230, **231**, 232, *232,*
　233–234
　Rigistān, Shīr Dār *madrasa*, **177**,
　232, **235–236**
　Rigistān, Ṭilā Kārī *madrasa, 232,*
　237
Shāh-i Zinda, general layout, *260,*
　262, 297, *539*
Shāh-i Zinda, mausoleum dated
　758/1360, **11**
Shāh-i Zinda, mausoleum of
　Chujuk Bīka, **265, 299**
Shāh-i Zinda, mausoleum of

Qāḍizāda Rūmī, **299**
Shāh-i Zinda, mausoleum of
　Shād-i Mulk, **13, 267**
Shāh-i Zinda, mausoleum of
　Shīrīn Bīka, **256**
Shāh-i Zinda, "mausoleum of
　Ustād ʿĀlim", **15**
Shāh-i Zinda, street in the
　necropolis, **301**
Sāmarrāʾ, al-Ḥuwaiṣilāt, 398
　al-Iṣṭabulāt, 398, 404, *575*
　al-Quwair, 398
　Ashnās, 398
　Balkuwārā palace, 381, 398,
　403–6, *575*
　Great Mosque, 53, 53, 74, **74**, 83,
　89,139, 146, *469*
　Great Mosque, minaret, *131*, 139,
　144–5, **146**, *499*
　Jausaq al-Khaqānī, 381, 398–404,
　400, **404**, 406, 421, *577*
　Jausaq al-Khaqānī, Bāb
　al-ʿAmma, 402, 407, 459
　Jausaq al-Khaqānī, Grand
　Esplanade, 402–3
　palaces, 395, 398–9, 403, 438
　private houses, 438
　Qaṣr al-ʿĀshiq, 398, **407**, 407–8,
　413, *575*
　Qaṣr al-Jiṣṣ, 398, 406–7, *575*
　Qubbat al-Ṣulaibīya, 254, **254**,
　255, *531, 546*
　Shīʿite shrine, 306
　site plan, *576*
　stucco dadoes, 399, **399**, *401,*
　403
　Zanqūr, 398
Sameh, tower, 138
Samīrān, anonymous mausolea, **276**
　minaret, 154
Ṣanʿāʾ, al-Jīla mosque, 91
　Great Mosque, 83, **91**, *91,* 92,
　481
　Great Mosque, minaret, *166*
　Masjid al-Abhar, minaret, *166*
Sangān-i Pāʾīn, Masjid-i Gunbad,
　104
Sangbast, caravansarai, **369**
　mausoleum, 293
Sanjar, tomb of *see* Marv,
　mausoleum of Sulṭān Sanjar
Saqqāra, monastery of Apā
　Jeremias, 46
Sar-i Pul, mausoleum of Imām-i
　Kalān, 258, *258, 533*
Ṣarafṣa Han, 347, *553*
Sarakhs, mausoleum of Abuʾl-Faḍl,
　291, *531, 532*
　mausoleum of Bābā Luqmān,
　291, 294
Sarcham, caravansarai, 360, *565*
Ṣarha, mosque, 92

Sarm, Friday Mosque, 114
Sasanian pavilion (Ṭāq-i Taqdīs?) on
    Berlin salver, *531, 572*
Sāva, minarets, 152
Schwetzingen, 10
Selcuk (Ephesus), mosque of ʿĪsā
    Beg, 98–9, *100*, 163, *484*
Seville (Ishbīlīya), Alcazar, 443, 446,
    450, 452–3, *593, 595*
  Alcazar, Room of the
    Ambassadors, 444
  Alcazar, Yeso courtyard, 450
  Great Mosque, **89**, 452, *475*
  Great Mosque, Giralda minaret,
    21, 129, **143**, 452, *499, 501*
Seyidgazi, *īwān* tomb, 311
Sfax (Sifāqis), Great Mosque, 77,
    475
  minaret, 138–9, 167, *499, 500*
Shāh-i Mashhad *madrasa*, Garjistān,
    182, *508*
Shahr-i Sabz, Ak Sarāy, **383, 385,
    422**, 423–6, **425, 427**, *583*
Shahūf, al-, Darb Zubaida,
    residential unit, 411, *577*
Shallāl, minaret, 165
Shibām, Friday Mosque, 91–2, *480*
Shiblī caravansarai, 366, *565*
Shīr Kabīr mausoleum *see* Marv,
    Shīr Kabīr, *mazār*
Shīrāz, Friday Mosque, 104, 110
  palace of ʿAdud al-Daula, 403,
    411, 428
Shīrdak Beg castle, *578*
Siirt, Great Mosque, *485*
Simnān, Friday Mosque, 104, *491*
Sīn, caravansarai, 360, **365**
  mosque, 104
Sinjār, minaret, 153
  niche, **420**, 421
Sīrāf, funerary structures, 276
  Friday Mosque, 101–2, *487, 489*
  Friday Mosque, minaret, 148
  mosque at site C, *491*
  mosque at site M2, *489, 491*
  mosque at site P2, *489*
Sivas, Buruciye *madrasa*, 214, *515*
  Çifte Minare *madrasa*, **9**, 162
  Gök *madrasa* 162, **213–214**, *515*
  Great Mosque, 95, *482*
  Great Mosque, minaret, **161**, 162
  "Güdük Minare", 164, 307, *540*
  Kaiqaʾūsīya, 208
  Saljūq *madrasa*, 208, 210
  Saljūq palace, 416
Sivrihisar, Great Mosque, 116, *486*
Siyāh Kūh *see* ʿAbbāsābād
Split, palace of Diocletian, *569*
Sujās, Friday Mosque, 102, **103**,
    104, 489
Sulṭān Han near Aksaray, 350, *552*
  miḥrāb, 467

Sulṭān Han near Kayseri, **347–348**,
    349, 552
Sulṭānīya, mausoleum of Chelebi
    Oghlu, 529
  mausoleum of Öljeitü, 155, 283,
    294, **295**, *295, 296*, 297, 302,
    305, *535*
  vanished twin-minaret portal, 155
Sūsa (Sūs) (Iran), mosque, 101, *488,
    489*
Sūsa (Sūs) (Tunisia), Great Mosque,
    32, *74*, 74, 77, *478*
  mosque of Bū Fatātā, 78, *478*
  ribāṭ, 331, *332, 548*
  manār, 138, *500*
Ṭabas, Madrasa-yi Dū Dār, **180**,
    181–2, *520*
Tabrīz, Masjid-i ʿAlī Shāh, 107, 424,
    491
  Masjid-i Muẓaffarīya (Blue
    Mosque), 112, *115, 492*
  mausoleum of Ghāzān Khān, 295,
    534
Ṭāfirṭāst, *ribāṭ*, 331
Tagisken, ancient Turkic mausolea,
    274, 275
Ṭāhart, *qaṣba*, 437–8, *590*
Taʿizz, al-Ashrafīya mosque and
    madrasa, 67, 91, *514*
  al-Muẓaffarīya mosque, **20**, 91,
    480
  Muʿtabīya *madrasa*, **193**, *514*
Takht-i Sulaimān, *muqarnas*, *583*
  palace, 415, 421–3, 440, *583*
  site plan, *583*
Ṭākistān, "Pir" mausoleum, 278,
    287, 535
Talkhatān Bābā, mosque, 104, *488*
Tamūr, mosque, 91, *480*
Tangiers, *madrasa*, 248
Ṭāq-i Kisrā *see* Ctesiphon
Ṭāq-i Taqdīs, 409, 454
  (?) on Berlin salver, *531, 572*
Tāsh Ribāṭ (Kyrgyzstan), 412, *550*
Tāʾūq, minaret, *152*, **153**
Ṭāybād, *buqʿa*, 297
Tāzā, Great Mosque, first state, 86,
    475
  Great Mosque, second state,
    86–7, *87, 475*
  Marīnid *madrasa*, 248
Tekor, Armenian church, drum, *541*
Temple, The *see* Jerusalem, Temple
    of Solomon
Tercan, mausoleum of Mama
    Hatun, *309*, 309, 311, 427, *540*
Termez *see* Tirmidh
Thulā, funerary *madrasa* of
    al-Hādī, 193, *513*
  Great Mosque, 91, *480*
  Masjid Ghurza, *480*
Thulaima, al-, Darb Zubaida, *551*

Tīm, mausoleum of ʿArab ʿAṭāʾ,
    288, 290–1, *531, 532*
Timbuktu, minaret, 142
Tīmūr, tomb of *see* Samarqand,
    Gūr-i Amīr
Tīnmāl, Great Mosque, 89, *474*
  miḥrāb, 467
Tirmidh, Char Sutūn mosque, 104,
    488
  Kirk-Kiz, 409–12, *580*
  Regent's Palace, 411–2, *580*
  Sultan Saʿādat ensemble, 266,
    268, *539*
Tīt, *ribāṭ*, 331
Tīthīd, mosque, 91, *480*
Tivoli, palace of Hadrian, 452
Tilimsān area, al-ʿUbbād, complex of
    Shaikh (Sīdī) Abū Madyan, 271
  area, al-ʿUbbād, mosque of
    Shaikh (Sīdī) Abū Madyan,
    475, 477
  area, al-ʿUbbād, mosque of
    Shaikh (Sīdī) Abū Madyan,
    qubba, 526
  area, al-ʿUbbād, Shaikh (Sīdī) Abū
    Madyan, *madrasa*, 247, *523*
  area, Manṣūra mosque, 89, *474*
  area, Manṣūra mosque, minaret,
    141, 144, *499*
  Agādir mosque, minaret, *499*
  complex of Sīdī al-Halwī, *91*, **127**,
    242, *477*
  funerary complex of Sayyidī
    Ibrāhīm, 242
  Great Mosque, 87, *475*
  Madrasa al-Qadīma, 242
  qubba of Sayyidī Ibrāhīm, *526*
  royal villa, 442
  Tāshfīnīya *madrasa*, 248, *523*
  "Tomb of the Sulṭāna", 271–2,
    272, 526
  Walad al-Imām mosque, 242
Tlemcen *see* Tilimsān
Tokat, Çukur (Yaghibasan) *madrasa*,
    208, 211, *517*
  Gök *madrasa*, **215**
  Khatuniye *madrasa*, *519*
  mausoleum of Nūr al-Dīn
    Sentimur, 306, **307**, *540*
  zāwiya and *khānqāh* of Sünbül
    Baba, 219, 333, *518*
Toledo (Ṭulaiṭula), Dhuʾl-Nūnid
    palace, 444
  mosque at Bāb Mardūm, **78**, *472*
  mosque at Bāb Mardūm, facade,
    472
  mosque at Bāb Mardūm, vaults,
    472
Tomb of Ghāzān *see* Tabrīz,
    mausoleum of Ghāzān Khān
Transoxiana, types of mosque and
    mausoleum, *530*

Tripoli (Ṭarābulus) (Lebanon),
    Khān al-Manzil, 356
    Madrasa al-ʿAjamīya, 203
    Madrasa al-Khātūnīya, 203
Tripoli (Libya), *funduq*, 358, *548*
    madrasa of ʿUthmān Pasha, 217,
    524
Tulūl al-Shaʿība, palace, 395, *577*
Tulūl al-Ukhaiḍir, 395
Tūnis, Dār al-Bāy, 442
    Dār Ḥasan, 442
    Great Mosque (Zaitūna), 60, 74,
    77, 81, **82**, 244, *474*
    Great Mosque (Zaitūna), minaret,
    138
    Madrasa al-Maʿriḍīya, 239
    Madrasa al-Muntaṣirīya, 241
    Madrasa al-Shammāʿīya, 239
    Madrasa al-Sulaimānīya, 241
    mosque of the Qṣar, *474*
    the Bardo, 442
Turbat-i Shaikh Jām, shrine
    complex, 106, **227**, 303
    madrasa of Amīr Fīrūzshāh, 227–
    8, *522*
    "Old Mosque", 277, *491*
Turkistān, *mazār* or shrine of
    Khwāja Aḥmad Yasavī, 108,
    297, *301*, 302, **303–305**, *539*
Turkmenistani buildings, joint
    plugs, *465*
Ṭūs, Hārūnīya mausoleum, 294
    Saljūq *madrasa*, 175
Tūva, *ordu* of Moyunçur Qaghān,
    410
Ūjān, Mongol palace, 428
Ukhaiḍir, Court of Honour, 398
    (cf. 391)
    palace, 144, 290, 334, **392,** *394,*
    395–8, **396–397**, 404, 410, 412,
    439, *574*
Ulukishla, caravansarai of Okuz
    Mehmed Pasha, 356, *561*
Umm al-Rasās, tower, 138
Umm al-Surāb, tower, 138
Umm al-Walīd, caravansarai (?), 334

Ummu Qurūn, Ḍarb Zubaida, 342,
    551
Urfa, Great Mosque, 95, *482*
    Khān al-Gumruk, 358
    Khān Shifta, **337**
    madrasa adjoining Great Mosque,
    196, 206, *516*
Urgench (Gurgānj), Masjid-i Jāmiʿ,
    minaret, *130*
    mausoleum of Tekesh, 280, *533*
    mausoleum of Turabek Khānum,
    297, 300, *300, 537*
Urmīya *see* Riḍāʾīya
Usais, palace, 385, *568*
Uskāf Banī Junaid, palace, 395,
    575
Uzgand, mausoleum associated with
    Naṣr b. ʿAlī, **294**, *530*
    mausoleum dated 1186–7, **263**,
    294, *530*
    mausoleum of Jalāl al-Dīn
    Ḥusain, **293**, 294, *530*
    minaret, **135**, 148, *503*
Uzgend *see* Uzgand
Vābkent, minaret, 148, **150**
Vagarshavan, caravansarai, *554*
Vakil Bazar, mausoleum of
    ʿAbdallāh b. Buraida, *532*
Van, Great Mosque, 98, *100*, *484*
Varakhsha, palace, 341, 409, *578*
Varāmīn, Friday Mosque, 14, *106,*
    106, 107, *490*
    Imāmzāda Ḥusain Riḍāʾ, *528*
    Shīʿite *madrasa*, 177
    tomb tower of ʿAlāʾ al-Dīn, 286,
    527
Warka, Parthian palace, 393
Wāsiṭ, mosque, 391, 393, *469*
    palace, 391, 393
Yarti Gunbad, mausoleum, 294, *532*
Yazd, Davāzdah Imām, 291, *291*,
    294, *535*
    Friday Mosque, **23**, 101, 106, **127**,
    487
    madrasa of Ḍiyāʾ al-Dīn, 225, *520*
    mosque of Mīr Chaqmāq, 110

mosque of Sar-i Rīk, 110
    Shamsīya *madrasa* (*madrasa* of Mīr
    Shams al-Dīn), **224**, 226, *520*
    Zindān-i Iskandar *see* Yazd,
    madrasa of Ḍiyāʾ al-Dīn
Yazd-i Khāst, *chahār ṭāq* converted
    into a mosque, 101, *487*
Yeni Han, 356
Yeniceköy Han, *553*
Yolcu Han, 353
Zaʿfarānīya, caravansarai, **366**
Zabid, Friday Mosque, 91
    Friday Mosque, minaret, 92, *502*
    Madrasa al-Jabartīya, *514*
    Madrasa al-Sikandarīya, *514*
Ẓafar Dhibīn, mausoleum in the
    mosque, 272, **273**
    mosque, 91–2, *93, 480*
    mosque, minaret, 92
Zain al-Dīn, *ribāṭ*, 366
Zaitūna *see* Tūnis, Great Mosque
    (Zaitūna)
Zaragoza (Saraqusṭa), Aljaferia
    (al-Jaʿfariya), oratory, 449
    palace, 443, 446–50, *447, 448,*
    593, 595
Zarand, Friday Mosque, minaret,
    153, 158, *504*
Zavāra, Friday Mosque, 104, *487*
    Masjid-i Pā Minār, minaret, **156**
Zazadin (Saʿd al-Dīn) Han, 350, *552*
Zibane, Walad Jalāl, minaret, 142
Zindān-i Hārūn, way-station, 334,
    338, *338*, 410, *550*
Zivarik Han, *553*
Ziyār, minaret, 154, *503*
Ziyāratgāh, Friday Mosque and
    madrasa, 107, *107*, 228, *493*
    Masjid-i Chihil Sutūn, 109
    Masjid-i Gunbad, 111
Zīza, *ribāṭ*, 366
Zora area, caravansarai, *554*
Zūr, caravansarai, 366
Zūzan, *madrasa*, **181, 182, 183,**
    182–3, *508*

Index of Terms in Foreign (Principally Islamic) Languages

ablaq, 206, 309, 318, 350, 355, 359, 419, 436–7
adhān, 129–34, 136, 155, 164, 213, 245
ʿaḍud al-Islām, 266
adventus, 385
ahl al-bait, 269
ʿalam/ʿalama, 134
ambo, 46–7
amīr al-muʾminīn, 246
amīr, 152, 186, 189–90, 195, 197, 200, 202, 205, 220, 266, 278, 283, 316, 340, 349, 351, 416, 437, 439
ʿanaza, 165
aqṣā, 73
artesonados, 457
asās, 134
astāna, 257
atābeg, 186, 349
atrium, 55–6, 97, 211, 453
auqāf see waqf
ʿaziza, al-, 442
bādgīr, 226
bādiya, 387
bait al-māl, 391
bait, 395, 397, 405, 413, 438–9
baraka, 63, 190, 204, 262, 266
barīd, 202, 351, 370
bayʿa, 48
bāzār, 32, 126, 158, 241, 244, 247, 361, 405, 414, 428
bedesten, 353
beg, 424
bimarhane, 208
bismillāh, 254
bīt hilānī, 385, 395, 402
caravansarai, 331–2
cardo, cardines, 404
castrum, 331, 334, 404, 406, 438
chahār sū, 244
chahār ṭāq, 101, 103, 276, 281, 290, 418, 422
chahār bāgh, 428–9
chemin de ronde, 396
chhatrī, 161
cordon sanitaire, 396
cuerda seca, 457
dāʿī, 176
dakhma, 269, 274, 276
dār, 40, 42, 391, 409–10
dār al-ḥadīth, 59, 222
dār al-ḥikma, 76

dār al-ḥuffāẓ, 59
dār al-imāra, 391, 409
dār al-qurʾān, 59, 222
dargāh, 219
dhikr, 60, 220
diaconicon, 211
dihqān, 342, 411
dikka, 55–6
dīnār, 60, 222
dīwān, 381, 453, 459
dīwān al-ʿāmm, 381
dīwān al-khāṣṣ, 381
durqāʿa, 435–6
duwaira, 219
duwīra, 250
faqīh (pl. fuqahāʾ), 204–5
fathnāma, 155
fiqh, 59, 173, 240
funduq, 331–2, 355
fuqahāʾ, see faqīh
futuwwa, 220
ghāzī, 264, 312, 331, 341
girikh, 412
guldasta, 159, 161
gunbad, 257
ḥadīth, 32, 39, 59, 61, 63–4, 126, 128–9, 156, 173, 191, 253, 260
ḥāfiẓ bilād Allāh, 266
ḥāfiẓ thughūr al-muslimīn, 266
ḥaidar, 18
ḥair, 403; cf. 390
ḥajj, 339, 342, 353, 374
ḥammām, 10, 220, 223, 254, 322, 361, 427, 440, 446, 460
han, 332, 338
ḥarim sarā, 430
ḥarīm, 10, 392, 401–2, 405, 413, 416, 424, 432, 453, 461
hasht bihisht, 279
ḥaush, 313
ḥazīra, 280, 313
hijra, 39, 274
ḥira, 387
ḥīrī, 405
ḥisba, 28
horror vacui, 457
hortus conclusus, 456
ḥujra, 231
ʿīd, 48, 55
ʿīdgāh, 48
idhiz eb, 147
ijāza, 372

imago mundi, 19
imām, 45, 48, 54, 56–7, 60, 83, 134, 182, 196, 262, 266, 278, 283, 375
imāmzāda, 254, 266, 273
imārat, 122, 162, 208, 341
imaret see imārat
impluvium, 55, 211
isfahsālār, 283
iwān, 24, 101–5, 107–8, 111–2, 126, 155–7, 159, 179–81, 183, 186–7, 192, 196–7, 202–4, 206, 211–2, 214–6, 220, 226–7, 234–5, 240–1, 306, 311, 335, 344, 359–60, 366–7, 390–1, 393, 395, 397–8, 402, 404–10, 413–4, 417–9, 421–7, 429–32, 435–6, 440, 442, 459–60
iwān, four-, plan see four-iwān plan
iwān, sanctuary see sanctuary iwān
iwān, two-, plan see two-iwān plan
jamāʿat khāna, 219
jāmiʿ (in general), 42, 44, 46, 48, 50, 52, 54, 59, 62, 64, 83, 86–7, 91, 100, 242, 245, 391
jāmūr, 248
jihād, 173, 264, 266, 274, 324, 331, 341
kākh, 257
kalām, 177, 220
kārbān, 331
kathisma, 49
khalqa, 59, 176
khān, 332
khānqāh, 7, 100, 108, 171, 173, 196, 227, 219–20, 316, 333, 341, 351, 409
khānqāh-cum-madrasa, 226
khaṭīb, 46, 48, 54, 61
khiyābān, 305
khuṭba, 46, 61, 68, 81
khwābgāh, 257
kilim, 59
kishlik, 347
kiswa, 322, 437
kubrā, al-, 241
külliye, 122, 460
kurgan, 275
kushk, 341–3, 409–10, 412–3
kuttāb, 59
lājvardīna, 423
lat, 147
limes, 144

mābain, 223
mabkhara, 171
madfan, 257
madhāhib *see* madhhab
madhhab, 44, 56, 60, 62, 175, 177, 183, 186, 188–9, 196–7, 200, 218, 220, 222, 237, 240, 242, 266, 271, 319
mafraj, 416
maidān, 112, 114, 429, 431
majana, 242
majlis, 444, 446
majma', 205
malqaf, 199
malwīya, 144–5, 322, 349, 421
mamlūk, 421
manār, 132, 138
manāra, 132–4, 138, 161
manzil, (pl. manāzil), 332, 373
maq'ad, 206, 436
maqṣūra, 3, 8, 16, 32, 45, 48–50, 52–4, 58, 81, 103, 246
marabūṭ, 268, 271
māristān, 195, 325
marqad, 257
martyrium, 36, 63, 121, 255, 268, 274, 281, 402
maṣāni'a, 373
mashhad, 258, 314
mashrabīya, 21, 199, 248, 330
mashwar, 453
masjid (in general), 31, 42, 44–5, 62, 64, 102, 116, 200, 216–7, 250, 254, 418
masjid and jāmi', 42, 44
maṣṭaba, 205, 353
mazār, 258
menorah, 133
mi'dhana, 132–3
miḥrāb, 5, 14, 16–7, 21, 24, 32, 34, 45–6, 48–50, 53–4, 58–9, 63, 74, 79–81, 83, 86–7, 93, 97–8, 101, 103, 106, 117–8, 120, 139, 144, 152, 159, 165, 180–1, 183, 188, 197, 205, 243, 247–8, 250, 254, 258, 278–80, 308, 311, 313, 322, 330, 369–70, 461
miḥrāb, external, 183
miḥrāb, types of 46
mīl, 134
milarion, 134
mīnā'ī, 417
minbar, 5, 16, 32, 34–5, 37, 40,44–9, 53–4, 58–9, 61, 63, 81, 130, 242, 246
mirador, 442, 457
mi'rāj, 63, 73
mizwār, 247
mu'adhdhin, 133
mudarrisūn, 205
mughaṭṭā, al-, 32

mu'īn al-dīn, 266
mujāhid, 173, 266
mulūk al-ṭawā'if, 446
munāẓara, 173
muqarnas, 17, 21, 24, 86, 104, 128, 148, 156–7, 164, 166, 183, 193, 203, 213, 223, 287, 308, 311, 316, 318–9, 323, 350, 355, 366, 377, 381, 416, 419, 422–3, 426, 428, 430, 432–3, 436, 439, 441–2, 444, 454, 457
murābiṭ, 266
muṣallā, 32, 40, 48
mutawaḍḍa', 205
muthāghir, 266
nār, 132
nāṣir al-mujāhidīn, 266
naskhī, 421
nūr, 132
omphalos, 393
ordu, 410
pandocheion, 334
paradeisos, 390, 418, 452; cf. 403
pisé, 406
pishṭāq, 24, 99, 158, 212, 290–1, 294, 297, 369, 398, 424
propylaeum, 69
prothesis, 211
protomai, 68
qā'a, 192, 199, 206, 359, 435–6
qabr, 257
qāḍī, 28, 60–1, 203, 205, 351
qal'at al-ḥamrā', 452
qamīṣ, 405
qandīl, 59
qaṣaba, 452
qaṣr (pl. quṣūr), 257, 381, 384–5, 411, 446
qātil al-kufra, 266
qātil al-mushrikīn, 266
qibla īwān, 107, 114, 116, 161, 180–1, 183, 195–7, 204, 206, 212, 218–9, 317, 319, 330
qibla, 14, 17, 31, 38, 40, 42, 46, 50, 53–4, 66, 68–9, 73, 77, 79–80, 86–7, 89, 98, 101, 116, 159, 171, 181, 183, 188, 196, 203, 212, 220, 227, 230, 247–8, 279, 294, 313, 318, 404
qishlaq, 416
qoruq, 277
qubba, 257
qubbat al-khadrā', 381
qubbat al-maẓālim, 61
qulla, 171
qurrā', 205
rab'/rub', 359
rabaṭ *see* ribāṭ
rabaṭa, 331
rāshidūn, 269
rauḍa, 24, 258, 453
ribāṭ, 26, 44, 173, 202–3, 219, 237,

260, 264, 266, 277, 331–2, 340–2, 366, 372–4, 429
riwāq, 32, 67, 91, 103, 126
riwāya, 241
ropat, 341
sābāṭ, 49
saḥā, 205
saḥāba, 40
ṣaḥn, 202, 452
saif al-Islām, 266
sajada, 42
ṣalāt, 44–6, 49, 52, 54–6
ṣami'a, 133
sarā'i, 332
ṣauma'a (pl. ṣawāmi'), 130, 132–4, 136–7
shādirvān, 97, 211, 437
shahāda, 18, 152, 156, 258
shaikh, 180, 204, 219–20, 278
simantron, 130
ṣinf, 220
sipahsālār, 349
sirdāb, 382, 387, 402–3, 408
spolia, 74, 77, 91, 330, 398
stambha, 147
stele, (pl. stelai), 253–4, 264, 280
stele, 320
stupa, 147, 175, 268
ṣughrā, al-, 241
sūq, 369
sūra, 87, 155, 427
tablinum, 453
tadrīs, 173
tafsīr, 59, 173
tālār, 432
tanūr, 59
ṭāq, 424
ṭārima, 206
ṭarīqa, 220
taswiya al-qubūr, 253
ṭawwāf, 275, 281
tekke, 219
tell, 419
temenos, 69, 71
tepe, 283
tholos, 171
tīm, 361
ṭirbāl, 144
topos, 390–1, 403
turba, 190–1, 202, 257, 272, 307, 323
'ulamā', 176, 208, 241, 247
vihara, 174
vijaya-stambha, 158
wakāla, 359, 361–2
waqf (pl. auqāf), 28, 173, 190–1, 195, 208, 220, 234, 240–1, 246–7, 250, 258, 260, 268, 325, 342, 349–50, 361, 369, 374
waqfīya, 28–9, 364
wuḍū', 55
yam, 370–2

yaylaq, 416, 421
yurt, 275, 277, 415
zāwīya, 100, 219, 271, 277, 314, 333

ziggurat, 145
zīlū, 59
ziyāda, 76

ziyārat, 258, 273
zoma, 133
ẓulla 40, 42

Index of Proper Names

N.B. In this index, noun and adjective are treated as a single entry, e.g. for Armenian *see* Armenia. Turkish names are given in their modern form, but the undotted i is not used.

Aachen, 83
Abāqā, 415, 421
Abarqūh, 297
ʿAbbāsids, 5, 14, 16, 59, 61–2, 71,
    84, 138, 144–5, 222, 224,
    253–4, 320, 341, 374, 377, 382,
    390, 392, 395, 403–4, 406,
    408–9, 417, 421, 426, 438, 440,
    444, 459
ʿAbd al-Laṭīf, 168
ʿAbd al-Malik, 71
ʿAbd al-Raḥmān I, 443
ʿAbd al-Raḥmān III, 379
ʿAbd al-Raḥmān III, 443
ʿAbdallāh b. Ṭāhir, 340–1
Abraham, 63, 72
Abū Bakr, 62
Abū Hammū I, 242
Abū Hammū II, 242
Abū Ḥanīfa Nuʿmān, 183
Abū Huraira, 32, 173
Abū ʿInān, 240, 242, 246
Abū Jaʿfar Aḥmad b. Sulaimān, 446
Abū Muslim, 409
Abū Yūsuf, 239
Abū Zakariyāʾ, 239
Abuʾl-Ḥasan, 240
Abuʾl-Muṭrif, 60
Abyssinia, 129
Achaemenids, 77, 274, 370–2, 393,
    426, 428
Ādharbāijān, 160, 370, 415
ʿAḍud al-Daula, 61, 373
Aegean, 370
Afghanistan, 65, 154, 174, 180, 182,
    273, 283, 342, 365, 411, 413
Afrāsiyāb, 411
Afrāvah/Farāvah, 341
Africa, 22, 64
Africa, North, 16, 26, 34, 132–3,
    142, 176, 373, 438, 442
Africa, sub-Saharan, 264
Africa, West, 142
Agadez, 142
Aghlabids, 16, 439–40
Ahlat, 306, 308
Aḥmad Shāh, 224
Aḥmadīlis, 278
Ahmed II, 458
Ahwāz, 64
Airtam, 175

Akhūr, al-, 341
Aksaray, 208, 349–50
Akşehir, 208, 311
ʿAlāʾ al-Dīn Kayqūbād, 377, 416
ʿAlāʾ al-Dīn Khaljī, 158–9
Alanya, 349, 416
Alberti, 12, 28
Aleppo, 68, 99, 138, 185, 188, 203,
    272, 323, 359, 361, 402, 419
Alexandria, 167
Algeçiras, Battle of, 454
Algeria, 66, 121, 142, 239, 242–3,
    437, 439
Algiers, 437–8
ʿAlī al-Tilimsānī, 242
ʿAlī b. Muḥammad al-ʿIyādī, 441
ʿAlī b. Yaḥyā b. Abī Manṣūr, 407
ʿAlī Muktafī, 145
ʿAlī Pasha, 241
ʿAlī, 49
Almohad, 21, 87, 140–1, 237,
    239–40, 243, 271, 439, 452
Almoravid, 87, 237, 239, 271
Amīr Māmāʾī, 436 (?)
ʿAmr b. al-ʿĀṣ, 34, 61
Andalus, al-, *see* Andalusia
Andalusia, 2, 35, 65, 86, 92, 140–1,
    236, 239, 271, 437, 442, 446,
    450
Antalya, 349
Aquarius, 440
Arabia, 22, 31, 44, 49, 61–2, 121,
    126, 128–129, 131–4, 138, 158,
    177, 254–5, 258, 272–3, 342,
    373–4, 377
Arabian Nights, The, 10
Arabic, 73,128–9, 131–4, 158, 258,
    331–2, 340, 349, 354, 384, 441
Araby, 10
Ardabīl, 430
Ardashīr Khurra, 393
Armenia, 99, 346, 349
Armenian architecture, 307–11, 346
Armenian caravansarais, 346
Armida, 456
Arrān, 307
Artuqids, 163, 207
ʿAsharī, 177, 220
Ashraf, 429
ʿĀshūrā, 266
Aśoka, 147

Aspendos, 416
Assyria, 391, 393
Aswān, 314
Ātur Gushnasp, 421
Aufī, 414
Āyat al-Kursī, 462
Ayyūbids, 99, 189–91, 202–3, 266,
    272, 306, 316, 318–20, 323–4,
    338, 351, 374, 419, 435
Azerbaijan *see* Ādharbāijān
Bābūr, 424
Babylon, 145, 391, 395
Baden, 10
Badr al-Dīn Luʾluʾ, 419, 421
Badr al-Jamālī, 166
Baghdād, 19, 21, 56–7, 61–2, 145,
    177, 220, 222, 224, 266, 332,
    342, 361, 382, 384, 390, 392–6,
    398, 405, 435, 459, 462
Bahrāmshāh, 412
Baḥrī, 203
Baibars, 193, 202–3
Baihaqī, al-, 59, 61
Baikand, 44, 340–1
Bain al-Qaṣrain, 316, 326
Bākū, 421
Balādhurī, al-, 134, 144
Balkans, the, 21
Balkh, 78, 175, 437
Bamiyan, 175
Banū Hūd, 446
Banū Marwān, 271
Bartolʾd, 174–5
Baṣra, 34, 38, 68, 83, 129, 136
Bāwandids, 278
Bedouin, 63, 144, 374, 384, 390, 392
Bel, 250
Bell, Gertrude, 361
Bengal, 22
Berbers, 439, 443
Berchem, van, 129
Bestiary, 16
Beylik, 207, 215
Beyşehir, 349
Beyşehir, Lake, 417
Bible, The, 63, 255, 267
Bijāpūr, 161
Bilāl, 129
Black Sea, 349
Black Stone, 31, 46
Blair, Sheila, 182

Bloom, Jonathan, 129, 134, 166
Book of Government, 340
Book of Kings, 453
Bosphorus, 122, 461–2
Brunelleschi, 28
Buckingham Palace, 377
Buddhism, 34, 147, 174–5
Bukhārā, 101, 226, 234, 340, 344
Bulliet, Richard, 173
Bundārī, al-, 373
Burjī, 171
Bursa, 56, 98, 356, 417
Buṣrā, 51, 187–8
Bust, 30, 413
Butler, 168
Būyids, 61–2, 177, 266, 316, 373, 382, 411, 428
Byron, Robert, 12, 431
Byzantium, 16, 44–6, 49, 53, 73, 83, 97, 118–9, 123, 130, 132–3, 167, 173, 211, 222, 268, 274, 281, 311, 346, 350, 388, 435, 438, 443–4, 457–8 254–5
Caesaropapism, 83
Caetani, 42
Cambaluc, 371
Carpini, John de Plano, 371
Caspian Sea, 283, 367, 426, 430
Castile, 424
Catholic, 371
Caucasia, 273
Caucasus, 391
Central Asia, 24, 44, 103, 147–8, 164, 174–5, 177, 220, 264, 273, 275, 291, 294, 309, 331, 339, 341–3, 375, 382, 391, 399, 408–9, 411–2, 416
Chardin, 433
Charlemagne, 390
Chief Eunuch, 459
China, 10, 19, 22, 33, 64, 128, 147, 282, 372, 411, 423
Chishtī, 220, 268
Christendom, 60
Christian, 8, 10, 14, 16, 19, 31–34, 36, 38, 45–6, 55, 59, 61, 63, 68- 69, 71–3, 77, 121, 129–31, 137–8, 140, 144, 190, 254, 266, 268, 274, 278, 281, 309, 398, 402, 435, 443, 446, 452, 457
Church, 33
Cilicia, 264
Circassians, 199, 349
Clavijo, Ruy Gonzales de, 424–5
Companions, 40, 42, 63
Constantine, 72
Constantinople, 51, 83, 119, 435, 457
Copt, 46–7, 73, 206
Cordoba, 60, 63, 71, 128, 237, 271,379, 413, 443, 456
Cordova *see* Cordoba

Creswell, 26, 40, 167, 183, 185–6, 207, 322, 395–6, 409, 667
Crimea, 349, 374
Crusaders, 324, 330, 435, 456
Ctesiphon, 390–1
Cyprus, 73
Dailamites, 393
Damascus, 21–2, 34, 68, 71–3, 99, 185, 187–8, 192, 203, 272, 323, 352, 355, 373
Dāmghān, 27, 47–8, 148
Dāmghānī, Ḥasan al-, 28
Dāmghānī, Muḥammad al-, 27
Dārābgird, 393
Ḍarb Zubaida, 144, 342, 373, 411
Darro, River, 452
Dawali, 342
Delhi, 6–7, 128, 158–9
Diyārbakr, 163, 208
Dome of Justice, 61
Dulac, 10
Dura Europos, 419
Dūst Muḥammad, 28
Dux Ripae, 419
Early Muslim Architecture, 26
East India Company, 359
Eastern Asia, 275
Edirne, 98, 311, 381
Egypt, ancient, 10, 166, 268
Eight Paradises, 433
Elbistan, 349
Eliming Tepe, 342
England, 9
English landscape garden, 461
Erivan, 462
Erzurum, 116, 208, 308
Etruscan 268
Euphrates, 388, 419, 441
Eurasia, 423
Eurocentricity 8
Europe, 7–8, 10, 12, 19, 21–2, 48, 62, 83, 126, 128, 133, 268, 359, 364, 372, 378, 428, 433, 442
European architecture, 9–10, 24, 71, 83, 378–9, 452; *see also* Western architecture
Evliya Chelebi, 417
Far East, 21–2
Fārs, 26
Fās, 48–9, 141, 239, 241, 244
Fāṭimid, 16, 21–2, 47, 54, 59, 61–2, 100, 176–7, 192, 220, 264, 275, 312, 314, 316, 318–9, 322, 393, 434–5, 438, 440–1, 444
Fīlālī, 241
Finster,Barbara, 395
First World War, 395
Fīrūzābād, 393
Fīrūzkūh, 155
Flecker, 10
Fletcher, 10
Forty Columns, 432

France, 9–10, 359
Franks, 359, 456
Friday mosque, 14, 16, 38, 44, 57, 144, 153, 179, 183, 245–6, 405, 413
Friday prayer, 16–7, 245
Friday travel, 375
Frye, Richard, 341
Fusṭāṭ, al-, 34, 38, 60, 63, 83, 129, 133, 136–7, 139, 311, 439
Gate of Knowledge, 18
Gemini, 459
Georgian architecture, 307
Germany, 9, 371
Ghardāya, 142
Ghazālī, al-, 133
Ghāzān Khān, 361
Ghazna, 155, 174, 177, 413
Ghaznavids, 155, 173, 177, 411–3, 415
Ghūr, 155, 173
Ghūrids, 155, 158
Ghuzz, 344
"Glory of Ardashir", 393
Godard, 175, 181
Gökböri, 220
Golden Horde, 421
Golden Horn, 379, 458, 461
"Golden Pen", 224
Gothic architecture, proposed Islamic origins of, 364–5
Gothic, 213, 350, 364
Graeco-Roman, 76, 457
Granada, 5, 10, 379, 452–3, 456
Grand Cairo, 10
Grand Vizier, 349–52
Gray's *Anatomy*, 10
Great Khan, 371–2
Greece, 73, 274, 371, 382
Ḥāfiẓ, 431
Hafṣids, 239
Ḥajjāj, al-, 44
Ḥākim, al-, 59, 62, 176
Ḥamā, 359
Hamadān, 393, 415
Hamadhānī, al-, 253
Ḥammādid, 440, 442
Ḥanafite, 44, 60, 183, 237
Ḥanbalī, 56, 177, 237
Ḥaram al-Sharīf, 204–6
Harāt, 157, 234
Ḥarīrī, al-, 64
Hārūn al-Rashīd, 342, 373
Haussmann, 6
Hebron, 60, 63
Hell, 63
Hellenistic, 222
Helmand, River, 413
Herbert, Sir Thomas, 428, 431
Herodotus, 370–1
Herzfeld, 180, 395, 399, 401, 404–6, 421

Ḥijāz, 73, 144, 166, 204, 384
Hindu, 34–5, 26
Ḥīra, 402, 405
Hishām, 390
History of Architecture on the Comparative Method, A, 10
Holy Cities, 144, 177, 342, 371, 373
Ḥudūd al-ʿĀlam, 341
Hülegü, 277
Huns, 147
Ḥusain, al-, 254, 266
Ibāḍites, 437
Iberian peninsula, 237
Iberian, 452
Ibn ʿAbdūn, 30
Ibn al-Athīr, 180
Ibn al-Bawwāb, 411
Ibn al-Faqīh, 68, 136
Ibn al-Jauzī, 384
Ibn al-Ṣaffāḥiya, 203
Ibn ʿAqīl, 177
Ibn Baṭṭūta, 60, 372, 416
Ibn Bībī, 377, 415–6
Ibn Gabirol, 452
Ibn Ḥamdīs, 381
Ibn Ḥammād, 440
Ibn Ḥauqal, 63, 332
Ibn Ḥazm, 271
Ibn ʿIdhārī, 443
Ibn Jubair, 30, 57, 220, 372
Ibn Khaldūn, 220, 377, 392, 406
Ibn Khallikān, 220
Ibn Khurdādhbih, 372, 403
Ibn Mardanīsh, 446
Ibn Muqla, 384
Ibn Saʿīd, 60, 239
Ibn Tafrājīn, 241
Ibn Ṭūlūn, 55
Ibn Tūmart, 237
Ibn Yāsīn, 271
Ibn Zamrak, 454
Idrīsī, al-, 372
Ifrīqiya, 438–9
Ikhshid, 54
Ilkhānids, 155, 178, 182, 225, 277, 283, 286, 294–5, 360–1, 370, 372, 415, 421–4
Iltutmish, 158
Imām Shāfiʿī, al-, 319
India, 10, 22, 56, 59, 66, 103, 147, 158–61, 219–20, 226, 268, 273, 279, 306, 371, 374
Indo-Pakistan sub-continent, 64, 267
Indonesia, 22
Ingelheim, 390
Inner Asia, 269
Iokapala, 147
Irbil, 220
Irving, Washington, 10, 457
Isaac, 72
Iṣfahān, 8, 48, 63, 152–3, 155, 174–5, 225–6, 234, 291, 370,

377, 381, 393, 428–30, 433, 459
Islam, 12, 32–3, 35, 42, 71, 73, 128–9, 131, 138, 152, 155, 182–3, 190, 222,, 253, 258, 262, 266–8, 272, 274, 280, 339, 393, 395, 454
Islam, popular 268
Islamic architecture as a field of study, 8
Islamicate, 8
Islamdom, 8
Islamisation, 220
Ismāʿīl b. Sāmān, 340–1
Iṣṭakhrī, al-, 341, 372
Istanbul, 118, 121–2, 163–5, 217, 356
Italy, 9, 167
Iznik tiles, 122, 462
Iznik, 122
ʿIzz al-Dīn Farrūkhshāh, 190
Jaihānī, al-, 372
Jain, 34–5
Jaipur, 429
Jala'irid, 361
Jāmī, 431
Janissaries, 459
Jannābī, al-, 276
Jazīra, 415, 417, 419, 421
Jedda *see* Jidda
Jehoseph bar Najralla, 452
Jerusalem, 14, 21, 30, 40, 61, 68, 73, 99, 202, 204–5, 372
Jews, 34, 72, 129, 133, 268, 452
Jidda, 8
John the Baptist, 254
Jordan, 373, 382
Judaism, 73
Julfa, 360
Jupiter, 393
Juzjani, al-, 413
Kanishka, King, 147
Karakorum, 371
Karrāmīya, 173, 219
Karbalā', 376
Kash, 423
Kāshān, 28, 152, 177
Kashmīr, 129
Kayseri, 116, 207, 306, 308, 349, 416, 418
Kew Gardens, 10
Khālisa, 63
Khaqān Urtugh Abu'l-Fatḥ b. Khaqān, 399
Khārijites, 437
Kharraqān, 277
Khaṭīb al-Baghdādī, al-, 434, 444
Khawarnaq, 377, 441
Khayyām, ʿUmar, 10, 12
Khiva, 234
Khorsabad, 145, 391
Khumarawaiḥ, 384, 406
Khurāsān, 59, 104, 110, 175, 148,

155, 158, 226, 291, 370
Khusrau II, 409, 422, 454
Khuttal, 173, 412
Khūzistān, 374
Khwārizm, 409, 412
Khwārizmshāh, 182
Khwarnaq *see* Khawarnaq
King of the Romans, 73
Kipchaqs, 349
Kipling, 10
Kirmān, 333, 371, 429–30
Kitāb al-Aghānī, 61
Kitāb al-Naqd, 177
Kitāb Manāsik al-Ḥajj, 372
Klingsor, 456
Konya, 97, 187, 207, 210–11, 311, 349–50, 417
Korea, 371
Kūfa, 34, 38, 62, 83, 144, 373
Kufic, 27, 63, 157, 181–2, 297, 320, 330, 421, 425, 440
Kuran, Aptullah, 207
Kurdistān, 421
Kurtly, 342
Kushans, 147
Kütahya, 349
Lane, 133
Leo, 443
Levant, 61, 65, 165, 254, 273, 312, 359, 434,
Lézine, 138
Libya, 47, 86, 371, 440
Loti, 10, 16
Louvre, the, 377
Luristān, 374
Lutyens, 6
Madina, 34, 39–40, 61, 64, 68, 129, 167, 192, 373
Mahdiya, 438, 440
Maḥmūd of Ghazna, Sulṭān, 174, 177, 413
Mahperi Khātūn, 349
Makdisi, George, 237
Makka, 10, 19, 32, 34, 39, 46, 61, 68, 73, 112, 167, 192, 205, 217, 253, 317, 342, 373, 393
Malik al-Amjad, al-, 190
Malik al-ʿAzīz ʿUthmān, al-, 320
Malik al-ʿAzīz Muḥammad, al-, 419
Malik al-Kāmil, al-, 319–20
Mālikite, 60, 197, 237, 240–1, 271
Malikshāh, 342, 370, 373
Mamlūks, 16, 20, 28, 99–100, 106, 137, 146, 165, 171, 179, 190, 192–3, 195–7, 202–6, 220, 242, 273, 312, 316, 318–9, 324–5, 338, 351, 356, 361, 373, 377, 421
Ma'mūn, al-, 59
Manichaeism, 219
Manṣūr, al- (ʿAbbāsid), 21, 71, 390, 392, 395, 409, 440

Manṣūr, al- (Aghlabid), 440
Manṣūr, al- (Umayyad), 379, 443
Maqāmāt (of al-Ḥarīrī), 64
Maqdisī, al-, 30
Maqqārī, al-, 443–4
Maqrīzī, al-, 134, 136, 197, 202, 405, 444
Marāgha, 307
Marand, 307, 360, 372
Marīnids, 239–41, 250–1
Marmara, Sea of, 458, 461
Marrākush, 48, 140, 247
Marv, 19, 342, 344
Mashhad, 234, 373, 430
Maslama, 130, 134
Master of Works, 121
Masʿūd III, 414
Masʿūdī, al-, 136, 391, 405
Maṭlaʿ al-Shams, 372
Mauṣil al-, 34, 419
Māzandarān, 287, 309
Mediterranean, 33, 45, 330, 452, 457
Mehmed Fatih *see* Mehmed the Conqueror
Mehmed I, 311
Mehmed the Conqueror, 217, 457, 459
Meinecke, Michael, 186
Meknes *see* Miknās
Mercury, Temple of, 10
Mesopotamia, 144, 146, 177, 290, 335, 370, 391, 393, 395, 434, 438
Middle Ages, 390
Miknās, 241
Mīr ʿAlī Shīr, 365
"Mirrors for Princes", 340
Miṣbāḥ b. ʿAbdallāh al-Yalsūtī, 241
Molotov cocktail, 350
Mongols, 8, 24, 108, 157, 179–80, 183, 220, 224, 277–8, 291, 348, 361, 370–2, 415, 421, 428, 440
Moorish, 8, 140, 452–3, 457
Morocco, 237, 239–44, 250–1, 267–8
Mosul *see* Mauṣil, al-
Muʿāwiya I, 48, 62, 129–30, 134, 392
Mudejar, 450
Mughals, 24, 159, 161, 226, 268, 279, 305–6, 351, 433
Muḥammad *see* Prophet Muḥammad, the
Muḥammad b. Sām, 155, 158
Muḥammad b. Tekesh, 182
Muḥammad I, 452
Muḥammad II, 452
Muḥammad the Mad, 311
Muḥammad V, 452
Muḥammadan, 8
Muḥarram, 266
Muhtadī, al-, 61

Muʿizz al-Daula, 62
Muʿizz, al-, 441
Mūlāy al-Rashīd, 247, 251
Muqaddasī, al-, 30, 44, 59, 64, 71, 73, 175, 316, 332, 340–1, 372, 374
Muqaṭṭam, 406
Muqtadir, al-, 444
Murād II, 311
Mūsā b. Nusair, 16
Mustaufī, Ḥamdallāh, 183, 372
Muʿtamid, al-, 407
Muʿtaṣim, al-, 399
Mutawakkil, al-, 402, 405
Muʿtazz, al-, 384, 405
Mycenae, 146
Mzab, 142
Naʿālī, al-, 60
Nādir Shāh, 303, 305
Nagari, 158
Najaf, 376
Narshakhī, al-, 340–1
Nāṣir Muḥammad, al-, sulṭān, 195, 436
Nāṣir-i Khusrau, 372–3, 403, 435, 444
Naṣrids, 5
Near East, 45, 131, 206, 267, 334, 348, 370, 398
Near East, ancient, 46, 144, 173, 395, 402, 406
Nero, 395, 454
New Testament, 254–5
Niğde, 116
Night Journey, 73
Nineveh, 391, 419
Nīshāpūr, 173, 175, 199, 237, 344, 411
Niẓām al-Mulk, 174–5, 178, 180, 234, 237, 240, 340
Niẓāmī, 431
Niẓāmīya *madrasas*, 175, 178, 180
Norman Sicily, 326
Normans, 441–2
Nubia, 264
Old Testament, 254–5
Ordericus of Pordenone, 371
Orthodox, 130
Ottoman, 5–6, 10, 14, 27–8, 48, 54, 56, 98, 111, 116–9, 121–3, 142, 155, 163–4, 171, 196, 203, 207, 210, 211–2, 216–9, 230, 234, 242, 306–7, 309, 338, 351–3, 355, 358–9, 361, 367, 373–4, 377, 433, 457–60, 462
Ottoman architecture before 857/1453, 116–9
Ottoman style, the mature, 119–23
Oxus, 175, 412
Ozymandias, 423
Pakistan, 158, 297
Palermo, 63, 83, 332, 441

Palestine, 177, 207, 220, 260, 351
Palmyra, 282
Pantheon, 53
Parthia, 274, 335, 341, 391, 393, 402, 415
Pax Achaemenica, 371
Pax Mongolica, 371
Pedro the Cruel, 452–3
People of the *suffa*, 42
Persian Gulf, 276
Persian poetry, 414
Persian, 257, 332, 340, 354, 423, 459
Peshāwar, 147
Pharaonic Egypt, 316
Plaster Castle, 407
Polo, Marco, 371–2
Portugal, 9, 271
Prophet Muḥammad, the, 17–8, 22, 31–2, 40, 42, 46, 48, 59–61, 63–4, 66, 68, 73, 91, 126, 129, 165, 248, 253, 260, 262, 264, 269, 393, 460
Provincia Arabia, 387
Qādir, al-, 60
Qafṣī, al-, 63
Qāʾim, al-, ʿAbbāsid, 177
Qāʾim, al-, Fāṭimid, 438
Qairawān, 34, 46, 78, 139, 142, 439–40
Qāʾit Bāy, 202, 204, 318
Qājārs, 6, 158, 235, 305
Qalāʾūn, 195, 330
Qalqashandī, al-, 374
Qarakhānids, 174
Qaraman, 98, 208
Qaramanids, 207
Qarasunqur, Amīr, 202
Qāsiyūn mountain, 323
Qawurt, 371
Qilich Arslan II, 416–7
Qilich Arslan IV, 416
Qiwām al-Dīn Muʾayyad al-Mulk Abū Bakr b. ʿAlī, 182
Qubādābād, 377
Qufṣ, 374
Qumm, 177, 234, 266, 286–7
Qurʾān readers, 316
Qurʾān, recitation of, 190, 205, 258
Qurʾān, 10, 17–8, 42, 49, 51, 59–60, 128, 155, 181, 183, 205, 218, 225, 241, 246, 253–4, 258, 266, 269, 278–80, 324, 375, 421, 427, 454, 456
Qūsūn, 436
Quṭb al-Dīn Aibak, 158
Qutham b. al-ʿAbbās, 262
Rabaḍ, al-, 271
Rabāṭ, 140, 250
Radāʿ, 193
Raj, 6
Ramaḍān, 59–60
Ramusio, 372

Raqqa, 419
Rāshidūn caliphs *see* Rightly Guided caliphs
Rasūlid, 92, 193
Ravenna, 51, 83
Rayy, 8, 175, 177, 334, 338, 415
Reception of the Ambassadors, 16
Reconquista, 446
Red Sea, 166
Renaissance, 7, 206
Ribāṭ, al-, 341
Rif, 250
Rightly Guided caliphs 19, 269
Roman, 16, 53, 69, 77, 138, 167, 211, 254, 334, 374, 385, 387–8, 404, 416, 438, 443–4, 452–3, 457
Roman architecture, 53
Romano-Byzantine, 78
Roman foot, 385
Rome, 371
Royal Road, 370–2
Rubruck, William of, 275, 371
Rubruquis *see* Rubruck, William of
Rufaida, 64
Russia, 9, 349
Russian chronicles, 341
Rustamids, 437
Saʿadians, 241
Sabian, 282
Sabīka, al-, 452
Sabzavār, 180
Saʿd b. Abi Waqqāṣ, 391, 409
Sadīr, 377
Ṣafar, 73
Ṣafavids, 4, 48, 112, 157–8, 181, 225–6, 234, 279, 303, 305–6, 351, 361, 365, 367, 370, 377, 381, 428–30, 433, 459
Saffārids, 411
Sagittarius, 18, 393
Sahara, 331
Saladin, 192, 319
Salakta, 138
Ṣalīḥiya quarter, Damascus, 323
Saljūq caravansarais in Anatolia, 346–50
Saljūqs of Rūm, 22, 116, 162–3, 180, 185–6, 196, 207–8, 214–5, 338, 348–50, 353, 356, 377, 381, 417
Saljūqs, 14, 24, 26, 102–7, 144, 148, 152–3, 155–7, 162–3, 171, 173–5, 177–8, 180–3, 185, 187, 206–7, 212, 219–20, 260, 275, 283, 287, 291, 294–5, 306–8, 311, 318, 341–2, 346–8, 370, 373, 411, 414–5, 421, 426, 428–9
Sāmān, 409
Sāmānids, 341, 409, 411, 428
Samarqand Gate, 340
Samarqand, 174, 234, 344, 425

Sāmarrāʾ, 76, 83, 379, 381–2, 402–4, 406–8, 411–3, 415, 443
Samarran stucco, 290
Samsun, 349
Sanīʿ al-Daula, 373
Sanjar, Sulṭān, 344
Sanskrit, 158
Saracenic, 8, 10
Saray Berke, 421
Sardis, 370
Sasanian, 38, 46, 78, 101–3, 144, 154, 173, 254, 268, 274, 276, 281, 290, 334, 347, 370, 390, 392–3, 402, 408, 412, 418, 421–3, 428, 432, 441, 444
Saturiq, 421
Saturn, 459
Saʿūdī Arabia, 31, 61, 342; *see also* Arabia
Sauvaget, 178, 218, 351, 370
Schacht, 133
Schmidt, Jürgen, 395
Schroeder, 146
Selim I, 460
Seraglio, 457, 460
Seven Heavens, 63
Seven Wonders, The, 132
Seville, 21, 30, 140,
Shāfiʿite, 60, 175, 220, 237
Shāh ʿAbbās I, 112, 305, 367, 374, 429–31
Shāh ʿAbbās II, 234
Shāhanshāh, 62
Shāhī Island, 277
Shāhjahān Khātūn, 309
Shāhnāma, 423
Shahr-i Sāmān, 409
Shaibānids, 226
Shīʿite, 61–2, 152, 176–8, 192, 240, 254, 258, 260, 262, 266–7, 275, 283, 286, 312, 376
Shīʿites, Sevener, 176, 279
Shīʿites, Twelver, 177, 269, 279
Shīrāz, 382
Shīrvānshāhs, 427
Shīz, 421
Sicily, 63, 167, 381, 441–2
Sidon, 359
Sierra Nevada, 452
Simnān, 149
Sinan, 118, 121–2
Sīstān, 338, 343
Sivas, 208, 210, 349, 356
Sivrihisar, 116, 208
Siyāsat Nāma, 340
Siyāvush, 266
Soghdia, 281
Solomon, 452–3
South-east Asia, 64
Soviet, 331, 342, 424
Soviet Union, ex-, 342
Sözen, Metin, 207

Stamboul, 10
Stone Carpet, 367
Strzygowski, 147
Subki, al-, 175
Sublime Porte, 431
Sudan, 129
Ṣūfīs, 12, 173, 204, 217–20, 240, 267, 316, 331, 341
Suger, Abbot, 28
Suhrawardī, al-, 220
Sulaimān b. ʿAli Pasha, 241
Süleyman the Magnificent, 217
Sullecthum, 138
Sulṭānīya, 155
Sunnī, 62, 152, 267
Sūra III, 185, 280
Sūra of Jonah, 427
Sūra XX:35, 253
Sūra XXI:35, 280
Sūra XXIII, 183
Sūrat Maryam, 155
Sūrat al-nūr, 17, 156, 278
Sūra of Light *see Sūrat al-nūr*
Sūsa (Iran), 370
Sūsa (Tunisia), 78
Suyūṭī, al-, 60
Syriac, 349
T-shape, 86, 117, 248, 404–5, 408, 438–9
Ṭabarī, al-, 62
Ṭabas, 182
Tabrīz, 311
Tafīlālet, 250
Taʿizz, 92, 193
Tāj Maḥal 268
Tales of the Alhambra, 10
Tangiers, 372
Teheran, 8, 181, 370, 373
Termez *see* Tirmidh
Thrace, 121
Tibet, 147
Tibetan monks, 371
Tigris, 56, 402, 404
Tilimsān, 89
Tīmūr, 423–4
Tīmūrids, 107, 109–10, 112, 157, 225–7, 234, 262, 278, 287, 302, 306, 415, 422, 425, 459
Tire, 208
Tirmidh, 409
Tirmidhī, al-, 64
Tokat, 356
Toledo, 237
Tower of Silence, 269, 276
Transoxiana, 226, 266, 288, 290, 318, 341
Travels of Marco Polo, 372
Tree of Life, 278, 309
Tripoli (Lebanon), 100, 203, 323, 359
Ṭughānshāh, 414
Ṭughril Beg, 174

Ṭūlūnids, 384, 406, 434
Tūnis, 142, 244
Tunisia, 132, 138, 142, 173, 242, 244
Turco-Mongol culture, 433
Turkic funerary practices 269, 277
Turkic, 147, 268–9, 275, 277, 309, 457
Turkish baroque, 6
Turkish language, 332, 354
Turkish triangles, 162, 164, 212
Turkmenistan, 342–3, 429
Ṭūs, 175, 180
Uighur, 382, 410
Ukraine, 349
ʿUmar, 49, 129, 391–2, 409
Umayyad desert residences, 4, 26, 183, 334, 346, 366, 384–90, 395–6, 413, 417, 437–8
Umayyads of Spain, 271, 379
Umayyads, 5, 18, 28, 44–7, 49, 51, 63, 68, 71–2, 84, 130–1, 136–8, 140, 144, 148, 253–4, 330, 333, 377, 382, 384, 387–8, 390, 392, 395–6, 398, 403, 407–9,

411, 413–4, 428, 438–40, 446, 450
Urmiya, Lake, 277
ʿUthmān, 49, 60, 62
Uzbekistan, 342
Van, Lake, 308, 373
Vasari, 28
Venice, 16, 359
Venus, 443
Villard d' Honnecourt, 27
Vishnu, 158
Vitruvius, 12
Volga Bulghars, 341
Wahhābis, 31, 129, 258
Walad Jalāl, 142
Walīd I, al-, 16, 68–9, 71–2, 91, 137–8, 204, 253, 340, 385
Walīd I, building programme, 68
Walīd II, al-, 385, 390
Wāsiṭ, 44
West, the, 6, 9–10, 12, 22,28, 60, 219, 248, 253, 266, 275, 377, 384, 415, 456–7
Western architecture, 16, 22, 26, 38, 44, 52, 74, 390, 441

Western art history, 7–8, 10, 14
Western scholars, 7–8, 20, 269
White Eunuchs, 459
White Palace, 423
William II, 441
Walid I, building programme, 68
Wren, Sir Christopher, 121
Yaʿqūb al-Manṣūr, 237, 239
Yaʿqūbī, al-, 402
Yāqūt, 144, 341, 372
Yazd, 297
Yazdigird, 276
Yazīd b. al-Walīd, 62
Yazīd III, 390
Yemen, 90–1, 193
Ẓāhir Ghāzī, al-, 419
Zaid b. ʿAlī, 62
Zangids, 419
Zīrī b. Manad, 438
Zīrids, 442
Ziyād b. Abīhi, 68, 83, 129
Zoroastrians, 34, 36, 38, 144, 254, 267, 269, 274–6, 281, 421
Zūzan, 183

Subject Index

ablutions 22, 25, 54–6, 91, 211, 242, 244, 250
abbot, 219
absolutism, 381, 390, 392
accessibility of ruler, 392
accommodation, 188, 199, 331–2, 334–6, 338–9, 344, 350, 352–3, 355–6, 359, 364, 366–7, 370, 374, 406, 415, 439, 453, 457; *see also* cells
acoustic, 48, 164
acropolis, 452
administration, 28, 364, 374, 382, 390, 392, 408, 426, 431, 435, 443, 452, 458–9
adoption of non-Islamic features, 35
aedicule, 55, 144, 154, 165
aerial photography, 51, 395, 398, 404, 441
aesthetic factors, 32, 110, 123, 153, 212, 240, 309, 421, 456
aesthetics, Muslim, 12, 14
agriculture, 384, 390, 395
aids for architects, 12
air-shaft, 188, 199
airholes *see* ventilation
aisles, 353
ajouré grilles, 83
alabaster, 21, 110, 453
altar, 45, 59
ambassadors, 42, 382, 424, 435, 460
ambiguity, 24–6, 32, 332, 435
ambulatory, 112, 226, 314, 330
animal combats, 384
animals, 14, 331, 334–5, 353, 355, 361, 371, 374–5, 384, 390, 402, 412, 414, 417–8, 421, 443, 452
  exotic, 434
ansate, 324
anti-Syrian, 145
anti-Umayyad, 145
antiquarianism, 457
apotheosis, 19
apotropaic, 18, 147, 412
appendages to mosques, 42
apse, 45, 211, 439
aquamaniles , 443
aqueduct, 77, 452
arabesque, 12, 22, 128, 166, 224, 290, 446
arcade, dwarf, 421
arcades, 31, 55, 67, 74, 77, 80, 87, 99, 103, 106, 109, 120, 126, 128, 144, 161, 164, 178, 181, 196, 204–5, 213–4, 216, 219, 242, 246, 248, 290, 308, 311,

330–1, 335, 338, 347, 365, 407, 409, 422, 426, 427, 437–40, 443, 446, 450, 459, 462
converging, 2, 38
  in hypostyle mosque, 2–3
  perpendicular to *qibla* wall, 2, 37
arch, 17–8, 24, 28, 99, 110, 122, 157, 166, 170, 192, 199, 203, 206, 212, 222, 241, 243, 283, 290, 307–8, 365, 398, 406, 409, 418, 423, 432, 436, 440, 442, 450
  ceremonial, 346
  forms, 87, 141, 158
  cusped, 87–8
  horseshoe, 330
  in Maghribī architecture, 86–7
  interlaced, 10, 87–8, 446, 450
  intersecting, 87
  keel-shaped, 318, 322
  lambrequin, 87, 450, 452
  lobed, 87, 407, 438, 446, 450
  multifoil, 87, 140
  pointed, 10
  segmental, 324
  shouldered segmental, 308
  stilted round-headed, 457
  strainer, 77
  trefoil, 87, 203, 291, 421
  triple, 187, 405, 438
  triumphal, 459
archaeology, 38, 101, 271, 331, 390
archaising tendencies, 140
archdeacon, 349
architect, 12, 14, 21, 24, 33, 36, 38, 54, 66, 69, 71, 77, 111, 116, 118, 121, 123, 126, 145, 157–9, 167, 171, 173, 190, 192, 205–6, 212, 217, 223, 228, 240, 243, 247–8, 277, 290, 294–5, 307–8, 316–9, 325–6, 335–6, 356, 401–2, 407–8, 413, 418, 422, 438, 456
architectural models, 12
archivolt, 311
arcuated niche, 16
armouries, 416, 459
arrow-slits, 334
arsenal 381, 419, 426
arterial routes, 349–50, 355, 371, 373; *see also* roads 14, 54, 67
articulation, 14, 54, 67–68, 73, 80, 83, 99, 102–3, 114, 122–3, 126, 139, 154, 157, 159–63, 165, 171, 182, 186, 199, 212, 214, 230, 294, 307–8, 313, 316, 318,

326, 331, 341, 360, 409, 419, 424, 440, 442
ashlar masonry, 307
assassination, 49
astrology, 308, 384, 423
astronomy, 208, 242
asylum, 62
atabeg, 186
atavism, 384
audience hall, private, 381, 398, 422, 424, 426, 432
  public, 19, 102, 381–2, 385, 397, 392, 395, 398, 402, 408, 412, 422–4, 432, 438–9, 441, 453, 458
awning, 244, 423, 432, 435, 460
axial nave *see* gabled transept
axiality, 2, 14, 16, 38, 45, 50, 53, 69, 72, 83, 87, 97, 101, 103–4, 111, 114, 117–8, 120, 122, 131, 139, 144, 146, 146, 181, 193, 195, 206, 212–4, 216, 225–7, 230–1, 235, 240–2, 247–8, 281, 311, 313, 320, 323, 330, 338, 362, 364, 366–7, 379, 392–3, 395, 398, 401–4, 406–7, 409, 411, 413, 418–9, 422, 427, 429–30, 432–3, 439–40, 442, 444, 446, 453
balcony, 21, 122, 142, 148, 154, 157–8, 159, 162–4, 214, 359, 364, 416, 419, 441, 459
baldachin, 19
balustrade, 141
banqueting-hall, 423–4, 435
baptistery, 281
barracks, 334, 381, 401–2, 411, 426, 453, 459
barrows, 268
basement, 439, 459
basic types of Iranian mausolea, 280–94
basilica, 33, 38, 72, 77, 346, 391–2, 402, 439, 444, 446
basin, 402, 440, 453
bastions, 62, 74, 162, 213, 215, 241, 331, 334, 339, 350, 360, 366, 369, 385, 414
bath, 208, 210, 352, 381–2, 387, 413, 456, 458; *see also* ḥammām
  hall, 392
batter, 142, 160, 290, 297
battle, 457
  scenes, 432
battlements, 441
bazaar see *bāzār*

beams, 457
behaviour in mosques, 63–4
belvedere, 453
bench, 205, 246, 331, 423, 437
bent entrance, 193, 244, 247, 317,
    366, 438–40, 453
bevelling, 163, 182, 231–2, 309,
    318, 330, 362, 366, 369, 430,
    433
birds, 91, 97, 226, 384, 412, 421,
    435, 441, 443
    of paradise, 18
bishop's palace, 51
blind arches, 153, 163, 166, 295,
    307, 309, 398, 409, 430–2, 438,
    441–2
block, 405
blue, 19, 22, 322
blueprint, 178, 190, 367
bodyguards, 381, 392–3, 402, 405,
    413
book painting, 271, 423, 425, 428,
    431
bookbinding, 320
booksellers, 63
booths, 353
boundary stone or marker, 132, 134
"brazen sea", 453
brick, baked, (decoration), 144,
    148, 153, 162–3, 185, 230,
    277, 286, 288, 290, 398, 413,
    417
    forms executed in stone, 307
bridges, 428
brocade, 443
bronze, 398, 443, 457
building programme, 204, 208, 237
    see also lost buildings
bull, 18, 68, 77, 308
burial close to saints, 266
    in houses, 253, 268
    in madrasas, 26
    in mosques, 253
    precinct, 313
    family, 313
buttress, 74, 118, 120, 123, 136,
    160–1, 164, 282, 297, 318, 330,
    387, 396, 407, 413, 416, 425,
    430, 438
calendar, 276, 308
caliph, 16–7, 19, 21, 44–5, 48–9,
    52, 54, 59–62, 68–9, 71–2,
    81, 129–30, 134, 145, 176–7,
    222, 224, 237, 246, 253, 312,
    320, 382, 387, 390–3, 395–6,
    398, 402, 405–7, 409, 415, 419,
    434–5, 438, 443–4
call to prayer see adhān
calligraphy, 28, 411
camel, 359
camp, Roman, 404; see also
    castrum

campanile, 24, 141
canals, 402, 413, 428, 454, 456
cannular niches, 440
canopy, 19, 48, 157, 264, 269, 311,
    442
    tombs, 311, 313
capital city, 44, 144, 153, 244, 273,
    314, 384, 390, 392–3, 398, 407,
    411–2, 415–6, 421, 425, 437,
    439, 443
capitals, 77, 83, 87, 91, 432, 457
    Corinthian, 330
caravan, 331, 344, 367, 371, 373,
    375–6
    travel, 154, 374–6
caravans, camel, 369–70
caravansarais in Ottoman Anatolia,
    353–4
    in Ottoman Syria, 352–3
    in the early Iranian world,
    338–46
    Anatolian, distribution of, 349–50
    etymology of, 331–4
    function of, 331, 370–4
caravansarais, general
    considerations, 336–8
    Īlkhānid and Jalā'irid, 359–65
    Iraqi, 338, 367, 369–70
    later Iraqi, 367–70
    medieval Syrian, 350–2
    octagonal, 366
    Ottoman urban, 354–6
    pilgrim, 352
    post-Mongol, in Iran, 365–7
    staff of, 350, 353
    suburban, 355
    urban, 331, 333, 336–7, 354–9
cardinal compass points, 393, 405–
    6, 409
carpet, garden, 429
carpets, 55, 59, 122, 206, 279, 433,
    458
cartouche, 457
caryatids, 432
castle, 338, 341–2, 384, 396, 419,
    426, 452
catacombs, 268
cathedral, 16, 21, 44–5, 74, 350
causeway, 367
cavetto cornice, 148
cedarwood, 454
ceilings, 83, 91–3, 101, 196, 199,
    206, 210, 242, 249, 412, 416–7,
    422, 432–3, 435, 443, 446, 454,
    456–7
cell, 133, 178, 180–1, 188–9, 191,
    193, 195–7, 203, 205, 208,
    211–2, 216–8, 220, 222–8,
    230–1, 234–5, 240, 242,
    247–50, 331–2, 335, 339, 347,
    353, 366
cemetery, 264, 266, 271, 316, 381

cenotaph, 311, 320, 330
central aisle, 16, 25, 50, 53–4,
    78–80, 83, 86, 91, 98
centralised plan, 121
ceramics display area, 431–2
ceremonies, princely, 16, 45, 50–1,
    130, 139, 165, 247, 266, 392,
    396–8, 402, 405, 413–4, 421–2,
    459
chain, 338, 342, 346, 353, 365–7,
    370, 373–4
chambers see cells
chambers within minarets, 136, 139;
    cf. 133–40
chamfer see bevelling
charitable foundations, 268, 350; see
    also waqf
chequered decoration, 307
choir screen, 49, 59
chronicles see literary sources
church, 14, 16, 31, 33, 36, 38, 45–6,
    51, 53, 55, 59, 62, 69, 71, 73,
    91, 97, 118, 121, 130, 133, 138,
    141, 191, 211, 244, 281, 307–9,
    398, 452
church bell, 129–30
circumambulation, 281
cistern, 331, 334, 342, 369–70, 427,
    440
citadel, 100, 155, 171, 411, 416–7,
    419, 437–8, 446, 452–3
cities of God, 215
city gates, Roman, 402
    miniature, 458
cityscape, 153, 171, 318
classical architecture, 33, 55, 255,
    274
    elements, 44–5, 77, 83, 173,
    254
classicism, 457
classification of mosques, problems
    in, 64
classrooms see lecture halls
clepsydra, 242
climate, 22–4, 73, 95, 211
clock, 242, 246
clockwork, 435, 444
closed and open spaces, 397, 408,
    452–3
cloth, 353
clothes, 416, 435, 441; see also
    textiles
cloverleaf race track, 403
clustering, concentration, 207, 230,
    234, 239–40, 262–4, 271, 280,
    311, 313, 316, 323, 377, 381,
    453
code of conduct, 219
coffee-houses, 369
coffering, 446
coffin, 253–4, 276
coins, 73, 130

colonialism, 6

colonnade, 171, 203, 240, 435, 453

colonnettes, 309
  engaged, 83

colour, 8, 14, 18–20, 22, 26, 56,
    112, 128, 206, 243, 248, 307,
    311, 322, 416–7, 425, 429–30,
    443, 456–7

column, 55, 76–7, 83, 87, 89, 91,
    95, 128, 158, 160, 166, 171,
    196, 206, 242–3, 318–9, 330–1,
    391, 412, 430–2, 437, 440,
    443–4, 453, 456–7, 459, 462
  bases, 432

columns, engaged, 123, 157–8, 164,
    282, 290, 307–8, 341
  iron, 158

commander-in-chief, 34, 46, 61

commemoration, 19, 46, 63, 73, 147,
    158, 255, 257, 260–1, 266, 268,
    278–80, 312

commerce see trade

communal prayer, 31–3, 35, 44, 50,
    59, 74, 106, 219–20

community centre, 40, 42, 73, 246

competition, emulation, 123, 189,
    200, 202, 262, 316, 393

complex of buildings, 59, 63, 100,
    106, 108–9, 122, 163, 171, 175,
    190, 194–5, 197, 199–200, 205,
    210, 215, 217, 220, 227–8, 230,
    242, 248, 260, 266, 271, 275,
    317, 319, 325, 330, 361, 379,
    381, 391, 396–7, 401, 404–5,
    409, 422–3, 426–7, 433, 435–6,
    438, 440, 446, 452–3

compulsory purchase, 69

concentric circles, 393

confiscation, 69

conical roof, 164, 277, 282–3, 286,
    307, 309, 311, 346

conscription of craftsmen and
    materials, 330

conservation, 71, 452

conservatism, 140, 142, 217, 234,
    239, 271–2, 280, 297, 351, 432

consoles, 416, 454

contamination caused by corpses,
    254, 269, 274

convent, 219

conversion of non-Islamic buildings,
    33, 38, 83, 91, 101, 126, 144,
    158, 191–2

cooking, 353

cooling devices, 382

copy, 167, 272, 408, 436

corbels, 162, 283, 308, 323, 436

corkscrew moulding, 158

corner, 71, 86, 109, 123, 134, 136,
    139, 159–61, 164, 166, 171,
    182, 196–7, 227, 230–1, 240,
    297, 331, 353, 360, 362, 366–7,

369, 382, 385, 393, 409, 413–4,
    418, 425, 427, 430, 433, 437,
    440–1, 446, 460

dome, 290
  tower, 134, 136, 139–40, 166

cornice, 148, 156–7, 164, 242, 283,
    286, 308, 311

corpse, 253–4, 269, 274, 276

corrals, 342, 396

correlations, 12, 14

corridor, 223–4, 234, 240, 244,
    248–50, 317, 354, 356, 366,
    396–7, 402, 407, 409, 412, 414,
    416, 424, 426, 435, 441–3

corvée see conscription of craftsmen
    and materials

cosmic associations, 409, 411, 454

cosmocrator, 19

cosmology, 454

cotton, 280

couriers, 371

court of honour, 391, 398, 453

courtyard, 14, 16, 22, 25, 31–2, 38,
    42, 44, 47–8, 54–6, 66, 68, 73,
    86–9, 91–3, 94–5, 97–8, 102–
    4, 107, 111, 114, 118, 120–2,
    126–7, 139, 159, 165, 175,
    178–82, 186–9, 192, 195, 197,
    199, 202, 206, 208, 210, 211–2,
    215–7, 220, 224–7, 231, 234,
    236, 240–4, 247–9, 250, 270,
    303, 314, 331, 334–5, 338–9,
    341, 344, 346–7, 350, 352–6,
    359–60, 362, 366, 368–70,
    373, 385, 388, 391, 393, 395,
    397–8, 402–14, 417, 419, 422–
    4, 426–7, 429–30, 435, 437–
    41, 443–4, 446, 450, 453, 457,
    459

covered area see sanctuary
  courtyard, 359
  hall, 347, 356, 362, 364–6
  market, 355–6, 358

craftsmen, named, 27–8, 446

cramped site, 99, 190, 192–3, 197,
    199, 203–4, 316–7, 336, 356,
    406, 419, 435–6

crenellations, 136, 141, 318, 326,
    350, 369, 398, 425

crescent, 165, 171, 248

cresting, 24

crown, 459

cruciform, 16, 19, 88, 111, 117,
    185–6, 196, 199, 205–6, 216,
    241–2, 255, 366, 395, 402,
    404–5, 407, 409, 413, 417, 427,
    429–30, 446, 459

crypt, 269, 275, 277, 309, 427

curriculum, 208

curses, 28, 61–2

curtain-raising devices, 407, 432

curtains, 24, 432

dadoes, 242, 247, 311, 402, 412, 414,
    423, 456–7

dams, 428

decagon, 157

decoration (or ornament), 8, 12, 14,
    16–18, 21, 24–6, 31–2, 46, 48,
    62, 65, 71, 73, 83–4, 91, 99,
    107, 118, 125, 152, 154–5, 157,
    162–4, 166, 170–1, 182–3, 190,
    193, 195, 203, 212–3, 215,
    223–4, 226, 230, 241–4, 247–8,
    250–1, 281, 286, 290–1, 293–5,
    297, 308–9, 311–3, 317–20,
    324, 326, 330, 344, 346, 350,
    359–62, 365, 367, 372–3,
    377–8, 388, 398, 406–7, 409,
    411–4, 417–9, 421, 423–5, 430,
    432, 438–9, 442–3, 446, 450,
    457, 459, 462

dependence on Syria in Spanish art,
    443

derivative nature of later Islamic
    architecture, 6

dervishes, 219–20

desert, 22, 144, 154, 341, 351,
    366–70, 373, 384, 413

despotism, 393, 396

destruction of buildings, 7–8, 266,
    409; see also lost buildings

devotional life, 316

diagonals, 12, 234–5, 331, 339, 366,
    407

diagrams, 12

dimensions, significant, 385, 437–8

direction of space, 405

discomfort, 387–8

disorientation, 410, 433

distances between stages, 371–2

distribution, 349

dockyard, 418

doctor, 349

dogleg passages, 427, 440

dome, 5, 8–9, 14, 16–8, 21, 23–5,
    32, 53–5, 78, 80–1, 84, 86, 91,
    93, 97–9, 108, 111–2, 116–9,
    121–3, 126, 155, 160–2, 165–6,
    168, 170–1, 187, 192–3, 202,
    210–2, 216, 220, 244, 257,
    281–2, 286–7, 290, 294, 297,
    302, 306, 311–3, 317–8, 320,
    323, 330, 354–5, 359, 365, 373,
    377, 391, 393, 395, 406,
    409–10, 417, 419, 422–3,
    425–8, 430, 432–3, 435–7,
    439–44, 446, 454, 456–7,
    459–62
  chamber, 14, 24, 38, 50, 97,
    101–4, 107–8, 110–2, 114, 116,
    120–2, 127, 141, 153, 164,
    182–3, 186, 196, 211–2, 215,
    220, 234–5, 244, 234–5, 244,
    294, 314, 316, 347, 366, 369,

392–3, 395, 402, 405, 409–10,
   422, 424, 437, 440
in front of *miḥrāb see* dome over
   miḥrāb
of Heaven, 18, 20
over entrance to sanctuary, 81
over *miḥrāb*, 41, 45, 50, 52–4, 79,
   81, 83, 98, 100, 165
  bulbous, 318
  decoration of, 318
  golden, 306
  keel-shaped, 166, 318
  melon *see* domes, ribbed
  ogee, 318
  shouldered, 318
  stilted, 317–8
domed octagon, 281–3
  square, 270, 280–3, 287–95, 297,
   311, 313–4, 316
  square, origins of, 281
  transept, 91
domes, in pairs or trios, 53
  pierced, 86
  ribbed, 86, 297, 311, 313, 318, 323
domestic architecture, 21, 26, 30,
   36, 39, 126, 133, 138, 173–5,
   181, 188–9, 191–2, 199, 200,
   206, 211, 213, 219–20, 242–4,
   253–4, 332, 334–5, 341–3, 385,
   387, 439
donkeys, 402
door, 49, 54, 59, 61–2, 133, 154,
   242, 248, 253, 311, 356, 375,
   391–2, 402, 411, 416, 419, 423,
   430, 435, 443, 457
doorknockers, 55
doorway *see* entrance
double courtyard, 338, 344, 370, 429
  dome, 271, 302, 319
double stretchers, 291
dragon, 18, 423
dragon-slayers, 417
drains, 402
drawbridge, 407
dressed stone, 366
drum, 11, 154, 164, 271, 286, 297,
   307, 311, 313–4, 317–8, 323,
   346
dry-dock, 350
dungeon, 439
duodecagon, 160, 279, 423
dynastic mausolea, 297, 320, 371
dynasties of the Islamic world, 4
eagle, 308, 421
  double-headed, 417
early domed Turkish mosques,
   114–6
earthquake, 167, 181
eaves, 462
ebony, 398, 443
education, 6, 59–60, 173, 176, 202,
   208, 215–8, 239

elephant park, 413
elephants, 384
embalming, 275
embassies, 46, 371, 427, 444
emerald, 452, 459
emperors, 444, 458
emphasis on interiors, 126–8, 243
empty space *see* open space
enclosure, 396, 398, 404–5, 413–5,
   429, 437
endowment *see waqf*
engravings, 428
ensemble, 122, 190, 195, 197, 395,
   397, 405, 411–4, 417, 419,
   424–7, 439, 446, 458
enthronement, 431
entrance, 74, 86, 98, 102, 144,
   154–5, 159–60, 171, 182,
   202–3, 205, 216, 246–7, 250,
   283, 286, 290, 308–9, 311, 313,
   323, 330, 331, 334, 339, 347,
   350, 353, 359, 362, 364, 381,
   387, 392, 398, 402, 405, 407,
   409, 413–4, 416, 418, 422,
   424–5, 432, 438, 446
  complex, 227–8
epic, 423
epigraphy *see* inscriptions
equilateral triangles, 14
esoteric, 20
ethnic factors, 12, 147
  mosque traditions, 64, 66
etymology, 131–4, 138, 331
eunuch, 220
ex-votos, 266
excavations, 90, 102, 138, 180, 206,
   237, 275, 290, 331, 341–2, 379,
   387, 390, 395–6, 398–9, 406–7,
   411–5, 417–9, 424, 437–44,
   446
executioner, 392, 459, 461
exotica, 10, 434–5, 443–4
experiment, 68, 92, 95, 102, 114,
   116, 121, 126, 154–5, 215, 227,
   280–1, 290–2, 294, 318, 402
exposure of corpses, 269, 274–5,
   277
extravagant design, 428
façade, exterior, 15, 17, 20, 25,
   78–9, 83–4, 86, 95, 98–9, 107,
   124–6, 152, 161–2, 166, 171,
   182–3, 190, 193–5, 197, 202–3,
   206, 208, 210, 212–3, 216, 222,
   226, 230–1, 242, 244, 246, 290,
   307–8, 317, 324–6, 335, 350,
   369, 402, 409–10, 413–4, 416,
   419, 424–5, 428, 431–2, 435,
   439–41
  interior, 51–2, 55, 76–7, 80–1,
   89, 94, 101, 103–5, 112, 126–8,
   157, 159, 174, 178–9, 181, 186,
   204, 227, 240–3, 246, 248, 250,

331, 335, 366, 398, 411–2, 414,
   422
factories, 359
falconers, 417
fantastic, 412
feasting, 431–3
feeling for space, 217
felt, 277
fenestration, 122, 206, 248, 317, 353,
   355
fertility, 18, 22, 454
festivals, 32, 48, 59, 171, 220, 250,
   266, 402, 431, 435
figural decoration, 128, 416, 418,
   421, 423, 431
finial, 84, 141, 164, 171, 248
fire, 132–3, 144–5, 421
fire temples, 26, 101, 276, 290
fireplace, 461
flanges, 153–4, 158–9, 164, 244,
   282–3, 286, 307–8
flexibility, 24, 42, 63, 71, 125–6,
   171, 202, 246, 353, 427, 432
floor covering, 59, 249
floors, 24, 59, 68, 71, 83–4, 206,
   242, 247, 249, 253, 406, 412,
   423–4, 426, 437–8, 453, 457
flower-beds, 279, 426, 428, 440, 456
fluting, 86, 122, 162, 164, 166, 170,
   339, 398
flying buttress, 119, 297
fodder, 384, 390
folk religion, 260
forest space, 87
formulae, 254
fort, fortresses, 132, 160, 333–4,
   340–2, 352, 387, 416, 438, 452,
   454
fortification, 44, 62, 166, 331, 333–
   4, 336, 338–9, 341–2, 361, 369,
   371, 381–2, 384–5, 387, 396,
   401, 404, 407, 411, 414, 419,
   422, 426, 437, 439, 446, 452,
   457
founder, 180, 183, 188, 190, 200,
   203, 225, 239, 260, 262, 319,
   325, 361
fountain, 22, 25, 27–8, 55, 97, 104,
   208, 211, 214, 216, 240–1, 244,
   250, 279, 352- 3, 359, 370, 374,
   381, 390, 402, 416–7, 424, 426,
   428, 432–6, 441–2, 453–4, 456,
   458, 461–2
four-*īwān* plan, 19, 103–4, 107–8,
   110, 112, 114, 175, 178,
   181–2, 186, 193, 196–7, 204–6,
   212, 214, 216, 222, 225–7, 232,
   235, 241, 366, 410–1, 413–4,
   417, 419, 422–4, 427, 433, 435,
   453
frailness, 433, 457
frescoes, 84, 91–2, 122, 193, 226,

278, 322, 398, 412–4, 416–7, 431–3, 435, 457
friars, 371
frontier, 167, 264, 266, 331, 340–1, 387
fundamentalism, 258
funerary complex, 161, 171
  compound, 280, 453
  customs, Mongol, 277
  mound, 275
  practices in the Islamic world, 253–4, 274–7
  furnishings, 57, 59, 387
gable, 14, 16–7, 78, 80–1, 83, 86, 126
gabled transept, 45, 50–3, 81
gadroon, 159, 163
gallery, 64, 112, 240, 248, 286, 290–1, 294–5, 297, 350, 352, 354–5, 412, 442, 453
game preserve, 390, 403, 443; see also paradeisos
garden, 10, 24–5, 34, 160, 234, 258, 279, 303, 306, 352, 381–2, 384, 390, 401–3, 406, 413, 416, 419, 425, 427–31, 433–5, 440–1, 443, 446, 452–4, 456, 458, 461–2
  walled, 428–9
gardens, European, 428
  informal, 428
  magic, 456
gargoyles, 308, 350
garrison cities, 34
gate, 19, 40, 48, 154, 341, 381, 392–3, 395–6, 398, 402, 404–7, 418–9, 422, 424–6, 437–8, 440, 452–3, 459–60
gatehouse, 160
gateway, 16–7, 171, 334
gazebos, 433, 461
geographers, 30, 59, 60, 63, 136
geographical factors, 12, 21–2, 65, 132, 140, 234, 254, 273, 275, 306, 316, 330, 332, 337, 340–1, 367, 371–4, 395, 414
  treatises, 26
geometry, 8, 12, 48, 83, 92, 128, 144, 148, 166, 171, 208, 224, 230, 242–3, 297, 303, 308, 318, 330, 346, 350, 359, 405, 416–8, 423, 438, 456–7
gigantic scale, 4, 83, 89, 107–8, 114, 155, 165–6, 183, 193, 196, 217, 226–8, 230, 283, 295, 297, 305, 316, 319, 330, 352, 360, 365, 369, 387, 390, 395, 399, 401–4, 413–4, 422, 424, 430, 435–6, 441, 452, 457, 459
gilding, 311, 330, 381, 398, 432–5, 443
glass, 59, 417, 441–2

glazed decoration see tilework
gold, 73, 253, 435, 443
good luck, 19
  works, 277
gout, 417
government communication networks, 371
governor, 44, 341, 351–2, 388
governor's palace, 51, 183
governor-generals, 351
grave, 253–4, 257, 271, 278, 280, 283, 319–20
graves, desecration of, 254
  visiting of, 266
green, 18, 22
grid, 222
grilles, 14, 22, 83, 199, 249, 330, 433, 457, 459
grooms, 331, 367
guard posts, 338
guard-room, 350, 424, 438, 453, 459
guards, 398
hadiths, 39
hall, triple-domed, 432
halls, transverse, 407, 422–3, 440
halva honey, 350
hangings, 443, 458
harbour, 406
heavens, 454, 459
height, 163, 165, 171, 271, 309, 311
helicoidal towers, 144–6
heraldic, 412, 421
herringbone, 318
heterodox, 240, 254, 271, 278–9
hexadecagon, 308
hexagon, 118, 121, 165, 311, 318, 360
hierarchy, 14, 16, 32, 54, 80, 86–7, 104, 159, 183, 196, 206, 212, 220, 365, 405–6, 413, 422, 426, 432, 443
high place, 437
holidays, 460
holy war see jihad
horoscope, 393
horses, 370–1, 459
horticulture, 446
hospitals, 14, 17, 60, 95, 195, 223, 342, 459
hostelries, 342
house see domestic architecture
house style, 358
hunting, 416, 431, 457
  lodges, 430
hyperbole, 428, 459
hypogea, 268
hypostyle, 66, 90–2, 97–8, 100–4, 109, 117
ice-house, 459
iconoclasm, 68
iconography, 165, 269, 418, 421
idolatry, 128

illumination, 59, 87, 132, 205, 258, 278
  manuscript, 297, 320
  Qur'an, 271
illusionism, 24, 196, 199, 212, 223, 286, 318, 433, 444, 450, 453
inaccessibility of key monuments, 8
  of ruler, 392–3
inauguration, 222
industrial quarters, 412
industrialisation, 7–8
influences, 5–6, 10, 36, 44, 137–8, 140, 142, 146–8, 162, 168, 192, 211, 237, 241–3, 275–7, 306, 308, 318, 343, 346, 350, 352–3, 378, 395, 408, 419, 423, 439–40, 450
informality, 33–4, 42
inhumation, 276
inkpot, 61
innovation, 24, 44–54, 65, 71, 83, 92, 110, 114, 130, 157, 173, 185, 216, 226, 280
inns, 332, 334, 358
inscription, trilingual, 349
inscriptions, 8, 10, 12, 17–8, 26–8, 62–3, 73, 91–2, 134, 137, 148, 152–3, 155–8, 163, 166, 180, 182, 190–1, 203, 218–9, 222, 224, 240, 242–6, 254, 257, 266, 276–80, 283, 286, 290, 297, 303, 307, 320, 324, 330–1, 344, 348, 350, 361, 364, 372, 412, 414, 416–7, 419, 421–3, 425, 427, 438, 440, 441, 444, 446, 452, 454, 457, 459, 462
  glorifying monarchs, 414, 419, 421
inspectors, 371
intarsia work, 318, 355
interchangeability of forms, 16, 24, 45, 173, 179, 191, 211, 234, 324, 334, 341, 359, 423, 438
inventories, 458
iron, 438
  rings, 331
ironwork, 330
irrigation, 384, 390, 413
ivory, 398
jasper, 453
joggled voussoirs, 309
joint foundations, 44, 100, 179, 187?, 190, 200, 210, 215, 219, 226, 235, 260, 277, 361
  plugs, 290
judge see qāḍī
jurisconsult, 205
jurisprudence, 60, 175
jurist, 220
justice, 42, 61, 427, 432, 437, 459
keep, 396, 452
khans as stores for food, 351

for munitions, 351
kilns, 423
kiosk, 129, 142, 144, 161, 279, 381,
    413, 415–6, 423, 428, 430, 435,
    461–2
kiosks of Anatolia, 416–7
    paired, 462
kitchen, 208, 220, 223, 250, 352,
    416, 418, 435, 459
Kufic, seal, 330
    square, 156, 330
labyrinth, 126, 409–11, 432, 453
ladies' quarters, 430
lake, 414, 418, 422–3, 429, 440
lamps, 17, 21, 59, 87, 132–3, 154,
    206, 278
landscaping, 122, 406, 413–4, 458
lantern, 166–8, 350
lapis lazuli, 398, 437
late antique traditions, 452
laterality, 14, 38, 81, 89, 104, 108?,
    110, 114, 116–8, 181, 187, 195,
    197, 199, 202, 205–6, 212,
    225–6, 230, 240–1, 248, 270,
    303, 323, 330, 334, 347, 360,
    366, 398, 404, 414, 432, 440–2,
    444, 446
latrines, 55, 126, 205, 212, 244, 352,
    359, 366, 369–70, 388, 413, 446
lattice, 48–79, 140, 148, 248, 277,
    318, 432, 451–2, 454, 456
"laundering", 200
lavatories see latrines
law court, 61, 437, 459
    school see madhhab
lead, 164, 206
lead frames, 457
leather, 350
lecture halls, 205, 210, 212, 219,
    227, 235, 240–1, 245
lecturers, 205
legends, 456
library, 60, 199, 212, 223, 240, 411,
    458, 460
light, 17, 24, 59, 74, 87, 112, 122,
    126, 132–3, 182, 216, 248, 326,
    330, 385, 410–1, 443, 453–4,
    456–7; see also lighting
light-house, 132–3, 138, 155, 167,
    366
lighting, 59, 87, 89, 95, 356, 359,
    410, 433
linen, 280
lintel, 307, 324
lion and the sun, 424
lions, 18, 308, 384, 417–8, 432, 435,
    453
literary sources, 8, 12, 16, 19, 24,
    26–8, 30, 38–9, 49, 68, 72,
    101, 129, 134, 136, 138, 145–6,
    148, 155, 167–8, 173, 175, 180,
    183, 185, 199, 205–7, 218, 226,

237, 257, 274–5, 290, 331, 344,
    370–1, 377, 393, 402, 405,
    408–9, 411, 413–4, 417, 424–5,
    427–8, 434–5, 440, 443–4, 457
liturgy, 31–3, 35, 39, 45–6, 49–50,
    53–4, 80, 139, 144, 152–4, 196,
    213, 408
living creatures, portrayal of, 68
living quarters, 199–200, 379, 387,
    392, 396–8, 402, 405–6, 412–3,
    439, 453
lobed plans, 153, 255
local see regional
local traditions, 8
location, 14, 18–20, 24, 33, 53, 61,
    68, 72, 86, 123, 136, 144,
    154–6, 158, 160, 162, 164, 171,
    174–5, 204, 212, 216, 239–41,
    243–4, 248, 264, 266, 271, 274,
    276, 279, 316, 335, 356, 381,
    395, 406, 409, 426–7, 429–30,
    444
lock-up khans, 349, 359
loggia, 206, 213, 423, 430–3, 436
longevity of architectural form, 348
loophole, 396, 410
lost buildings, 7–8, 26, 30, 206–7,
    242, 428, 435, 452
    property, 64
lozenge grid, 157, 163
lustre tiles, 398, 418
lyric, 423
machicolation, 350
"machine for living", 395
madrasa adjoining mosque, 196–7
    and mosque, shared functions of,
        212, 218–9
    design influencing mosques, 192,
        196
    Anatolian, in the Saljūq and
        Beylik periods, 206–15
    early history, 173–4
    four-rite, 185–6, 188, 192, 196–7,
        214
    two-rite, 188
    added to mosques, 179
    in Egypt, 192–202
    in the Yemen, 193
    Anatolian courtyard, 212–5
    diet in, 249–50
    discomforts of life in, 248–50
    domed Anatolian, 210–2
    fashion for building, 183, 185,
        189–90, 194–5, 200, 207–8,
        239
    fittings of cells in, 249
    function of Syrian, 188–90
    funerary, 190–2, 195, 200, 215,
        241, 277
    hanging, 199, 205
    "hidden", 218
    Īlkhānid to Ṣafavid, 225–235

Īlkhānid, 225–6
Iraqi, 220, 222–5
Maghribī, 235–51
Moroccan, 242–51
Moroccan, capacity of, 249
Ottoman, 215–7
paired, 193, 230, 242
pre-Īlkhānid Iranian, 180–3
problems of classification, 212
Ṣafavid, 234–5
staff of, 173, 197, 208, 212, 219,
    223, 241, 246, 250
State-sponsored Saljūq, 175–80
Syrian to 648/1250, 186–92
Tīmūrid and Shaibānid, 226–34
magic, 418
mannikins, 421
manor house, 343, 421
map of the Islamic world, 2–3
marble, 46, 48, 71, 84, 157, 206,
    243, 246–7, 307, 311, 318, 330,
    355, 398, 403, 414, 416–7, 423,
    435, 437, 440, 442–3, 453, 457,
    462
marker, 5, 133, 137, 144, 154, 159,
    165, 171, 244, 280, 282
markets, 32
marquetry, 432
martyr, 2, 254, 258, 264, 266
mathematics, 12, 14, 208, 222
matting, 24, 59
mausolea, 7, 11, 13, 15, 19–20, 24,
    33, 44, 46, 91, 126, 152, 160–1,
    164, 171, 188, 190, 192, 195,
    197, 199–200, 202, 205, 208,
    211, 253–330 passim, 351
as supplementary places of
    worship, 277–8
in Ayyūbid and Mamlūk Egypt,
    general considerations, 316–9
in Ayyūbid Cairo, 319–22
in Ayyūbid Syria, 323–4
in Mamlūk Cairo, 324–30
in Egypt and Syria, 311–30
in Iran, 273–306
in mosques, 272
'Alid, 316
Anatolian, 306–11
dynastic, 262, 427
Fāṭimid, 311–6
Islamic, forms of, 268–73
justification for, 278, 325
Ottoman, 311
paired, 190, 208, 316
religious and symbolic aspects of,
    277–80
sanctification of secular, 260
Turkish elements in Iranian,
    276–7
two-tier, 269
uneven spread of, 271
attached to palace, 325

in Islam, role of, 260–4, 266–8
Islamic terminology for, 255, 257–8
maze, 410
medical school, 208
memorial structures, Christian, 254–5
menagerie, 384, 434
menstruation, 64
mensuration, 12
merchandise, 331
merchants, 331, 336, 340, 344, 349–52, 355, 359, 371–2, 374, 384
metalwork, 61, 171, 225, 241–2, 249, 330, 435, 443
metaphors, 393
method, 1–5, 64–5
mezzanine floor, 442
miḥrāb, external, 213, 416
horseshoe shaped, 330
triple, 319
milestone, 134
military camp, 334
factors, 34, 62, 73, 132, 147, 166, 213, 266, 324, 339, 341, 350–1, 373, 387, 396, 405, 409, 416, 436, 441, 459
intelligence, 370
millefiore glass, 398
minaret, 5, 16, 18, 22, 24, 27, 56, 71, 86, 91–2, 95, 101, 104, 106, 109, 119, 122, 129–71 *passim*, 182, 192, 200, 203, 205, 208, 213–4, 230–1, 242, 244, 322, 461
etymology of, 131–4
Maghribi type, 133, 136
rooms in, 140, 173; cf. 133
in Iran, 146–8, 150–8
in Iraq, 144–6
or towers, context of the earliest, 129–31
or towers, helicoidal, 144–6
Almohad, 140–2
earliest, 129–30, 134, 136–8
earliest in Iran, 148
five-tiered, 160
four-tiered, 157, 159, 168
general considerations, 129
Īlkhānid, 155–7
Indian, 158–61
Ottoman, 164–5
paired, 154–5, 158, 164–5, 171, 213
Rūm Saljūq and Beylik, 161–4
Tīmūrid and Ṣafavid, 157–8
West African, 142
Yemeni, 166
mint, 459
missionary, 173, 176
models, 107, 122, 142, 144–5, 226,

242–3, 254, 273, 281–2, 290, 306–8, 352, 387, 396, 412, 437, 442
modules, 12, 14, 22, 48, 74, 93, 216–7, 222, 243, 347, 385, 421, 431–2
monastery, 46, 53, 133, 138, 175, 219, 248, 331, 341
monastic foundations, 266
morgue, 60
mortuary, 246
mosaic, 22, 46–7, 71–3, 84, 137–8, 311, 318, 324, 330, 398, 417, 437–8, 442–3
mosque, cathedral, 44
design, foreign elements in, 35–6, 38, 44–54
early history of, 5, 33–6
mosque, eight-bayed, 409–10
exterior, 398
madrasa connections, 192, 196–7, 215, 227, 235, 242, 244
nine-bayed, 78, 104, 117
mosque-*madrasa*, 195–7, 199
mosques built in foreign styles, 66
circular, 68
for specific crafts, 62
for specific quarters, 62
in Anatolia, covered, 95, 97–8
of Arab plan, 66, 68, 74, 83–4, 94–5, 100–2, 117
ʿAbbāsid, 73–4
Anatolian hypostyle, 92–9
burial in, 253
early, 34–5, 61, 66–8, 74, 76, 83, 138
early, in Iran, 100–2
functions of, 5, 31, 40, 42
funerary, 63, 91, 202, 277
hanging, 199
Īlkhānid, 106–7
Iranian Saljūq, 102–6
Maghribī, 52–3, 85–9
memorial, 62–3
neighbourhood, 244–5
pavilion, 347, 353
post-mediaeval, 65
private, 60, 63, 387
Ṣafavid, 112–4
Tīmūrid, 107–12
transept, 2, 5
tribal, 62
Umayyad, 68–73
Yemeni, 90–2
mother of pearl, 330, 398, 437
mouldings, roll, 318
mourning customs, 253, 266
mud brick, 46, 48, 134, 142, 152, 166, 180, 225, 297, 390, 398, 406, 410, 412–4
compressed, 342
muezzin, 56

multi-functionalism, 6–7, 42, 361
multi-partite elevation, 165–8
multifoil plans, 255
multiple foundations, 7
functions, 59, 76, 132, 195, 197, 202, 208, 246, 331, 341, 347, 361, 384, 409, 415, 433
hostelries, 369
music, 59, 246, 382, 432–3, 460
mystical orders, 219
mystics, 26; *see also* Sūfīs
myth, 262, 390
naphtha pots, 352
narthex, 118, 187, 426
naval arsenal, 350
tournaments, 440
nave, 353, 404
necropolis, 262
need for survey work, 7
niches in pottery shapes, 431–2
nimbus, 393, 421
nomads, 275, 277, 341, 344, 387, 392, 415–6, 421, 423, 457
numerology, 19, 421
oath, 48, 60–1, 322, 390
observatory, 208, 212
oculus, 359
office (i.e. Office of Works), 367
official audiences, 344
couriers, 351
oil-lamp, 132
onyx, 243
open and covered spaces, 429, 433
open (empty) space, 21–2, 24, 32, 34, 39–40, 42, 44, 55, 66–9, 76, 83, 101, 104, 122, 126, 139, 197, 211, 217, 313, 316, 332, 334–6, 338, 347, 350, 352, 366–7, 393, 396–7, 402, 404, 406–7, 410, 413, 416, 419, 423, 427–9, 432, 440, 459
oratory, 44, 100, 112, 189, 242, 244, 247–8, 250, 413, 440, 446, 450, 453
orb, 165
orchard, 424
orientation, 31–2, 35, 46, 112, 114, 181, 183, 193, 247, 250, 253, 317, 393, 401, 414, 425, 433
originality of Anatolian *madrasa*s, 214
Moroccan *madrasa*s, 243–51
Anatolian mosques, 92–3
architectural features, 114
Ayyūbid *madrasa*s, 191
caravansarai, 334–6, 342
decorative schemes, 442
emphasis on the sanctuary, 80–3
game park, 390
mausolea, 254–5, 274–7
minaret, 144–8, 165, 168, 170
palaces, 412, 418, 457

Syrian *muqarnas* domes, 323–4
the *madrasa*, 173, 175, 185–6,
    211–3, 218
the *maqṣūra*, 49
the mausoleum, 254–5
the *miḥrāb*, 45
the *minbar*, 46–7
the mosque, 32–6, 39, 45, 63
tomb towers, 282
foreign, 46, 50, 54, 308, 330,
    402
orthodox, 126, 152, 177, 192, 200,
    222, 239, 240, 253–4, 257–8,
    268, 271, 274, 280, 313, 320,
    324, 352
ossuaries, 274, 276, 281
oxen, 453
pagan, 33, 71, 138, 155, 173, 182–3,
    254, 277, 341, 421
pages, 460
pagodas, 147
palace adjoining mosque, 83, 393,
    395
    city, 408, 415, 435, 443, 452, 457
    mosque, 416
    school, 460
    multi-storey urban, 435
palaces, 3–5, 16, 21, 24, 26, 44–5,
    48–9, 51, 53–5, 72, 101–3,
    111, 126, 144, 158, 188, 254,
    257, 279, 325, 332, 341, 344,
    347, 351, 361, 377–462 *passim*
    'Abbāsid, 390–408
    Anatolian, 415–8
    burial in, 278
    early Iranian, 411–5
    in later medieval Syria and Iraq,
        418–21
    in Sicily, 441–2
    in Spain, 442–57
    in the Maghrib, 437–42
    in the medieval Iranian world,
        408–15, 421–3
    later Maghribī, 442
    loosely planned, 426–7, 458
    medieval, in Egypt, 434–5
    of Sulṭān 'Alā' al-Dīn Kayqubād,
        417–8
    or royal residences in the 13th
        century, 415–8
    Parthian, 402
    Ṣafavid, 428–33
    Ṣafavid, in Iṣfahān, 431–3, 459
    Ṣafavid, outside Iṣfahān, 430–1
    self-contained, 381, 392–3, 395,
        415, 426
    Umayyad, 381, 384, 390, 395,
        397, 407
palatial compounds, 381
palatine chapel, 83
palm, date, 40, 76, 142, 384, 434,
    442–3

panegyric, 414, 452
panorama, 437
parade ground, 42, 401, 458–9
paradise, 17, 19, 24, 128, 258, 264,
    269, 278, 280, 381, 428, 456,
    459
parapet, 318, 326, 355
park, 441, 452, 458–9
parody, 51
parrots, 421
parterre, 456
partridges, 421
passion plays, 266
pastiche, 10
patio, 442–3
patron, 18, 26, 28, 44, 68, 100, 103,
    136, 145, 152–3, 171, 174,
    185–6, 189–90, 195, 199, 202,
    204, 208, 210, 217, 222, 234,
    240–1, 247, 257, 262, 268, 271,
    277, 283, 297, 312, 342–3, 346,
    348–9, 351, 365, 367, 373–4,
    378, 385, 387–8, 452, 454
pattern books, 12
pavilion, 4, 55, 111, 142, 161,
    165–6, 170–1, 268–9, 381, 406,
    415–6, 418, 423, 425, 427–30,
    434, 438, 441–4, 446, 456–7,
    459–60
paving *see* floor
peacock, 18, 278, 442
pearl, 452
pearl, suspended, 443
pendentives, 112, 122, 461
    pyramidal 323
perfume, 59, 64, 241, 258
peripatetic court, 429
"peripheral" areas, 65
phoenix, 423
piazza, 21, 122, 126, 405
piers, 77, 83, 87, 95, 112, 120, 122,
    205, 243, 297, 330, 407, 412,
    433, 444, 452, 456
    crystal, 443
pietism, piety, 31, 73, 153, 240, 271,
    277–8, 320, 374, 376
pigeon, 443
pilasters, 411
pilgrim route, 342, 370, 373; *see also*
    Ḍarb Zubaida
pilgrimage, 60–1, 63, 68, 142, 144,
    220, 255, 258, 266, 271, 273,
    282, 312, 314, 352, 367, 370,
    373–5
pillars, 422
    of the faith, 19
plaque, 423
platform, 331, 366–7, 369–70, 406,
    414, 418, 436
plaza, 405
plinth, 153–4, 156, 159, 164, 283,
    286, 308, 331, 342, 425–6

podium, 430, 462
poem, 26
poetry, 64, 246, 257, 395, 414, 423,
    441, 443–4, 452, 454, 459
police, 62
politics, 33, 46, 48, 51, 53, 61, 63,
    72–3, 81, 103, 130–1, 134, 140,
    147, 165, 173–7, 187, 194, 204,
    207, 210, 217, 222, 241, 244,
    262, 266, 268, 272, 278, 316,
    322, 324, 330, 374, 384, 393,
    411, 426, 435
polo, 403, 405
polyhedral, 286
pond, 432, 434–5
pool, 22, 24, 55–6, 104, 107, 181,
    216, 240, 247, 250, 390, 406,
    412–3, 416–7, 419, 422, 424,
    426–8, 430, 432–3, 436, 439,
    441–3, 446, 450, 453–4, 456,
    458, 461–2
popular architecture, 314
porcelain, 458
porch, 74, 97–8, 126, 171, 205, 212,
    244, 416, 436–7
portal, 15, 17–8, 43, 46, 56, 74, 83,
    97, 99, 104–5, 107–8, 112, 114,
    156, 158, 162, 166, 182, 183,
    193, 196, 202, 204, 211, 212–4,
    220, 224, 226–7, 230, 233,
    238–9, 241–2, 244, 290, 297,
    330, 350, 353, 356, 359–60,
    366, 369, 375, 411, 419, 424,
    436, 440, 442
    complex, 369
    twin minaret, 105–7, 154–5, 159,
        162, 182, 196, 214; *see also*
        minarets, paired
portcullis, 396
portico, 55, 67, 98, 117–8, 120, 204,
    211, 250, 311, 314, 385, 406,
    412, 432, 435, 438–9, 441, 450,
    459–60
portraits, 414
ports, 349
post-houses, 334, 371
post-medieval Islamic architecture,
    6
postern, 412
prayer hall in Maghribī *madrasa*s,
    247, 249
    hall, laterally developed, 187, 192,
        202
    hall, triple-bayed, 187, 189
    mat, 61
prayers answered, 271
    for the dead, 266
pre-Achaemenid structures, 146
pre-Buddhist Indian structures, 146
precinct, 4, 165, 279, 311, 313, 381,
    393, 396, 405, 411–3, 424,
    426–9, 432

pressure on space, 316–7; *see also* cramped site
princely lifestyle, 47, 387
  tent, 275, 277
prison cells, 427
privacy, 49, 81, 126, 247, 381, 387–8, 392, 404, 409–10, 415–6, 431, 433, 435, 438, 443, 453, 457
private quarters *see* living quarters
processions, 16, 51, 83, 253, 266, 275, 322, 393, 402, 406, 418
professors *see madrasas*, staff of
projecting *see* salient
propaganda, 33, 44, 71, 131, 176, 188, 192, 217, 316, 319, 352, 374, 409
proportional ratios, 12, 14, 74, 76, 141, 154, 159, 222, 226, 404, 407, 421
prospect *see* vista
proverbs, 10
province, 121, 134, 163–5, 173, 175, 202–4, 264, 272, 314, 316, 338, 342, 367, 371, 430–1, 436
public and private, division between, 381, 393, 395, 429, 433, 453
publication, medieval, 60
pulpit, 46, 48
puns, 18
pylon, 153, 166
pyramidal roof, 244, 248, 307
pyramids, 268
quadrant, 366, 404, 407
quarter (in a town), 44, 62–3, 241–2, 323
quarters for servants, 459
quicksilver pond, 434, 443
quincunx, 118
radial, 281, 322, 425, 429–30
ramp, 140, 144–5, 402, 437, 439, 442
ramparts, 443
rams, 280, 308
ratio of width to height, 282–3
ratio *see* proportional ratios
re-use of earlier buildings, 421–3
rear façade, 303
reception hall, 359, 405, 408, 410, 419, 424, 427, 433, 435, 439, 444, 446, 453, 460
receptions, public, 381, 442
recitation, 266
reconquest, 452
refuge, 342
refurbishing and extension, 110, 112, 152, 416–7
regattas, 418
regents, 351
regional schools, 8, 64–6, 211, 270, 307, 332–3, 352, 382, 421, 435

relics, 60, 255, 267, 460
religious sciences, 173, 240
repetition, 122, 128, 205, 430
reservoir, 254, 413, 442
restoration, 452
retiral rooms, 382, 387
re-use of sacred sites, 267
revenue, 361
revivalism, 31
ribāṭs, urban, 332, 351
ribbed roofs, 308–9
ribs, 86–7, 277, 365
riding schools, 416
rights of way, 20, 30
riparian, 404, 404, 413, 419
ritual, 31, 81, 126, 129, 133
river, 405–6, 413, 419–20
roads, 342, 344, 346, 349, 370–1, 429; *see also* arterial routes
rock reliefs, 154
  tombs, 154, 274, 276
rooms *see* cells
rosettes, 412
royal aloofness, 392
  associations, 16–7, 52–4, 78, 81, 83
  box, 49
  central tract, 404–8
  city *see* palace city
  quarters, 414, 416, 422, 461
rubble, 350, 365–6, 419, 438
ruler as architect, 416
sacred rocks, 271
  versus secular, 32 (cf. 83)
safe travel, 371
saint, 19, 60, 63, 255, 260, 266–7, 271, 278, 303
salient, 74, 99, 166–7, 213, 216, 226, 241, 244, 250, 331, 360, 366, 369, 387, 404, 407, 412, 414, 416, 423, 431, 438–41, 460
sanctuary, 14, 16–7, 20, 22, 32, 38, 44, 50, 54–6, 59, 63–4, 66, 68, 73–4, 78–81, 83, 87–8, 91, 93, 97, 102–5, 107–12, 114, 121–2, 126, 139, 154, 165, 174, 186, 192, 196, 203, 216, 220, 266, 314
  accentuation of, 78
  entrance, 86
  iwan, 103–4, 108, 111, 113, 154, 161
  roofing systems, 50, 53, cf. 74, 77, 80
  transformation of, 79–83
sarcophagi, 281, 427
school, 458
screen, 435, 452, 459
screening, 392, 398, 424
screens *see mashrabiya*
sculpture, 8, 16, 59, 91, 97, 99, 214,

253, 280, 308, 346, 350, 414, 417–8, 421
seal of the Prophet, 460
seclusion, 392–3, 395, 406, 431, 453, 456
secret burial, 277
secular and sacred, 86, 244, 262, 361, 393
security, 396, 402, 404–5, 426
self-image, 415
semi-dome, 118, 120–3, 439
sentry-box 133, 137
serpent, 18
setting, 277, 279, 303, 306, 311, 337, 381, 390, 428, 433, 452, 458
setting, sensitivity to, 230, 234–5
shade, 19, 22, 74, 126, 242, 269, 279, 335, 425, 456
shah, 102, 112, 431–3
shamanism, 146, 308
shops, 21, 28, 30, 246, 352–3, 356, 361, 364, 366, 405, 413–4
shrine, 21, 55, 106, 108, 147, 158, 227, 250, 258, 262, 266–8, 271, 273, 280, 294, 303, 306, 330
shroud, 253–4, 280
shutters, 24
signal towers, 133, 155, 157
signpost, 132, 134, 154
silk, 280, 353, 371, 458
  workshops, 416
silver, 59, 73, 435, 443
site, 19, 21, 63, 68–9, 71–3, 90, 138–9, 145, 155, 165, 167, 175, 182, 190, 192–3, 195, 197, 199, 204–6, 216–7, 227–8, 234–5, 243, 249, 251, 262, 267, 271, 276, 283, 302, 305, 316–7, 320, 325, 332, 342, 349, 354–5, 356, 362, 378–9, 390–1, 398, 402, 404, 406, 413, 422–3, 426, 429, 431,435, 437, 439–40, 443, 452, 454, 458–9
skylight, 56, 97–8, 211, 417, 456
skyline, 205
slave trade, 351
slaves, 349
sleeping, 331, 361, 367, 369–70, 423
solar motifs, 18
solids and voids, 428
songs, 246
soup kitchen, 60, 352
speed of building, 325, 398
spices, 59
sport, 462
spymaster, 392
square, 21, 112, 119, 403, 431, 441
squinch, 291, 318, 323, 438
  net, 302
  zone *see* zone of transition
stables, 331, 333–4, 338–9, 344,

346–7, 350, 353, 355–6, 366–7, 381, 403, 436, 453, 459
staff of the Prophet, 460
stages of mourning, 275
stained glass, 59, 206, 320, 330, 412, 437, 457
staircase, 129, 134, 137, 140, 144, 148, 154, 159, 166, 200, 205, 240, 244, 246, 309, 317, 374, 416, 422–4, 426, 432–3, 435–7, 459
stalactite vaulting *see muqarnas*
star, stellate, 18, 147, 157, 203, 255, 282, 313, 395, 412, 440–1, 454, 456
statues, 253
stencils, 297
stepping, 318, 407, 426, 438, 459
stereotomy, 119, 190, 213, 307, 346, 416, 419, 427
"stone of warning", 459
stopover, 331, 334, 344, 370, 429; *see also* way-station
storage space, 356, 359, 361–2, 364, 405
store-room, 416, 439, 459
street, 56, 61, 126, 190, 195, 202–3, 230, 244, 249, 297, 316–7, 325, 356, 359, 404- 5, 413, 428, 436
stretchers, 290–1
striped masonry, 164
structure and ornament, role of, 83–5
stucco ornament, 27, 86, 91, 148, 193, 242–3, 247, 290, 297, 307, 312, 320, 324, 402, 408, 411–3, 417–9, 421, 423, 438, 442, 457
stylistic change, 12
sub-continent *see* India
subsidiary functions, 76
suburb, 409
successive subdivision, 405
summer-houses, 433, 461
summer pastures, 416, 421, 457
sunburst designs, 322
sunlight, 22, 24
superposed arcades, 77
supervising construction, 180, 247
suspended buildings, 21, 416
symbol, 68, 244, 248, 260, 278–80, 283, 393, 412
symbolism, 5, 14, 16–20, 33, 42, 44–6, 49, 53, 59, 97, 128, 132, 139, 147, 152, 155- 6, 158, 161–2, 164–5, 171, 205, 213, 215–6, 222, 269, 277, 374, 417, 419, 425, 431, 443, 454
symbolism of numbers, 279; *see also* numerology
symmetry, 202, 215–7, 222, 228, 230, 250–1, 335, 364, 366–7,

393, 397, 409, 412, 418, 425, 429–30, 438, 446, 459
synagogues, 33, 91
systems of communication in the Mongol empire, 370–2
taboo, 277
talisman, 457
tank, water, 188
taper, 148, 154, 159, 165–6
tax, 62, 72–3
tea-houses, 369
teacher/teaching, 5, 40, 60, 173, 176, 190–2, 197, 199, 203, 218, 220, 226, 237, 241, 243–4, 246, 266
teak, 320
temples, 33, 36, 45, 71, 91, 145, 147, 158, 175, 267, 282
ten-sided, 307
tenement block, 359
tent, 32, 268–9, 275, 277, 282, 384, 387, 393, 415, 422–3, 425, 433, 459
funerary, 275
tent-inspired buildings, 19, 268, 275, 277, 421, 425, 433, 457, 460
tents, Mongol, 5, 158
terminology of Islamic architecture, 7–10, 8–10, 24, 179, 190–1, 219, 255, 257–8, 333, 340, 354
terrace, 205, 361, 381, 406, 414, 416, 428, 440, 443, 446, 458, 462
terracotta, 183, 224, 290, 297, 414
tetrapylon, 160
textiles, 54, 61, 382, 405, 412, 442
and architecture, 405
texture, 8, 12, 17–8, 26, 128, 153, 243, 277, 291
theatre, 402, 462
theologians, 177
theophany, 255
three-tier elevation, 138, 148, 154, 157–8, 163, 166–7, 286–7, 293, 309, 312–3
throne, 45–6, 48, 247, 412, 435, 437, 446
apse, 81
iwan, 411, 418
room or hall, 45, 51, 395, 402, 404–7, 413–4, 423, 439, 454, 458
tiles, overglaze painted, 311
tilework, 8, 12, 19, 22, 24–5, 48, 112, 122, 141–2, 156, 158, 163, 183, 185, 220, 230, 242–3, 247, 295, 297, 303, 307, 311, 398, 412, 416–8, 422–3, 425, 430,
titles, 18, 62, 155, 182, 203, 245–6, 266, 324, 419, 421, 443
tomb towers, 27, 153, 262, 268–9, 275–7, 280–7, 291, 294–5, 306–7, 309, 316
tombstones, 278–9

topography, 190–1, 262, 406, 413, 443, 461
totemism, 308
tower, 71, 129–30, 132–3, 136–40, 144–5, 147–8, 159, 161, 166, 170, 182, 342, 369, 385, 396, 404, 407, 409, 414, 416–7, 419, 439, 441, 446, 452–3, 459, 462
tombs, Palmyran, 282
towers of skulls, 160
trabeate, 76, 93, 95, 425
tracery *see* lattice
tracts, 438, 446
trade, 63–4, 334, 336, 338, 340–1, 344, 349–50, 353, 355–6, 358–9, 367, 369, 374
transept, 50–1, 53–4, 81, 91–2, 98, 347
raised gabled, 45, 50–3
translucence, 443
transversal grouping, 446
transverse aisle, 86–7
anteroom, 439, 446
axis, 406
qibla aisle, 86
vestibule, 440, 444
transversely vaulted halls, 429, 438
travel by day, 366
travellers, 42, 57, 60, 66, 220, 275, 331–3, 342, 344, 350, 353, 355, 361, 366–7, 369, 374–5, 427–8, 433, 456
treasurers, 351
treasures, 444
treasury, 42, 55, 60–1, 126, 391, 401–2, 426
treatises on architecture, 28
tree, artificial, 435
trees, 71, 104, 107, 147, 181, 217, 226, 271, 278–9, 374, 382, 390, 428, 434, 438, 459
evergreen, 278
trellis *see* lattice
triangle, 364
tribe, 44, 62, 264, 384, 392
tribunal, 453
triconch, 16, 45, 402
hall 439
trilobe, 318, 320, 407
tripartite layout, 453
sanctuary, 214, 250
sub-division, 438
triple-aisled hall, 402
gate, 405
iwan, 402, 406, 420, 424
opening, 439, 446
tract, 439
triple-domed sanctuary, 225
triumph *see* victory
tufa, 307
tulip garden, 462
tunnels, 402–3

turquoise, 459
twelve-sided, 279, 282, 286
tombs, 269, 307
twin minarets, 114
two-*iwān* plan, 104, 109, 182, 187–8, 192, 195, 199, 202, 206, 212, 225
undercrofts, 407–8
underglaze, 418
underground chambers, 427
channels, 427
passages, 402, 435
units of measurement, 222
university, 60, 217, 244
urban setting, 20–1, 53, 129, 138, 156, 243, 316
vaulting, 17, 24, 53, 74, 77–80, 86–7, 95, 98–9, 101–4, 110, 116–7, 128, 140, 154, 164, 183, 185, 187, 190, 196, 202, 205, 210–2, 216, 223–4, 229, 244, 287, 297, 302, 311, 313–4, 319, 323, 331, 338, 344, 347, 350, 352, 361, 364–5, 377, 390–1, 396, 398, 407–8, 410–2, 416, 418–9, 422–3, 426–7, 430, 433, 436, 439, 441
transverse, 79, 110, 199, 225
vaults, barrel, 416
cross, 410
four-sided, 365
membrane, 365
net, 431, 459
rib, 10
transverse, 365
tunnel, 313–4, 353
ventilation, 89, 95, 223, 352, 359, 377, 385, 388, 410, 417, 419, 427

veranda, 460
vernacular architecture, 8, 433, 438
vestibule, 16, 107, 114, 116, 187, 191, 196, 202, 204–5, 212, 231, 235–40, 331, 366, 398, 409–10, 413–4, 418, 426, 437, 440, 442, 444, 446
victory, 51, 71, 120, 155, 158, 160, 183, 246, 462
monuments, 71, 462
view *see* vista
villa, 442–3, 452, 456
visibility, 56, 196, 244, 278, 302, 391
vistas, 74, 87, 122, 205, 217, 359, 406–7, 413, 416–7, 419, 423, 426, 431, 433, 437, 440, 443, 456, 459
vizier, 175, 210, 241, 365, 384, 392, 446, 452, 459
voussoirs, 446
walkway, 338
warehouse, 361
warren, 426
washroom, 205
wasted space, 395–6
watch-towers, 132, 136, 144, 147, 155, 282, 338, 370–1, 406, 416, 418
water, 30, 240, 242, 246, 279, 331, 352, 374–5, 379, 382, 388, 402–4, 413–4, 416–7, 419, 425–6, 428–9, 432–3, 435, 440–2, 452, 454
channels, 279, 403, 424, 435, 446
spouts, 308, 350
sports, 418

way-station, 332, 338, 342–3, 351, 371–3, 414, 429
weapons, 322, 458
weavers, 437
welfare, 22, 260, 268, 339–40, 373–4
wells, 188, 331, 334, 339, 434
wider central aisle *see* central aisle
window frame, 311
of appearances, 385, 402 (see also *bit hilāni*)
windows, 14, 24, 83–4, 99, 122, 137, 141, 165–6, 180, 203–4, 206, 213, 216, 249, 276, 290, 313, 316, 318, 320, 326, 330, 353, 359, 385, 388, 406, 409, 416–9, 426, 430–1, 433, 454, 457, 459
twin, 308
wine, 382
winter prayer hall, 110, 126
quarters, 416, 457
women, 64, 89, 182, 190, 202, 234, 239, 251, 278, 309, 312, 320, 322, 342, 344, 349, 373, 439, 443
wood, 8, 30, 46–7, 49–50, 81, 83, 91–2, 140, 199, 206, 240–1, 244, 247, 249, 253, 277, 319, 330, 375, 398, 422, 430, 433, 435–7, 442, 446, 454, 457
wooden-roofed hall, 95, 97–8, 121
zodiac, 418
zone of transition, 13–4, 18, 24, 103, 106, 112, 164, 282, 291, 297, 308, 313, 318- 20, 322–3
zoo, 384